errors

p 35

p 43

p 54

239

245-

291

D1209089

The
WIZAR
of
ARMA

SIMON AND SCHUSTER · NEW YORK

DS

GEDDON

FRED
KAPLAN

Published by Simon and Schuster
A Division of Gulf & Western Corporation
Simon & Schuster Building
Rockefeller Center
1230 Avenue of the Americas
New York, New York 10020
SIMON AND SCHUSTER and colophon
are registered trademarks of Simon & Schuster.
Designed by Edith Fowler
Manufactured in the United States of America

10   9   8   7   6   5   4   3   2   1

Library of Congress Cataloging in Publication Data

Kaplan, Fred M.
    The wizards of Armageddon.

Includes bibliographical references and index.
    1. Atomic warfare.   2. Strategy—History—20th
century.   3. Atomic weapons.   4. United States—
Military   policy.   5.   Military   research—United
States—History—20th century.   I. Title.
U263.K36   1983   355'.0217   83-369
ISBN 0-671-42444-0

FOR MY PARENTS

CONTENTS

1	Year Zero	9
2	Living with the Bomb	24
3	Planning for War	33
4	On the Beach at RAND	51
5	The Superbomb	74
6	The Vulnerability Study	85
7	The Hydra-Headed Monster	111
8	The Gaither Committee	125
9	The Report of Maximum Danger	144
10	The Missile Gap	155
11	The Massive-Retaliation Speech	174
12	The Limited-War Critique	185
13	Counterforce	201
14	Dr. Strangelove	220
15	The Real Rivalry	232
16	The Whiz Kids	248
17	Two Briefings	258
18	The SIOP and the Road to Ann Arbor	263
19	The Gap That Never Was	286
20	The Crises	291
21	Shelter Mania	307
22	Damage Unlimited	315
23	Vietnam: Stalemate	328
24	The ABM Debate	343
25	The New Generation	356
26	Dancing in the Dark	385
	Notes	392
	Interviews	431
	Acknowledgments	435
	Index	439

1 YEAR ZERO

IT WAS AUGUST 7, 1945, a cool but sticky Tuesday morning in Bethany, Connecticut, a sleepy suburb resting on the northwestern edges of New Haven. Bernard Brodie, a brilliant new addition to the Yale University political science faculty, went driving with his wife, Fawn, to buy *The New York Times* at a drugstore in the neighboring village of Woodbridge, roughly halfway between the Brodie home and the Yale campus.

Bernard Brodie was fascinated by the weapons of war, especially the weapons of naval warfare and how they affected the tactics and strategies of those great battles on the high seas that had proved so decisive to the outcomes of war over the past few centuries. For most of the present war, World War II, Brodie had worked for the Navy in Washington, D.C., where he had been given, among other assignments, the task of ghostwriting the biannual report of Admiral Ernest J. King, Chief of Naval Operations and commander of the entire U.S. wartime fleet. Brodie's book, *A Layman's Guide to Naval Strategy*, first published in 1942, was in its third edition. The Naval War College had persuaded the Princeton University Press to drop the word *"Layman's"* from the title so that the school could assign the book as a standard text for officers without embarrassment. Now, at age thirty-five, Brodie was acquiring a solid reputation as one of the nation's foremost naval strategists.

Stepping inside the pharmacy, Brodie picked up a copy of the *Times*. The banner headline riveted his attention: "First Atomic Bomb Dropped on Japan; Missile Is Equal to 20,000 Tons of TNT; Truman Warns Foe of a 'Rain of Ruin.' " His eyes moved quickly down the right-hand column of the page, scanning smaller headlines reading: "New Age Ushered," "Day of Atomic Energy Hailed by President, Revealing Weapon," "Hiroshima Is Target," " 'Impenetrable' Cloud of Dust Hides City After Single Bomb Strike."

Brodie read just two paragraphs of the story that followed,

9

looked up for a few seconds, turned to his wife and said, "Everything that I have written is obsolete."

Brodie was not the only one for whom everything turned obsolete that morning. The whole conception of modern warfare, the nature of international relations, the question of world order, the function of weaponry, had to be thought through again. Nobody knew the answers; initially, not many had even the right questions. From these ashes an entire intellectual community would create itself, a new elite that would eventually emerge as a power elite, and whose power would come not from wealth or family or brass stripes, but from their having conceived and elaborated a set of ideas. It was, at the outset, a small and exceptionally inbred collection of men—mostly economists and mathematicians, a few political scientists—who devoted nearly every moment of their workaday thoughts to thinking about the bomb: how to prevent nuclear war, how to fight nuclear war if it cannot be deterred.

In the first months following Hiroshima and Nagasaki, Yale University would become a prime mover on the thinking about how to live with the bomb, and Bernard Brodie was at the center of that movement. When the Yale group started to split up around the end of 1950, Brodie spent a few months near the heart of the war machine, in the Air Staff of the United States Air Force, where he examined the nation's war plans, the targets inside enemy Russia that the U.S. would incinerate in the event of another war. From there, Brodie moved to Southern California, to the RAND Corporation.

RAND was where the ideas came together. It was an Air Force creation, independent in title but contracted to do research for the Air Force. The Army and Navy had their bands of hired intellectuals too, but through the 1950s American military policy and defense budgeting emphasized nuclear power, and the Air Force had the big bomb. The Air Force was where the money was funneled and the thinking was concentrated; RAND was where the thinkers coalesced.

They were rational analysts, and they would attempt to impose a rational order on something that many thought inherently irrational—nuclear war. They would invent a whole new language and vocabulary in their quest for rationality, and would thus condition an entire generation of political and military leaders to think about the bomb the way that the intellectual leaders of RAND thought about it.

The themes of such classic films of the nuclear age as *Dr. Strangelove* and *Fail Safe*, the catch phrases of the popularized strategic debates of the 1960s and 1970s—"counterforce," "first-strike/second-strike," "nuclear war-fighting," "systems analysis," "thinking about the unthinkable," "shot across the bow," "limited nuclear options"—would all have as their source the strategists of the RAND Corporation in the 1950s.

In the sixties, with the inauguration of President John F. Kennedy and the appointment of Robert S. McNamara as Secretary of Defense, the new "defense intellectuals" would move into positions of power, either as administration officials or as influential consultants. One British journalist would describe them in the London *Times Literary Supplement* as men who "move freely through the corridors of the Pentagon and the State Department rather as the Jesuits through the courts of Madrid and Vienna, three centuries ago, when we in Europe were having our own little local difficulties."

By the 1970s and especially into the eighties, the ideas of these thermonuclear Jesuits would have so thoroughly percolated through the corridors of power—and through their annexes in academia—that, at least among fellow members of the congregation, their wisdom would be taken almost for granted, their assumptions worshiped as gospel truth, their insight elevated to an almost mystical level and accepted as dogma.

Throughout this period, most of the defense intellectuals—with a few notable exceptions—would stay out of the limelight, preferring the relative anonymity of the consultant, the special assistant. Yet this small group of theorists would devise and help implement a set of ideas that would change the shape of American defense policy, that could someday mean the difference between peace and total war. Though virtually unheard of by most of even the very well read among the general population, they knew they would make their mark—for they were the men who pondered mass destruction, who thought about the unthinkable, who invented nuclear strategy.

Bernard Brodie hardly seemed the type to become the pioneer of nuclear strategy when he walked through the portals of

the University of Chicago in 1933. He was twenty-three, the product of an upwardly mobile but still quite poor Jewish family on
Chicago's South Side. He was rather short, with glasses and wavy
hair, very bright but awkward, unmannered, badly dressed.

Brodie had gone to work for the Weather Bureau, which had
barometers stationed in the University of Chicago quad. He had
thought he would make a career of meteorology, but after one look
at the grandeur of that campus, he changed his mind. Still working for the Bureau to support himself, he made plans to enroll at
the University of Chicago. The early years of Robert Hutchins' influence as university president were heady ones and during them
Brodie inaugurated a lifelong love of classical music, art, fine literature and history. He courted a fellow student, Fawn McKay, a
Mormon girl from the backwaters of Utah, for whom the university was equally liberating.

Brodie loved horses and at sixteen lied about his age to join
the National Guard, which trained its soldiers on horses. ("Horses
will always be used to tow the artillery," his officers proclaimed.)
While there, he grew increasingly fascinated with the technology
of weapons, particularly firearms, and read as much about their
history as he could find.

Brodie graduated in 1938 with a degree in philosophy, high
marks and a reputation as an outstanding student. In March, two
months before Brodie received his baccalaureate, Hitler's troops
crossed into Austria. Earlier in the decade, Japan had invaded
Manchuria and fascists had taken over the republic of Spain. Like
many aware young men of the day, Brodie grew concerned about
world affairs. That, combined with his military interests, led him
to enter the university's graduate school of international relations.

The social science departments at Chicago were widely considered to be among the nation's finest, certainly the most innovative. And in the interwar period, they were virtually an anomaly on
the American intellectual scene. It was a time of isolationism for
the United States, a sentiment embraced by masses, politicians
and intellectuals alike. The European war of 1914–1918 had been
a bleakly disillusioning experience. Woodrow Wilson had sent
American boys off to fight for democracy and freedom; they helped
win the war for the Allies, but the aftertaste was sour. War had not
been the glorious affair it was promised to be. After the war, the
Senate voted down American entry into the League of Nations,
refusing to soil once more the country's unique brand of democ-

racy in the brutish dirt of the Old World's balance-of-power politics.

In the 1930s, when war loomed again on the European horizon, most Americans wanted no part of it. In 1928, Secretary of State Frank Kellogg and French Foreign Minister Aristide Briand were the first to sign the Kellogg-Briand Pact, a multilateral agreement that outlawed war.

In the years between the two world wars, most American universities reflected the popular notion that America was a unique creation, something apart from and beyond the politics of its European ancestors. Political science was taught as if politics were composed of organization charts, venerable static institutions and the Articles of the Constitution. International relations was considered synonymous with international law, its curricula crowded with summaries of peace-treaty provisions and the message that peace and world order were essentially the products of well-drafted international legislation and mutual good will.

Against this rather bland and abstract tradition that contradicted everything that was going on in the world, the Chicago school splashed a bracing tonic of realism. Charles Merriam led the way with his provocative discourses on American politics, expounding on the now common but then utterly earthshaking thesis that the essence of all politics lay not in structures of organizations or the Bill of Rights or the Electoral College, but in *power*—who uses it, for what ends, in what political context, against whom.

The Merriam school of thought carried over into Chicago's department of international relations, mainly through Professor Quincy Wright, an institution all to himself. In 1926, Wright commenced a study on the causes of war that would not be published for sixteen years. The very existence of such a project at a major American university was astonishing. Even at Chicago, there were, as late as the mid-1930s, professors of international relations who would not allow war to be discussed in class because its very mention as a serious topic violated the spirit of the Kellogg-Briand Pact, implied that war might not be illegal.

The Wright project was a major departure, a huge endeavor entailing a vast collection of data not just from international law but from every field of scholarship imaginable—anthropology, economics, sociology, psychology, geography, biology, data on technological change, the balance of power (loathed phrase of the day), the history of armaments, public opinion and the press. Wright liked numbers: public-opinion poll data, excursions on a quantitative model of the arms race developed by mathematician Lewis Richardson, quantitative analyses of the contents in mass media.

When completed, the two-volume work, called *A Study of War*, had about it a dazzling sense of unity. It was heavy going and turgid, but it was so comprehensively interdisciplinary that it represented a quantum leap for the study of international relations.

Bernard Brodie was Quincy Wright's star student in his graduate-school days. In 1939, the year that he began his dissertation, Brodie won the department's only fellowship, an award of $350, and was assigned to assist Professor Wright, then in the final phase of his leviathan. The next year, when Brodie was about to face the job market, Wright sent well over a dozen letters to acquaintances in top-notch colleges across the country advertising "an A-number-one man, Bernard Brodie."

Brodie also greatly admired Jacob Viner of the economics department, another new thinker. Viner was physically small but intellectually towering. Once a star student at McGill in Canada, then at Harvard, he joined the Chicago faculty and introduced a course new to the field of economics—the politics of international economic relations. Viner had been a consultant in Franklin D. Roosevelt's first Administration, and was profoundly struck by how rare it was that economic theory alone provided an answer to any serious problem. As a scholar, he was interested in the history of pamphleteering, which naturally led him to a study of mercantilism, the relations between the free market and the state. This interest, combined with his Washington experience, inspired Viner to see the true nature of economics as an interdisciplinary subject—and one dominated by considerations of political power. While many of his colleagues went thrashing about in the new-fangled field of econometrics—an attempt to predict economic behavior by the imposition of vast mathematical models—Viner, in part because he never was much of a mathematician, liked to say, "After all, this subject was originally called *political* economy."

From Wright and Viner, Brodie learned some valuable lessons that Brodie's contemporaries in other universities were, in the main, not getting even by the end of the 1930s. From Wright, Brodie learned about the multiple causes and complexities of war.

He picked up a well-blended mix of realism and idealism: a view that peace relies on more than provisions of international law, but also that, as Wright said, "opinions and ideas are an element in political power no less, and perhaps more, important than armies, economic resources and geographic position."

Wright founded the Study of War project on the belief that by better understanding war one could better ensure the keeping of peace. At the same time, he had a *Realpolitik* view of national security and was no pacifist when it came to defending what he saw as national interests. He was a major figure in the Hyde Park branch of the Committee to Defend America by Aiding the Allies, an anti-appeasement organization of some influence in 1939 and 1940 that favored repealing the Neutrality Act so that the United States could ship arms to Britain and France. Wright petitioned several senators on this cause.

The lessons from Jacob Viner reinforced those of Wright's and added a new dimension. Power, thought Viner, could be surrendered only to something more powerful still. Governments will not lay down their swords before a world government simply out of good will or in the name of international cooperation. Doing so would violate their sovereign interests, and no nation could be expected to submit voluntarily to so clear a request of surrender.

In 1938, his senior year as an undergraduate, Brodie wrote a term paper for Quincy Wright titled "Can Peaceful Change Prevent War?" The paper was prompted by a popular thesis held by many political scientists and statesmen of the day: that, given the decay of the postwar settlements of 1919 and a resurgence of international violence, a method must be devised of establishing procedures for allowing changes in the international system, of avoiding war by accomplishing peacefully the ends for which nations might otherwise despairingly resort to war. This would serve the cause not only of peace but also of justice.

In a particularly Viner-esque passage, Brodie responded: "If change is to be effected to correct an injustice, or to rectify disequilibrium, it necessarily follows that states will find themselves called upon to make material concessions without receiving any material compensation, which they cannot be expected to do willingly. . . . Are we to expect the state yielding its territories to be entirely appeased by the proud contemplation of the generosity of its contribution to world order? These are questions which cannot

be glossed over. If the problems they entail cannot be satisfactorily
solved, we need concern ourselves no further with the idea of
peaceful change."

Brodie absorbed from the University of Chicago two great
lessons: that political change in international relations is likely
and, therefore, so is war; that there are ways to reduce the chance
of war, but short of drastic and unprecedented changes in the distribution of global power, a world government is destined to remain a feckless and ephemeral vehicle. These were new lessons in
the study of politics in America, and their impact would be deeply
felt when, a few years later, Brodie began to ponder the consequences of the atomic bomb.

It was 1939, Brodie was a star student, but he did have a wife
to support (he'd married Fawn three years earlier, before entering
graduate school). He was writing a dissertation about the impact
of naval technology on nineteenth-century diplomacy and it would
no doubt be lauded by his professors. But then what? Hardly any
universities in the United States had room for a teacher with this
peculiar specialization.

On September 1, 1939, fortune struck, in a sense. Hitler's
invasion of Poland marked the beginning of a world war unprecedented in scope, destruction, horror and conflagration; but it also
launched the career of Bernard Brodie. The job market would now
be considerably brighter for a smart young scholar who knew a
great deal about the nature and the machinery of warfare.

A year later, his doctoral dissertation complete, Brodie wrote
to his mentor, Quincy Wright: "As you already know, the skies
have finally opened for me, and both my wife and myself are
thrilled no end at our unexpected good luck." Wright had strongly
urged his old friend Edward Mead Earle of the Institute for Advanced Study at Princeton to take Brodie on for a year as a research fellow. Earle read Brodie's dissertation, was impressed, arranged for Brodie to win a Carnegie Corporation fellowship of
$1,800, and suggested that the Princeton University Press might
publish the dissertation if Brodie were to write an additional chapter on naval inventions of the early twentieth century for topi-
cality.

Brodie felt very much at home in Princeton, especially with
his sponsor, Ed Earle. Like Quincy Wright, Earle involved himself
in the study of war. More like Brodie, he was mainly interested in

strategy and military history. Earle was just beginning to organize a project on the evolution of strategic thinking. The result, published in 1943, was *Makers of Modern Strategy,* a collection of twenty-one essays by various scholars on "Military Thought from Machiavelli to Hitler," the standard textbook in the field for the next fifteen years.

From Earle, Brodie learned that strategy is "not merely a concept of wartime but an inseparable element in statecraft at all times," that military policy must be firmly linked with national politics and foreign policy. "The truth of the matter," wrote Earle in a 1940 article that Brodie marked up with underlinings, brackets and check marks, "is that, in a democratic society, it is imperative that we have the widest possible discussion of military problems, conducted on the highest possible plane." Most important was "a long-term program of research and, ultimately, of teaching which will enable the United States in times of peace as well as in times of crisis and war to build up a body of knowledge, and a corps of scholarly experts who can help in the formulation of public policy and who can contribute to an understanding of the military problems and the military power of the nation." Brodie would draw inspiration from that passage for years.

Brodie made a fine impression at Princeton. The Ford Foundation awarded him $200 to do research on the sociological consequences of peacetime military inventions. And Nathan Leites, a scholar at Princeton with whom Brodie would become close later in life, urged him to write a paper for the "Public Policy Pamphlet" series on the strategic consequences to the United States of a German victory over Britain. Brodie was following Wright's footsteps in his work on the Committee to Defend America by Aiding the Allies.

Brodie was also checking over the galleys of his revised-dissertation-turned-book, to be called *Sea Power in the Machine Age.* The Japanese attack on Pearl Harbor on December 7, 1941, brought America into the war—and created a fair demand for books about sea power that the Navy could store on board its ships. *Sea Power in the Machine Age* was just rolling off the presses, and the Navy instantly snatched up 1,600 copies—in those days, a best seller by most university-press standards.

By this time, thanks largely to recommendations from Ed Earle, Brodie was teaching in the political science department at Dartmouth College. He titled his first course "Modern War Strat-

egy and National Policies," the outline for which took several
leads from his training at Chicago. The topics of the lectures included: "The politics of power," "Pressures short of war," "War as
a continuation of policy," "Ubiquity of war in the modern state
system," "The causes of war," "The meaning of war," "The quest
for 'national security,' " "The diplomacy and legalisms of war,"
"Economic warfare." As Brodie wrote in a letter to Wright, he was
trying to integrate in such a course the disciplines of anthropology, geography and economics—precisely the Chicago approach.

Meanwhile, the Princeton Press was so thrilled by the success of Brodie's book that it commissioned him to write another, *A
Layman's Guide to Naval Strategy.* By the time it appeared in
1942, thousands of students were pouring into the U.S. Navy's re-
vitalized Reserve Officers' Training Corps. In early October, the
Navy ordered 15,000 copies of the book for its ROTC courses. Bernard Brodie, who had never seen an ocean much less been on a
battleship, was coming into a sort of fame as one of the very few
American civilians making a name for himself in the realm of contemporary strategy.

Brodie's appointment at Dartmouth was coming up for review in the spring of 1943, and the political science department—
much more in the stodgy American tradition than Brodie had been
accustomed to at Chicago or Princeton—chose not to renew. College dean E. Gordon Bill wrote Brodie: "There is a rather unani-
mous feeling in the Department of Political Science that you are
too much of a specialist and, in fact, too big a man in your field to
fit into any future plans of the Department . . . as they are now
being envisioned."

Even before receiving this rejection slip, Brodie had taken a
leave of absence from Dartmouth to enlist in ordnance school at
the Navy Yard in Washington, and by March gained a job at the
Navy's Bureau of Ordnance. That fall he was promoted to full
lieutenant, and in November got transferred to the Office of the
Chief of Naval Operations, where he wrote "Combat Narratives,"
short books distributed as confidential documents to all fleet officers describing various campaigns in the war. He served also as
chief ghostwriter of the King Report, the biannual statement of
Chief of Naval Operations Admiral Ernest J. King.

Good writers were hard to come by, so the Navy also assigned
Brodie tasks in the Office of Naval Intelligence. Together with a

wild Hungarian named Ladislas Farago, who would later author several popular war biographies and adventures, Brodie wrote propaganda tracts that were broadcast to German U-boats in an effort to get their crews to surrender or be less aggressive. Some were effective. One of the first requests that many captured U-boat crewmen made upon surrender was whether they could meet "Captain Norton," the name used by the man reading the Brodie-Farago scripts.

The war was nearing its end, and Brodie was weary of ghostwriting. As early as September 1943, he wrote Earle: "So far as my own preferences are concerned, I couldn't get back to the academic life too soon to suit me." Two months later he wrote, regarding his ghostwriting for King, "My voice is getting more and more sepulchral, and I expect soon to be able to walk through closed doors without opening them."

In August 1944, Brodie spent an afternoon leading the weekly round table of the prestigious Institute of International Studies at Yale University, speaking on military technology and peace planning. Brodie impressed his audience. A few months later, William T. R. Fox, a professor on the Institute's staff and also a former student of Quincy Wright's and Jacob Viner's at Chicago, recruited Brodie to join him at Yale the following summer. In mid-March the official letter of reception from Frederick Sherwood Dunn, director of the Yale Institute, arrived: "We have an urgent need for you both for researching and teaching."

In the 1940s, there was no more exciting and stimulating place in the academic world for an international relations scholar to reside than at the Institute of International Studies at Yale. It began life in 1935, the brainchild of the three Yale professors who were then teaching international relations—Nicholas Spykman, Arnold Wolfers and Frederick ("Ted") Dunn. "It was not by accident that Yale embarked on a program of this kind when it did," wrote Dunn in an annual report some years later. "The early thirties were a time when storm clouds were gathering on the international political horizon and when the impact of foreign conflicts on the security of the United States was becoming more manifest every day."

Arnold Wolfers was a Swiss lawyer who emigrated to Germany after World War I, eventually assumed the directorship of Berlin's finest institute of political studies, managed to get a vis-

iting professorship at Yale in 1933 and, rather than go back to living under the new Nazi regime that was elected to power while
Wolfers was away, simply stayed on. Wolfers wrote books on international economics and politics with a decidedly *Realpolitik* view.
For a man who grew up in the neighborhood of one world war and
barely escaped before another was about to begin, the turbulences
of global power politics were as natural to Wolfers as they were
unseemly and avoidable to most political scientists in America.

Nicholas Spykman was a Dutch sociologist who came to Yale
via California. At one time a Wilsonian idealist in his thinking,
Spykman received a private lecture on the role of power and force
in international relations from his friend Wolfers, and promptly
underwent a dramatic conversion—frequently going too far in the
other direction even for Wolfers's taste. In a 1942 book called
America's Strategy in World Politics, Spykman assumed an almost brutal view of the world: "The international community is a
world in which war is an instrument of national policy and the national domain is the military base from which the state fights and
prepares for war during the temporary armistice called peace."

Ted Dunn had been a lawyer in the State Department who
gradually realized that legal considerations rarely played any role
in the way nations behave. Legal norms were shaped by dominant
ideas of capitalist Europe and so could not be separated from—in
fact, must be considered subordinate to—political and economic
factors. Dunn thought that international treaties played a vital
role, but only so long as all parties to them had incentives to carry
out their provisions. He found chimerical and counterproductive
the ideas of most liberal intellectuals of the day, with their proposals for peace treaties or world-order blueprints that had no foundation in the independent interests of sovereign nations in the real
world. Dunn came to Yale in the mid-1930s, switched from international law to politics and diplomacy, and fell under the spell of
Spykman and Wolfers.

In one fundamental respect, the aim of the Yale Institute
bore similarities to that of Quincy Wright's at Chicago: "to supplement the traditional legal and institutional description of international events with a broader approach that included the best of
the political, historical, geographical and economic skills." But
whereas Wright attempted to improve the future by studying the
past, the Yale group went about its mission by studying and attempting to influence the decisions of the present. The Yale group

sent hundreds of copies of its various studies to well-placed government officials, who frequently read them.

The Institute had the strong support of Yale president Charles Seymour and was initially fueled with a $100,000 grant dispensed over a five-year period by the Rockefeller Foundation. By the mid-1940s, the Institute had clearly taken off. The number of international relations majors at Yale had jumped more than fivefold since 1937—up from seventeen to eighty-eight. This meant more faculty slots and more power for the Institute within the political science department.

Nicholas Spykman fell ill from cancer in 1940 and died three years later, but the Institute lived on in good health for another decade under the directorship of Ted Dunn. One booster was the creation of an Advisory Council in the mid-1940s consisting of Yale alumni high up in the corporate world—Henry Luce, Prescott Bush, Frank Altschul, Stanley Resor and others. With the influence and prestige of those names, the Institute could replenish its coffers with money from not only Rockefeller but also J. P. Morgan, Union Carbide, Shell Oil, Pan Am, J. Walter Thompson, IBM, Socony, U.S. Steel and many more.

Another source of health in the early 1940s was the influx of several students of Quincy Wright's and Jacob Viner's from Chicago. William T. R. Fox came in 1943, mainly on the recommendation of Wright. Fox recruited Brodie. Brodie recruited his friend Klaus Knorr a few months later. Jacob Viner himself came every few years as well, taking a leave of absence from Chicago to come take part in whatever was going on at the Institute of International Studies.

There was a heady feeling at the Institute in those heydays, an *esprit de corps* bordering on elitism, a shared conviction that its members were pioneers of a new age, riding on a crest that most others of their profession—including many of their non-Institute colleagues down the hall—chose not even to paddle through. Their offices were all close to one another, crammed along one segment of a wing on the second floor of the Hall of Graduate Studies.

Every Wednesday afternoon, the Institute staff held a formal round-table discussion on a particular topic, sometimes with an outsider as the main speaker (as Bernard Brodie had been that day in August 1944). Every day, they were constantly in touch with each other, batting around ideas, reading each other's manu-

scripts, commenting and criticizing in a completely collegial
manner.

As one political scientist from down the hall described the Institute's atmosphere, "they work under the influence of a group
pressure to produce and with the stimulation that comes from
give-and-take within the group about their individual undertak-
ings. They have created something of an 'island' within Yale in
which a tighter group discipline prevails and a sharper drive to
produce exists than I sense in the university community as a
whole."

Indeed, a small community of power-conscious international
relations scholars had emerged from a few universities around
this time. And it was not without influence. As a result of a conference held in Rye, Westchester County, in the spring of 1945,
Dunn, Fox, Wolfers and a Yale China specialist named David
Rowe—together with Ed Earle and Harold Sprout of Princeton
and Grayson Kirk of Columbia—wrote a twenty-three-page paper
called "A Security Policy for Postwar America," which declared:
"The day when the United States can take 'a free ride' in security
is over." Referring to the emerging domination by the United
States and the Soviet Union, they dubbed the new era "the age of
the Big Two." (Bill Fox had, just before, written a book called *The
Super-Powers,* the first usage of that phrase.) They urged that the
good relations of the World War II alliance be maintained, but
cautioned that conflict between the two great powers over the political destiny of Germany could spark renewed conflict. Two generals and an admiral on the Joint Strategic Survey Committee of
the U.S. Joint Chiefs of Staff read the paper, promptly classified it,
and distributed it as an official JCS document. One of the generals
told Earle, "There is a desperate need for civilian contribution to
this type of thinking and strategic planning."

Yale was starting to provide such a contribution, not only in
the Institute's faculty but also through the students it was graduating. As early as 1942, the number of Yale students entering the
Foreign Service had increased dramatically.

The most long-lasting influence, however, was yet to come.
Bernard Brodie joined the Yale faculty on August 1, 1945. Five
days later, the United States dropped the atomic bomb on Hiroshima. When Brodie came to his office at the Institute the next
day, Bill Fox greeted him with the same question that Brodie had

essentially posed to himself only a few seconds after glancing at the front page of the newspaper earlier that morning.

"Where does this leave you with your battleships?" Fox asked.

Brodie, still somewhat baffled, just shrugged.

2 LIVING WITH THE BOMB

A BUZZ OF EXCITEMENT dominated most discussions on the second floor of the Hall of Graduate Studies at Yale for the next month, all of it about the atom bomb. The significance of the weapon—that, with a single blow, it could destroy an entire city—sunk in quickly. Pondering the implications took longer. It was evident that the prevention of war between the Big Two now took on an even greater magnitude of importance, but how would that be accomplished? Does the bomb make war more likely or less? How would it be used in a war, to what end? Is it possible to impose international controls over the production and storage of these new weapons? What would World War III be like? Does the atom bomb mean the obsolescence of all other forms of military force?

The training in politics acquired at Chicago and Yale provided some guidelines. The first display of Yale thinking on the matter revealed itself back in Chicago. Just weeks after Hiroshima, Bill Fox talked with Edward Shils, a University of Chicago sociologist with whom Fox had once shared an office in the Social Science Research Building. Along with Chancellor Robert Hutchins and Eugene Rabinowitch, a physicist at the University of Chicago's Metallurgical Lab, Shils was organizing a conference on the control of atomic energy. Hutchins was proud of the lab's role in ending the war, but also felt disturbed by the enormous power of this weapon and how it might affect all humanity in any future war.

Some of the nation's leading scientists would be there—Leo Szilard, a Met Lab physicist who had voiced his dissent against using the bomb before the war was over; David Lilienthal, director of the Tennessee Valley Authority and later chairman of the Atomic Energy Commission; Joyce Stearns, former director of the Chicago Met Lab; Harold Urey, physical chemistry professor at Chicago; Eugene Vigner, physicist at Princeton's Institute for Advanced Study, to name a few. There would also be some government officials, most notably Henry Wallace, who promised to report back on the conference to President Harry Truman himself.

It was an impressive list, but the organizers needed some political scientists, and they did not want to invite the older professors in Chicago's departments. This was a new weapon, a new age, and they wanted new thinkers. Shils asked if Fox would like to come. He also asked Harold Lasswell, Edward Mead Earle, Jacob Viner and Bernard Brodie.

Brodie had already begun to investigate. For a man with training in the humanities, he was extremely adept at picking up technical concepts by quickly perusing scientific books and journals. He carefully read the *Smyth Report,* an official volume written by H. D. Smyth, a Princeton physicist who had worked on the Manhattan Project at the Chicago Metallurgical Lab. The report, issued by the War Department only days after the atomic bombing of Japan, explained in general terms the structure of the bomb, what elements it contained and how it exploded. Sensing that the size of an atomic arsenal would dictate the strategy surrounding the weapon, Brodie also studied such arcane sources as the most recent volumes of the U.S. Bureau of Mines' *Minerals Report* to learn whether critical uranium-ore deposits were scarce or plentiful. To compare the atomic bomb with war inventions of the past, he referred back to his first book and to the early official reports on the strategic bombing campaigns of World War II.

His first conclusion was that the A-bomb changed not merely the destructiveness but the very nature of war. Military inventions of the past, Brodie had reasoned, were always limited enough in scope and consequence to permit timely measures of adaptation by an opponent. Not so with the atom bomb: the war would probably be too brief to allow the time needed for developing those countermeasures or building up a force powerful enough to alter the course of the battle. This fact alone minimized the value of historical precedent.

Brodie had figured naval strategy would be his life's work, but he was now forced to conclude that the Navy would play only a minor role in any future war. It wasn't that ships would be destroyed by A-bombs; they could easily enough disperse and keep moving about on the vast ocean surface. More pertinent was that historically, navies have had value primarily in long wars, and the atom-bomb war would not last very long. The Navy would still be useful in maintaining foreign bases and in transporting the

Army—which would still exist, though in streamlined form—to decisive points. And given America's postwar commitments, the fleet could serve well as a policing force, a mission for which the A-bomb was superfluously destructive. However, the days when naval supremacy and wartime control of the seas dominated considerations of the balance of power were over.

The age of defenses was probably also finished. Brodie recalled that the defense of London against German V-1 rockets during World War II was considered remarkably effective. Yet from British Information Services bombing reports, Brodie knew that in one eighty-day period, 2,300 of those missiles hit the city. The peak effectiveness of defenses came on August 28, 1944, when out of 101 bombs that approached England, 97 were shot down before reaching London. This was indeed spectacular, but Brodie projected that figure into the future and thought, "If those four had been atomic bombs, London survivors would not have considered the record good." To be effective, a defense against an atomic attack must be *completely* successful, and the annals of military history provided no encouragement for believing such perfection possible.

Finally, Brodie's reading of the *Smyth Report* and the mineral yearbooks led him to deduce that the explosive materials necessary for A-bombs would remain scarce: not so scarce that an aggressor could not destroy all the cities he might want to, but scarce enough to make it wasteful to use the weapon against any but the most valuable targets. The most valuable targets, Brodie figured, were not the enemy's military forces, which were widely scattered and (some of them) mobile, but its cities, in which the economic power and political machinery of a nation were greatly concentrated.

From this, Brodie inferred important political implications. First, a nation must remain constantly prepared for war; there will be neither the time nor the surviving industrial machinery to mobilize once atom bombs start exploding. This constant readiness may encourage aggression, exacerbate world tension or possibly even spark in some men's minds the luring temptation of "preventive war." Then again, the calamity that would certainly ensue if the other side struck back with its own atom bombs would be so grimly devastating that its very anticipation might deter a potential aggressor from attacking in the first place. Brodie wrote up a three-page outline summarizing these thoughts and took it with him to Chicago. The conference was held at his alma mater from Wednesday, September 19, through Saturday the 22nd.

On the question of whether the A-bomb would deter or foster war between the great powers, Brodie had still not made up his mind. At the conference, he simply laid out the arguments that would support either side of the question. Nor had Brodie decided on an answer by the beginning of November, when the Institute of International Studies published his twenty-eight-page monograph, *The Atomic Bomb and American Security,* essentially an elaboration of his informal talk at Chicago.

However, Brodie's Chicago mentor, Jacob Viner, had made up his mind. In the course of his Chicago Conference talk on the economic implications of the bomb, Viner flatly stated, "The atomic bomb makes surprise an unimportant element of warfare. Retaliation in equal terms is unavoidable and in this sense the atomic bomb is a war deterrent, a peace-making force."

Viner, who was visiting Yale that fall, accepted Brodie's assumption that cities were the only efficient target of an atom-bomb attack. With that premise in mind, Viner kept repeating to Brodie, over and over, a point that he found irresistibly logical. If a country has made all the obvious preparations for a possible attack from the enemy, Viner reasoned, it could certainly retaliate with an atomic attack of its own. Since all the cities on both sides will be destroyed in the aftermath, going first holds no advantage. As Viner put the case to the American Philosophical Society in Philadelphia on November 16, "What difference will it then make whether it was Country A which had its cities destroyed at 9 A.M. and Country B which had its cities destroyed at 12 A.M., or the other way around?"

The logic was indeed unassailable, and Brodie was finally convinced.

Bill Fox came back from the Chicago Conference with a deep feeling that most of the professionals thrashing about in the realm of atomic-energy control were off in a forest of ideals and assumptions uninhabited by real leaders of real nations in the real world. Most of the scientists talked about creating an establishment for controlling atomic energy as if the task were not much less mechanical than that of building an atomic bomb—as if the overwhelming problems of national power and of creating political incentives for convincing nations to submit to such a program entailed no uniquely insuperable difficulties.

Even his friend Ed Shils, in a speech at the conference, had
gone on about how an "agreement not to use atomic bombs . . .
can never be . . . successful unless it exists on a foundation of
moral consensus among the major states of the earth," and that
the problem is "how, in the time that remains to us, before the
knowledge and technique required to construct atomic bombs
is so widely diffused as to produce an 'arms race'—how can we
promote by education and propaganda, and by the partial modifications of existing institutions, the state of mind without
which there will be neither demand for nor acceptance of a World
State."

Fox thought it might be feasible to develop some sort of international inspection system to regulate or prohibit the manufacture of atom bombs, and he thought that the United States, having been the only country to have thus far used the weapon, must
assume the moral leadership to take the first bold steps in offering
such a plan to the world. But all this talk about a "World State"
was for dreamers. Maybe in several decades, maybe after the system of nation-states had been thoroughly jolted and scrambled
and knocked out of place by some cataclysmic series of events, but
it was not the sort of thing that sounded at all practical or even desirable to someone trained in thinking about these matters by the
likes of Quincy Wright, Jacob Viner and the group at Yale.

"Proposals for the short-run and middle-run future must operate within the existing multi-state system," Fox cautioned his
listeners during his Chicago Conference talk. "Other things being
equal, proposals which promise least disturbance to the existing
balance of interests between and within states will find more general acceptance."

Calls for a world government were widespread among serious-minded people. Norman Cousins' words in *The Saturday Review of Literature* of August 18 were typical of these expressions:
"There is no need to discuss the historical reasons pointing to and
arguing for a world government. There is no need to talk of the
difficulties in the way of world government. There is need only to
ask whether we can afford to do without it. All other considerations become either secondary or inconsequential."

Fox and his colleagues at Yale disagreed, not because they

were opposed to the control of atomic weapons but because they thought that if the elusive path to world government was the only one followed by the community most immersed—and probably most influential—in the business of controlling the new weapon, then all such efforts would be doomed, from their irrelevance, to failure.

Ted Dunn liked to quote a Robert Browning poem that made the very same point:

> The common problem, yours, mine, everyone's,
> Is not to fancy what were fair in life
> Provided it could be,—but, finding first
> What may be, then find how to make it fair
> Up to our means—a very different thing!

Fox and Dunn decided that the Institute should put out a book through a commercial publisher, a collection of essays by a few members of the staff that would make a firm case for the control of atomic weapons, but that would also lay out the facts about the nature of the bomb, its political implications and how ideas about the avoidance of its use might fit into what they saw as a more realistic view of world politics.

The book was eventually called *The Absolute Weapon* and subtitled *Atomic Power and World Order*. An internal copy was privately circulated to a small number of specialists in February 1946 and appeared under the Harcourt, Brace imprint in June. The title was taken from a passage in the essay by Bill Fox, explaining that, unlike all other weapons, any numerical advantage that one side might possess in atomic bombs has little impact on the balance of power as long as the other side has enough weapons to destroy any enemy's cities. "When dealing with the absolute weapon," Fox wrote, "arguments based on relative advantage lose their point."

Dunn appointed Arnold Wolfers to write on "The Atomic Bomb in Soviet-American Relations," Percy Corbett (an international lawyer on the Institute's staff) to analyze the "Effect on International Organization," and Bill Fox to expound on "International Control of Atomic Weapons," an essay that especially took after those who rallied behind the slogan "World Government Now." Ted Dunn wrote the introduction. Its title: "The Common Problem," named after his favorite Browning poem.

The bulk of the book Dunn turned over to Bernard Brodie.

Yale's president, Charles Seymour, especially admired Brodie's work on *The Atomic Bomb and American Security,* calling it "one of the coolest as well as most comprehensive discussions of what the world must now face." The monograph was admired by high-ranking officials in the Departments of State and War; Brodie was, along with Dunn and Fox, made consultant to the State Department on methods of controlling the A-bomb, and he was appointed chairman of an atomic-energy committee of the Social Science Research Council.

Brodie wrote two chapters for *The Absolute Weapon,* and was therefore arbitrarily anointed the book's "editor." The first was called "War in the Atomic Age," the second "Implications for Military Policy." Both elaborated on the themes introduced in Brodie's earlier monograph—the alteration caused by the bomb in the very nature of the war, the obsolescence of the traditional functions of the Navy, the futility of defense, the scarcity of atomic materials in the foreseeable future to the point where cities (i.e., large targets of concentrated value) would remain the uniquely optimal targets for the atomic weapon.

But his chapters in this new book went beyond merely re-hashing those already-developed themes. They also contained new material, reflecting the resolution of Brodie's earlier ambivalence about the impact of the bomb's existence on the likelihood of war or peace, the synthesis of his own thinking with Viner's insight about surprise attack, and the fitting of these ideas into an intellectual construction grounded in lessons about power that he had learned in his school days at Chicago and that every day were reinforced in the halls he occupied at Yale. The product was a pair of essays that would be heralded for many years as the first fully developed, sophisticated treatise on the subject of an appropriate military policy for the nuclear age, the first conception of nuclear deterrence.

In these chapters, Brodie made three essential points. First, "superiority"—either in number of air forces or in number of bombs—"is not itself a guarantee of strategic superiority in atomic bomb warfare." This conclusion was based on the assumption that fissionable materials were relatively scarce and that, therefore, "the primary targets for the atomic bomb will be cities. One does not shoot rabbits with elephant guns, especially if there are elephants available." The destructive power of each bomb, given the technology of the day, was too great "to warrant its use against any target where enemy strength is not already densely concentrated."

From this premise flowed a novel conclusion: "the number of *critical* targets is quite limited. . . . That does not mean that additional hits would be useless but simply that diminishing returns would set in early; and after the cities of, say, 100,000 population were eliminated, the returns from additional bombs would decline drastically." Brodie had learned about "diminishing returns" from economics; it was a concept indicating the point at which the demand for a certain good begins to fall off with each additional unit supplied. "If 2,000 bombs in the hands of either party is enough to destroy entirely the economy of the other, the fact that one side has 6,000 and the other 2,000 will be of relatively small significance." Bill Fox coined the term "the absolute weapon," but the elaboration was Brodie's.

Second, *deterrence* of war is the only rational military policy for a country in the nuclear age. Brodie had by now accepted Viner's argument about the futility of surprise attack. If one side, wrote Brodie, "must fear retaliation, the fact that it destroys the opponent's cities some hours or even days before its own are destroyed may avail it little. . . . Under those circumstances, no victory, even if guaranteed in advance—which it never is—would be worth the price."

From that observation, Brodie outlined the essence of a national-security policy for the future: ensuring that the strategic retaliatory arsenal survives an enemy attack. The airplanes or rockets designed to deliver the retaliatory blow must be completely separated from the cities that would be targeted in nuclear war; they must be placed on "dispersed reservations," stored underground, in any case sharply isolated from urban centers for supply or support. The implications for the future of warfare were profound:

> The first and most vital step in any American security program for the age of atomic bombs is to take measures to guarantee to ourselves in case of attack the possibility of retaliation in kind. The writer in making that statement is not for the moment concerned about who will *win* the next war in which atomic bombs are used. Thus far the chief purpose of our military establishment has been to win wars. From now

on its chief purpose must be to avert them. It can have almost no other useful purpose.

The implications for world order were as considerable as those for military policy. If a world government can exist only in fantasy because no nation has incentive to join or obey it, then the threat of atomic retaliation will in effect serve as a substitute for world government, as the force from above looming over all international activity, working itself into every calculation of the risks and benefits of aggression, at least between the great powers. Efforts to outlaw the use of the bomb through treaty might still be worth working for; but "without the existence of the state of balance—in terms of reciprocal ability to retaliate in kind if the bomb is used—any treaty . . . would have thrust upon it a burden far heavier than such a treaty can normally bear."

The nature of war had changed drastically, and so had the conditions of peace. The atomic bomb would forevermore dominate both. "Everything about the atomic bomb is overshadowed by the twin facts that it exists and that its destructive power is fantastically great," wrote Brodie. Key here was the phrase "it exists." To Brodie and the others at Yale, a plan for ensuring peace had first to come to grips with the fact of everyday living with the bomb.

3 PLANNING FOR WAR

THE WORLD was a turbulent place those first few years after the end of the Second World War. Western Europe lay exhausted from the convulsions of battle, its economies in disarray, local Communist parties growing in strength as a consequence. Inspired by nationalist independence movements, the old colonies were rebelling, inspiring into vogue the term "power vacuum." In 1947, under the by-line "X," George Kennan, the nation's foremost Soviet expert, wrote an article in the widely read journal *Foreign Affairs* arguing that the Soviet Union was governed by an intrinsically expansionist ideology, and that the United States must adopt "a long-term, patient but firm and vigilant containment of Russian expansive tendencies." In 1948, the Soviets toppled the democratic government of Czechoslovakia and, later that year, attempted a blockade of Berlin. Tensions between East and West mounted. The "Cold War" was on.

Living with the bomb suddenly became more awkward, difficult and perturbing than ever. The Soviets were too far away to launch a direct attack against the United States and, for the moment anyway, there was only a small chance of their invading Western Europe. For one thing, the United States had the bomb—not many, but some—and the Soviets did not. However, it would only be a matter of time before they too started assembling an arsenal of atomic weapons. Meanwhile, almost immediately after World War II, the United States had rapidly demobilized its non-nuclear military might. As Bernard Brodie wrote in the fall of 1948, "the fact remains that the atomic bomb is today our *only* means for throwing substantial power immediately against the Soviet Union in the event of flagrant Soviet aggression." The atom bomb would still serve as a powerful deterrent to Soviet aggression, but things do sometimes get out of hand, conflicts do escalate. The international situation, wrote Brodie, "requires appraisal of the atomic bomb as an instrument of war—and hence of international politics—rather than as a visitation of a wrathful deity."

An epigram Brodie had composed two years earlier was immediately relevant: "War is unthinkable but not impossible, and therefore we must think about it."

Moreover, it seemed that one of Brodie's main assumptions in *The Absolute Weapon* was now unraveling—the notion that superiority in atomic weapons offered no strategic advantage. Brodie read articles in *The New York Times* by military correspondent Hanson Baldwin, and heard corroborating reports from some military friends, that the materials for making atom bombs might be even scarcer than was previously thought. There was no way for an outsider to know this for sure; the size of the atomic stockpile was among the most highly classified bits of data in government files. But it was known that only eight bombs had been tested since the bombing of Nagasaki, and it was now widely rumored that uranium ores were extremely scarce.

Clearly, a three-to-one superiority in atomic bombs would not have much meaning if each side had thousands of bombs, enough of them to blow up the other's major cities and then some. But, Brodie began to ask himself, what if each side had only hundreds of bombs? Then a three-to-one margin might have significance. Moreover, this margin, if it did exist in the near future, would no doubt favor the United States, which certainly could manufacture far better airplanes and missiles than the Soviet Union, and which would still be producing bombs when the Soviets only started to produce their first.

Given the possibility of Soviet aggression, the bomb assumed enlarged importance in American policy. And given a supposed condition of even greater atomic scarcity than previously imagined, the question of how to use the bomb, if it came to that— which targets to strike, in what order, for precisely what desired effects—suddenly emerged, at least in Bernard Brodie's mind, as a vexingly pertinent problem.

At the same time, Brodie realized that virtually nobody in any position of responsibility seemed to be thinking along these same lines. In 1947, under the auspices of the Library of Congress, he conducted a survey of military thinking on the bomb, reading the official literature and interviewing officers in the Navy and the War Department. The level of thinking, he discovered, was shockingly shallow. One War Department paper referred to the need for "a significant number of bombs," defined as the number that would "provide an important military capability." Yet nowhere

had anyone given much thought to figuring out what "a significant number" or "an important military capability" might mean.
Certainly much would depend, in assessing these matters, on how
the weapons were used; but to evade the issue of numbers was to
miss the whole point, for the number available would in large part
govern the way in which they could be used.

"What we need to know," wrote Brodie, "is: 'How many
bombs will do what?' " And, significantly, "the 'what' must be
reckoned in overall strategic results rather than merely acres destroyed." Under the new political and technical circumstances,
indiscriminate bombing would not be enough.

Brodie had only the faintest glimmerings of an answer to all
these questions, but he figured the best way to focus on the problem would be to undertake a comprehensive study of the effects of
strategic bombing in World War II and, from that, produce an
analysis that might have relevance for the latest phase of the new
atomic age. Sometime in 1949, Brodie decided to write a book on
the subject and to call it *Strategy of Air Power.*

Brodie carefully studied the *United States Strategic Bombing
Survey,* a multivolume report on the effects of the bombing on the
German and Japanese economies, war machines and civilian morale, the product of a massive research effort undertaken just after
the war by a group of economists, among them John Kenneth Galbraith, George Ball, Paul Nitze, Burton Klein and Henry
Alexander. Brodie also held lengthy conversations with General
Orvil Anderson, commander of the Air War College at Maxwell Air
Force Base in Alabama, and Carl Kaysen, a young economist who
during the war had helped pick European bombing targets while
working in a London-based unit of the OSS known as the Economic Objectives Unit.

An intense controversy had already surrounded the strategic
bombing campaign, with detractors and advocates mustering various statistics from the enormous body of available data to prove
that the bombing had either been decisive or a miserable failure.
One thing was clear, however: the bombing, especially of Germany, had not been nearly so crucial as proponents of "air power"
had predicted before the war. In the 1920s and 1930s, air corps
training schools in Britain and the United States had become enthralled by the theories of Italian Brigadier General Giulio Douhet
and American General Billy Mitchell, visionaries who saw air
power as the decisive vehicle of future wars, superseding and ren-

dering marginal or superfluous the clashes of armies on the ground, flying above and beyond those brutal skirmishes to strike directly at the heart of the enemy's industrial strength and its civilian morale, without which national leaders could no longer wage war.

At the start of the war, the British Royal Air Force went after the "vital nerve centers" of the German economy, but that meant flying in daylight in order to see the targets. As a result, German fighter pilots and antiaircraft gunners could see clearly the British bombers and shoot them out of the sky. Attrition was terrible. The RAF started flying at night, but could barely find the right city, much less individual factories. So they made a virtue of necessity and proclaimed—along Douhet's lines—that the main target of attack was the "morale" of the German people, that the massive bombing of their towns, houses and workplaces would accomplish that goal. Nearly one-fifth of German houses were destroyed or heavily damaged, 300,000 civilians were killed and 780,000 wounded; but this "area bombing" had virtually no effect on the German war effort.

The U.S. Army Air Forces stuck with a doctrine of "precision bombing" against particular targets, but met with only slightly better success. One problem was that the pilots could not drop bombs very accurately, owing to bad weather, industrial haze, deliberate smoke screens, antiaircraft barrage, simple incompetence, the occasional unreliability of weapons or some combination of these factors. Only 20 percent of bombs aimed at precision targets fell within the "target area," that is, within 1,000 feet of the target.

Moreover, the German economy had a tremendous capacity for expansion. Hitler went into the war with great optimism, feeling it unnecessary to gear up for an all-out war economy and sacrifice the production even of such luxury items as lace. As a result, the German industrial economy was extremely resilient. Damage could readily be repaired, losses replaced, new factories dispersed. Bombers went directly after the German aircraft-frame industry, tank and truck plants, and the various industries that supported these war supplies—steel, oil, rubber, ball-bearing plants and the like. Nevertheless, in 1944, the peak year of the Allied bombing effort, production of all German military hardware *exceeded*—in some instances, far exceeded—the output of previous war years when the bombing was not so intense.

Brodie saw that bombing, at least toward the very end of the war, did knock out two vital German industries—liquid fuel and chemicals—as well as the transportation services. But he also saw that those results came too late to matter much. The Russian Army had begun its counterattack from the east, and the other Allied forces had broken out west of Saint-Lô. By the time the bombing really began to be felt, "the Battle of the Bulge was a thing of the past and the Allied armies were well into Germany." In short, strategic bombing played its greatest role not as some cosmically independent force from above, but as a highly useful adjunct to the war primarily being fought—as all other wars of the past had been—below on the ground.

Still, Brodie figured that unavoidably, in a future hypothetical war fought directly against the Soviet Union, "strategic bombing would be our chief offensive weapon." And the atomic bomb would certainly deal a mightier blow to any particular target than ordinary high-explosive bombs had delivered in the last war. One thing that struck Brodie dramatically was that until quite late in WW II, the U.S. Army Air Forces "had given very little systematic thought to the problem of target selection." Whatever equipment an air force might have, it "can be no more effective than the logic that governs its choice of targets."

The most wasteful aspect of the strategic bombing, and to Brodie "the biggest single factor in delaying useful results," was the effort devoted to the area bombing of cities—a waste of bombs and lives that had no payoff militarily. But even in the precision bombing of particular targets, the Air Force frequently chose illogical points at which to aim. For example, in striking rail transportation, the bombs were usually aimed at the center of freight-car marshaling yards. However, that usually left "stump yards" near the yard's entrance, which the Germans could use for high-priority traffic. Perhaps better targets would have been the entrances rather than the centers. Similar statements could be made about the bombing of most sectors of the German economy. Possibly, Brodie thought, only a moderate improvement in planning, testing and flexibility of doctrine might have led to a decisive effect much sooner.

That point was debatable, but the significant implications of the argument lay in planning for the next war. The Soviet economy seemed far less resilient than Germany's. If atomic bombs were so scarce, their targets must be chosen much more carefully and systematically if the United States were not to squander its superiority. Above all, the bombing of cities for its own sake—the most ineffective element of bombing in World War II—should not dominate the strategic bombing of World War III.

Brodie wrote up these preliminary thoughts in the August 15, 1950, issue of *The Reporter,* under the title "Strategic Bombing: What It Can Do." Brodie's main point was that "we cannot accept the conclusion that because atomic bombs are a convenient way of destroying cities, it is a sound strategy to use them for that purpose. Even narrow military considerations might dictate other targets, and strategy cannot be guided exclusively by narrow military considerations." He recognized that an atomic-bombing campaign might "quickly degenerate into pure terroristic destruction." But if this possibility slackened incentives "to choose targets shrewdly and carefully . . . such an event would argue a military failure as well as a moral one. . . ."

None of this explicitly contradicted the fundamental points that Brodie had made nearly five years earlier in *The Absolute Weapon,* but it certainly did mark a departure into a new dimension. Brodie was beginning to think in operational terms, was beginning to think through the problems of the bomb not just in peace but also in war, not just how to live with the bomb but how to use it.

Possibly the most avid reader of Bernard Brodie's piece in the August 15 *Reporter* was General Lauris Norstad, the Air Force Vice Chief of Staff, who in turn showed a copy to his boss, Chief of Staff General Hoyt Vandenberg. During the war, Vandenberg had commanded the Ninth Air Force, the largest assemblage of aircraft ever deployed in military history. His primary mission was not strategic bombing, but providing close air support for General Omar Bradley's ground troops as they plowed across the plains of Europe. An officer's attitude about war often grows out of his wartime experiences, and so Vandenberg had no sentimental attachment to the grand dogmas surrounding the massive bombing of cities.

Norstad was a brilliant staff planner who worked on targeting during the war, became the first Air Staff's deputy chief of staff for operations shortly afterward and was now serving as Vandenberg's chief intellectual. Like Vandenberg, he had no firm attachments to any one school of thought about how to use air power.

These were nerve-racking times in the Air Force. One year earlier, at the end of August 1949, the Russians had set off their first atomic explosion. Six months later, the Joint Intelligence Committee, an interservice office that reported directly to the Joint Chiefs of Staff, had predicted that the Soviets would build up an atomic arsenal large enough to attack the United States and that they "may attack . . . at the earliest possible moment . . . at any time they assessed that it was to their advantage" to do so.

In June 1950, the Korean War broke out. The Joint Chiefs firmly believed that North Korea's invasion of the south was merely a Soviet ploy, a trick to force the United States to divert its limited military resources to some remote and relatively unimportant peninsula in the Pacific, while in the meantime the Red Army prepared to invade Western Europe, and perhaps the Middle East too. That would mean general war, and atomic bombs would inevitably be used, almost certainly at the very start of the war. The approved JCS war plan stated that a "strategic air offensive with atomic and conventional bombs will be initiated at the earliest possible date subsequent to the outbreak of hostilities." The Joint Chiefs thought that atomic war with the Soviets was not merely possible but almost certain.

Meanwhile, the Chiefs were not in terribly good shape to deal with such an event. In December 1949 they had approved an emergency war plan called "Offtackle," and they had attached to it an appendix listing the specific types of targets inside the Soviet Union that the bombers of the U.S. Strategic Air Command should attack. However, the JCS had not yet approved the appendix. There were still major arguments, mostly between Air Force planners and SAC operators, over which targets were feasible and appropriate to strike. Some officers and special ad-hoc panels questioned whether an atomic air attack would really bring the Soviet war machine to a grinding halt before it had already accomplished its war aims. Two things were certain: first, the United States had slightly fewer than 300 atom bombs; second, the Air Force office of plans and operations had calculated, in April 1950, that if war came before the year was out, the U.S. Air Force "could complete only the atomic phase" of Offtackle. That "atomic phase," therefore, had better work. The targeting plan had to be re-examined and made as effective and efficient as possible. Outside advice and criticism were needed—and fast, before the war began.

It was this strange convergence—the Air Force Chief of Staff's lack of enthusiasm for city bombing, the outbreak of the Korean War with general atomic war undoubtedly on the horizon, and the appearance of Bernard Brodie's article in *The Reporter* magazine—that prompted General Vandenberg, at General Norstad's urging, to ask Brodie to come serve as a consultant in the Air Staff, to examine and comment on the target list of the war plan.

Brodie was flabbergasted, but embraced the opportunity. He was tiring of Yale and tiring of political science. His colleagues at the Institute of International Studies were still interested in the ramifications of the atom bomb, but Brodie was heading into questions of military strategy, which did not interest them or many others in his profession very much at all. Moreover, he was beginning to feel a great need for access to classified information. Essential issues of strategy were very much bound up with such matters as the size of the atomic stockpile, the strengths and vulnerabilities of the Soviet Union and the U.S. targeting plans— none of which could be known with any confidence if he stayed on the outside.

By 1950, the Air Force was riding high. At the start of the war, it was a fledgling subservice of the U.S. Army; by the end of the war, it had monopoly control over the weapon that finally brought Japan to its knees. In 1946, the Strategic Air Command was created as guardian over the new weapon, and shortly thereafter the Air Force was made an independent service. In the early years of postwar demobilization, the Air Force was the only service of the armed forces to get practically as much money from the President and Congress as it wanted.

Arguments were breaking out, however, over just what the nature of air power was and how it should be used in the next war. Military planning was essentially Air Force planning, and Air Force planning was still very much dominated by putative lessons of World War II. Conflicts over planning were rooted in disagreements over what those lessons were. And those disagreements were based on the different wartime experiences of the various planners involved in the intramural fighting.

General Vandenberg and many of his aides on the Air Staff were trying to devise a targeting plan that would aim at destroying particular types of industries, the specific sectors of the Soviet economy on which the war machine uniquely and critically depended. Vandenberg's assistants in the Air Intelligence Division devised a concept called "killing a nation." On how to pull it off, they had taken a few pages from the *U.S. Strategic Bombing Survey,* the most comprehensive study on the effects of the strategic bombing of the last war.

The *Survey* pointed to two industries that looked promising for the future: liquid fuel and electric power. The bombing of liquid-fuel plants toward the end of the war made it impossible for Nazi panzer divisions to move their tanks or for the Luftwaffe to fly its planes. From an airman's point of view (and this view almost always ignored the tremendous pressures on the demand for fuel created by the Allied invasion *on the ground*), the bombing of liquid-fuel targets knocked the German war economy flat on its back.

The German electric-power system was never made an explicit target by the Allied air forces, partly because they assumed that the German power grid was highly developed, that losses in one area could be regained by switching over to the power source of another. However, the investigation by the *Strategic Bombing Survey* economists revealed that this assumption was wrong. The "electric power situation was in fact in a precarious condition from the beginning of the war and became more precarious as the war progressed. . . . Fears that their extreme vulnerability would be discovered" were constantly expressed in sessions of the Nazi Central Planning Committee. An explicit emphasis on bombing these power plants, concluded the *Survey,* "would have directly affected essential war production."

Then there was a third critical target, unique to the atomic age—the Soviet Union's atomic-energy plants; their destruction would ensure that the Russians could no longer produce the decisive weapon.

The Air Intelligence Division worked out a targeting plan for the Air Force that would emphasize blowing up those three critical types of targets, which they thought constituted the vital center, the *solar plexus,* of the Soviet war-supporting economy.

This effort was one facet of a targeting plan that had been approved by the Joint Chiefs, known in shorthand as "Delta-Bravo-Romeo." The critical industries fell under Delta, "the *disruption* of the vital elements of the Soviet war-making capacity." Bravo called for "the *blunting* of Soviet capabilities to deliver an atomic

offensive against the United States and its allies." Romeo stood for
"the *retardation* of Soviet advances into Western Eurasia." Destroying the critical targets of each category would destroy the Soviet war effort.

The officers of the Strategic Air Command, the airmen who
would have to fly or coordinate the mission, had no objection to
the Delta-Bravo-Romeo categories. But they thought the idea of
separating out specific industrial sectors in some delicate and discriminating fashion was a disastrous notion. To SAC, that simply
was not the way to fight a war.

General Curtis E. LeMay, the commanding general of SAC
and its living personification, fought this targeting battle against
the Air Staff with determination. LeMay had the ultimate clout.
The Joint Chiefs might toy with fancy ideas and theories, but
LeMay was the one who would route the bombers to their destina-
tions; he was the one who would be pressed to deliver; he had the
bombs. And most of the Air Force officers knew that, on a tactical
level anyway, LeMay pretty much did as he pleased.

During the final phase of World War II, LeMay commanded
the XXI Bomber Command, part of the Twentieth Air Force, planning the bombings and fire bombings over Japan. They were terrifying raids, almost unimaginably massive. One attack over Tokyo,
delivered March 9, 1945, involving incendiary bombs dropped
from 334 B-29s, burned to a crisp nearly sixteen square miles of
territory, leveling 267,171 buildings, killing 83,793 Japanese,
wounding 40,918 others. During the month of March alone,
LeMay's crews poured a similar rain of destruction upon thirty-
three cities across the Japanese map. The Joint Chiefs had sent
LeMay a target priority list earlier that spring. Heading the list
were select aircraft plants, followed by other particular industrial
factories; at the bottom of the list were industrial *areas*. But the
weather was terrible in Japan, even worse than it had been in Europe, and a bombardier had to see specific targets before he could
hit them. During the best month for bombing Japan, visual bombing was possible for seven days. The worst had only one good day.
LeMay struck a deal with a Chinese insurgent named Mao Tse-
tung to set up a radio station and report on the weather. That
helped, but not enough.

LeMay had the tool, air power; he could hit industrial areas,
but not precision targets; so he threw out his instructions and did
what he could. He looked up the size of the large Japanese cities in

the *World Almanac* and picked his targets accordingly. Square miles—that's all he could hit, and he figured if he hit enough of them, that would do the trick.

By late spring the results were pretty clear. Fire bombing had been particularly effective, since so many Japanese buildings were made of wood. The fire took hold, and the flames spread, toppling buildings like a blaze of dominoes. General Henry "Hap" Arnold, commander of the Army Air Forces, visited LeMay in the Pacific and, after hearing a briefing, asked him when the war would be over.

LeMay assembled his officers and ordered them to count how many square miles they had left to hit, how many bombs it takes to cover that much area and how long it would take, given logistics and so forth, to get to them. "The war will be over the first of September," LeMay told Arnold. That would be when the XXI Bomber Command would run out of targets to hit.

To LeMay, demolishing everything was how you win a war. He thought that strategic bombing in Europe had been handled all wrong, too much fussing with "bottleneck" targets and "precision bombing," that the whole point of strategic bombing was to be massive, a campaign of holy terror. The atom bomb only made this point stronger. LeMay thought that the advent of the atomic bomb blasted all doubts that air power could win a war by itself.

LeMay kept three big pictures framed next to one another on the walls of his office at SAC headquarters. The first was a painting of Napoleon's army retreating from Russia. The second was a painting of Hitler's armies retreating from Russia. The third displayed a passage from Winston Churchill's 1949 speech delivered at the Mid-Century Convocation of the Massachusetts Institute of Technology, proclaiming, "For good or ill, air mastery is today the supreme expression of military power, and fleets and armies, however necessary and important, must accept subordinate rank."

LeMay took over SAC in 1948 from General George Kenney, who was retiring. LeMay's first job, as he saw it, was to show his crewmen that they didn't know the first thing about what they were doing. He planned an exercise. All the bombers from all the SAC bases across the country would launch a full-scale simulated attack on Dayton, Ohio. The result was devastating: not a single airplane finished the mission, not a single crew demonstrated competence at finding specific targets or "dropping" bombs. Just two years later, LeMay had whipped SAC into a formidable force that trained with a fair degree of realism, displayed high morale, and could probably complete some sort of mission.

In short, LeMay owned the bomb. And he did not like the ideas going on inside the heads of planners in the Air Staff. A strategic air offensive against Soviet Russia would best be handled like his air war against Japanese cities—by attacking industrial *complexes,* which in effect meant cities. He had no objection to the Air Staff's predilection for destroying liquid-fuel industries, for that seemed to have been effective in Germany and, besides, there were many other choice targets by those factories. But atomic-energy facilities and electric-power plants? Who knew how many the Soviets had or where they all were? Even if somebody did know, they would be difficult for pilots to find. Most of the plants that anybody did know something about were sited outside cities, some of them out in the middle of nowhere. What was the point of dropping something as *big* as the atom bomb just to hit one target? LeMay's proposed war plan, called SAC Emergency War Plan 1-49, was to "deliver the entire stockpile of atomic bombs . . . in a single massive attack," pounding 133 A-bombs on seventy cities within thirty days.

The Air Staff intelligence analysts were persistent. At one point, they succeeded in moving the aim point of one bomb targeted on the Kremlin a half mile to the south to make it explode halfway between the Kremlin and an electric-power plant just outside Moscow. LeMay convinced the Joint Chiefs, though, that striking the Soviet atomic-energy and electric-power industries was not feasible. It would require far greater prewar reconnaissance than LeMay could provide with existing technology and resources.

LeMay was not the only internal critic of the Air Staff plan. Officers on the interservice Joint Intelligence Committee were coming to the conclusion that the whole basis of the JCS war plan might be resting on shaky foundations. Nobody could quite figure out what targets corresponded to the Bravo and Romeo missions, to the ideas of "blunting" the Soviet Union's nuclear-weapons force and "retarding" a Soviet invasion of Western Europe. These missions might, by definition, involve "targets of opportunity," objects at which a pilot could only "see and shoot" once he flew over them. If so, as one Joint Intelligence Committee report put it to the JCS, this "condition precludes a specific appraisal of intelligence adequacy"—jargon that, coming from an intelligence officer, could be translated as meaning, "Quit wasting your time, this mission is impossible."

It was in this context that Bernard Brodie's *Reporter* article—the article talking about the fatuousness of bombing cities indiscriminately and the importance of selecting targets judiciously—caught General Lauris Norstad's eye. This was the setting when General Hoyt Vandenberg asked Professor Bernard Brodie to take a step into the savage jungle of nuclear war planning.

Brodie read the targeting plans—SAC's and the Air Staff's—and was appalled by the loose, illogical, second-rate thinking that had gone into both. The Air Staff's seemed a bit better since it talked about specific targets instead of blasting brick walls; but both hinged on the notion that somehow the bombing campaign would, just like that, force the Soviet Union to "collapse." Brodie thought that the Air Staff was profoundly misreading the *Strategic Bombing Survey*. To the degree that the bombing of Germany in World War II had been effective, it took the additional pressures from the Allied ground forces to make it in any way decisive to the outcome of the war. Yet this future war that the Air Force was planning involved no ground forces; it would be waged entirely through air power. The apotheosis of Douhet had been realized.

Brodie went around town—inside Pentagon conferences and briefings, over to the Target Divisions branch of Air Intelligence in an office hidden away in a building on the corner of 12th and Constitution in downtown Washington—basically making a pest of himself. A man of no small ego, who had made a name for himself as the leading civilian military thinker of the day, Brodie felt no qualms about letting majors and colonels and generals know what he thought of their work.

He particularly annoyed the Target people downtown, telling them that LeMay was right, they *didn't* know where all the Soviet electric-power plants were; how could they hope that such an attack would have any effect at all?

On a broader level, Brodie had serious questions about the assumptions underlying the whole war plan. He told General Charles Pearre Cabell, director of the Air Intelligence Division, that he simply could not figure out this business of "killing a nation," how the process of "collapse" would take place, just what would happen to the Soviet economy, how that would ruin the Soviet war effort and how that would in turn doom the Soviet regime. He kept hearing the phrase "Sunday punch" tossed around casually.

Finally, Brodie did not see why SAC had to hit the Soviet Union with all its atom bombs at once, why it had to be in such a hurry when the Soviet Union had hardly any bombs at all. He posed this question directly to LeMay, but LeMay found it a bit daffy. LeMay had no use for ideas such as a "reserve force." The notion violated one of the "principles of war," the principle of "concentration of attack." These principles had been around for centuries. Nobody violated them lightly, and if someone did, it shouldn't be a civilian who, as a basic rule, had no business fooling around with the military's war plans.

LeMay's plan came down, in the final analysis, to city bombing, the very type of strategic bombing that Brodie had labeled as utterly ineffective in his *Reporter* article. As early as 1948, Brodie had pinned the critical question as being "How many bombs will do what? And the 'what,' " he continued, "must be reckoned in overall strategic results rather than merely in acres destroyed." Now, inside the war machine, Brodie observed that SAC was still thinking basically about destroying acres; and while Air Staff officers were talking about specific targets, they had only the vaguest ideas about *what* it was they thought these bombs would do.

Two years earlier, at a conference on technology and international relations, held at the Shoreland Hotel in Chicago, Brodie speculated about how the strategic situation might change once the Soviets acquired their own atomic arsenal. He thought American policy might adapt in one of two directions. The existence of even *some* Soviet atom bombs "may, on the one hand, put a greater urgency upon our using those [bombs] we have in order to anticipate [the U.S.S.R.'s] attack and to weaken the potential strength of that attack; or it may, on the other hand, cause us to hold our bombs as a threat to induce him to hold his."

The key point was the idea of *holding* the release of American atom bombs as a bargaining lever, as a measure of coercion, as a way of threatening the Soviets to back down. The idea did not loom large in Brodie's speech; he was not forcefully arguing a case for adopting such a strategy; he was merely presenting it as a possibility. Yet now, in 1950, looking at the SAC and Air Force war plans—which involved the release of the entire atomic arsenal, as quickly as possible, against every target on the target list—and

seeing just how senseless those plans were, made that passage
from Brodie's 1948 essay sparkle.

Brodie wrote two reports for Vandenberg, one after his first
two weeks on the job, the other in March 1951. The second concentrated on the idea of slowing down the proposed delivery rate
of atomic bombs, of deliberately *avoiding* the destruction of Soviet
cities, at least in the first phase of the war. The reasoning harkened back to Brodie's 1948 speech in Chicago: there was "more
strategic leverage to be gained in holding cities hostages than in
making corpses."

Brodie reasoned that the final surrender of the Japanese in
the Pacific war resulted not from the atom bombs dropped on
Hiroshima and Nagasaki, but from the *implicit threat* of more
atom bombs on their way if the Japanese did not give up then.
(That the United States actually had no more bombs beyond the
first two was inconsequential, since the Japanese could not possibly have known this.) Likewise, the Soviets would more likely stop
fighting after receiving *some* destructive blows, knowing that if
they did not stop, their cities would be the next targets to get hit.
If, however, we blew up their cities at the very outset of the war,
the bargaining lever would be blown up along with them. Hostages have no value once they are killed. Consequently, the Soviets would feel no inhibitions about blowing up American cities
in return, hardly an outcome that would serve the interests of
American security.

Finally, Brodie connected these ideas with a theme he had
developed in *The Absolute Weapon*—that for this strategy to work,
SAC must survive an enemy attack. If after a war has broken out,
the United States tries to threaten the Soviets with weapons yet
undelivered, there must be absolute assurance that the Soviet
Union cannot destroy those weapons before they are used.

Brodie admitted that this whole concept would mean "sacrificing the prospect of total victory, but," he added, "for the future
that might be a small price to pay for the sake of avoiding total
war."

Brodie was not opposed to the use of atomic weapons. On the
contrary. In December 1950, not long after he arrived in the Pentagon, before the Chinese entered the Korean War, Brodie wrote
in a memo: "We have thus far given the Chinese every possible assurance that they could intervene with impunity . . . [We] should
begin publicizing right now the fact that strategic bombing does

not necessarily mean mass slaughter. All the gasping of horror which occurs every time the use of the atomic bomb is mentioned is extremely harmful to us politically and diplomatically."

In short, Brodie's ideas about the bomb were meant as suggestions on how the bomb might be used more *effectively*. His Vandenberg memorandum presented the first analytical case for limitations on the use of the atomic bomb in a war against the Soviet Union. It was the first suggestion that nuclear deterrence does not necessarily end once war begins; that if threatening the destruction of Soviet cities tends to deter Soviet aggression (as he had argued in *The Absolute Weapon*), then the same threat might deter the Soviets from attacking American cities even once a war has broken out. It marked the beginnings of a formulation of a military *strategy* that fully took into account the fact that an atomic war would be a *two-way* affair—that destroying the enemy would very likely prompt the enemy to destroy us—and that, therefore, the horrendous magnitude of the A-bomb imposed as many limitations as it created opportunities. In criticizing the official target plans, Brodie offered no new wisdom on what better targets SAC might hit. However, he saw "an enormous area for wisdom and science in determining what *not* to hit" and "in determining what can be achieved by war, and in what way, other than by unloosing destruction on an unlimited basis."

More than a quarter century later, Brodie would look back on the reports he wrote for Vandenberg as "the most important and best thought out documents I ever wrote." In 1950, however, inside the Pentagon, the documents were not so roundly admired. In most quarters, Brodie and his reports were scorned. First, most military officers generally thought that outside civilians had no business looking at targeting plans, much less tampering with them. Second, the idea that all future wars would not necessarily be total wars, that in a war with the Russians, total war was something to avoid rather than to "prevail" in, the idea that you might not want to tear up as much Soviet property and kill as many Communists as you possibly could, seemed naïve and foolish. That they violated just about every "principle of war" devised was the reception given Brodie's memoranda by most true-blue SAC and Air Force types.

It is unclear what Vandenberg thought of the substance of Brodie's work, but he sufficiently admired Brodie's intelligence to ask him, on March 23, 1951, to organize and chair a Special Advisory Panel on Strategic Bombing Objectives. The panel would study the issue for four months, with a possible extension at Vandenberg's request. Brodie readily accepted the task, but before the end of May, six months sooner than originally planned, Brodie was out of the Pentagon, his employment for Vandenberg—as Brodie put it in a letter many years later—"rather abruptly terminated."

Brodie was never popular with most of the Air Force officers with whom he had to work. His job with Vandenberg was made possible by the urgings of Larry Norstad. Toward the last days of Brodie's Pentagon period, Norstad was transferred from Vice Chief of Staff to Commander of the U.S. Air Force in Europe, then headquartered at Fontainebleau, just southeast of Paris. With Brodie's chief sponsor out of the country, Vandenberg's other principal aides—including General Charles Pearre Cabell, the director of Air Intelligence, whose analyses Brodie had dared to criticize—had Vandenberg's ear and confidence to an even greater degree than before.

The Special Advisory Panel on Strategic Bombing Objectives, to be chaired by Bernard Brodie, was aborted. Brodie saw Vandenberg for the last time as a special consultant on the morning of May 18, and was out of the Pentagon before the end of the month.*

Brodie could have gone back to Yale to teach international relations again, but he chose not to. For one thing, the Institute of

---

* Another likely reason for Brodie's departure was the lobbying efforts of his old friend and adviser from Princeton, Edward Mead Earle. Earle did not like Brodie's article in the August 15 *Reporter*. He thought it underestimated the impact of the bombing in WW II, as well as the intelligence of those who planned the bombing. As an aide on targeting issues to General Hap Arnold during the war, Earle undoubtedly took Brodie's criticisms personally. Even earlier, Earle had criticized Brodie's talk at the September 1945 Chicago Conference on Atomic Energy Control for its omission of any reference to air power.

On April 30, 1951, Earle wrote to his friend Secretary of the Air Force Thomas Finletter that he would be in Washington the week of May 7 and would like to "have a word with you" about some news that he had heard "from various sources" that Bernard Brodie, "whom I have known for about twelve years," was "about to undertake a study [for the Air Force] of very considerable importance."

Earle presumably saw Finletter on May 7 and at half past noon definitely talked with General Vandenberg. There is no record of what was said, but it seems unlikely that Earle would be placed on the busy calendar of the Air Force Chief of Staff just to recommend Brodie for a project to which Vandenberg had already appointed him in mid-March. Eleven days later, Brodie saw Vandenberg for the last time.

For the ten years since Brodie had been at Princeton, he and Earle had been frequent correspondents. After Brodie left the Pentagon and for the next three years, until Earle died, they never exchanged a single letter.

International Studies had broken up. Whitney Griswold had replaced Charles Seymour as Yale president the previous fall, and
almost immediately let Ted Dunn, director of the Institute, know
that he disapproved of the Institute's sort of work. In April, Griswold abolished the Institute.

Ted Dunn arranged with the Milbank Foundation an endow-
ment that would allow him and five other Institute faculty members to move *en masse* to Princeton. On April 2, 1951, Princeton
University announced the creation of the new Center of International Studies. An editorial in the next day's New York *Herald Tribune* noted that the whole affair "calls up memories of medieval
days, when scholars wandered from university to university amid
the free cities of Europe."

Bernard Brodie turned his back on this academic chaos. He
had seen the secrets and could not imagine now returning to the
outside, especially to the comparatively staid existence of campus
life. In 1949, while still at Yale, he and some others at the Institute—Bill Fox, Ted Dunn, Bernard Cohen and a young political
scientist who had only recently received a Ph.D. from Yale, William Kaufmann—had done some consulting work on psychological warfare for the RAND Corporation, a nonprofit research institute in Santa Monica, California, that worked on many classified
projects for the Air Force. Brodie had made an impression, and
Hans Speier, the head of RAND's social science division, recruited
him. Brodie joined up—and stayed for the next fifteen years.

Five and a half years earlier, at the Chicago Conference on
Atomic Energy Control in September 1945, Ed Shils, the Chicago
sociologist who delivered one of the opening addresses, raised the
question of how the existence of the atom bomb and the secrecy it
entailed would affect intellectual life in America. "What kind of
men," he said, "will be willing to work in this centrally important
field in peacetime when they know that all they do is intended for
war and that all they can do can confer on mankind only the dubious benefits of a victory in an atomic bomb war?"

In the 1950s, nearly all these men that Shils talked about
would find themselves writing, thinking and calculating in the
RAND Corporation.

4 ON THE BEACH AT RAND

ALONG THE jagged coastline of Southern California, past the green hills and forests of Malibu, five miles down and across from the Santa Monica Mountains, beyond the Pacific Palisades, just short of Muscle Beach and the small town of Venice, there sits some of the most quaintly decrepit oceanside property in America. The Santa Monica Beach hardly looks different from the way it appeared only a few years after World War II: the same huge archway along the entryway, the same calliope with the lighthouse-shaped apartment on top, the same small seafood diner.

At the edge of this underdeveloped strip of land, between Ocean Park Avenue and Main Street, stand two adjoining pink-and-white buildings—one two-storied, the other five—that, from the outside, appear as if they might hold nothing less innocuous than the business offices of the local telephone company. Once inside, appearances change: the security guard at the desk in the lobby, the locked doors that open only with the flashing of a special pass, the dimly lit corridors, the offices with papers and books and reports piled on desks and strewn all about, blackboards crammed with diagrams and complex mathematical equations, the library with its Top Secret section, the special-clearance room in the basement where war games are played.

This is the RAND Corporation, and during the peak of the Cold War, most of its occupants did little but sit, think, talk, write, pass around memos, and dream up new ideas about nuclear war. Isolated from the hurly-burly of the rest of the world, the men and women (mostly men) of RAND nurtured an *esprit de corps,* a sense of mission, an air of self-confidence and self-importance. It was, in large measure, this atmosphere, this intoxication, that induced the gradual creation of a *doctrine* concerning nuclear weapons, nuclear deterrence, nuclear war-fighting; that identified this doctrine with RAND, and that propagated the notion that "the RAND way" was the only legitimate way of thinking about the bomb.

•

RAND had its origins in the military planning rooms of World War II. It was a war in which the talents of scientists were exploited to an unprecedented, almost extravagant degree. First, there were all the new inventions of warfare—radar, infrared detection devices, bomber aircraft, long-range rockets, torpedoes with depth charges, as well as the atomic bomb. Second, the military had only the vaguest of ideas about how to use these inventions; thinking about new problems was not an integral feature of the military profession. Someone had to devise new techniques for these new weapons, new methods of assessing their effectiveness and the most efficient way to use them. It was a task that fell to the scientists.

The result was a brand-new field, called "operational research" in Britain, "operational analysis" when it was picked up in the United States. The sorts of questions its practitioners had to answer were crucial to the war effort: How many tons of explosive force must a bomb release to create a certain amount of damage to certain types of targets? In what sorts of formations should bombers fly? Should an airplane be heavily armored or should it be stripped of defenses so it can fly faster? At what depths should an anti-submarine weapon dropped from an airplane explode? How many anti-aircraft guns should be placed around a critical target? In short, precisely how should these new weapons be used to produce the greatest military payoff?

The operational research groups were composed of scientists from all fields—physics, astronomy, chemistry, physiology, zoology, economics, mathematics—and thus were called "mixed teams." When P. M. S. Blackett, one of the founders of operational research, explained the British experience to American officers in the early years of the war, he told them that every type of profession had been tried for the job except lawyers. Misunderstanding the gist of the remark, the U.S. Army Air Force hired as its first OR chief John Marshall Harlan, a lawyer who later became an associate justice on the Supreme Court.

The scientists working on OR carefully examined data on the most recent military operations to determine the facts, elaborated theories to explain the facts, then used the theories to make predictions about operations of the future. In looking at the air campaign against German U-boats, for example, they analyzed past campaigns, looking at the number, tactics, defensive strength, of-

fensive armament, geographic distribution, and state of training of
the crews of the U-boats; the number and duration of sorties,
search tactics, height of patrol, attack tactics, bomb load, accuracy, geographic distribution, performance, camouflage, radar
performance, and training of the crews of the aircraft, and at the
various weather conditions. By calculating the effect and importance of each of these variables, the scientists could predict what
effect a change in any one of them—a new kind of radar, better accuracy, better camouflage, different altitude—might have on the
outcome of the campaign.

For example, when Blackett first joined the British Coastal
Command in the spring of 1941, the air campaign against U-boats
was curiously unsuccessful. Command officers had observed,
prior to this time, that as soon as a U-boat captain spotted an aircraft he dived as deep as possible to avoid getting hit. In reaction,
the Coastal Command set the depth charges on its weapons to explode 100 feet below the surface of the water, assuming that the
U-boat could sight the airplane two minutes before the attack and
could, in that period, dive 100 feet. Yet they were damaging only a
few submarines.

Blackett and some colleagues discovered from combat data
that the Command's assumptions were true *on average,* but not
nearly all the time. Furthermore, in those cases where the U-boat
dived 100 feet, the airplane pilot could no longer tell just where
the submarine was and would, therefore, almost certainly be
bound to miss. In some cases, however, the warning time was
much less than two minutes, and the U-boat could descend only
about 20 feet before the aircraft dropped its load; in those cases,
the sub could still be located and hit. Therefore, if the depth
charges were set at 20 feet, instead of 100, the percentage of submarines actually damaged or destroyed would be much higher.

The Coastal Command implemented the recommendations.
The results were so spectacular that captured German U-boat
crews thought that the British had started to use a new and more
powerful explosive. Yet the cause of greater damage was simply a
slight change in tactics, systematically calculated by OR scientists
engaged in nothing more complicated than standard scientific
methods of investigation—with the difference being that, for the
first time in history, they were being applied to military tactics in
wartime.

Similar techniques were developed to show that, contrary to

conventional military wisdom, large naval convoys are safer than small convoys, that bombers should be diverted from strategic bombing of German cities to going after German U-boats, that fighter planes should fly every day they are serviceable regardless of whether enough can be put up in the air to fight in large formations.

By the end of the war, every U.S. Army Air Force unit had its own operational analysis division. The scientists not only worked on calculations in the home office, but went out to the fronts, primarily to gather data, but also to make suggestions on how new tactics might be applied to the new weapons. Toward the latter part of the war, scientists were not just asked for advice; they were invited to sit alongside the generals and colonels in Washington headquarters and participate directly in war planning.

A key player in this new phase of civilian involvement was Edward Bowles. Bowles had come to the Office of Scientific Research and Development from the MIT Radiation Lab at the start of the war, then transferred to the War Department to serve as special consultant to Secretary of War Henry Stimson and General George Marshall. Starting in 1943, he worked with General Hap Arnold in adapting techniques of air warfare to the possibilities offered by the new scientific devices. Bowles had a tremendous faith in the power that comes from the fusion of military might with scientific brilliance.

Bowles was practically an agnostic in this faith compared with General Henry Harley Arnold. Everyone called Arnold "Hap" because of his amiability and the broad smile that nearly always crossed his face. Yet lurking behind the smile was a man obsessed with destructive power and with the role that scientists might play in making future weapons still more destructive. When he heard that Secretary of War Stimson had doubts about the bombing of Dresden, Arnold wrote a memorandum: "We must not get soft. War must be destructive and to a certain extent inhuman and ruthless." He wanted his scientists to invent "explosives more terrible and more horrible than anyone has any idea of."

Arnold was a devoted disciple of General Billy Mitchell, who was court-martialed in 1925 for proclaiming, against all orders, that in the next war battleships and land armies would be vulnerable to attack from the air. Arnold flew his first plane in 1910, when Harry Atwood, a famed cross-country barnstorming pilot, landed on a parade ground on Governors Island and asked then-

Second Lieutenant Henry Arnold to take a spin. Many air officers of Arnold's generation—the founders of the independent Air Force, Ira Eaker, Carl Spaatz, George Kenney, Jimmy Doolittle—first thrilled to the romance and derring-do of human flight in this fashion. Arnold was hooked on air travel from that moment on. One year later, he took flying lessons in Dayton, Ohio, from Orville Wright himself, and in 1912 earned his military pilot license.

That same year, he first met Billy Mitchell. Arnold was twenty-six, working in the office of the chief signal officer; Mitchell was thirty-two and on the command staff. The idea of a full and independent air force was just a dream in those days, but Arnold and Mitchell were among the dreamers. During Mitchell's court-martial, Arnold testified on his behalf. At one point while he was on the stand, some planes could be heard flying over Washington. Pointing upward, Arnold solemnly said, "There goes all our air force. It has thirty-five planes, the largest number we could muster to defend Washington." When World War II started and Arnold was commander of the Army Air Forces, he insisted on mass production of B-29 bombers.

Arnold considered himself a visionary. Four months before Germany was defeated, seven months before Japan surrendered, he called in his top officers and said, "We've got to think of what we'll need in terms of twenty years from now. For the last twenty years we have built and run the air force on pilots. But we can't do that anymore." Arnold told them that he foresaw an age when intercontinental missiles would dominate warfare, that the Air Force would have to change radically to confront the challenges of this new age. His small audience was stunned into silence. Every man in the room was a pilot.

Meanwhile, Hap Arnold was worried. He was fifty-five when the war began. He was among those responsible for making something of air power, and he wanted to leave a legacy. The future would be an age of intercontinental missiles, robots, super destructiveness, but what would happen to all the scientists who would be necessary for the challenge, the scientists who were proving so valuable to the present war effort? After the war, peacetime demobilization would quickly spread to their ranks as well; they would go back to lucrative jobs in universities and industry; certainly the meager salaries of civil service would hardly serve as incentive for them to stay in and help their country prepare for World War III.

On November 7, 1944, Arnold wrote a memo to his chief scientific adviser, a brilliant Hungarian refugee named Theodore Von Karman. Arnold's opening words: "I believe the security of the United States of America will continue to rest in part in developments instituted by our educational and professional scientists. I am anxious that the Air Force's post war and next war research and development be placed on a sound and continuing basis.

"I am asking you and your associates," Arnold continued, "to divorce yourselves from the present war in order to investigate all the possibilities and desirabilities for post war and future war's development," as they concern the Army Air Force.

Over the next thirteen months, Von Karman and his Army Air Force Scientific Advisory Board produced—and distributed piecemeal—a lengthy multivolume report called *Toward New Horizons*. Its message read like music to Hap Arnold's ears. "The scientific discoveries in aerodynamics, electronics and nuclear physics open new horizons for the use of air power," the report began. Even greater advances, including the development of intercontinental ballistic missiles, lie just over the horizon. Therefore, the Air Staff must "be advised continuously on the progress of scientific research and development in view of the potentialities of new discoveries and improvements in aerial warfare." The important thing is to maintain "a permanent interest of scientific workers in problems of the Air Forces." Doing so involves the creation of "a nucleus for scientific groups such as those which successfully assisted in the command and staff work in the field during the war. In these studies experts in statistical, technical, economic and political science must cooperate."

In these words, Von Karman laid out the blueprint for what would be called Air Force Project RAND.

In this respect, however, he only reinforced a movement already afoot and under the sturdy guidance of Hap Arnold, Ed Bowles and a few others, most notably Arthur Raymond, chief engineer at the Douglas Aircraft Company in Santa Monica, and his assistant Frank Collbohm.

Collbohm's introduction to Arnold came in 1942, when Douglas Aircraft was building A-20 airplanes for the British. The British wanted some night-flight capability, but had only primitive radar installations, which could barely make out the targets that pilots needed to see. Collbohm, who told Donald Douglas, president of the company, that he had heard something about a radar project going on at MIT, went to its Radiation Lab in Cambridge. Ed Bowles and Lee DuBridge, two scientists at the lab, took Collbohm up on the roof, where they had the radar operating. The sky was extremely foggy. All pilots were grounded, except for David Griggs, a physicist at the lab who owned a private plane and who had been given an exemption. He was at the moment flying over the MIT campus. Collbohm could not see him, but the radar was tracking him perfectly.

Collbohm repeated the tale about the MIT radar to Douglas and General Arnold, who were highly impressed. From that point on, Ed Bowles and the MIT Rad Lab were in with the Army Air Force, and so was Frank Collbohm. He was already a dollar-a-year consultant to the Secretary of War. Now he started to consult for Arnold, too, mostly on tactics and economics.

In 1944, Ed Bowles organized the first experiment in direct civilian scientific participation in American wartime planning, the B-29 Special Bombardment Project. He chose Arthur Raymond and Frank Collbohm to direct the effort. The Army Air Force was facing a severe logistical problem in the Far Eastern theater. Given the distances involved from accessible bases, it was very difficult to fly very many bombing sorties over Japan. Using OR techniques, Raymond and Collbohm and their team discovered that the range, speed and bomb-load capacity of the B-29 could be vastly increased by stripping away most of the plane's heavy defensive armor. They also calculated that doing so would make the B-29 fly much faster than any known Japanese fighter plane; hence the armor plating would not be missed. They recommended retaining only a tail gun and some armor in the rear to guard against possible random dive-bomb attacks from above. In the last weeks of the Pacific war, one wing of B-29s was stripped down in this fashion. General Curtis LeMay, commander of the XXI Bomber Command, reported to headquarters that never before had bombing been so precise.

As Collbohm gained a broader perspective on the war planning, he grew disturbed that many high-ranking military officers were winning the military phase of the war but losing sight of the larger objectives. For example, in their obsession with measuring effectiveness by gauging damage of production facilities, many officers wanted to bomb the coal mines of the Ruhr Valley. Collbohm and many other civilian consultants argued that the Germans were practically defeated, and that such rich resources should now be protected, not destroyed. Collbohm talked the situation over with Dave Griggs, Ed Bowles and others. They all agreed that the military could not afford to lose the technical and scientific community after the war.

When Collbohm aired his concerns to Arnold, the general agreed. "We have to keep the scientists on board," he said. "It's the most important thing we have to do."

Arnold immediately sent Collbohm back to Santa Monica to calculate how much money and what sorts of facilities and personnel would be needed for a new organization of scientists, similar to that urged by Von Karman, that would work for the military.

Throughout the summer of 1945, Collbohm made frequent trips to Washington to discuss the new organization with Arnold, Bowles, and Secretary of War Robert Patterson. In Santa Monica, he and Douglas talked a lot about it as well.

On September 30, Collbohm came to Arnold with a proposal from Don Douglas: Douglas Aircraft would agree to house an independent group of civilians to assist the Army Air Force in planning for future weapons development. Arnold was excited by the idea. Douglas had served the nation well in war. By the war's end, it was one of the largest aircraft manufacturers in the nation. And Don Douglas was a man Arnold could trust. They were longtime hunting-and-fishing friends and, two years earlier, Arnold's son had married Douglas' daughter. Arnold had already concluded that this new scientific organization probably could not be set up at a university, owing to the need for classified information; nor could it be inside the government, due to the relatively low pay scales of civil service. He had thought that industry was out of the question too, that possible conflicts of interest would make life difficult for the fledgling outfit. But if Don Douglas was willing and eager to take this thing on and get it moving, then maybe an industry connection would work after all.

Arnold called for a lunch meeting to be held the very next day at Hamilton Field, an Air Force base just outside San Francisco. Arnold and Collbohm, who were in Washington, borrowed President Truman's private plane to get there. Present at the meeting were Arnold, Collbohm, Ed Bowles, Don Douglas, Arthur Raymond and a few other representatives of Douglas Aircraft. The meeting was to the RAND Corporation what the Continental Congress had been to the United States. Years later, the comparison would be made self-consciously; the group that met at Hamilton

Field would be referred to in RAND folklore as "the founding fathers."

Arnold announced to those assembled that he had $30 mil-
lion left over, unspent, from his wartime research budget. He
wanted to divide that into three packages of $10 million each for
projects that would study techniques of intercontinental warfare.
He pledged one of the packages to Douglas: that would be enough to
finance the new group and to keep it standing on its own feet for
a few years, free from pressures to exhibit its achievements prematurely. Douglas wanted to start quickly, before the inevitable peacetime economy measures drastically reduced the output of his
company. Frank Collbohm said that he would hunt around for someone to direct the outfit and would lead it himself in the meantime. Arthur Raymond came up with the name RAND, standing
for "Research and Development." (Later, Curtis LeMay, noting
that RAND never produced any weapon, would waggishly say that
it should have stood for "Research and *No* Development.")

On December 1, 1945, General LeMay was appointed head of
a new directorate, Deputy Chief of Air Staff for Research and Development. The idea of establishing a separate high-level office to
deal with all R&D projects had been recommended by Theodore
Von Karman's *Toward New Horizons* report. Among LeMay's
tasks would be to watch over, provide guidance to, and protect
from all obstacles the new Project RAND. One of the first things
LeMay did was to call the representatives from all relevant commands into his office to determine the precise wording of the
RAND contract. Nobody was to leave the room until the language
was composed.

The job did not take long. The charter of RAND read:
"Project RAND is a continuing program of scientific study and research on the broad subject of air warfare with the object of recommending to the Air Force preferred methods, techniques and in-
strumentalities for this purpose." On March 1, 1946, Army Air
Force contract number MX-791 was signed. Project RAND was
born.

RAND started life as a four-man outfit housed in a walled-off
section on the second floor of the main Douglas Aircraft building
in Santa Monica. At the outset, they worked—along with some
Douglas engineers—strictly on technical and engineering problems: comparisons of rockets and ramjets, the use of titanium

alloys on supersonic airplanes, aerial refueling, bomber and fighter designs, nuclear propulsion, upper-atmosphere physics, new mathematical and statistical techniques. The project was attracting top-notch scientists and mathematicians, many of whom had worked during the war in OR divisions or on radar technology.

RAND's first report, released May 2, 1946, was called *Preliminary Design of an Experimental World-Circling Spaceship*, and it predicted that the launching into outer space of what would later be called a satellite "would inflame the imagination of mankind, and would probably produce repercussions in the world comparable to the explosion of the atomic bomb." Few paid attention in 1946, but eleven years later, when the Soviet Union put Sputnik in the sky, those words eerily rang true.

RAND was expanding. In March 1947, it was too large for the Douglas building so Douglas rented an abandoned newspaper plant in downtown Santa Monica and, soon after that move, portions of the buildings on all four corners of the intersection at Fourth and Broadway. (In 1953, RAND would build and move into the two-story pink building on the beach; in 1961, the five-story annex would be added.)

However, the connection with Douglas Aircraft was cracking. The company lost a few contract bids in the early days of RAND, and Don Douglas started to think that the Air Force might be leaning over backward to avoid the appearance of favoritism. RAND was becoming a financial liability, and Douglas' initial enthusiasm was rapidly cooling. By September 1946, Ed Bowles, still an "Expert Consultant" to the Secretary of War, complained to Hap Arnold that Project RAND "has been moving very, very slowly—so slowly, in fact, that the opposition in the Air Forces is sitting by, if I may say so, gloating over [its] impending failure. . . ." Especially concerned about these problems was Frank Collbohm, temporarily in charge of RAND. Collbohm started to look for a way that RAND might escape the clutches of Douglas Aircraft.

He called on Rowan Gaither, a wealthy San Francisco lawyer whom Collbohm had met during the war when Gaither was business manager of the MIT Radiation Lab. Gaither sat down with Collbohm, systematically listed the pros and cons of various ways to set up a reborn RAND, and concluded that the best technique was to establish RAND as an independent, non-profit corporation.

The idea met with Don Douglas' approval, and on January 26, 1948, Arthur Raymond and Larry Henderson of RAND asked for the legal consent of the Air Force general counsel. Raymond had been with Douglas since the war, had worked on the B-29 Special Bombardment Project with Collbohm. Henderson, another of the original RAND staff and now its Washington representative, had been in the Office of Scientific Research and Development as well as the MIT Rad Lab during the war and, before that, had picked up legal and business experience at Harvard Law School, Harvard Business School and, just before the war broke out, as assistant to the vice-president for foreign affairs at Chase National Bank.

After discussions with the RAND guardians, Air Force Chief of Staff General Carl Spaatz wrote to Douglas on February 10, granting consent "when we are satisfied that the new corporation is in existence and is capable of discharging the contract obligations as effectively as the Douglas Company."

Gaither advised Collbohm, Henderson and Raymond that they would need about $1 million to start a corporation. With the respectable Rowan Gaither as an active backer, they were promised a $600,000 line of credit from the Wells Fargo Bank of California as long as RAND came up with an initial $400,000.

Around this time, the Ford Foundation was in a state of flux, going through a major reorganization. Gaither knew this because of his connections with the foundation. (He would later become its chairman.) One Ford trustee, Donald David, was dean of the Harvard Business School and a former professor of Larry Henderson's. Gaither, Collbohm and Henderson traveled to Cambridge, Massachusetts, and persuaded David and a much more influential Ford trustee, Dr. Karl Compton, a famed MIT physicist, of their cause.

As a result of this lobbying effort, a meeting was arranged with Henry Ford II himself. Ford was enthusiastic and promised a $100,000 interest-free loan (which was later converted to an outright grant) and an additional $300,000 credit guarantee. They then returned to the Wells Fargo Bank, which now reduced its offer of credit from $600,000 to $150,000. Still, it was enough. An eminent board of trustees was established, chaired by Rowan Gaither. On May 14, 1948, RAND became an independent, nonprofit corporation, but of a rather strange breed—all of its contracts would still come from the Air Force. Collbohm, for the time being anyway, resisted suggestions even to broaden RAND's base to include contracts from the Office of the Secretary of Defense.

"Civilians come and go," Collbohm said. "The Air Force stays forever."

Even while RAND was still operating under Douglas Aircraft, even when things were far from smooth for top management, the civilian analysts of Project RAND were having a wonderful time. By the fall of 1947, they numbered 150. For anyone interested in some vague combination of mathematics, science, international affairs and national security, RAND offered a nearly ideal setting. There was an intense intellectual climate, but no teaching obligations or boring faculty meetings. There was access to military secrets, but no military officers from whom to take direct orders. There were brilliant minds working to solve fascinating problems. It was freewheeling, almost anarchic, virtually without hierarchy or separation among disciplines. One man invited to RAND in 1947 wrote in a memo, "I have been at RAND for three exciting days and I would like to become part of it. Right now RAND is part solid, part liquid, and part gas. . . ." It was run under Air Force contract, but that was all right. The Air Force was the only service that had the atom bomb; American security policy was based almost entirely on the bomb; therefore, Air Force policy essentially *was* national security policy, and Project RAND was the Air Force center of ideas.

Early in 1947, Olaf Helmer of the RAND mathematics division came up with an idea that would change the complexion of the Project. Helmer was a German refugee with two Ph.D.s, in mathematics and in logic, who emigrated to the United States in 1936, taught mathematical logic at the New School for Social Research and City College of New York, and during the war worked for a group on 57th Street in New York called the Applied Mathematics Panel, the OR unit of the Office of Scientific Research and Development. Helmer had been at RAND for a short time when he reflected on the possibility that RAND might be too limited in its outlook. Military problems, after all, were not just engineering or mathematical or physics problems; they involved questions that might better be investigated by economists or political scientists as well.

John Davis Williams, head of RAND's math division and a former colleague on the Applied Mathematics Panel, liked

Helmer's idea, made it his own and set off to persuade Frank Coll-bohm that RAND should have two new divisions, one in econom-ics and the other in social science.

Williams had come to RAND in 1946—he was the fifth RAND employee—on the recommendation of Warren Weaver, director of the Applied Math Panel during the war and social sci-ence chairman of the Rockefeller Foundation shortly after.

John Williams weighed close to 300 pounds. Trained as an astronomer, he was also an excellent pool shark, he would later write an article on TV wrestling for the promotional issue of *Sports Illustrated,* and he loved to supercharge and drive fast cars. He had loaded a Cadillac engine in his brown Jaguar sports coupe, and relished few things more than taking it out on midnight test runs at 155 miles per hour. (Williams might also be credited as the man who first applied radar to automobiles, building his very own "fuzz buster.")

Williams loved mathematical games and had for some time been particularly keen on a new chain of ideas called the "theory of games" or "game theory," devised by a mathematician named John von Neumann. Von Neumann was possibly the most brilliant man—certainly among the broader intellects—of the twentieth century. He was a cheery, roly-poly man, short and round-faced like a cherub. As a teen-ager, he was known to his friends as "Mr. Miracle" because of his great love for inventing mechanical toys. During World War II, he was chief mathematical wizard at the Manhattan Project. After the war, he taught at Princeton, but re-mained at Los Alamos as a consultant in the Theoretical Division, or T-Division, where—along with Edward Teller, Enrico Fermi, Lothar Nordheim and others—he became enraptured with the problems and principles of fusion energy and the hydrogen bomb.

Von Neumann grew up in Hungary, coming to the United States in the 1930s, retaining a bitter hatred of Communism, an uncharacteristically fervid emotion about the subject which lasted the rest of his days and which also allowed him—in contrast with J. Robert Oppenheimer and many other leading scientists of the day—to work enthusiastically on the H-bomb project with no moral qualms. "I think," von Neumann wrote to Lewis Strauss in November 1951, "that the USA-USSR conflict will very probably lead to an armed 'total' collision, and that a maximum rate of ar-manent is therefore imperative."

In 1951, fusion experiments were bogged down by the almost impossibly complicated mathematical calculations that the scientists had to work out. For assistance, they had only the ENIAC computer, whose memory could hold a mere 27 words and which was constantly on the blink. Von Neumann invented a new electronic computer that could hold 40,000 bits of information, recall them later, identify errors in the instructions that anyone fed it and correct the errors. When von Neumann displayed the machine to the Atomic Energy Commission, he gave it the high-sounding name of "Mathematical Analyzer, Numerical Integrator and Computer." Only later did officials see that von Neumann, forever the practical joker, had dubbed the machine with a name whose acronym spelled MANIAC.

A problem that previously would have taken three people three months to solve could now be worked out by the same three people in ten hours. The research on the H-bomb was, thanks to MANIAC, lifted out of its slump.

Through the late 1940s and early 1950s, von Neumann made frequent trips to RAND. John Williams, head of RAND's math division, adored Johnny von Neumann, and was thrilled when, in December 1947, he convinced von Neumann to join RAND as a part-time consultant. Williams would frequently try out immensely difficult math problems on von Neumann during his visits, but never stumped him. Von Neumann had the sort of mind that could routinely solve in his head the most elaborate calculations to the second or third decimal point.

In 1928, when he was twenty-four, von Neumann had sat in on a fateful poker game that set in motion a remarkable train of logical observations. First, he noted that a player's winnings and losses depended not only on his own moves, but also on the moves of the other players. In devising a strategy, he had to take into account the strategies of the other players, assuming that they too were rational; that, therefore, the essence of the good strategy was to win the game, regardless of what the other players did, even though, paradoxically, what the other players do determines, in part, the playing of the game.

Von Neumann then realized that the game of poker was fundamentally similar to the economic marketplace. Economists had been attempting to impose mathematical models on classical economic theory, but with no success. The reason for their failure, von Neumann reflected, was that the theory assumed an independent consumer trying to maximize his gains and independent sellers trying to maximize theirs—whereas, in fact, just as in the game of poker, the consumer and the seller formed a unit, competing but interdependent, and their moves could not be systematically analyzed or strategically planned except in the context of each other's moves. So it goes with any situation in which two or more players have a conflict of interest and in which a good deal of uncertainty is involved.

Von Neumann developed what ultimately came to be called "game theory" as a mathematically precise method of determining rational strategies in the face of critical uncertainties. The classical case of game theory is the Prisoners' Dilemma. Two prisoners, arrested on suspicion for the same crime, are kept in separate cells with no chance to communicate. They are separately approached by guards and given the following proposition: if neither squeals on the other, they will both serve brief sentences; if Prisoner A tells on B, but B keeps quiet, then A will be let free and B will serve maximum sentence; likewise, if B talks but A remains silent, then B will be freed and A forced to serve full sentence; if both A and B rat on each other, then they will serve half sentences. On the surface, it seems that it would serve both their interests to remain silent. However, there is a great deal of uncertainty. Prisoner A worries that Prisoner B might feel compelled to talk, since it would be to B's advantage to do so; if, under such circumstances, A does not talk, A serves a full jail sentence. Prisoner B is, of course, thinking similar thoughts about Prisoner A's possible moves. Therefore, both prisoners will talk and both will serve half jail sentences, even though both would have been better off keeping quiet.

According to game theory, moreover, both prisoners would be perfectly *rational* if they did talk. Both have to assume that the other prisoner, the other player, will play his best move; thus, each has to play the move that would be best for himself *given the best move of the other player*. That is the essence of game theory: find out your opponent's best strategy and act accordingly. Such a strategy may not get you the maximum gain, but it will prevent you from taking the maximum loss.

Von Neumann proved his theory with highly complex mathematics, which have never been disputed, and also illustrated his proof with some lower-level matrixes. The Prisoners' Dilemma can be outlined in a rather simple diagram.

PLAYER B

		TALK	SILENCE
	TALK	-.5,-.5	1,-1
PLAYER A			
	SILENCE	-1,1	.7,.7

The rows represent A's possible choices; the columns represent B's. The numbers in the boxes represent the values that they each place on the possible choices, with A's value cited first. If they both talk (-.5,-.5), they both serve half sentences; if one talks and the other remains silent (1,-1; -1,1), one goes free and the other serves full sentence; if both remain silent (.7,.7), they serve brief sentences.

If Player A is rational, he will scan his possible strategies and pick the one that gives him the least-worst payoff, no matter what strategy B picks. Talking could give him -.5, but remaining silent might give him -1, if B decides to talk. So A will go with the strategy of talking. Similarly, B's silence might give him a negative payoff of -1, whereas talking will reduce that loss by half. He too will talk. Von Neumann called that the "minimax solution"—the lowest maximum, the highest minimum.

Von Neumann wrote a scholarly paper on game theory in 1928 and created a minor sensation in the scientific and mathematical communities of Europe. The sensation exploded in 1944 when he and a Princeton economist named Oskar Morgenstern collaborated to write an enormous volume in English called *Theory of Games and Economic Behavior,* laying out the theory systematically, offering the mathematical proofs, suggesting applications of the theory to economics and the entire spectrum of social conflict.

It was a conservative theory and pessimistic as well. It said that it was irrational behavior for one to take a leap, do what is best for both parties and trust that one's opponent might do the same. In this sense, game theory was the perfect intellectual rationale for the Cold War, the vehicle through which many intellectuals bought on to its assumptions. It was possible to apply the Prisoners' Dilemma, for instance, to the Soviet-American arms race— substituting "Build More" for "Talk" and "Stop Building" for "Silence." It made sense for both sides to stop building, but neither could have the confidence to agree to a treaty to stop building arms (.7,.7), suspecting that the other might cheat, build more and go on to win (-1,1). Distrust and the fostering of international tensions could be elevated to the status of an intellectual construct, a mathematical axiom.

Game theory caught on in a very big way at RAND in the late 1940s. John Williams was particularly entranced with it, and wrote a very lively compendium of dozens of situations and anecdotes in which game theory could play a valuable role in guiding decisions. But there was a major limitation to game theory. For it to be used precisely, as a science, the analyst had to have some way of calculating what numbers should go in the matrixes. This would be particularly true in games not just of two-by-two matrixes—such as Prisoners' Dilemma—but three-by-three or five-by-five or ten-by-ten or any number of combinations. And then what about those games that involve not just two players but three or four or more? Then there were games where both players did not settle on the same box in the matrix, or had no logical reason to do so—where certain moves might be optimal 60 percent of the time, but other moves 40 percent of the time. In these cases, the players would have to play according to a mixture of random selection and the laws of probability, just as a good poker player bluffs systematically but randomly, so that his strategy is not discovered.

The numbers in each matrix box reflect a set of values that each player holds. Even in the simple Prisoners' Dilemma game, it is difficult for Player A to formulate strategy unless he knows the values of Player B. If B makes few distinctions between spending half his life in jail and all his life in jail, or if spending only a year or two in jail is practically as decent as being let free, then Player A would play a different strategy from the one played under the assumption that both sides had the same values.

In short, Williams realized that if game theory were to grow and have true relevance to economics problems or international conflict, and if RAND were to lead the way in this intellectual movement, then RAND would have to hire social scientists and economists who could study the "utility functions" of consumers and the actual behavior and values of various nations. The mathematicians, who certainly know nothing of such things, could then incorporate their findings into the matrixes of game theory.

So it was that John Williams—through the combination of

Olaf Helmer's suggestion and his own fascination with game theory—proposed that two new divisions that would broaden the
range and scope of RAND be created, one for social science and
the other for economics. At first, Collbohm failed to see much use
in having such divisions, nor could many of the RAND scientists,
especially the engineers, to whom the social sciences represented
something soft and unscientific. But Williams was brilliant, no
doubt about that, so Collbohm listened, became convinced and
agreed to set up a meeting in Washington with RAND's immediate Air Force boss, General Curtis LeMay. Attending the meeting
were Williams, Larry Henderson, LeMay and one of his aides,
General Tommy Power.

LeMay initially scoffed at the idea, but Williams patiently explained his idea and eventually won approval for his departments.
The task now was to find someone who could staff them. Allen
Wallis, a friend of Williams' from Applied Math Panel days and
now an economics professor at Stanford, suggested that he get in
touch with a fellow named Leo Rosten.

Rosten was leading one of the most varied careers in
America. He later acquired fame as the author of such books as
The Joys of Yiddish, Captain Newman, M.D., and the best-selling
novel *The Education of H*Y*M*A*N K*A*P*L*A*N*. Rosten had
been trained in political science and economics, mainly under
Jacob Viner, at the University of Chicago (where he and Wallis
were classmates) and the London School of Economics. Shortly
after graduating, he was awarded one of the first fellowships
granted by the Social Science Research Council. After that, he
moved to Beverly Hills and, under the name Leonard Ross, wrote
screenplays for Hollywood studios.

When the war broke out, Rosten joined the Office of War Information and supervised analyses of public opinion, enemy morale, how to deal with enemy interrogation if captured, the sociology of Nazism and other aspects of psychological warfare. But his
most important position, taken mostly at his own initiative, was
key point of liaison between Washington and Hollywood, convincing the government to use the expressive medium of the movies to
educate the public on what the war was all about, and persuading
studio executives to join the effort as well. Dozens of talented
screenwriters and cinematographers joined the Signal Corps' film

unit, making training films for soldiers and aircraft companies and shooting battle scenes of the war itself for documentary shorts.

Rosten also got Walt Disney to make animated propaganda and instructional films. Disney had refused all previous efforts to get him involved in government projects, but he liked Leo Rosten, the only intellectual he knew who had not criticized Disney for making movies that frightened small children. Disney's grandest war film was *Victory Through Air Power,* an extraordinary display of Giulio Douhet's theories of air power captured in animation. The climax was powerful: Japan becomes a monstrous octopus, its gigantic tentacles unfurled across the Pacific; American B-29 bombers turn into bold eagles, spitting out hundreds of bombs, sinking the octopus to the depths of the ocean floor.

Rosten seemed the perfect man to help coordinate the beginnings of a RAND social science division. He could write well, he had been trained in the social sciences, he had wartime experience, worked with propaganda and public opinion, knew civilian and military officials in Washington, and had contacts with the aircraft industry. Rosten agreed to come work for RAND part-time, joining the mathematics division until the social science unit was established.

By day, Leo Rosten was writing a screenplay called *The Velvet Touch,* a murder mystery slated to star Rosalind Russell. When night fell, Rosten worked on the psychological and political uses of an earth-circling satellite for Project RAND. Nobody in Hollywood knew anything about the nocturnal side of Rosten's life—not his agent, not his studio, not the stars or producers or directors with whom he worked all day.

Meanwhile, along with a logician in the math division named Abraham Kaplan (who would later write one of the seminal books on logical exposition), Rosten was also drawing up a list of social scientists who might be invited to a conference that RAND was planning to hold. The conference was John Williams' idea. The purpose was to gather together some of the nation's most promising, if not already prominent, social scientists, to discuss how they might apply the techniques of social science to problems of national security.

In August 1947, Rosten and Williams traveled from Santa Monica to New York by train. (Williams, for all his derring-do as a road speedster and for all his futuristic visions of intercontinental

missiles and interplanetary travel, was deathly afraid of airplanes.) For the next few days, bright young professors from Columbia, Princeton, Yale and other top-notch universities from
around the area came to be interviewed by Leo Rosten about a social science department at some place most of them had never
heard of before called Project RAND.

Rosten had already decided on whom he wanted as director
of the social science division, a German refugee named Hans
Speier. Rosten knew Speier from the Office of War Information,
where Speier had worked in the overseas branch of the propaganda policy administration. Speier had come to the United States
from Germany in 1933 and joined the sociology department at the
New School for Social Research in New York, often called the
"university in exile" because of all the German refugees who
taught there. Speier worked on a Rockefeller Foundation project
analyzing totalitarian propaganda and, during the war, published
a widely read book on German radio propaganda. Speier was somewhat shy and self-effacing, but he matched Rosten's conception
of what kind of person should be leading the new division at
RAND.

Meanwhile, John Williams was tracking down a few people
himself. For the director of the new economics division, Williams
was drawn to Charles Hitch. In 1947, Hitch was settled and comfortable teaching economics at Oxford, and was spending the
summer at the University of São Paolo in Brazil, when Williams
tracked him down and invited him to a RAND Conference of Social Scientists, to be held in New York from September 19 to 24.

Hitch was instinctively attracted to the idea. During the war,
he had done OR work in an Anglo-American section of the OSS
called Research and Experiments Department Number 8 (or RE-
8, for short), under the direction of RAF Wing Commander Dun-
can Dewdney, who had been an oil engineer before the war broke
out. Housed in wooden shacks in the small village of Princes Risborough, twenty miles east of Oxford and not far from RAF headquarters at High Wycombe, RE-8 was in the business of assessing
the effects of the strategic bombing campaign against Germany.
They were given photographs of roof damage taken from airplanes
flying directly over the bomb targets after each raid. RE-8 analyzed the photos, used various statistical techniques to calculate
the effects of the bombing on the German war economy, civilian

casualties and enemy morale, and then filed reports to the RAF and the United States Eighth Air Force stationed in England.

RE-8's techniques were clever, if nothing else. Its analysts first obtained overhead photos of *British* buildings that had been bombed by Germany. They analyzed the roof damage, correlated that with readily available data on the economic effects of the bombing—in terms of decline in war production, casualties and worker absenteeism—and, from all this, worked out a mathematical formula that would translate an assessment of roof damage into an estimate of the bomb's overall effect.

When analyzing the bombing over Germany, they reversed the procedure. They had the roof damage from the photoreconnaissance flights. They assessed that damage, and then plugged in the formula that they had worked out from the British data to estimate the probable effects of the bombing on the German economy. They coupled this with a statistical index devised by R. E. Fisher, an Oxford don and prominent biological statistician. Called the "mean area of effectiveness," this index used the estimates of bomb damage to measure how far from the target a bomb had exploded.

It was hardly the most reliable or solid statistical technique ever conceived, but it was the best that RE-8 could do under the circumstances. Many of their reports foretold what the *U.S. Strategic Bombing Survey* would more conclusively observe after the war: that, in the British night bombing over Germany, only between one-third and one-half of the bombs dropped hit the right city, much less any particular industrial complex; that, except for the bombing of transportation and liquid fuels toward the very end of the war, those bombs that did strike targets damaged the German war economy only slightly. (Years later, after reading the *Bombing Survey*, Hitch would judge that in retrospect RE-8, for all its pessimism, had generally *over*estimated the effects of the bombing.)

From this experience, Hitch learned that there was a role for this sort of analysis outside the classroom, that even fairly crude economic and statistical computations could contribute substantially to the formulation of strategic military policy. It was with this in mind that Hitch accepted John Williams' invitation to come to New York in September.

•

There was a good turnout at the New York Economic Club the first day of the RAND conference. Thirty scholars of various sorts showed up, along with several RAND employees. Among the curious were Bernard Brodie, Bill Fox and Harold Lasswell of Yale, Charles Hitch, Hans Speier, political scientist Franz Neumann and anthropologist Ruth Benedict of Columbia, Jacob Viner, then at Princeton. Leo Rosten, who planned the conference, could not make it: he had to attend a sneak preview of *The Velvet Touch*.

John Williams saw the conference as a way of sizing up people who might be good for RAND and then trying to recruit them. It would also be an opportunity, as he put it, "to discuss any research relevant to the broad topics of the identification, measurement and control of factors important in (1) the occurrence of war, and (2) the winning of war if it should occur."

John Williams' mentor and idol, Warren Weaver, who was also a RAND consultant, delivered the opening address. He talked about his having spent nearly one-fourth of his life working for the military in two world wars. He talked about the work in operations research during the last war. He explained that RAND was greatly interested in the concept of "military worth," in seeing "to what extent it is possible to have useful quantitative indices for a gadget, a tactic or a strategy, so that one can compare it with available alternatives and guide decisions by analysis. . . ."

After the conference, John Williams urged Hans Speier and Charlie Hitch to join RAND and become the first directors of the social science and economics divisions, respectively. Speier agreed. Hitch was more difficult, but after what he would later call the most agonizing decision in his life, Hitch agreed to quit academia in December and come to RAND.

At that conference the previous September, there was one particularly revealing remark that Warren Weaver made very early on in his opening address. "I assume that every person in this room is fundamentally interested in and devoted to what can broadly be called the rational life," he said. "He believes fundamentally that there is something to this business of having some knowledge . . . and some analysis of problems, as compared with living in a state of ignorance, superstition and drifting-into-whatever-may-come."

"The rational life" might have served well as an emblem of the RAND style. And with a social science and an economics divi-

sion, RAND was about to start pursuing it along a slightly different dimension. Before, RAND had confined itself essentially to
studying the technical aspects of the instruments of warfare.
Now, some of those at RAND, anyway, would start to study the
strategy of warfare, would try to impose the order of the rational
life on the almost unimaginably vast and hideous maelstrom of nuclear war.

5 THE SUPERBOMB

LATE IN 1951, a very small number of physicists at the RAND Corporation started to learn a great deal about a new and fantastic weapon that would dwarf all weapons before it. Some called it the "Super," because it could release 1,000 times as much explosive energy as the atomic bombs that were dropped over Hiroshima and Nagasaki at the end of the war. It was a thermonuclear weapon, the hydrogen bomb.

Only through a great deal of effort and a bit of luck did RAND learn of this development at all. Information about anything related to atomic weapons was tightly held. A "Q" clearance—the very restrictive Atomic Energy Commission code word for all atomic-energy data—was required before one could even hear the magic phrase "intercontinental ballistic missile." Special subsets of Q were needed to learn much more. Before 1947, the AEC denied these special clearances to anyone at RAND, a state that would have made research in the area of atomic bombs impossible. In July of that year, however, after General LeMay turned on some pressure, the AEC gave in and granted clearances to a few analysts. By October, the Air Force made it clear to the AEC that RAND would be increasingly active in studies on weapons design, weapons effects and targeting. The restrictions were loosened still further.

Early in 1948, a physics division was set up at RAND, with initially a staff of three—the director, David Griggs, Ernst Plesset and Sam Cohen. Shortly after, Griggs went to teach at UCLA (though he stayed at RAND part-time), Plesset took over the division and others joined. During the war, Plesset had done instrumentation work at Douglas Aircraft and was the only physicist in the company. He joined RAND in its all but earliest days. In 1949, he took some time off to work at the JCS Weapons Systems Evaluation Group in Washington. Plesset was in Washington the day the Russians exploded their first atomic bomb. So, by coincidence, was Edward Teller, a brash, brilliant, charismatic Hungarian émigré who had been a physicist on the Manhattan Project, and who was devoting most of his time trying to convince people that the United States should actively pursue research on fusion technology, the process that would make a hydrogen bomb implode. It was Plesset who brought Teller in touch with several high-ranking Air Force officers, just after the Soviet explosion, to talk about atomic energy and the Super.

Plesset remained close friends with Teller, and—like most of the RAND physicists—had fairly close contacts at the Los Alamos weapons laboratory. Through these connections, and especially through Teller, Plesset learned in 1951 that the H-bomb appeared feasible; that Teller and another physicist, Stanislaw Ulam, had worked out its physics and its design, at least theoretically; that certain implosion devices had been tested; that it would almost certainly be only a matter of time (and money) before an operational Superbomb became a major part of the U.S. Strategic Air Command arsenal.

Plesset knew that Frank Collbohm, RAND's president, loved a good secret and this was the greatest of the decade, maybe the century. Plesset told Collbohm that the H-bomb was soon to be a reality. Then he made a proposition. What if a few RAND analysts got together and analyzed the implications of such a weapon—its physics, its destructive magnitude, its technical and strategic and military implications. RAND could time the study so that it would be ready for briefings at just the moment that Los Alamos officially announced the weapon's feasibility to the Administration. Everyone would be interested in hearing the briefing—the Air Staff, the Secretary of Defense, the Secretary of State, probably the President of the United States. RAND could make a substantial dent on the course of history.

Plesset had already arranged such a deal with Los Alamos director Norris Bradbury, using a similar sort of appeal. When you announce the bomb's feasibility, Plesset had told Bradbury, Los Alamos should be in a position to interpret its implications, and that's where RAND comes in.

Bradbury had agreed. So, predictably, did Collbohm.

The physics division was generally not on good terms with much of the rest of RAND. For security reasons, an electronic door separated the physicists from all the other divisions. Physi-

76   FRED KAPLAN

cists looked down on social science and economics: their attitude
was that doing things like designing a bomb was real science, and
that the business about analysis was peripheral at best.

By the early 1950s, even John Williams was disappointed
with the social science division. It wasn't turning out to be what
he had envisioned its becoming. He privately referred to Hans
Speier, the division's director, as "that Prussian staff officer." He
thought that Speier was running the place too much like some
Teutonic library, that too many of the people Speier hired were
using RAND as a base from which they could research their doctoral dissertations.

The physicists were particularly scornful. They had no use
for even the best material produced by the social science group.
Once, Hans Speier approached Herman Kahn, a frantically voluble analyst in the physics division, thinking he would score points
on Kahn by raising the subject of a book that Nathan Leites of the
social science division had written, *The Operational Code of the
Politburo,* which had been hailed by reviewers as the first systematic analysis of how the Kremlin makes the decisions.

"Doesn't something like the Leites book change your opinion
of the social science division?" Speier asked.

"I read *The New York Times,*" Kahn responded. "What the
hell should I read Nathan Leites for?"

In return, many of the social science and economics divisions
looked upon the physicists as arrogant elitists who knew nothing
about politics, who foolishly thought that all problems could be
solved by hardware, and whose inbred tendencies and extreme secrecy were inimical to the pursuit of scholarship and to the very
purpose of RAND.

Still, for this project on the implications of the hydrogen
bomb, Plesset knew that the other divisions of RAND would be of
invaluable assistance. He picked three other analysts to work on
the project with him: Charlie Hitch, head of the economics division; Jim Lipp, head of the missiles division; and Bernard Brodie, a
new employee with social science.

The choices were the obvious ones to make. Hitch had assessed bomb damage in World War II. He would be ideal for calculating how much damage the hydrogen bomb could do to the
Soviet economy. Brodie had written *the* book on the strategic implications of the atomic bomb, *The Absolute Weapon,* and had
done targeting analysis for General Vandenberg. He would be best

for thinking through this new weapon's strategic impact. Lipp, a highly competent scientist who had directed RAND's project on earth-circling satellites, was assigned the task of figuring out the tactical implications of the H-bomb in a European war. Plesset gave himself the job of presenting details on the Super's technical aspects, with assistance from others in the physics division who would do some calculations for him without knowing of this particular project's existence. It was a very secretive affair.

In December 1951, the four-man team began work. At the beginning, it was a rather mechanical task. Plesset knew from Los Alamos scientists that the H-bomb could release the explosive energy of one million or five million or ten or twenty million tons of TNT. The Nagasaki bomb, by comparison, had released the equivalent of twenty *thousand* tons—or twenty kilotons. A new term had been invented for the grander scale of the H-bomb: *megaton*. Plesset and some others in physics drew some "lay-down" circles, indicating the radius of various types of damage—blast, heat, prompt radiation (nobody as yet knew about fallout)—produced by bombs of one to twenty megatons. Hitch, Brodie and Lipp took these circles and laid them over maps of various kinds of targets—cities, built-up industrial complexes, battlefields—scaled to the same dimension as the circles.

Suddenly the work was not so merely mechanical anymore. It became, for some on the project, the most dissettling and gruesome work they had ever encountered.

Charlie Hitch had grown somewhat inured to looking at the consequences of strategic bombing while working at RE-8 in England during World War II. But the analysts at RE-8 had measured the damage in terms of thousands of square feet. Plesset's damage circles showed that a five- or ten-megaton hydrogen bomb would kill people within 50 square *miles* of ground zero, and would severely burn people's skin and topple buildings within 300 square miles. At RE-8, Hitch had dealt with bombing raids involving hundreds of airplanes, producing thousands—at the very most, tens of thousands—of civilian casualties. Laying Plesset's circles on various maps revealed that a mere fifty-five H-bombs of twenty megatons each would completely wipe out the fifty largest cities of the Soviet Union, killing *thirty-five million* Russians, all in a matter of minutes. And that assumed that the urban population would have the protection of World War II-type shelters. Even when Hitch, along with Brodie, tried to simulate attacks that would damage the most important industrial complexes while minimizing casualties, ten or eleven million Soviet civilians would die.

A later generation of defense analysts would toss these figures around with casual aplomb; but in early 1952, nobody had ever dreamed of such massive destruction. Nobody had ever killed 35 million people on a sheet of paper before. To those who did it for the first time, the experience was shocking, disturbing and painful.

Charlie Hitch's wife called John Williams' wife one morning and asked, "What's happening at RAND? Charlie comes home, he barely says hello, he's uncivil, and after dinner he just locks himself up in his study. Something terrible is going on there."

For Jim Lipp, it was too much to bear. He was a gentle man, the sort of person who told friends that when it came to nuclear weapons, he cared about his grandchildren and his grandchildren's grandchildren. Lipp laid Plesset's damage circles over a map of Western Europe to see how many soldiers and civilians would be killed if H-bombs were used on the battlefield. After doing some calculations, he discovered that, even under the best of circumstances, nearly two million people would be killed. He nearly threw up. After three weeks of this sort of work, lasting late into the night nearly every night, Lipp dropped out of the project. (His work was taken over by Ed Paxson of RAND's mathematics division, and was eventually incorporated into Brodie's portion of the briefing.)

Bernard Brodie was supposed to think about the strategic implications of all this. The calculations of bomb damage done by his colleagues pushed Brodie even further along a line of thinking that he had begun to pursue one year earlier while examining the U.S. targeting plans for General Hoyt Vandenberg, Air Force Chief of Staff. At that time, Brodie had concluded that the indiscriminate bombing of Soviet cities would be militarily ineffective and would only prompt the Soviets to destroy American cities in return; that damaging *some* Soviet targets, while leaving their cities intact, could give the United States some bargaining power after a war had already started; that we could threaten the Soviets by saying, "Back off or we'll hit your cities with our remaining weapons"; that those remaining weapons would not only serve to *deter* the Soviets from destroying American cities, but might also *compel* them to come to the peace tables.

The hydrogen bomb reinforced Brodie's thinking and also stretched it. At least with the A-bomb there were still a few restraints. To destroy some targets, the bombs would have to be fairly accurate, and that posed several problems. But the RAND team's calculations revealed that the *hydrogen* bomb was so powerful that it could miss targets by two miles or more and still destroy whatever target anyone might want to hit. With the A-bomb, there was the problem of scarcity of fissionable materials. Even before the H-bomb, this problem was gradually being solved by an acceleration in the production of these materials. But the H-bomb eliminated the problem entirely: just one bomb could destroy the largest Soviet or American city, along with every important industrial target in it.

Before this project, Brodie had decided that the atomic bomb was "not so absolute a weapon that we can disregard the limits of its destructive power," and that, therefore, the "problem of target selection, for example, [was] still important." The hydrogen bomb, however, "makes strategic bombing very efficient, perhaps all too efficient. We no longer need to argue whether the conduct of war is an art or a science—it is neither." A theme that Brodie had composed during his Pentagon days emerged much more clearly: "The art or science comes in only in finding out, if you're interested, what *not* to hit."

A few months earlier, Brodie had not understood the famous dictum of Karl von Clausewitz, the nineteenth-century Prussian warrior-philosopher—the much-cited expression, "War is a continuation of policy by other means." Brodie had thought, and had even written, that a war fought with atomic bombs would be "much too violent to fit into any concept of a continuation of diplomacy." However, since learning of the H-bomb's enormously destructive power, Brodie came to see that Clausewitz was saying something extraordinarily profound—"that war is violence . . . but it is planned violence and therefore controlled. And since the objective should be rational, the procedure for accomplishing that objective should also be rational, which is to say that the procedure and the objective must be in some measure appropriate to each other."

Applying this to the new age of the hydrogen bomb, Brodie concluded that there could no longer be anything rational about the strategic bombing of any target that lies inside the Soviet Union. That would only spark Soviet retaliation, with monumentally destructive effect in the United States. Brodie realized that "national objectives cannot be consonant with national suicide"—and "there is no use talking about a mutual exchange of nuclear weapons, including the type of the future [the H-bomb], as being anything other than national suicide."

Still, in the evolution of his thinking over the past six years, Brodie came to see that war must have objectives, and while he was never among those who thought war with the U.S.S.R. imminent, he did think it was possible. In that case, how could a nation use something like the hydrogen bomb in such a way that the "procedure" would be commensurate with the "objective"? One thing seemed clear at the time to Brodie and to nearly all of his contemporaries: "We seem to be destined or doomed," as Brodie put it, "to a permanent inferiority [to the U.S.S.R.] in numbers of men on the ground in Western Europe." One way of compensating for this inferiority was through superior firepower, and it was "quite clear that weapons of this sort plus the conventional nuclear weapon introduce a fantastic augmentation of firepower.

"Strategic bombing has been defined as that action which destroys the war-making capacity of the enemy," Brodie said in a top-secret Air War College lecture, delivered in April 1952. "But I have the feeling that burning up his armies, if you can accomplish it, does the same thing. One may be as easy as the other, and certainly we shouldn't have to do both." A problem with battlefield use of atomic weapons was trying to locate precisely where the opposing armies might be. With the H-bomb, the point became moot. You could wipe out entire rear areas of whole divisions. Thus, "if . . . nuclear weapons would actually enable us to break and burn the Soviet armies on the ground wherever they might commit aggression, we might decide that it was possible, I won't say to win a war, but to secure our objectives without bombing enemy cities."

It wasn't that Brodie was wildly enthusiastic about the prospect of fighting a thermonuclear war in Europe. Who could be after examining those sickening circles of damage that Jim Lipp had laid down on a map of the Continent? Brodie's advocacy was more an argument of desperation. The Soviet Union appeared to have preponderance in non-nuclear forces. If the Red Army did start moving across the plains of West Germany, there was, to Brodie's mind, nothing to be done except to start dropping nuclear bombs.

The argument was similar to the one made by J. Robert Oppenheimer, the great physicist and director of the wartime Manhattan Project, the "father of the atom bomb," as he was often called. In the fall of 1951, Oppenheimer had been involved in a study at the California Institute of Technology called Project Vista. Its basic conclusion: "bring the battle back to the battlefield"—essentially for the same reasons that Brodie outlined in his H-bomb study the following winter. With something so powerful as the H-bomb, strategic bombing of Soviet cities made no sense, it was immoral, and it was probably also suicidal.

Brodie knew Oppenheimer. They first met in September 1947, when Oppenheimer delivered a lecture at the National War College in Washington, D.C., and Brodie introduced him. In February 1951, while Brodie was working for General Vandenberg, he and Oppenheimer talked at least three times, mostly about the nation's nuclear targeting plans and how they might be changed. It is unclear whether either of the two influenced the other, but they were certainly thinking along the same track.

Brodie would later change his views on the feasibility of battlefield nuclear war—and then he would change his views again, for a variety of intellectual and personal reasons. But one problem that Brodie would continue to grapple with, and one that would come to preoccupy the minds of other RAND strategists a few years later, was the dilemma of how in the thermonuclear age to integrate the enormous power of the hydrogen bomb with a set of sensible war aims and national objectives, how to impose force effectively without committing "national suicide," how to use the H-bomb *rationally*.

For all the horror surrounding the hydrogen bomb, Brodie, Hitch and Plesset all agreed that the nation had to go ahead and build the new weapon. There was hardly any discussion of the issue. The Russians had the atom bomb; they could probably build the hydrogen bomb at some point if they wanted to do so; we had to get it first. That was the basic line of thinking. The Cold War was heating up; the Korean War was being waged (and almost everyone assumed at the time that it was being directed from the Kremlin); not very many, in this environment, were thinking about starting disarmament talks or unilaterally holding back on developing a major new weapon of unprecedented power.

The Plesset-Hitch-Brodie briefing on the "Implications of

Large-Yield Nuclear Weapons" was a hit on the Washington national-security circuit. As Plesset had predicted, nearly everyone with a "need to know" wanted to hear it—members of the Air Staff, Secretary of the Air Force Finletter, Chief of Staff Vandenberg. It was an extremely secret and sensitive matter. In March 1952, after the briefing had been delivered a few times, Brodie discreetly wrote to Air Force General Roscoe Charles Wilson, who knew about the project: "Ernie Plesset and I have been on the road with a show advertising the merits of Supersuds Soap. There has been a large demand for both our act and our product among those who need the latter for polishing considerable brass fittings."

That month, without the presence of Hitch or Brodie, Ernie Plesset briefed Secretary of Defense Robert Lovett and, after that, Secretary of State Dean Acheson and AEC Commissioner Gordon Dean. Plesset gave them the entire briefing, and then told them something that made the H-bomb more attractive still: that the weapon did not require tritium, the heavy hydrogen isotope, H_3, which was so difficult and expensive, at the time, to squeeze out and which most people with some knowledge of the H-bomb thought was absolutely critical to its workings. (Plesset had not told this to Hitch or Brodie: their security clearances did not entail access to information so sensitive as that.)

Acheson had previously opposed the H-bomb, but now—after realizing the magnitude of it and hearing that it would work and be relatively cheap to manufacture—changed his mind. Later that month, Larry Henderson, RAND's vice-president in Washington, who had sat in on several of the briefings and by now knew it very well, delivered the briefing to President Harry Truman.

Few who heard the briefing took to heart Bernard Brodie's deepest point—that strategic bombing no longer had any purpose. However, many were quite taken with his idea that the thermonuclear weapon could be invaluable in stopping the Red Army on the battlefield. The portions by Plesset and Hitch were seen as nothing less than stunning: the calculations revealing the immense blast damage, the fireball that could burn up an entire city, the intense heat, the incredibly massive damage that could be done to a modern industrial economy by just a few dozen bombs in a few short seconds.

The briefings constituted a major coup for the fledgling RAND Corporation. They helped muster a great deal of support for a go-ahead decision on the H-bomb, and also helped to overcome a major obstacle. The obstacle, curiously, was Los Alamos. The scientists at the weapons lab were unenthusiastic about the H-bomb. They held Robert Oppenheimer in almost godlike awe, and Oppenheimer, as head of the AEC's General Advisory Committee, had recommended halting the hydrogen-bomb project, believing that the H-bomb would be far more destructive than any military considerations might require and that it might prompt the Soviets to build one, too.

In battle with Oppenheimer was Edward Teller, pushing the case *for* the H-bomb as if his life depended on it. Teller was a Hungarian refugee, an almost fanatical anti-Communist with particular loathing for the Soviet Union. He was an ingenious man, impatient, furious, driven, constantly seeking the bigger-than-life problems, the ultimate mind-bending puzzle. In the early 1930s, when Teller was in his twenties, he and fellow physicist and friend Otto Frisch spent a weekend in the country with physicist Niels Bohr. On the train ride back, Teller—not having worked for two days—grew extremely restless. He kept pestering Frisch: "Have you got a problem for me to solve?" Finally, Frisch gave him a problem: put eight queens on a chessboard in such a way that none could take another. Teller thought for twenty minutes, then called out the squares on which the queens should be placed. "Do you have another problem for me?" he asked Frisch. Then another, and another.

Teller was almost obsessively attracted to the grand problem of fusion, the process that would make a bomb of theoretically limitless size implode. Teller had worked on the Manhattan Project. By 1944, the physics of the A-bomb had essentially been solved; the rest was an engineering problem. That held no fascination for Teller. At his own initiative, against the wishes of his colleagues, Teller started a project experimenting with fusion, many months before even the *fission* bomb had proved successful.

After the war, Teller continued to lobby hard for fusion, making important connections within the Air Force and key congressional committees. Teller was still at Los Alamos, but finally quit, disturbed by the lab's slow progress on the H-bomb. Teller decided to launch a second weapons lab, one that could competitively force Los Alamos into the H-bomb business or, failing that, develop the H-bomb all on its own.

Ernie Plesset was an ally of Teller's in this endeavor, as were

84

84 FRED KAPLAN

many in the RAND physics division. A split was rupturing the entire nation's scientific community—big bomb versus small bomb, Teller versus Oppenheimer. The RAND physicists, respectful as they were of Oppenheimer, sided with Teller. The rupture came to a climax in 1953, when Oppenheimer was declared a "security risk," and had his clearances stripped. This scandalous blackballing was set in motion initially by Air Force reaction to Oppenheimer's stance against the H-bomb and his opposition to bombing Soviet cities, in short his opposition to *the* mission of the U.S. Air Force.

When Oppenheimer demanded hearings the following year and the Atomic Energy Commission obliged, two of the main witnesses testifying against him were Edward Teller and the former director of the RAND physics division, David Griggs. It was Griggs who, as Air Force chief scientist in 1951–52, had first found out about what Oppenheimer's Project Vista was up to ("bring the battle back to the battlefield"), a discovery that—as Griggs testified at Oppenheimer's hearings—prompted him to entertain "serious questions as to the loyalty of Dr. Oppenheimer."

Ernie Plesset, Charlie Hitch and Bernard Brodie were horrified by the implications of this new weapon that they were the first to analyze systematically. Yet their study and their briefings helped build and solidify political support for the approval of the H-bomb and of Teller's proposal to build a special laboratory to manufacture it. If, as Robert Oppenheimer had remarked, "the physicists have known sin," the social scientists now became active collaborators.

In September 1952, the new lab was established in Livermore, thirty-three miles southeast of Berkeley, under the auspices of the University of California. On November 1, the first hydrogen bomb—produced at Los Alamos—was exploded, as part of codeword Operation Ivy, off the Eniwetok atoll in the Pacific. They called the bomb Mike. It exploded with the power of twelve megatons, causing the tiny island of Elugelab, the site of the blast, to vanish from the face of the earth.

Teller "watched" the explosion on a seismograph machine at Berkeley. In a fit of joy, he wired a three-word telegram to Norris Bradbury, director of Los Alamos: "It's a boy."

6 THE VULNERABILITY STUDY

For Bernard Brodie, as well as many others who examined its effects and implications, the hydrogen bomb made nuclear war between the superpowers a most unlikely event. If in 1946 Brodie had concluded that the atomic bomb would deter aggression so long as the United States maintained an ability to "retaliate in kind," then the H-bomb, compressing as much as 1,000 times the explosive power of the Nagasaki bomb into a single weapon, would deter nuclear aggression to a still greater degree.

The key condition, however, was assuring "retaliation in kind." In *The Absolute Weapon,* Brodie wrote that doing so meant keeping the atomic arsenal far away from the targets of an atomic attack. Through the late 1940s, Brodie had thought that the logical targets to attack would be a nation's large cities, since the materials needed for making a bomb were too scarce for hitting much else. By 1952, it was clear that the United States would have an abundance of bombs and materials with which to manufacture more. But the strategic concepts from the brief period of atomic scarcity had struck, as if by analytic habit.

Brodie was hardly alone in his thinking. The U.S. Air Force was concentrating its air-defense weapons around the large cities of the northeast. When the Joint Chiefs contemplated the most likely targets of a Soviet attack against the United States, they listed the nation's most critical industrial plants. When war planners thought about which targets to hit inside the Soviet Union, which routes the SAC bombers should fly and how they should be refueled, they always assumed that SAC would be able to use its entire force of bombers, minus a few that would probably break down or get shot down along the way. They always assumed —sometimes tacitly, often explicitly—that the United States would naturally get in the first blow.

But around the same time that Ernie Plesset, Charlie Hitch and Bernard Brodie were contemplating the implications of the H-bomb, another RAND analyst was mulling over a different set of questions. What if the *Soviets* got in the first blow? And what if instead of heading toward American cities, the Soviet bombers set out to destroy the American SAC force, which at the time was concentrated on a small number of air bases overseas? If the Soviets chose that tactic and succeeded, then the United States might not have very many weapons surviving the attack for "retaliation in kind," meaning that the Kremlin might see some incentive—and some possibility of winning a nuclear war—in launching a surprise attack, *à la* Pearl Harbor, catching all of SAC on the ground. If they could pull off such an attack, then all previous calculations about the costs and risks of starting a nuclear war would be toppled completely and American security would suddenly appear to be in a grim state.

The analyst pondering all this was Albert J. Wohlstetter, a mathematical logician only recently hired as a consultant by the RAND economics division. Wohlstetter did not reach that conclusion, or even that particular formulation of the problem, all at once. It came through a series of reactions to other studies going on at RAND about the same time—a historical study by Wohlstetter's wife, Roberta, in RAND's social science division, some military applications of John von Neumann's theory of games by the mathematics and economics divisions, and, especially, some work in an entirely new field called "systems analysis" being done by a RAND mathematician named Edwin Paxson.

Ed Paxson had come to RAND in 1947, invited by John Williams, who worked with him during World War II at the Applied Mathematics Panel in New York. Paxson was ingenious, rude, abrasive, a driven man, hardworking, hard-drinking, chain-smoking. A RAND analyst would typically brief his colleagues about a project on which he was working before writing it up as a formal report. It was great sport to sit around and blast holes in the briefer's analysis, one of RAND's favorite intellectual games. But Paxson was brutal at it. At one briefing, the poor object of his scorn and derision grew so nervous that he finally fainted.

At RAND, Paxson invented the term "systems analysis." It differed from the "operational research" of World War II in one critical respect. An operational researcher answered the question: what is the best that can be done, given the following equipment having the following characteristics? The systems analyst, as Paxson conceived of the notion, would answer a more creative question: here is the mission that some weapon must accomplish—

what kind of equipment, having what sorts of characteristics, would be best for the job? In short, the systems analyst becomes a military planner in his own right.

When Paxson first came to RAND, the management decided not to put him in any single division. Instead, they dubbed him "The Systems Analyst," and allowed him to dream up his own projects and borrow assistants from any of the various departments. Paxson was the numbers-cruncher *par excellence.* He loved to devise and try to solve equations of gargantuan dimension, the more numbers and variables and mathematical complexities the better. His dream was to quantify every single factor of a strategic bombing campaign—the cost, weight and payload of each bomber, its distance from the target, how it should fly in formation with other bombers and their fighter escorts, their exact routing patterns, the refueling procedures, the rate of attrition, the probability that something might go wrong in each step along the way, the weight and accuracy of the bomb, the vulnerability of the target, the bomb's "kill probability," the routing of the planes back to their bases, the fuel consumed, and all extraneous phenomena such as the weather—and put them all into a single mathematical equation.

Paxson had boundless faith in the potential of systems analysis. For several years, his enthusiasm was contagious in many of the corridors at RAND. For an organization dominated by mathematicians, systems analysis appeared to be *the* way to get the scientific—the right—answer. Projects that involved no systems analysis, such as most of the work produced by the social science division, were looked down upon, considered interesting in a speculative sort of way at best.

However, there was one aspect of systems analysis that, some soon began to realize, considerably reduced its value as a panacea. It may have been more creative than operational research; but during World War II, OR analysts were continuously working with *real* combat data, altering their calculations and theories to be compatible with new facts. Yet there was, of course, no real combat data for World War III, the cosmic "nuclear exchange" that the systems analysts of RAND were examining. The numbers that fed into the equations came from speculation, theories, derivations of weapons tests results, sometimes from thin air—not from real war. Since they were analyzing primarily weapons of the future, not even something as simple but absolutely crucial to the analysis as the weapon's price tag could be fully trusted; it could only be predicted, and then just roughly.

In 1949, Ed Paxson and another early systems analyst at RAND, Edward S. Quade, worked for many months on mathematical models of hypothetical air duels fought between fighter planes and bombers. After trudging through a tremendously large series of complicated equations, Paxson and Quade concluded that, with the right kind of fire-control systems, a fighter pilot could close in on a bomber at a certain optimal point, fire his weapon, and shoot the bomber out of the sky in six out of every ten confrontations. After doing these calculations, Paxson and Quade compared their findings with real combat data from World War II. They found that in those cases where the fighter and bomber were in roughly the same geometric position that Paxson and Quade figured would give the fighter a 60 percent probability of kill, the fighter pilot actually downed the bomber only 2 percent of the time. Why the huge difference between theoretical calculation and reality? They puzzled over this disparity for a few disturbing days, and finally conceded that a real pilot in a real airplane shooting real bullets does not so eagerly or easily close in on a big bomber. He takes a couple of shots perhaps, then veers off. Doing anything more would be too dangerous.

In short, war involved a lot of uncertainties, and if the systems analyst failed to take at least the most important ones into account (and who knew just what those were in any particular case?), the conclusions and recommendations might be way off the mark.

This realization marked the discrediting of one of Paxson's first and most ambitious pieces of systems analysis at RAND—his attempt to design the "best" bomber for the U.S. Air Force to use in a strategic atomic-bombing campaign against the Soviet Union. In many ways, it was an impressive effort. Using a combination of economic and mathematical analysis, Paxson drew up a list of the 100 "best" industrial target complexes to hit inside the U.S.S.R. He pulled together more than a dozen variables describing features and profiles of a bombing campaign and a bomber, put them into a single analysis and demonstrated how they interacted with each other, trying out different combinations to see which performed the best under a variety of circumstances. And he devised a way of defining effectiveness, a standard by which one weapon might be judged "better" than another. His measure was simply the number of targets a bomber could destroy for every million dollars spent. This was a new and unique way of taking into account, simultaneously, the war plan and the defense budget. You could ask, "If I have a fixed budget, which bomber could destroy the most targets?" or "If I must destroy a fixed number of targets, which bomber can do the job most cheaply?"

Paxson concluded that the Air Force should build a turbo-prop airplane rather than one with a turbojet engine. Not going with a jet meant sacrificing some quality in performance, but performance was merely a means to the end of bombing Soviet targets. And Paxson calculated that for the same price a larger number of fairly cheap turboprop bombers would do more damage than a smaller number of highly expensive turbojet bombers.

Air Force officers, almost all of whom were pilots, hated the study. They didn't care about systems analysis. They liked to fly airplanes. They wanted a bomber that could go highest, farthest, fastest. And that obviously meant some sort of turbojet model. Some at RAND felt the same way, especially those in the aircraft and engineering divisions who sympathized with the Air Force.

But there were others who felt there was something else wrong with that Paxson study, something more fundamental. And that was where Albert Wohlstetter entered the picture. As a mathematical logician, Wohlstetter greatly admired some aspects of Paxson's work—the elegant modeling, the manipulations of all those variables, how he made them interact in a single piece of quantitative analysis. But Wohlstetter also noted some peculiarities in some of Paxson's major assumptions.

Most glaringly, there was a chart in Paxson's study comparing turboprop and turbojet bombers in terms of cost and combat radius. The SAC operational plan in the early 1950s was to fly bombers from the United States to overseas bases and then to mobilize and launch the attack against the Soviet Union from there. In his study, Paxson had arbitrarily picked for his staging area a base in Newfoundland, about 3,600 miles from his proposed set of targets in the U.S.S.R. According to Paxson's chart, a turbojet plane operating at a 3,600-mile combat radius would cost almost three times as much as a prop plane of equal range—$32 million, compared to about $12 million. Yet the chart also revealed that at 3,000 miles or less, a turboprop and a turbojet plane were about evenly priced. Upon further analysis, it appeared that for the state of the art of that period, an airplane traveling at high speeds or at very low or very high altitude—things that a jet-powered plane could do—hit their maximum range at about a 3,000-mile radius, beyond which a much bigger, heavier and, therefore, more expensive airframe would be needed. Indeed, according to Paxson's chart, the cost of a jet bomber rose very gradually up to 3,000 miles and then shot up dramatically—in fact, doubling between 3,000 and 3,600 miles.

Wohlstetter had recently been assigned by Charlie Hitch to do an Air Force-commissioned study on the selection and use of overseas bases. It hadn't struck Wohlstetter as being very interesting at all. But now, looking at this diagram in Paxson's study, he saw that the location of a base—particularly its distance from the target—made a critical difference in determining what sort of bomber might be best for the Air Force. The turboprop looked good for longer-range missions; but had Paxson examined operations from bases much closer to the Soviet Union (and most bases were within 2,500 miles), he might have come up with an entirely different conclusion. From this, Wohlstetter realized that the issue of base selection was vital.

Wohlstetter's first task was to find the right questions to ask; clearly, Paxson had missed a few. He started by doing essentially what Paxson had done—considering the bombing campaign as if it were a sort of transportation problem, getting the airplane from the U.S. to the target and then destroying as many targets as possible. But he centered the analysis on an issue that Paxson had not considered: where were the best places to put overseas bases? Then he broadened the problem to ask where the best places would be if the Soviets had air-defense weapons protecting the targets. How would that alter the flight path of a SAC bomber, and how might that affect the choice of bases?

Shortly after embroiling himself in the mathematics of the problem, Wohlstetter detected a major dilemma lying at the heart of the whole matter. On the one hand, as bases are moved farther away from the target, costs rise considerably: aircraft must be larger and heavier, so that they can travel great distances. That alone makes them more expensive, but there are also related rises in costs for longer runways, more fuel and fuel storage, increased stock and maintenance, and greater manpower requirements.

On the other hand, a close look at a map revealed a severe disadvantage to basing the bombers closer to the target, a disadvantage that the more traditional methods of bombing analysis might have detected but did not begin to analyze: when the base is close to the Soviet Union, the Soviet Union is also close to the base. In other words, SAC might more swiftly and easily strike the Soviets; but the Soviets might also more swiftly and easily strike SAC.

The significance of this dilemma struck Wohlstetter primarily because of two other streams of thought running through various RAND corridors, quite separate from the sorts of analyses done by Ed Paxson and his fellows in systems analysis.

The first was the spread of game theory throughout the mathematics and economics divisions of RAND in the early 1950s. The Fourth Annual Report of RAND, published in March 1950, exclaimed in its section on the mathematics division that in "the analysis of systems for strategic bombardment, air defense, air supply, or psychological warfare, pertinent information developed or adapted through survey, study or research by RAND is integrated into models, largely by means of mathematical methods and techniques. . . . In this general area of research . . . the guiding philosophy is supplied by the von Neumann-Morgenstern mathematical theory of games."

There is no doubt that Wohlstetter was exposed to principles of game theory in his early days at RAND. His good friend J. C. C. McKinsey was heavily immersed in game theory, writing an introductory text on the subject and publishing more arcane articles in *The Annals of Mathematics Studies,* a highly technical journal published at Princeton by Johnny von Neumann. Ed Paxson was also intrigued, as were many in the systems-analysis field. Wohlstetter had several conversations with a RAND economist named Kenneth Arrow, who was writing a treatise that applied principles of game theory to questions of social choice. (The resulting book, *Social Choice and Individual Values,* published in 1951, became an instant classic and later won Arrow the Nobel Prize in economics.)

Wohlstetter had doubts about how far one could go with a strictly mathematical exposition of game theory, but he was certainly taken with its fundamental guiding point: that in planning one's own tactics and strategies, one had to take into account systematically the actions that an enemy might take if that enemy were a completely rational player.

Up to this point, most military applications of game theory had focused on tactics—the best way to plan a fighter-bomber duel, how to design bomber formations or execute antisubmarine-warfare campaigns. But Wohlstetter would carry it further. It was this insistence on figuring one's own best moves in light of the enemy's best moves that provoked Wohlstetter to look at a map and to conclude that the closer we are to them, the closer they are to us—the easier it is for us to hit them, the easier it is for them to hit us.

Finally, there was the influence of Wohlstetter's wife, Roberta. Andrew Marshall, an analyst in the social science division who had a deep fascination with the techniques of intelligence, suggested to her that she look at Pearl Harbor from an intelligence perspective—to ask what was it about American intelligence in 1941 that prevented anyone from foreseeing the Japanese attack right up to the last moment.

Roberta Wohlstetter spent the next seven years on this project, finishing it in 1957 and publishing a declassified version in 1962. (The book would be called *Pearl Harbor: Warning and Decision,* and would win handsome praise and a number of historians' awards.) Even in the early phases of the study, by 1951, she could see, in a very rough way, how the United States had missed out on adequate warning of the attack: it was not so much that the nation lacked intelligence as it was that the military was unable to separate the relevant information from many other messages that had no particular relevance.

And so, Albert Wohlstetter, in addition to detecting the fatal flaw in Ed Paxson's bomber study and looking at a map with the principles of game theory in mind, was also getting from his wife a heavy dose of information on the issue of surprise attack, a feeling of how even a powerful nation might not see an attack coming. The Pearl Harbor fleet had been remarkably vulnerable. The Japanese had their eyes set on oil in the South Pacific. They had no desire to occupy Pearl Harbor, but saw the American presence there as an obstacle. They noticed the fleet's vulnerability, and so disposed of it. Wohlstetter projected a similar situation to the mid-1950s, imagining the Russians as the Japanese and SAC's overseas bases as Pearl Harbor. If a crisis seemed about to turn into war, or if the Russians, say, wanted to invade Western Europe, their chief worry would be SAC—which had, after all, been designed primarily to counter a Soviet attack against Europe. (At the time, almost nobody even pretended that the Soviets had much ability to attack the United States directly.) If the Soviets, under such circumstances, saw that SAC was vulnerable, they might feel tempted to knock it out so that the European grab could succeed more assuredly. The realization that SAC might be vulnerable to a direct Soviet attack put a whole new spin on the notion of deterrence.

For Wohlstetter, what began as a seemingly boring study, and then as the discovery of a fatal flaw in Ed Paxson's earlier study on the ideal bomber, was unexpectedly turning into a critical analysis not just of overseas bases but of the foundations of SAC policy, of the resistance that the United States could muster in the face of a direct attack, of the nation's ability to deter Communist aggression and nuclear war.

Wohlstetter, although he did not know this at the time, was not the first to point out the vulnerability of U.S. overseas bases. As early as February 1950, the Weapons Systems Evaluation Group, the Pentagon think tank of the Joint Chiefs of Staff, wrote in its very first report that the overseas bases in England were vulnerable and that they might be " 'Pearl Harbored' at the outset of future hostilities." The Joint Intelligence Committee, responding to this report, affirmed that "Soviet forces are considered adequate to launch D-day attacks which, if consummated, would be in sufficient strength to cause serious damage to the bases under consideration" in the SAC program. In June 1950, SAC commander General Curtis LeMay told the Air War College: "We would be foolhardy to risk, on other than unavoidable emergency basis, the deployment to forward airdromes within range of enemy attack of the tremendous investment in national resources represented by even a few atomic bombs."

Even at this early date, LeMay eventually wanted to have an intercontinental bomber force, one that would require no foreign bases at all. LeMay distrusted and disliked most foreigners. As far as he was concerned, the command of SAC and the delivery of nuclear bombs over Russia were the main ingredients of victory, and it was just too important for SAC to depend so critically on a bunch of foreigners.

Still, it was clear that through the 1950s, the technology for intercontinental bombers would remain rather primitive; overseas bases of one sort or another would still be needed. It was also clear that, even while paying lip service, few in military command took seriously the notion of base vulnerability. In devising war plans and assessing threats, most officers and analysts fell back on the traditions of OR-style analysis of World War II, in which the main goals were to penetrate enemy defenses and destroy enemy targets. In that tradition, the vulnerability of air bases was viewed as just another in a series of things that might go wrong, as perturbations that might require some minor adjustments in the analysis, but certainly nothing that should attract center-stage attention. Taking the *offense* and the *initiative* was all-important.

Wohlstetter saw vulnerability as the centerpiece of the strategic problem largely because he knew absolutely nothing about the traditions of strategic-bombing analysis and, therefore, was not blinded by their assumptions. Likewise, he had no preconception that cities were the logical targets of an A-bomb attack because, unlike Brodie and the others, he had done no serious thinking about the bomb during the late 1940s, the period of atomic scarcity. As a result, Wohlstetter came up with a set of conclusions that would revamp the way that "defense intellectuals" would view nuclear strategy for decades to come.

Before coming to RAND, Albert Wohlstetter had no experience and not much interest in military matters or strategic thought. For most of his life, he had been a rather otherworldly figure. He was born in 1912, in New York, to a family of well-to-do Viennese extraction. His father, a lawyer by profession, owned a phonograph company on the side and, through that enterprise, made many friends who performed at the Metropolitan Opera.

During World War I, the conversion from civilian goods to war production—and the consequent competition for labor and scarce materials from Du Pont and other large corporations—wiped out his father's fledgling recording business, and he died shortly afterward, when Albert was just four. An older brother of Albert's soon struck it rich in investment banking, however, and the family's standard of living was back on the track—until the Depression, when it was reduced to straitened circumstances once more.

Amid this turmoil, Albert Wohlstetter turned inward, and discovered and immersed himself in the formal beauty of logic and mathematics. As a young teen-ager, he perused Bertrand Russell's *Principia Mathematica*. At the City College of New York he studied math and philosophy. After graduating, realizing there were few jobs to be found in the field he loved, he enrolled very briefly in Columbia Law School but, quickly bored, switched departments to study mathematical logic and the logic of science.

Even in his college years, Wohlstetter was flamboyant and eccentric, smooth and suave in an affected sort of manner, however genuine the flavor might have been. In 1934, his senior year, the City College newspaper selected him "Most Sophisticated" member of his class.

During the 1930s, Wohlstetter's college years, City College and Columbia University were hotbeds of student radicalism, among the most intensely political campuses in the nation. Wohlstetter toyed a bit with socialism, but he never grew enthusiastic about it. He considered himself a logician, not an activist. His mind was more comfortable with methodology than ideology. When the Depression stimulated an interest in studying economics, he read Karl Marx, John Maynard Keynes and the free-marketeer Alfred Marshall, then systematically formulated their statements and propositions in the symbolic language of mathematical logic. He concluded from this exercise that Keynes was the least plausible of the three (too many tautologies), Marshall the most plausible, and Marx (too many logical contradictions) somewhere in between.

That was how Albert Wohlstetter learned new things and made political judgments amid the political dynamite of the thirties. For Wohlstetter, the criterion of acceptability for a book or thesis or statement was whether it was symbolically satisfying, whether it was mathematically logical, whether it fit into the highly abstract universe of *Principia Mathematica*.

In his first venture into the outside world, Wohlstetter could remain on theoretical territory. With a grant from the Social Science Research Council, he worked at the Department of Agriculture and then the National Board of Economic Research, working on such recondite matters as the impact of random variables on statistical analysis.

Then came the war. Like most pure mathematicians of the pre-computer age, Wohlstetter felt that it was stooping himself to work on projects that might have some relevance in solving problems of the real world. That was the sort of thing that *applied* mathematicians did. The logic could no longer remain pure, the models were less elegant. But this was war, and if Wohlstetter wanted to remain gainfully employed, he would have to learn to like it.

Living off another fellowship, this from the Carnegie Corporation, Wohlstetter became a consultant on the Planning Committee of the War Production Board, and soon one of its quality-
control managers, supervising inspections of motors, generators,
electronic circuitry and other war equipment. The task was much
more up his alley than it might have seemed at first glance. Scientists at Bell Labs had developed a theory of quality control within
the framework of probability analysis. The idea had grown out of
the recognition that, for many items, it was impossible to test
every unit that came off the production line. (A good example was
the time that it took for a fuse to blow.) One had to select a sample
of units and infer from that the quality of the entire line, and Bell
had calculated how to do that scientifically. Wohlstetter, in fact,
had analyzed these sorts of theories in his doctoral dissertation at
Columbia. Working in the war, it seemed, would not require an
entirely new angle on life after all.

However, the experience did give Wohlstetter a chance to
apply the math that he had been studying in theory all these years,
and it gave him a technical education. He frequently had to talk
with engineers and machine-shop foremen about how machinery
worked. He had to find out how and what sorts of things could go
wrong, and how to improve them.

After the war, Wohlstetter spent a brief time in private business in New York, then moved back to Washington to work for the
National Housing Agency. A housing shortage was in the makings
and new ideas were welcome. One particularly innovative engineer at the agency, Paul Weidlinger, had worked during the war
for a small aircraft company owned by Wohlstetter's brother,
Charles, designing such things as airplane hangars that could be
assembled instantly. At the National Housing Agency, Wohlstetter helped Weidlinger apply a similar concept to housing—prefab
modular units that could easily be transported and pieced together
at low cost and minimal construction time.

Wohlstetter then got the idea to start a housing firm that
combined the prefab ideas of his work in Washington with the ar-
chitectural designs of the International Style or Bauhaus movement. In 1947, he and his wife, Roberta, moved to Los Angeles,
found a modern split-level house in the hills of Laurel Canyon,
and set up his company. Not long after, the firm folded—some of
its ideas, such as assembling houses without nails, were too much

at variance with the L.A. housing code—and Albert contemplated moving back east to teach.

But Roberta convinced him to take a look at the RAND Corporation. Shortly after they had moved to Los Angeles, they ran into some of Albert's old friends—Abe Girschick, his old boss from the Agriculture Department; Olaf Helmer, a mathematical logician whom Wohlstetter had met in New York while Helmer was teaching at the New School for Social Research; and J. C. C. McKinsey, a friend from his math days at Columbia. All three were now working in Santa Monica for Project RAND. It was through their efforts that Roberta got a job in the social science division, and now, with Albert's firm having folded, she convinced him to come talk with Charlie Hitch, head of the economics division. Wohlstetter went to look at the place and found he liked its atmosphere, the brilliant people, the diverse interests and especially the predilection that many of the top analysts had for mathematical models. Early in 1951, Albert Wohlstetter joined the RAND economics division as a consultant.

The study on the selection and use of overseas bases was Wohlstetter's first major project at RAND. By the beginning of 1952, he had made his novel, if then still somewhat tentative, discovery that the entire Strategic Air Command might be dangerously vulnerable to a surprise Soviet attack.

At this point, Wohlstetter's technical training during World War II started to show its usefulness. He stalked the RAND corridors, staking out every expert on radar, air defense, aircraft technology and logistics that he could find, asking them frankly naïve questions about how things worked, how they might work better, how things could go wrong.

While touring the RAND hallways, Wohlstetter ran across a young economist-engineer named Henry (or, as his friends called him, Harry) Rowen. Rowen was bored with his work—fairly tedious and mechanical numbers-crunching, involving no imagination or creativity. Wohlstetter began trying out some of his ideas on Rowen, who became increasingly intrigued with the project and who joined it full-time in December 1951.

Wohlstetter also received assistance from Robert J. Lutz, a former MIT aerospace engineer who had worked for Consolidated Aircraft in San Diego during the war and who joined the aircraft division at RAND in 1949. Like most of the rather sober crowd in the aircraft shop at RAND, Lutz thought that Wohlstetter was more than just a little eccentric: voluble, keeping as high a profile as possible, running around the corridors as if there were no to-morrow. He had an almost monomaniacal sense of urgency: some thing or another *had* to be done tomorrow or that night. Ideas kept popping out of his head. Lutz found it hard to believe that Wohl-stetter could possibly have control over all this information he was gathering. But as Lutz became more involved in the project, he found to his amazement that he did.

Still, Lutz found problems. Wohlstetter was making the anal-ysis too abstract. He was starting to do what Paxson and most other systems analysts did: come up with some amorphous, hypo-thetical bomber force that would do the "best" job. Lutz put the project on a more concrete basis, doing what a SAC planner might have done if ordered to change Air Force operations along Wohl-stetter's tentative recommendations, analyzing not some ideal bomber of the future, but the airplanes that the United States ac-tually possessed at the time—mainly B-47 and B-36 bombers and KC-97 refueling tankers. He also got Wohlstetter to analyze not some imaginary set of targets, but the 100 industrial-complex tar-gets that Ed Paxson had used in his bomber study.

As Wohlstetter went about his business, discovering the vul-nerabilities of SAC and peering into the most arcane detail, he had Lutz and Harry Rowen—and later, toward the end of the study, another young RAND economist named Frederic S. Hoffman—do the more classical analysis of bombing campaigns: designing bomber-penetration tactics, gathering data on fighter-bomber duels, figuring out precise flight paths from various bases to vari-ous targets, timing the attack so that as many SAC planes as pos-sible—coming from several different directions—would show up on Russian radar screens all at once, calculating the attrition rates resulting from estimates of Soviet bombers and air-defense weap-ons. Rowen and Hoffman, as members of the RAND cost-analysis division, also put price tags on the various systems.

Wohlstetter, meanwhile, was discovering that SAC was sit-ting in a house of cards. He was looking at the period from 1956 to 1961, four to nine years into the future. By then, SAC would have about 1,600 B-47 bombers with a combat radius of 1,700 miles, 300 vintage B-36 bombers with a 2,950-mile radius, perhaps a wing of 3,060-mile B-52s, and 720 KC-97 tankers. SAC operations involved flying the bombers from thirty bases in the United States to eighty-two bases overseas. (In 1952, when Wohlstetter began looking at the data, SAC had only thirty-two of these overseas bases.) SAC crews would set up replicas of the bases back home, then load the planes with bombs and send them off to the targets from the overseas bases. This operation would take about a week to get off the ground.

The practice came from World War II, when bombing was merely part of an overall campaign and the bomber bases were rarely in danger of being destroyed. But this was the atomic age; the Soviets had exploded an A-bomb in 1949. Yet SAC had not adjusted to the changed situation; the commanders were still, almost unconsciously, planning for a World War II-type operation.

Moreover, most of the bases were very close to the Soviet Union—one-third of them within the combat radius of Soviet lightweight bombers, all of them within reach of their medium bombers. Many were so close that Soviet bombers could attack them with no U.S. radar warning. Also, for economizing measures, the airplanes were parked close to spare parts and repair facilities; most fuel-storage tanks were built above ground; no attempt had been made to disperse the storage of critical items. A few bombs could knock out not only the airplanes but also everything that could fix the planes that were merely bruised and all the supplies and fuel that might allow other bombers from other bases to fly over and to carry out the bombing mission as planned.

In fact, Wohlstetter and his team estimated that a mere 120 bombs—forty kilotons each, with average miss distances of 4,000 feet—could destroy 75 to 85 percent of the B-47 bombers while they casually sat on overseas bases. The Strategic Air Command, seemingly the most powerful strike force in the world, was appearing to be so vulnerable in so many ways that merely putting it into action—moving it overseas in accordance with the official Mobility Plan—created a target so concentrated that it invited preemptive attack from the Soviet Union.

The conclusion, by this point, was clear. But Wohlstetter and company thought that they might not be readily believed. They spent all of 1952 exploring every conceivable way that they might be proved wrong and trying to come up with their own solution to the problem. They examined everything from the effectiveness of air-defense fighters deployed to protect SAC bases from attack to the rate at which hydraulic faucets on SAC bases could pump water. Their conclusions were left essentially unaltered.

They recommended that early-warning radar systems should be improved, so that the bombers could evacuate their bases more quickly; adequate warning alone reduced the percentage of bombers a Soviet attack could wipe out from 75 or 85 to only 20 percent. More drastically, they recommended that overseas bases be used only for refueling, not as a base of complete operations in their own right. This would minimize both the amount of material overseas and the time that each airplane would have to spend on the ground. On each base, furthermore, supplies should be dispersed and, where possible, hardened to resist blast. Air-defense squadrons should be strengthened. Repair facilities should be better protected.

The conclusion that these refueling bases would be the best way to go emerged from a standard systems analysis, asking the Paxson-inspired questions, "Which system more cheaply destroys a given number of targets?" and "For a given budget, which system destroys the most targets?" However, the Wohlstetter analysis carried an unusual twist: instead of comparing different bombers, it compared different basing schemes—an air-refueled system, the Air Force-programmed operating base system, and (the one that Wohlstetter eventually favored) a ground-refueled system. They also compared these three systems under three different assumptions concerning the size of the Soviet bomber force as of 1956—higher than that expected by Air Force Intelligence, the expected number, and some number lower than that expected.

The results of the analysis determined the choice of system. In all cases, the ground-refueled system—using overseas bases only to refuel bombers—was by far the cheapest. Operating from these sorts of bases, B-47s could destroy the same number of targets for nearly one-third the cost of the Air Force system. And for a hypothetical $40 billion budget, they could destroy about twice as many targets—300 to about 1,200 (depending on the size of the Soviet bomber force), compared with fewer than 100 to about 600. On this score, the purely intercontinental operation—refueling the bomber in the air all the way, with no overseas bases at all— would be much too expensive. Since so much of such a plan's budget would have to pay for more tankers, SAC would have only enough bombers to destroy 350 or so Soviet targets under the best of circumstances and fewer than 50 under the worst.

The results surprised nearly everyone. After Wohlstetter circulated around RAND a draft of the team's tentative findings, he was approached by Herman Kahn, a nuclear physicist at RAND who was becoming increasingly interested in nuclear strategy. Kahn thought that Wohlstetter had overdone it, that this "programmed system," against which Wohlstetter's preferred system looked so good by comparison, was too obviously rigged and exaggerated.

"Albert, this programmed system that you've demolished," he said, "is a straw man."

"Herman," Wohlstetter calmly replied, "that *is* the system that SAC has programmed." Kahn was aghast.

By the fall of 1952, if there were any doubts left in the Wohlstetter team's minds about the vulnerability of SAC, they were dispelled at once by a strange twist of fate. On September 1, a tornado unexpectedly swooped down upon Carswell SAC Air Force Base in Texas. Wind gusts approached 125 miles per hour. The storm demolished one B-36 bomber and heavily damaged eighty-one more, putting both wings on the base out of commission for a month. Further damage was done by flying debris from nearby repair docks. One fighter airplane was blown into the air and carried several hundred feet. One hangar collapsed. Gasoline spilled from many of the wrecked airplanes, some of them frighteningly close to broken electrical circuits. If some Carswell crew members had not quickly shut off all electrical current, blazing fires would have caused still greater damage. As it was, no electrical equipment was allowed on the runways until three days after the storm.

General Hoyt Vandenberg, Air Force Chief of Staff, ordered a team to investigate the causes and extent of the damage, and then had another board of inquiry, composed of senior officers, determine "whether, as a result of the lessons of the experience, changes of policy concerning the dispersion of aircraft may be advisable."

To Wohlstetter, the storm confirmed the team's conclusions about SAC vulnerability, plus some. A forty-kiloton bomb could have produced that tornado's wind gusts even if it missed the base by 9,000 feet. It would also have created a powerful explosion of blast, intense heat and radiation, and it all probably would have happened so quickly that nobody would have had the time—

maybe they would not even have been alive—to shut off the electric power, meaning that fire would have engulfed the base as well.

Not only did the storm confirm the RAND group's findings, but it would also make its conclusions appear more credible—and many of its recommendations more compelling—to Air Force officers when they would hear them in the months to come.

By January 1953, Wohlstetter felt sufficiently confident of the study's conclusions to start lining up briefings throughout the Air Force hierarchy. Over the next two months, he, Rowen, Hoffman and Lutz prepared a paper, numbered RAND Report R-244-S, the S signaling that this was a special report not even to be listed in the RAND index of publications. It would, for the time being, do the Air Force, RAND's sole sponsor, no good to have some congressman or reporter discover the existence of a study suggesting that SAC, history's most powerful fighting force and the very rationale of the Air Force's independent existence, could easily be wiped out on the ground.

The team's first out-of-town briefing came in March, at SAC headquarters at Offutt Air Force Base in Omaha, Nebraska. Everyone was nervous. There was some doubt as to whether General LeMay, SAC commanding general, would even stay in the room after listening to the first few minutes of so critical an assessment of his operations. As it turned out, LeMay did not show up at the briefing, but his deputy, General Tommy Power, and most of the other top SAC officers did.

Wohlstetter went through the briefing, flipping over one chart after another, holding discourse on the dilemmas of base location, describing the vulnerability and concentration of the programmed bases, the inadequacy of the early-warning net, the attrition that the Soviets could impose with a surprise attack, the enormous differences in cost and effectiveness among various alternative bases, and the case for having only refueling bases overseas.

Power sat through the briefing without expression. At its conclusion, he stood up, said, "Very interesting," turned around and walked out the door.

Power's subordinates sat silent for a moment, not knowing just what to do. Finally, a few of them gingerly stepped up to the podium and asked Wohlstetter and his team a few questions.

Some of them expressed frank amazement. In SAC's own analyses, the staff had never considered the impact that a Soviet attack against the bases might have on SAC's ability to launch a devastating "Sunday punch" of its own. They had always assumed that SAC would have enough warning to get off the ground, that the Russians would never lay a finger on any of the bombers while they were still on the ground.

Next stop on the circuit was the Pentagon in Washington. The first audience there was a group of about forty senior staff Air Force colonels, among them the assistant for development planning, Bernard Schriever; the executive assistant to the director of operations, L. C. Coddington; executive assistant to the director of plans, Jim Whisenand; assistant to the director of installations, C. A. Eckert; and executive assistants in nearly all the other commands within the Air Staff.

Colonel Coddington was the most articulate of the group, a laconic, no-nonsense fellow. He had also previously been deputy to General Harold Maddux, who had ordered the RAND basing study in the first place, a fortuitous connection since Coddington most enthusiastically touted the study's findings.

Some of the others were not so enthusiastic. The installations command had spent all of the previous week, including all weekend, working up their budget for overseas bases for the next fiscal year. Its officers were in no mood to face something that might force them to start all over again. Colonel Eckert, representing installations at the Pentagon briefing, tried to shunt the RAND study off.

"I hope none of you are taken in by all this slide-rule razzmatazz," he scoffed, noting that the kinds of bases these RAND guys were advocating would cost "millions."

Coddington sharply interrupted. "Look," he said, "you're talking millions. *He's* talking billions. You're talking about spending another weekend redoing the budget. *He's* talking about the survival of the United States strategic force."

But there were more briefings to come before policy could be changed. They had to talk to the general officers for plans, for operations, for logistics, for intelligence, for communications, all the different commands. In the process, an Ad Hoc Committee of the Air Staff was appointed to examine the RAND study independently. They had to brief this committee and all of its constituent offices.

Wohlstetter, Rowen, Hoffman and Lutz would spend virtually the entire summer of 1953 in Washington. In all, they would deliver the overseas-bases briefing ninety-two times.

After a while, it became clear that the main obstacle to any action's being taken on the RAND proposals lay in the Strategic Air Command. LeMay and his disciples disliked the notion of spending a lot of money on protecting the bomber force. If the bombers were vulnerable, that only meant that SAC should get more bombers so that the number surviving would be higher. More to the point, it meant that SAC should make sure to get in the initial blow instead of waiting around for the Soviets to strike first.

There was a political reason for SAC's resistance, as well. Although SAC was a command of the Air Force, it took orders only from the Joint Chiefs of Staff. Yet the RAND study grew out of the Air Staff. If SAC succumbed to RAND's recommendations, it might mean the first in a series of Air Staff incursions into SAC plans and operations. LeMay was fiercely jealous of any trespassing. SAC was a fiefdom all to itself in those days. LeMay tried to keep all SAC planning to himself. There was the issue of security as well. Who knew whether someone—maybe even the President of the United States—could really be trusted? LeMay often said, "On some Mondays I don't even trust myself."

The Ad Hoc Committee of the Air Staff, appointed to study the RAND briefing and present its independent findings to the Air Force Council, was proving to be another obstacle. The committee, by its rules, had to reach a consensus before passing recommendations to the top-level Council. This rule of consensus allowed some of the more reluctant commands to use the study as a delaying tactic, to refuse to join any consensus for as long as they felt like holding out—which could, theoretically, be forever.

Wohlstetter was growing frustrated. He had convinced himself that those charts and diagrams and calculations proved that unless his recommendations were implemented, the Soviets could engulf the United States in a nuclear war before the end of the decade, and that the West would lose. He went over to RAND's downtown Washington office, a cramped, windowless basement in the Cafritz Building on Eye Street near Eighteenth, to talk with RAND's D.C. representative, Larry Henderson. Henderson suggested that they line up an interview with General Thomas D.

White, who was acting Air Force Chief of Staff while Hoyt Vandenberg lay dying of cancer. This would be a major step, the highest-level end run around the Air Force bureaucracy that anyone could imagine. But Henderson and Wohlstetter thought it was worth the attempt.

In August, the meeting with White took place. Attending were General White, Wohlstetter and the top management echelon of RAND—president Frank Collbohm and vice-presidents Larry Henderson and J. R. Goldstein. White became convinced of the study's importance and assured them that it would be placed on the Air Force Council agenda.

That same month, Wohlstetter was given an additional boost by the Russians. Soviet Premier Georgi Malenkov announced on August 8 that the Soviets had exploded their first hydrogen bomb. As it turned out, it was not remotely of the same design as the American H-bomb and carried an explosive punch of about 400 kilotons—hardly small, but no larger than the mightiest *fission* weapon detonated by the United States. Still, at the time, the mere existence of a Soviet H-bomb, of whatever design, heightened most Air Force officers' apprehensions about possible Soviet aggression, a point that Wohlstetter unabashedly exploited in subsequent briefings.

By October, the Ad Hoc Committee, under General Tommy White's orders, presented its analysis of the RAND basing study to the Air Force Council, with separate comments from the director of plans, the director of operations and SAC. On October 29 and 30, the Council made its own report to General White and Acting Secretary of the Air Force Jim Douglas. It recommended:

"a. That the vulnerability of Air Force facilities be recognized in all Air Staff planning and actions.

"b. That specific vulnerability factors be developed on a zonal basis [within each air base].

"c. That a program of hardening bases to atomic attack be initiated. . . . Also, a capability for achieving rapid recuperability of attacked bases shall be developed.

"d. New advanced bases shall be constructed and stocked to ground refueling standards with atomic toughening and rapid refueling capacity unless construction to other standards is required either by national or political agreements or overriding operational requirements. . . .

"e. That the material resources in overseas areas be reduced to the minimum extent possible consistent with the planned utilization. . . ."

General White and Secretary Douglas approved the Air Force Council's decision.

In April 1954, Wohlstetter, Rowen, Hoffman and Lutz expanded their briefing into a massive 424-page top-secret study, RAND Report R-266, entitled *Selection and Use of Strategic Air Bases*. By the time of its release, the Air Force was already implementing some of the recommendations that Wohlstetter had made in his briefings. References to the "programmed system" were thus tactfully changed to read the "formerly programmed system."

Nevertheless, the RAND recommendations were never put in full force. For one thing, while the Soviet H-bomb heightened the urgency of doing something about vulnerability, it also made RAND's alternative proposal somewhat obsolete. When Wohlstetter and his team talked about hardening and dispersing airplanes and various facilities on overseas bases, they were assuming Soviet bombs in the tens or low hundreds of kilotons. At one point during Wohlstetter's research, Charlie Hitch—who, at the same time, was working on the highly secretive H-bomb study with Bernard Brodie and Ernie Plesset—discreetly told him, without any elaboration, that he should make sure that the overseas-base study's conclusions were not sensitive to nuclear explosions of one megaton or so. Wohlstetter, not knowing of the RAND H-bomb study but respecting Hitch's judgment, made some alterations in the proposed base design to deal with one-megaton explosions. But now that the Soviets appeared to be on the verge of having an arsenal of H-bombs, *multi*megaton explosions would have to be anticipated. No overseas base, not even the truncated one proposed by Wohlstetter's team, could survive an attack employing weapons that powerful.

Moreover, LeMay was still determined to solve the problem through acceleration of a new intercontinental bomber—the B-52—that would depend on no overseas bases at all. Anything making medium-range bombers, like the B-47, seem more attractive would only delay the day that LeMay was waiting for.

A compromise came in almost accidental fashion, thanks to a fortuitous error in SAC communications and some ingenious planning by a B-47 Wing Planner at MacDill Air Force Base, near

Tampa, Florida, named Colonel Ed Jones. SAC had two sets of basic flight plans—the "40 Series," which covered the flight from the United States to the overseas bases, and the "50 Series," which was the strike plan for the first missions flying from the base to the targets. At about the time of the RAND study's approval, the B-47s at MacDill were being fed into the new SAC Emergency War Plan, and SAC sent out a rather puzzling communiqué. The B-47s in Tampa were accidentally put into the "50 Series," the attack phase of the bombing mission.

Nobody had given much thought before to flying B-47s straight from the United States—or the ZI, standing for Zone of the Interior, as the Air Force called the U.S. in those days—but Colonel Jones had his orders, and that is what he would try to do. Jones locked himself away for a few days and emerged with a plan calling for refueling the bombers in the air over Iceland, proceeding toward the North Sea, bombing targets around Leningrad and then recovering on overseas bases.

Jones's wing commander delivered the briefing to planning and operations officers at SAC—to, predictably, rancorous response. "You know," one colonel said after the shouting had died down, "there's this nut from RAND who's been going around briefing everybody about the vulnerability of our bases," pronouncing "vulnerability" with a heavy dose of sarcasm. "We've been getting a lot of static on this from Washington. Gentlemen," he continued, "*this* is our answer."

The Jones flight plan became Air Force policy. Developed in 1954, it was called the Fullhouse Concept, and was later refined and modified and given such names as Leap Frog, High Gear, Air Blast and Hot Point. The basic idea behind all these concepts was the same: "to limit the importance of the overseas areas as pre-strike bases and [reduce] their role to principally that of en route *aerial* refueling bases and *post*-strike support." As a result, "targets could be attacked from the ZI, with minimum reliance on overseas bases, in a matter of hours after the initiation of hostilities."

Wohlstetter and his team had rejected this type of plan because it would cost too much. So many additional tankers would have to be bought that, for the same amount of money, SAC would have fewer bombers than it would have under the RAND concept. To that argument, SAC's response was simply that the Air Force would have to get more money.

Furthermore, there were few in Omaha who supported the nub of Wohlstetter's argument—the idea that SAC had to sit out a surprise attack from the Russians. Instinctively, the men of SAC still could not conceive of the Russians' one-upping the U.S. If they were worried about vulnerability, they thought that the way to solve that problem was to destroy the enemy before he destroys them. Concepts such as Fullhouse and its successors were planned not just to reduce vulnerability, but to get SAC bombers over their targets more quickly, to get in a better, faster preemptive strike. The RAND study on overseas bases prompted a series of events and coincidences that finally led SAC to reduce its dependency on elaborate overseas bases, but its precise recommendations were not the ones that SAC actually adopted.

The main impact of the Wohlstetter study was much larger and of broader importance. Among its more enthusiastic supporters in the Air Staff and especially among many of Wohlstetter's colleagues at RAND, it fostered the notion that imbalances and vulnerabilities that were revealed through complex calculations changed everything about the likelihood of war and the meaning of victory. It helped reinforce the assumption that once the Soviets acquired a theoretical capability to launch a dazzling, partially disarming first-strike, they might very well launch one, despite the many uncertainties and risks involved.

More crucially, the study marked the beginnings of a formal separation of strategic thinking from questions of national objectives. Bernard Brodie had observed that, given the enormously destructive power of the atomic bomb and especially the hydrogen bomb, a relatively small number of weapons could accomplish whatever strategic mission one might have in mind, and that beyond a certain point more weapons made increasingly little difference. Wohlstetter did not know of the feasibility of H-bombs when he began work on the overseas-base study, but both the United States and the Soviet Union had tested some by the time it was published. The analysis by Plesset, Hitch and Brodie on the implications of the H-bomb had revealed that a mere fifty-five H-bombs could destroy the fifty largest Soviet cities and kill 35 million civilians.

In the worst case of Wohlstetter's analysis, the Soviet Union was estimated as being able to destroy 85 percent of the SAC bomber force. But SAC would have, by 1956, 1,900 B-47 and B-36 bombers, and 15 percent of 1,900 is 285 bombers, each carrying from two to four bombs. Thus, after absorbing a Soviet first-strike, and with no alterations in the SAC basing system at all, the United States could still have destroyed roughly 600 Soviet targets.

Wohlstetter said that he was more interested in deterring nuclear war than in figuring out how to fight one. Yet nowhere did he or any of his associates ask if, in the 1950s when the Soviets had very few strategic weapons, destroying 600 targets was enough to deter—or whether one really needed to destroy, as Wohlstetter's preferred basing system would have allowed, 1,200 targets.

Albert Wohlstetter made much of the Pearl Harbor analogy. It inspired the scenario that made his discovery of SAC vulnerability so realistic. But he never did consider whether the Japanese would have attacked Pearl Harbor—no matter how temptingly vulnerable the fleet there might have appeared—if they thought that the United States could have retaliated with 600 or even 100 or even 10 Nagasaki-size, much less multimegaton, nuclear explosions.

The Wohlstetter study set the model of what strategic analysis should be. It was the study that, for years after, almost everyone in the quantitative quarters of RAND would instantly cite when asked to name the most impressive systems analysis they had produced. It imposed a much higher premium than had previously existed on the claim that good strategic analysis meant quantitative analysis with elaborate calculations and "hard" data. And since most of this data came from Air Force Intelligence—which, curiously, this group of analytic skeptics accepted without much question—quantitative analysis tended to paint a very scary picture of the Soviet threat.

Aside from contributing to and intellectually justifying the Air Force Intelligence estimates (which were consistently more pessimistic than those of the CIA and the other military services), the study was among the first attempts to abstract the "nuclear exchange," to place it, like one of Wohlstetter's exercises in mathematical logic from earlier days, in a rarefied universe all its own, apart from the world of political leaders and their appreciation of horrible risk, apart from the broader issues of how nuclear weapons fit into an overall strategy and of how many weapons were needed before their further accumulation no longer much mattered.

Specifically, Wohlstetter made the issue of calculated vulnerability the central focus of strategic analysis generally. In the early 1950s, SAC's overseas bases were bizarrely complicated, horrendously inefficient and vulnerable. Whether the vulnerability was truly critical, given the enormous size of the American arsenal, is another question; but there can be little dispute that it was a sound idea to rely much less on these bases, since the mere act of mobilization, of preparation for war, would put the SAC force in greater danger than it had been prior to mobilization. There is no question that the Wohlstetter study helped reduce this reliance.

But Wohlstetter then made his reputation on examining vulnerability and, in later years, he would continue to impose the concept on nearly everything he analyzed. As the theory trickled down not just through the corridors of RAND but also in Washington and other sectors of the "strategic community," the concern about vulnerability grew into an infatuation, then an obsession and finally a fetish of sorts. Eventually, it would wend its way into the political realm and—apart from Wohlstetter's original intentions or logic—become entangled with claims of a "missile gap"; it would sit at the center of grisly scenarios about Soviet first-strikes and American weakness; it would provide the rationale for a host of new weapons that the military wanted to build; and it would serve as a powerful engine driving at least the American side of a nuclear arms race over the next quarter century and beyond.

7 THE HYDRA-HEADED MONSTER

IN THE SUMMER of 1953, while Albert Wohlstetter was away in Washington, pushing his overseas-base briefing on anyone in the Pentagon who would listen, some of the RAND physicists in Santa Monica were fiddling with calculations about the hydrogen bomb that would eventually alter the entire picture of nuclear weaponry and, on the face of things, invest in Wohlstetter's worries about the vulnerability of SAC a still greater sense of urgency.

From their sources at the Los Alamos weapons lab, Ernie Plesset and David Griggs were learning that there was something highly significant about the hydrogen bomb other than its tremendous explosive power. The physics of the weapon meant that a relatively small amount of fissile uranium or plutonium was all one would need to trigger the fusion implosion of hydrogen isotopes that produced the bomb's extremely high yield. Meanwhile, the weapons scientists were designing bombs of astonishing efficiency. They were getting to the point where they could pack a bomb with the explosive power of 500 kilotons into a device substantially smaller than the bulky atom bomb dropped over Nagasaki, which had set off an explosion only 4 percent as powerful.

Plesset and Griggs realized that this meant that the hydrogen bomb, along with the new weapons technology that accompanied it, could be made small enough and light enough to fit on top of an intercontinental ballistic missile. The ICBM—that had been General Hap Arnold's dream when he conceived of Project RAND, that was what RAND's mission was all about.

In the fall of 1950, RAND had produced a series of studies for the Air Force, concluding that long-range ballistic missiles would be of military value. In January 1951, the Defense Department reactivated Project MX-774, which had been eliminated from the budget in 1949, and renamed it the Atlas Missile Project. It was still a program with low priority, the aim of which was to determine whether a large, 5,000-mile ballistic rocket was within the state of the art. Up until this point, the technical obstacles were

111

too great. The pure fission weapon was too heavy and large for a worthwhile payload to be positioned on the nosecone of a rocket and fired to some point halfway around the globe. But now, the H-bomb—small and light yet massively destructive—might make Hap Arnold's dream come true.

Yet there were still some major problems. The most troublesome involved meeting the requirements that had been imposed on the missile's technical performance by its program managers at Convair Missile Division, the aerospace company that had won the Atlas contract. They wanted Atlas to have a 3,000-pound warhead that would re-enter the atmosphere at six times the speed of sound (without burning up) and that would land within one-quarter to one-half mile of the target. All these requirements were clearly far beyond the "state of the art" in 1953. Even the Convair managers were not expecting such a missile to be ready for operation until 1965.

The slow pace at which Convair was moving the ICBM program particularly concerned an aeronautical engineer in the RAND missiles division named Bruno Augenstein. In early 1948, Augenstein had come to RAND as a subcontractor for the North American aircraft company, doing analyses of satellites and preliminary design work on what in the late 1950s would become the Navaho cruise missile. After a brief respite teaching in the Aeronautics Department at Purdue University, he joined RAND full-time in 1949.

On August 8, 1953, the Soviets set off their first hydrogen bomb. One of Augenstein's friends in the intelligence community contacted him to talk about some of its details. It seemed that this Soviet bomb bore little resemblance to the American H-bomb. For one thing it was less powerful, something of a relief. But there was also something ominous. The H-bomb that the United States had set off was not really a practical bomb; it was more like a "device." It required a huge refrigeration system to keep it cool, something that could not be sent up on a rocket, or even, very easily, on a bomber. Yet analysis of fallout samples from the Soviet explosion indicated the presence of lithium, a chemical that made refrigeration unnecessary.

The implication was sensational. It meant that the Soviets could conceivably build an ICBM with an H-bomb on board much earlier than the United States. Like most weapons scientists of the day, Augenstein thought that if the Soviet Union beat the United

States in a race for the ICBM, the consequences would be catastrophic. The Atlas project had to be pushed along at a much faster
clip.

The Convair requirements for Atlas were certainly extreme.
The trick was to find some technically feasible way of relaxing
them without degrading the missile's capabilities. Using the same
evidence about lighter and smaller warheads that Plesset, Griggs
and others had obtained from Los Alamos scientists, Augenstein
figured that the Atlas warhead could be made half as heavy as the
3,000 pounds that Convair was requiring, with no reduction in its
explosive punch. On the requirement that the warhead re-enter
the atmosphere and head toward the target at six times the speed
of sound, Augenstein's own research suggested that an object
moving at merely the speed of sound would be difficult enough for
Russian air defenses to track and shoot down; therefore, such
high speeds were, for the time being, unnecessary. Given that, the
problem of re-entering the atmosphere without burning up the
warhead became simpler to solve.

His most critical discovery, however, concerned the missile's
accuracy, its CEP ("circular error probable"), indicating the distance from a given point within which a weapon lands 50 percent
of the time. Convair wanted the Atlas CEP to be somewhere between one-quarter and one-half mile—which would require
highly sophisticated inertial guidance systems that nobody had as
yet come close to inventing.

Augenstein examined some mathematical models of bomb
destruction that others at RAND had devised. Extrapolating from
these models, Augenstein calculated how many 500-kiloton warheads would be needed to attack the industrial target complexes
in the 20 largest Soviet cities (containing 55 percent of the
U.S.S.R.'s industrial capital), the next 50 top cities (another 32
percent) and the next 110 urban areas (an additional 17 percent)—assuming different CEPs ranging from one to five miles.

Compared with missiles having a one-mile CEP, it turned out
that the United States would need only 1.6 times as many missiles
with three-mile CEPs to destroy the 20 largest Soviet cities, twice
as many to attack the 70 largest and 2.5 times as many to target
the 180 largest cities. Since fissile materials were now quite plentiful, getting the additional weapons would be no problem. In fact,
with the bigger bangs that the H-bomb could produce—blasts in
the megaton range—CEPs as high as five miles would still be

adequate for destroying all the urban targets one might want to hit in a retaliatory strike. Therefore, Convair could relax its absurdly difficult CEP requirements to as high as three or five miles, and Atlas could still perform its essential retaliatory mission.

The upshot of Augenstein's analysis was that with accessible technology, and only more money and a higher priority given to the Atlas project by the Defense Department, the United States could have an operational ICBM by 1960—five years sooner than the Convair planners were shooting for.

Augenstein finished his report late in November of 1953. His boss, Jimmy Lipp, head of RAND's missiles division, who had been working with Augenstein as the study had progressed, was tantalized. Lipp had been appalled by the death and destruction wreaked by a twenty-megaton bomb during the brief period when he was working with Ernie Plesset, Bernard Brodie and Charlie Hitch on the H-bomb study. But as efficient as weapons technology may have been by 1953, it was not yet so developed as to allow a bomb anywhere near twenty megatons to fit onto the tip of an ICBM. More than that, there was something so technically challenging and politically grand about a workable ICBM—and arriving at it before the Russians—that an attempt to achieve it was cause for excitement.

On December 11, Lipp took the results of Augenstein's study to Frank Collbohm, who was enthralled with the analysis. This study that Lipp was laying out before him could put RAND way out in front of the competition from other groups and ad hoc panels also working on the ICBM.

Collbohm went to Washington the next day to brief the study to senior Air Staff officers, indeed telling virtually every general he found roaming the Pentagon's hallways that the ICBM was now a practical goal, that RAND had discovered the solution.

His audiences were intrigued, but many were skeptical. The Air Force still meant, by and large, the big-bomber force. Even the more interested officers preferred to reserve judgment until hearing from other quarters—the most distinguished of which was the Strategic Missile Evaluation Committee, code named the Teapot Committee, chaired by John von Neumann. In June of 1953, von Neumann and Edward Teller told the Air Force Scientific Advisory Board that it was possible to manufacture a one- or two-megaton thermonuclear warhead that weighed a mere 3,000 pounds or less. The Teller-von Neumann presentation had been lined up by Colonel Bernard Schriever of the Development Planning Office in the Air Force. The DPO was also the specific office that monitored the RAND contract. Ernie Plesset and David Griggs knew that von Neumann and Teller had done some calculations suggesting the feasibility of a small thermonuclear warhead—indeed, von Neumann and Teller, both frequent visitors to RAND, were the ones from whom Plesset and Griggs first heard of such news. Plesset convinced Schriever, who was also quite keen on accelerating an ICBM program, to journey to Princeton and try to get von Neumann to be chairman of an ad hoc panel of the Scientific Advisory Board that would evaluate the issue.

On June 16, with this knowledge in hand, Secretary of Defense Charles Wilson ordered a review of the guided-missile program to identify and eliminate duplication. He assigned responsibility for the project to his assistant secretary for research and development, Trevor Gardner. Gardner, in turn, placed a special panel to look at strategic missiles under the administrative authority of General Schriever. Von Neumann had recently been diagnosed as having terminal cancer, but he accepted Schriever's request that he head the Teapot Committee. Others on the committee included Herbert York of Livermore Lab; George Kistiakowsky and Jerome Wiesner, who would later serve as Presidential science advisers; Simon Ramo and Dean Wooldridge, who would form the Ramo-Wooldridge Corporation, manager of the first ICBM project; Clark Millikan of Cal Tech—in short, some of the nation's most brilliant weapons scientists.

On December 12, Frank Collbohm briefed Air Staff officers on the Augenstein report demonstrating the feasibility of the ICBM. Around this same time, the Teapot Committee was meeting in Los Angeles. Sometime between December 17 and 19, Bruno Augenstein briefed the committee, telling its members— with the same charts that Collbohm had used as illustration—that the Atlas missile could have a 1,500-pound warhead and that its accuracy could be as poor as three or five miles and still perform its mission. Von Neumann had heard a similar analysis two months earlier, when Ernie Plesset briefed the committee in Colorado Springs. Plesset had given them the H-bomb briefing that he had developed with Charlie Hitch and Bernard Brodie—which also made the case, though Augenstein did not know about the H-bomb briefing, that the fantastic explosive power of the hydrogen bomb made the question of CEP far less relevant than many believed.

At a meeting of the Air Force Scientific Advisory Board on October 21, von Neumann talked of the possibility that the accuracy requirement for Atlas might be relaxed, but he was still tentative on this matter. "There is no doubt," he said, "that this subject should be examined much more carefully." Bruno Augenstein's briefing before the committee in late December describing the precise guidance system that could be used, portraying the precise trade-off curves between CEP and the number of weapons necessary, provided the more careful analysis and reinforced the direction in which von Neumann was headed from the start.

Augenstein's formal RAND research memorandum, RM-1191, titled *A Revised Development Program for Ballistic Missiles of Intercontinental Range,* was delivered to the Air Force on February 8, 1954. Collbohm wanted above all to beat the Teapot Committee to the punch. He did. Two days later, von Neumann filed his report with the Air Force Chief of Staff. It concluded that the ICBM was feasible, that twenty launching sites with a stockpile of 100 missiles could be established by June 1960 if the requirements for the warhead's weight and accuracy were substantially modified, and that modifying them would in no way reduce the missile's effectiveness.

On March 11 and 14, the Air Force Council met and "agreed that it is possible to broaden CEP requirements immediately" and noted that doing so "will simplify the problems of developing adequate guidance systems for all strategic missiles." The Council ordered that the Atlas "should be given a high priority" and "extraordinary action be taken to accelerate the revised program . . . so as to achieve the early establishment of an optimum intercontinental ballistic missile system." On May 6, General Hoyt Vandenberg, Air Force Chief of Staff, approved the Council's recommendations.

In July, Trevor Gardner directed General Schriever to take charge of the newly created Western Development Division of the Air Research and Development Command. The organization was so highly secretive that its very initials, WDD, were classified beyond top secret, and its headquarters were located in an abandoned parochial schoolhouse on the edges of Los Angeles, with frosted and heavily barred windows, locked doors, a chain-link-fenced parking lot, and an armed guard sitting inside. Simon Ramo and Dean Wooldridge banded together to form the Ramo-Wooldridge Corporation (later TRW, Inc.), whose sole task was to provide technical assistance to the ICBM program.

The age of the strategic missile, "the hydra-headed monster," as those working on it liked to call it, had begun.

Albert Wohlstetter was still briefing his overseas-base study in the fall of 1953 when he heard about Bruno Augenstein's analysis on the feasibility of the ICBM. Wohlstetter's first reaction was minor panic. He had spent nearly two years working on the vulnerability of SAC's bombers. First, the hydrogen bomb came along and threw off his calculations about how vulnerable his proposed basing system might be, and now the intercontinental ballistic missile threatened to make his whole study irrelevant.

His worries were alleviated, however, by two considerations. First, bombers would still comprise the vast bulk of both sides' strategic arsenals for years to come. Second, the ICBM would make SAC vulnerable in ways completely different from those that Wohlstetter was describing in the overseas-base study. Furthermore, the protective schemes proposed in that study would be inadequate against ICBMs, which reach their targets so quickly that in a surprise attack there would be virtually no warning time at all.

In short, the ICBM would allow Albert Wohlstetter the perfect opportunity to be commissioned a follow-on study to the overseas-base study, an update given the new technological situation. Wohlstetter was making the vulnerability of SAC his own little cottage industry.

Wohlstetter had also acquired a singular reputation with RAND management. The base study was a great success. He had delivered it ninety-two times—*ninety-two*, beyond most people's comprehension, much less endurance. And it worked. General Tommy White pushed it; the Air Force Council endorsed it; RAND saved the world—that was how management felt. Wohlstetter wanted this new project, on SAC vulnerability in the new age of ICBMs, to be grand and comprehensive. More than twenty RAND technicians and consultants ended up working on specialized studies within the project—on early-warning lines, on infrared detection of missiles, on fallout estimates, on the practicality of bomb-alarm systems, on the hardening of aircraft shelters, on possible anti-missile defenses. It was a high-priority RAND project, and Wohlstetter could pick his team as he wished, even raiding other projects while doing so.

Just after the start of the project, in January 1954, Wohlstetter and Fred Hoffman, his assistant, who had also worked on the overseas-base project, laid out their basic assumptions and a few tentative conclusions in an internally circulated RAND document called *Defending a Strategic Force After 1960*. Their first observation: "The defenses programmed, or recommended, to protect SAC in the Fifties will be entirely ineffective against an [ICBM] which would deliver bombs with essentially no warning," and the ICBM "*may* be feasible for the Russians by the end of this period." If the United States cannot protect SAC from a Soviet ICBM threat, they continued, reflecting a principle that went back to Bernard Brodie's 1946 essay, "then our advertised capability for retaliation will be fictitious." SAC could not "hurt the Russians very much."

A few rudimentary calculations revealed to Wohlstetter and Hoffman that the Soviets could destroy at least 80 percent of SAC bombers with a force of about 150 missiles, less than one-third the number of missiles that Air Force Intelligence was predicting the Russians would have by 1960. It was the same problem that they faced in the overseas-base study—a surprise attack that could decimate SAC and thus wipe out the deterrent force.

But the ICBM had limitations, and if SAC were to be protected, there must be a way to exploit them. These limitations were poor accuracy and a payload too small to deliver—at the time, anyway—more than a couple of megatons of explosive power. The solution, then, was to put the bombers in blast shelters. This could be done, they reasoned, by placing them on top of hydraulic elevators that could sink into a pit shaped like the contours of the airplane itself and then sliding massive concrete doors over the pit. Unsheltered, a bomber will be destroyed by a 500-kiloton bomb exploded as far away as three miles. A bomber placed in a shelter hardened to resist fifty-five pounds per square inch (psi) of blast overpressure, however, will not be destroyed by 500 kilotons unless the bomb lands 3,600 feet from the plane. A much tougher shelter still, one hardened to resist 200 psi, is destroyed only if the bomb lands within 600 feet. The destructive power of a bomb depends on its explosive yield and its accuracy. The ICBM would already be quite inaccurate; and hardening the target to resist the force of blast would have the same effect as reducing its explosive yield considerably. As a result, Wohlstetter and Hoffman noted in their initial calculations, a Russian attack with 300 ICBMs directed against SAC bases would probably destroy only 30 percent of the bombers if they were hardened to resist 55 psi, and only 2 percent if they were hardened to 200 psi.

Wohlstetter was inspired toward this solution by his old friend Paul Weidlinger, the civil engineer who had worked on quickly assembled hangars for the aircraft company owned by Wohlstetter's brother, and who had hired Albert to work with him at the National Housing Agency after the war. Wohlstetter had talked with Weidlinger about the vulnerability problem, and thought that as a structural engineer, he might have something to offer. Weidlinger discovered, among other things, that the Air Force assumed that objects could be hardened to resist a maximum of twenty psi. Examining the assumptions behind these Air Force calculations, Weidlinger guessed that it was possible to do better. The Air Force, it turned out, had been relying on calculations by very conservative engineers who, noting that normal buildings collapsed at five psi, thought that it was really going out on a limb to speculate that one might build something that could resist twenty.

Twenty psi might indeed have been an upper limit for many objects in civilization: nobody wanted airplanes or bridges that sagged or buildings that were half-collapsed. But with something like a shelter for protecting a missile or a bomber, all that was necessary was for the thing inside to survive and to be used once; aesthetic virtues were utterly unimportant. With this in mind, the hardness of a structure could be extended well beyond twenty psi.

Paul Weidlinger spent that summer at RAND as a consultant, and with some help from Herman Kahn—who, while in the RAND physics division, was becoming increasingly interested in strategic issues and was gradually allying himself with Wohlstetter—concluded that a 200-psi shelter was quite feasible. Indeed Weidlinger designed on paper just such a shelter, suitable for the B-52. Wohlstetter was now satisfied that his and Hoffman's theoretical observations about hardening shelters were technically feasible.

For nearly nine months, the Wohlstetter-Hoffman team slaved away on calculations, conceiving the most ingenious ways that the Soviet combined bomber and missile threat—based on

Air Force Intelligence projections—could do SAC in with as little warning as possible. Detailed map exercises were conducted, with Soviet bombers refueling in midair and going way around U.S. radar-warning nets to maximize surprise. Two-wave attacks were assumed—the first wave against the small number of SAC bases inside the United States (twenty-nine when Wohlstetter and Hoffman began their study, with fifty-five planned by 1962), the second wave nabbing those bombers that managed to survive the initial attack and fly on to dispersed bases. Air Force Intelligence was assuming a ferocious Soviet strategic buildup of 500 ICBMs and 500 Bear and Bison intercontinental bombers by 1960. Wohlstetter and Hoffman thought that they were making a very dramatic point when they illustrated how SAC could be devastated even assuming a very "low" estimate of Soviet forces—a strike of 250 or even 150 heavy bombers and the same number of ICBMs.

As for the American ICBM force, the plans for deploying it involved placing the missiles so close to one another and leaving them so unshielded that a mere 24 Soviet nuclear missiles would destroy 96 of the 120 that might be deployed by the early 1960s.

The Wohlstetter-Hoffman team came up with fifty ways to help solve the problem—among them hardening bombers inside shelters (the Weidlinger solution, which Wohlstetter considered most important), dispersing and hardening critical facilities on each base, adding more recovery bases inside the United States, building up active defenses around SAC bases, extending the perimeter of radar-warning nets, constructing long-range bomb alarms that would alert all SAC bases when one of them is hit by a nuclear bomb, allowing ambiguous warning signs of an attack to provoke preliminary bomber-evacuation measures.

Just as in the overseas-base study, the existing SAC system was compared with the proposed system through Edwin Paxson's systems-analysis technique—asking which system can destroy a given number of targets more cheaply and which system can destroy the most targets for a given amount of money. And again, the RAND system looked better. To destroy 85 percent of the 270 Soviet urban targets, "in the face of moderately high Soviet offense and defense capabilities" (defined as 500 Soviet ICBMs, 500 Soviet bombers, 295 air-defense fighter regiments, 225 local-defense-missile sites), SAC's system would cost nearly $35 billion, whereas RAND's would cost about $10 billion. RAND's proposal would cost more money than SAC was spending, but in terms of cost per target destroyed, it would be much cheaper. Likewise, in the face of an attack composed of 300 Soviet bombers and 250 ICBMs, with a second wave of 500 additional bombers, SAC's planned system could kill about 15 percent of the population in the 270 largest Soviet cities, given a $3.4 billion budget, whereas the RAND system could kill about 90 percent.

The exercise was complex but fundamentally mechanical: conceive the cleverest Soviet attack; punch in the Air Force Intelligence estimates on Soviet strategic forces and air defenses; from the yield and accuracy of Soviet offensive weapons and the psi-resistance of U.S. SAC targets, compute the weapons' "kill probability," the chance that they destroy the bombers or crater the runways or gut the support facilities. Then make the hypothetical improvements in SAC and do the calculations again. Keep doing the calculations over and over, adjusting them to slight improvements in the force, until nearly the entire SAC force is, on paper, able to survive even the most ingenious of Soviet surprise attacks and deliver the most powerful of retaliatory blows.

The results were presented in a RAND study, Staff Report R-290, entitled *Protecting U.S. Power to Strike Back in the 1950s and 1960s*. There were a few at RAND, most notably in the social science division, who had some doubts about R-290, who thought it lacked a political dimension, who wondered whether the Kremlin leaders really were prone to such risky maneuverings, who were skeptical that war would come with a bolt-from-the-blue surprise attack, as R-290 assumed. But the social science division was removed from the rest of RAND—literally, 2500 miles away, in Washington, D.C. Most were figuratively removed, too: quantitative analysis had triumphed at RAND, through the spread of systems analysis and game theory and—until the Wohlstetter studies, which put the economics division on top of the strategic business—through the domination over the rest of RAND by the mathematics division. These sorts of studies were scientific, so it was thought; there were numbers, calculations, rigorously checked, sometimes figured on a computer. Maybe the numbers were questionable, but they were tangible, unlike the theorizing, the Kremlinology, the academic historical research and interpretation produced by social science. Wohlstetter snootily denigrated all such works as being in "the essay tradition."

And within this newly triumphant time for the economics division, Wohlstetter established himself as the self-styled intellec-

tual leader, the man who had calculated the essence and requirements of deterrence in the nuclear age. Few of Wohlstetter's
thoughts were wholly original. The idea of a surviving second-
strike force as the essence of deterrence came from Bernard
Brodie; the systems analysis he took from Ed Paxson, E. S. Quade
and others; the historical parallel of Pearl Harbor was inspired by
his wife, Roberta Wohlstetter; much of the actual quantitative
work in his two big studies was handled by his colleagues, Fred
Hoffman, Harry Rowen, Bob Lutz and dozens of others. But
Wohlstetter expanded on that which he borrowed. Brodie, assuming that nuclear weapons would be used against cities, never
thought that protecting the second-strike force would take very
much imagination. Paxson, creative as he was, failed to include
some important factors, such as the location of air bases, in his
conception of a "system." Wohlstetter, coming to the field of
national security with no background in it, was able to view things
from a novel perspective and to synthesize its elements into a new
package. Through Wohlstetter's own personal influence within
RAND, vulnerability began to loom as the preoccupying issue, the
virtual obsession, of strategic analysis.

It was not so much analytic prowess that gained Wohlstetter
his eager following at RAND, especially among some of the younger economists. More, it was his tone, style and manner that
seemed cultivated to convey the image of a man on top of *everything.* Even his office was designed to be distinctive, decorated in
stark black with silk wallpaper and an Eames chair behind his
desk. He knew math and statistics and economics, but he also
knew about wine and fine food and he could talk about art, philosophy and classical music. To the amusement of many onlookers, a
fair number of RAND economists—previously quite humdrum in
life-style—started acquiring a taste for obscure and expensive
vintages and had their wives trained as gourmet cooks because
Albert's wife, Roberta, was a gourmet cook.

The Wohlstetter home was the frequent scene of late-night
dinners and strategic rap sessions, the RAND coterie and occasional outside guests and distinguished RAND visitors attending.
Albert was the guru, Roberta the den mother, Albert holding court
on his views of the world, Roberta dishing out delectable soufflés
and not missing a beat of the conversation. For a RAND economist
or engineer who had spent much of his career crunching numbers for dry, dull estimates of how much a weapon will cost or fig-

uring out how to stretch titanium over the cockpit of a jet fighter, those drives up the winding, hilly roads of Laurel Canyon, toward the Wohlstetter house, were the closest that any of them would ever come to approaching Mecca.

Outside the coterie, many at RAND thought Wohlstetter was something of a phony, pretentious, amusing at best. Many of the engineers and physicists particularly looked down on Wohlstetter. For one thing, they found his work much less important than he claimed. To them, strategic matters were ancillary to the real issues of science; the fact of the bomb's existence and how it worked were considered much more important than the esoterica of how it might be used. They thought he talked in tones far too authoritative and even condescending about things he really did not know. Ernie Plesset, head of the physics division, came away from a Wohlstetter briefing at RAND muttering, "You'd think he was reciting from the Sermon on the Mount in there."

Among Wohlstetter's following he was indeed on the mount; and the sermon they embraced told of the coming vulnerability of the strategic retaliatory force.

Within the strategic set at RAND, there were some who had problems with the way that Wohlstetter did business, especially his sharp sensitivity to any criticism and the absolute loyalty he demanded from anyone who worked with him. Among the RAND strategists of an independent bent—Herman Kahn, Daniel Ellsberg, William Kaufmann, Andrew Marshall and others—admiration for Wohlstetter was genuine but grudging. They hesitated before depending too heavily on Wohlstetter's work for the formulation of their own assumptions and conclusions. However, they could turn to Roberta Wohlstetter and her just-finished study of Pearl Harbor, which revealed how a surprise attack might be executed, how the absence of its detection might reflect not simple blindness or stupidity but careful measures taken by the aggressor and the confusion of the relevant intelligence traffic amid the "noise" of other, less relevant, perhaps even deceptively transmitted signals. Everyone liked Roberta Wohlstetter. She was wonderfully gracious, very bright but with a subdued ego.

In any event, by 1957 or 1958, a definite strategic community had formed within RAND. It had reached—by dint of small numbers, a common outlook, a (mostly) common academic background in mathematics and economics, and the forcefulness of a few strong personalities—a fairly tight consensus on the major

issues, the most solidly held of which was the not unlikely prospect of a Soviet surprise attack against the increasingly vulnerable
Strategic Air Command. For this new strategic community, these
were heady days at RAND. They knew—some of them had invented—the tricks of the trade, the systems analysis, the method
of calculation, that allowed them to deal rationally with the biggest
issue of all time, the hydrogen bomb.

But these were grim times, as well. Wohlstetter and Hoffman
may have written at the end of one chapter in R-290 that they "do
not, of course, imply that a Russian attack is imminent"—only
that "it is a painful fact that the risks to the Soviets of attempting a
surprise attack on the United States are much lower than generally estimated." The atmosphere at RAND, however, indicated
differently. Many rational analysts were spending typically sixty-
or eighty-hour workweeks frantically writing reports and comput-
ing calculations. To many, it appeared that the Russians might indeed attack sometime in the near future. The calculations indicated that it would soon be possible and even profitable for them to
do so; therefore, given their aggressive aims and our vulnerability,
that would be their rational strategy.

Alain Enthoven and Daniel Ellsberg were two of the brightest of RAND's young economists who joined the Wohlstetter strategy clique. They both came to RAND in their mid-twenties in the
immediate wake of Wohlstetter's R-290 report. Both decided not
to sign up for RAND's highly lucrative retirement plan. They figured that, along with much of the rest of the Western world, they
might not be around long enough to enjoy its benefits.

8 THE GAITHER COMMITTEE

IN THE LAST HALF of the 1950s, the specter of a Russian surprise attack against a vulnerable America became the central threat in the eyes of the strategic community not only in Santa Monica, but also in Washington, D.C., Cambridge, Massachusetts, and their surrounding environs. In this environment, Albert Wohlstetter and his R-290 report were a perfect fit, and played a critical role in the development of the consensus. R-290 legitimized a basic fear of the enemy and the unknown through mathematical calculation and rational analysis, providing the techniques and the general perspective through which the new and rather scary situation— the Soviet Union's acquisition of long-range nuclear weapons— could be discussed and acted upon.

R-290 was top secret, like most of RAND's more intricate analyses, but it was read by those, especially in the Department of Defense, with access to such information. The chief impact of R-290, however, came with the formation of a special blue-ribbon commission, under the auspices of the National Security Council but outside any staff or line command. Formally, the commission was called the Security Resources Panel of the Science Advisory Committee of the Office of Defense Mobilization. More commonly, it was called the Gaither Committee, named for its designated chairman, H. Rowan Gaither.

The Gaither Committee began life in the spring of 1957, when the National Security Council met to evaluate a proposal made the previous January to spend $32.4 billion over the next eight years, $28.6 billion of it in federal money, on a massive blast-shelter and fallout-shelter program that could save millions of American lives in the event of a Russian nuclear attack. Civil defense was becoming a *cause célèbre* among many who looked closely at defense problems generally, but this concern was fairly recent, dating back only a few years earlier when scientists started to learn about radioactive fallout. Calculations now suggested that about 20 percent of all deaths in nuclear war would be caused by blast and heat; the rest, by the *residual* radiation known as fallout. Suddenly, the notion of the Soviet Union's amassing its own substantial arsenal of H-bombs took on a more menacing character: a nuclear attack would kill not just a few million Americans, but tens of millions, more than 100 million, maybe everybody—unless we buried ourselves in fallout shelters and stayed there, nourished by prestocked supplies, for weeks or months.

Scientists, especially at Cal Tech and MIT, spent their summers in the early and mid 1950s working out the civil-defense problem. Project East River and the Summer Studies at MIT's Lincoln Laboratory were the most notable, recommending elaborate and expensive nationwide shelter programs as essential elements of an overall defense program.

By the beginning of January 1957, enough analysis had been made of civil defense for the FCDA, the Federal Civil Defense Administration, to urge a massive shelter program for protection in the event of nuclear attack. It recommended that the federal government spend from fiscal years 1958 through 1965 $28.6 billion, and state and local governments another $3.8 billion, on shelters. The Federal Housing Administration would provide mortgage insurance for privately built backyard shelters, up to $2,500 per shelter, and tax codes would be changed to allow taxpayers to deduct up to $2,500—$500 a year spread out over five years—for expenses incurred in home-shelter construction. With these incentives, the FCDA estimated, another $15 billion or more might be spent privately, in addition to the $32.4 billion spent with public revenue.

On March 29, the NSC Planning Board told James Lay, the NSC's executive director, that the board was "unable at this time to make a recommendation which would enable the Council and the President to act upon any shelter proposal on the basis of an informed judgment." It recommended that various executive agencies carry out studies, to be presented to the NSC. Among the assignments was: "A study by the Science Advisory Committee of the Office of Defense Mobilization as to the relative value of various active and passive measures to protect the civil population in case of nuclear attack and its aftermath, taking into account probable new weapons systems." On April 4, the NSC approved the Planning Board's recommendation; on April 8, President Eisenhower signed the NSC's approval.

Not quite two weeks earlier, on March 26, just three days before the NSC Planning Board made its report on the FCDA recommendations, Nelson Rockefeller met for lunch with President Eisenhower, the President's chief of staff, Sherman Adams, and the budget director, Percival Brundage. At the time, Rockefeller was chairman of Eisenhower's Psychological Warfare Panel and was obsessed with civil defense. At the luncheon, Rockefeller stressed that "the will to resist" was central in deterring the enemy. He said that the Russians might start a war without warning; that some of their planes and missiles would get through, no matter how good our continental defenses might be; and that "the side preserving its manpower resources and maintaining its will to resist would have a major advantage."

Rockefeller urged Eisenhower to establish a Presidential commission to examine in detail the whole civil-defense issue, a commission composed of "men who believe in the importance of having an optimum defense for the United States and who are open-minded about how that is to be achieved." Eisenhower had no particular penchant for civil defense, but so many reputable people whom he knew did have an intense feeling about it that he decided to turn one of the studies proposed by the NSC on April 4—the one by the Science Advisory Committee of the Office of Defense Mobilization—into the Presidential commission that Rockefeller advocated.

One prominent member of the Science Advisory Committee, and later Eisenhower's chief science adviser, was James R. Killian, Jr., president of MIT. Robert Cutler, Eisenhower's national security adviser, asked Killian for names of prominent people who might head up this special committee. Killian recommended H. Rowan Gaither, whom Killian knew from the days when Gaither was business manager of the MIT Radiation Lab during World War II and, more recently, from some "future studies" on American society that Gaither had sponsored as president of the Ford Foundation. Eisenhower formally invited Gaither to direct the special committee on May 8, 1957; one week later, Gaither accepted "with humility and with a full sense of the magnitude and urgency of the task."

Gaither's deputy would be Robert C. Sprague, president of the Sprague Electric Company in western Massachusetts and a man with active interest in defense. Sprague had worked on two highly classified studies evaluating U.S. continental defenses, the first in 1953 for the Senate Armed Services Preparedness Sub-

committee, the second in 1955 for a special committee headed by
James Killian on the possibilities of a Soviet surprise attack.

Gaither, Sprague, Gordon Gray, and national security adviser
Robert Cutler listed other names to serve on the panel. They chose
William C. Foster, deputy secretary of defense in the early 1950s;
James Phinney Baxter III, president of Williams College, former
member of Killian's committee, and author of *Scientists Against
Time,* a history of operations research during World War II; Wil-
liam Webster and James Perkins, who had both worked on civil-
defense studies; Jerome Wiesner of MIT, a participant in many
studies on weapons analysis; Robert Prim and Hector Skifter of
Bell Labs and Airborne Instruments; Robert Calkins and John
Corson, two economists; and the panel's technical adviser, Edward P. Oliver, an engineer from RAND.

Rowan Gaither had been the wealthy San Francisco lawyer
who, not quite a decade earlier, helped Frank Collbohm turn
RAND into an independent nonprofit corporation. Now he was
chairman of the board of the Ford Foundation and chairman of
the board at RAND. After accepting Eisenhower's offer, he called
on several of the top analysts at RAND for advice on how to pursue
the matter at hand.

One of those he called upon was Albert Wohlstetter. Wohlstetter had only recently begun to brief R-290 around the Pentagon, and firmly believed that the issues raised in that study were
the most important in the entire realm of national security. This
round of briefings was progressing more briskly than had been the
case with the early months of his overseas-base study of a few
years earlier. Already, he had briefed R-290 to Defense Secretary
Charles Wilson, and accompanying him to that briefing had been
not only a fair number of Air Force generals but also General
Nathan Twining, Chairman of the Joint Chiefs of Staff. But now
Gaither was talking about something potentially larger—a Presi-
dentially appointed commission, packed with prominent names,
that might change the whole focus of the Eisenhower Administration's skimpy and unimaginative defense policies.

Wohlstetter tried to convince Gaither that civil defense did
not lie at the heart of the matter. He reminded Gaither of the
R-290 and overseas-base studies, which Wohlstetter had briefed to
him as chairman of RAND's board of directors. Wohlstetter suggested that the vulnerability of SAC was the most critical issue
facing the country, far more critical than civil defense, and that

perhaps Gaither should broaden the terms of his mandate to include the problem of maintaining a ready and effective second-
strike capability in the face of a Soviet surprise attack.

Gaither agreed and when the panel began to meet very secretly that summer in the Executive Office Building next door to
the White House, he had little trouble convincing the other members that they should perhaps consider civil defense in the context
of broader security issues. Certainly Robert Sprague and Phinney
Baxter had no problems with the idea, having served just two
years earlier on Killian's surprise attack panel.

By August the project was under way. An advisory panel of
still more prominent men had been established to give the committee greater prestige and credibility—Ernest Lawrence of Livermore Lab, former Defense Secretary Robert Lovett, John
McCloy of Chase Manhattan Bank, Frank Stanton of CBS, Mervin
Kelly of Bell Labs, General Jimmy Doolittle, General John Hull,
former Chief of Naval Operations Admiral Robert Carney. And the
steering panel—the original group composed of Gaither, Sprague,
Baxter, Foster and the rest—organized a team of seventy-one scientists, economists, weapons experts, and past and present government officials to serve as a vast research staff.

Early in September, just as the committee started working
heavily on analysis of the problem, Rowan Gaither fell ill with
cancer and had to enter the hospital. Robert Sprague and William
Foster took over as co-chairmen; but by this time, certainly by no
later than mid-August, Gaither's early proposal to broaden the
mandate of the so-called Gaither Committee had taken hold.

The influence of Wohlstetter's R-290 did not stop with the
expansion of the Gaither Committee's mandate. Herman Kahn,
the jolly, corpulent RAND physicist who by this time had heavily
immersed himself in the strategic side of the nuclear-weapons
business, was a consultant to the Gaither Committee. Originally,
he was to be one of the seventy-one project researchers, but he
was denied the special security clearance required because of his
wife's Communist Party relatives. (This once-removed Communist connection, in fact, was on the verge of jeopardizing Kahn's
career at RAND, until a security hearing, demanded by Kahn,
cleared up the whole business and allowed him to carry on.)

Kahn was mainly working on the civil-defense side of the
Gaither Committee, but he was also very keen on Wohlstetter's

R-290, and pushed that report within the lower levels of the committee as best he could. One man he talked to about R-290 was Spurgeon Keeny. Keeny had been one of the few men in all of the United States to be drafted into the military in the few years following World War II. Having studied Russian and physics at Columbia University, he was able to talk the Air Force into giving him an officer's commission and putting him in the intelligence division, where he spent the next six years trying to locate atomic-energy plants inside the Soviet Union and integrating that intelligence with nuclear-war targeting plans. Keeny came to the Gaither Committee as the atomic-energy specialist in the office of the Assistant Secretary of Defense for Research and Engineering. He started working with the committee part-time, but soon became so engrossed that, throughout the summer and early fall of 1957, he made it his full-time task.

Keeny was not involved in top-level meetings, but he did a great deal of staff work for Jerry Wiesner and Hector Skifter, helping to write the supporting analysis papers on passive defense, active defense and especially strategic policy. Herman Kahn acquainted Keeny with the shocking findings of the report by Wohlstetter and Fred Hoffman. The paper that Keeny finally wrote on strategic policy was essentially a distillation of R-290, incorporating its basic points.

The steering panel of the committee spent most of its time reading the reports written by the project staff and listening to dozens of briefings from Air Force generals about how badly the Air Force needed more weapons and more money, from intelligence officers on the growing magnitude of the Soviet long-range missile and bomber threat, from the Army's Operations Research Office on how the Army's wonderful proposed air-defense missiles would shoot down 98 percent of incoming bombers and missile warheads.

And they received a briefing from Albert Wohlstetter on the findings of R-290. The briefing had a particularly galvanizing effect on Robert Sprague, who since Gaither's hospitalization had become the committee's co-chairman. Sprague was naturally receptive to the ideas of R-290, for many of them had been expressed earlier in the Killian Panel on surprise attack, on which Sprague had been chief consultant.

Formally called the Technological Capabilities Panel and, like the Gaither Committee, created under the auspices of the Science

Advisory Committee of the Office of Defense Mobilization, the Killian Panel turned in to Eisenhower, in February 1955, a lengthy
two-volume report called *Meeting the Threat of Surprise Attack*.
The report called for improving intelligence technology both for
seeing what the Soviets were up to and for warning of an impending attack, strengthening defensive measures (both anti-missile
missiles and civil defense), improving communications and,
"through innovation in technology," improving U.S. retaliatory
power by making SAC less vulnerable to surprise attack. This
would be done mostly through a strengthened continental air-
defense force, but also through some of the measures that Wohlstetter quite independently urged in the overseas-base study of
1953–1954 and in the R-290 report of 1956—greater warning
time, more bases and dispersal of equipment on those bases.

The TCP recommended doing just about everything that
could be done through science and technology—a crash program
on ICBMs, on intermediate-range missiles based in Europe, on
new military communications systems, intelligence systems, new
weapons of all sorts. Its overall impact was enormous. It helped accelerate the ICBM and IRBM programs, it sparked Presidential
endorsement of the Navy's Polaris submarine program, it led to
the development of the U-2 spy plane (thanks to Edwin Land's
photographic genius), and it spurred Eisenhower to establish his
own office of the special assistant for science and technology.

More generally, it added scientific legitimacy to the general
feeling among many in government that the arms race must be
continued and accelerated at all costs. Even after both the United
States and the Soviet Union reach the stage where each could destroy the other with multimegaton bombs, where, in short, "the
contest is drawn and neither contestant can derive military advantage," that would be no reason to stop. "We need not assume
that this stage is unchangeable or that one country or the other
cannot move again into a position of relative advantage." The
search for "technological breakthroughs" must continue.

But that was for the future. For now, Sprague was intrigued
and slightly infuriated by what Wohlstetter had to say. Nothing
seemed to have happened to SAC's readiness between the time
that the TCP filed its report in 1955 and now, more than two and a
half years later, when the Gaither Committee was sitting and listening to Wohlstetter. The committee had been told by Air Force
officials that SAC had developed a plan that would ensure getting

25 percent of the bombers off the ground in the event of a surprise attack, that, in effect, the criticisms made by the TCP more than two years earlier had now been taken care of.

In the month of September, the Gaither Committee's steering panel and some of the staff members made trips to various military facilities—SAC headquarters in Omaha, NORAD in Colorado Springs, several radar sites, and so forth. Most appalling to the members was the trip to SAC. General LeMay told the panel that SAC was second to none, that they were wasting their time, that this business about a missile threat was nothing to worry about, that missiles would have no real significance in his military lifetime, that the manned B-52 bomber could solve any problem.

Back in Washington, Robert Sprague approached Robert Cutler, Eisenhower's national security adviser, and told him that the session with LeMay was entirely unsatisfactory, that he would not deal with any of their questions seriously and gave them nothing of value generally. After conferring with Eisenhower, Cutler gave four of the top steering panel members—Sprague, Bill Foster, Jerry Wiesner and Bill Webster—authority to go back to SAC headquarters and get more information from LeMay. A few days later, the four men made their journey.

On September 16, they flew with LeMay to headquarters of the North American Air Defense Command, NORAD, in Colorado Springs. Sprague and Bill Foster had asked LeMay to stage a spontaneous alert of the entire SAC force, to see if the planes could indeed take off in time. The alert signal was sent out to all bases. Over the next six hours, the amount of warning time the United States might receive in the event of a surprise Soviet bomber attack, not a single airplane was able to take off from the ground; only a few that happened to be on a test flight at the time of the alert were airborne.

That was appalling enough to the panel. More shocking was that LeMay seemed totally unimpressed by the exercise. He simply grunted, said the Soviets could never coordinate the sort of attack that could bring all their bombers over all the SAC targets simultaneously, that SAC would always get off the ground in time. Beyond that, he explained no more.

Back at SAC, LeMay showed Robert Sprague a huge map depicting the location of all the SAC air bases and how long it would take the bombers on each of these bases to get off the ground, combat ready, if they received "tactical warning" only—that is, if the first sign of a Soviet attack were the warning flash that appeared on NORAD screens once the Soviet airplanes passed through the Distant Early Warning Line, the DEW Line, up around the North Pole.

Sprague had served on surprise-attack panels before, and knew roughly the time it would take for a Russian bomber to get from the DEW Line to each SAC base in the United States. The bombers could take off with fairly short notice, at least theoretically, and each SAC base was assigned three auxiliary civilian bases where the bombers could land and disperse in the event of warning. But Sprague also knew that the bombers would have only limited crews, limited fuel loadings and no atomic weapons on board. The bombs were stored on the SAC bases, separated from the planes; they were not protected from the overpressures of blast, and it would take some time to load them onto the bombers. In other words, they were highly vulnerable. And there were no atomic bombs on the auxiliary bases. In short, the SAC bombers might get off the ground, but they would have nothing to drop on Russian territory, nothing with which to carry out the national policy of "massive retaliation."

Looking at the numbers on the big map at SAC headquarters, which showed the time it would take for the bombers to get off the ground fully loaded, Sprague calculated that in nearly every instance they exceeded the time it would take for a Russian bomber to fly from the DEW Line to the bases. The only exception was the base in Morocco, holding about a dozen SAC bombers. Sprague was genuinely frightened. That exercise in Colorado Springs was no anomaly; the conclusions of Wohlstetter's R-290 were not theoretical; a surprise Soviet attack might very well destroy America's ability to retaliate in kind, and therefore, once the Soviets acquired the means to launch such an attack, the United States might no longer be able to deter nuclear war and win the war if the Soviets provoked one.

Sprague pointed all this out to LeMay, who calmly responded that this didn't scare him. He told Sprague that the United States had airplanes flying secret missions over Soviet territory twenty-four hours a day, picking up all sorts of intelligence information, mostly communications intelligence from Soviet military radio transmissions. He offered to take Sprague into the office where this data was sent and stored. All those statements the Soviets periodically made about American spy planes penetrating Russian airspace were true. We always said the incidents were accidental, but they were not; they were very deliberate.

"If I see that the Russians are amassing their planes for an attack," LeMay continued, "I'm going to knock the shit out of them before they take off the ground."

Sprague was thunderstruck by the revelation. This was knowledge that only a very, very small number of Americans possessed or knew anything about. Most startling was LeMay's final bit of news, that he would order a preemptive attack against Soviet air bases.

"But General LeMay," Sprague said, "that's not national policy."

"I don't care," LeMay replied. "It's my policy. That's what I'm going to do."

Sprague was both relieved and stunned. He was relieved that at least the United States would not allow its bombers to be destroyed on the ground on the opening day of a nuclear war, that there were spy planes continuously relaying communications intelligence to SAC headquarters about Soviet military moves, that therefore the country could rely on something more timely than mere tactical warning. Nevertheless, he was stunned that under the assumptions that most people talked about, a surprise attack with tactical warning only, the United States did not have the ability to retaliate massively, hardly the ability to retaliate at all, and that to the extent we did have this ability, it was only because of a preemptive-strike war plan that SAC held secretly, separate from the war plans developed by the Joint Chiefs of Staff and signed by the President of the United States.

This was why LeMay seemed unfazed by that exercise at NORAD, where not a single SAC plane could take off the ground during the entire period of tactical warning, and why LeMay was unimpressed with all the studies—the one that Sprague had worked on for the Senate Armed Services Subcommittee, the Killian TCP study, Wohlstetter's overseas-base study and R-290—that concluded that SAC was devastatingly vulnerable.

Sprague decided that no staff member of the Gaither Committee, or anyone else he ever talked with, would know anything about it.

By October 1957, the steering panel of the Gaither Committee had decided that a massive civil-defense program—the one

they were assigned to evaluate originally—should take a back seat
to what they saw as the much more pressing need of building up a
much larger offensive missile force and protecting it from an attack through dispersal and hardened shelters, so that SAC might
survive an attack without having to implement LeMay's secret
war plan.

Then on October 4, as the committee was near completion of
its work, something happened that rocked the nation into a state
of near panic: *Sputnik*. The very word was enough to send shivers
up just about every American's spine. For Sputnik was the name
of the 184-pound satellite that a Russian rocket launched into
orbit in outer space that day. A Russian rocket! The very notion
that the Russians, previously thought of as primitive Asiatics
when it came to advanced technology, could beat the United
States of America in something so ultimately technological as the
launching of an object into outer space was absolutely horrifying,
a threat to national security in its own right.

It was an event that evoked hysterical public pronouncements. John Rinehart of the Smithsonian Astrophysical Observa-
tory proclaimed that "no matter what we do now, the Russians
will beat us to the moon. . . . I would not be surprised if the Russians reached the moon within a week." Edward Teller, father of
the H-bomb, declared on national television that America had lost
"a battle more important and greater than Pearl Harbor." In the
U.S. Congress, Clare Boothe Luce called Sputnik's beep "an intercontinental outer-space raspberry to a decade of American preten-
sions that the American way of life was a gilt-edged guarantee of
our national superiority." Senator Lyndon Johnson's aide, George
Reedy, summed it up in a memorandum to his boss written two
weeks after the launch: "the American people are bound to become increasingly uneasy. It is unpleasant to feel that there is
something floating around in the air *which the Russians can put
up and we can't*. . . . It really doesn't matter whether the satellite
has any military value. The important thing is that *the Russians
have left the earth and the race for control of the universe has
started*."

To some, the directly military implications of Sputnik were
also haunting. A few months earlier, Nikita Khrushchev had
boasted that the Russians had developed an intercontinental-
range rocket. Now he was demonstrating to the world that the
Russians could launch such a rocket. The rest of the argument

seemed, at the time, all too clear. If the Russians could put a satellite on the tip of that rocket, they might also load a nuclear warhead; if they could send it up into outer space, they might also be
able to make it come back down to earth—specifically, down to
American territory—and all this a few years before the United
States would even have an ICBM ready for deployment.

To the members of the Gaither Committee, who had spent
the past few months doing nothing but dwelling on every frightening scenario of a Soviet nuclear attack imaginable, Sputnik
seemed to confirm the worst of their suspicions about Russian
military might. A new sense of urgency, on top of one that was already quite intense, consumed the committee's final efforts. The
various staff groups had turned in their papers on civil defense, on
missiles, on anti-missile missiles, on strategic calculations, on
strategic policy generally. The steering panel knew that the final
condensed report would have to pack a powerful enough wallop to
galvanize the Eisenhower Administration—which many of them
considered passive and complacent—into decisive and immediate
action.

Robert Sprague and James Phinney Baxter took on the task
of boiling down the staff papers and the panel's own collective
thoughts into a tight, logical draft, Sprague because he was the
committee's co-chairman since Gaither had been hospitalized,
Baxter because he was an eloquent and skilled historian who
wrote well. In the end, Sprague let the task of most of the writing
fall into Baxter's lap. Baxter felt the task was a bit beyond his own
talents and so privately recruited the assistance of another member of the committee, one of the staffers subordinate to the steering panel, a former State Department official from the days of the
Truman Administration, a good friend of Baxter's, a controversial
figure named Paul Nitze.

Paul Henry Nitze had kept a low profile on the Gaither Committee, at least to the outside world of the Eisenhower Administration. He might as well have been on the steering panel—he attended most of its meetings—but he wasn't. He was a Democrat
and was well known as a sharp critic and personal antagonist of
Eisenhower's bristly and domineering Secretary of State, John
Foster Dulles. It would do the committee's credibility no good to
have his name formally signed on a report that was bound to be
somewhat critical of the Administration's defense efforts. So his

name was entered as one of the committee's staff members, but
was given no highlight.

But Nitze contributed a great deal of energy to the project,
coming up with dozens of ideas on how the West could wage the
Cold War with greater enthusiasm and success. One of the most
well considered and original was the need for a buildup of conventional, non-nuclear forces to meet Soviet aggression on the pe-
ripheries, the "gray areas," that part of the globe that would later
be called the "third world," without having to escalate the conflict
to a nuclear level. Among the more eccentric of his ideas was that
we should develop a "love gas," as he called it, some chemical
substance that could be sprayed all over the Soviet Union, especially over the Kremlin, that could induce its inhabitants to become more peaceful, complacent, unaggressive, acquiescent . . .
loving.

Nitze joined the Gaither Committee as an active Cold Warrior who had already done a great deal of thinking about how civil
defense and the prospect of a Soviet nuclear attack fit into the
broad scheme of foreign policy.

As Secretary of State Dean Acheson's policy planning director in the previous Administration, Nitze—along with Assistant
Secretary of Defense Frank Nash and Richard Bissell of the
ECA—drafted a lengthy paper entitled *Reexamination of United
States Programs for National Security.* Acheson and Defense Secretary Robert Lovett signed it and presented it to the National Security Council, as NSC-141, on January 19, 1953, one day before
Harry Truman left office to make room for Dwight David Eisenhower.

The paper touched on virtually every topic that fell under the
rubric "national security," mainly on the need for a buildup of
conventional, non-nuclear military forces. The Eisenhower Administration, upon entering office, had rejected its findings because the program would cost far more money than the President
was willing to spend. Yet a major part of the paper also focused on
the merits and functions of civil defense. The "willingness of the
United States . . . to initiate an atomic attack in the event that the
Soviet rulers take certain actions which we would regard as a
casus belli will be significantly affected by the casualties and destruction which the Soviet system could inflict in retaliation. Even
at the present time, these casualties and this destruction would be

very high and the prospect, under a continuation of our present programs, will rapidly worsen. There is an increasing danger that unless a large-scale civil defense program and measures to improve greatly our own defense against air and sea attack are undertaken, the United States might find its freedom of action impaired in an emergency."

If the Soviets developed their own hydrogen bomb, Nitze and his associates foretold, "this would present an extremely grave threat to the United States, notwithstanding our own thermonuclear capability. It would tend to impose greater caution in our cold war policies to the extent that these policies involve significant risks of general war." Thus, an "adequate civil defense is of utmost importance because the freedom of the United States Government to take strong actions in the cold war, which may carry with them serious risk of violent Soviet reactions, will depend in increasing measure upon firm public morale in the United States." Paul Nitze had the right temper for the times.

There was another reason why Phinney Baxter could hardly have chosen a more suitable man for the task at hand. When it came to writing official, top-secret reports that combined sophisticated analysis with a flair for scaring the daylights out of anyone reading them, Paul H. Nitze had no match.

Nitze had done yeoman's work on this score seven and a half years earlier, in April 1950, with the composition of a report submitted to the National Security Council, under the signatures of Secretary of State Dean Acheson and Defense Secretary Louis Johnson, called *United States Objectives and Programs for National Security*—labeled, and known more widely ever since, as NSC-68.

The Cold War was mounting in those years. The previous half decade had witnessed a severe corrosion in the Western world and an expansion of the U.S.S.R., the political take-over of Eastern Europe, the Berlin blockade, the civil war in Greece. Yet President Harry Truman, bolstered by a cautious team of economic advisers, refused to raise the $15 billion ceiling that he had imposed on defense spending. George Kennan, the powerful director of the State Department's policy planning staff, worried about the need to contain Soviet expansionism, but believed that a "containment" policy should emphasize political and economic bolstering of the West, rather than "war scare" hyperbole or a massive military buildup. And Defense Secretary Louis Johnson, a former campaign manager of Truman's, loyally supported his commander in chief's budget ceiling.

Dean Acheson became Secretary of State in 1949; he and Kennan continually clashed over the nature of the Soviet threat and how the U.S. should respond to it. In January 1950, Acheson fired Kennan from the policy planning office, made him counselor and sent him off on a month-long fact-finding mission to South America. Acheson believed that America's attitude toward defense had to take a much harder line, and he appointed in Kennan's place at policy planning one of Kennan's assistants, Paul Nitze. Throughout his clashes with Kennan, Acheson had found a sympathetic ear in this young former Wall Street banker. Nitze, he recalled in his memoirs, was "a joy to work with because of his clear, incisive mind."

NSC-68 was written chiefly as a memorandum to guide policy in light of the explosion of a Soviet atomic bomb the previous August. But it was used by Acheson and Nitze as a vehicle for pushing their own, more militaristic views into official parlance.

A special interagency committee was established to work on NSC-68, but Nitze drafted most of the paper in the early spring of 1950. It was a long-winded memorandum, melodramatic and spooky. It foretold that when the Kremlin "calculates that it has a sufficient atomic capability to make a surprise attack on us, nullifying our atomic superiority and creating a military situation decisively in its favor, the Kremlin might be tempted to strike swiftly and with stealth." The year of maximum danger was 1954. By that time, the Soviets could amass 200 atomic bombs, enough to deliver a surprise attack "of such weight that the United States must have substantially increased . . . air, ground and sea strength, atomic capabilities, and air and civil defenses" if it is to survive.

Throughout, Nitze wrote of the "Kremlin's design for world domination," intrinsic to the Soviet system, fatal to the West. "The Kremlin is inescapably militant . . . because it possesses, and is possessed by, a worldwide revolutionary movement, because it is the inheritor of Russian imperialism, and because it is a totalitarian dictatorship. . . ." Its system "requires a dynamic extension of authority and the ultimate elimination of any effective opposition." Since the U.S. is "the principal center of power in the non-Soviet world," it "is the principal enemy whose integrity and vitality must be subverted or destroyed . . . if the Kremlin is to achieve its fundamental design."

Meanwhile, Nitze continued, the military strength of the West was "becoming dangerously inadequate." In a hypothetical 1950 war, the U.S. could protect the Western hemisphere, Pacific bases and most essential supply lines—but now *global* power was necessary. The Kremlin's "assault on free institutions is worldwide now, and in the context of the present polarization of power a defeat of free institutions anywhere is a defeat everywhere."

Nitze's prescription: a scheme for *Pax Americana*—"to foster a world environment in which the American system can survive and flourish." The requirements: higher military spending, more military aid, improved internal-security measures, civil defense, a psychological-warfare campaign, more intelligence activity, reduced spending on nondefense programs, higher taxes.

The language of NSC-68 was deliberately hyped. Acheson explained in his memoirs: "The purpose of NSC-68 was to so bludgeon the mass mind of 'top government' that not only could the President make a decision but that the decision could be carried out." The "task of a public officer seeking to explain and gain support for a major policy," he wrote, "is not that of the writer of a doctoral thesis. Qualification must give way to simplicity of statement, nicety and nuance to bluntness, almost brutality, in carrying home a point." He recalled of the NSC-68 paper, "If we made our points clearer than truth, we did not differ from most other educators and could hardly do otherwise."

In making things "clearer than truth," in "bludgeoning the mass mind of 'top government,' " Paul Nitze found his calling. When Truman received NSC-68 on April 7, 1950, he gave a copy to his chief domestic adviser, Charles Murphy, who took it home that night to read. It scared him so much that he didn't go to the office the next day, but just sat at home, reading the memorandum over and over. Two weeks later, Truman called Louis Johnson into his office and told him that the economy-in-defense policy was dead. Although some in the government opposed the massiveness of the effort proposed in NSC-68, criticism vanished on June 25, when the North Korean Army spilled over the border and the Korean War was on. Limited and localized, the Korean War was hardly the sort of war for which the NSC-68 programs were designed. But the war forced many to think about the need for long-range strategy; NSC-68 was there and, on the face of things, prophetic. On September 30, the NSC officially adopted it as a statement of policy. The defense budget climbed from $13.5 billion to $48.2 billion for fiscal year 1951. Prewar levels were never approached again.

Nitze's memo helped determine the missions and assumptions shaping this higher spending and more active Cold War policy. Its most enduring legacy was the view of the world that it projected: the "underlying conflict" between the "free world" of the West and the "slave society" behind the Iron Curtain, the equation of "free world" with any regime that harbored anti-Communist sentiments, the reduction of the complexities of what would later be called the third world to a simple Manichean vision, the highly pessimistic image of Soviet military might, and the idea that the only real answer to the Soviet challenge lay in the construction of a gigantic, worldwide U.S. military machine. In NSC-68, Nitze systematized the uneasy feelings that many harbored about the Russians, gave them the ring of historical truth and political analysis, and provided a prism through which all Soviet activity could be viewed.

When James Phinney Baxter asked him to draft the report of the Gaither Committee in the fall of 1957, Paul Nitze faced another golden opportunity. Here again was an Administration that refused to sacrifice old-fashioned notions of balanced budgets for the needs of national security in the face of a menacing Soviet threat. Here again was a specially appointed committee that just might change things all around. It was time to write another hair-raiser.

The report was handed to President Eisenhower on November 7. It was entitled *Deterrence and Survival in the Nuclear Age*, a much shorter document than NSC-68, only twenty-nine pages of text, but nearly as gripping. "The evidence clearly indicates," the first page proclaimed, "an increasing threat which may become critical in 1959 or early 1960." The U.S.S.R.'s gross national product was growing, with particular emphasis on heavy industry, allowing the Kremlin "to finance both the rapid expansion of their impressive military capability and their politico-economic offensive by which, through diplomacy, propaganda and subversion, they seek to extend the Soviet orbit.

"The singleness of purpose with which they have pressed their military-centered industrial development," the report continued, "has led to spectacular progress." The Soviets had "produced fissionable material sufficient for at least 1,500 nuclear weapons," along with a sizable long-range air force, intermediate-range missiles, a mighty air-defense system, the development of cruise missiles and intercontinental ballistic missiles, in which, the report asserted, they have "probably surpassed us."

The report drew special attention to the "current vulnerability of SAC to surprise attack during a period of lessened world tension," a situation that calls for "prompt remedial action . . . to secure and augment our deterrent power." For by 1959, "the USSR may be able to launch an attack with ICBMs carrying megaton warheads, against which SAC will be almost completely vulnerable under present programs. . . . The next two years seem to us critical. If we fail to act at once, the risk, in our opinion, will be unacceptable."

Nothing was said about those spy planes that gathered communications intelligence over the Soviet Union, the planes that LeMay told Sprague about, the planes that would allow the United States to know quite a while before the period of "tactical warning" that Soviet bombers would soon be on their way.

All in all, it was a stark, broad-brushed portrait of the Soviet threat, dauntingly unequivocal in nature and magnitude. Some of the staffers were a bit disturbed with the direction the final draft was heading. They agreed with the conclusions of the growing strength of Soviet military might and the vulnerability of SAC, but the papers they had written for the steering panel had been less firm. There were caveats, qualifications; the language was more guarded, the assumptions behind the assessments explicitly spelled out. But the leading voices on the Gaither Committee were adamant in sticking to the more aggressive line of argument. Jerry Wiesner of the steering panel and Herbert York of Livermore Labs and the Gaither staff had a constant line on the issue: "What's important," they would say, "is not what the Soviets *might* do; it's what they *could* do." And there was a very palpable sense, a sense of dread urgency, that once the Soviets obtained the ability to launch a first-strike, they might very well go ahead and launch.

In this sense, the committee reflected the basic assumptions of Air Force Intelligence, especially SAC Intelligence. LeMay had a phrase for the concept—"the gnome in the basement." The gnome was Khrushchev or whoever might be dominating the Kremlin, aided by his own military planners. LeMay told his staff that they should picture their counterparts in Russia doing analyses, comparing forces, seeing what they could do, then coming outside, looking at the light, and saying, "No, we won't attack today." But one day, the gnome might step out and say, "Yes, the correlation of forces is right today. Let's go."

LeMay used the image primarily as a device to keep SAC crews ready at all times. It was a great device for maintaining morale at a constantly high level. But LeMay and his aides also believed it. And, for all their disdain toward Curtis LeMay, so in effect did most of the members of the Gaither Committee.

9 THE REPORT OF MAXIMUM DANGER

THAT THE RUSSIANS were gaining on the United States and were about to overtake us, that the age of the missile gap was upon us, that we were frightfully vulnerable, that the Russians might therefore one day threaten us with their nuclear weapons or actually fire them our way—these were the profound feelings, the firm convictions of the steering panel of the Gaither Committee. The report that they delivered to the White House in early November, entitled *Deterrence and Survival in the Nuclear Age,* outlined the threat as they saw it and also some military programs to relieve the present danger.

Many of the recommendations were taken from Albert Wohlstetter's influential R-290 report for RAND. But the committee went further than Wohlstetter and urged stepping up the nation's missile programs, increasing the number of Atlas and Titan ICBMs to be initially deployed from 80 to 600, making them operational by 1959. They also wanted the Thor and Jupiter intermediate-range ballistic missiles, IRBMs, placed in Europe by 1958, with an initial deployment of 240 instead of the 60 that were planned.

At RAND, Albert Wohlstetter heard that the committee was going to urge accelerated IRBM programs, and was disturbed. Wohlstetter thought that IRBMs were weak and even dangerous weapons for shoring up nuclear deterrence. It was the overseas-base problem, which Wohlstetter had diagnosed in 1953, all over again: the IRBMs would be close to the Soviet Union, but then so would the Soviets be close to the IRBMs; missiles in Europe, therefore, might weaken deterrence by presenting yet another temptingly vulnerable target for the Soviets to destroy preemptively. Wohlstetter and another RAND analyst, William Kaufmann, wrote the committee a letter, urging it to abandon the IRBM proposal, explaining the reasons why. But the letter went largely ignored. Maybe they would be vulnerable, the committee's reasoning went, but if the Soviets had ICBMs and we had none, then we would have to have *some* sort of missile. The gap had to be closed, and quickly, before the year of maximum critical danger was upon us.

The committee also recommended a nationwide fallout shelter program. However, the committee divided its recommendations into two groups—"Highest Value Measures" and "Lower Than Highest Value Measures." The steps to reduce SAC vulnerability and build more missiles—as well as to "augment forces for limited war capability," one of Paul Nitze's more forceful contributions to the group's efforts—were classified "Highest Value"; the civil-defense program was ranked "Lower Than Highest Value."

In all, the Gaither Committee proposed spending an additional $44,220,000,000 over the next five years—$19,090,000,000 for the Highest Value Measures, $25,130,000,000 for civil defense. The only question that remained was what the President of the United States, the man who ultimately would decide on all this, would say.

In the eyes of the Gaither Committee, things did not seem exceedingly hopeful. Dwight Eisenhower was famously tight with money—his own and the public's. He was especially tight with money for defense. Shortly after he entered office in January 1953, Eisenhower cut the Truman defense budget for fiscal year 1954 from $41.3 billion to $36 billion, taking the largest share of the cut out of the Air Force. Most people did not know that Eisenhower was acting on the basis of a remark made in April 1953 by General Lauris Norstad, head of U.S. Air Forces in Europe, to the effect that Air Force personnel could be cut by 10 or 12 percent with no detriment to national security. But the Eisenhower cut set the tone for how his Administration would be perceived by those, like many on the Gaither Committee, who thought the United States should be spending much more.

Still, the cut did reflect Eisenhower's basic attitude. He was on record as disparaging the sorts of analyses that geared the defense effort to some "single critical 'danger date' and . . . single form of enemy action. . . ." Rather, defense must be developed over the long haul, requiring a "strong and expanding economy, readily convertible to the tasks of war." He consistently opposed building up armed forces "excessively under the impulse of fear," for that "could, in the long run, defeat our purposes by damaging the growth of our economy and eventually forcing it into regimented controls." Privately, he often emphasized that the nation had to distinguish between "a respectable posture of defense and an all-out military buildup," and that "an attempt to be completely secure could lead only to a garrison state, and even then could not succeed."

A large meeting of the National Security Council, to consider the contents of the Gaither Report, was scheduled for Thursday morning, November 7, 1957. Three days before that session, Eisenhower and a few of his top security aides—Gordon Gray and Robert Cutler of the NSC staff, James Killian of the Science Advisory Committee, and Eisenhower's staff secretary, General Andrew Goodpaster—met with the Gaither Committee's advisory board and the three top members of the steering panel, Robert Sprague, William Foster and Rowan Gaither himself. Gaither had not served much on the committee since September, when he was hospitalized with cancer, but he had returned for the last few weeks of steering-panel sessions, and he presented the major findings of the committee at this relatively small November 4 conference with the President.

Eisenhower seemed interested, but said he thought Gaither was exaggerating the threat. Gaither had said, among other things, that a Soviet attack could kill or seriously wound half of the American population. Eisenhower remarked that when each superpower can inflict that sort of damage on its opponent, "we are getting close to absolutes," and in those circumstances, the active defenses and civil-defense program urged by the Gaither Committee would probably serve little purpose, for "there is in reality no defense except to retaliate." Eisenhower also said he thought SAC was stronger than the committee indicated, that the bases overseas provided a great capacity for dispersion, and that the free world held the periphery around the Soviet Union and could pose a threat from a multitude of points, whereas the Soviets had no such advantage in their ability to threaten the United States.

It was a curious sort of performance for a President of the United States to display. Eisenhower did agree with Gaither that the country would have to start investing more money in military technology five years hence, and that in the interim the people would have to be educated so they would support what was required. But he declined to take on the burden himself. William Foster and John McCloy, one of the committee's advisory board members, urged Eisenhower to take on this task, McCloy telling him that he could "blow the opposition out of the water."

But Eisenhower demurred. "I'm a minority President in the Congress," he said. "I can't alienate the Democratic Party by attacking some of its leading members."

Then Eisenhower made a more revealing, more thoughtful remark. Someone, he said, had advised him recently to describe the defense problem in more lurid terms than he had previously—not to say that it was a problem to be dealt with over the next forty years, but to call for a major spurt of activity now. But Eisenhower refused to go down that road. It wasn't accurate, he said, it would be misleading. The true task was for the nation to carry the load, over the long haul, until the Soviets change internally. And he would be endangering and unnecessarily frightening the public to say anything different.

But, as of November 4, Eisenhower was generally supportive, and finished the meeting with the comment that it might be good for the Gaither group to be kept together to review the matter every now and then.

Sprague, Foster and the rest were pleased by Eisenhower's favorable comments, but there was a sense of unease about it. On the specific points—the nature, magnitude and immediacy of the Soviet threat, as they saw it, the need to do something big now—the President had shown himself utterly unaffected.

Over the next two days, Sprague would feel still more ill at ease. On Wednesday, November 6, at 11 A.M., Eisenhower met in the Oval Office with about fifty of the Gaither Committee's staff scientists. It was a courtesy meeting, called at the suggestion of Eisenhower's national security adviser, Robert Cutler, just to express appreciation for all the work the staff had done. Eisenhower thanked them very much, told them it was a very interesting report, but then said something that seemed to come out of nowhere.

"You know, you recommend spending a billion dollars for something in here," Eisenhower said, pointing at the report. "But do you know how much a billion dollars is? Why, it's a stack of ten-dollar bills as high as the Washington Monument."

He paused for a few seconds, thanked the group again, and they all left. If Eisenhower is so awed by a billion dollars, some of them thought, how could he ever be persuaded to spend the $44 billion that their report recommended?

Just after the meeting with Eisenhower, a luncheon was held for the committee's steering panel. Robert Sprague was seated just to the right of Jim Douglas, Secretary of the Air Force, and Curtis LeMay was sitting on Douglas' left. Sprague was growing nervous about the NSC session of the following day. He had asked Cutler to schedule fifteen minutes afterward for a private meeting to include just Sprague, Foster, the President and his closest military advisers; Sprague had something to say that was so sensitive he could not allow anybody else—not even his own colleagues—to hear it. Sprague had decided to tell Eisenhower what he had learned from LeMay on that second visit to SAC. Not the information about LeMay's preemptive war plan—Sprague figured he had no business telling the President what one of his own military commanders was up to—but rather the startling news that, even by SAC's own numbers, not enough bombers could get off the ground fully loaded in time to deliver a devastating retaliatory blow in response to a Soviet attack, and that therefore the Administration's policy of "massive retaliation" was, in the event of a surprise attack with tactical warning only, unworkable.

After sitting in on the two preliminary meetings leading up to the November 7 session, Sprague wondered just how much the Administration really knew. So, during lunch, Sprague conducted a test. He casually leaned over to Jim Douglas and said, "I assume that you're familiar with the fact that if the Soviets attacked us and we had tactical warning only, virtually none of our aircraft could retaliate."

Douglas looked at Sprague incredulously. "You're crazy," he said. "Even under the worst of circumstances, one hundred and sixty-seven planes would not be destroyed." Douglas then turned to LeMay on his left. "You heard Mr. Sprague, General. Isn't it so that . . ."

"Wait, that's not the right question," Sprague interrupted. "The right question is: assuming tactical warning only, how many airplanes will we have available with full crew, fuel load and atomic weapons on board? And the answer to *that* question is: practically none."

Douglas turned hesitantly to LeMay. "Mr. Sprague is correct," LeMay stated. Douglas sat silent through the rest of the lunch.

Now Sprague was alarmed. If the Secretary of the Air Force had been asking the wrong question and thus getting an irrelevant answer, then no doubt the President had not been properly informed, either. In a way, though, Sprague was not surprised. When he had served as a one-man commission to the Senate Armed Services Preparedness Subcommittee in 1953, looking into the issue of continental defense, he checked out dozens of highly classified documents, including such crucial ones as the estimate of the likely result of a nuclear exchange three years hence. The thing that shocked him most was that this particular document had not been checked out previously by any high officials in the White House, the office of the Secretary of Defense or the State Department. Rather, the Secretaries of State and Defense, the national security adviser and the President had been briefed by staff officers. And, as Sprague well knew from his own experience, briefers are not necessarily paid to tell the truth. He had seen enough briefings by Navy officers on how the aircraft carriers could survive in wartime, and then read the actual study on which the briefing was supposedly based, only to find out that the study had come to exactly the opposite conclusion. Similar instances of deception had occurred with the Air Force and the Army.

The next day's meeting was enormous, one of the largest of the NSC ever—sixty-nine attendants, including the President, Secretary of State John Foster Dulles, Defense Secretary Neil McElroy, the civilian service secretaries, the Joint Chiefs of the Staff, nearly the entire Cabinet, all the relevant deputies and special assistants on security matters, twenty members of the Gaither Committee and advisory board.

One by one, Sprague, then Jerry Wiesner, then William Foster, John Corson, then William Webster got up before the large group to discuss the sections of the report that they had supervised, graphs and charts used extensively. Above all, they emphasized the vulnerability of the SAC force and the supreme importance of a program to disperse the bombers (and ICBMs, when they entered the force) and to harden them in protective shelters. All listened attentively, Eisenhower with a copy of the report sitting on one knee, following along while he listened.

Eisenhower's response, when it was all over, was roughly the same as his response to Gaither's less formal presentation the previous Monday: very interesting, but would the American people really foot the bill? John McCloy and Robert Lovett, prominent financiers as well as members of the Gaither Committee's advisory board, contended that the economy could sustain the measures recommended. Indeed, one entire section of the Gaither Report was devoted to illustrating just that point, through various assumptions and calculations about economic growth and taxation. Still, Eisenhower had his doubts.

Then there was John Foster Dulles, Eisenhower's highly vocal Secretary of State. He didn't like the report one bit, indeed kept interrupting during the discussion period when anyone seemed on the verge of making a decent argument on its behalf. The recommendations, he said, were unnecessary, they would cost too much, would take away too much funding from the more vital programs, such as foreign aid, and this business of civil defense would regiment the country, frighten our allies and drive the Soviets into a still more massive arms buildup besides. In the end, the meeting resolved nothing.

Then came Sprague's big moment. As the meeting broke up, Eisenhower headed toward the Oval Office, and Robert Cutler led a dozen men in the same direction. They were Sprague and Bill Foster, along with John Foster Dulles, his brother and Director of Central Intelligence, Allen Dulles, Defense Secretary Neil McElroy and his assistant for R&D, Don Quarles, Air Force Secretary Jim Douglas, Air Force Chief of Staff Tommy White, JCS Chairman Nathan Twining, AEC Chairman Lewis Strauss, Gordon Gray of the Office of Defense Mobilization, which sponsored the Gaither Committee, and Eisenhower's staff secretary and ubiquitous notetaker, General Andrew Goodpaster.

Sprague had briefed Eisenhower forty-five or fifty times in the past few years as a consultant to the NSC. The reception had always been friendly. This one, he feared, probably would not be.

Sprague began by explaining the extreme sensitivity of what he had to say, that the Gaither Report had not contained much of the information that followed because very few members of the committee knew about it. First, he noted that the committee had studied SAC's response capability under three broad conditions. In a situation of world tension, when SAC would be in a "readiness state," the bombers could respond quickly and successfully in the event of a Soviet attack. If the Soviets initially attacked the NATO allies but saved the attack on the U.S. for later, SAC would also be sufficiently ready to respond. But, he continued, if the attack occurred at a time of low international tension, when SAC was on a normal alert status, and if there were up to five hours of warning time, SAC could scarcely respond at all.

He told Eisenhower of the September 16 alert exercise from NORAD, when not a single SAC airplane was able to take off with six hours' warning. Remembering Eisenhower's remarks about how easy it was to disperse SAC to overseas bases at the November 4 meeting, Sprague noted that very few SAC planes were actually on overseas bases because they were more vulnerable still. The SAC plan was to use those airfields as *post*-strike recovery bases. Furthermore, the Navy's aircraft carriers, which had atomic weapons on board, were also highly vulnerable to attack.

In all, Sprague summed up, America's retaliatory force presented some sixty targets for the Soviets to hit. If one assumed four airplanes per target to give a reasonable chance of destruction, the Soviets would need 240 aircraft to knock out the retaliatory force—and intelligence estimates indicated they would have far more than that number. At best, the United States might get off 50 to 150 large weapons, but the Soviets had invested a great deal on air defense, and they have a very large number of radars and fighters. In short, even under optimistic circumstances, we cannot assume we could lay down a substantial retaliatory attack.

Afterward, Sprague considered the meeting an abysmal flop. He told Andy Goodpaster that he thought he had failed to convey the sense of urgency that the committee felt. He thought that his words would startle and shock the President, but instead Eisenhower just sat there, silent, expressionless, that was the most disturbing thing about the whole episode.

But Sprague did not really know Eisenhower, and so could not have known that he played the scene all wrong. Eisenhower disdained hype, and hype was precisely what Sprague created.

The substance of Sprague's briefing made little impact, as well. In fact, in Eisenhower's eyes, he presented the best argument against the basic conclusion. Sprague had said that if the war began after a period of high international tension or if the Soviets attacked our allies first, if SAC had more than five or six hours' warning, if it had "strategic warning" instead of just "tactical warning," then SAC would be able to get off a good retaliatory blow in the event of Soviet attack. Eisenhower had enough background in military history and military affairs to know that wars tend not to start with a "bolt from the blue," that they arise out of extremely high tension; and that being the case, SAC was probably in pretty good shape.

There was another factor that Sprague probably could not

have known. Eisenhower took an enormous interest in all intelligence affairs, dating back to World War II when he was Allied commander, through his days as SHAPE commander in Europe, and including his tenure as President. Eisenhower may not have known about LeMay's preemptive war plan, but he almost certainly knew about those airplanes flying over the U.S.S.R. twenty-four hours a day gathering all sorts of military intelligence. In short, he knew that SAC would probably have more than just tactical warning, more than five or six hours of warning time.

Ultimately, he did take some of Sprague's comments to heart. He initiated a program requiring that one-third of SAC bombers either be airborne or be on a fifteen-minute alert. He took the Gaither Report seriously enough to ask for detailed commentary from the Secretary of Defense, the Joint Chiefs of Staff, the Treasury Department, the Budget Bureau and the Council of Economic Advisers. The report was the subject of at least three NSC meetings over the next five months.

However, Eisenhower did not take Sprague's comments enough to heart, did not take the Gaither Report so seriously, as to believe that their fears warranted spending tens of billions of dollars, on top of an already-expanding budget, to shore up a deterrent that he thought was, for the time being, already quite adequate.

On the evening of December 9, 1957, a dinner was held at the Georgetown home of William Foster, Robert Sprague's deputy on the Gaither Committee. Attending were fellow Gaither members Paul Nitze, CBS president and Gaither advisory-panel member Frank Stanton, Wall Street lawyer and former Air Force Undersecretary Roswell Gilpatric, Laurence Rockefeller, pollster Elmo Roper, New York management consultant Franklin Lindsay, John Cowles of the Cowles Newspapers chain, and—reportedly with President Eisenhower's permission—Vice-President Richard M. Nixon.

The dinner was Foster's and Nitze's idea. Their purpose was to figure out some way of breaking through the apparent indifference and apathy that the Administration was thus far displaying toward the Gaither Report, to come up with some way to convey the message and urgency of the report to the public and, at the same time, to keep battling on its behalf within the government. Foster was keen on trying to convince Eisenhower to issue a sanitized version of the report. Others liked the idea of forming a committee similar to the ones that alerted fellow countrymen to the dangers just before World War II and that helped sell the Marshall Plan to the public. Very gingerly, some talked of leaking its findings to the press.

Eventually, Foster and Sprague did make the Establishment lecture-circuit rounds, talking very broadly and generally about the present danger before such groups as the Business Round-table, the Council on Foreign Relations, the various War Colleges, each of them delivering forty or fifty speeches in all, Foster frequently conferring with Richard Nixon on what he could and should say. Nixon had virtually no say on defense issues with Eisenhower at this point; he had not even been invited to the November 7 NSC meeting at which the Gaither Report was discussed, even though forty-nine other government officials had attended, including a representative from the Justice Department. Still, at the Foster dinner, Nixon expressed agreement with the committee's conclusion, and the group was pleased to find someone so high up in government in sympathy with their concerns.

Nitze and Foster had both approached Sprague to join them in this more intimate effort to go public with the report itself, but Sprague declined, thinking it was improper for a group appointed by the President to make end runs and report to anyone else.

Two days later, on December 11, a story about the Foster dinner appeared in *The New York Times,* with another, more detailed story appearing the next day, as well. They were only the beginnings of the press leaks. Before the dinner, only one story had appeared: on November 23, just more than two weeks after the big NSC meeting, the headline "U.S. Report Urges Atomic Shelter at 20 Billion Cost" graced page one of the *Times.* But it was not until after the Foster dinner that the big stories appeared.

The biggest came under Chalmers Roberts' by-line in the December 20 *Washington Post.* The headline: "Enormous Arms Outlay Is Held Vital to Survival." The lead paragraphs read powerfully, if luridly:

> The still-top-secret Gaither Report portrays a United States in the gravest danger in its history.
> It pictures the Nation moving in frightening course to the status of a second-class power.
> It shows an America exposed to an almost immediate threat from the missile-bristling Soviet Union.

It finds America's long-term prospect one of cataclysmic peril in the face of rocketing Soviet military might and of a powerful, growing Soviet economy and technology which will bring new political, propaganda, and psychological assaults on freedom all around the globe.

On it went like that for nearly a page.

Eisenhower was furious. The *Post* story embodied everything that he hated: leaks to the press, attempts to pressure him into doing something that needed careful deliberation, exaggerations of the dangers to national security. And he knew there would be political heat to take, as well. The Democrats were already making successful capital of the Sputnik affair, claiming that the Republican Administration was behaving too complacently, was endangering the nation by not spending enough money on more bombers and missiles. Now the Gaither Report was turning into another cause for political jubilation among the opposition. Almost at once, after the *Washington Post* story appeared, dozens of Democratic senators and congressmen took the floor to request or demand that President Eisenhower release the report to the public, which had a right to know the facts on which their lives as Americans were hanging. Lyndon Johnson, Hubert Humphrey, Henry Jackson, Mike Mansfield, John Sparkman, William Proxmire, Stuart Symington and others all eagerly boarded the Gaither bandwagon.

All these demands and all the panic, over Sputnik and over the Gaither Report, conveniently fed into another phenomenon that the Democrats were simultaneously doing their best to exploit—a sharp turn inside the American intelligence community that produced what came to be known as the "missile gap."

10 THE MISSILE GAP

IN THE MONTHS leading up to Sputnik and the Gaither Report, but following the transmittal of Albert Wohlstetter's R-290 report for RAND, Air Force Intelligence was predicting the end of deterrence for the United States in a matter of a few years. On September 30, 1957, a special Air Force panel delivered a report to General Thomas White, Air Force Chief of Staff, noting that the Soviet Union's major objectives were "first, destroy or neutralize U.S. capabilities and nuclear retaliatory forces; and second, to deliver an attack on urban, industrial, political and psychological targets in the U.S. so as to prevent mobilization of the U.S. weapons potential."

Having a substantial ICBM force would give the Soviets the means to fulfill their objectives, and the panel predicted that by 1963 a Soviet attack that aimed three missiles at each SAC air base and missile site would destroy so much of America's nuclear strength that "the Soviets might well consider that they would be in a position to initiate general war with very little risk of retaliatory major destruction to their national strengths."

On November 12, the intelligence community's official National Intelligence Estimate stated that the Soviets could have 500 operational ICBMs by the end of 1962 or, if they built their program on a crash basis, by the end of 1961. Some officers in SAC Intelligence figured that the Soviets might have many more than that, perhaps up to 1,000. Meanwhile, the United States was scheduled to have only twenty-four Atlas missiles ready to go by 1960 and only sixty-five by 1961. This estimate was not a matter of controversy within the intelligence community; it was a position held by Air Force Intelligence and by estimators inside the CIA alike.

Yet there was no hard evidence for these claims of a missile gap. The estimate sprang from the demise of worries about a "bomber gap," which the intelligence community had also commonly predicted a few years earlier, but which was now commonly agreed to have been a gap that never was and that almost certainly would never be.

By 1954, it was clear that the Soviets had built a prototype design of a bomber with potential intercontinental range that the United States dubbed the Bison. After surreptitiously observing from afar an April rehearsal for the May Day air show, American air attachés in Russia reported seeing at least twelve and maybe twenty Bison planes in the air. Intelligence analysts in the U.S. Air Force reasoned that if the Russians were putting that many in the air at one time, then they could have something like twenty-five to forty Bisons off the production line.

The real intelligence scare came a year later, on July 13, 1955, the U.S.S.R.'s Aviation Day, when the Russians proudly display their air power. American attachés reported seeing ten Bisons flying by, then another formation of nine Bisons, then still another nine—twenty-eight planes in all. Again, Air Force Intelligence reasoned that the Soviets must have about twice that number actually built, which meant that the production lines were cranking out many more Bisons than they had previously guessed. The intelligence estimates for what the Soviets would have a few years hence began to explode. The 1956 National Intelligence Estimate, known as the NIE, predicted that the Soviets could have 500 bombers with the range to attack the United States four or five years into the future; at one point, Air Force was predicting as many as 600 to 800 Bisons.

The air attachés' reports did not form the basis of these projections; they merely provided what seemed to be concrete evidence supporting a massive array of data that was beginning to come in. The plant that produced all the Bisons, called the Fili Plant, happened to be in Moscow. Americans naturally were not allowed to enter the plant, but they could fairly easily observe activities going on around it. They could hear and often even see the planes taking off from the runway; and since they knew that the planes flew from the plant to a nearby military air base and never came back, they were not faced with the problem of distinguishing takeoffs from landings. From captured German reconnaissance photos taken from the air during World War II, analysts back in the U.S. could calculate the plant's size and floor space, as well as the most efficient use of that space and, from that, infer some numbers on likely production rates. The attachés in Moscow could report the approximate size of any expansions or new annexes to the plant.

Air Force Intelligence also knew of a measure devised by American aircraft companies called the "learning curve," which assumed that over time, and with greater efficiencies gradually built in, production of aircraft would grow at a certain, calculable rate. Air Force Intelligence also assumed that the plant had two labor shifts, and that sometime in the next couple of years, after the Fili Plant had reached the peak of its "learning curve," the Soviets would have constructed a second plant to build still more Bison bombers.

When all these factors were taken into account, it appeared that the Soviets could have built 500 or so intercontinental bombers by the early 1960s.

Yet there was another assumption that entered into these calculations, something less tangible but, in the eyes of intelligence analysts of the day, far more real and certain. The Soviet Union's primary goal was to attack a large number of strategic and urban-industrial targets inside the United States. U.S. targeting studies had revealed that the Soviets would need something like 500 bombers of intercontinental range to accomplish the goals that intelligence had imputed to them. Therefore, any evidence that seemed to confirm the assumption about Soviet aims—regardless of evidence that might point to other conclusions—was viewed as truth.

At that time, the Central Intelligence Agency had no charter to do military analysis; that job was assigned to the intelligence staffs of the individual services. However, there was an oversight board, the Office of National Estimates, ONE, headed by a veteran intelligence analyst, Sherman Kent. ONE was responsible for producing the annual National Intelligence Estimate, and so had the authority to look into intelligence in all fields, including military. While technically independent of the CIA, it was housed in the Agency's headquarters. Still, ONE had to rely almost entirely on Air Force Intelligence for analysis and estimates of Soviet long-range missiles and bombers.

However, there was a division of the CIA in charge of economic intelligence, headed by a young analyst named Ed Proctor, who managed to grab one slice of military intelligence: trying to calculate how much money the Soviets were spending on their armed forces. This task allowed Proctor and his staff to obtain as much data as they wanted on Soviet bombers, which allowed them to get heavily involved with the whole question of bomber production and production rates. In short, through a cleverly roundabout route, the CIA's economic division got into the business of analyzing all the technical and arcane issues that lay at the very heart of the Strategic Forces section of the NIE—formally the exclusive province of the military services, especially the Air Force.

From their studies of other economic sectors of the U.S.S.R., the analysts in Proctor's shop knew practically everything there was to know about Soviet factory markings—things like how serial numbers on manufactured goods can reveal what year and month a particular item was produced. In this sense, airplanes were just like any other manufactured goods, and the serial number, so to speak, was the tail number on each plane, which the CIA could detect on a few of the many photographs taken with long-range lenses by the American air attachés observing the goings-on at the Fili Plant in Moscow.

Not long after they began amassing this sort of data, Proctor and his team began to conclude that the Air Force estimate—the official National Intelligence Estimate—could not be right. One of the assumptions behind that estimate was that the Bison bombers were produced in batches of ten. The assumption was integral to all the other assumptions and, thus, to the overall estimate. Ten was the logical number, given the Air Force estimates of the Fili Plant's floor space, of the plant's "learning curve," of the number of labor shifts working on production. And ten was the absolutely necessary number, given the more basic assumption that the Soviets wanted to be able to attack a whole variety of American targets as soon as possible. If the number were significantly less than ten, then all the other assumptions were wrong, including the basic one concerning Soviet aims and intentions.

And yet the CIA was coming to believe that the Soviets were producing the Bisons in batches of only five. The analysts would see Bisons marked with tail numbers ending with 10, 11, 12, 13, 14 or 20, 21, 22, 23, 24 or 30, 31, 32, 33, 34—but not a single plane ending with 15, 16, 17, 18, 19 or 25, 26, 27, 28, 29. . . . Moreover, there was another set of numbers on the plane indicating when it was manufactured. As it turned out, about as much time elapsed between the plane with numbers ending in, say, 22 and 24 as between planes ending in 24 and 31. In other words, there probably would not have been enough time to produce 25, 26, 27, 28, 29 and 30 in the interim.

Thus, if no airplanes with higher end numbers existed, then that clearly meant they were being produced in batches of five, not ten; and that clearly meant that the estimate was all wrong, that the Soviets were producing only about half as many Bison bombers as the NIE projected, and that meant that all the other assumptions behind the NIE—from the efficiency of a Soviet aircraft plant to the objectives of the Kremlin—were also wrong.

By 1957, not only was Proctor's shop convinced that the NIE was wrong, but so were a number of analysts on the staff of the Office of National Estimates.

Allen Dulles was in a spot. As manager of the entire intelligence community, he was reluctant to abandon the estimate of the Air Force, the source of all the data that the community was receiving on Soviet bomber production. He was also reluctant to accept immediately the critique made by Proctor's shop. That division might know a lot about economics and factory markings, but could he really believe that the men who worked there knew as much about airplanes as the Air Force did? They had never even looked much at airplanes before they got involved in this exercise. Furthermore, if the NIEs that the Agency had been supporting the past few years were based on totally faulty data and assumptions, how would they come up with a new estimate—who could produce one—and what would that say, politically, about the wisdom of the CIA?

So, a fight broke out between Air Force Intelligence and the CIA. The Air Force had stakes beyond merely protecting its reputation as a reliable intelligence agency: a large Soviet strategic air force meant guaranteed support for a large American strategic air force, which meant more prestige and a greater share of the defense budget than for the Army and the Navy. Not surprisingly, in this internal clash, Army Intelligence sided with the CIA's economic division.

The Air Force response to the CIA critique sounded entirely reasonable. The Air Force, its intelligence officers pointed out, made a logical estimate. It accorded with everybody's perception of Soviet intentions; it accorded with their estimates of the Fili Plant's floor space, with the July 1955 air display over Moscow and with their judgment that the Soviets produced ten planes per batch. All that the CIA analysts had was the *absence* of any data that proved conclusively the estimate of ten per batch. The Air Force didn't think that the sample size was large enough to conclude that the Soviets produced only five per batch, at least not in the face of all the other conflicting information.

The CIA economic division's response was equally logical, but in precisely the opposite direction. The five-per-batch number that they had come up with was absolutely solid, they said, and the confidence levels were very high. This meant that the Fili Plant was not producing to what the Air Force thought was full capacity, that the plant did not work in two shifts, that its learning curve had not yet peaked, that the Soviets were not planning to build a second Bison plant. The air show of July 1955 was a bit tougher to challenge, but all the other bits of data suggested either that it had been a fluke or that the Soviets must have been flying every single bomber in their inventory, not, as the Air Force had assumed, half of them.*

The dispute reached a bitter stalemate—when along came Khrushchev's belligerent bragging about the U.S.S.R.'s terrifying ICBM program and then, on October 4, the launching of Sputnik. That settled the great dispute over the bomber gap. The CIA's economic analysts won. The big bomber projections were dropped from the NIE. But they were dropped only because Sputnik allowed all of the broad assumptions about Soviet behavior and intentions to be preserved. The intelligence community could still argue that the Soviets wanted a big nuclear force aimed at the United States, but that they had now decided to build one in the form of ICBMs, not bombers. The NIE could still be judged fundamentally sound in its assessment of the nature and magnitude of the Soviet threat. And the U.S. Air Force could still use the estimates as its rationale for a gigantic fleet of long-range bombers and missiles of its own.

A new consensus was reached. And the consensus included not just Air Force Intelligence officers but also CIA analysts. Very few, even among the CIA skeptics, had ever altered their assumptions about the nature of the Soviet threat. They had been a bit puzzled by their own discoveries. But they viewed themselves as independent analysts, not attached or beholden to any military service—unlike their adversaries in Air Force Intelligence, who

* Years later, some intelligence analysts would speculate that the same planes might have been flying around the display area twice, but the theory has never been confirmed.

were under constant pressure to make their estimates of Soviet forces consistent with the budgetary desires of the Air Force proper. And they were eager to get into the strategic-estimates game, where all the big action and excitement lay. Challenging the predominant strategic estimators, the officers of Air Force Intelligence, and doing so with solid evidence and creative but logical analysis, was the best way to go about getting there. But when it came to thinking about Soviet aims and intentions, there was no question in 1957, even among the skeptical economists in the CIA, that the Reds were out to clobber America.

And so, as the bomber gap ended, the missile gap began.

The members of the Gaither Committee, the analysts at the RAND Corporation, the Democrats in Congress who criticized Eisenhower's defense programs, had no way of knowing that the missile-gap intelligence estimates virtually appeared out of thin air, supplanting the bomber-gap estimates as the latter proved illusory.

The first NIE ascribing a huge missile arsenal to the Soviet Union was released in November 1957, and projected that the Russians would have 500 ICBMs by the end of 1962 or, if they embarked on a crash program, the end of 1961. There was no solid evidence for this estimate. All the earlier intelligence assumptions had led to the conclusion that the Soviets could have 500 intercontinental bombers by that date. When that projection proved false, Air Force Intelligence essentially changed "bombers" to "ICBMs," but retained the original number 500.

By 1958, mainly with the aid of photographs taken from U-2 reconnaissance airplanes, which had begun flying spy missions over Russia in 1956, the Air Force had enough data to estimate the floor space of factories producing missiles. As with the bomber-gap estimates, they could figure the most efficient use of that floor space, assume a "learning curve" in the production, go on to assume that additional production plants would be utilized once the "learning curve" peaked, and infer from all this some figures on production rate.

From these extrapolations, the Air Force essentially confirmed the NIE of the previous year. The NIE of 1959 also concluded that if the Soviets decided to start a general nuclear war, their first move would be to destroy the Western nuclear forces in order to minimize or prevent retaliation. Since the 100 ICBMs that the Soviets could have by 1959 or 1960 would be enough to demolish almost all of SAC's air bases, the situation seemed very grim.

However, by mid-1958, something seemed to appear not quite right with this estimate, and the early skeptics came once again from the inner corridors of the CIA—this time from the science and technology division headed by Herbert (Pete) Scoville, Jr., and his specialist on missiles, Sidney Graybeal. Just as the CIA's economic division got involved with the NIEs during the bomber-gap period because of its experience in examining factory markings, the CIA science and technology office became involved during this period in the late 1950s because it knew about missiles.

No American had ever laid eyes on an actual Soviet missile, but these CIA scientists came up with some ingenious methods for essentially reconstructing one. The method involved monitoring Soviet missile test flights—originally with radar technology, later with acoustic, telemetric, optical, and infrared sensors. From the data intercepted, Scoville, Graybeal and their staff could infer rough estimates of a missile's size, weight, fuel loading, inner workings, accuracy and (based on its weight) explosive power.

In the course of monitoring these tests, however, the CIA scientists began to notice that the rate of Soviet ICBM testing had slowed down considerably. The Soviets were still testing plenty of short-range missiles; by the summer of 1958, they had tested a dozen medium- and intermediate-range missiles; but they had fired only six intercontinental-range missiles, and they had not fired any for quite a while. Still, the CIA stuck to its original estimate. Again, it was the dilemma of negative evidence: how long do you wait for something to happen before you conclude that it isn't going to happen? It was too early to draw conclusions.

Still, officers in Air Force Intelligence thought that the CIA was vastly underestimating the Soviet ICBM test program, and began to worry that if the CIA were allowed to dominate on this issue, the estimate on Soviet missile production might eventually change—thus endangering the massive missile program that the Air Force was advocating. Word began to get around that the Soviets were doing a lot more testing than the CIA was reporting; that this information was being systematically suppressed and kept away from Allen Dulles; that in fact Soviet missile production was also a lot more vigorous than the NIEs suggested.

Finally, the word trickled down to Stuart Symington, the Democratic Senator from Missouri. Symington was the ideal man to take on the job of pushing the Air Force's case. A senior member of the Armed Services Committee, former Secretary of the Air Force in the Truman Administration, sharp critic of Eisenhower's defense policies, the most vocal advocate of the Gaither Report's public release, the most spirited warning siren on the missile gap and clearly laying the groundwork for his ambitions in the upcoming 1960 Presidential election, Symington was a man who was eager to jump on board any claim or statistic bemoaning America's military weakness or decrying Russia's military strength.

Symington heard about the reports of underestimating in the CIA from Colonel Thomas Lanphier, a man well plugged into the Air Force gossip network, having ridden for more than a decade on his fame as the war hero who directed the air ambush that trapped and shot down Japanese war leader Admiral Yamamoto during World War II. Lanphier had also been Symington's executive assistant when he was Secretary of the Air Force; he was president of the Air Force Association shortly after that, and he was now assistant to the president of Convair, manufacturer of the Atlas ICBM. Lanphier had his own stakes in beating down the CIA, since a large Soviet ICBM program made it more likely that his own company would be awarded a large ICBM production contract.

Symington, meanwhile, saw in Lanphier's report the makings of a terrific scandal that would work to his own political favor. Symington requested a personal briefing from Allen Dulles at CIA headquarters in late July 1958. The data that Dulles gave him on Soviet missile testing differed so considerably from Lanphier's data that Symington requested another session with Dulles on August 6, this time bringing Lanphier with him. Dulles brought in Howard Stoertz, the Soviet specialist on the ONE staff, to comment and take notes. Lanphier's basic message to Dulles was that he, the Director of Central Intelligence, was being misled by his own people on the number of ICBM tests the Soviet Union was conducting, that the real number was much higher than six. Stoertz and Dulles both said they had never heard anything like this before, but would investigate the matter.

A new interagency intelligence committee had recently been established under the supervision of Air Force Colonel Earl McFarland, called the Guided Missiles Intelligence Committee, or

"Gimmick," for short. Dulles had McFarland look into Lanphier's claims. Over the next couple of weeks, GMIC hunted but found nothing. One reasonable hypothesis it came up with was that Lanphier's sources in Air Force Intelligence were counting a lot of intermediate- and medium-range missile tests, in addition to ICBM tests. The U.S. had a radar in Turkey that looked out across the Black Sea toward the Caspian Sea. Both Soviet missile test ranges—one of which tested ICBMs, the other IRBMs and MRBMs—were within view of this radar.

In any event, another meeting was held with Dulles, Symington and Lanphier in mid-August. McFarland was also present and reported there was nothing to substantiate Colonel Lanphier's report; that, as Dulles had told him on August 6, the Soviets had fired only six ICBMs, four of which were believed to have landed in the target area.

To Lanphier, it didn't add up. If the Soviets were going to deploy 100 ICBMs by 1959 or 1960, much less 500 by 1961 or 1962, then they had to have fired more than six test missiles by August of 1958. There were lead times involved. In Convair's experience, a missile had to be tested at least twenty times before it could be declared operationally ready and reliable; then there was the additional time it would take to transport the missiles to their bases, set up launching sites, command-control centers and so forth. If the testing data were correct, then the National Intelligence Estimate must be wrong.

Over the next several months, Dulles and his staff reached the conclusion, hesitantly but inexorably, that the estimate must indeed be wrong. There simply were not very many more Soviet ICBM tests being conducted. It was the dilemma of negative evidence again, but they had waited a long time now and the evidence was still negative. Yet, as in the bomber-gap period, the estimate they had was all there was. If the CIA and the ONE denied its validity, where would they find the data for a new one?

Moreover, over the past year, much more had been learned about the technology of missiles. The scientific analysts realized, to a much greater degree than before, how complicated it was to set up an operational missile site. Before, they had just considered the task to be one of building and deploying missiles; now they realized that the support equipment—the launchers, the communications system and the like—was much bulkier, more complex, more time-consuming to set up. They realized that even if the Soviets had a lot of missiles, they might not have so many of them on launchers, ready to be fired in the event of war.

Then there were the U-2 photographs that were coming back. The U-2 was a super-secret program. Outside the intelligence community, only slightly more than a handful of Pentagon, White House and State Department officials knew of its existence. Certainly nobody in Congress was aware of it. The plane flew at 80,000 feet, was "armed" with a very long range lens camera with remarkably good resolution (developed by Edwin Land, inventor of the Polaroid), and had been making spy sorties across the Russian border since 1956.

The interagency Guided Missiles Intelligence Committee had developed criteria on where to look for ICBMs: for example, it figured they would have to sit not very far off the tracks of the Soviet Union's huge railroad systems, the only network that could move the missiles around. But, even with the U-2, there were some uncertainties. The plane had not yet been flown over all the area around the tracks. More particularly, it had not yet reached Plesetsk, in northern Russia, where the Soviets had been test firing (and perhaps getting ready to deploy) their ICBMs.

The end of the year was approaching; the negative evidence was still negative. The NIE for that year was delayed, deliberately, the analysts racking their brains, going over the data again and again, looking for something that might be interpreted as a *positive* sign of more ICBM testing, some ICBM deployment. But there was nothing.

Finally, on February 9, 1960, two months late, the NIE was released. It was a hodgepodge. It offered no consensus, and the bottoms of the pages were filled with dissenting footnotes signed by the intelligence agencies of the various services. The date by which the Soviets could have 500 ICBMs was pushed back to mid-1963, perhaps even further back than that. They would have only 50 ICBMs by mid-1960, only 35 of them on launchers. By mid-1961, they would have between 175 and 270 missiles, 140 to 200 of them on launchers. By mid-1962, they would have 325 to 400, with 250 to 350 on launchers. By mid-1963, 450 to 650, with 350 to 450—still fewer than 500—on launchers.

The differences in the numbers reflected the differences between the CIA, which picked the lower numbers, and the Air Force, which estimated the higher numbers. And in the footnotes were the Army and Navy intelligence services' dissents, which—

using the same data available to the CIA and Air Force Intelligence—arrived at still lower numbers. The Soviets, they said, would have only 50 missiles by mid-1961, only 125 by mid-1962 and 200 by mid-1963.

At this point, very few in the CIA or the Air Force were willing to take these extraordinarily low estimates seriously. For one thing, the politics of the situation seemed clear: the Army and the Navy competed against the Air Force for scarce budgetary resources; if the Soviets had only a few ICBMs in the works, that would deny the Air Force its chief rationale for building several thousand ICBMs and would, thus, leave more for the non-nuclear forces of the Army and the Navy.

Second, Navy Intelligence was automatically suspect. Keith Brewer, head of ONI, the Office of Naval Intelligence, had not believed the Soviets had set off an atomic bomb, and for many years after the fact. The Navy was always estimating, since that time, that the Soviets had only about one-fifth the fissionable material that the rest of the intelligence community was estimating. Brewer had worked at the Oak Ridge nuclear laboratory in Tennessee during the war, and simply could not believe that any other nation, especially the Soviet Union, had the collective brains and know-how to do what he and his associates had done.

There was a third reason why the Army-Navy numbers were rejected, and this was most critical. With the Air Force numbers, the Soviets could still damage or destroy most of the American SAC bases by mid-1961. The CIA numbers were only slightly less pessimistic, pushing the danger date back to late 1961. Whatever the fine differences, SAC still seemed dangerously vulnerable.

By this time, for all their earlier objections, top Air Force officers had come to accept the assumptions about SAC vulnerability laid out by the Wohlstetter-Hoffman R-290 report from RAND and by the Gaither Report. In the few years since, Air Force Chief of Staff General Tommy White and the new SAC Commander, General Tommy Power (LeMay left SAC around the time of the Gaither Committee and came to the Pentagon to become Vice Chief of Staff), had put in motion several programs on dispersal of bases and airborne alert of the bombers themselves, all with the purpose of reducing their vulnerability to attack.

Yet the Air Force was compelled to take these steps only after realizing it would be in its interest to do so. If the policy-makers were assuming that a certain percentage of the planes would get destroyed on the ground, that meant still more bombers for the Air Force—to allow for the attrition and still be able to fulfill the "military requirements." And if SAC bombers were up in the air flying around all the time, that yielded two bonuses: higher morale for the pilots, who loved to fly, and a better chance of getting "modernized" bombers sooner, since already-deployed ones will be worn out much sooner. In short, some of the R-290 and Gaither recommendations provided perfect intellectual rationales for a more steadily funded and larger Strategic Air Command.

Significantly, the only portion of the R-290/Gaither program that the Air Force consistently and successfully resisted was the notion of putting the bombers inside underground hardened shelters. Officers argued that it would be too expensive, maybe $10 billion or more, and that it might not protect, ultimately, the bomber against radiation effects. But the real reason had more to do with Air Force interests. With hardening, the dispersal and airborne-alert programs, so advantageous to the Air Force budget, might be cut back. To spend money on offense, not defense, was practically dogma in Air Force circles.

SAC was even more eager to use intelligence estimates as a method of advancing its own interests. The forceful leaders of SAC's own intelligence agency at the time were Generals James Walsh and George Keegan. Keegan was the more fiery of the two. He received his first training in intelligence as a member of a small advisory group to the Air Force Assistant Chief of Staff for Intelligence in the early 1950s. Keegan's boss was Professor Stefan Possony, an extremely right-wing Russophobic Sovietologist with a particular penchant for conspiratorial views of history. This advisory group's mission was to brainstorm on what kinds of horrifying things the Russians might be doing, and then to find the evidence.

Keegan had learned his job well, and was a full believer in the technique. He was a forceful speaker, a master showman, a superb briefer. Around the late 1950s, as even Air Force Intelligence was giving way on high Soviet ICBM estimates, SAC kept a full steam blowing. Keegan and Walsh had briefings, charts, diagrams, photographs *proving* that the Russians were already fielding ICBMs but that they were hiding them—in barn silos, medieval monasteries, mysterious-looking buildings out in the middle of nowhere.

With so many Soviet missiles that you could never know precisely how many there were or where they were located, arguments for an enormous SAC force could proceed indefinitely. The military requirements worked both ways: the large number of Soviet ICBMs meant a large number of targets to hit, which required a large number of SAC bombers and missiles; likewise, with so many Soviet missiles that might attack SAC, America needed hundreds and hundreds more to allow for heavy attrition. The Air Force proper finally agreed officially with the view that the Soviets were probably engaging in deceptive practices in their ICBM program. But not even Air Force Intelligence was willing to go as far as Keegan.

Still, with SAC or Air Force or even CIA intelligence estimates on the size of the near-future Soviet ICBM arsenal taken as the truth, the fundamental assumptions about the nature and magnitude of the Soviet threat could still be retained as legitimate.

On the other hand, if the Army and Navy numbers were treated seriously, the Soviets would appear to pose essentially no great threat to SAC. They would not have enough missiles to do so until mid-1963; and by that time, the Navy would have several new Polaris submarines, nuclear-powered, each carrying sixteen nuclear-tipped missiles, based underwater and virtually invulnerable to attack. Moreover, thanks in part to such studies as R-290 and the Gaither Report, the Air Force would have started to field its new Minuteman ICBMs in dispersed and hardened shelters.

The Army-Navy numbers, in other words, said there was no great danger to SAC, and no missile gap.

Throughout this period, nobody in the Senate knew the origins of the missile gap, knew that it sprang from the failure of the bomber gap to materialize. Nobody knew of the wide disagreements among the intelligence agencies as to the number of ICBMs the Soviets might have in place by the early 1960s. Nobody knew about the U-2 flights. Symington and most of the other Democrats, many of whom took their cues on this point from him, heard only about the Air Force Intelligence estimates, which (next to those of SAC Intelligence) were most pessimistic of all. Thus, when they heard Allen Dulles or Defense Secretary Neil McElroy or his successor as of December 1959, Thomas Gates, or even President Eisenhower say that there would be no missile gap, the Democrats and other critics of the Administration felt that these officials must be knaves or fools, that they were deluded or misled, that they were endangering the nation merely by their presence in high office.

But Eisenhower did know the background of the bomber gap and the missile gap. When charges of the missile gap began to circulate widely among political opponents in 1958, he assigned his staff secretary, Brigadier General Andrew Goodpaster, to find out whatever happened to the mysteriously vanished bomber gap. Goodpaster went through all the old NIEs, talked with intelligence officers, and learned how the NIEs had assumed that another Bison plant would be built, how they relied on a host of assumptions concerning production rates that turned out to be false. When he reported his findings to Eisenhower, the President felt secure in resisting all the fuss about a new gap. And when, in 1959 and 1960, the CIA started to back off somewhat, when the year of maximum danger started to recede into the distant future, Eisenhower felt his judgment vindicated.

On August 29, 1958, *after* he had met twice with Allen Dulles, Symington met with Eisenhower and gave him a letter, telling him that the intelligence community was wrong, that he was being misled. Eisenhower told Symington that whoever his sources were in Air Force Intelligence, they could not possibly know everything that those in the upper levels of the agency knew. Eisenhower never told Symington or anyone else in Congress about the U-2 or the Turkish radar site, but that was what he was talking about.

The missile gap also dominated the discussions of the day at the RAND Corporation. But there it was a more sophisticated conceptualization than the simple bean-count comparisons tossed around by Symington and his followers. The strategists of RAND preferred to call it a "deterrence gap." The issue was not so much that the Russians had more missiles as it was that SAC was so vulnerable that even the low side of the official intelligence estimates indicated that the Soviets would have enough missiles to knock out America's power to strike back—in Bernard Brodie's by-now ancient phrase, "to retaliate in kind"—after an aggressive first-strike. That being so, the nation's and thus the free world's ability to deter Soviet aggression was on the verge of being shattered.

Still, this more sophisticated view was the product of quantitative analysis, and the numbers came from the National Intelligence Estimates that foresaw an impending missile gap. And like the Stuart Symingtons of the world, most of the RAND strategists knew much less about those estimates than they thought they did. CIA policy on the distribution of the annual NIEs had changed after 1958: henceforth, no contracting firms—and that included RAND—were to receive copies. By coincidence, the 1958 NIE represented the peak year of the missile gap. It was not until 1959 that the estimated numbers of future Soviet missiles began to go down and the Army and the Navy began to add their footnotes. But almost none of the RAND analysts knew anything about this. They received intelligence estimates only from the Air Force Chief of Staff, and did not know that, from 1959 on, the Air Force numbers were considerably higher than those of the rest of the intelligence community. If RAND got any dissenting data at all, it came from SAC Intelligence, whose officers thought that the Air Force estimates were on the low side.

In quantitative studies, there is a technique known as "sensitivity analysis": the idea is that in a world of uncertainties, an analyst should test the validity of his conclusions by altering the key assumptions; if within a reasonable range of assumptions the conclusions remain roughly the same, then they could reasonably be considered correct. Having read only intelligence estimates estimating 500 Soviet ICBMs by the early 1960s, the RAND strategists thought they were being more than reasonable to do sensitivity analysis assuming that the Soviets attacked the U.S. with only 150 or even 250 ICBMs. They had no way of knowing that some intelligence agencies were predicting only 50.

At the height of the missile-gap period, Albert Wohlstetter decided to go public. It was an unusual thing to do among the RAND strategists. With few exceptions, they had stuck to the more restricted world of top-secret studies and high-level briefings. First, there was the matter of security: not much could be said without broaching regulations on classified materials. Second, there was the elitist notion, pervasive at RAND, that influencing military officers and Pentagon officials was what really counted, that airing views to the general public served little purpose and might, in fact, be seen as stepping out of bounds or displaying disloyalty to RAND's sponsor, the U.S. Air Force. Third, at least in Wohlstetter's case, there was the condescension toward "the essay tradition," toward popular articles that lacked or failed to reflect the rigors of systems analysis.

Still, in May 1958, Rowan Gaither, Phil Mosley, a professor at Columbia who also sat on RAND's board, and Jim Perkins, a former adviser to the Gaither Committee, asked Wohlstetter to give a talk on SAC vulnerability to the prestigious Council on Foreign Relations in New York. Naturally, Wohlstetter accepted. Among the attendants was Hamilton Armstrong, editor of the Council's influential quarterly, *Foreign Affairs*. Armstrong was impressed with the talk and asked Wohlstetter to write it up for the journal.

The article appeared in the January 1959 issue, and was titled "The Delicate Balance of Terror." It was essentially a distillation of the two major works that Wohlstetter had directed at RAND, the overseas-base study and R-290. Yet unlike those analyses, "The Delicate Balance of Terror" was aimed at the "outsiders" taking part in the defense debate, the civilian "defense-intellectual" community in Washington and at Harvard and MIT, the denizens of the foreign-policy establishment who read and wrote for magazines like *Foreign Affairs* and who influenced the tenor and substance of the general discussion of all such issues.

It had been a nearly universal assumption among this outside community, even among those who vigorously disagreed about much else, that America's ability to retaliate after a Soviet first-strike was pretty well assured. Wohlstetter's article challenged that assumption. Without quantifying the argument, as he had in the classified report, he made the basic point that SAC was terribly vulnerable, that the U.S. might not be able to retaliate with enough power to deter Soviet aggression. The public debate, he wrote, was misleading on this score, tending to confuse deterrence "with matching or exceeding the enemy's ability to strike first," when the critical element was to build a nuclear force that could survive a Soviet first-strike and proceed to carry out a devastating second-strike.

That thesis had been around ever since Bernard Brodie wrote *The Absolute Weapon* in 1946, but it was news to most readers when Wohlstetter wrote that the "notion that a carefully planned surprise attack can be checkmated almost effortlessly, that, in short, we may resume our deep pre-Sputnik sleep, is wrong. . . ." Correcting the problem of vulnerability and maintaining the delicate balance of terror will involve measures that "*are* hard, *do* involve sacrifice . . . and, above all . . . entail a new image of ourselves in a world of persistent danger." He concluded, "It is by no means certain that we shall meet the task."

The article created a huge sensation among the defense intellectuals along the Washington-New York-Cambridge corridor. Its language was somber, its logic compelling, its tone and argument confirming the general feeling among the foreign-policy establishment that Eisenhower was bungling the job miserably and putting the nation at great risk.

More critically, at a time when many feared that the Russians were surpassing the United States, Wohlstetter's article helped create an intellectual framework in which this fear could be stated respectably. The danger was not the "international Communist conspiracy" or anything of an embarrassingly ideological or, for that matter, political nature. Rather, it was this almost mechanical concept of a very delicately balanced set of scales that once tipped even slightly off balance, threw the entire order of international relations out of kilter, placed the West in supreme danger, wiped out the deterrent power of America's nuclear weapons and slid the world toward the precipice of a calamitously destructive war that the Soviet Union would almost certainly win.

Wohlstetter had diligently sought to avoid any connection between his article and the missile-gap thesis. Indeed, he explicitly stated in the piece that numerical comparisons between Russian and American missile arsenals were beside the point, that it was how much strength we had *after* a Soviet first-strike that counted. But his views were actually much closer to those of the missile-gap doomsayers than he cared to acknowledge. They were subtler and more sophisticated, but the assumptions in both were identical. They were based on the highly pessimistic intelligence estimates that lay at the heart of the missile gap. And they contained the same assumptions about Russian intentions, the same judgment that the Soviets would very likely threaten to attack the United States once they had, on paper, the technical ability to do so.

Wohlstetter's contribution to the period was an escalation of the intellectual plane on which the missile gap could be blithely assumed and seriously discussed. The very phrase "missile gap" was coming to symbolize everything complacent, stultified, unforward-looking about the Eisenhower Administration. For those who sensed that merely comparing missile numbers might be a popularly potent but intellectually inadequate critique of Eisenhower's defense programs, "The Delicate Balance of Terror" provided a new platform for attack. Among the critics who would inevitably have great influence in the next Democratic Administration, the RAND technique of how to assess the strategic balance and how to deter nuclear war—developed and calculated in detailed studies over nearly the past decade—triumphed.

Over that same decade, another thread of ideas was being spun at the RAND Corporation—ideas about not only how to deter nuclear war, but also how to fight one.

11 THE MASSIVE-RETALIATION SPEECH

O N JANUARY 12, 1954, almost exactly one year into the Eisenhower Administration, John Foster Dulles, the Secretary of State, delivered what was announced ahead of time as a major address before the Council on Foreign Relations in New York. For many years after, it would be known simply as "the massive-retaliation speech," and would serve as the fulcrum around which a great debate would revolve for at least the rest of the decade.

The speech began by criticizing the Truman Administration for having created a foreign policy geared almost entirely toward reacting to emergencies. "Emergency measures are costly; they are superficial; and they imply that the enemy has the initiative." More important, Dulles said, was to look at national security from the perspective of a "long haul." The "Soviet Communists are planning for what they call 'an entire historical era,' " Dulles said, "and we should do the same. They seek, through many types of maneuvers, gradually to divide and weaken the free nations by overextending them in efforts which, as Lenin put it, are 'beyond their strength, so that they come to practical bankruptcy.' Then, said Lenin, 'our victory is assured.' Then, said Stalin, will be 'the moment for the decisive blow.' "

Thus, said Dulles, "in the face of this strategy, measures cannot be judged adequate merely because they ward off an emergency danger. It is essential to do this, but it is also essential to do so without exhausting ourselves."

More specifically, it is neither sound foreign policy nor sound economics "to commit U.S. land forces in Asia to a degree that leaves us no strategic reserves . . . [or] to support permanently other countries . . . [or] to become permanently committed to military expenditures so vast that they lead to 'practical bankruptcy.' " In short, the Truman policy had to be changed "to assure the stamina needed for permanent security."

Permanent security, Dulles continued, requires above all a

complete change in the attitude toward local, non-nuclear defenses. There "is no local defense which alone will contain the mighty landpower of the Communist world." Therefore, if the U.S. continued to go about the world, committing ground troops here and there to stave off piecemeal Communist aggression, as it had in Korea, then we would soon be exhausted to the point of bankruptcy, leading ultimately to the decay of our true security. In fact, such a policy might tempt an aggressor such as the Soviet Union, which is "glutted with manpower," to "attack in confidence that resistance would be confined to manpower"—in short, "to attack in places where his superiority was decisive."

Rather, Dulles maintained, in a passage that would be frequently quoted, "the way to deter aggression is for the free community to be willing and able to respond vigorously at places and with means of its own choosing." And that meant reinforcing local defenses with "the further deterrent of massive retaliatory power," the power of America's strategic nuclear arsenal.

"If an enemy could pick his time and place and method of warfare—and if our policy was to remain the traditional one of meeting aggression by direct and local opposition—then we needed to be ready to fight in the Arctic and in the Tropics; in Asia, the Near East, and in Europe; by sea, by land and by air; with old weapons and with new weapons." But now, with the new policy—what Eisenhower called the "New Look"—"the Department of Defense and the Joint Chiefs of Staff can shape our military establishment to fit what is *our* policy, instead of having to try to be ready to meet the enemy's many choices. That permits a *selection* of military means instead of a multiplication of means," a reliance on the terror of our atomic arsenal instead of on millions of soldiers and weapons deployed all around the globe. "As a result, it is now possible to get, and share, more basic security at less cost."

Relying chiefly on the bomb would keep the economy from collapsing under the weight of excessive conventional arms and soldiers, hold off Communist aggression where it counts, and thus, due to the combination of those efforts, be sufficient, indeed ideal, for maintaining the peace and protecting freedom's security. So thought John Foster Dulles.

Dulles was the chief articulator of the New Look, but he was by no means its sole architect. Sharing his views entirely, and contributing to the formulation of the policy, were Admiral Arthur

W. Radford, Chairman of the Joint Chiefs of Staff, Treasury Secretary George Humphrey, Budget Director Joseph Dodge and, above all, President Dwight David Eisenhower.

Although a former Army general—and, therefore, a man who might be expected to support extravagant defense budgets—Eisenhower was a penny pincher, perhaps especially when it came to overseeing the military establishment that he knew so well. As early as 1946, he frequently lectured fellow officers on the need to pay close attention to what "the economy can stand." During the 1952 Presidential campaign, he declared that "the foundation of military strength is economic strength" and that a "bankrupt America is more the Soviet goal than an America conquered on the field of battle."

Eisenhower had an almost mystical attachment to the unfettered free market and a loathing toward any tampering with it. Like most Republicans, he despised taxation, debt and inflation, feeling that if they were allowed to spiral out of control, the free economy, and with it, the free society, would collapse.

On May 4, not quite four months after taking office, Eisenhower wrote a confidential letter to his good friend General Alfred Gruenther, Chief of Staff of SHAPE, the Supreme Headquarters, Allied Powers Europe. "As you know," he began, "we are trying to bring the total expenditures of the American Government within reasonable limits. This is not because of any belief that we can afford relaxation of the combined effort to combat Soviet communism. On the contrary, it grows out of a belief that our organized, effective resistance must be maintained over a long period of years and that this is possible only with a healthy American economy. If we should proceed recklessly and habitually to create budget deficits year after year, we have with us an inflationary influence that can scarcely be successfully combatted. Our particular form of economy could not endure."

Two and a half months earlier, Eisenhower's Budget Director, Joe Dodge, had produced a report that must have disturbed Eisenhower greatly. The size of the federal debt, Dodge noted, was $267.5 billion, more than five and a half times the debt held just before World War II. If the spending policies of the Truman Administration were continued, the debt would reach $307 billion by 1958, $33 billion beyond the statutory limit. Thirty percent of national income was currently being snatched by government; more than two-thirds of that revenue was being taken by the federal

government, and two-thirds of that went toward foreign aid and
military spending. Foreign aid had the full support of Eisenhower;
he considered it the program in which "the United States is getting more for its money than in any other." Therefore, given the
statistics and given Eisenhower's economic philosophy, holding
the line on military spending seemed mandatory. And since a
huge conventional force of troops, tanks, ships, fighter planes, artillery and so forth needed for large-scale combat was most expensive of all, Eisenhower was determined to cut back on this non-
nuclear side of the military.

There was something else besides economic concerns that
drove Eisenhower to this position, however, and that was Korea.
The Korean War had been trudging along for nearly two and a half
years when Eisenhower took office, and it seemed to be heading
nowhere, toward neither victory nor defeat. By the following July,
when an armistice would finally be signed, more than 33,000
Americans would have died in the war, and for a purpose that few
back home could figure out. "No More Koreas" became a popular
slogan, especially among politicians who liked to boost the Air
Force, whose philosophy of Air Power saw no need to slug things
out in a messy ground conflict, at the expense of the Army, whose
mission involved precisely that. Retired Army General Eisenhower
certainly had no favoritism toward the Air Force, but, perhaps
with convictions more sincere than most, he joined in with the
"No More Koreas" cry.

Eisenhower's hesitation to get involved in small, distant battles, especially battles fought in Asia, antedated Korea by many
years. In the early-to-mid-1920s, Eisenhower was an Army major
assigned as chief aide to General Fox Conner, commander of U.S.
forces in Panama. Conner taught him how to think about military
decisions systematically, according to the logic of the standard
five-paragraph field order—assessing Mission, Situation, Enemy
Troops, Our Troops, Plans, Logistic Support and Communications, in that order.

Conner talked a great deal with Eisenhower about the critical
importance of the second paragraph, the Commander's Estimate
of the Situation—assessing each course of action open to the
enemy and each corresponding move available to you, examining
each action and response in combination to see what was the
worst thing that could happen and, in that context, which opportunities to best exploit.

The technique was in many ways like John von Neumann's Theory of Games, the art and science of calculating the best strategy assuming a rational opponent who is doing his best to do you in under all circumstances. In fact, when Eisenhower was President and the Atlas ICBM program was under development, he met von Neumann, grew to admire him greatly, became fascinated with Game Theory, and told von Neumann of its amazing similarity to the commanders' guidelines taught to him thirty years earlier.

When President Eisenhower applied Conner's method to the question of fighting small conventional wars, especially in Asia, he could only be dubious about any chance of military success. The "Estimate of the Situation" required knowing fairly well how the situation looked in the mind of the enemy, and Eisenhower simply did not believe that any Westerner could truly comprehend the Oriental mind. To Eisenhower, via Conner, the less one knew about where the successive steps of a battle might lead, the less one could formulate a sensible strategy and, therefore, the less willing one should be to jump into a violent fray of mystery.

Still, while all these influences shaped Eisenhower's judgments about what not to do, they provided little guidance for a positive defense policy. He was still lost on how to solve what he frequently called "the great equation"—how to maintain a strong defense over "the long haul" without wrecking the free economy in the process. Guidance was where John Foster Dulles came in.

Dulles' idea of massive retaliation did not originate with his January 1954 speech before the Council on Foreign Relations. For several years, Dulles had accepted the use of nuclear weapons in war as an almost foregone conclusion. As early as October 1948, at the height of the Truman-Dewey campaign, Dulles, speaking as the Republican Party's official foreign-policy adviser, told General George Marshall, at the time Truman's Secretary of State, in a private conversation, "Why, the American people would execute you if you did not use the bomb in the event of war."

A coherent outlook had developed in his mind by 1951 at the latest, when on February 2, after working on the Japanese peace treaty, he sought to assure an audience in Tokyo that the United States would protect Japan by the threat to destroy any aggressor with "a striking power, the immensity of which defies imagination."

On May 5, 1952, he suggested to the French National Political Science Institute in Paris that "we might consider whether open military aggression by Red armies could not best be prevented by the readiness to take retaliatory action, rather than by attempts to meet the aggression on the spot where it occurs." In a passage most foretelling of the Council speech, Dulles stated, "So long as the Soviet and Chinese Communist leaders can pick the time, place and method of aggression . . . and so long as we only rush ground troops to meet it at the time they select, at the place they select, and with the weapons they select, we are at a disadvantage which can be fatal.

"On the other hand," he continued, "the free world possesses, particularly in air and sea power, the capacity to hit an aggressor where it hurts, at times and places of our own choosing. If a potential aggressor knew in advance that his own aggression would bring that answer, then I am convinced that he would not commit aggression."

Dulles' position on the atomic bomb and its use took on an almost religious quality. In the mid-1940s, he had been chairman of the Commission on a Just and Durable Peace, an organization established in the early days of World War II by the Federal Council of the Churches of Christ in America. On August 9, 1945, immediately after the United States dropped the A-bomb on Hiroshima, Dulles released a nationwide press release urging Truman to suspend the air attack for a long enough time to give the Japanese leaders a chance to react. To do otherwise would be to tell the world that "we, a professedly Christian nation, feel morally free to use atomic energy in that way." That being the case, "men elsewhere will accept that verdict. Atomic weapons will be looked upon as a normal part of the arsenal of war and the stage will be set for the sudden and final destruction of mankind."

Similarly, exactly five months later, in a speech published in *The Christian News Letter,* Dulles warned that a failure of the United States to turn over custody of atomic weapons to "the dictates of . . . world opinion" would "wholly destroy our moral influence in the world and seriously set back the possibility of developing the greater fellowship we need." We would then live in a world in which, when war occurs, "nations avail themselves of any weapons which they think will make the difference between victory and defeat."

Before long, it was clear that the United States had no such intention of sharing its ownership of nuclear power. Gradually,

Dulles began to embrace the negative side of his earlier predictions—that the bomb "will be looked upon as a normal part of the arsenal of war" and that nations will use "any weapon which they think will make the difference between victory and defeat"—with equal moralistic fervor.

At first, Eisenhower felt uncomfortable with the idea of massive retaliation. When he discovered in the summer of 1952 that the Republican platform statement on defense policy contained the phrase "retaliatory striking power," a phrase composed by Dulles, he had it removed, finding it offensively cold-blooded.

Eventually, however, Eisenhower caught on to just how nicely the concept fit in with his own ideas about defense and economy. It all came together during the transition period between Eisenhower's victory in November 1952 and his inauguration the following January. During the campaign, Eisenhower had dramatically promised to visit the front lines of Korea as the first step toward ending the war. On November 29, carrying out his commitment, Eisenhower embarked on the trip, taking along his designated Defense Secretary, Charles Wilson, head of General Motors. The plane stopped for refueling at Iwo Jima, where Admiral Arthur Radford, Commander in Chief of the Pacific Fleet, was brought on board at the request of Wilson, who wanted to size him up as possible Chairman of the Joint Chiefs of Staff.

After the tour of Korea, the group flew to Guam, picked up a group of Eisenhower's advisers who had flown there from New York, and headed back to the United States aboard the cruiser U.S.S. *Helena*. Among them were the future Treasury Secretary, George Humphrey; the designated Budget Director, Joseph Dodge; and Eisenhower's natural choice for Secretary of State, John Foster Dulles. In the relaxed atmosphere, out in the Pacific Ocean, they talked about how to solve Eisenhower's "great equation," how to protect the national security without wrecking society in the process.

It was here that the ideas came together, that Eisenhower's concerns blended in with Dulles' solution. Radford backed Dulles up from a military point of view; Dodge and Humphrey readily saw the economic advantages; Eisenhower saw a mixture of both. The Eisenhower defense policy took formal shape. Eisenhower suddenly saw the virtue of relying primarily on the "retaliatory striking power" that he had rejected as distasteful only a few months earlier. The "New Look" in national defense policy was born.

Eisenhower started to believe, and maintained the belief throughout his two terms as President, that any military action that grew to the scope of the Korean War or beyond "would become one for use of atomic weapons." He adamantly felt that any direct clash between the U.S. and the U.S.S.R. would undoubtedly involve nuclear weapons used in full force at the outset; that it was "fatuous" to believe that any such "life and death struggle" between these two great nations would develop in any other fashion.

Dulles was more aggressive about broadcasting this policy than Eisenhower. Dulles viewed the superpower competition as a titanic struggle between freedom and slavery, the shining beacon and the web of darkness, God and the Devil. Eisenhower approached the New Look mainly as a technique of saving money, keeping the country out of faraway wars against enemies about whom we knew nothing, and convincing the Russians that we would destroy their country in retaliation to serious aggression as a means of deterring such aggression in the first place. Nevertheless, Eisenhower bought the fundamental premise of his Secretary of State's thinking: referring to nuclear weapons, he wrote Dulles in the spring of 1955 that it was necessary to "remind individuals that we are really regarding these weapons as 'conventional.' "

The speech that Foster Dulles delivered to the Council on Foreign Relations in January 1954, that made "massive retaliation" practically a household phrase, was, in short, the culmination of top-level thinking inside the Eisenhower Administration, a carefully worked-out position that completely reflected the views not just of the Secretary of State but of the President of the United States as well.

And yet, whether they knew it or not, the Dulles speech merely codified the military policy that the U.S. Joint Chiefs of Staff had already formulated in the late Truman Administration. The Air Force, dominated by Curtis LeMay's Strategic Air Command with its almost theological worship of Air Power, naturally disdained reliance on the old-fashioned tools of warfare; this was the Atomic Age, and the atomic weapon should dominate. The philosophy was clearly spelled out as early as 1948 in the official top-secret Air Force guidance, *Doctrine of Atomic Air Warfare*: "Progression from the spear through the bow, musket, rifle and

artillery to the weapons of World War II was simply a matter of
ever-increasing firepower. . . . The atomic bomb does not appear
to have deviated from this evolutionary trend."

Once the Navy began to acquire atomic weapons of its own in
1951, fleet officers started to spout the same doctrine: "It is in our
interest," wrote L. D. McCormick, Acting Chief of Naval Operations in July of that year, "to convince the world at large that the
use of atomic weapons is no less humane than the employment of
an equivalent weight of so-called conventional weapons. The destruction of certain targets is essential to the successful completion of a war with the U.S.S.R. The pros and cons of the means to
accomplish their destruction is purely academic."

The Army, assigned the chore of fighting out battles on the
ground, sought to dispel these grandiose theories of Air Power. In
September 1952, Army General Omar Bradley, who was then
Chairman of the Joint Chiefs of Staff, told newsmen at NATO
headquarters that "it would be premature for any planners to attempt to substitute atomic weapons for sound balanced forces.
Actually, no matter how many atomic weapons or bombs the collective NATO defense may eventually have on hand, there will always be a need for sufficient ground strength to force the enemy
to concentrate for attack." Bradley was trying to get the West European nations to build strong conventional armies, dozens of divisions on top of the four that the United States already had deployed there. The plan was being severely undermined by those
who claimed with total confidence that the U.S. nuclear shield
was sufficient. "In my opinion," Bradley stated, "no tested knowledge of atomic weapons to date indicates any reason to let up in
our efforts to build up our collective security forces to at least
those that we are planning for the next few years."

Indeed, an Army study completed the previous summer concluded that the bombing operations against the Soviet industrial
potential, as planned by the Air Force, would not prevent the Soviets from successfully mounting a ground attack across the
plains of Western Europe. In the intricate intramural schemings
and competitions permeating the Joint Chiefs, the Navy sided
with the Army on the conclusions of that study—but only to bolster its own claims that the Navy's attack-aircraft carriers could do
the job better than the Air Force. On the fundamental issue of
whether large ground forces were needed or whether air (and

sea) power could savage an enemy without much assistance from the more traditional tools of warfare, the Navy, for its own budgetary reasons, sided with the Air Force.

With the Army outnumbered, a JCS statement of December 1951 declared, "It is United States policy on atomic warfare that, in the event of hostilities, the Department of Defense must be ready to utilize promptly and effectively all appropriate means available, including atomic weapons, in the interest of national security and must therefore plan accordingly." Throughout the early 1950s, the official war plans ordered that a "strategic air offensive with atomic and conventional bombs will be initiated at the earliest possible date subsequent to the outbreak of hostilities"—a notion remarkably similar to the ideas laid out in the mid-1950s by Dwight David Eisenhower and John Foster Dulles.

The basic effect of the new Administration's New Look was that the Air Force-Navy position was sanctified, given the seal of total legitimation at the highest level. In the Truman Administration, the Army dissent was frequently supported, directly or indirectly, by many top officials who believed that large conventional forces were necessary, among them Secretary of State Dean Acheson and his policy planning director, Paul Nitze. Now they were out and all progress made toward building a case for massive conventional forces received a powerful setback. With the entire Joint Chiefs of Staff replaced, and with Admiral Radford at the helm as Chairman—the first JCS Chairman never to have served previously as a service Chief—the conventional-force argument was set back further still.

Before the first year of the Eisenhower Administration was over, it was very clear in the White House, the State Department, the Office of the Secretary of Defense, and the Joint Chiefs of Staff that the United States was unambiguously relying on its atomic arsenal to counter all but the slightest motions of Communist aggression. With Foster Dulles' Council speech in January of the second year, it was also very clear to the general public.

Admiral Radford put the thesis even more bluntly than Dulles in a confidential speech delivered to the Naval War College in Newport, Rhode Island, on May 25, 1954: "What does all this mean?" he asked of the New Look policy. "It means that atomic forces are now our primary forces. It means that actions by other forces, on land, sea or air are relegated to a secondary role." It "means that nuclear weapons, fission and fusion, will be used in the next major war. Availability of fissile material, the economy of its use, the magnitude of its destructive effects, and the flexibility of its use makes it the primary munition of war. Victory will come to the side that makes the best use of it."

12 THE LIMITED-WAR CRITIQUE

VIRTUALLY THE ENTIRE foreign-policy establishment turned out that cold January evening in New York to hear what Foster Dulles had to say before the august Council on Foreign Relations. And they were nearly all horrified. Part of their revulsion was toward the self-righteousness of the speech, the condescending tone which said in effect that Dulles was wiser, more morally sensible, more sensitive to the nation's true security interests than were the men of Truman and Acheson, many of whom were sitting in the audience. The Marshall Plan, the Berlin Airlift, the formation of NATO—all considered noble achievements by those who participated in them—were dismissed by Dulles as mere reactions to emergencies, unaffected by broader strategic interests or a sense of the initiative.

What appalled them more was the substance of the speech— its lack of clear economic thinking, its failure to think through the dilemmas of using the atom bomb as either a threat or an instrument of war. Particularly astonished by the speech was Paul Nitze, chief author of NSC-68, the paper that served as the Truman Administration's blueprint for rearmament after the Korean War broke out. Nitze never did like Dulles. They worked at rival Wall Street firms in the 1930s, and Nitze thought Dulles all too eager to do whatever clients wanted regardless of considerations of sound finance. When Eisenhower took office, Dulles asked Nitze to stay on at the State Department for six months, but then let him go, telling Nitze that he essentially agreed with his policies but they had raised such a fuss about Truman's foreign policy in the campaign that personnel simply had to be changed. In short, Nitze viewed Dulles as an opportunist and a charlatan.

To Nitze, the speech simply made no sense. The very next day, he wrote a ten-page critique for Robert Bowie, his successor at the Policy Planning Staff. Dulles had raised the Korean War as the sort of thing we must avoid in the future. But to Nitze, the Korean War only demonstrated that reliance on the atomic bomb alone—and then the U.S. had an atomic monopoly—would not deter the Soviets from aggression; and yet it was such a reliance that Dulles proposed to bring back.

Nor could Nitze fathom the economic analysis furnished by Dulles, the notion that raising defense spending would "bankrupt" the economy. "Can one say today," wrote Nitze, "when our population is living better than any people on earth have ever lived, when our steel plants are only being used to 75% of their capacity, when we feel threatened by the magnitude of our agricultural surpluses, that we are even close to the economic limits of what we could do if we were called upon with clarity of purpose and nobility of vision to do it? Are we facing 'practical bankruptcy' with average consumer expenditures five times those of the average Soviet citizen while the Russians are not?"

Finally, to Nitze, Dulles seemed to lack an understanding of just how powerful the bomb was. The Soviets had the bomb, too, and if we massively retaliated against them, they would almost certainly massively retaliate against us.

On the basis of these arguments, a general critique of the Dulles speech—and, by implication, the Eisenhower defense policy—began to emerge within the foreign-policy establishment, among certain prominent newspaper columnists and in Democratic Party circles. But the most powerful critical blow, the line of argument that was most articulately formulated and that would have the greatest influence, came ten months after the Dulles speech in the form of a twenty-three-page mimeograph released by the Center of International Studies at Princeton University. The essay was entitled "The Requirements of Deterrence," and its author was a Princeton political science professor named William W. Kaufmann.

William Weed Kaufmann was a short man, with a slightly high-pitched voice and moods alternating between a dour, even sour cynicism and a wry, contagious mirth punctuated by a chuckling giggle. After age ten, when his father died, Kaufmann attended boarding schools, then prep school in Switzerland and at Choate (where one of his classmates and friends was Jack Kennedy), then Yale, where he graduated in 1939. War was distinctly hovering over the horizon in his undergraduate years. The Yale Institute of International Studies—the academic bedrock of *Realpolitik* thinking founded four years earlier by Nicholas Spykman, Arnold Wolfers and Ted Dunn, and later joined by Bernard Brodie—was having an impression on the campus. But New Haven was also a center of the isolationist movement, and several of the faculty—including Whitney Griswold and Kingman Brewster, later university presidents—were active in the America First organization. The *Yale Daily News* and the Political Union served as frequent forums for the great interventionist versus isolationist debate in those years.

The times and the Yale climate naturally pushed several students in the direction of international affairs as life's work. The class of '39 grew up to be an uncannily illustrious group, its alumni including Cyrus "Spider" Vance, campus hockey-team star and future Deputy Secretary of Defense and Secretary of State; William Bundy, conservative leader of the Political Union and later Assistant Secretary of State in the Lyndon Johnson Administration (with his brother, McGeorge, Kennedy's National Security Adviser, one class behind); Stanley Resor, later Secretary of the Army and Undersecretary of Defense; William Scranton, future governor of Pennsylvania and a Presidential candidate at the 1964 Republican convention.

For many of these alumni, political interests were combined with a strong flavor of *noblesse oblige*. Yale was a bastion of upper-class education, and in the wake of the Depression and on the eve of World War, many were uncomfortably conscious of their own wealth and (in numerous conscience-stirring *Daily News* editorials, it was spelled with a capital *M*) Materialism. Bill Bundy represented the apotheosis of this tendency. In an oration delivered to his fellow Yale seniors on Class Day, 1939, he passionately told them, "If we are to consider ourselves as a group and a class of special significance, we must get right down to earth and perform special services, for it is only on that basis that the idea of class can be tolerated in a democracy."

Bill Kaufmann was wealthy, but not that wealthy. He was not a part of the gala-party social set at Yale, nor a prominent campus politico. He was a prize-winning orator, a very diligent student, one of the academic stars in diplomatic history. But two years before America's entry into the war, he didn't take the international storm clouds too seriously. He joined a spirited group of campus anarchists called the Veterans of Future Wars, which morbidly but good-humoredly paraded around the campus grounds carrying placards demanding their veteran payments now since they would not likely be alive to collect them after the war was over.

After graduation, Kaufmann moved to Manhattan and worked for a year on Wall Street. He then returned to New Haven for graduate school in the department of international relations, but within a couple of months was drafted into the Army and assigned to a Medical Corps training battalion in Camp Lee, Virginia. Private Kaufmann hated the Med Corps, felt unqualified for his tasks and longed for a more exciting post in the Army Air Corps or the Intelligence Service. Eventually, his application to the Air Corps was accepted.

After the Germans seized Crete, the Army had embarked upon an enormous glider-plane program. Gliders were great fun to fly, almost anyone could get into the training program, and about 20,000 joined up, including Kaufmann. After a year, however, with the Normandy invasion in the works, the Army decided that gliders would not be so great for combat after all, and Kaufmann was retrained first as a bombardier and then as a radar instructor. In April 1945, he was finally assigned to an operational unit that was scheduled to join the Eighth Air Force in England. When they got to the East Coast, they found themselves put on hold for two weeks at Roosevelt Island in New York, during which V-E Day was celebrated.

For Kaufmann, the war in the Pacific was equally eventful. He was sent to Arizona to train on a new navigational radar system invented by the MIT Radiation Lab, and before he could be sent out to join the Twentieth Air Force, the Japanese surrendered.

Kaufmann re-enrolled in the graduate school of international relations at Yale and was soon recognized as the department's brightest postwar graduate student. His doctoral dissertation—on British foreign policy toward Latin America and balance-of-power politics in the nineteenth century—won Yale's annual historian's prize even though Kaufmann was not in the history department. After completing his Ph.D., he joined the Yale faculty and the Institute staff, the first staff member to have emerged from the ranks of Institute students.

It was the start of the postwar peak for the Institute of International Studies when Bill Kaufmann returned to graduate school. Besides Ted Dunn and Arnold Wolfers and Percy Corbett, there were also the Chicago émigrés—Klaus Knorr, William T. R. Fox, Gabriel Almond, Jacob Viner on occasion, and especially Bernard Brodie. Brodie was already attracting attention as one of the few civilians to think about the strategic implications of the atom

bomb in a sophisticated way. And it was under the influence of
Brodie, who became friend and mentor, that Kaufmann grew serious about the study of international relations and national-security problems. His perspective became the same as Brodie's—the
Chicago/Yale School of International Realism, with its focus on
the causes of war, the inevitable failure of all peace plans that rely
on dreams of world government, the essential role that power
plays in all political systems, and the peculiar twist that the existence of the atomic bomb, "the absolute weapon," puts on all
these maxims.

In 1949, a group of six Institute professors, including Bernard Brodie and Kaufmann, was hired by the social science division of the RAND Corporation in Santa Monica to do part-time
work analyzing psychological warfare. At Yale's Sterling Library,
Kaufmann had one day run across a set of the Nuremberg war-
crimes hearings and read them with fascination. He grew particularly intrigued with what the transcripts revealed about the
Barbarossa campaign, Nazi Germany's massive June 22, 1941, invasion of Russia that took Stalin so much by surprise. Kaufmann's
contribution to the Yale group's RAND work was a case study on
Barbarossa.

Kaufmann's paper was one of the few admired by Hans
Speier, director of RAND's social science division, and Speier
asked him to come spend the summer of 1951 in Santa Monica as
a consultant. At the end of the summer, Speier offered Kaufmann
a full-time job. Kaufmann was about to take it, but was talked out
of the idea by Ted Dunn, director of the Institute of International
Studies. The Institute had just left Yale the previous April—owing
to disagreements between Dunn and Yale's new president, Whitney Griswold—and was now taking up a new residence at Princeton under the new name of the Center of International Studies.
Bernard Brodie had already taken off, first to the Air Force Staff on
leave, then to RAND for good; if Kaufmann left too, it could mean
the beginning of the Institute's ultimate splitting up. Out of loyalty to Ted Dunn, Kaufmann stayed.

At Princeton, besides teaching history and associating with
his fellow Yale refugees, Kaufmann began to elaborate on the
work that he had started at RAND. His research on the Nazis'
Barbarossa plan led him to formulate general propositions on the
various ways in which nations respond to military threats and the
specific circumstances under which they tend to respond. From

this approach, he began to rethink the basic question that he had picked up from Bernard Brodie at Yale: how does one deter an enemy from aggression in an age when both sides would have plenty of atomic bombs?

Kaufmann toiled with the dilemma off and on through the early 1950s, and then in January 1954 came the massive-retaliation speech by John Foster Dulles. Because that speech so comprehensively summarized a strategy that almost blithely relied on nuclear weapons to deter aggression—and, therefore, utterly neglected the dilemmas of the atomic age that Bernard Brodie and Bill Kaufmann had pondered—Kaufmann considered it the ideal foil to attack, the perfect vehicle through which he could clarify and express his own thinking.

In *The Absolute Weapon,* Brodie's seminal work of eight years earlier, Kaufmann's mentor had concluded that nuclear war could be deterred by the threat to "retaliate in kind" in the event of direct attack on the United States. Now, when both the U.S. and the Soviet Union were acquiring a formidable arsenal of atomic—and soon thermonuclear—weapons, Kaufmann saw, in a twist on Brodie's reasoning, that if Soviet aggression in, say, Asia provoked the United States to retaliate massively against Soviet territory with our full atomic arsenal, then the Soviets would almost certainly launch an atomic volley of their own right back against the United States. "As a consequence of these developments," Kaufmann would write, "it may no longer be desirable to treat nuclear weapons as adjuncts to conventional military power; nor may it be possible for us to consider using them without anticipating retaliation in kind."

A policy of deterrence, Kaufmann recognized, inevitably carried a potentially costly risk—"that, despite our best efforts, the antagonist will challenge us to make good on our threat. If we do so, we will have to accept the consequences of executing our threatened action. If we back down and let the challenge go unheeded, we will suffer losses of prestige, we will decrease our capacity for instituting effective deterrence policies in the future, and we will encourage the opponent to take further actions of a detrimental character." If the threat is massive retaliation and if deterrence for some reason fails, then the only way to avoid perilous humiliation is to go ahead and drop atom bombs; yet the Soviet Union can also massively retaliate in return. "In other words," Kaufmann concluded, "we must face the fact that, if we are challenged to fulfill the threat of massive retaliation, we will be likely to suffer costs as great as those we inflict." And that is unacceptable.

Kaufmann's basic conclusion was identical to that reached two years earlier by Bernard Brodie when he and his RAND colleagues, Charlie Hitch and Ernie Plesset, examined the implications of the hydrogen bomb. Brodie had drawn insight from the nineteenth-century Prussian warrior-philosopher Karl von Clausewitz, who argued that war is violence but controlled violence in pursuit of some national objective. Brodie, realizing that "national objectives cannot be consonant with national suicide," thus concluded that "there is no use talking about a mutual exchange of nuclear weapons," especially in the age of the H-bomb, "as being anything other than national suicide." Brodie had spelled out these basic thoughts publicly in the January 1954 issue of *Foreign Affairs,* which Kaufmann must have read.

From that general observation, however, Kaufmann branched off into a series of arguments and conclusions quite different from Brodie's. In 1951, while working for General Hoyt Vandenberg on the Air Staff, and in 1952, in connection with the H-bomb project at RAND—and, though much less explicitly, in the 1954 *Foreign Affairs* article, entitled "Nuclear Weapons: Strategic or Tactical?"—Brodie had found a solution to the dilemma in the controlled use of nuclear weapons on the battlefield. Brodie did not embrace this idea with joy or enthusiasm, but he felt—in the early 1950s anyway—that it was the only alternative, given the Soviet Union's putative superiority in manpower and conventional arms.

Kaufmann, on the other hand, thought it was unwise and dangerous, except under the most extraordinary of threats to America's security, to use nuclear weapons at all. If the Soviets outnumbered us on the ground, then that meant only that the United States, even if at great expense, had to build up a vastly strengthened conventionally armed military force. The essential aspect of deterrence is that the threat be credible, to the enemy and to ourselves. An examination of American foreign policy over the years would suggest that "it is quite out of character for us to retaliate massively against anyone except in the face of provocations as extreme as Pearl Harbor." In a democratic country especially, the potential costs of an interventionist policy "must seem worth incurring." In short, "there must be some relationship be-

tween the value of the objective sought and the costs involved in
its attainment. A policy of deterrence which does not fulfill this
requirement is likely to result only in deterring the deterrer."
Especially as more becomes known about the effects of nuclear
weapons, Kaufmann observed, "we must immediately face the
prospect that the leaders of the Soviet Union and Red China
would hardly endow . . . a doctrine [of massive retaliation] with
much credibility."

Indeed, Kaufmann maintained, a policy of massive retaliation
encourages the Soviets to engage in this sort of piecemeal aggression. As long as each side has enough nuclear weapons to destroy
the other, the threat of massive retaliation to small-scale conventional aggression lacks credibility. Thus, the side with overwhelming conventional forces can go about making incursions and disrupting stability as it pleases, as the Communists appeared to be
doing, at the time of the Dulles speech, in Indochina.

It was on the ground that Communism was making its advances in the "gray areas." It was *without* nuclear weapons that
the United States had been establishing its most successful containment policies—the Berlin Airlift, the founding of NATO, intervention in Korea. All have "suggested rather strongly that the
United States is willing—and, it should be added, able—to meet
[Soviet] moves successfully on the ground and according to the
rules set by the opponent," to "limit and contain Communist
thrusts by means of local applications of counterforce." It was this
"credit . . . that we have at our disposal in making credible any
policy of deterrence, and as such it will have much to do with the
effectiveness of our program," Kaufmann noted. The Dulles policy
of massive retaliation, utterly at odds with this record and lacking
in credibility on other grounds as well, will thus be an ineffective—indeed, counterproductive—deterrent in the face of most
types of Communist aggression. Dulles was attempting to build a
deterrent "on the cheap" and yet it could only lead to "despair . . .
futility and . . . recklessness. . . ."

The proper deterrent would be one that tries "to fit the pun-
ishment to the crime," that prevents—and if that fails, defeats—
aggression at all levels. "If we show a willingness and ability to intervene with great conventional power in the peripheral areas,
after the manner of Korea," Kaufmann would write, "we will have
a reasonable chance of forestalling enemy military action there."
This would mean competing with the Communists on their own

terms, which is exactly what Dulles was trying to avoid. But Kaufmann wondered whether those terms were so favorable to the enemy after all: "Our effort in Korea was smaller in size and probably less costly in terms of human and material resources than the Communist commitment. And it was the Communists who finally became eager to terminate the conflict." In any event, a policy of credible deterrence was the main goal. And to Kaufmann's mind, the "outbreak of World War II, Pearl Harbor, the loss of Eastern Europe, and the Korean War itself resulted in part from a failure by the United States to institute adequate policies of deterrence."

In the summer of 1954, Kaufmann completed a paper outlining his thoughts on this matter, and sent it off to RAND for possible publication. The review committee at RAND did not care for it at all and sent it back to Kaufmann, telling him that if he wanted to publish it on his own it was all right with them. RAND, after all, was financed almost entirely by the Air Force. And 1954 was still a time when, especially among the Air Force and its minions, the idea that the next major war might not be a "total war"—the notion of a "limited war" waged directly between the United States and the Soviet Union—was considered a bit of lunacy almost beneath consideration. The Korean War was commonly judged a failure to be avoided in the future, the "wrong war fought at the wrong place at the wrong time"—not the politico-military success story, the exemplary case of limited warfare matched to limited objective, that Kaufmann wished the nation to emulate.

So it happened that on November 15, 1954, the Princeton Center of International Studies published a monograph called "The Requirements of Deterrence" by Professor William W. Kaufmann. That same week, Bernard Brodie published an article in *The Reporter* called "Unlimited Weapons and Limited War," which made essentially the same point as Kaufmann's "Requirements of Deterrence." Evidently, in the few months since his *Foreign Affairs* article, Brodie, like Kaufmann, was coming to the conclusion that even battlefield nuclear weapons were perhaps too dangerous, that "conventional" defenses better fit the threat. And, like Kaufmann, Brodie invoked the success of Korea as proof of his point's plausibility.

One year later, when Kaufmann was compiling a collection of essays by himself and some colleagues at Princeton, which included his "Requirements of Deterrence," he sent a draft to his old mentor Brodie for comment. Brodie exploded. Either he had never read Kaufmann's original version of "Requirements," or he had forgotten about it, for he accused Kaufmann of stealing him blind, of plagiarizing his "Unlimited Weapons and Limited War." Brodie was very well liked and admired by former students and academic colleagues, but they also knew that he occasionally displayed a savage temper and a bristling ego, especially if he thought others were robbing his ideas. Rather than point out that the essay in question originally appeared at almost exactly the same time as Brodie's article, Kaufmann wrote him a very humble note, asking if he could "intrude upon you simply to offer an apology for having failed to document adequately my great dependence upon your work in the papers which I sent you. The failure was inexcusable and I shall not even attempt to explain it away. Let me say only that it will be rectified immediately. . . . I shall always want it to be known how indebted I am to you for friendship, knowledge, and advice." Kaufmann slapped three footnotes referring to the Brodie article onto the book version of "Requirements of Deterrence," fifteen more references to other Brodie articles in the two other essays that Kaufmann wrote for the anthology, and hoped the matter would be forgotten.

But the incident would mark the beginning of a decline in the Brodie-Kaufmann friendship. Even though Kaufmann would move out to RAND in 1956 and work in the social science division, where Brodie also resided, the two did not talk very much and only rarely socialized. The falling-out was ironic, for it only reflected how close the two men were to each other. It was only natural that Kaufmann, an intelligent student and colleague of Brodie's, who had been taught in the same tradition of international relations and who had been instilled with the same Clausewitzian principles by which Brodie abided, would formulate a highly similar critique.

When Kaufmann's Princeton monograph was released in November 1954, its most avid readers were a group of high-ranking Army officers in the Pentagon. The Army was particularly despairing over massive retaliation. Admiral Radford, Chairman of the JCS, was ordering substantial cuts in ground forces, the instruments of warfare on which the Army depended and which many Army officers sincerely believed were vital for defense.

An aide to General Matthew Ridgway, Army Chief of Staff,

was the first to come across Kaufmann's booklet, and was over-
joyed with it. These were the arguments and ideas that Army officers had been trying to articulate at JCS meetings and inside their
own councils. The idea of large conventional forces certainly
wasn't new. The Army had been arguing its case for years on more
traditional, strictly military terms: you can blow up huge chunks
of territory with the big bomb, but you need ground forces to occupy that territory. Nor was the Army the only advocate of conventional defense. As early as 1950, a group of eleven Harvard and
MIT faculty members—including McGeorge Bundy, John Kenneth Galbraith, Arthur Schlesinger, Jerome Wiesner and Jerrold
Zacharias—had written a long letter to *The New York Times,* criticizing on moral and strategic grounds the military establishment's predominant reliance on atomic warfare. Then there were
the papers written by George Kennan and Paul Nitze in the State
Department, during the Truman Administration, arguing along
similar lines. But those days were over. And this unclassified essay
by this unknown Ivy League professor seemed more powerful: not
only had he spelled out the arguments concisely and dramatically,
he fused them with broader issues of foreign policy and of pre-
venting—not just fighting—wars. And he had done all this as a direct rebuttal to the Dulles/Radford/Eisenhower policy which was
at that moment placing the Army in serious shackles.

Kaufmann's monograph was circulated widely in the Pentagon. Top Air Force officers heard about the report and obtained
copies too. From their point of view, Kaufmann didn't understand
what they liked to refer to as the "flexibility of Air Power." But
they were worried. As one colonel, a special assistant to Vice Chief
of Staff General Tommy White, said in a memo to his boss, "Kaufmann's contentions are well written and will be persuasive to
readers who, like him, are only partially informed on this important security question."

From 1955 on, in JCS meetings and in public relations campaigns, the Army took a much more aggressive stance against the
Air Force-Navy position. Nuclear war, Army generals began to say
publicly, was becoming "increasingly impossible," given the
"stalemate" in strategic forces between the U.S. and the U.S.S.R.
This condition gives the enemy every incentive to concentrate its
efforts in small, local, limited wars; and, unlike the Air Force,
which only wants to make "the biggest bang or the biggest hole in

the ground," the Army is interested in having "the means to apply the exact amount of force required, and at the exact spot, to accomplish a specific task."

However, throughout the decade, the Air Force consistently won the interservice contests on this issue: not only did the Navy side with the Air Force, but so did the JCS Chairman, the Secretary of Defense, the Secretary of State and the President. When in 1956, Admiral Radford found out that the proposed JCS war plan for that year—the Joint Strategic Capabilities Plan, or J-Scap—contained compromise language suggesting that nuclear weapons might not be used in conflicts short of "general war," he fired off a memo to all the Chiefs, telling them that this was "a radical departure from the present approved policy," which "clearly states that atomic weapons can and will be used in military operations short of general war as authorized by the President"; that "our national policy regarding use of atomic weapons has been recently reaffirmed, and this policy does provide that atomic weapons will be used not only in general war but in local war if the situation so dictates."

Each year, from 1956 till the end of the Eisenhower Administration, Army Chief of Staff General Maxwell Taylor—Matthew Ridgway had resigned in protest in 1955—would insist on meeting in the Oval Office with the President and the rest of the Chiefs to make his case against the predominance of Air Power and big bombs in the war plan. And each year, Eisenhower would insist to Taylor, over and again, with growing impatience, that those war plans reflected national policy approved by him, the President. Once, to Taylor's astonishment, Eisenhower told him, "The Army will be truly vital to keeping order inside the United States. The Army will be the stabilizing thing after the big war, the force that pulls the nation together again."

In the last few years of the decade, some of the Army's arguments began to take hold—inside the National Security Council, the President's Science Advisory Committee, more far-flung quarters of the Pentagon, and especially within the Democratic Party. As the Soviet Union began to acquire its own nuclear arsenal, and as tensions began to mount in various "hot spots" around the globe, most notably in Southeast Asia, the Army's arguments grew increasingly compelling. And they were compelling largely because of what the Army took from the writings of the most articulate of the civilian strategists—Bernard Brodie, George Kennan, Paul Nitze and, perhaps most directly, William Weed Kaufmann.

Behind Kaufmann's own arguments for a large conventional-force buildup, however, was an intellectual edifice that military men of all stripes found utterly foreign, but that would have profound influence on the civilian community of defense intellectuals for the next decade and beyond. It was a philosophy not only of using limited weapons, but of limiting, controlling, rationally calculating the very process of making war. The tenets of this new philosophy were spelled out at great length in two other essays that Kaufmann wrote for a symposium that he edited in 1955–1956 at Princeton called *Military Policy and National Security*.

The basic problem, as Kaufmann saw it, was not only that the United States would have to build the means for fighting limited wars, but that in these wars, we would somehow have to compel the Soviets to keep their efforts confined to fighting a limited war, to refrain from expanding it into a nuclear war as well. Imposing such mutual restraints would require altering the very nature and purpose of warfare. Kaufmann saw the future of Soviet-American relations as one of "continuing competition . . . as full of hairpin curves, of sudden rises and declines, of agreeable prospects and impending catastrophes, as the classic Alpine roads." We must, therefore, view all Soviet efforts at infiltration and aggression in the "gray areas" in terms of their effect on this grand competition. "Whatever the nature of the particular situation, we will therefore want to ensure our ability to go on playing the game."

Fighting wars becomes, in an almost too Clausewitzian sense, an extension of Cold War politics by other means. Such wars "perform a function midway between the abstractness of a show of force and the terrible concreteness of annihilative conflict," Kaufmann noted. "They become partial or token tests of strength" or represent "indices of relative power" in the competition.

It was an unorthodox conception of strategy, Kaufmann readily acknowledged, but "it must be remembered that the type of war envisaged is quite unorthodox, too." Traditional strategy, along with its weapons and axioms, held that the idea of war was to destroy the enemy's will to fight, essentially his capabilities,

which therefore must be smashed. In an era when both combat-
ants have long-range multimegaton nuclear weapons in their arsenals, however, the traditional military objectives could not be
gained without committing national suicide in the process, thus
nullifying whatever Pyrrhic victory might have been achieved.

Nobody desires self-annihilation, so both sides have an incentive to keep the war limited. It is important, therefore, to keep
the terms of battle confined, from the outset, to conventional
weapons and within a circumscribed area. For "the scope and
method of the initial attack will tend to define the minimum limits
of the ensuing conflict and the possibilities of controlling it." Limited wars should be fought, or rather "managed," in such a way as
to send "messages" to "the other belligerent," which would "have
a good chance of inducing him to accept limitations of geography,
weapons and possibly time." Indeed, the role of force under these
circumstances lies in its "great value as a counter in the bargaining process" that shapes the "continuing competition." Thus, one
reason for building up conventional forces is that they are the
weapons that the Soviets will be using, and, "as in poker, the
game will be far easier to play when everyone is using the same
kind of chips."

Nuclear weapons must, therefore, be avoided in limited war
because they are "new and strange. They have about them all and
more of the sinister psychological connotations of gas or dum-dum
bullets. . . . They have tended to fall into that very arbitrary category of weapons that are regarded as uncivilized to use." Finally,
"because of their capacity for large-scale slaughter, they may be
able to cause such sudden and startling reversals of military fortune as to increase the uncertainty and irrationality that are always so pervasive in conflict situations. If we employ them on the
enemy, we invite retaliation, shock, horror, and a cycle of retaliation with an end that is most difficult to foresee." The critical element of keeping limited wars limited—their predictability, controllability, rationality—becomes completely unhinged, and so
therefore does the very purpose of waging limited wars.

For victory in the traditional sense cannot be a proper goal.
"Limited war cannot be a means of bringing about a radical alteration in the distribution of power. . . . Nor can it be a method of obtaining overwhelmingly favorable resolutions of outstanding
issues." If those were the aims, then it would by definition no
longer be a "limited war." A more proper aim on the battlefield is

sustained stalemate. Once "the lines of battle have been drawn," from Kaufmann's frame of mind, "the chances of an inconclusive result would seem very good indeed." As long as "both sides will have ample reserves to pump into the conflict, playing for such a stalemate . . . would thus seem to be desirable." The war would end in the same rational fashion by which it had begun and been waged: whenever the enemy—assuming it is he who pulls out—calculates "that the costs of fighting to him outweighed the costs to the United States, and consequently that the advantages of terminating the conflict were greater than the advantages of continuing it."

It would be a completely different sort of war not only for the military to fight, but for the American people to support. "All the emotions traditionally associated with war must be inhibited," Kaufmann realized. "We are flung into a straitjacket of rationality, which prevents us from lashing out at the enemy. We are asked to make sacrifices and then to cheer lustily for a tie in a game that we did not even ask to play."

It was a conception very similar to John von Neumann's Game Theory—the "calculating individual," the elements of value, cost and risk, the premise of rationality, of violence on the battlefield elevated to a jousting tournament or a chess game.

Kaufmann had little knowledge or interest in Game Theory, but he did come out of an intellectual tradition whose principles and perspectives—while not at all mathematical—produced preferences and conclusions quite similar to those of von Neumann's theory. First, from his training at Yale, Kaufmann was an internationalist and a Realist. He saw rivalry and conflict as unavoidable, usually predominant features of world politics. Second, mainly from his association with Bernard Brodie, he was a Clausewitzian in his outlook on the nature of war: wars were fought over political objectives, and the means of violence, the costs risked, must be commensurate with the political benefits to be potentially gained. In an age of nuclear weapons, wars could not be fought in their traditional manner without upsetting the chief Clausewitzian principle: there simply were no objectives commensurate with the horribly destructive magnitude of all-out nuclear war. Yet it was nevertheless a world of overwhelming tension and lurking Communist aggressiveness. Therefore, warfare had to be "returned to its traditional place as politics pursued by other means." That meant, in the nuclear age, creating new rules for fighting wars.

On a more personal level, Kaufmann never really felt quite at home in the twentieth century. "We may not be able to create the refined distinctions that characterized the politics of the seventeenth and eighteenth centuries, when two powers could be friends on one side of a line while fighting bitterly on the other side," Kaufmann wrote in one of his Princeton essays on limited war; "but we may at least be able to approach the relatively compartmentalized pattern of the nineteenth century, and that itself would be a significant gain."

Shortly before *Military Policy and National Security* went to press, Kaufmann wrote Bernard Brodie that he was "rather unhappy with a number of the chapters—my own included." He had, consequently, "been hoping to get sufficiently authoritative confirmation of my doubts to support the case for cancellation or postponement of publication." He feared—unjustifiably, as it turned out—"the book will get a bad reception."

Still, what Kaufmann had written was the product of extensive thinking and did constitute a coherent framework in which to view the problem of modern limited war. And it would serve as the foundation of his thinking on *nuclear* war when he turned his head in that direction over the next few years after returning to the RAND Corporation, where the art of imposing rationality on nuclear war was well under way.

13 COUNTERFORCE

IN FEBRUARY 1956, three months after reluctantly turning in his final manuscript to the Princeton University Press, William Kaufmann ditched academic life altogether and moved to Santa Monica and the RAND Corporation. The Yale refugees from the old Institute of International Studies, of which Kaufmann was a member, were not finding Princeton the compatible home they had optimistically anticipated. The new Center of International Studies, which they created there, never achieved the same coherence that had been so vital to their spirit, indeed existence, back in New Haven. Its members were now scattered across the Princeton campus in various departments, forced to do more teaching than researching, not allowed the sense of elite separateness that Charles Seymour had given them in his tenure as Yale president. So when Hans Speier, RAND's social science chief, who had always been impressed with Kaufmann and who—unlike some at RAND—liked "The Requirements of Deterrence" very much, asked Kaufmann to take a permanent position at RAND, Kaufmann leaped at the chance.

Back in Santa Monica, one of the first activities in which Kaufmann became involved was one of the simulation games, or "diplomatic exercises," that were the rave in the RAND social science division at the time. The game would set up a situation; players would divide up into "Red" and "Blue" teams; the managers of the game would provoke a conflict, and the players would act out their respective roles to see what happens. The mathematicians and economists at RAND thought this was foolishness, perhaps fun but not at all scientific. The leaders of the social science division, on the other hand, especially its director, Hans Speier, thought that the simulations run by the mathematicians, involving nuclear-exchange calculations with estimates of kill probability, weapons reliability and so forth, were devoid of history or politics, that they left no room for the exigencies of chance, the moves and countermoves and other real-life phenomena which they thought their own games represented. In the mid-to-late 1950s, the issue of political games and their relevance was one that symbolized and further sharpened the rift between the social science division and the rest of RAND.

The particular game in which Kaufmann participated in his very early days at RAND in 1956, a game managed by Speier and fellow RAND sociologist Herbert Goldhamer, concerned NATO military policy. Kaufmann was initially intrigued with the game because it started with a premise quite similar to his analysis in "The Requirements of Deterrence." Speier and Goldhamer asked whether—now that the Soviets were building up their own nuclear arsenal—our NATO allies could really trust us to drop nuclear bombs on Russia in response to a Soviet ground invasion against Western Europe, knowing that the Soviets would almost certainly drop bombs on the United States in return. Although in "Requirements of Deterrence" Kaufmann had focused mainly on the defense of Asia, these were precisely the sorts of questions that had driven him to his advocacy of a massive conventional-force buildup.

Yet the upshot of this game at RAND, as concluded by most of its players, was that the United States should supply the NATO allies with their own nuclear weapons. Kaufmann was appalled. He had concluded in his Princeton work that nuclear retaliation, in an age of potentially mutual destruction, was a fatuous response to conventional aggression; that all Clausewitzian principles of war would be thrown to the winds, that the scope of violence would exceed any objectives to be gained, that the war would no longer be subject to strategy in the traditional sense.

Kaufmann argued strenuously against the nuclear-sharing solution in the course of this game, but he had little to offer in the way of an alternative. The game did show Kaufmann just how serious was the issue the nuclear plan's advocates were raising—not merely for Asia and the other "gray areas" of the world, but also for Western Europe. From that point on, Kaufmann felt that he had to find some way to maintain NATO's credibility without having to resort to spreading nuclear weapons all over the globe.

It was through this concern that Kaufmann met Albert Wohlstetter. Wohlstetter had just completed his R-290 study, which revealed that SAC was highly vulnerable to an attack from the Soviet Union, a conclusion having enormous implications for the future of nuclear deterrence and the likelihood of war. Wohlstetter was passionately opposed to spreading nuclear weapons to allies abroad, but for reasons different from Kaufmann's. He thought that such weapons would be exceedingly vulnerable to preemptive attack because of their proximity to Soviet territory. Still, their analyses mutually reinforced each other's conclusions, and so a friendship was struck.

First with Wohlstetter and then with others, Kaufmann began increasingly to hover around the economics division at RAND. When Kaufmann first came to RAND, he thought that he would elaborate further on his ideas about limited war. At the time, he found nuclear war uninteresting: it seemed an almost totally unlikely event, given the massive nuclear arsenals on each side, which would deter the other from entertaining ideas of starting such a war; and if it did erupt, it could only lead to an "all-out war of nuclear annihilation," he had written, for which "it is difficult to visualize any strategy at all, in the traditional sense." But now he discovered, mainly within the economics division, a whole cadre of smart analysts working on the deterrence, targeting and strategy of nuclear war. They had fashioned the technique of "systems analysis," which uncovered a new set of problems that practically redefined the nature of strategy in the nuclear age. In the mid-1950s, within this small strategic community, there existed that effervescent enthusiasm and intellectual excitement that Kaufmann remembered from his postgraduate days at Yale and that he had missed in his less happy tenure at Princeton. Moreover, the very existence of so talented a group within RAND suggested that maybe there was something worth exploring in the bizarre business of nuclear weapons after all.

Kaufmann began to immerse himself slowly in the mind-boggling morass of nuclear strategy. Yet, while doing so, he remained firmly anchored to the intellectual framework that he had constructed two years earlier in his Princeton essays on limited war, and he never veered too far from the problem that puzzled him in the Speier-Goldhamer game: how to assure the NATO allies of America's commitment to their defense without either committing national suicide or spreading nuclear weapons abroad.

Over the next few years, Kaufmann was eventually to find the answer to the puzzle in a fusion between his own ideas on limited war and a tradition of thinking that had evolved at RAND among a mere handful of analysts since the very early 1950s. The result would be a fully formulated doctrine known variously as "no-cities strategy" or "war-fighting" or "counterforce."

The pioneer in this RAND tradition was Bernard Brodie. Actually, the pioneering took place just before he went to RAND, in 1951, while working as special consultant to General Hoyt Vandenberg in the Air Force Staff. Reacting in horror to the purposeless destructiveness of the Strategic Air Command's "Sunday Punch" war plan—essentially a swift, all-out atomic blow against every target in the Soviet Union, not much different from the "massive retaliation" doctrine that John Foster Dulles would advocate a few years later—Brodie devised a war plan that would be at once less destructive and more congruent with rational war objectives. The idea was that if the Soviets invaded, say, Western Europe, and if the United States were forced to use atomic weapons in response, the U.S. should avoid hitting any Soviet cities, at least in the first round. Instead, we should fire only a small number of our nuclear weapons on nonurban targets, maintaining a highly protected U.S. reserve force of atomic weapons, and using that reserve force as a bargaining lever, as an implicit threat to the Russians that unless they quit the war, we would up the ante and start destroying their cities, one by one, until they gave up. The important aspect of strategy, then, was not so much what to hit as what *not* to hit, and to use this combination of sticks and carrots as a means of coercing the Russians to surrender.

When Brodie got to RAND and told some of his new colleagues of his Air Staff work, he found some receptive listeners. In 1950, a few members of the social science division had done a study entitled "Warning and Bombing," known as "The Warbo Study," for short. The idea started with W. Philip Davison, a corporal in the Army's psychological warfare branch during World War II who, when he first came to RAND's Washington, D.C., office in late 1949, started poring over voluminous files at the National Archives on Nazi SS reports describing the popular mood in German-occupied territories. Davison came across one extensive report by the secret police stationed in a small Czech town in which almost everyone worked at the town's single factory. One day, rumors spread that the British were about to bomb the town, and despite everything that the factory managers and town authorities could do to suppress the rumor, almost everyone evacuated. A couple of weeks after they all returned, the same rumor spread and nearly everyone evacuated again. In neither instance was the town attacked, and yet production had been slowed down considerably.

Davison was intrigued with this obscure wartime incident, and thought it suggested a policy that the United States might adopt deliberately in a future war: that warning the population before bombing it might be more humane but no less effective. In some instances, the act of warning alone could cause enough disruption that bombing would not be necessary. Davison composed a memo on the subject to Hans Speier, who was quite taken with the notion and assembled a team composed of himself, Davison, Andrew Marshall, Victor Hunt—all of the social science division—to look into it further.

When Bernard Brodie came to RAND and discussed his Air Staff work with Andy Marshall and Victor Hunt, it was only natural that they found his ideas attractive. Brodie had gone considerably beyond the ideas of the Warbo Study, in that he was proposing not hitting cities at all, while Warbo still assumed bombing factories in cities. Still, they were favorably disposed to the notion that not bombing certain areas might be equally important to bombing others.

Victor Hunt was associate director of RAND social science and, along with Brodie and Marshall, one of the few from that division to reside full-time in Santa Monica rather than at RAND's Washington office. A humanist historian by training, an anti-militarist in sentiment, Hunt was particularly intrigued with Brodie's idea of sparing cities in the initial phases of a war and of using the withheld reserve force to exert bargaining leverage over the enemy. But Hunt went a bit further than Brodie and suggested not only what targets should be avoided but also what targets should be hit. To Hunt, simply restraining from striking Soviet cities might impel the Soviets to show similar restraint toward American cities, but then again it might not. To ensure further that damage to our cities would be minimized, we should try to destroy those weapons that could do such damage, namely, the long-range bomber force of the Soviet Union.

Victor Hunt was perhaps the only person at RAND whom nobody disliked. He scored very highly in the game of composing blistering critiques of reports he deemed inadequate, a favorite RAND pastime; but unlike almost everyone else who competed at this sport, Hunt could do so without personally offending the objects of his wrath. Colleagues commonly referred to him as "a

prince of a man." So it was that when, in 1952, Hunt wrote and
circulated a six-page internal memorandum outlining the ideas
that he and Marshall had discussed with Brodie, and adding to
them his own anti-military, or "counterforce," targeting twist, the
memo was closely read and widely commented on.

Targeting had been a topic of great interest at RAND since
the late 1940s. RAND hired several targeteers from World War II
strategic-bombing campaigns as consultants or full-time employees. Most notable were Charlie Hitch from Princes Risborough,
now head of the RAND economics division, and John Williams
from the New York Applied Mathematics Panel, now head of the
math division. But there were also Carl Kaysen from the Economic Objectives Unit of the OSS, Burt Klein from the postwar
U.S. Strategic Bombing Survey, and others. They led several projects that attempted to quantify data from the war and to assess
various theories of strategic bombing, calculating whether it was
more efficient to attack concentrated industries or urban-industrial complexes, devising measures by which to judge what sorts of
bombs were best to use against specific targets, figuring out how
to locate the most vulnerable bottlenecks in a national economy.

When he first came to RAND in the summer of 1950, Andy
Marshall worked on some of these studies, calculating the effects
of a strategic-bombing campaign against the Soviet economy. And
two years later, with RAND economist Jack Hershleifer, he un-
dertook an enormously elaborate campaign analysis, simulating
an actual bombing attack, laying out a Soviet target system and air
defenses, routing the planes from base to target in such a way to
go around or destroy the defenses, flying the remaining bombers
back to base, doing reconnaissance on what targets were not hit
the first time, flying the surviving bombers back over those targets
and striking them again, and so forth.

These sorts of studies focused on war as a problem of arith-
metic, calculus and probability. They served as inputs to many of
the broader "systems analyses" turned out by Ed Paxson, E. S.
Quade and, later, Albert Wohlstetter—the studies that asked what
was the best type of bomber or the best basing mode in terms of
which system could destroy the most targets for a given amount of
money or which would cost less given a certain number of targets
destroyed.

Victor Hunt's short memorandum interested the specialists
in this tradition of RAND analysis because it dealt with targeting.

But it especially grabbed their attention because it suggested two ways in which their discipline could be expanded in scope: first, it talked about targeting the enemy's military forces, whereas virtually all previous RAND efforts in this field concentrated on economic targeting; second, through Bernard Brodie's insight, it attached the whole question of targeting to the broader questions of war objectives and strategy—connecting the intensity with which the war is waged to the task of bringing the war to a successful conclusion with minimal damage done, in the process, to American cities.

Within a few months of the Hunt memo's dissemination, some of the analysts within RAND's strategic community began to meet on a fairly formal basis every two or three weeks to discuss the relationship between nuclear weapons and strategy, strategy and war, war and deterrence. Calling themselves the Strategic Objectives Committee, they included Bernard Brodie, Andy Marshall and Victor Hunt of the social science division, John Williams of the math division, Jimmy Lipp of the missiles division, Herman Kahn of physics on the periphery and, as rapporteur for the group, a young engineer named James Digby. Charlie Hitch, head of the economics division, also sat in occasionally.

Among the specific issues discussed were those that had been raised by Bernard Brodie and Victor Hunt. In the spring of 1953, Brodie wrote a paper called "Must We Shoot from the Hip?," arguing for a reduction in the vulnerability of the Strategic Air Command. His reasoning was not so much to make it more difficult for the Soviets to launch a successful first-strike but to allow the United States to use nuclear weapons, if it had to, with deliberation and restraint, to make possible the retention of a reserve force as a bargaining lever without having to worry that the Soviets might knock out the reserve force. It was essentially the same argument that Brodie had made in his Air Staff report for General Vandenberg. Brodie, Charlie Hitch and Andy Marshall also wrote a paper called "The Next Ten Years," which laid out these ideas.

At this stage, however, ruminations on counterforce were fairly theoretical; the concept was explored, but not its feasibility. That task was taken up late in 1954 by Jim Digby, the engineer who served as rapporteur in the Strategic Objectives Committee and who became increasingly intrigued with the practical side of the Brodie-Hunt-Marshall-Hitch thinking. A few years earlier,

Digby had worked with fellow RAND engineer Ed Barlow on an air-defense study commissioned by the Air Force—an elaborate systems analysis simulating a Soviet bomber attack, running their planes (on paper) along various flight paths, testing through various statistical techniques the effectiveness of proposed U.S. fighter-interceptor planes and surface-to-air missiles in their attempts to shoot down the approaching bombers, and then assessing how much industrial capital the penetrating bombers would destroy and how many people they would kill.

The main conclusion of the Barlow-Digby study was that air defense could not cope with a large-scale concentrated attack, that enough bombers would get through and inflict devastating damage. Digby was interested in counterforce as an alternative method of destroying Soviet bombers before they could destroy American cities. Or, if counterforce could not permanently destroy the bombers, then perhaps it could delay and disrupt their operations so heavily that the Soviets would have to divide their attack into several waves, each containing a much smaller number of bombers so that air defenses might shoot down a much higher percentage of the bombers that did survive the counterforce strike.

For the counterforce study, Digby assembled a large team of technical analysts to do a systems analysis similar to that done for the air-defense study, but running the simulation in reverse—from U.S. bombers taking off in the United States to their dropping bombs over airfields in the Soviet Union. The purpose was to discover just how effective a counterforce campaign might be. They took Air Force Intelligence data on the general area where Soviet forces were believed to be located, laid out map exercises on flight tactics to avoid Soviet defenses and when to refuel, calculated how many bombers and weapons were needed given the performance of the airplanes and bombs of the day. It had earlier been believed that if SAC tried to attack the Soviet long-range air force, the Soviet planes would merely take off. One discovery that Digby made, through talking with Air Force Intelligence officers, was that Soviet planes were not on alert at all, that moving them would take a great deal of time, and that in any event they would have to fly back somewhere to reload and refuel if they wanted to make subsequent attacks.

The Digby team was about halfway done with its work, and in fact had presented a preliminary briefing to some Air Force offi-

cers, when Albert Wohlstetter conducted a raid on Digby's operation to assemble a group of analysts to help him and Fred Hoffman
with their next project on SAC vulnerability, which when finished
in 1956 would be numbered R-290. Wohlstetter, who had been
busy in 1953 and 1954 briefing the overseas-base study in Washington, had not been a part of the Strategic Objectives Committee,
and so had little interest and only scant awareness of the rationales for a counterforce strategy. Indeed, one premise of R-290
was that our "principal deterrent . . . must be our ability to destroy
their [Soviet] *cities.*" As Wohlstetter's raid decimated Digby's
ranks, the counterforce project slowly ground to a halt, and further elaboration or systematic thinking on the counterforce idea
fell into a state of limbo.

Two people at RAND who did try to keep the flame burning
were Andy Marshall and a man who joined RAND's economics division just as Digby began his study, Joseph Loftus. Before coming
to RAND, Loftus had for four years been civilian director of the
Target Programs office in Air Force Intelligence. The Air Target
Division, of which Target Programs was a part, was filled with military targeteers busily applying to the atomic age the principles
that they had pursued in the strategic-bombing campaigns of
World War II. It was these officers who came up with such atomic
targeting concepts as "the Sunday Punch" and "killing a nation."

Loftus found himself growing skeptical of these strategic-
bombing concepts. When he came on board in June 1950, the
SAC Emergency War Plan (EWP) in effect had only twenty-four
weapons allotted to Bravo targets, and most of them aimed so that
they could pick off Bravo and Delta targets—airfields and cities—
at once, with the emphasis on Delta. In fact, the whole EWP was
geared primarily to Delta, far more than Loftus thought necessary
or wise.

The atomic-energy division of Loftus' office, run by a young
nuclear physicist and Russian expert named Spurgeon Keeny,
was finding evidence of a growing Soviet atomic-energy industry,
suggesting that the Soviets would soon be amassing their own
atomic arsenal. With that in mind, Loftus figured that the number
of Bravo targets would soon be expanding and that, therefore, Air
Intelligence would have to devote far more careful attention to
collecting and analyzing data on such targets as air bases.

Loftus was not entertaining no-cities concepts, nor was he
mulling over the implications of a Soviet atomic force on the credi-

bility of the U.S. deterrent, as Brodie and Bill Kaufmann did later. Loftus would have considered those lines of thinking too abstract, irrelevant to his own concerns. To Loftus, the issue was simpler: the Soviets were soon going to build more A-bombs, those bombs would be able to destroy America; as a target planner, he had to develop better intelligence on Bravo targets so that SAC could destroy the airplanes carrying those bombs first in the event of war.

The problem was that the officers in the Evaluation Division of Air Targets were thoroughly ingrained in the LeMay/World War II tradition and thus thought that airfields were inappropriate targets for bombing, especially for the big blasts that blew out of the A-bomb. And as it happened, all intelligence tasks concerning Soviet airfields were assigned to Evaluation.

In a bureaucratic end run around this obstacle, Loftus set up within his own Targets Program shop something he called a "Research Unit." Surreptitiously, Loftus put the Research Unit to work on determining the physical vulnerability of an airfield—not only of the runway and the bomber themselves, but also of essential supplies, fuel and tools—and on figuring out which airfields could support the long-range Soviet air force. Obviously, SAC had to get in the act to provide much of the data. Eventually, General Jim Walsh, head of SAC Intelligence, became actively involved in the effort—mainly because, once Walsh and LeMay discovered what was going on, they didn't want it to be left under the control of a civilian like Loftus. A study finally emerged out of the joint SAC-Target Programs effort. SAC insisted on controlling distribution and no more than a dozen copies were made.

The study was numbered ATD-751, and it was an outline of a war plan that would emphasize counterforce targeting much more heavily than prior EWPs had done. The basic idea behind the study, and formulated as a result of the Research Unit's computations, was that a 500-kiloton weapon exploded high above an airfield could not only make a big mess but leave the base inoperative for roughly a week: even if the landing strip could be repaired before then, simple items like screwdrivers and other essential supplies would have been destroyed.

Loftus worked like a madman on the study all through 1952, frequently staying up all hours making sure that everything was just right. To some analysts in Target Plans, the job was routine and mechanical—Kharkov today, Kiev tomorrow. . . . But Loftus behaved as if the war were starting tomorrow. He was a moody man, with a black sense of humor and a grim seriousness. He worried about the problem all the time. He had nightmares that war had come and he had not properly counted all the Soviet airfields. Loftus also had great faith in the power of analysis, that if you worked long and hard enough at it, you could solve any problem. And so Loftus worked long and hard at making sure he knew every Bravo target in the U.S.S.R.

A lot of data was available even as early as 1952, much more than SAC wanted anyone on the outside to know. There were aerial photographs taken by German pilots during World War II, interrogations of captured German scientists who had worked on Soviet military projects, reports from spies and émigrés, communications intelligence (known in the trade as COMINT) intercepted by the supersecretive National Security Agency. Since prior to this time not very many in SAC or Air Intelligence paid close attention to the Bravo mission, Loftus and his Research Unit were the first to examine this enormous haystack of intelligence data systematically, at least in the context of atomic-weapons targeting.

ATD-751 was completed late in 1952. Somewhat to Loftus' surprise and much to his delight, it was implemented the next year as an integral part of SAC's Emergency War Plan. The EWP written in 1953 called for nearly 200 sorties devoted to the Bravo mission. All the Delta targets would also be attacked at the same time, according to the EWP. But that didn't bother Loftus. He wanted to cover the targets of a soon-expanding Soviet long-range bomber force; he was interested in counterforce, in war-fighting, not in no-cities. And here were his ideas, virtually unaltered, set down in the official EWP.

As the EWP guidelines were translated into actual operational plans at the beginning of 1954, however, Loftus noticed something strange. The programming people in Air Targets were changing the desired "aim points" on the target maps—just slightly, but enough to compromise Loftus's objectives. Many Soviet airfields were situated within five miles of cities, a degree of proximity tempting to military targeteers trained in the World War II style of strategic bombing. They moved the aim points slightly away from the air base and closer to the city, trying to "kill" both with the same big shot. They called this "Bonus." Still more disturbing to Loftus was that, in case killing both proved technically difficult, the targeteers would put far greater emphasis on Bonus than on counterforce.

The more Loftus thought about it, the more he realized that the Air Force, and especially SAC, were interested not in counterforce, but in mass destruction. The first time Loftus went out to SAC Headquarters in Omaha, General Jim Walsh, director of SAC Intelligence, had invited him over to his house for cocktails. As they entered the foyer, Loftus noticed a huge Bible on an end table just to the side of the entrance. Walsh was in the middle of a frequently delivered mini-lecture, explaining to Loftus that the big bomb was meant for big damage.

"Goddammit, Loftus," he screamed, "there's only one way to attack the Russians, and that's to hit them hard with everything we have and"—at this point, pounding his fist on top of the Bible—"knock their balls off!"

That's all they were interested in, Loftus realized—knocking the Russians' balls off. Meanwhile, Loftus was also finding himself pushed out of control at Target Programs. From the time he had first joined Air Intelligence, military officers were nominally in charge, but bright civilians were given the run of the lot. Around the same time that the targeteers began corrupting Loftus' counterforce dreams, the heads of Air Intelligence started to think that it was time that the military officers start taking over. Most of these officers were captains and majors, bomber pilots, fly-boys, not keenly interested in intelligence and not very smart.

By April 1954, Loftus realized that the EWP was completely out of his hands, and everything else was slipping away too. In July, he quit.

Almost at once, he got a job offer from the RAND Corporation. Loftus had frequently sat in on Air Force briefings given by various RAND analysts and had come to know a few of them fairly well. Until the end of the year, Loftus hung around RAND's Washington office, perusing internal reports and memoranda. Just before leaving for Santa Monica, he found out about Jim Digby's counterforce study, and was delighted and surprised that someone else was taking an interest.

In Santa Monica, Loftus introduced himself to Digby right away. While he did not work directly on Digby's project, he did put him in touch with people in Air Intelligence who could aid him in getting up-to-date intelligence on the location of Soviet military targets. Through this connection with Digby, he first met Andy Marshall. Marshall had worked on a study concerning early warning a few years earlier and, ever since, was utterly fascinated with the techniques of intelligence. It was only natural that Marshall and Loftus struck up a close friendship.

Digby's ill-fated study notwithstanding, few RAND analysts in the mid-1950s thought about counterforce, and those who did considered it chimerical and impractical, believing it impossible to know where Soviet military targets were or how to hit them if their location were somehow discovered. One thing Marshall learned from Loftus was that this simply was not true. Loftus told him about the World War II photographs, the analysis that he and his associates in Targets had done, most of all about communications intelligence, COMINT, intercept technology that nobody else at RAND knew anything about. Marshall would occasionally tell a colleague or two that the United States did have the intelligence data to wage a counterforce campaign, but when asked for substantiation, he stayed mum.

In the summer of 1957, Marshall was tapped to go to Washington to work on the staff of the Gaither Committee. Marshall, a statistician by training, did quantitative operations-research analysis of problems fed to him by the committee's steering panel. But he also kept informed on the general direction of the committee's analysis and conclusions. He was extremely disappointed with what he saw. The committee was utterly unimaginative on the issue of what to do with nuclear weapons if the nation had to use them. It simply assumed, almost tacitly, in accordance with the conventional wisdom of the day, that they would be used to strike back at the cities of the Soviet Union. There was not even remotely any consideration of the idea of going after enemy military forces or of withholding a large segment of the arsenal, that he, Brodie, Digby, Loftus and Victor Hunt had discussed back at RAND. While many of the Gaither Committee's members had been sharply critical of John Foster Dulles' "massive retaliation" doctrine, and while the committee did recommend the expansion of conventional military forces, their collective view on the use of nuclear weapons was no less oriented to massive retaliation than the Secretary of State's.

With RAND sociologist Herbert Goldhamer, Marshall's mentor while a student at the University of Chicago, and with a little help from RAND's chief Kremlinologist, Nathan Leites, Marshall spent the next four months working out a highly elaborate study systematically analyzing various possible strategies, in the face of various likely Soviet threats, that would prove the virtues of counterforce and, more important, discredit population-targeting as a reasonable strategy.

Published and stamped top secret on April 30, 1959, the study was called *The Deterrence and Strategy of Total War, 1959–61: A Method of Analysis,* and to Marshall's colleagues, it could only be judged an ambitious, analytical *tour de force.* Its premises and conclusions, with slight variations, synthesized the two strands of strategic thinking then prevalent at RAND. It assumed that the Soviets launch a "surprise ('sneak') attack" against SAC targets with at least 200 ICBMs, a few hundred bombers, or both. In the end, it called for the protective measures to reduce SAC's vulnerability, as prescribed in the Wohlstetter-Hoffman-Rowen studies; and it called for the counterforce and withholding targeting strategies thought up by Bernard Brodie, Victor Hunt and the old Strategic Objectives Committee.

To one trained in the RAND style of strategic analysis, the study was ingenious. The logic was presented in the form of Game Theory, with the possible strategies of the U.S. and the U.S.S.R. laid out on giant matrixes. The preferable U.S. strategy was determined by calculating which moves and countermoves produced the highest value under a broad range of circumstances, depending on such variables as the proportion of SAC surviving a first-strike, the Soviet estimate of this proportion, Soviet choice of targets, U.S. choice of targets, Soviet estimate of U.S. choice, estimates of military or population damage done by each of these possible choices, the availability of warning of a Soviet attack, and the "utilities or values attached by the Soviet Union and the United States to various outcomes of the war anticipated on the basis of the initial moves of the war and their outcomes."

Their conclusion after 195 pages was that the population-targeting strategy, which lay at the heart of the Gaither Report as well as of the Wohlstetter-Hoffman R-290 study, produced the worst value in most cases. The best values were produced by one of two alternative strategies, depending on the circumstances: either firing at military targets with very high yield weapons, exploding them near the ground, thus spreading radioactive fallout to nearby cities, destroying the Soviet military *and* killing some people as a "bonus"; or, if SAC had enough forces surviving a first-strike to do so, firing some weapons at military targets, but withholding a large reserve force, as well, aimed at Soviet cities and used as a bargaining lever to try to bring the war to a swift and successful conclusion. And to be able to pull off such a strategy, the U.S. should adopt many of the protective measures recommended by Wohlstetter and Hoffman in R-290: putting bombers and missiles in hardened shelters, dispersing them more widely, improving early-warning systems.

The study was laid out in systematic, logical order, and above all it was quantitative. Again and again, Marshall and Goldhamer warned that the numbers that they put in the matrix boxes were hypothetical, illustrative. They even conceded at one point, "Very likely a decision to initiate nuclear war cannot be made on the basis of strict calculation"—an observation quite contrary to the foundation of the entire study, which was that the "utility to the Soviet Union of starting a war" is "based on the utilities of the [Soviet] matrix, the probabilities of the different results of a Soviet first-strike, and the probabilities attached to the various U.S. countermoves," in short "an average of the possible war outcomes weighted by their probabilities." But such concessions could easily be glossed over. However arbitrary the numbers, they *were* numbers. Unlike the work of, say, Bernard Brodie or Victor Hunt, written in what Albert Wohlstetter scorned as "the essay tradition," Marshall and Goldhamer were speaking the right language. Their study could be taken much more readily as serious analysis in the RAND universe.

Marshall did not choose the quantitative Game Theory approach as a clever tactic to suit his audience. Marshall, in this sense, was as much a part of this audience as anyone. The approach represented the way that he truly did think through problems. Marshall and Goldhamer only briefly acknowledged once that it "might be worthwhile investigating whether there are idiosyncratic Soviet dispositions that can be expected to increase the deterrent effect of various measures (or to suggest quite new ones)." In the main, they rested the study on the premise that in "trying to estimate possible U.S. courses of action, the Soviets would presumably attempt to construct their own version of the U.S. utility matrix"—in effect, on the premise that the Kremlin thinks about the bomb in much the same way as the RAND Corporation.

One upshot of the Marshall-Goldhamer study was that, because of its methodology and seemingly scientific approach, a broad segment of the RAND strategic community began to enter-

tain counterforce and withholding strategies more seriously than
at any time since Jim Digby's aborted study four years earlier.
Still, there were major doubts on the part of many that the U.S.
lacked the intelligence data to find and destroy Soviet military targets. The only reassurance on this point that Marshall and Goldhamer offered in their study was the single sentence: "We believe
that the United States has relatively good knowledge of the location of operational bases in the Soviet Union." Ever discreet, Marshall made no reference to all the types of data that Joe Loftus had
told him about—the World War II information, the aerial photographs from balloons and the U-2 aircraft, the COMINT inter-
cepts, the spies and, in the near future, reconnaissance satellites.

Marshall and Loftus were frustrated by the skepticism, but
did little to quash it. The information was just too sensitive to
spread around indiscriminately. Their frustration heightened,
however, in 1959–1960, during the biggest group project in
RAND history, the Strategic Offensive Forces, or SOF, study.
General Tommy White, Air Force Chief of Staff, asked RAND to
undertake the project. He had read all the papers and monographs
on the nature of deterrence, but he wanted analysts to start thinking about what we should do if deterrence failed, what were the
objectives of war under those circumstances, and how do those objectives fit in with the weapons that the Air Force was planning to
build in the 1960s. (White asked RAND to do this before the Marshall-Goldhamer study was issued.)

Tommy White was a peculiar Chief of Staff, more intellectual
than most of his predecessors. The son of a Presbyterian minister,
fluent in seven languages, White worked his way through military
ranks as an attaché in Russia and China and then spent ten years
inside the Pentagon—not as a commander in the field—before
becoming Chief. He was genuinely interested in ideas, and had
come to look toward RAND as a source of many.

The SOF study was supervised by Ed Barlow, who was
Director of RAND Projects. Nearly everyone worked on some aspect of the study—the cost-effectiveness of bombers versus missiles, examinations of ballistic-missile defense and air defense,
studies of Air Force research and development efforts, the vulnerability of SAC, different approaches to targeting, every topic one
could possibly imagine that might concern the modern Air Force.

The man picked to analyze counterforce strategies was Ed
Oliver, an engineer and technical adviser to the Gaither Commit-

tee of 1957. Oliver produced an anti-counterforce report arguing that however desirable such a strategy might be, it was unfeasible, given intelligence technology. Marshall and Loftus approached Oliver shortly after he completed his first draft and questioned his assumptions, his calculations and especially the degree of access he had to data on the most modern reconnaissance technology. Oliver delved into the matter again, and came up two weeks later with the confession that a fuller study should be conducted.

Marshall and Loftus wondered whether Ed Oliver was up to the task. Both felt that somebody had to do an analysis so compelling that skepticism at RAND, and perhaps in the Air Staff, would be overcome. Marshall and Loftus started to engage in intensive conversations with Bill Kaufmann in the social science division, a man they both liked from the time he came to RAND in 1956 and who seemed intuitively sympathetic to the counterforce idea.

Kaufmann had spent his first few years at RAND mainly as a student of sorts. He had done a few studies on his own, but they were "in the essay tradition." Providing a political scientist's perspective, he had served as one of several assistants on a few major projects. But he was still on the sidelines of RAND's strategic community, still learning about weapons and technology and systems analysis, still absorbing this new methodology and new focus on national security. In this course of re-education, he was still trying to find the answer to the problem—how to convince the allies of America's commitment to their defense without either committing suicide or spreading nuclear weapons in the process—that he had faced in that "diplomatic exercise" game on NATO during his early RAND days.

Kaufmann and Loftus got along quite chummily. When they talked about strategy, counterforce frequently came up. Kaufmann had heard about counterforce, but like most of the others at RAND, he had casually dismissed the matter from his mind, believing that the concept was impractical. Loftus set out to dispel this skepticism by telling Kaufmann of the highly secret techniques by which the intelligence agencies could know the location of the important counterforce targets. Andy Marshall instructed Kaufmann about the work that Jim Digby had partially completed in his counterforce study of 1955, and convinced him that going after the Soviet military targets was operationally feasible.

The more he thought about it, the more Kaufmann began to

realize that counterforce went a long distance toward solving the NATO problem, that counterforce in fact fit quite nicely into the scheme of limited war that he himself had outlined in his Princeton essays of 1954–1956. Massive retaliation was an inadequate policy once the Soviets had amassed their own nuclear arsenal, because destroying their cities would provoke the Soviets to destroy our cities. The RAND game on NATO concluded that we should give the allies their own nuclear weapons because the Europeans could not reasonably trust the United States to blow up Russian cities in retaliation to a Soviet attack on Europe, thus sacrificing New York for Paris, Chicago for Bonn.

But what if we didn't blow up Soviet cities at all? What if we executed a *counterforce* attack in retaliation to a Soviet invasion of Western Europe? Not only would that strike at the very heart of the Soviet military power, but it might also serve as a more credible deterrent to such an invasion in the first place. If we did not strike at Soviet cities, perhaps the Soviets would strike back at something other than American cities. And if, therefore, American cities were not placed so much at risk in the act of defending Western Europe, then America's commitment to the NATO alliance could once more be made credible, which was to Kaufmann the objective of preeminent importance.

In the Princeton essays, Kaufmann had argued the case for restraint of force in future limited ground wars with the Soviet Union. The continuing competition with Communism was going to have its violent moments in the coming decades, and it was important to meet the challenges without provoking nuclear holocaust. Limited wars should be "managed," Kaufmann had written in 1955, in such a way as to send "messages" to "the other belligerent," which would "have a good chance of inducing him to accept limitations of geography, weapons and possibly time. The scope and method of the initial attack will tend to define the minimum limits of the ensuing conflict and the possibilities of controlling it."

Kaufmann now saw in counterforce a chance for these principles of limited war to be carried over into the arena of nuclear war. If the U.S. confined the "scope and method of the initial attack" to a purely counterforce strike, then perhaps the Soviets, if they retaliated at all, would follow in suit and keep their strikes purely counterforce in nature as well. He was also attracted to the idea of preserving a large, nearly invulnerable reserve force, to be used as a bargaining lever. He had written in 1955 that nuclear weapons were the "Constant Monitor"—in the words of his mentor, Bernard Brodie—that loomed over all limited war, providing the incentive for both powers to keep the conflict limited. Now, Kaufmann saw the reserve force, aimed at enemy cities, as the Constant Monitor that might keep both sides playing a game of limited nuclear war, constraining their strikes to counterforce targets only.

In this sense, Kaufmann went further than Loftus or Marshall. In *The Deterrence and Strategy of Total War,* Marshall and Herbert Goldhamer had concluded that, under several circumstances, an attack on Soviet military targets with high-yield, ground-burst nuclear weapons—spreading radioactive fallout to nearby cities, killing people as a "bonus"—would be the preferable strategy. To Kaufmann, killing civilians was not a "bonus." The point of the counterforce attack was to set precedent, to define limits under which the rest of the war would be waged. Kaufmann saw a need for an *ability* to destroy enemy cities, but only as a reserve force, to be used only in the last resort, in case the Soviets attacked American cities.

To Kaufmann, the NATO riddle was solved, and to Marshall and Loftus the doctrine of counterforce had found an articulate spokesman. Kaufmann was not the only one who was formulating new ideas at RAND in the late 1950s. It was a time of great excitement and urgency, the giant Russian bear looming over the West with its threatening missile gap. The hallways, blackboards, seminar rooms of RAND, arsenal of the U.S. Air Force, were filled with syntheses of concepts, calculations, notions of sending signals and bargaining with force, of ultimately imposing order on the Bomb. The man who most fiercely sought to make nuclear war rational and reasonable, and who, more than anyone else from RAND, gained global fame for his efforts, was a mordantly jolly physicist named Herman Kahn.

14 DR. STRANGELOVE

HERMAN KAHN had reached essentially the same conclusions about nuclear strategy that William Kaufmann did, but the two could not otherwise have been more different. Kaufmann, born and raised on Manhattan's Upper East Side, educated at prep schools, trained in history and political science at Yale, mild-mannered, well ordered; Kahn, born of Jewish emigrants in Bayonne, New Jersey, reared in the Bronx, majored in nuclear physics at UCLA and Cal Tech, brazenly theatrical, long-winded, overflowing with a thousand and one ideas.

At age ten, Kahn's parents divorced and he moved with his mother and sister to Los Angeles. Several years later, he enrolled at UCLA and, later, graduate school at the California Institute of Technology. Needing money, he planned a career in real estate, when in 1948, a friend of his from junior-high days, a fellow physicist named Sam Cohen, told him to apply for a job where he was working, a place in Santa Monica called Project RAND. Cohen urged Ernie Plesset, director of the RAND physics division, to hire Kahn. At first, Plesset couldn't tell whether Kahn was a genius or just crazy, but he gave in to Cohen's request.

Kahn first knew that he had come to the right place in 1950, when he served on a technical advisory board studying nuclear-powered airplanes. It was in these sessions, he wrote later, that he "first came in contact with the philosophy which is willing to ask any question and tackle any problem." The more exotic and unimaginable the technological wonders involved, the more eager Kahn was to jump in and apply his peculiar brand of logic, mathematical calculation, rationality.

In 1952, the Livermore Laboratory outside Berkeley—Edward Teller's living dream of a second national weapons lab to compete with Los Alamos, which Teller feared was deliberately dragging its feet on fusion research—was just getting under way. Through their intimate contacts with John von Neumann, Edward Teller and Hans Bethe, three of the giants in nuclear physics, the physicists at RAND were among the few anywhere who knew anything about fusion. During Livermore's first year, a group of these scientists—among them Ernie Plesset, David Griggs, Albert and Richard Latter, and Herman Kahn—commuted to Berkeley every week to lead the way on calculating how to design an H-bomb.

Herman Kahn played a major role in this effort. His earliest work at RAND had involved mathematical theory, an attempt to simplify Monte Carlo calculations, a technique of statistically systematizing random variables so that they can be taken into account in the analysis of physical properties. In connection with his work for Livermore, Kahn applied Monte Carlo techniques to calculations on the workings inside a hypothetical hydrogen bomb, especially the diffusion of heat and the collision of neutrons.

At one point, Kahn had calculations on bomb designs plugged into all twelve high-speed computers then operating in the United States. Acquiring a *Wunderkind* reputation as a mathematical physicist both at RAND and among weapon scientists at Oak Ridge, Los Alamos and Livermore, Kahn frequently held court among interested colleagues for hours at a time on the wonder of calculations, and how they could solve every problem. He left Cal Tech before finishing his Ph.D. He dropped all plans of going into real estate.

More gregarious and interdisciplinary than most of his colleagues in the physics division, Kahn roamed the RAND hallways in search of other interesting activities. One thing he noticed was that many of the engineers in various other departments were making egregious errors in dealing with nuclear weapons. Some in the RAND aircraft division, for example, were working on the design of an airplane that could carry a five-foot-long 100,000-pound bomb. Kahn knew that this could be done in a much smaller airframe and tried to convince his friend Sam Cohen, who was the aircraft division's liaison in the physics division, to inform them. Cohen refused: the physics division was operating under regulations of the Atomic Energy Commission, which had an entirely different system of classified information from that of the Air Force contract under which the rest of RAND was operating. Ernie Plesset told Kahn the same thing.

But Kahn had no tolerance for such rules. He moved around the building on his own, telling other analysts where they were going wrong in certain assumptions. He became more intensely involved with studies utilizing the systems analysis that Ed Paxson and others had innovated, eventually presenting a series of lectures that many who had been practicing the art for much longer heralded as the best lectures ever given on the subject.

And from his interest in systems analysis, Kahn fell in quite naturally with the crowd contemplating nuclear strategy. He was enthusiastic about Albert Wohlstetter's method of analysis in the overseas-base study, and grew to adopt Wohlstetter's conclusions on SAC vulnerability and his recommendations on dispersing and hardening bomber and missile bases. He began to sit in on the sessions of the Strategic Objectives Committee, became close friends with Andy Marshall, and talked at great length with Bernard Brodie about the latter's work on nuclear targeting for General Hoyt Vandenberg and his study, with Charlie Hitch and Ernie Plesset, on the implications of the H-bomb.

Brodie had first conceived the idea of avoiding Soviet cities in nuclear strikes, but when Victor Hunt and others on the RAND Strategic Objectives Committee extended that concept to avoiding cities *and* going after Soviet military targets, Brodie expressed pessimism about its feasibility. Calculations suggested that even with a purely countermilitary attack, two million people would still die, a horrifyingly high number.

But Kahn, by this time fully participating in committee sessions, put a novel twist on this observation. To Kahn, such a calculation made the two types of targeting all the more distinctive: as Kahn phrased it, *only* two million people would die. Alluding almost casually to "only" two million dead was part of the image that Kahn was fashioning for himself, the living portrait of the ultimate defense intellectual, cool and fearless, asking the questions everyone else ignored, thinking about the unthinkable.

Kahn's specialty was to express the RAND conventional wisdom in the most provocative and outrageous fashion imaginable. At a briefing to high-level SAC officers, Kahn flailed away at their official war plan, with its "Sunday Punch," the all-out nuclear holocaust, the absence of any conception of a reserve force or the city-avoidance and force-withholding strategy worked out by Bernard Brodie and others at RAND. Brodie, deeply fascinated with Freud and undergoing psychoanalysis himself, had written a short, internally circulated memorandum on the analogies between war plans and sex—the no-cities/withhold plan that he had conceived was likened to withdrawal before ejaculation, while the SAC war plan was like going all the way.

With this in mind, Kahn told the assembled officers at SAC, "Gentlemen, you don't have a war plan, you have a war orgasm."

Brodie, Marshall, Loftus, Digby, Kaufmann and other RAND analysts had already talked and written about the dangers of a massive-retaliation war plan in an age when the Soviets had their own nuclear arsenal. Kahn tried to express the critique more graphically. With mock sincerity, Kahn proposed what he called a "Doomsday Machine." It would be a vast computer wired up to a huge stockpile of H-bombs. When the computer sensed that the Soviet Union had committed an act defined as intolerable, the machine would automatically set off the Doomsday bombs, covering the earth with sufficient radioactive fallout to kill billions of people. Along with an engineer at RAND, Kahn had figured out on paper that such a Doomsday Machine was technologically feasible.

As Kahn half expected, not a single military officer liked the idea. Yet the Doomsday Machine was only a slightly absurd extension of existing American and NATO policy: the Soviets do something provocative, and we blow up most of their citizens, which provokes them to blow up most of ours.

To Kahn, the answer was clear. The war plan should contain many options other than the all-out strike. The U.S. had to be able to "control" the war, to exercise "intrawar deterrence," to deter the enemy from advancing its aggression after the war had started (a concept taken from Bernard Brodie's early work). In later years, during the early-to-mid 1960s, Kahn would work out an elaborate theory of "escalation," conceiving of 44 "rungs of escalation" from "Ostensible Crisis" to "Spasm or Insensate War," with the rungs in between including "Harassing Acts of Violence," "Barely Nuclear War," " 'Justifiable' Counterforce Attacks," "Local Nuclear War—Exemplary," "Constrained Disarming Attack," and "Slow-Motion Countercity War."

Kahn saw himself as the grand systematizer, the one-man think tank, the high priest of nuclear rationality.

To "control" the war, the military needed above all what Kahn called a Credible-First-Strike Capability (which he later semantically modified to Not-Incredible-First-Strike Capability), so that we could suppress Soviet strategic forces in the event of a

Warsaw Pact invasion against Western Europe that conventional forces alone could not repel. And it needed Tit-for-Tat capability, the ability to launch very small nuclear salvos in the event of Soviet provocations of a lesser order.

With his penchant for labels, Kahn called the pure-deterrence strategy Type I Deterrence, the Not-Incredible-First-Strike Capability Type II Deterrence, the Tit-for-Tat Capability Type III Deterrence. In an era of continuing crises, Types II and III Deterrence were, to Kahn's mind, essential. Without them, the U.S. would be terribly vulnerable to "nuclear blackmail" by the Russians.

"If the Soviet [aggressor] is reasonable," Kahn would write, "he will avoid the defender's cities, civilians and recuperative capability in order to maximize his postattack blackmail threats." He will attack, or threaten to attack, America's SAC bases. Then, he would use his remaining weapons as blackmail devices, telling us, in effect, that if we fired back at Soviet cities he would use the Soviet reserve force to clobber our cities, which is all we could do if we had only Type I Deterrence.

In short, Kahn's view of the nature of the Soviet strategic threat was the mirror image of the counterforce/no-cities/bargaining-lever strategy that Bernard Brodie and others in the RAND Strategic Objectives Committee had suggested as the rational nuclear strategy for the *United States* to employ in dealing with the Russians.

In the late 1950s, when it was popular to speak of a missile gap, Kahn called the threat of Soviet nuclear blackmail a "Deterrence Gap" or an "Operational Gap." These gaps were highly dangerous because, to Kahn, a perilous world of crisis after crisis lay ahead, a series of Soviet-imposed Munichs or Pearl Harbors. With Type I Deterrence only, the U.S. would try to get the Soviets to back down in a crisis of the early 1960s, Kahn imagined in the late 1950s. But "our negotiators would be afraid to spell out our threat, for nothing that they could present would be both credible and effective." Indeed, Kahn predicted that "however the next crisis is touched off, the Soviets do not have to back down because of fear of an attack by the United States—but we may."

Kahn was not advocating preventive war or surprise attacks on the U.S.S.R. However, he was very explicitly promoting the *first use* of nuclear weapons in the face of provocations that could not be deterred or answered by means short of that. Doing so would require a crash buildup of (Air Force) missiles and bombers, more "limited-war" forces as well, and a massive civil-defense program.

It was the civil-defense proposal that gained Kahn his most scabrous notoriety. To Kahn, the purpose of a gigantic civil-defense system was not so much to protect civilians against a Soviet first-strike, which was how many other civil-defense advocates of the day viewed such a program. "The whole purpose of the system," he wrote, "is to enable the U.S. to take much firmer positions" in hot and cold wars, to allow the President to engage in first-strikes (Type II Deterrence) and tit-for-tat threats (Type III Deterrence) of his own.

"Any power that can evacuate a high percentage of its urban population to protection," Kahn wrote, "is in a much better position to bargain than one which cannot do this." Indeed, international politics of the 1960s and beyond would be so racked with tension and crises that, to Kahn's mind, it was "perfectly conceivable . . . that the U.S. might have to evacuate two or three times every decade."

In fact, Kahn felt that having a good civil-defense system made the act of going to the nuclear brink an altogether salutary thing to do on occasion. To those, both in and out of RAND, who objected that this Credible-First-Strike Capability might convert a limited, peripheral war into a strategic nuclear war, Kahn responded: "Insofar as the civil defense program gives us the ability to convert *at our discretion,* it should be a good thing."

Kahn's interest in civil defense began in 1956, but picked up considerably in 1957, when he went to Washington to serve as a consultant to the Gaither Committee. There, Kahn dreamed up an awesome vision of a nationwide shelter program for the future. Kahn calculated that "an adequate civil defense program" could be bought for $200 billion to be spent over a fifteen-year period. For concentrated cities, about fifty million "very high-quality" shelter spaces could be built at $700 per space. They could be 1,000 feet underground, with fast-closing doors at the surface, hardened to resist 1,000 pounds per square inch of blast. On Manhattan Island, these doors could be spaced within 2,000 feet of one another for something between $500 and $900 per shelter space. Less elaborate shelters for another 150 million Americans could be built for $400 to $500 per space. Kahn envisioned spending another $5 billion to provide space in the nation's mine shafts,

$30 billion to protect industrial capital, and $25 billion to buy a three-year food supply with which to stock the shelters.

Even the staff of the Gaither Committee considered Kahn's vision out of bounds.

Back at RAND, Kahn assembled a team of seventeen analysts to study the civil-defense issue more intensely. Kahn kept the discussion on a more modest scale, proposing to spend $500 million per year to buy twelve million radiation meters, stock existing shelter spaces with supplies, train a cadre of civil-defense educators, and do further systems analysis of the problem before embarking upon a full-scale multibillion-dollar effort.

Kahn and his team measured the likely effects of nuclear explosions in blast damage, roentgens of radiation and economic dislocation. Their conclusion was that a huge civil-defense program, consisting of evacuation and shelters, was feasible, and would save tens of millions of lives in a nuclear war, thus deterring Soviet blackmail and giving America a strong bargaining position in the crises ahead.

Kahn was not so fundamentally different from the other RAND strategists whose ideas inspired him. Bernard Brodie had advocated controlled responses in the use of nuclear weapons; Herbert Goldhamer and Andy Marshall had written of the need for counterforce capability; William Kaufmann had supported a "winning," "war-fighting" strategy that "can support a dynamic foreign policy for the United States." However, Brodie and Kaufmann especially approached the business of first-use and counterforce strikes uneasily, as acts of desperation among a terrible set of choices. Kahn, on the other hand, dived in eagerly.

More than this, Kahn went public with his ideas. He delivered dozens of lectures, not only to Air Force generals and War Colleges but to community and civic groups. They seemed endless, these talks, running up to six or eight hours, three days' worth of such talks when delivered to the War Colleges, Kahn standing before a podium, briefing stands at either side of him, flipping one chart over another, talking at a maddeningly fast pace, interjecting jokes, chuckling, pointing to charts, tables, graphs comparing the number of fatalities under various wartime conditions, illustrated under such captions as "Will the Survivors Envy the Dead?" and "Tragic but Distinguishable Postwar States."

More than 5,000 people heard these talks before Kahn finally compiled them into a 652-page tome called *On Thermonuclear War*. It was a massive, sweeping, disorganized volume, presented as if a giant vacuum cleaner had swept through the corridors of RAND, sucking up every idea, concept, metaphor and calculation that anyone in the strategic community had conjured up over the previous decade. The book's title was an allusion to Clausewitz's *On War*, and was Kahn's way of saying that he considered it to be the comprehensive, perennial classic on the subject. Published in 1960 by the Princeton University Press, it sold an astonishing 30,000 copies in hardcover, quickly became known simply as *OTW* among defense intellectuals, and touched off fierce controversy among nearly everyone who bore through it.

Kahn either delighted or repelled, and he meant to do both. He knew that, especially to a lay audience, these ideas about nuclear war-fighting were strange and new; the notion of thinking about mass destruction was grotesque. To break through the cultural barrier, Kahn sought to amuse, shock, titillate, outrage. Kahn's lectures gripped his audiences. Ordinary businessmen and housewives would stroll out of an auditorium after listening to a Herman Kahn lecture, carrying on in rapt conversation about "intrawar deterrence," "Credible-First-Strike Capability," and the dialectics of nuclear blackmail.

For many, however, Kahn's nonchalant approach to a subject so murderous and grim seemed obscene. Kahn practically asked for such a response. He filled his lectures with such descriptive passages as this:

> Now just imagine yourself in the postwar situation. Everybody will have been subjected to extremes of anxiety, unfamiliar environment, strange foods, minimum toilet facilities, inadequate shelters and the like. Under these conditions, some high percentage of the population is going to become nauseated, and nausea is very contagious. If one man vomits, everybody vomits. It would not be surprising if almost everybody vomits. Almost everyone is likely to think he has received too much radiation. Morale may be so affected that many survivors may refuse to participate in constructive activities, but would content themselves with sitting down and waiting to die—some may even become violent and destructive.
>
> However, the situation would be quite different if radiation meters were distributed. Assume now that a man gets

sick from a cause other than radiation. Not believing this, his morale begins to drop. You look at his meter and say, "You have received only ten roentgens, why are you vomiting? Pull yourself together and get to work."

Nuclear war, Kahn would say, will increase the number of children born with genetic defects, but 4 percent of all children are born defective now. Thus, he concluded, "War is a terrible thing, but so is peace. The difference seems in some respects to be a quantitative one of degree and standards."

Kahn would say that after the war, human tragedy would surely increase, but "the increase would not preclude normal and happy lives for the majority of survivors and their descendants." Indeed "we can imagine a renewed vigor among the population with a zealous, almost religious, dedication to reconstruction, exemplified by a 50- to 60-hour work week."

It was this sort of language that provoked the mathematician James R. Newman to write in a review of Kahn's *On Thermonuclear War* for *Scientific American:* "This is a moral tract on mass murder: how to plan it, how to commit it, how to get away with it, how to justify it."

Kahn was appalled by Newman's review, thought it maliciously misinterpreted his argument, and wrote to Dennis Flanagan, editor of *Scientific American,* asking if he would be interested in printing a rebuttal by Kahn, to be titled "Thinking About the Unthinkable," defending his approach "in coming to grips with this unpleasant problem" of nuclear weapons.

Flanagan responded, "I do not think that there is much point in thinking about the unthinkable; surely it is much more profitable to think about the thinkable. . . . I should prefer to devote my thoughts to how nuclear war can be prevented. It is for this reason that we must decline your offer to give us your article."

This was precisely the sort of attitude that Kahn, in his own rather perverse fashion, was trying to overcome. The exchange of correspondence provoked Kahn to start writing a book by the same title, *Thinking About the Unthinkable.* To Kahn's mind, unless you were willing to believe that nuclear war was impossible, you had to start thinking about it.

Yet many of Kahn's critics, including those in the social science division of the RAND Corporation, thought that Kahn's particular fashion of thinking about nuclear war would, if taken seriously by policy-makers, only make the possibility of such a war more likely. Even Kahn admitted, "The one circumstance under which almost all Soviet experts agree the Russians might strike is the one in which they feel they are anticipating a strike by us." Yet wasn't that just what Kahn was advocating with his business about Types II and III Deterrence—creating a defense "posture" that would allow the U.S. President to threaten the Russians with a first-strike in the event of a crisis?

There was also a pseudoscientific element in Kahn's analysis. The civil-defense study examined the relationship between radiation dosage and human fatalities and crop damage, shelter preparations and the number of survivors, blast and the survival of the national economy. Kahn and his associates went through dozens of possible scenarios, effects and consequences, working through the problem in the most meticulous quantitative detail. But examined closely, the optimistic conclusions that Kahn reached hardly met the standards of realistic, systematic analysis.

First, Kahn employed "seven optimistic assumptions" about the postwar conditions, on which his conclusions critically depended: "Favorable political environment," "Immediate survival and patch-up," "Maintenance of economic momentum," "Specific bottlenecks alleviated," " 'Bourgeois' virtues survive," "Workable postwar standards adopted," "Neglected effects unimportant."

If any of these assumptions didn't hold in the real world, all of Kahn's bets were off. Yet none of the assumptions were subject to analysis; they were all held on faith. It was part and parcel of Kahn's long-held, almost dogmatic belief in the free-market system, inculcated since his early teen-age years when he taught himself economics by perusing the works of the classic eighteenth-century free-market philosopher Adam Smith. Kahn admitted that his estimates of economic recovery did not take into account bottlenecks that would likely occur. "However," he wrote, "experience has shown that entrepreneurs and engineers are very capable at 'making do' when necessary."

Even the recuperative phases of the postwar world would be run according to the principles of the free market. Foods contaminated with strontium 90, for example, would be classified into five grades—from less to more contaminated, A, B, C, D and E. "The A food would be restricted to children and to pregnant women. The B food would be a high-priced food available to everybody. The C food would be a low-priced food also available to everybody. Finally, the D food would be restricted to people over age forty or fifty," whose bones would not pick up so much strontium anyway. (E food would be given to animals.)

The price difference between B and C food "comes from assuming some sort of free market mechanism." For, "If there were no free market, some sort of rationing of B food would be required, but this could introduce all kinds of serious administrative, political, and ethical difficulties and would not encourage expanded production of B food unless some subsidy were granted—implying further complications."

Had Kahn really taken into account all the complications of nuclear war? He reported that his team's civil-defense study concluded that "a nation like the United States or the Soviet Union could handle each of the problems of radioactivity, physical destruction, or likely levels of casualties, *if they occurred by themselves.*" But they "did not look at the interaction among the effects [they] did study." If "all these things happened together and all the other effects were added at the same time," Kahn conceded, "one cannot help but have some doubts" as to the conclusion's validity. "How much confidence did our researchers have in these recuperation calculations? In the sense of having taken account of *all* factors, not too much . . . our study was not complete enough to be a full treatment of this complicated problem."

Kahn's 56-page chapter on civil defense in *OTW*, called "Will the Survivors Envy the Dead?," began with an air of scientific rigor and mathematical precision. It ended with rambling, uplifting rhetoric: "We may not be able to recuperate even with preparations, but we cannot today put our finger on why this should be so and I, for one, believe that with sufficient study we will be able to make a very convincing case for recuperation, if we survive the war, and, more important, that with sufficient preparation we actually will be able to survive and recuperate if deterrence fails."

The rest of Kahn's book crucially depended on the feasibility and success of a nationwide civil-defense program. Yet, in the final analysis, proof of this feasibility rested not on the rigorous thinking that Kahn elsewhere celebrated, but on faith in the basic goodness of the free market even under the most catastrophic circumstances, faith in the ability of quantitative analysis to solve problems even when faced with unpredictable, largely unquantifiable variables.

•

In 1964, film-maker Stanley Kubrick released a brilliant black comedy about a nuclear confrontation between the U.S. and the U.S.S.R. called *Dr. Strangelove: Or How I Learned to Stop Worrying and Love the Bomb.*

Strangelove, the character and the film, struck insiders as a parody of Herman Kahn, some of the dialogue virtually lifted from the pages of *On Thermonuclear War.* But the film was also a satire of the whole language and intellectual culture of the strategic-intellectual set. Kahn's main purpose in writing *OTW* was "to create a vocabulary" so that strategic issues can be "comfortably and easily" discussed, a vocabulary that reduces the emotions surrounding nuclear war to the dispassionate cool of scientific thought. To the extent that many people today talk about nuclear war in such a nonchalant, would-be scientific manner, their language is rooted in the work of Herman Kahn. And to the extent that people have an image of defense analysts as mad-scientist Dr. Strangeloves who almost glorify the challenge of nuclear war, that image, too, comes from Herman Kahn.

Kahn was more extreme in his tone and views than many of his RAND colleagues. But he was only pushing the strategic postulates, the analytical techniques, the underlying world view of the RAND conventional wisdom to their logical limits. He was the ultimate creature and creation of the rational life at RAND, the desperate, at times fervid effort to find, as Kahn phrased it, "more reasonable forms of using violence."

15 The Real Rivalry

THE VIEWS THAT Herman Kahn, Bill Kaufmann, Andy Marshall and a few others at RAND held on counterforce strategies struck a live chord at the very end of the 1950s. For the Air Force was locked in ferocious battle with the Navy, and counterforce seemed just the weapon to help them win the war.

Air Force-Navy rivalry had a long history. Its first major instance had broken out in 1949 during the "Admirals' Revolt," when in reaction to severe cuts in the Navy's budget, the entire top echelon of naval officers broke all tradition of subordination and publicly testified against the official emphasis being placed on the atom bomb, on the Strategic Air Command, on the Air Force's B-36 bombers, at the expense of more traditional modes and weapons of combat, as represented by the Army and the Navy, especially the Navy's aircraft carriers and their task groups. The chief testimony came from Rear Admiral Ralph Ofstie. Ofstie had served on the U.S. Strategic Bombing Survey shortly after World War II and had been among those who concluded from the study that the Army Air Force's strategic bombing had accomplished little for all the resources and lives that the effort had cost.

In public congressional hearings held in 1949, Ofstie condemned Air Force-style strategic bombing as "ruthless and barbaric . . . random mass slaughter of men, women and children . . . militarily unsound . . . morally wrong . . . contrary to our fundamental ideals. . . ." Admiral Arthur Radford, then Vice Chief of Naval Operations, backed up Ofstie's testimony, adding that attack aircraft flying off Navy carriers could more readily and precisely strike the enemy's military targets than could the B-36 bombers.

The Navy attacked the A-bomb, then sole property of the U.S. Air Force, not only as immoral but also as ineffective. One unfortunate Navy commander told Congress that if an A-bomb exploded at one end of Washington's National Airport and you stood at the other end with nothing more protecting you than the clothes on your back, you would not be hurt.

The Air Force won the great battle between the B-36 and the supercarrier. Support for SAC Air Power within Congress was too strong to be crumbled.

Then in 1951, the Navy started to assemble its own atomic arsenal. Suddenly, only a few years after the Admirals' Revolt, the atomic bomb was no longer so "barbaric." Some naval officers began to argue, along Air Force lines, that atomic bombs should be used at the outset of a conflict. Admiral Radford, as Eisenhower's JCS Chairman, suddenly became the most vociferous proponent of "massive retaliation." Most of the Navy, however, distinguished itself from the Air Force by officially advocating the "tactical" bombing of military targets, as opposed to SAC's strategic bombing, which the Navy now decried as "rigidly pre-planned."

The typical Navy officer continued to believe that the most important function of his service was to engage in tactical strikes supporting *limited,* not atomic, wars. But A-bombs were where the money was in the early 1950s, and so the Navy dived into the atomic competition.

Through the 1950s, the Navy tried to prove the superiority of attack-aircraft carriers to Air Force bombers by pointing out the vulnerability of fixed SAC bases and, conversely, the mobility of carriers on the high seas. This tactic proved less than totally successful, as the Air Force could usually well argue that, with electronic intelligence and other devices, airplanes could locate and track ships with little difficulty.

But then in the mid-1950s, the Navy began work on a project that truly would prove threatening to the Air Force—the Polaris submarine. Each Polaris could hold sixteen nuclear missiles. Not only could the subs move continuously, but they could do so underwater, making them virtually impossible to detect or track. And by this time, due in no small part to Wohlstetter's and Hoffman's RAND studies, the Air Force was coming to recognize the vulnerability of its SAC bases. The Polaris was something the Navy could stab at the very heart of Air Force operations and budgets.

By 1958, the Polaris project looked technically feasible: a solid-fuel missile had been developed; an underwater missile-launch system had been demonstrated. One Navy captain told an

Air Force friend, Colonel Richard Yudkin, Assistant Director of Air Force Plans, "We've got something that's going to put you guys out of business."

On January 15, 1957, Admiral Arleigh Burke, Chief of Naval Operations and the driving force behind the Polaris program, approved a study composed by the Naval Warfare Analysis Group (NAVWAG), an organization that had grown out of the Navy's World War II operations-research panels. The study was called NAVWAG Study #1, *Introduction of the Fleet Ballistic Missile.* In the approving cover memorandum to NAVWAG-1, Burke wrote that the mission of this new Navy missile, to be loaded onto the Polaris submarine, was to be "expressed as a deterrent capability" with strategic targets, thus placing the Navy, for the first time, in direct competition with the Air Force. The aircraft carriers had also been placed in the role of striking strategically, but their primary mission was still "control of the seas."

One year later, the Navy went further in its attack on the Air Force, attempting to formulate a new strategic doctrine that would denigrate the value of land-based missiles and bombers in favor of submarines. This new view was articulated in NAVWAG Study #5, *National Policy Implications of Atomic Parity.* The NAVWAG analysts, led by a civilian named John Coyle, took the RAND R-290 and Gaither Committee reports as a premise, but then twisted their conclusions into quite a different shape. Drawing attention, as the two earlier studies had, to the emerging vulnerability of the U.S. strategic force, NAVWAG-5 predicted that, with continued SAC dominance, "we shall soon find ourselves in the new uncomfortable position of relying largely on the *size* of our striking forces to offset their *vulnerability.*" This could only be seen as "a prescription for an arms race, and also an invitation to the enemy for preventive-war adventurism."

The R-290/Gaither solution of hardening missiles into shelters and surrounding them with anti-missile batteries similarly "promotes an arms race." According to NAVWAG, it "challenges the enemy in an area (endless mass production of higher-yield, more accurate missiles) where he is ready and able to respond impressively." Thus, this "fortress concept to achieve security against surprise" commits us only "to an eternal, strength-sapping race in which the Soviets have a head start."

NAVWAG's answer for "get[ting] off the arms-race treadmill" was to secure the strategic force through "mobility and concealment" in submarines, rather than in the "hardening and active defense" of bombers, missiles and anti-missile missiles. And, to avoid "the provocative over-inflation of our strategic forces, their size should be set by an objective of generous *adequacy for deterrence alone* (i.e., for an ability to destroy major urban areas), not by the false goal of adequacy for 'winning.' "

There was nothing really new about this doctrine. It was a return to Bernard Brodie's earliest conception of deterrence as expressed in his 1946 *The Absolute Weapon*—the concept of deterring the enemy by threatening to destroy his society, the corollary notion that this can be accomplished with a relatively small number of weapons, that as the number of major targets run out, so too do "diminishing marginal returns" begin to set in on the effectiveness of each additional weapon.

The Navy, in its new official line, had come full circle: from an abhorrence of city destruction in 1950 to its doctrinal glorification in 1958. The one consistent element in this 180-degree shift, and that ultimately underlay all the phases of strategic rhetoric, was opposition to whatever the Air Force happened to be plugging at the time. In the early 1950s, the Air Force had the bomb, and the Navy did not, so the Navy made a moral case against the mass destructiveness of these evil weapons. In the late 1950s, both sides had the bomb, but the Air Force had far more, and the Navy had the new Polaris, with which the admirals now wanted to supplant the Air Force from the strategic arena altogether. Moreover, submarine-launched missiles would lack the accuracy to hit anything but enemy cities. So a case was made for keeping the necessary number of strategic weapons to a minimum, restricting targets to major enemy cities (of which there were only a couple of hundred) and thereby making a strong case for putting all the strategic weapons underwater.

NAVWAG-5 also pointed out that with the money saved from not having to build an "excessive" number of nuclear weapons, the U.S. conventional force could be built up, so that in the age of "atomic parity," Soviet aggression at "lower levels of conflict" would not result in the free world's getting "nibbled to death."

It was this sort of argument that frightened Air Force officers to distraction. There was a genuine logic to the Navy case and it was just the sort of thing that could do the Air Force in.

Meanwhile, the Navy was promulgating the message of NAVWAG-5 through all available channels. Admiral Burke delivered speeches on the virtues of a mobile deterrent geared to the threat to destroy enemy cities ("mutual deterrence") and the dangers of relying on the current vulnerable land-based force. An unclassified version of NAVWAG-5 was sent out in a letter to all retired naval officers with instructions to speak out on these issues in public as much as they could. General Tommy Power, Commander of SAC (Curtis LeMay had been moved up to the Pentagon as Vice Chief of Staff), obtained a copy of this letter and sent it on to General Tommy White, Air Force Chief, adding that "we would be well advised to match this action in concept and to exceed it in distribution."

"There is an all-out battle going on right now," the director of Air Force Plans and Policy, General Hewitt Wheless, wrote to his SAC counterpart, General Charles "Westy" Westover, in May 1959. Wheless, like most of his colleagues, saw the Army and Navy aiming to reduce Air Force—especially SAC-related—programs, so that more money could be spent on Army and Navy programs. "Because of SAC's public acceptance as *the* deterrent," Wheless continued, "they must have an acceptable rationale, and to this end, they're leaning awfully hard on this new targeting concept, i.e., 'city' destruction, to prove that SAC is excessive."

More disturbing to the Air Force Staff, including the Chief of Staff, Tommy White, was that the Air Force, especially SAC, in the construction of its own targeting plans and philosophy, was setting itself up for this Navy onslaught. The Air Force war plan involved destroying an "optimal mix" of urban and military targets. The report of an April 1959 "Coordination Conference" between SAC and Britain's Bomber Command referred to city destruction as the "Primary Undertaking" and destruction of military targets as the "Alternative Undertaking."

The labeling of city bombing as the "Primary Undertaking," General Wheless noted in his letter to General Westover of SAC, "will be pointed out to us as an example of SAC (and Bomber Command) agreement with the Army and Navy concept." Tommy White conveyed the same concern to Tommy Power: "This would lead to the conclusion . . . that attacking 'cities' constitutes the most important segment of the strategic effort. This conclusion would not only be used as further justification of Polaris but . . . would be used as a strong position (which is already emerging) to eliminate virtually any strategic requirement other than Polaris, i.e., SAC."

Back at the RAND Corporation, things were in flux. The enormous Strategic Offensive Forces project was falling apart. Disagreements were breaking out among the team's leaders; some of the systems analyses were producing results clearly displeasing to the Air Force (for example, that the newly proposed B-70 bomber was a failure); disorganization was rampant. Several individual memorandums and papers came of the project, but no overall report. And amid the fray, several in the strategic community were finding an opportune moment to take leaves of absence.

Still, RAND *did* work for the Air Force and this was the sponsor's time of need. Several RAND analysts came up with ideas to help out in the great battle with the Navy and its much loathed Polaris. Bruno Augenstein, the engineer who in 1953 helped solve the problem of designing a quickly feasible ICBM, came up with the notion of a 1,000-megaton, or "gigaton," bomb: if SAC was vulnerable, just having twenty or so of these weapons surviving would be more than enough to deter and defeat.

Albert Wohlstetter, on leave at the Council on Foreign Relations in New York, called one of his assistants, Dave McGarvey, and, in response to the Navy's claim that land-based missiles attract the enemy's fire and thus needlessly kill millions of American civilians as well, had McGarvey calculate how many Americans would die from the fallout produced by a nuclear attack on Navy installations in the continental U.S., including on the Navy shipyard in Brooklyn.

Herman Kahn's marathon lectures and his book, which had just been published, with their discussions of Types II and III Deterrence and Credible-First-Strike Capability, were providing useful ammunition in the great battle, even if many officers were slightly put off by Kahn's tone and by his infatuation with civil defense.

But a small group of Air Force officers found most helpful of all William Kaufmann and his newly emerging ideas on counterforce. On February 1, 1960, as a visiting professor at Yale, on leave for a term from RAND, Kaufmann sent a brief memo to George Tanham, vice-president of RAND and head of RAND's Washington office. The memo, entitled "The Puzzle of Polaris," argued that, while the Polaris might "constitute a valuable supplement to our land-based strategic force," it could never serve as the back-bone of the deterrent. The main reason for its limitations was that, unlike the land-based forces, the Polaris would lack the explosive yield and accuracy to allow the U.S. "to pursue meaningful coun-terforce and damage-limiting strategies."

Tanham, who was also RAND's liaison with the Air Staff's plans office, sent copies of Kaufmann's memo to various generals and colonels whom he had befriended. The memo circulated all the way up to General Tommy White, who was much impressed. (Clearly, by this time, White must have forgotten that this same W. W. Kaufmann had six years earlier composed an essay called "The Requirements of Deterrence" that he, White, had disliked and that the Army had latched on to in its raging mid-fifties battle against the Air Force.) White had Kaufmann write a letter ex-pressing his views in language suitable for publication, private distribution on Capitol Hill and possible excerption for congres-sional testimony.

On February 18, Kaufmann, in the capacity of a recently elected member to the Air Force Scientific Advisory Board, wrote in a more polished, seven-page letter to White:

"A strategic force primarily or totally dependent on Polaris would increase the difficulty of defending allied areas, particularly Western Europe. . . . In fact, placing our bets essentially on Po-laris would appear almost to invite the Soviets to engage in limited aggression. Certainly the risks would look far less against a sub-merged, city-busting system than against a widely dispersed, pro-tected, land-based system which appeared capable of conducting a counterforce campaign." The "Minimum Deterrence" strategy favored by the Navy, in short, "would hardly be a winning one."

The letter was a synthesis of Kaufmann's old views on limited war, the counterforce legacy passed on by Andrew Marshall and Joseph Loftus, and Herman Kahn's conception of Type II Deter-rence. It fit very nicely into the framework of what General Tommy White and others in the Air Staff had loosely and sporadi-cally been thinking about. The memo and its eager reception marked the first steps in Kaufmann's move toward the center stage of RAND's strategic community and, in some Air Staff quar-ters, toward the official adoption of a pure-counterforce strategy.

The next big step came in June when Kaufmann got a call from George Tanham, asking him to stop in Washington before returning to Santa Monica. Tanham had been talking with an Air

Force general named Noel Parrish, who was worried that the Air Force was about to take a beating from the Navy. Tanham had told Parrish that Kaufmann had some reassuring ideas.

Noel Parrish was an Ichabod Crane sort of figure, with a wiry physique, long head, pointed nose. He was thoughtful, more genuinely interested in ideas than many of his fellow officers. In 1946, he had been a member of the first graduating class of the Air Command Staff College at Maxwell Air Force Base, and wrote a dissertation promoting integration of blacks into the Air Corps, which was considered quite provocative in its day. At the Air War College, he listened to some of the earliest lectures and discussions on the implications of the new atomic bomb, including those by Robert Oppenheimer and Bernard Brodie.

In the early 1950s, Parrish was a speechwriter for General Hoyt Vandenberg when he was Chief of Staff and then for General Nathan Twining, who followed after Vandenberg died. Then he spent three years as the American representative to NATO's defense college. In the course of all this, Parrish grew more convinced that conventional armies could not stop a Red invasion, that the A-bomb (and then the H-bomb) was the weapon of wars in the future, and that the Air Force was the only outfit that really knew how to use it.

Parrish, who had been involved in some of the earlier disputes over the worth of aircraft carriers versus land-based bombers, hated the Navy. However, he was hardly a SAC lackey either. As early as 1950, he wrote speeches for Vandenberg and Twining that entertained the notion of using the bomb against military targets only. Vandenberg and Twining had both done tactical, not strategic, bombing during World War II—Vandenberg providing close-air support for Omar Bradley's armies in Europe, Twining as an air commander in the Mediterranean theater. Neither was wedded to the all-out philosophy that SAC, under Curtis LeMay, adopted after the war.

So it was only logical that when, in June 1960, Kaufmann told Parrish that his solution to the "Polaris Puzzle" was to alter SAC's strategy to attacking military targets only, avoiding destruction of enemy cities at least so long as the enemy avoids destruction of our cities, Parrish's eyes lit up.

Parrish was Assistant Deputy for Coordination under the Director of Air Force Plans. His job was to make sure that all statements coming out of the Air Force were consistent, but Parrish was a bureaucratic hardballer, a supreme manipulator, and he used the office as a means of controlling and censoring information that went out as well. He had just put together a briefing, a compilation of all Air Force statements over the past year on targeting and strategy, to show just how inconsistent they were, to show that the Air Force really didn't have a strategy strong enough to beat the Polaris. When he had shown the briefing to LeMay, then the Vice Chief of Staff, LeMay tried to dismiss all the references that various officers had made to pure-counterforce strategies. LeMay said that SAC studies showed that no matter what our targeting or Russian targeting might be, the number of people killed on both sides remained about the same. LeMay, still very much a SAC man, wanted least of all to see the "max effort" strategic-bombing tradition of World War II diminished. Parrish went to Tommy White after the briefing and opined that targeting *did* make a difference in the level of casualties, but he had no proof.

Listening to Bill Kaufmann talk about counterforce campaigns and city avoidance as strategies for the battle against Polaris, Parrish realized that the winning weapon in his battle with SAC officers might be right before him. Parrish made arrangements to contract RAND to do a study on counterforce, with particular concentration on comparing the outcomes of the war given differing targeting plans on each side. William Kaufmann would direct the study.

Kaufmann returned to Santa Monica with orders and a mission. His friend and counterforce mentor, Joe Loftus, introduced him to two young econometricians who could aid him on the project, David McGarvey and Frank Trinkl. Both had been crunching numbers for Albert Wohlstetter, who in the final days of the Strategic Offensive Forces study had written, along with Harry Rowen, a letter to General White saying that in the event that nuclear weapons had to be used, America's strategy should be to "limit damage" to the U.S. homeland. Kaufmann had thought this a bit vacuous, unrelated to considerations of warfighting and strategy. If you want to limit damage, Kaufmann had told Wohlstetter, don't drop the bombs in the first place. Kaufmann proposed to Frank Collbohm a different sort of letter to White, stressing that the point of counterforce was not merely to limit damage, but to bargain the enemy into surrender, to attack military targets and avoid urban targets as a means of coercion.

The Wohlstetter-Rowen letter won out in Collbohm's judgment; but now, with walking orders from Noel Parrish, Kaufmann had his chance.

When Kaufmann came along, McGarvey and Trinkl were sitting in a back room at RAND working on damage-limiting calculations, drawing circles on maps representing where the bombs drop in a nuclear attack, then, utilizing theoretical models of the distribution of radioactive fallout from a one-megaton weapon, calculating the area of contamination at various dose levels, calculating how many people would die as a consequence. The work that McGarvey and Trinkl were doing constituted the first full-blown effort, outside the government anyway, to simulate mathematically the effects of a nuclear exchange between the U.S. and the U.S.S.R.

To work out these calculations, they used a technique developed by various RAND mathematicians called the "Uniform Random Drops Model." For mathematical convenience, the model assumed that the population of both countries was distributed uniformly across the map. The model also assumed that bombs are dropped at random in a uniform distribution. Into this model, the analyst plugs a calculation of how many megatons of fission energy are released per thousand square miles by the nuclear attack under analysis. And from all this, one can derive an estimate of the resulting casualties.

McGarvey and Trinkl modified the model to make it slightly less crude. They divided the U.S. and the U.S.S.R. into different regions, corresponding to how the various military targets in each country were distributed, and then calculated the results according to the Uniform Random Drops Model in each region. They both knew that this still missed the true picture by some distance, but it was as close as they could get.

For Kaufmann's purposes, McGarvey and Trinkl were the ideal collaborators for his counterforce study. Kaufmann would formulate the philosophy and the scenarios; McGarvey and Trinkl would crunch them into numbers and calculate the comparative casualty estimates that Parrish wanted.

McGarvey, Trinkl and Kaufmann slaved away on their model and calculations for weeks in the early summer of 1960, working through the numbers and taking them through dozens of permutations. Their mathematical war game was set for 1963. The data on U.S. and Soviet strategic forces came from the Air Force. In the

summer of 1960, Air Force Intelligence was predicting that by
mid-1963 the Soviets would have 500 long-range bombers and 700
ICBMs—300 more ICBMs than the CIA was then predicting, 500
more than Army and Navy Intelligence were counting on. Air
Force Intelligence, mainly to justify the large ICBM force that the
Air Force proper wanted to build, was still operating at the peak of
missile-gap period, even while the other intelligence agencies
were revising their estimates downward. Like almost all of the
RAND analysts, Kaufmann had access only to Air Force Intelligence, and that served as the basis for his study.

The team's initial findings in July were dramatic. One scenario, corresponding to the Navy's city-destruction strategy
(Kahn's Type I Deterrence), had the Soviets launching a surprise
attack against U.S. SAC and submarine bases, and the United
States ordering a full-scale retaliatory strike against Soviet urban-
industrial targets with the small number of Atlas and Titan
ICBMs, Polaris missiles and alert B-52 bombers that survived. The
Soviets react by destroying our cities. The war is over. The results:
three-quarters of the American population, 150 million people,
dead; 60 percent of U.S. industrial capacity destroyed. By comparison, 40 million Russians, less than 20 percent of their population, are dead; and about 40 percent of their industries are ruined.

In the second scenario, corresponding to SAC's Optimal Mix
strategy, the Red Army attacks Western Europe. Conventional
NATO forces cannot contain them, so SAC launches a full-scale
attack against Soviet cities, airfields, missile sites, rail centers,
shipyards, factories, all the targets. Several Soviet missiles and
bombers escape the attack and rain destruction on as many
American cities as they can. The results: half the industrial base
of both countries is destroyed; 75 million Russians are dead, 110
million Americans.

The third scenario, the counterforce/no-cities strategy, pro-
duces entirely different results. The Soviets attack Western Europe. Conventional forces cannot hold them; the U.S. launches a
nuclear attack against the U.S.S.R. but restricts the targets of attack to bomber fields, missile pads, submarine pens and control
centers associated with the Soviet Strategic Rocket Forces. The
Soviets retaliate against the United States, but, seeing that we
have avoided their cities, find it in their interest to avoid ours as
well, and so likewise confine their attack to SAC striking forces.

We "mop up" their remaining air defenses and strategic forces, holding some of our weapons in a reserve force. We then send a message to the Russians, telling them to stop or else we will start picking off their cities one by one. The Soviets, clearly outgunned, surrender. The war is over. Only three million Americans have died, and only five million Russians.

In short, the work by Kaufmann, McGarvey and Trinkl revealed that if counterforce works, it could save 100 million lives in the event of nuclear war.

Parrish was thrilled. Kaufmann worked up a briefing and headed off to Washington for a two-week stint, delivering a summary of the study to a larger, broader and higher-level group of Air Force officers. Some of the officers had problems with Kaufmann's conception of counterforce. What if our bombers are much less accurate than we think—won't their explosive power kill more people? What if the Russians don't fight according to the counterforce rules? What if the "loser" uses his remaining weapons to destroy the "winner's" cities? If we emphasize counterforce in a second-strike, won't many of our weapons hit empty air bases and launch pads, since the Soviets will already have fired their weapons? Won't counterforce weaken the bedrock of nuclear deterrence and stimulate an arms race, with the results of heightened suspicion on both sides, higher danger of war by accident, miscalculation or preemption?

Many of these same questions had been posed at RAND by analysts in the social science division, who felt that Kaufmann's emphasis on quantitative measures and nuclear-exchange scenarios ignored such important political issues as how the war began, over what sorts of political goals or values it is being fought. These were the very questions with which Kaufmann, in an earlier period, was preoccupied.

It was a "rolling briefing," Kaufmann fielding these sorts of questions from Air Force officers, relaying them back to McGarvey and Trinkl for further calculation, formulating new rhetorical arguments on his own.

To the argument that counterforce weakens deterrence by making the costs and risks of attacking seem more acceptable to an aggressor, Kaufmann conceded the risk but contended that a policy of counter-city retaliation frightens us as much as it does the enemy, and that, therefore, such a policy is inadequate, especially for deterring attacks against allies. In this sense, counter-force could make deterrence more credible—the conclusion that so attracted Kaufmann to counterforce in the first place.

On the matter of accelerating the arms race, Kaufmann, fa-miliar only with Air Force Intelligence numbers on the rate of So-viet missile production, could only argue that we were in an arms race already, with the Russians leading the way. Similarly, an-swering the problem of hitting lots of empty Soviet missile holes, Kaufmann reasoned that the Soviets would logically retain a sub-stantial reserve force, and that therefore many live military targets would be hit.

Perhaps the most pertinent question was whether the Soviets would play along with the rules. On this, Kaufmann could only hope that the Soviets would see that their own best rational inter-ests of saving their own cities from annihilation would prompt them to do so.

The issues were hardly settled. Kaufmann was the first to admit to a whole series of uncertainties over how the war would actually proceed or end. But he was convinced that the threat of blowing up Soviet cities was inappropriate and not very credible, now that the Soviets also had the power to blow up American cities. And in that context, counterforce appeared as the best hope in an awful situation.

Debate within the Air Staff came to a halt when General Tommy White, Air Force Chief, embraced Kaufmann's briefing wholeheartedly. As late as June 1958, White had told an audience of national-security specialists that he was "disturbed" by the re-cent tendency among some analysts "to consider seriously self-restraints in nuclear weapons planning in the face of sure knowl-edge that no such restraints will be applied by the enemy. Our pre-occupation with niceties in nuclear warfare . . . would, I am sure, delight the Kremlin."

Only two years later White was endorsing without reserva-tion a strategy that imposed just such "self-restraints" and that elevated to high wisdom the "preoccupation with niceties in nu-clear warfare." The key difference between the summer of 1958 and the summer of 1960 was that the Polaris had evolved into a much more serious threat to the Air Force. Since the Polaris could not perform counterforce missions and could do well only against cities, the counterforce/no-cities doctrine appeared suddenly very attractive.

White struck up a rather avuncular relationship with Bill Kaufmann, encouraged him to think through the issues further. He traveled out to Santa Monica when Kaufmann delivered the briefing before a RAND audience, his presence serving as a bulwark of official support.

On October 1, copying the Navy's public relations strategy of propagating the "city-destruction" doctrine, the Secretary of the Air Force sent a "policy letter" to all Air Force commanders, urging that "your public speeches, briefings, Commander's Calls and other presentations should (1) strongly stress the importance of our maintaining a proper strategy and (2) thoroughly explain counterforce."

The briefing papers on positions to take at the upcoming Air Force Commanders' Conference in mid-November stressed that "effective deterrence is achievable only through possession of a striking power that threatens destruction of substantially all of the enemy's long-range nuclear delivery capability. . . . A threat to destroy a large number of Soviet citizens does not represent effective deterrence of a Soviet attack against the U.S. and it provides no deterrence to other forms of Soviet aggression such as an attack against another NATO country."

Meanwhile, Noel Parrish, as the man through whom all public statements by Air Force officers must first filter, censored anything inconsistent with counterforce and, with White's tacit permission, leaked to the press the findings of the Kaufmann briefing. Kaufmann's philosophy emerged as official Air Force policy.

There was still one major obstacle: the Strategic Air Command. On paper, SAC was merely one of several commands under the Air Staff's wings; in truth, it was a fiefdom, not easily challenged much less defeated. And the commander of SAC in 1960, General Tommy Power, abhorred any departure from the strategic-bombing traditions of World War II. Power, too, had flown bombing sorties over Japan in 1945, and when LeMay was appointed SAC Commander, he selected Power as deputy. Power saw the virtue of the H-bomb in its stupendous size and power, and any strategy that deliberately diminished that was perverse, almost traitorous.

Power was a brutal, easily angered man who struck Air Staff officers outside SAC as dim-witted and insensitive to the dilemmas that the bomb raised. Once, when Herman Kahn was briefing Power on the long-term genetic effects of nuclear weapons, Power suddenly chuckled, leaned forward in his chair and said, "You know, it's not yet been proved to me that two heads aren't better than one." Even Kahn was outraged, and sternly lectured Power that he should not discuss human life so cavalierly.

At Tommy White's repeated urgings, General Power finally agreed to hear Kaufmann's counterforce briefing. It took place at SAC Headquarters in Omaha on December 12, 1960. Not two minutes into the lecture, Power interrupted with a long, angry tirade against everything that Kaufmann was saying.

"Why do you want us to restrain ourselves?" Power bellowed. "Restraint! Why are you so concerned with saving *their* lives? The whole idea is to *kill* the bastards!" After several minutes of this, he finally said, "Look. At the end of the war, if there are two Americans and one Russian, we win!"

Kaufmann—his patience exhausted—snapped back, "Well, you'd better make sure that they're a man and a woman." At that point, Power stalked out of the room. The briefing was over.

Several weeks later, Power cabled White to make sure that the Kaufmann briefing did not represent the Air Force position on strategy or targeting. White cabled an appeasing note back to Power, assuring him that in a briefing to President Eisenhower in February 1960, "I endorsed the 'optimum-mix' concept . . . a target system consisting of a mix of vital military and important urban-industrial targets, including all vital strategic elements of the enemy's known nuclear offensive capability." White gave only conditional endorsement of Kaufmann's briefing as presenting the case for an improvement "to provide a wider range of options in the future, while continuing to deny a potential aggressor any comfort regarding the possible magnitude or objectives of our response."

It was a tepid response, not scornful but not terribly supportive. White viewed the job of Chief of Staff as a unifier of the Air Force Commands, especially in these tough times of a joint Army-Navy offensive. SAC was the most powerful of the commands, and White could not afford to jump into a big fray with Tommy Power. In a crunch, Tommy White backed away.

But that was not the end of the counterforce/no-cities strategy. There were still higher authorities to consult and advise, and after the 1960 election, with a new Administration in office, a new Secretary of Defense controlling the Pentagon, the Kaufmann briefing and the RAND version of counterforce would achieve their crowning glories.

16 THE WHIZ KIDS

BY THE TIME of the 1960 Presidential campaign, defense intellectuals were riding high. The missile gap was very much on everyone's mind, as well as an image of a sagging defense posture and eight years of a complacent Republican Administration. The marketplace was filled with books and articles on how to solve the problems of national security in order to meet the crises that lay ahead.*

Onto this stage stepped John Fitzgerald Kennedy. Vigor, youth, the "New Frontier," "getting the country moving again"—these were the themes of Kennedy's Presidential campaign, and not least on the subject of national security. As much as anyone, Kennedy had milked the missile-gap phenomenon for political capital. From his days as a congressman in the early 1950s, Kennedy had hooked himself to the advocates of Air Power. As early as February 1956, he was warning that "the United States might well be behind the Soviet Union" in missilery. A year later, he stated that if present trends were not reversed by 1960, "this nation will have lost its superiority in strategic air power."

His most dramatic missile-gap speech was delivered on the Senate floor August 14, 1958. Its impact was so potent that Republican Senator Homer Capehart of Indiana threatened to clear the galleries on grounds that Kennedy was disclosing information harmful to the national security.

"We are rapidly approaching that dangerous period which

* There were Albert Wohlstetter's "Delicate Balance of Terror" article in *Foreign Affairs,* Herman Kahn's *On Thermonuclear War,* William Kaufmann's Princeton essays, Thomas Schelling's *The Strategy of Conflict,* Bernard Brodie's *Strategy in the Missile Age,* Charles Hitch and Roland McKean's *The Economics of Defense in the Nuclear Age.* Other works and documents included the leaks on the Gaither Report, a similar but unclassified report issued in 1958 by the Rockefeller Brothers, Harvard Professor Henry Kissinger's best seller, *Nuclear Weapons and Foreign Policy,* studies directed by Paul Nitze at the Johns Hopkins Washington Center for Foreign Policy Analysis, scores of articles and books by disgruntled Army officers, including Maxwell Taylor's *The Uncertain Trumpet,* James Gavin's *War and Peace in the Space Age,* and the much-praised work by British soldier-strategist B. H. Liddell Hart, *Deterrent or Defense.*

General [James] Gavin and others have called the 'gap' or the 'missile-lag' period," Kennedy proclaimed. Sometime between 1960 and 1964, "the deterrent ratio might well shift to the Soviets so heavily . . . as to open to them a new shortcut to world domination." The Soviets' "missile power will be the shield from behind which they will slowly but surely advance—through Sputnik diplomacy, limited brushfire wars, indirect non-overt aggression, intimidation and subversion, internal revolution, increased prestige or influence, and the vicious blackmail of our allies. The periphery of the Free World will slowly be nibbled away. The balance of power will gradually shift against us."

In a speech delivered in April 1959, Kennedy pinpointed the main problem in our defense posture as "the problem of protecting our striking power, making it more secure against enemy attack." He emphasized that "even if the missile gap were somehow ended and our supply of ICBMs equaled that of the Soviets, we would still be on the short end of the *deterrent* ratio. . . ." Taking a page from Wohlstetter's "Delicate Balance of Terror," the candidate noted that "there is no security in merely matching . . . the 'first-strike' forces of the Soviets. . . . The real question is how large will [our] force be after the first Russian strike? How secure is it against destruction?" Taking another page from the RAND studies (and the Gaither Report, which they influenced), Kennedy urged the hardening of SAC bases (including putting bombers and missiles in "underground hangars covered by very thick, reinforced concrete roofs"), dispersing the bases and making some weapons mobile.

Surreptitiously, a small team of RAND analysts was aiding the Kennedy campaign. The connection was made by Daniel Ellsberg, who, while taking a leave of absence at Harvard to finish his Ph.D., met Dierdre Henderson, coordinator of an "Academic Advisory Group" for the Kennedy campaign. The group was composed mainly of Harvard and MIT professors—among them Henry Kissinger, Arthur Schlesinger, John Kenneth Galbraith, Paul Samuelson, Archibald Cox, Carl Kaysen, Barton Leach, Jerry Wiesner—as well as such outsiders as Paul Nitze and General James Gavin. The purpose of the group was to provide Kennedy with advice, but, much more than that, to lend him the prestige of association with the nation's intellectual heavyweights. Ellsberg stayed in touch with Henderson and convinced a segment of the strategic community back at RAND to enlist in the cause.

John Kennedy was RAND's nearly ideal candidate—energetic, urbane, active and genuinely interested in bolstering national security. From his articles and speeches, he seemed familiar with the issues, and like the men of RAND, he opposed massive retaliation, favored the buildup of "limited-war" forces, recognized the dangers of SAC vulnerability and the accompanying missile gap—or "deterrent gap."

Beginning late in 1959, on the firm condition that their involvement not be revealed to anyone outside the campaign, some of the RAND strategists—Ellsberg, Albert Wohlstetter, Alain Enthoven, Harry Rowen, Andrew Marshall, Fred Hoffman—regularly passed along ideas and helped draft speeches for the Kennedy brigade. Their ideas caught on with some leaders of the Academic Advisory Group, passages from their drafts found their way into some of the candidate's speeches. But throughout the campaign, the RAND strategists were players on the remote sidelines. They had no direct contact with Kennedy himself.

After the election, however, the leading RAND strategists moved to the forefront and found themselves with the opportunity to translate their theories directly into policy. Their agent to power, the man who would be at once their liberator and captive, was John Kennedy's choice for Secretary of Defense, Robert McNamara.

Robert Strange McNamara was a rather unlikely candidate for the job. At age forty-four, he had only months before Kennedy took office been made president of Ford Motors. Other Secretaries of Defense had been corporate executives; one, Charles Wilson, had been head of GM. But McNamara was different: he was an innovator, an intellectual, a liberal. He contributed money to the ACLU and the NAACP. Ford Motors was in Detroit, but McNamara lived in nearby Ann Arbor, where he could be closer to the academic community at the University of Michigan. He worked eleven hours a day, then came home to read books or attend meetings with a dozen or so other intellectuals and discuss national and international issues or new literary works.

During World War II, McNamara worked in the Statistical Control Office of the Army Air Corps as part of an operations-research group from the Harvard Business School that applied new management theories and techniques to make the war effort more efficient. Among his tasks was to figure out the logistical requirements and schedules of the Eighth Air Force, calculating how to mesh the right number of men with the right amount and types of equipment at the right time. Later, with the 20th Air Force in the Far East, he worked on the enormously difficult problem of getting B-29 bombers from India to forward bases in China and then on to their targets in Japan without running out of fuel. McNamara's techniques were credited with giving the airmen of Curtis LeMay's XXI Bomber Command 30 percent more flying hours.

After the war, McNamara and nine others from the Stat Control Office banded together to sell themselves as a group to some manufacturing firm eager to buy their collective skills. Henry Ford II, who had recently taken over the company from his father, took the gamble, and the group became known as the "Quiz Kids" or the "Whiz Kids." They turned management practices at Ford Motors upside down, rationalized the place, swept the company's finances out of debt. McNamara was central in this process, and later he helped design Ford's first compact car, the Falcon. In November 1960, capping a meteoric rise through corporate ranks, McNamara was promoted to company president.

His experiences in the war and at Ford provided McNamara with the confidence that he could gain command of any situation and that he could do so more quickly and proficiently than the conventional experts in the field, whether they be auto executives or Air Force generals. McNamara was coldly clinical, abrupt, almost brutally determined to keep emotional influences out of the inputs and cognitive processes that determined his judgments and decisions. It was only natural, then, that when Robert S. McNamara met the RAND Corporation, the effect was like love at first sight.

John Kennedy formally introduced McNamara as his Pentagon chief on December 13. McNamara had been recommended by Robert Lovett, the venerable banker-statesman who had been civilian director of the Army Air Corps when McNamara was making his remarkable impression in Stat Control. When Kennedy and McNamara met, McNamara warned that he hadn't really kept up with military affairs since shortly after World War II and therefore had doubts as to whether he could handle the job. Kennedy told him that there wasn't any training school for Presidents either, but that after having talked with Dwight Eisenhower, he was certain he could handle his post. McNamara went to talk with Thomas Gates, Eisenhower's Secretary of Defense, and came back with the same conviction. McNamara was in.

McNamara forced one condition: he could choose his own subordinates. For the next week, McNamara holed himself up at a room in the Shoreham Hotel with a telephone and hundreds of three-by-five note cards, gathering information on an equal number of possible candidates for various positions. For the job of Pentagon comptroller, several people were mentioning the name of Charles Hitch, director of the economics division at the RAND Corporation and, by this time, a well-known economist and president of the Operations Research Society of America. McNamara had never heard of Hitch, but was urged to read his new book, *The Economics of Defense in the Nuclear Age.* McNamara was startled. Here was someone who was doing the same sort of thing that McNamara had done during the war—applying principles of microeconomics, operations research and statistical analysis to defense issues—but doing it on a much broader scale, covering the whole gamut of national security, including comparing and choosing weapons systems, restructuring the defense budget, formulating military strategy.

McNamara called Hitch on the phone and offered him the job of Pentagon comptroller. Hitch at first refused. For Hitch, it was a situation similar to that December thirteen years earlier when Johnny Williams had torn him away from the peaceful environs of Oxford University to come to RAND. McNamara's was another all-too-tempting offer and Hitch ultimately accepted.

Hitch asked Alain Enthoven, a former fellow RAND analyst who had been working at the Pentagon's R&D directorate for a year, to come join him as his Deputy Assistant Secretary for Systems Analysis. It would be a new office, Hitch's own creation, that would apply the techniques of analysis that RAND had been practicing for longer than a decade.

Meanwhile, Paul Nitze, scribe of NSC-68 and the Gaither Report, critic of Dulles' massive-retaliation policy, whom McNamara had chosen as Assistant Secretary for International Security Affairs, called Harry Rowen, Enthoven's fellow Wohlstetter acolyte from RAND, to be his deputy. Both Rowen and Enthoven would frequently ask Wohlstetter for advice and consulting. Enthoven picked Frank Trinkl, Bill Kaufmann's numbers-cruncher on the counterforce study, to be his deputy in charge of strategic offensive forces; when Trinkl left in 1964, Fred Hoffman, Wohlstetter's partner on R-290, replaced him. Harry Rowen had Dan Ellsberg and Kaufmann do some consulting as well. Kaufmann resigned from RAND to spend half his time in Washington and the other half as a professor of political science at MIT.

Almost immediately after Kennedy took office, McNamara assigned several special task forces to do studies on various aspects of defense policy with an eye toward formulating a supplemental appropriation to the fiscal 1962 defense budget that Eisenhower had left behind. Paul Nitze would direct the project on conventional forces; the project on strategic nuclear forces would be handled by Charlie Hitch, Alain Enthoven and Marvin Stern, a young weapons scientist in the Office of Defense Research and Engineering. Hitch suddenly caught pneumonia, so Stern and Enthoven took over the study, with Enthoven reporting directly to McNamara.

Enthoven, a devout Roman Catholic, was almost broodingly intense about everything that occupied his mind. In his final days at RAND, he wrote a report on SAC vulnerability, a follow-up study to Wohlstetter and Hoffman's R-290. Like Wohlstetter, whom Enthoven practically worshiped, he deeply felt that SAC vulnerability was the most important danger facing the Western world. When both Charlie Hitch and Bernard Brodie mildly criticized Enthoven for being too pessimistic, for giving the tone of his report "a certain accent of hopelessness and tragedy," Enthoven replied, "Fundamentally I do believe that the situation borders on the hopeless and the tragic . . . I plead truth as my defense."

Enthoven left RAND out of frustration and impatience, bitter and indignant that his report was all but ignored by RAND management. "I have lost patience with the whole climate that fosters the treatment of subjects of the utmost gravity and complexity in a slick 45-minute briefing," he wrote to Bernard Brodie shortly after leaving RAND for the Pentagon. "Quite frankly I am sick of RAND's emphasis on communicating everything in this fatuous way. My favorite caricature of RAND has Herman Kahn finishing a two-hour briefing full of important and exciting new ideas only to have one prominent member of the management say 'Why is your fly open?' while another says 'You'll have to cut it to a half hour.' "

Robert McNamara hit it off with Enthoven as well as he had with Hitch. Even more than Hitch, Enthoven was a numbers

man. He was thirty when he took charge of Systems Analysis in
the Pentagon and had the systems analyst's obsessive love for
numbers, equations, calculations, along with a certain arrogance
that his calculations could reveal truth. And so Enthoven and
McNamara got along splendidly, seeing each other nearly every
day, an honor that McNamara bestowed to no other Pentagon official below the rank of assistant secretary.

For the same reasons that McNamara liked him, Enthoven
drove most military officers, especially Air Force officers, half
crazy. First, it was his arrogance that bothered them. Arguing
with one general about nuclear war plans, Enthoven finally
stated, "General, I have fought just as many nuclear wars as you
have." To another, one of the senior generals in the U.S. Air Force
Europe, who started to give Enthoven a briefing one day, he
sharply said, "General, I don't think you understand. I didn't
come for a briefing. I came to tell you what we have decided."

It wasn't just Enthoven who angered the military; it was
McNamara's whole entourage of young, book-smart, Ivy League,
think-tank civilian assistants, who soon earned the appellation
given to McNamara's band of statisticians in the Army Air Corps
and at Ford Motors—the "Whiz Kids." Hitch and Enthoven, with
the assistance of Kennedy's Budget Director, David Bell, re-
vamped the entire defense budget. Before, each service was dealt
with separately, little attention paid to overlap or lack of coordination among them. Henceforth, the budget would be organized by
"mission" categories—Strategic Nuclear Forces, General Purpose
Forces, Research & Development, Operations & Maintenance,
and so forth—cutting across the separate branches of the armed
forces. For the first time, then, Air Force bombers and missiles
were compared directly with Navy Polaris submarines and missiles. And everything was scrutinized with the cost-benefit and
cost-effectiveness analysis that Charlie Hitch had done for years at
RAND, asking the questions, "What weapon system will destroy
the most targets for a given cost?" or "What weapon system will
destroy a given set of targets for the lowest cost?" assuming that
the Soviets have first launched a preemptive strike attempting to
destroy those forces.

Using this sort of analysis, McNamara's Whiz Kids, only
weeks into their occupancy of the Pentagon, started to whack
away at such precious Air Force projects as the B-58 and B-70
bombers, the Skybolt, Snark, Jupiter, Regulus and Hound Dog

missiles. Their analysis told them that bombers were less "survivable" than ICBMs in hardened silos, and that the Minuteman ICBM was, by most standards, more "cost-effective" than other alternatives. At the same time, while they expanded the Minuteman production line beyond that of the Eisenhower plan, they decided to buy at first only 1,200, then 1,300, then 1,400, and finally 1,000 Minuteman missiles, instead of the 3,000 that the Air Force wanted, to say nothing of the 10,000 on which SAC was counting. They also gradually phased out all of the 1,500 B-47 bombers that, in early 1961, comprised the backbone of SAC, reasoning that B-52s were better than B-47s and missiles better than bombers.

Moreover, the Whiz Kids tended to favor accelerating the Navy's Polaris submarine program and putting more money into the Army's conventional forces—an effort that was especially pushed when Kennedy appointed as Chairman of the Joint Chiefs his favorite military man, Army General Maxwell Taylor, who had been frustrated in his attempts to strengthen the Army during Eisenhower days.

During the first couple of years of the Kennedy Administration, the Air Force could not win a single battle with McNamara. And all the blame fell on the Whiz Kids, who, except for the relatively low-keyed and gentlemanly Charlie Hitch, practically shoved their victories and their youthful civilian power in the military's face.

General Tommy White, now retired Air Force Chief of Staff and once an enthusiastic supporter of RAND when its analysts worked strictly for the Air Force, wrote a cutting piece in *The Saturday Evening Post,* which began, "In common with many other military men, active and retired, I am profoundly apprehensive of the pipe-smoking, tree-full-of-owls type of so-called professional 'defense intellectuals' who have been brought into this nation's capital. I don't believe a lot of these often overconfident, sometimes arrogant young professors, mathematicians and other theorists have sufficient worldliness or motivation to stand up to the kind of enemy we face. War is a brutal, dirty, deadly affair. Our enemy is a coarse, crooked megalomaniac who aims to kill us. . . . Perhaps the most dangerous aspect of American strategy-making today is that military influence is so disparaged by the so-called intellectuals."

General Curtis LeMay, who succeeded Tommy White as Air Force Chief of Staff, absolutely despised the Whiz Kids. He was horrified when Harold Brown, McNamara's thirty-four-year-old R&D director, tried to tell him which bomber the Air Force should really want. "Why, that son of a bitch was in junior high school while I was out bombing Japan!" LeMay said. After McNamara killed the B-70 and a host of other Air Force weapons, and then stopped building Minuteman after reaching 1,000 missiles, LeMay would often ominously inquire of his Air Force friends, "I ask you: would things be much worse if Khrushchev were Secretary of Defense?"

The Whiz Kids were well aware of their low popularity among military officers; indeed, they thrived on their reputation, seeking battle with the Joint Chiefs whenever they felt it appropriate to do so. Once, Charlie Hitch, Harry Rowen, Alain Enthoven and Bill Kaufmann were flying back to Washington from Army Headquarters at Fort Leavenworth. Suddenly Kaufmann started to chuckle, turned to his friends and said, "What would the Air Force do if they knew we were all in the same airplane together?" They laughed uproariously.

From the Whiz Kids' point of view, military officers were riled because they were being outsmarted. The military had never before been pressured to justify its weapons programs; the President, especially Eisenhower, had cut or modified their budgets on the margins, but they had pretty much been left alone to devise their own independent plans. They wanted more, bigger, better— setting their "requirements" at whatever levels their budgetary wish lists could absorb, never asking how much was enough to perform a certain mission, and certainly never comparing their own forces with those of the other services. The politics of the defense budget was composed almost entirely of the internecine warfare waged among the Army, Navy, Air Force and Marines, with the Secretary of Defense almost powerless to step in and impose ultimate authority.

McNamara could absorb, memorize and synthesize vast arrays of numbers, facts, analytical concepts with amazing speed and comprehension, and frequently embarrassed colonels and even some generals by knowing more about the weapons under discussion than they did. So McNamara, with the help of his Whiz Kids, *told* them what to do. And Jack Kennedy, who was enamored of McNamara's brilliance, almost always backed him up.

In December 1961, some of the brightest Air Force officers met at Homestead Air Force Base in Florida to figure out what they were doing wrong, how they could deal with McNamara and win a few bureaucratic battles. They concluded that they would have to work up their own analytical corps. No longer could they justify a weapon merely by saying, "There's a military requirement for it." They too would have to learn the lingo of "scenarios," do "cost-effectiveness" analysis, become their own "systems analysts." Smart colonels were assigned to "murder boards," which tried to pick apart Air Force rationales before McNamara and his assistants could. In short, they would try to beat McNamara at his own game.

Especially in the first few years of this experiment, their analyses were usually pretty bad, often blatantly tendentious. Not that McNamara's squad always analyzed with total objectivity, either. On many occasions, McNamara first came up with the conclusion and then ordered analysis to support it. The initial decision to build 1,200 Minuteman missiles, for example, was essentially a political compromise. With the aid of analysts in the Budget Bureau and the President's Science Advisory Committee, NSC analyst Carl Kaysen, using Enthoven's brand of systems analysis, demonstrated that the U.S. could get along just fine with only 600 Minutemen. Kennedy found Kaysen's arguments persuasive, but McNamara told the President that 1,200 was the least he could get away with and still maintain a credible relationship with Congress and the Joint Chiefs. Kennedy, the cautious politician, went with McNamara.

As a result of the McNamara-Hitch-Enthoven years, systems analysis became accepted as the buzz word, the way that decisions were rationalized, the currency of overt transactions, the *lingua franca* inside the Pentagon. In his *Saturday Evening Post* diatribe, Tommy White wrote, "The term 'defense intellectual' conveys a nice, cozy, unwarlike and non-military feeling, as though modern war could be settled on a chessboard in an ivy-covered Great Hall." General White had a point more profound than he might have known. The Whiz Kids had transformed not only the vocabulary and procedural practices of the Pentagon, but also the prevailing philosophy of force and strategy—not only the way that weapons are chosen, but also the way that war should be fought. In this dimension William Kaufmann and his counterforce briefing made their deepest marks.

17 TWO BRIEFINGS

ROM THE BEGINNING of his tenure in the Pentagon, Robert McNamara was fascinated with nuclear weapons—horrified by their awesome destruction, yet eager to find a way to bring them under some sort of rational control.

One week into the Kennedy Administration, he heard about a report by the Weapons Systems Evaluation Group (WSEG) called WSEG-50, its full title *Evaluation of Strategic Offensive Weapons Systems*. It had been completed just one month earlier, and those officials in the White House and the Pentagon who had seen it briefed were full of praise for it. McNamara figured he should make some time to listen to this briefing himself.

On January 26, George Contos, a weapons scientist who had supervised WSEG-50, and a few of his colleagues who had co-authored the study presented a briefing to McNamara that was scheduled to last for ninety minutes. McNamara grew so fascinated with their report, however, that the briefing lasted all day. It was just the sort of analysis that would appeal to McNamara. Every long-range bomber and missile program that the U.S. military wanted as of 1964–1967 was systematically and mathematically evaluated and compared for their cost-effectiveness, given likely Soviet nuclear forces during the same period. The study also examined the feasibility of a counterforce targeting strategy.

It was a huge report, ten thin volumes in all, the product of thirty WSEG analysts working for just over a year. Its chief conclusions, buttressed by hundreds of charts, graphs and tables, were that the B-47 and B-58 bombers should be scrapped; that the newly proposed B-70 bomber was too costly, too vulnerable on the ground and too easily shot out of the sky by surface-to-air missiles that the Soviets could readily develop; that the new, smaller Minuteman ICBMs were more cost-effective than their huge, bulky Atlas and Titan predecessors; that missiles were better than bombers generally; that great emphasis should be placed on the Navy's

Polaris submarine and missile, since their underwater mobility made them least vulnerable of all to Soviet attack.

McNamara emerged from the briefing excited. This was just the handle that he had been looking for, the integration of all the strategic weapons programs that the military was requesting into a single overall perspective. He told Charlie Hitch and Alain Enthoven that he was very impressed with the WSEG-50 study. Hitch and Enthoven looked dismayed; they hadn't cared for it at all. On most of the points concerning specific weapons systems, they agreed. But WSEG and RAND differed radically on one critical point, and that was on the question of counterforce.

Counterforce occupied only one section of WSEG-50, but its conclusion was that such a strategy would not be effective, would not significantly limit the damage that the Soviets would wreak on the United States in a retaliatory strike. The key problem, according to WSEG, was that the Soviets would have substantial strategic forces that the U.S. simply could not target—perhaps a few missiles and bombers on bases that our reconnaissance intelligence could not find, and several submerged submarines. WSEG calculated that, even if the U.S. destroyed all of the targetable forces, the non-targetable weapons could, depending on the circumstances, deliver 1,000 to 2,000 megatons, killing at least half of the American population. Even if the people were fully sheltered by a comprehensive civil-defense system, around sixty million Americans would still die if the Soviets released all of their remaining weapons. Furthermore, the WSEG team argued, an attempt to gain a counterforce advantage would only spark an arms race that the U.S. could not win. It takes more than one weapon to destroy another one; therefore, for every missile that the Soviets add, the U.S. would have to add more than one.

In the end, WSEG recommended a strategy that harkened back to Bernard Brodie's earliest formulation of deterrence in *The Absolute Weapon,* a strategy similar to that emerging from the Navy*—a doctrine of "finite deterrence," stating that "once an effective basic force level consisting of the more promising weapons systems is deployed, it does not make much difference whether

---

* This was no mere coincidence. WSEG's director in 1960 was John "Savvy" Sides, an extremely shrewd Navy admiral.

increments of one system or another are added in the retaliatory force." One of the analysts on WSEG-50, an engineer named Larry Deane, privately referred to counterforce as "dynamic disarmament." Since they had concluded that counterforce and other war-winning and damage-limiting strategies were essentially futile, the only alternative was to maintain a strategic retaliatory force so invulnerable and so horrifying in its destructive power that no aggressor would dare launch a first-strike. That was the essence of deterrence. To the WSEG analysts, any effort to minimize the destructiveness of the retaliation would weaken the deterrent power of the strategic arsenal.

This philosophy went deeply against the RAND tradition that Hitch and Enthoven represented—not so much because it hurt the Air Force (Hitch and Enthoven were no longer working for the Air Force), but because Hitch had been seriously convinced from the days of the RAND Strategic Objectives Committee, and Enthoven persuaded after hearing Bill Kaufmann's counterforce briefing, that all-out city destruction was immoral and strategically unwise. However difficult the effort might be, it would be worthwhile to try to control the escalation of nuclear war, to restrict attacks to military targets, to withhold a reserve force with which to coerce the Soviets to do the same, to end the war before cities were destroyed. Hitch and Enthoven told this to McNamara in very brief terms, and urged him to hear Kaufmann's briefing too. McNamara agreed.

The meeting was held on Friday, February 10, at 3 P.M., with McNamara, Kaufmann, Enthoven and Marvin Stern attending. McNamara was the only one who had not heard it before. By this time, Kaufmann had perfected the briefing. It contained fifty-four charts and, for most audiences, took four hours to go through. With McNamara it took only an hour. He grasped the meaning of nearly every chart at once.

McNamara was fascinated by the briefing. The idea of restricting the initial attack to military targets and using a withheld reserve force to bargain with the enemy, of trying to rationalize conflict, made sense to McNamara, the anti-emotional economist. Still, there was something about it that bothered him. Kaufmann anticipated some of his doubts with a reservation of his own: while the counterforce/no-cities idea served as a good guide on how to play the first round or two of a nuclear war, it left the question of how to end the war very much open. This issue had recently begun to bother Kaufmann considerably. He had discussed it with one of his assistants, Frank Trinkl, and was frustrated that Trinkl didn't even see the problem. Trinkl, ever the econometrician, reasoned that once the Soviets saw that launching more nuclear weapons would only hurt them more than it would help them, once they saw that the cost-benefit calculus went against them, they would stop. The notion of things in war getting out of hand, which Clausewitz had called "friction," and of which Kaufmann the political scientist and historian was acutely aware, simply struck Trinkl as irrational and, therefore, nearly impossible.

Kaufmann had brought up the same point with his Air Force sponsor, General Noel Parrish, and had met the same resistance. Parrish was uninterested in attacking anything but military targets, no matter how the war progressed, and thought that would force the Soviets to surrender, automatically. Kaufmann and Parrish once had a big argument over this, with Kaufmann finally challenging, "Suppose we do knock out most of their counterforce targets. What do we do then—go buzzing about in bombers and shouting 'Quit'?"

McNamara caught the significance of this problem right away, but he saw another that bothered him still more. McNamara had liked the WSEG-50 briefing not least because it specified a point at which he could justify telling the Joint Chiefs "No more nuclear weapons"—and that was the point at which all major Soviet cities could be devastated by an American retaliatory blow even after a fairly successful Soviet first-strike. But where was the cutoff point in Kaufmann's scheme? It seemed to McNamara that as long as the other side kept building nuclear weapons, then the military's "requirements" for more and more nuclear weapons for the U.S. could be endless.

Kaufmann responded with a chart that had been drawn by Norman Hanounian, a RAND specialist on nuclear weapons' effects, which showed that after 8,000 to 10,000 megatons had dropped on the United States, the radioactive fallout would be so great that fatalities would be roughly the same no matter whether cities or military bases had been targeted. Kaufmann suggested that a cutoff point be drawn at 8,000 to 10,000 megatons. That didn't satisfy McNamara. With that much megatonnage, an attack would kill nearly everyone. McNamara wanted something with which he could control much more tightly the appetites of the Joint Chiefs.

Meanwhile, once exposed to Kaufmann's briefing, McNamara, for the time being anyway, could not help but accept its logic. True, he wanted to put a strap on the Joint Chiefs, hungry for more nuclear weapons, and the WSEG-50 solution nearly was an ideal way to do that. At the same time, Kaufmann's briefing, with prodding assistance from the three key RAND analysts in the Pentagon, Enthoven, Rowen and Hitch, persuaded McNamara that if nuclear war did come, the U.S. should at least *try* to keep it from getting completely out of hand, that it was his responsibility as Secretary of Defense to provide the President with "options" from which to choose.

Everyone knew about how the inflexibility of each combatant's war-mobilization plans had inexorably sparked the opening volleys of World War I, against the desires and better judgments of all political leaders concerned. "Options," "flexible response," "controlled escalation" became buzz words of the Kennedy Administration. It was only natural that Kaufmann's counterforce briefing would have an irresistible, if somewhat desperate, appeal.

There was another reason why McNamara latched on to the counterforce/no-cities idea. Between the WSEG-50 and Kaufmann briefings, McNamara had journeyed to the headquarters of the Strategic Air Command at Offutt Air Force Base, outside Omaha, Nebraska, to be briefed by General Tommy Power and his staff on the Single Integrated Operational Plan—the SIOP, the U.S. military's general nuclear war plan. What he saw and heard in Omaha was so macabre, shallow and horrifying that by the time he got back to Washington, he was eager to find some way not only to control the Joint Chiefs' appetite for more nuclear weapons, but also to control the pace and scope of a nuclear war. Some combination of WSEG-50's weapons recommendations and William Kaufmann's no-cities strategy seemed just the recipe.

18 THE SIOP AND
THE ROAD TO ANN ARBOR

O
N THE SURFACE, the SIOP was a creation of Thomas S.
Gates, Jr., Secretary of Defense in the last year of the Eisenhower
Administration. By mid-1960—Gates ordered the establishment of
a SIOP on August 16—it was becoming all too clear that nuclear
weapons were multiplying out of control. Each Air Force Command had control over the detailed war planning of its own nuclear arsenal, as did the Navy fleets and the Army units with their
battlefield weapons. With the Navy's Polaris submarine about to
come on line, the confusion would worsen.

Gates believed it was dangerous, foolish and wasteful for the
United States to have so many different plans for the straightforward and relatively inflexible mission of nuclear retaliation. As
things stood, many targets in the Soviet Union would be struck by
American weapons twice, three times, or more. All strategic nuclear weapons, Gates thought, should be integrated under a single
planning command and targeted according to that command's direction. Hence, the Single Integrated Operational Plan.

In fact, however, the idea of a SIOP originated not with Gates
but with the Air Staff. While some Air Force officers too were worried about duplication of targeting in the war plans of the day,
their main motivation in promoting the idea of a SIOP was the
same as their reason for suddenly adopting Kaufmann's counter-
force/no-cities strategy—to fight off the Navy, to maintain SAC's
preeminent position in the strategic-nuclear business in the face
of the challenge from Polaris. By 1960, it was clear that Polaris
could not be stopped. So the strategy behind SIOP was to co-opt
the Polaris, to take it out of the hands of the Navy and place it
firmly under the wings of SAC.

The Air Staff's original position, ardently advocated by General Tommy White, Air Force Chief of Staff, was to create a unified
"Strategic Command," putting SAC in charge of all the strategic
weapons of all the Air Force commands *and* of the Navy fleets, including the new Polaris missiles. By June 1960, White was con-

263

vinced by his staff that the Strategic Command notion would not wash: resistance from the Army and the Navy in the working committees of the JCS was too heated, too adamant. White adopted what he had previously planned as a "fallback position" for the Air Force: creating a Joint Strategic Target Planning Agency, which would maintain the separate services but which would integrate the targeting of all their weapons and designate the Commander in Chief of SAC as the Director of Strategic Targeting. On June 14, SAC gave Tom Gates a briefing called "Unity in the Strategic Offensive." It argued the case for such an agency, which would produce a National Strategic Target List (NSTL) and a Single Integrated Operational Plan (SIOP) under the direction of the SAC Commander.

Gates was easily persuaded that military planning needed integration. In his brief tenure as Secretary of Defense, he was finding the behavior of the Joint Chiefs increasingly appalling. They seemed incapable of arriving at common decisions. Even their intelligence estimates of Soviet military strength wildly differed from one another's, and were obviously geared to justify their own parochial interests at the expense of the nation's. In August 1959, the Chairman of the JCS, General Nathan Twining, had asked the Chiefs for answers to eighteen basic questions—"The 18 Questions," they came to be called—on nuclear targeting. By the time of the SAC briefing ten months later, the Chiefs had yet to agree on answers to any of them, which to Gates made the SAC presentation all the more compelling.

On July 6, Gates met with Eisenhower to recommend the creation of a SIOP just as the SAC briefing of three weeks earlier had outlined. Present nuclear targeting plans, he told Eisenhower, were a mess. There was duplication, triplication of coverage on 200 or 300 targets in the Soviet Union. The Navy did not plan to deliver some of its nuclear weapons on board aircraft carriers until fifteen days into the war. Also like the briefing, Gates argued that SAC should serve as SIOP center. SAC had the resources, the methodology, the computers already at hand.

By early August, Admiral Arleigh Burke, Chief of Naval Operations, got wind of what the Air Force was up to. One of his aides happened to be over at the Weapons Systems Evaluation Group to transmit some technical data, at the group's request. Two Air Force officers also happened to be there, and they started to tease him. "At last," one of them said, "we've got control of the Polaris."

"What are you talking about?" Burke's man asked.

"We've got it in the bag. The decision's been made," the Air Force rep snickered. "All you have to do is find out about it."

After hearing this report, Burke did some investigating and found out about the SIOP and the real purpose behind it. When it came to protecting the Navy, Arleigh Burke had no match. When it came to fending off threats from the other services, Burke was even more sensitive, protective, and paranoid than his Air Force counterpart, Tommy White. And when it came to the Polaris submarine, these sorts of dangers and threats made Burke's blood boil. The Polaris was Burke's conception: he had pushed it through an unwilling Navy bureaucracy, he had calculated the technical requirements, he had helped devise the doctrine that justified it strategically, he had led the assault on the Air Force, using the Polaris as the opening wedge of the attack. Burke knew he was in a bureaucratic shooting war, and he wasn't about to let the Air Force get hold of his Polaris.

Arleigh Burke counted a few Air Force officers among his friends, but he hated the Air Force as an organization. "This is just like Communism being here in the country," he said after catching on to the Air Force's SIOP ambitions. "It needn't have happened that Lumumba can take over a country, or that Castro, with a very few people and no following at the beginning, can take over a country, with a well-disciplined force, small but well-disciplined. It doesn't have to happen that way. It just does." To Burke's mind, that was just what was happening now, with the Air Force doing to national security what Castro had done in Cuba. "They're smart and they're ruthless," he warned Navy secretary William Franke. "It's the same way as the Communists. It's exactly the same techniques."

When one of Burke's aides remarked that the Air Force's motives were decent, that "they think they are doing the best thing they know how for the country," Burke replied, "You're more generous than I am. . . . They're dishonest. They're dishonest and they know it." In Burke's mind, "they have no feeling at all that they are responsible for anything but the Air Force. . . . They have no responsibility for anything else, and they will wreck the United States. They are perfectly willing to wreck the JCS and they're doing the best to wreck it."

"This is the Communist thing," said the aide, now doing his best to go along with the Chief.

"The Communist thing," Burke chimed in, "to wreck it."

Gates and Eisenhower certainly had a point in endorsing integration of the nuclear war plans. The Air Force and the Navy would soon be adding thousands of new weapons to their arsenals; operational planning was getting far too loose and way out of control. But Burke understood—and knew that White and Power also understood—the politics underlying war plans in a way that Gates and Eisenhower apparently did not. Burke knew that whichever service controlled the target list, made the rules and defined the criteria of what degree of damage must be inflicted on what targets with what probability, would in effect be the service that decided how those weapons would be used, how many weapons of what type the nation should buy, how much money should be spent on each service's nuclear weapons.

Burke feared that if SAC were allowed to invent the definitions and criteria, "then our budget is going to be in a very sad way indeed. We'll be buying B-70s." He feared that SAC would invent "damage-expectancy" numbers that required SAC to build a lot more bombers. If, for example, they said that a certain target had to be destroyed with 90 percent probability and if the calculations showed that one bomb could destroy it with only 65 percent probability, then SAC would have a reason to drop more than one bomb on the target and, therefore, would "need" to buy another bomb for each target. He also feared that SAC would give the Polaris missiles such tasks as destroying Soviet air-defense sites, "paving the way for the B-52s," or hitting highly blast-resistant targets, which the inaccurate Polaris missiles could not destroy, thus proving "that it takes sixty-seven of them to knock out this target." In other words, if the Air Force had failed to eliminate the Polaris or to steal it away under the guise of a "unified Strategic Command," then through the SIOP they would assign it to trivial targets or to targets that it could not hit, further reinforcing SAC's domination in the strategic-warfare game.

Burke's predictions and fears came close to the truth. From the first SIOP Planning Conference, chaired by Tommy Power on August 24, it was clear that SAC was very much in control and intended to remain there. Army and Navy officers were assigned to certain billets, but SAC had 1,300 men in Omaha who could work on SIOP, a presence with which the other services could not hope to compete.

Moreover, from day one, Power and his staff began to fiddle

with the "damage-expectancy" numbers. On August 19, the JCS had issued a National Strategic Target and Attack Plan (NSTAP), commonly called the N-Stap, which laid down the criteria and definitions for the Target List and the SIOP. In one passage, the NSTAP stated that the National Strategic Target List (NSTL) "will consist of a *minimum number* of specific targets whose timely and assured destruction will accomplish the specific objectives. . . ." It had been the Navy's interpretation that the NSTAP meant for there to be a "minimum number" of targets specified on the Target List, just enough to "accomplish the specific objectives." However, at the August 24 SIOP conference, General Bob Smith, SAC Intelligence chief, directed that the NSTAP would be interpreted to mean that there was a "minimum number" below which the SIOP committee could not go; that, in other words, the NSTAP specified no upper limit, that the list could specify as many targets as the U.S. had strategic weapons to hit.

It was a subtle distinction, but a critical one. By the Navy's definition of "minimum number," the SIOP would be a war plan that allocated just enough weapons to "accomplish the specific objectives," and no more. Consistent with the Navy's own doctrine of "finite deterrence," it would suggest an upper limit to the number of nuclear weapons that SAC could build and deploy. By SAC's definition, on the other hand, the SIOP would amount to firing off all the weapons at once, with no logical limits on how many targets the U.S. would have to destroy to accomplish those objectives and, therefore, no limit on the number of weapons needed. From the beginning, then, the most important definition of all tilted very much in SAC's favor.

As the months transpired, there was more of the same. Everywhere SAC Intelligence looked, they found targets, thus justifying the need for more weapons. They thought the Soviets would have 700 ICBMs by 1962, the Navy thought there would be only 200; the Air Force won the battle, to the extent there was one, with the result of 500 extra targets, requiring more than 500 extra weapons. Similarly, SAC listed 1,115 airfields that should be targeted; the Navy analysts found only 770. SAC also assumed a very high attrition rate for their bombers that would be destroyed on the ground, those that would be shot down by Soviet missiles and interceptors, and those that would fail to perform or miss their targets. If, subsequently, the operational alert force were only one-third the size of the total force, then that meant that the total

SAC bomber force would have to be tripled. Meanwhile, as Burke anticipated, most Polaris missiles were shunted off to hit surface-to-air missile sites or wasted on targets that they had scant chance of destroying alone.

The NSTAP had specified that there be at least a 75 percent chance of destroying certain targets. Power and his staff pounced on those magic words "at least." They initially specified that the 202 most important targets be destroyed with 97 percent probability, the next 400 targets with 93 percent. Eventually, this was modified, but in the final result of the first SIOP, 7 targets had to be destroyed with 97 percent assurance, 213 with 95 percent assurance, 592 with at least 90 percent, and 715 with at least 80 percent. This meant, just as Burke had predicted, that a lot of targets would be hit with a lot of weapons. For example, nine weapons were to be "laid down" on four targets in Leningrad, twenty-three weapons on six target complexes in Moscow, eighteen on seven target areas in Kaliningrad. The average target would receive 2.2 weapons, almost all of them several megatons in explosive power.

Moreover, the calculations that produced these "requirements" took into account only the effects of blast, not the other effects of a nuclear explosion, such as heat, fire and radiation. Blast was much easier to calculate than the other effects; but omitting the others altogether drastically understated the damage done by a single bomb and, therefore, overstated the number of weapons needed to do the damage specified.

Meanwhile, naval analysts on the scene calculated that even if only one weapon were exploded over each target area in the SIOP, the radioactive fallout produced over Helsinki, Berlin, northern Japan and South Korea by such an attack would exceed the maximum safety limits established by the JCS. As one Navy officer put it, "our weapons can be a hazard to ourselves as well as to our enemy."

From beginning to end, the SIOP sharply exaggerated the number and size of bombs needed to damage all types of targets. On November 3, George Kistiakowsky, chairman of Eisenhower's Science Advisory Committee, traveled to SAC headquarters for three days, at the request of the President, to be briefed on the status of the SIOP. Arleigh Burke had planted suspicions about SAC's manipulations through Eisenhower's naval aide, E. P. Aurand, arousing Eisenhower to have Kistiakowsky check out the rumors. "Kisty" brought along one of his aides, a weapons scientist named George Rathjens, and the Deputy Director for Science and Technology of the CIA, Herbert "Pete" Scoville. In Omaha, Rathjens looked through SAC's atlas of Soviet cities, searching for the town that most closely resembled Hiroshima in size and industrial concentration. When he found one that roughly matched, he asked how many bombs the SIOP "laid down" on that city. The reply: one 4.5 *megaton* bomb and three more 1.1 *megaton* weapons in case the big bomb was a dud. The explosive yield of the atomic bomb that destroyed one-third of Hiroshima on August 6, 1945, was a relatively puny 12.5 *kilotons*.

SAC—or its SIOP incarnation, the Joint Strategic Target Planning Staff, the JSTPS—finished the SIOP on December 14, 1960, just as Eisenhower had ordered. It was labeled SIOP-62, meaning that it was to go into effect in fiscal year 1962, which would begin June 1961. It called for shooting off, as quickly as possible, the entire portion of the U.S. strategic nuclear force that was on alert, 1,459 nuclear bombs, ranging from ten kilotons to twenty-three megatons, totaling 2,164 megatons in all, against 654 targets—military and urban-industrial, simultaneously, in accordance with SAC's "optimum-mix" strategy—in the U.S.S.R., Red China and Eastern Europe. China was targeted because it was part of the "Sino-Soviet Bloc," Eastern Europe because it hosted hundreds of Soviet air-defense radar and missile sites, which had to be "taken out" so that SAC bombers could fly safely through the corridors leading to the Russian heartland. JSTPS calculated that the U.S. alert force alone would kill 175 million Russians and Chinese.

If the entire force were launched—and this is what was called for if the U.S. fired a preemptive first-strike—the attack would involve 3,423 nuclear weapons, totaling 7,847 megatons; it would kill 285 million Russians and Chinese and severely injure 40 million more. None of these figures included the millions of casualties in Eastern Europe or the fallout victims in the free world.

In mid-December, Secretary of Defense Tom Gates, along with several Pentagon officials and the Joint Chiefs, listened to one of Tommy Power's aides run down all the facts and figures of SIOP-62 in a lengthy briefing. They heard it two days in a row— the first by themselves, the second with a slightly broader audience including the service secretaries. After the second presentation, Gates asked the Chiefs what they thought. Tommy White of the Air Force, naturally, thought it was splendid. The Army and Navy Chiefs, George Decker and Arleigh Burke, privately thought it excessive, but they knew when they were outgunned and Burke personally was contemplating how to take over the SIOP when the new Kennedy Administration came into office; so they too, though less enthusiastically, expressed general approval.

Then General David Shoup, Commandant of the Marine Corps, spoke up. The Marines had virtually no involvement in the nuclear game, so Shoup could take a position as close as possible to that of an outsider while still sitting on the JCS. The day before, during the first JSTPS briefing, Shoup had been bothered by a graph that showed tens of millions of Chinese being killed by the U.S. attack. He had asked General Power what would happen if the Chinese were not fighting in the war. "Do we have any options so that we don't have to hit China?" he inquired.

"Well, yeh, we *could* do that," Power reluctantly replied, squirming in his front-row seat, "but I hope nobody thinks of it because it would really screw up the plan."

As the nation's military leaders endorsed SIOP-62 before the Secretary of Defense, David Shoup stood and said, "Sir, any plan that kills millions of Chinese when it isn't even their war is not a good plan. This is not the American way."

This was the SIOP on which Robert McNamara was briefed when he journeyed to SAC headquarters for the weekend of February 3, 1961, two weeks into the Kennedy Administration, one week after he had heard the WSEG-50 briefing, one week before he would hear the Kaufmann no-cities briefing. Traveling with McNamara were his Deputy Secretary of Defense, Roswell Gilpatric; Chairman of the JCS, General Lyman Lemnitzer; Marvin Stern; and Herbert York, Eisenhower's Director of Defense Research & Engineering who had agreed to stay on for the first two months of the Kennedy Administration.

If Tommy Power and his aides had hoped to faze or dazzle McNamara, as they had others, with their vast array of charts, detail, numbers and "computer science," they came away from the briefing disappointed. McNamara knew numbers and statistics better than any of them, and his experiences in World War II had convinced him that the military hardly held a monopoly on military wisdom. He quickly grasped the connection between the extremely high "damage-expectancy" numbers and the "requirements" for an immense arsenal of strategic weapons, especially of SAC bombers. He realized, and pointed out, that firing four weapons on a single "designated-ground-zero" to ensure that at least one weapon would wreak the desired damage was wasteful, and that the fallout produced by such an attack would be "fantastic." The whole way that the JSTPS had done the calculations, he said, was excessively conservative; the number of Soviet casualties and the destruction of Soviet industry would actually be much higher than SIOP-62 suggested. McNamara said all of this unabashedly.

In an effort to prove his point, he asked a question only slightly different from that which George Rathjens had posed when he toured SAC with George Kistiakowsky the previous November: using the JSTPS methodology, how much was "needed" to do the same damage that a 12.5-kiloton bomb had done against Hiroshima at the end of World War II? A quick calculation revealed that SIOP-62 would have "laid down" three eighty-kiloton weapons. Herbert York, a physicist who had been involved in work on the H-bomb during the early days of the Livermore Lab, interjected to explain that three eighty-kiloton bombs carried about the same explosive power as a single half-megaton bomb.

There was something else that troubled NcNamara. What SAC labeled "Plan 1-A" of SIOP-62—suggesting that it was the basic plan—called for an all-out preemptive first-strike against the U.S.S.R., Eastern Europe and Red China, in response to an actual or merely impending Soviet invasion of Western Europe that involved no nuclear weapons at all. That was the crux of SIOP: a first-strike plan that held back nothing, that killed hundreds of millions of people, just because they lived under Communist rule, without any Communist government's having so much as scratched a square inch of the United States. As much as anyone else who had witnessed this spectacle, if not more so, Robert McNamara was horrified.

The capper came from General Tommy Power. Not the least appalling detail of SIOP-62 was the virtual obliteration of the tiny country of Albania—even though it had dramatically dissociated itself from the policies of the U.S.S.R.—simply because within its borders sat a huge Soviet air-defense radar, which, according to the SIOP, had to be taken out with high assurance. As Power was leading McNamara and his entourage outside the briefing room after finishing the presentation, he smiled at McNamara and said, with a mock straight face, "Well, Mr. Secretary, I hope you don't have any friends or relations in Albania, because we're just going to have to wipe it out."

McNamara stopped in his tracks for a moment and glared at Power with all the contempt he could muster.

The close look at SIOP-62 made McNamara far more receptive to William Kaufmann's no-cities briefing one week later than he might otherwise have been. Kaufmann briefed McNamara on February 10. In the next few days, Charlie Hitch, Alain Enthoven and Marvin Stern gave McNamara the paper on strategic-nuclear-war forces and policy that McNamara had assigned them almost immediately upon arriving at the Pentagon. Their proposals included placing a premium on "survivable" forces and thus accelerating a program of hardening Minuteman ICBMs and building mobile Polaris missiles; slowing the procurement of—in some cases, phasing out—bombers; placing a higher percentage of bombers on airborne alert or in protective shelters; comparing the merits of forces generally according to their cost effectiveness; and, not least, adopting a new nuclear war plan that would emphasize destroying enemy military forces, avoiding their cities and protecting a ready reserve force aimed at their cities but withholding this force as a bargaining lever with which to coerce the enemy to end the war and come to terms favorable to the United States.

In short, the Hitch-Enthoven-Stern paper represented an amalgamation of the three main intellectual strands that had developed inside the strategic community at the RAND Corporation over the previous decade: the studies on SAC vulnerability by Albert Wohlstetter and his clique, of which Enthoven was a devoted member; the work in systems analysis started by Ed Paxson and elaborated extensively by, among others, Hitch; and the counterforce/no-cities strategy that grew out of Bernard Brodie's work in the Air Staff in 1951, evolved through the sessions with Brodie, Hitch, Andrew Marshall and others in the RAND Strategic Objectives Committee through the mid-1950s, and climaxed with the counterforce briefing by William Kaufmann.

McNamara approved the whole package, using it as the basis for his first five-year plan on nuclear weapons systems, called "The General War Offensive Package," written in late February. At this stage, however, the counterforce/no-cities idea was still little more than a piece of paper in the Office of the Secretary of Defense, and quite contrary to the spirit and substance of the official SIOP. Now the guidance for a new war plan had to be extended throughout the military.

Dozens of unsettled issues about defense policy were darting about in McNamara's mind. On March 1, McNamara issued to the service secretaries, the Joint Chiefs, his own assistant secretaries and special assistants, his counsel and his director of research and engineering a thirteen-page document, which he drafted personally. It was a list of ninety-six projects and questions that McNamara wanted completed and answered, each assigned to a particular office, many of them with an unreasonably early due date specified. At the time, the Whiz Kids were known in military circles as "McNamara's Band," and so the list of assigned projects came to be called "The 96 Trombones." (One week later, McNamara issued a revised list with only ninety-two questions, but the name "96 Trombones" stuck.)

The first two projects on the list were directly responsive to the issues raised in the Kaufmann briefing. The first: "Prepare a draft memorandum revising the basic national security policies and assumptions, including the assumptions relating to 'counterforce' strikes. . . ." The second: "Prepare a 'doctrine' which, if accepted, would permit controlled response and negotiating pauses in the event of thermonuclear attack." The first, due May 1, was sent to the Chairman of the JCS and to the office of the Assistant Secretary of Defense for International Security Affairs. The second, due April 17, was tasked only to the JCS Chairman, General Lyman Lemnitzer.

Lemnitzer replied to Project No. 2 on April 18, one day late, reporting "that we do not now have adequate defenses, nor are our nuclear retaliatory forces sufficiently invulnerable, to permit us to risk withholding a substantial part of our effort, once a major thermonuclear attack has been initiated." Therefore, he concluded, "attempts at the present time to implement such a doctrine, or to declare such an intent, would be premature and could gravely weaken our deterrent posture."

McNamara was in the process of ordering steps to make the strategic forces less vulnerable. Indeed, his motivation for doing so was not only to deter a Soviet first-strike, but also to do just what Lemnitzer said was nearly impossible to do in early 1961—

"to permit us to risk withholding a substantial part" of the nuclear force as part of a "controlled response," or "counterforce/no-cities," doctrine.

But these fine points were not of much concern to Lemnitzer, nor to most other military officers dealing with nuclear policy. In truth, they simply wanted no part of, and wanted to do their best to frustrate, any work on doctrines promoting "controlled response" and "negotiating pauses." The whole idea went against the grain of military thinking, which was much more in accord with the philosophy of SAC and SIOP-62: the bomb was massive and raw; that was its chief virtue; and you don't frighten or, if necessary, destroy the Communists by restraining its power. Project No. 2 made some of the Chiefs and their aides uneasy, made them wonder whether this Secretary of Defense, as well as the President of the United States, who was also suspected of harboring queasy feelings about the massive destructiveness of the H-bomb, would really be man enough to use the thing if the Free World's survival depended on it. The image that Kennedy and McNamara intellectualized war accentuated the feelings of distrust already alienating the military establishment from the Pentagon Whiz Kids. The distrust worked the other way, as well: McNamara and his assistants were contemptuous of the military mind for treating the mind-boggling topic of nuclear war so crudely, for failing to comprehend that any such war would be a two-way war.

Lemnitzer had another objection to the "controlled response" notion: "the advantages to be achieved by limiting our responses, under such conditions, could only be realized by the enforcement upon the Soviets of a degree of tacit 'cooperation' which does not now appear realistic." This had troubled McNamara, too, during the Kaufmann briefing: it takes two to fight a controlled nuclear war, and how would we know that the Soviets, contrary to everything that their leaders said on the subject in public, would play along? In the meantime, however, SIOP-62 had to be replaced with something more controlled, more discriminating, so that McNamara—and the world—could avoid being plagued with its excessive "requirements" for more nuclear weapons and, in the event of "general war," its monstrously catastrophic consequences.

Project No. 1 of McNamara's 96 Trombones—"Prepare a draft memorandum revising the basic national security policies and assumptions, including the assumptions relating to 'counterforce' strikes. . . ."—elicited a much more sympathetic response. In the International Security Affairs office, the Assistant Secretary of Defense, Paul Nitze, turned the project over to Harry Rowen, who in turn gave it to his very close friend from RAND, now a Pentagon consultant, Daniel Ellsberg. To Rowen, Dan Ellsberg was the ideal man to work on Project No. 1. Just out of Harvard graduate school, before joining RAND full-time, Ellsberg had made something of a splash in the academic world with a series of lectures on "The Art of Coercion," which used Game Theory to illustrate how nations bluff, coerce and blackmail one another in wars, crises and diplomacy. At RAND, Ellsberg came under the wings of the Wohlstetter clique on SAC vulnerability and firmly attached himself to elements of the Kaufmann philosophy as well.

More than this, Ellsberg was one of the very few civilians anywhere who was intimately familiar with the military's war plans. In the fall of 1959, RAND had loaned Ellsberg to the Office of Naval Research, under Admiral Harry Felt of the Pacific Command, to do a study on the security and efficiency of command-control-communications systems for nuclear war. Ellsberg felt that to do the study well he had to see the war plans, and got permission from Felt to go into the Top Secret cage at the Command and look at anything he wanted. He read all the war plans that affected the Pacific Command, not just the high-level JCS directives but the operational plans and procedures affecting individual fleets and carriers. No one had ever read the plans beyond one level above and below that of his own set of instructions. Thus no one had any idea of the enormous discrepancies between the basic guidance furnished by the Joint Chiefs of Staff and the orders as they finally emerged in the specific instruction to the ship's commanding officer in the fleet.

The basic mission of the Pacific Command, or PacCom, in the event of nuclear war, was to bomb cities in Red China. For one thing, those were the easiest targets to hit for attack airplanes flying off carriers based in the Pacific Ocean. One of Ellsberg's most shocking discoveries was that if the JCS instructed PacCom to hit military targets in Russia instead, the fleet would almost certainly end up hitting cities in China anyway. A particular command's war plans are only consistent with its geographic deployment, training practices and alert procedures. And all of these were geared to hitting cities in China. In the cascade of messages that would be sent down from the top level to the next level to

headquarters to command to carrier, there was no easy way to
alter the Emergency Action Message so that the mission could be
so radically changed.

In the spring of 1960, Ellsberg spent a good deal of time in
Washington, D.C., exploring the war plans even more deeply.
While visiting the National Military Command Center, the War
Room in the Pentagon, he discovered that the officers transmit-
ting the alert codes did not have copies of the messages that were,
in turn, being sent to lower levels of command. When Ellsberg
asked the Duty Officer to see the book that decoded the messages,
the officer could not find it. At every level of the war plan, then,
Ellsberg found a rote set of reactions, confusion, inflexibility, virtually no practical way to modify the all-out, hit-everything-at-once
character of the official war plan.

It was also in Washington that Ellsberg met a group of fairly
like-minded colonels in the Air Force Staff—especially Glenn
Kent, Russell Dougherty, Ernie Cragg and Bob Lukeman—who,
after hearing Ellsberg describe the shocking state of affairs in the
Pacific, let him in on some of the official JCS and Air Force war
plans as well, and talked with him about these plans for several
days, six to eight hours at a time. It turned out that these plans
were terribly inflexible as well.

SAC had always insisted that there be essentially one war
plan—a few "options" to adjust for differences in the weather or
various conditions of warning time, but fundamentally a single
plan. Especially in the days before very fast computers, devising
one war plan was difficult enough. Every detail had to be pre-
planned so that bombers would hook up with in-flight refueling
tankers at just the right time, go on to destroy their targets at just
the right time, and return to base. In all of this, there was a phenomenon to be avoided called "interference." When one airplane
dropped its bombs, SAC wanted to make sure that another pilot
would not be flying just overhead, only to be killed by the bomb's
blast or blinded by the flash of the fireball. Avoiding this "interference" required very complicated flight paths; the timing had to be
precise, down to the minute.

Yet Ellsberg also learned some facts that made SAC's rationale for having just one war plan appear ludicrous. The communication of Emergency Action Messages often got so scrambled in
exercises that different SAC bases would receive the message to
"Go" as much as four hours apart from one another. Then the

wind differed from place to place and day to day, which also affected flight times. These two factors alone would completely wreck all efforts by the war planners to set off explosions over Russian targets simultaneously and to avoid the "interference" that might prevent a few bombardiers from executing their missions. The finely detailed coordination built into the war plan in fact had little bearing on what would actually happen in a nuclear war. Ellsberg also knew that the SAC planners themselves must realize this, suggesting that all the talk about avoiding "interference" was a ruse, a way of excusing SAC and the Air Force from working so hard on devising alternative war plans, a further barrier justifying the all-out, max-effort, bomb-everything philosophy of nuclear war deeply embedded in SAC's collective psyche.

The Air Force colonels also showed Ellsberg one of the most tightly held documents in the JCS files—the JSCP, the Joint Strategic Capabilities Plan, referred to as the J-Scap. The JSCP was the war plan; Annex C of the JSCP, the Atomic Annex, specified the guidance for nuclear attacks. No civilian had seen the JSCP before—not the Secretary of Defense, not the President. They were shown something called the JSOP, the Joint Strategic Operational Plan, which was similar but not precisely the same. One feature of the JSCP, but not the JSOP, was a definition of "General War": "A general war is an armed conflict in which Armed Forces of the U.S.S.R. and those of the United States are overtly and directly engaged." In 1958, the Army had tried to add to this sentence the phrase, "as principal protagonists with the national survival of both deemed to be at issue," but the Air Force succeeded in removing the amendment. And in general war, the U.S. Emergency War Plan—the nuclear war plan, which was superseded in late 1960 by the SIOP—would be executed.

To Ellsberg, the implications were staggering. The military's nuclear war plan was a single war plan, calling for blowing up all enemy targets in Russia, China and Eastern Europe as quickly as possible, with the chances of restraining or redirecting the attack remote at best. Ellsberg saw that the JSCP, the terms defining the overall war plan, called for carrying out this nuclear attack whenever the U.S. and the U.S.S.R. directly engaged in battle, however tentatively, over however grand or trivial a cause. Ellsberg, at this time, was an extremely hardline Cold Warrior. After taking his doctorate exams at Harvard in 1953, he had enlisted in the Marine Corps (hardly typical for a budding Ivy League Ph.D. candidate), became a company commander and, in 1956, extended his duty when his battalion was sent to the Mediterranean, savoring the prospect of possible combat in the Suez crisis. Ellsberg truly believed, as did most of his comrades at RAND, that some sort of armed conflict between the superpowers would erupt in the coming decade. Seeing that the military planned on automatically escalating the conflict to all-out nuclear war terrified him.

When Ellsberg returned to RAND, Kaufmann was just beginning work on his counterforce/no-cities study. Ellsberg played no role in it, but he recognized its significance. He disagreed with one crucial aspect—the degree to which Kaufmann was emphasizing the counterforce element of the strategy. Ellsberg agreed that the targets hit should be counterforce in nature, but he knew that several Soviet air bases and command centers lay near cities; trying to destroy *all* the counterforce targets would therefore wreck the attempt to avoid damaging enemy cities. And it was the no-cities aspect of the strategy that caught Ellsberg's eye. He saw it as the one hope of avoiding the murderous and suicidal policy of the JSCP.

On April 7, 1961, Ellsberg's thirtieth birthday, and eleven days before Lyman Lemnitzer turned in his dissent against a "controlled response" to Robert NcNamara, Ellsberg finished a draft of the revisions for a basic national security policy that McNamara had requested as Project No. 1 of his 96 Trombones five weeks earlier. Ellsberg's draft suggested a strategy for achieving U.S. wartime objectives "while limiting the destructiveness of warfare. . . . Specifically, the United States does not hold all the people of Russia, China or the [East European] Satellite nations responsible for the acts of their governments. Consequently, it is not an objective of the United States to maximize the number of people killed in the Communist Bloc in the event of war." In fact, "attacks against high governmental and military command centers, or indiscriminate initial attacks on all major urban-industrial centers would fail to inhibit punitive retaliation by surviving enemy units, but would instead eliminate the possibility that enemy responses could be controlled or terminated to U.S. advantage." Over and again, Ellsberg stressed the need for a durable reserve force and an enduring command-control apparatus, which had no place in the JSCP's Atomic Annex or in the subsequent SIOP-62. "In particular," he wrote, in a passage that most reflected the Kaufmann briefing, "alternative options should include counterforce operations carefully avoiding major enemy cities while retaining U.S. ready residual forces to threaten those [urban-industrial] targets."

In May, one month before SIOP-62 was scheduled to go into effect, McNamara signed the Ellsberg memorandum as his own and sent it to the Joint Chiefs as his basic initial guidance for a revised SIOP-63.

Meanwhile, Ellsberg was crusading all over official Washington, telling McGeorge Bundy at the NSC, Walt Rostow at the State Department, Paul Nitze and Roswell Gilpatric at the Pentagon all about the horrors of the JSCP, urging them to change its definition of "general war" so that an armed conflict between the U.S. and the Russians would not inevitably escalate into nuclear war of any sort. With practically every national security adviser in the Administration—and the President himself—keen on building up non-nuclear forces, this effort succeeded and the following year's JSCP was changed accordingly.

Over the summer, Alain Enthoven and Frank Trinkl took Ellsberg's revised SIOP guidance and elaborated it into greater detail, ordering that Soviet targets be divided into five separate categories: (1) strategic forces, meaning air bases, missile sites and submarine pens; (2) air-defense sites away from cities; (3) air-defense sites closer to cities; (4) command-control centers; and (5) the all-out strike against Soviet cities. The revised SIOP-63 was to allow for options successively combining these categories. Only the least destructive, most purely counterforce option would be exercised in the initial U.S. strike; then, if the war escalated beyond that level, that option would be combined with the second, and then with the third, then the fourth—and finally, but only if all other options had been exhausted and if the war could not be kept under control, or if the Soviets did not follow our signals of restraint and "controlled response," Option Five, the all-out strike that dominated the existing SIOP. There were also to be suboptions, providing for a choice on whether the weapons should be airburst or groundburst, high yield or lower yield, "clean" or "dirty." Finally, Enthoven and Trinkl, under McNamara's signature, directed that there should be "country withholds," allowing the President to hit or avoid hitting any targets at all in China or Eastern Europe or both. The watchwords were those that informed the Kaufmann briefing: control, flexibility, discrimination, options.

Some features of certain weapons systems would have to be changed to make all this practical—not only a new emphasis on hardened and mobile missiles rather than more vulnerable bombers, but also fine tuning command-control mechanisms governing the launching of the missiles, making it possible to fire only a few of them, or even a single missile, at a time, and building "options" into each missile's computer program so that it could be fired at one of several possible targets. Under the existing Minuteman ICBM program, the President would have to launch missiles in multiples of fifty if he wanted to launch any, and each ICBM was inflexibly programmed to strike one preselected target.

Marvin Stern, the Assistant Director for Strategic Systems in the Pentagon's R&D office, was ordered to see that the Air Force changed the Minuteman ICBM program accordingly. Stern, co-author of the Hitch-Enthoven-Stern "General War Offensive Package" of the previous February, had worked on the Atlas ICBM program at Convair in the mid-1950s, served on several expert panels dealing with the problems of early warning and accidental nuclear launches in the late 1950s, and accompanied McNamara and the others to SAC for the SIOP-62 briefing. He firmly believed that the changes should be made, and he knew that they were technically feasible. The Air Force, however, wanted no part of this "controlled response" business and simply refused to spend money on it, arguing that it was infeasible. Stern approached McNamara's general counsel, Cyrus Vance, and asked what could legally be done to prod the Air Force into action.

"Anything you can get away with," Vance replied.

Against all regulations and laws, Stern canceled Minuteman funding for one month, pending a commitment by the Air Force to improve command-control and develop a rapid retargeting program for the missile. In justifying the action, Stern spoke before a group of high-ranking military officers that Secretary of the Air Force Gene Zuckert and the new Air Force Chief of Staff, General Curtis LeMay, who had moved up when Tommy White retired, assembled to respond to Stern's fiscal pressure. Stern explained the changes that McNamara was making in the SIOP in a way that he thought would most logically appeal to his audience.

"If you really believe in the present SIOP," Stern told them, "then you agree that we should fire all the generals, because everything's worked out ahead of time. We're just going to fire off everything, and no generals have to be around to make decisions.

But as you know, wars don't happen that way. We need generals to make decisions."

The appeal was transparent to the entire audience but it worked. Besides, they knew that they would get no more money for Minuteman until they did what Stern—and, obviously, McNamara—wanted. They gave in, changed the command-control electronics and added "selective-launch" and eight "target-selection" features to each Minuteman, at a total cost, eventually, of $840 million.

Early that fall, to help him justify his defense budget to President Kennedy, McNamara asked Alain Enthoven to compose what he called "Draft Presidential Memorandums," or DPMs, one crisply written, fully detailed Top Secret exposition for each major segment of the budget. In 1961, there were only two DPMs—one for Strategic Nuclear Forces, one for General Purpose (non-nuclear) Forces. By 1968, there would be sixteen, including Mobility Forces, Land Forces, Tactical Air Forces, Theater Nuclear Forces and so forth. Throughout the McNamara years, the DPMs represented the most authoritative, analytical articulation of the rationale behind the defense budgets, policies and strategies. When a reporter once asked him if he planned to write memoirs, McNamara replied that he had already done the DPMs. "They're a far better source than any personal memoirs," he said.

The first DPM sent to President Kennedy, dated September 23, 1961, urged halting production of the B-52 bomber after 630 had been built and phasing out the B-47s and B-58s entirely, reasoning that missiles were more cost-effective than bombers, that missiles also had "greater survival potential and endurance in the wartime environment," and that because of their higher vulnerability, bombers "cannot be held in reserve to be used in a controlled and deliberate way." He lauded the Polaris submarine-launched missiles as weapons "ideal for counter-city retaliation" that "do not have to be launched early in the war . . . [and that therefore] can be held in reserve and used in a controlled and deliberate way. . . ."

In general, he rejected both "the extremes of a 'minimum deterrence' posture on the one hand"—which WSEG-50 had promoted—"or a 'full first-strike capability' on the other"—which Plan 1-A of SIOP-62 had so explicitly ordered. Rather, wrote Enthoven, with McNamara's approval, "The forces I am recommending have been chosen to provide the United States with the capability, in the event of a Soviet nuclear attack, first, to strike back against Soviet bomber bases, missile sites and other installations associated with long-range nuclear forces, in order to reduce Soviet power and limit the damage that can be done to us by vulnerable Soviet follow-on forces, while, second, holding in protected reserve forces capable of destroying the Soviet urban society, if necessary, in a controlled and deliberate way." These forces and this strategy, he continued, "should provide us with a capability to achieve a substantial military superiority over the Soviets even after they have attacked us." He made the same points one month later in a shorter budget memorandum to Kennedy that was also Top Secret but circulated more freely in the White House and Bureau of the Budget.

Several of Kennedy's White House and budget aides opposed the counterforce/no-cities idea, thought it would lead to an excessively large arsenal, and leaned instead toward a "minimum deterrence" position. But Kennedy had nearly absolute trust in Bob McNamara and shared his horror at the military's all-out SIOP-62 and the casual attitude that many military officers displayed toward the prospect of global destruction. Kennedy's brother Robert, who also tremendously admired the Secretary of Defense, once remarked only half jokingly, "Bob McNamara is the most dangerous man in the Cabinet because he is so persuasive and articulate."

By early 1962, McNamara and associates were ready to make the new strategy public. A few of the Whiz Kids, with some aid from McNamara himself, had already leaked its general outlines to Richard Fryklund, a reporter from *The Washington Star* to whom General Noel Parrish had leaked the Kaufmann briefing in 1960. In January, McNamara testified before congressional committees that a "major mission of the strategic retaliatory forces is to deter war by their capability to destroy the enemy's warmaking capabilities," and that the forces were being programmed so that Russian cities could be hit or spared.

On February 17, before the Fellows of the American Bar Foundation in Chicago, McNamara described his plan to protect command-control facilities, which would allow nuclear forces to "be used in several different ways. We may have to retaliate with a single massive attack. Or, we may be able to use our retaliatory forces to limit damage done to ourselves, and our allies, by knocking out the enemy's bases before he has had time to launch his second salvos. We may seek to terminate a war on favorable terms by using our forces as a bargaining weapon—by threatening further attack. In any case, our large reserve of protected firepower would give an enemy an incentive to avoid our cities and to stop a war."

The ultimate triumph of the RAND philosophy came in the spring and summer of 1962. It began when McNamara made plans to deliver a major policy address before the semiannual meeting of NATO's foreign and defense ministers in Athens on May 5. McNamara gave the job of writing the speech to Harry Rowen, who turned it over to his friend and consultant Bill Kaufmann. The only guidance Kaufmann received was that it should deal with initiatives in U.S. defense policy that concerned Europe, but he felt emboldened by McNamara's increasingly open advocacy of his own counterforce/no-cities strategy and so decided to base the speech on that theme.

There was another reason Kaufmann wanted to focus on counterforce. The British and especially the French were making loud noises about building their own independent nuclear-deterrent forces. French President Charles de Gaulle, in particular, was publicly raising disturbing doubts as to whether the United States could really be trusted to protect Western Europe with nuclear weapons if need be. The Russians, too, now had a nuclear arsenal. If the Soviets overwhelmingly invaded Europe, and if the U.S. responded by attacking Soviet cities with nuclear weapons, the Soviets would strike back at American cities. De Gaulle wondered whether the American President really would sacrifice Chicago for Bonn, New York for Paris. He doubted they would, and so sought to build up his own national arsenal, independent of the U.S. or NATO.

General de Gaulle's plans to let the Europeans have control over their own bombs reminded Kaufmann of the Speier-Goldhamer NATO game that he had played at RAND when he first came to Santa Monica in 1956. It was during that game that Kaufmann first found himself attracted to the counterforce/no-cities strategy: if we attacked the Soviets in such a way that we hit their military forces and explicitly avoided their cities, then the problem of America's credible commitment to NATO might be brushed aside; we wouldn't be sacrificing American cities for European cities because we would be trying to keep cities out of the war altogether. Kaufmann felt that McNamara's speech in Athens would be the ideal forum for conveying this same message to NATO ministers.

Just minutes into the speech, Kaufmann had McNamara explaining that "the U.S. has come to the conclusion that to the extent feasible, military strategy in general nuclear war should be approached in much the same way that more conventional military operations have been regarded in the past. That is to say, our principal military objectives, in the event of a nuclear war stemming from a major attack on the Alliance, should be the destruction of the enemy's military forces while attempting to preserve the fabric as well as the integrity of allied society. Specifically, our studies indicate that a strategy which targets nuclear forces only against cities or a mixture of civil and military targets has serious limitations for the purpose of deterrence and for the conduct of general nuclear war." Conversely, if deterrence fails and if the U.S. engaged "in a controlled and flexible nuclear response," the Kremlin would have "very strong incentives . . . to adopt similar strategies and programs," thus saving tens or hundreds of millions of lives on all sides and bringing the war to a rapid conclusion.

The problem, Kaufmann/McNamara concluded, with the notion of the Europeans building their own small, independent nuclear forces is that these arsenals would only be able to strike Soviet cities. (Indeed, statements by de Gaulle and such French strategists as André Beaufre and Pierre Gallois, among others, suggested that this was the essence of the French philosophy of deterrence.) And it would be "intolerable to have one segment of the Alliance force attacking the urban-industrial areas while, with the bulk of our forces, we were succeeding in destroying most of the enemies' nuclear capabilities. Such a failure in coordination might lead to the destruction of our hostages—the Soviet cities— just at a time at which our strategy of coercing the Soviets into stopping their aggression was on the verge of success." In sum, independent nuclear forces within NATO would, by nature, wreck the delicate strategy underlying the counterforce/no-cities concept.

Kennedy had emphasized to McNamara that in the speech he should "repeat to the point of boredom" that we would use nuclear weapons only in response to a major attack against the U.S. or the allies; that we were not contemplating preventive war; and that the Europeans should not believe that by firing off their own nuclear weapons they would drag the United States into a war, that we would withdraw our commitment to NATO first.

The British and especially the French found McNamara's speech interesting but less than persuasive. They didn't think that merely adopting the no-cities policy changed the new strategic equation that compelled them to deter war with their own nuclear forces; they didn't really believe that the Soviets would play along with McNamara's limited-nuclear-war game. De Gaulle had personally remarked to Paul Nitze, when Nitze had visited France nearly a year earlier, that the whole concept of "nuclear strategy" was absurd: nuclear weapons, he said, were bombs of mass destruction; you couldn't rationally fight a war with them; you could only deter war. McNamara's speech did not change many minds of that conviction.

Still, they were enthralled by the detailed rendering of U.S. strategic thought. So, when the University of Michigan in Ann Arbor invited McNamara to deliver the commencement address that June, he decided that he would read a trimmed-down, unclassified version of the Athens speech.

McNamara's special assistant, Adam Yarmolinsky, prepared a first draft, Dan Ellsberg revised it considerably, and Bill Kaufmann added some final touches. Ellsberg and Kaufmann did their work reluctantly: they didn't think that nuclear strategy should be discussed in detail so publicly; it would sound too grisly and macabre to the untrained ear. Also, along with many White House advisers, they thought it unwise to criticize the British and the French so directly in public. But McNamara was adamant on both counts. The gist of the counterforce/no-cities doctrine remained.

The days of massive retaliation and SIOP-62 were decisively finished. The age of flexible and controlled response and counterforce/no-cities options had unambiguously commenced. William Kaufmann, Charles Hitch, Alain Enthoven, Henry Rowen, Daniel Ellsberg and their colleagues in Santa Monica were gratified. More than a decade of development in the style of thinking at RAND, the attempt to impose order on the cataclysmic chaos of nuclear war, had been crowned with success.

But their triumph was short-lived. Over the next few years, the sharp vision of the New Strategy would gradually blur into an uncertain haze.

19 THE GAP THAT NEVER WAS

EVEN BEFORE Robert McNamara transformed the RAND philosophy into official U.S. policy, its underpinnings were beginning to collapse. The first sign that the RAND strategists may have been seeing things all wrong appeared in the very early days of the Kennedy Administration, when McNamara started to realize that the much vaunted and feared missile gap, which John F. Kennedy had ruthlessly exploited in the 1960 Presidential campaign, just might be a myth.

In the last year of the Eisenhower Administration, a great debate had erupted inside the intelligence community over the size of the Soviet ICBM force in the next few years, with estimates ranging from 50 to 200. Even these figures were little more than speculation, for the U-2 flights were picking up no evidence of ICBM deployment. Intelligence officials figured that there had to be some long-range missiles somewhere because they had long ago assumed that the Kremlin's objective in nuclear war would be to launch a devastating attack, probably a preemptive one, against major urban and military targets in the United States. They attributed the lack of evidence of Soviet weapons to the U-2's having photographed only a fraction of the Soviet landmass, and to the clouds and bad weather that often obscured a clear view.

On August 10, 1960, the U.S. launched the first fully successful orbit of a new strategic-reconnaissance satellite called the Discoverer. Many more launches followed. The Discoverer could take photographs from outer space, and its camera was so powerful and precise that when the pictures were dropped to earth, recovered and developed, an experienced photoanalyst could identify objects as small as thirty-six inches. The first photos were processed in November. They revealed the presence of four operational Soviet ICBMs at the missile-testing site at Plesetsk, in northern Russia. Communications intelligence and reports from spies had suggested that missiles were being deployed there, but the U-2 flights never had the chance to detect them; pilot Francis

Gary Powers had been on his way to Plesetsk on May 1, 1960, when a Soviet surface-to-air missile shot him down. Aside from these four ICBMs at Plesetsk, however, the Discoverer found nothing. Through the winter and spring, Discoverer snapped thousands of photos, but still found nothing.

Among the very first things that Robert McNamara did upon being sworn in as Secretary of Defense on January 20 was to go with his Deputy Secretary, Roswell Gilpatric, a former Undersecretary of the Air Force and a true believer in the missile gap, up to the Air Force photo-intelligence office on the fourth floor of the Pentagon. They spent hours at a time, for several days over a period of three weeks, scrutinizing the Discoverer photos. Even Air Force analysts were embarrassed by the pictures. The images starkly rebutted the estimates of Air Force Intelligence. The Soviet ICBM, the SS-6, was monstrously huge, heavy, cumbersome, required an equally enormous support and security apparatus, and would have to be transported on railroad tracks or extremely heavy roads. Discoverer was peering all along and around the railroad tracks and major highways throughout the Soviet Union, and finding nothing.

By early February, McNamara concluded that there was no missile gap. Still unfamiliar with many aspects of Washington ways, he said as much to a group of reporters, in what he thought were off-the-record remarks, the evening of February 6. Headlines appeared the next day. Not three weeks into office, the Kennedy Administration that was propelled into office partly on accusations of a missile gap now appeared to be acknowledging what President Eisenhower had told the nation all along—that, in the words of his last State of the Union Address, "The 'bomber gap' of several years ago was always a fiction, and the 'missile gap' shows every sign of being the same." McNamara responded to the headlines with qualifications and caveats, Kennedy announced that studies were still under way and it was too early to tell whether there was a missile gap or not, but the denials were rather tepid.

By early spring, the Discoverer had photographed virtually every square foot where the Soviets might possibly be testing, deploying or supporting ICBMs. In June, the CIA issued a National Intelligence Estimate concluding that the Soviets might already have 50 or 100 ICBM launchers and that they could have 100 to 200 by the following year. There was no evidence supporting this claim in the Discoverer photos or elsewhere. However, such an estimate still allowed the intelligence community to maintain its assumption concerning the basic Soviet strategy. With that many missiles, the Soviets could still destroy virtually all of the bases of the Strategic Air Command. However, the Army and the Navy footnotes to the Estimate, even more dramatically than before, contested that assumption, dissenting that the Soviets had "no more than a few" ICBMs either in mid-1961 or in the coming year.

Finally, by the end of the summer, the CIA and even Air Force Intelligence were forced to give in entirely. The assumption that the Soviets were planning to use their nuclear weapons to launch a devastating preemptive strike against SAC and other important targets in the continental United States had corrupted intelligence estimates for six years. In 1956, when some CIA economic analysts had challenged the NIEs that predicted a "bomber gap," their evidence was dismissed, largely because it failed to conform to this basic assumption about Soviet strategic goals— until, one year later, the Soviets appeared to shift tactics from bombers to ICBMs, at which point Air Force Intelligence could admit that the CIA was correct but that the basic assumptions of the Air Force, indeed of the entire intelligence community, were still valid, and that the Soviets would now pursue their aims through a massive missile buildup. As evidence of a missile buildup failed to materialize, the analysts made excuses. But then came the Discoverer satellites and still nothing materialized. Now they had to admit there was no bomber gap, no missile gap, no gap.

Only the officers of SAC Intelligence held out, for they had a critical interest in depicting an enormous Soviet threat. Without it, they would have a harder time justifying their own plans for thousands of U.S. bombers and 10,000 Minuteman ICBMs, plans that McNamara and his Whiz Kids were already jeopardizing. General James Walsh, SAC Intelligence chief, and his assistant, General George Keegan, put together a briefing meant to frighten the daylights out of anyone who heard it. Tommy Power himself delivered the briefing several times to Pentagon officials and panels composed of weapons scientists. On these occasions, Power unilaterally downgraded the classification level of some Discoverer photos to illustrate his point that the Russians were hiding ICBMs all over Russia. Photos of medieval towers, agricultural silos, a Crimean War memorial were depicted as cleverly disguised missile sites.

Right, Toward the end of World War II, General of the U.S. Army Air Forces Henry H. "Hap" Arnold organized a think tank that would let the military retain the permanent services of talented scientists who had contributed greatly to the war effort and who would otherwise return to civilian life once the peace was signed.

Above, The think tank became Air Force Project RAND, later the RAND Corporation, and over the next three decades would be considered the nation's leading center for intellectuals who based their careers on thinking about the bomb—how to deter nuclear war, how to fight nuclear war if it could not be deterred.

Bottom right, General Curtis LeMay, who led the bombing raids over Japan during the war, was RAND's first protector inside the Air Force bureaucracy. After he became Commander of the Strategic Air Command in the late 1940s and as RAND grew in power later on, he came to resent the "defense intellectuals" he once had overseen.

Left, Bernard Brodie, whose love of horses drove him to join the National Guard at age 17 (in 1927), later joined the Yale University faculty and became renowned as the first nuclear strategist. In his influential 1946 book, *The Absolute Weapon,* Brodie wrote that deterring—not fighting—wars was the military's main function in the atomic age, and that this was best accomplished by keeping the nation's atomic arsenal invulnerable to attack and threatening potential aggressors with "retaliation in kind."

Below left, Over the next few years, however, first as consultant to the Air Force and then as an analyst at RAND, Brodie began thinking about how to fight wars with the bomb—how to use the bomb rationally—as well. Part of this new concern was prompted by the invention of the much more powerful hydrogen bomb (seen here in a test, obliterating the tiny island of Elugelab).

Below right, Also influential in RAND's early days was John von Neumann (pictured with his wife and his dog, "Inverse"), a brilliant mathematician whose invention of "game theory" provided what seemed to many at RAND a scientific technique for analyzing nuclear war—and the Cold War.

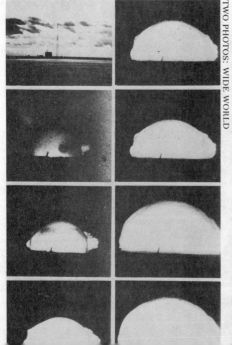

Right, Albert Wohlstetter, a flamboyant mathematical logician, discovered in the early 1950s that the bombers of the U.S. Strategic Air Command were vulnerable to Soviet attack. His two influential RAND reports—based on the technique of "systems analysis"—concluded that as a result, the ability of the United States to deter nuclear war was in danger. In the late 1950s, his analyses helped shape perceptions of a "missile gap" (which later proved mythical). *Below,* Wohlstetter *(back to camera)* was a guru to many younger RAND analysts. Among them were Henry Rowen *(second from left)*, who later, as a Kennedy Administration official during the Berlin Crisis of 1961, helped devise a contingency plan for launching a first strike against the U.S.S.R.; and Andrew Marshall *(third from left)*, who became an influential Pentagon official in the 1970s and '80s.

Some at RAND were rankled by Wohlstetter's style and were reluctant to depend too heavily on his studies. They could turn to his wife, Roberta Wohlstetter *(right center)*, a woman of subdued ego, whose RAND study of Pearl Harbor contained many of the same lessons.

Above left, John Foster Dulles, President Eisenhower's Secretary of State, delivered a speech in January 1954 proclaiming "massive retaliation"—the act of responding to Soviet aggression anywhere with atomic war against the Soviet homeland—as official policy.

Above right, William Kaufmann, then a Princeton professor, criticized Dulles in a monograph—highly influential among Army officers in the Pentagon—that formulated a theory of "limited war." In 1960, at RAND, building on theories of nuclear warfighting formulated a few years earlier by Bernard Brodie and others, Kaufmann composed a briefing that advocated a strategy of "counterforce" or "no-cities targeting."

Left, Herman Kahn, a RAND physicist-turned-strategist, gained the most fame for his voluble excitement about nuclear warfare. In three books and hundreds of public lectures, Kahn created a self-image as the man who could "think about the unthinkable," arguing the case for a Credible First-Strike capability, limited nuclear war and a massive fallout-shelter program.

In the late 1950s, the U.S. Navy challenged Air Force dominance over the nuclear world with development of the Polaris missile, to be fired from submarines (*right*) which—unlike SAC air bases— were virtually invulnerable to attack. Admiral Arleigh Burke (*above left*), Chief of Naval Operations, also supported a strategy, called "finite deterrence," that directly criticized the counterforce idea then being adopted—with RAND assistance— by the Air Force.

Generals Thomas White (*above center*), Air Force Chief of Staff, and Thomas Power (*above right*), Commander of SAC, fought back by persuading the Eisenhower Administration to establish the SIOP—the Single Integrated Operational Plan —a unified nuclear war-plan that would secretly give SAC control over how all nuclear weapons, including the Polaris, would be used in war. The first SIOP, signed December 1960 as SIOP-62, still called, however, for a shoot-everything "massive retaliation" policy.

Running for President in 1960, John F. Kennedy (*above*) promised to get the country moving, fight for freedom anywhere and restore the national defense. He was the RAND man's ideal candidate, and several RAND-sters advised his campaign.

Paul Nitze (*with Kennedy*), who became an assistant secretary of defense under JFK, was not from RAND, but was a hawkish defense intellectual of long repute—author of NSC-68, an official "Cold War blueprint" of 1950, and of the Gaither Report, a 1957 blue-panel paper heavily inspired by Albert Wohlstetter's studies. In the 1970s, Nitze would organize the Committee on the Present Danger, an anti-détente group many of whose members joined the Reagan Administration.

Other key Pentagon officials under Kennedy were Alain Enthoven (*below left*) and Charles Hitch (*below right, with wife*), both from RAND, who brought into government the technique of systems analysis, the emphasis on curing SAC vulnerability and the strategy of counterforce—all creations of RAND. Enthoven became head of a new Pentagon office called Systems Analysis and antagonized Air Force generals with his arrogance. Hitch, as Pentagon comptroller, was more mild-mannered.

Above, Robert McNamara, Kennedy's Secretary of Defense, had a dazzling grasp of numbers and abstract concepts. He was initially fascinated with the RAND theories and accepted them as official policy. Later, he became disillusioned—concluding that the nuclear warfighting strategy was impractical, would not soften the devastation of a nuclear war and only gave the Joint Chiefs of Staff more excuses to request new nuclear weapons. However, he remained sufficiently impressed by the theories of "sending signals with force"—the underpinnings of counterforce—to help plan the U.S. entry into the Vietnam War. When that war turned into a nightmare, McNamara's disillusionment was total.

Below left, playing war game at RAND, another devotee of warfighting theories turned sour by Vietnam was Daniel Ellsberg, a RAND analyst weaned on game theory. As a Pentagon consultant in 1961, he wrote the guidance for a new SIOP that conformed to a counterforce/no-cities strategy similar to William Kaufmann's 1960 briefing.

Above left, James Schlesinger refined theories still further in a 1960s RAND study called NU-OPTS, or Nuclear Operations, which advocated small-scale nuclear strikes. NU-OPTS had much impact on a few Pentagon analysts working on nuclear-targeting studies. When Richard Nixon appointed Schlesinger Secretary of Defense in 1973, he could implement the ideas as policy, through a document called NSDM-242. President Jimmy Carter's PD-59 and Ronald Reagan's "Defense Guidance" were mainly modifications of NSDM-242—which was, in turn, modeled after McNamara's revised SIOP, in turn based on the ideas of RAND in the 1950s.

Above right, Thomas Schelling, a Harvard professor and former RAND strategist, inspired Schlesinger to think about "limited nuclear options." His ideas about sending signals with force also influenced the U.S. strategy in Vietnam.

Below, Bernard Brodie, in the 1970s, toward the end of his life, criticized the notions of nuclear warfighting that he had helped to create, and called into question the legitimacy of the entire profession of "nuclear strategy." He died in 1978, a pariah among most of his former RAND colleagues.

Nobody was convinced. All the hard evidence contradicted SAC's claims.

On September 6, the CIA issued a special NIE reporting new data leading the CIA to "believe that our present estimate of 50–100 operational ICBM launchers as of mid-1961 is probably too high." The Agency now believed that the Soviets "deliberately elected to deploy only a small force of first-generation ICBMs in 1960–1961, even though they had the capability to deploy ICBMs in considerably greater quantity." Finally, the special NIE admitted that "the present Soviet ICBM capabilities, along with those of bombers and submarines, pose a grave threat to U.S. urban areas, but a more limited threat during the months immediately ahead to our nuclear striking force."

How many ICBMs were the Soviets now thought to have? Not 500 or 200 or 100 or even 50, but *four*—just four SS-6 missiles. Another twenty newer SS-7 and SS-8 sites were under construction, but none of them, nor any more SS-6s, would be deployed for the rest of the year. In other words, there *was* a missile gap, even a deterrent gap, and the ratio in forces was nearly ten to one—but the gap was in *our* favor.

The official intelligence estimates and the nation's leading strategic analysts who relied on these estimates had consistently made a whopping error. It was an error not merely of degree, but of fundamental, central importance to the conclusions of their analyses and studies. Four missiles meant that the Soviets could have done virtually no damage to SAC, and suggested that they had decided to forgo a first-strike capability.

In short, the Discoverer photos shattered the assumptions underlying the NIEs of more than half a decade, as well as the assumptions underlying many of the strategic analyses produced over the same period by the RAND Corporation.

The end of the missile gap crushed the assumptions behind much of the theorizing about counterforce strategies as well. The counterforce/no-cities idea, at least by the time it fell into William Kaufmann's hands, had been seen as a strategy that could cleverly exploit the vulnerabilities of an enemy with a superior force. Had it been known that the Soviets possessed only a handful of missiles with intercontinental range, virtually no one would have stopped to wonder whether the threat of "massive retaliation" or SAC's "optimum-mix" strategy could serve as a sufficiently "credible" deterrent or a devastatingly "war-winning" policy.

Yet in another sense, the disappearance of the missile gap suddenly made the counterforce strategy much easier to execute than anyone had previously imagined. With so few Soviet missiles—that is, so few counterforce targets—a successful attack would require far fewer American weapons and could tolerate much less thorough and precise coordination. In the first major crisis that faced the Kennedy Administration, several high-ranking officials in the Pentagon and the White House viewed a disarming, damage-limiting counterforce strike as an attractive option indeed.

20 THE CRISES

A s EARLY AS 1959, in the opening period of his run for the Presidency, Senator John Kennedy predicted that sometime in the next few years, the Soviets would stage an ultimatum over Berlin that would climax in a "test of nerve and will" between East and West. Since the hottest days of the Cold War, Berlin had served as the main arena of conflict in the continuing struggle between the superpowers. And it certainly appeared, by the time Kennedy took office, that that struggle was about to intensify.

Shortly after the Allied powers defeated Germany near the end of World War II, they divided the country into four zones separately occupied by the U.S., England, France and the U.S.S.R., corresponding to the position of each nation's land armies at the time of Nazi surrender. They likewise divided the capital city of Berlin into four separate sectors. As Soviet-Western relations worsened and tensions flared, the administrative arrangements in Germany were strained to intolerable degrees. Finally, Germany was divided into two nations—a Communist-ruled East Germany in what had been the Soviet zone of occupation, and a West Germany created by the merger of the three Western zones. When the Soviets blockaded all roads and waterways leading into West Berlin in 1948, the United States mounted a massive airlift, dropping packages of aid into the city by parachute for more than 300 days. The airlift forced the Soviets to halt the blockade, and the four powers signed an agreement allowing the Western nations free access to West Berlin.

In 1955, West Germany joined the North Atlantic Treaty Organization, provoking the Soviets to form the Warsaw Pact. In December 1957, NATO agreed to put U.S.-controlled intermediate-range ballistic missiles, IRBMs, in West Germany, which the Soviets regarded as a threatening move. Meanwhile, attracted to the pleasures of Western life, East Germans were emigrating to West Germany in droves, using West Berlin as the readily accessible transfer point. By September 1958, East Germany had lost two million people, many of them young and technically skilled, with continued losses of more than 10,000 per month.

Soviet Premier Khrushchev was under agonizing pressure— from his foes in the Kremlin, from the East German regime, from Chinese hardliners—to do something about the increasingly peril- ous Berlin problem. In November 1958 he announced that within six months he would sign a peace treaty with East Germany, de- claring the final borders of World War II permanent and handing East and West Berlin, including the issue of Western access rights, over to the sovereignty of East Germany, declaring that if the West tried to interfere, there would be war. In messages to for- eign ambassadors and official notes to the three Western powers controlling West Berlin, Khrushchev and his diplomats declared that they intended "to liquidate the occupation statutes concern- ing Berlin," to declare "null and void" the arrangements that had existed since World War II.

Eventually, this Berlin crisis of 1958–1959 was settled pretty much without incident. East German authorities occasionally held up Western military traffic on the *Autobahn;* the U.S. sent in very-high-altitude transport planes, which Soviet fighters at- tempted but failed to intercept. Finally, Khrushchev won a few in- ternal victories in the Kremlin; the U.S. demonstrated both its mil- itary superiority and its will to use it if necessary; and Khrushchev, in a meeting with Eisenhower at Camp David in Sep- tember 1959, toned down his rhetoric and dropped his already- extended deadline on signing a treaty with East Germany.

However, that did not mark the end of the Berlin crisis. On January 6, 1961, Khrushchev delivered a speech to the U.S.S.R.'s leading ideological institutes, declaring that his policy of "peaceful coexistence" would in no way interfere with the "intensive eco- nomic, political and ideological struggle" between East and West, that "national wars of liberation" were "sacred," to be supported by Communists "wholeheartedly and without reservation." Fi- nally, he talked about Berlin, where "the positions of the United States of America, Britain and France have proved to be especially vulnerable. . . . These powers cannot fail to realize that sooner or later the occupation regime in that city must be ended. . . . And should they balk, then we will take resolute measures, we will sign a peace treaty with [East Germany] ."

Kennedy reacted grimly but resolutely to the speech, inter- preting it as Khrushchev's outline of a grand strategy for Commu-

nist subversion and expansionism, not just in Berlin but throughout the world, especially in the "gray areas" of Indochina, Africa,
Latin America. He circulated the speech to his staff, instructing
them to "read, mark, learn and inwardly digest." He frequently
read excerpts from it aloud at NSC meetings. It spurred Kennedy
on in his fascination with counterinsurgency and counterguerrilla
forces, reinforced general suspicions that "national liberation
movements" in the underdeveloped world acted in effect as Soviet
agents, convinced him that a new period of heightened danger in
the Cold War lay before him, and seemed to confirm his earlier
prediction that Berlin would serve as the main object of contention
in the battle of wills.

In June, Kennedy journeyed to Vienna to meet on neutral territory with Khrushchev. The idea was to relax tensions, but it
wasn't to be. On Berlin, Khrushchev bluntly stated his position.
The German situation was a mess that had to be resolved. A peace
treaty with East Germany, ending the wartime occupation zones,
would be signed by the end of the year, whether or not the Western powers wanted to join the U.S.S.R. in doing so. From that
point on, all access to West Berlin would have to be settled with
the East German authorities, who would wield sovereignty over all
Berlin. The Soviet Union would certainly not allow the U.S. to
maintain its present rights there. And if the U.S. tried to act as if it
still owned West Berlin, that would violate East Germany's sovereignty and be a cause for war.

The Vienna meeting profoundly disturbed Kennedy. As the
two parted, Kennedy predicted, "It will be a cold winter." He was
shaken by the implacable stance that Khrushchev took. That the
Cold War might become a hot war by the end of Kennedy's first
year of office seemed possible.

Three weeks after Kennedy returned to Washington, he received a paper on the Berlin crisis that he had assigned the previous March to Dean Acheson, Secretary of State in the Truman
Administration and progenitor of the NATO alliance. Acheson
thought that Berlin itself was more the pretext than the problem.
Khrushchev's intention was not to do something about the German problem but to test America's will to resist aggression. By
forcing the U.S. to back down on the commitment to Berlin,
Khrushchev could destroy our commitments elsewhere, our general influence in the world. Khrushchev had dared to force the crisis because he felt that the United States was too fearful to use nu-

clear weapons—which we would have to use if the Soviets insisted on occupying all of Berlin to the bitter end of what might start out as a conventional conflict. Acheson's solution was to avoid any sort of negotiations; they would only divert attention from the real issue. Instead, Kennedy should order a massive buildup of conventional forces, enough to hold out in conventional conflict for several weeks—not so much to defeat the Communists on the ground, but to persuade the Kremlin that we had the resolve to carry the conflict to whatever level it would take to keep West Berlin free, to affirm to the world that we honored commitments. Ideally, such resolution might persuade Khrushchev to back down. However, Acheson fully acknowledged that such a strategy might very well result in nuclear war.

Several White House and State Department advisers argued that Acheson went too far, that Khrushchev's objectives might be more limited, that the President should seek out proposals to settle the crisis through negotiation. Kennedy sided with his advisers on negotiations, but agreed with Acheson's fundamental approach. Indeed, the memo helped Kennedy define the terms and nature of the crisis. During a visit to the White House later in the year by Finnish President Urho Kekkonen, Kennedy described Khrushchev's pressure on Berlin as part of a campaign "to neutralize West Germany as a first step in the neutralization of Western Europe." Kennedy explained, "It is not that we wish to stand on the letter of the law or that we underestimate the dangers of war. But if we don't meet our commitments in Berlin, it will mean the destruction of NATO and a dangerous situation for the whole world. All Europe is at stake in West Berlin."

Earlier that spring, as Khrushchev began turning the screws on Berlin, William Kaufmann, consulting for Harry Rowen in the Pentagon, made an astonishing discovery while looking over some new intelligence data. By this time, thousands of photographs taken by the Discoverer reconnaissance satellite had been analyzed by the CIA, and while officials still proclaimed a missile gap, its unraveling was clearly under way. Moreover, the analysts had obtained highly detailed information about the Soviet missiles—their readiness, how long it would take the Soviets to launch them, the readiness of ancillary forces of the Soviet strategic arsenal, such as the air-defense and early-warning networks, the command-control facilities and all the rest. Kaufmann was one of the first civilians in the Pentagon to examine these recent findings closely, and their implications were stunning.

The intelligence analyses disclosed that the Soviet strategic forces were in awful shape. The ICBMs and IRBMs were not loaded with warheads, and it would take at least six hours to get them loaded. None of their bombers were on any sort of alert. Almost all of their nuclear-missile submarines were in port, and those at sea had to surface before launching. Moreover, the Soviet early-warning network was riddled with gaps that would make it very difficult to detect a less-than-massive U.S. bomber attack, especially if the bombardiers flew in at low altitudes. Not only that, but the much-celebrated air-defense forces had little value: for all the surface-to-air missiles and fighter-interceptors, the Soviets lacked the ability to coordinate an air-defense campaign and shoot down very many bombers, especially if flight tactics were carefully planned.

The existing U.S. war plan required coordinating a massive attack, first knocking out air-defense sites, paving the way for the follow-on B-47 and B-52 bombers to strike their designated targets in the Soviet heartland unimpeded. But if those air-defense sites posed little danger to the U.S. bombers, as now seemed the case, then a relatively small U.S. bomber fleet could go in and virtually devastate the entire Soviet strategic force on the ground. And since the mission would require such a small number of airplanes, the U.S. could probably devise flight tactics that avoided tipping off Soviet early-warning radars to the attack. In short, the classic surgical strike might be feasible. The Kaufmann counterforce option took on an air of practicality that not even its progenitor could possibly have foreseen.

Nearly every high-ranking White House and Pentagon official was searching desperately for attractive options that spring, some stratagem that would, as Kennedy often phrased it, avoid the twin perils of "humiliation or holocaust." It was clear that if the Soviets went all out in defending Berlin with conventional forces, they would win: they were much closer to the theater of battle, they could amass far more divisions, they could fight in tandem with the East German military, in whose borders West Berlin was trapped. NATO would have to launch what amounted to an invasion; and if it came to that, the Western powers simply lacked the conventional forces necessary to carry out an offensive of that scope.

On the other hand, Robert McNamara learned from the JCS in May that the U.S. military's official contingency plans for Berlin called for sending a few brigades down the *Autobahn* from West Germany to Berlin. If the Warsaw Pact resisted those troops, the U.S. would move immediately to the all-out nuclear strike envisioned in the JSCP's Annex C and in SIOP-62.

When Kaufmann showed the new intelligence data to Harry Rowen and carefully explained their significance, Rowen reacted very excitedly. Nobody had yet found the magical option that combined credibility and effectiveness, that could be presented to the President as something that he could *do* if the tentative probes of a confrontation exploded into full-scale war with the U.S.S.R.

Rowen took Kaufmann to meet Carl Kaysen, McGeorge Bundy's assistant in the National Security Council, with whom Rowen had previously discussed the vexing challenge of credible options over Berlin. Kaysen too found Kaufmann's discoveries most intriguing. He and Rowen spent hours discussing how the details of such an operation might be worked out.

In June, the Berlin crisis began to heat up. Kennedy and Khrushchev had their tense confrontation in Vienna during the first week of the month. At an NSC meeting on June 14, McNamara informed Kennedy that U.S. military forces in Berlin had enough ammunition and combat rations to hold out in a conventional conflict for only eighteen days. On the twenty-eighth, Dean Acheson's get-tough memo, urging a strategy that by his own admission might result in nuclear war, was circulated throughout the national security bureaucracy.

The next day, Rowen and Kaysen met with Colonel DeWitt Armstrong, Paul Nitze's Berlin adviser in the Pentagon's International Security Affairs office, and Harvard Professor Henry Kissinger, a consultant in the NSC, to discuss the military contingency plan that the JCS had recently given McNamara. Kaysen described the plan in a memo to McGeorge Bundy written shortly after the meeting: "It is clear that the 'general war' which the JCS discussed is exactly the one-sided response with all our nuclear forces envisioned in SIOP-62." Reporting on the meeting with Rowen, Armstrong and Kissinger, Kaysen continued, "The planning for several alternative limited target lists which might be relevant to the Berlin crisis has not begun. Rowen is drafting a request for such planning, a copy of which I expect to receive, but I think this should be considered as an urgent matter at higher levels."

Some plan had to be devised quickly to create some limited nuclear options for dealing with the contingency of a Berlin crisis gone out of control, a plan quite free from the straitjacket of SIOP-62. The memo that Harry Rowen sent Kaysen was essentially an elaboration on the Kaufmann counterforce/no-cities option, based on the discoveries in the new intelligence data that Kaufmann himself had discovered a couple of months earlier.

On July 7, Bundy wrote a memo to Kennedy, noting that he, Kaysen and Kissinger "all agree that the current strategic war plan is dangerously rigid and, if continued without amendment, may leave you with very little choice as to how you face the moment of thermonuclear truth. We believe that you may want to raise this question with Bob McNamara in order to have a prompt review and new orders if necessary. In essence, the current plan calls for shooting off everything we have in one shot, and it is so constructed as to make any more flexible course very difficult."

The next day, Saturday the eighth, Bundy, McNamara and Secretary of State Dean Rusk met with Kennedy at his weekend beach house in Hyannis Port, Massachusetts. Kennedy asked McNamara to draw up plans to mobilize one million ground troops for a Berlin contingency.

On Tuesday night, July 25, Kennedy delivered a dramatic radio and television speech to the nation about the dangers facing freedom in Berlin. Based partly on McNamara's answers to the questions he had posed at Hyannis Port, Kennedy said that he would ask Congress, the next day, for a $3.3 billion supplement to the defense appropriations bill, half of which would go for procurement of non-nuclear weapons and ammunition, an increase in the Army's authorized strength from 875,000 to one million men, an increase of 29,000 and 63,000 in Navy and Air Force strength respectively, a doubling and tripling of draft calls, authority to call up the ready reserves and the National Guard, a delay in the deactivation of B-47 bombers and an acceleration in the nation's civil-defense programs.

The emphasis was on building up conventional forces, but Kennedy realized their limitations in an area such as Berlin, where the Warsaw Pact would have the advantage of geography. When he had asked McNamara to draw up non-nuclear war plans for Berlin, he noted that the forces should be sufficiently large to indicate American resolve and to give the Russians time for second thoughts, to allow for what many called a "negotiation pause," before the conflict escalated to nuclear war. He knew that if the Soviets did not balk, nuclear war was the only alternative to surrender.

On July 7, Bundy had advised Kennedy to broaden the options that would be available to him at his "moment of thermonuclear truth." The next day at Hyannis Port, Kennedy read a critique of Dean Acheson's report by Kissinger, State Department Counsel Abe Chayes and Kennedy adviser Arthur Schlesinger, Jr., noting that Acheson's paper "hinges on our willingness to face nuclear war" although "this option is undefined. Before you are asked to make the decision to go to nuclear war," the critique continued, "you are entitled to know what concretely nuclear war is likely to mean. The Pentagon should be required to make an analysis of the possible levels and implications of nuclear warfare and the possible gradations of our nuclear response." McGeorge Bundy's notes on "JFK's Berlin Agenda," taken at a meeting of Kennedy's Berlin Steering Group on July 19, indicate that there was discussion of "nuclear war—its flexibility."

On August 13, a few minutes past midnight, East German troops occupied the border line separating East from West Berlin and constructed the first layers of brick and barbed wire that built the Berlin Wall. In retrospect, the Wall represented, in some ways, a solution to the crisis, especially to the refugee problem that plagued East German authorities. But it came as a complete shock and surprise to the West, and American officials took the move as antagonistic, another escalation in the spiralling crisis.

The next day, Kennedy wrote a memo to McNamara: "With the weekend's occurrences in Berlin there will be more and more pressure for us to adopt a harder military posture. . . . I would appreciate it if you would plan to discuss this matter with me this week. . . ."

It was around this time that Kennedy asked McNamara to look into the question of "flexible response" with nuclear as well as non-nuclear weapons—not necessarily to advocate their use, but to examine the possible consequences if they were used. When McNamara turned to his Whiz Kids for assistance, Rowen already had something of a plan in the works.

It was in August that the fascinating intellectual puzzle took on more serious and official overtones. Kaysen consulted with General Maxwell Taylor on getting the Joint Chiefs on board this sort of operation. Rowen set up a small task force in the Pentagon to deal with the details of the contingency plan. It was a very tightly held business. Henry Kissinger was not involved at all. Kaufmann was shunted off to the far sidelines. Enthoven, Hitch, Nitze, Seymour Weiss and one or two other officials from State, McGeorge Bundy of NSC and Dean Acheson, as a senior consultant in the White House, played very peripheral roles. General David Burchinal and a few others in the Air Staff fed Rowen information on the precise location of Soviet counterforce targets and on how many bombers, carrying what kinds of bombs, it would take to destroy them with high confidence. Frank Trinkl cranked Burchinal's numbers into a mathematical model that calculated how many Americans the surviving Soviet forces would kill, using the same methodology that he and Dave McGarvey had employed in the summer of 1960 back at RAND to support Kaufmann's counterforce study. Only now the exercise was for real, having an impact on high-level analysis and, if the worst came, maybe on policy.

The study was finished in mid-September, shortly after release of the special National Intelligence Estimate revealing that the Soviets had only four operational ICBMs. The paper was written mostly by Rowen, who passed it on to McNamara, who in turn gave it to Kennedy. Only five names appeared on the memorandum—Kennedy, McNamara, Maxwell Taylor, McGeorge Bundy and Carl Kaysen. It was highly detailed, down to specifying the altitudes and general flight tactics of the attacking bombers. It concluded that a counterforce first-strike was indeed very feasible, that we could pull it off with high confidence.

Ted Sorensen, the chief White House counsel and speech writer who had been with Kennedy since his earliest Senate days, was outraged when Kaysen told him about the study, shouting, "You're crazy! We shouldn't let guys like you around here." Even more appalled was a friend of Kaysen's on the NSC staff named Marcus Raskin. Raskin had served as foreign policy adviser to a few liberal Democratic Senators and had been hired by Bundy as the token leftist. Raskin was horrified by the very existence of such a study. "How does this make us any better than those who measured the gas ovens or the engineers who built the tracks for the death trains in Nazi Germany?" he hollered at one point. Raskin never spoke with Kaysen again.

Not just the liberals and leftists on board found the study dissettling. For the study also concluded that a few Soviet bombs and missiles would almost certainly survive—owing to the inaccuracy or failure of some of our own bombs, the chance that a few of the bombers might crash before making it to the target or, especially in the case of the few nuclear-missile submarines that the Soviets had, the chance that we might not be able to find all the targets. Frank Trinkl calculated that in the best case, if the Soviets retaliated, two or three million Americans would die; in the worst case, as many as ten or fifteen million might die.

At the RAND Corporation, the attack plan would have been heralded a monumental success. Not just Herman Kahn but virtually the entire strategic community would have considered two, three, or even ten million fatalities, in the abstract, "acceptable," or anyway certainly not "unacceptable," losses under the circumstances. But now, in the real world, in the context of a real crisis with real political decision-makers, the reaction was much different. Nearly everyone was aghast.

Among the most fiercely opposed was Paul Nitze. It was, in some ways, ironic. Nitze, author of NSC-68, coauthor of the Gaither Report, was certainly a hardliner. He had swung back and forth on the issue of counterforce. In a speech that he wrote in April 1960, for a major national-security conference at Asilomar in Monterey, California, Nitze concluded that the U.S. should develop a secure mobile deterrent force, scrap the land-based missiles once that's accomplished, then "multilateralize the command of our retaliatory systems by making SAC a NATO command," and finally "turn over ultimate power of decision on the use of these systems to the General Assembly of the United Nations," inviting the Soviets to do the same, specifying that a U.N. order to use the weapons would be honored only in retaliation to a direct nuclear attack by an enemy. The speech stood out from the annals of Paul Nitze's writings as an anomaly. Nobody at Asilomar liked the speech. All of his friends in the Air Force, at RAND, in the academic and think-tank world hated it. One month after writing the speech, he delivered another at the Air War College at Maxwell Air Force Base, Alabama, concluding quite differently that we had to develop a first-class counterforce capability.

Like many others in the national security field in the late 1950s and very early '60s, Nitze was searching for an alternative to the suicide of massive retaliation, the dreamworld of "general and complete disarmament," and the potential infeasibility of a totally disarming first-strike. In the winter of 1960, just before Kennedy took office, Nitze heard Bill Kaufmann's counterforce/no-cities briefing, and was impressed with the possible solutions it offered.

Now, in the early autumn of 1961, when the United States had preponderant nuclear superiority over the Soviet Union, when a virtually disarming counterforce strike appeared technically feasible and when it looked like the United States might have to bring atomic weapons into play, Paul Nitze balked. What if things didn't go according to plan? What if the surviving Soviet weapons happened to be aimed at New York, Washington, Chicago—in which case, even under the best of circumstances, far more than a few million would die? There were just too many things that could go wrong. And even if they went right, two or three million were a couple of million too many.

Then there was Western Europe to consider. The memo on the first-strike plan conceded that the location of all the short- and medium-range nuclear missiles, of which the Soviets had hundreds, was a much less certain matter. We would certainly miss many of these, and the number of European fatalities could be as high as in the "low tens of millions." To Nitze and to his mentor, Dean Acheson, who considered NATO his own personal creation, that was an even stronger reason to reject the first-strike option entirely.

If ever in the history of the nuclear arms race, before or since, one side had unquestionable superiority over the other, one side truly had the ability to devastate the other side's strategic forces, one side could execute the RAND counterforce/no-cities option with fairly high confidence, the autumn of 1961 was that time. Yet approaching the height of the gravest crisis that had faced the West since the onset of the Cold War, everyone said, "No."

At the same time that a handful of high officials were contemplating the Rowen-Kaysen first-strike study, the Pentagon was

sponsoring a huge simulation war game at Camp David, run by
Thomas Schelling, a RAND strategist and Harvard professor. Two
games were played, over the weekends of September 8–11 and
September 29–October 1. Several high government officials
played the leaders of "Blue" (representing the U.S.) and "Red"
(the U.S.S.R.)—among them Rowen, Kaysen, John Mc-
Naughton, Henry Kissinger, Alain Enthoven, DeWitt Armstrong,
McGeorge Bundy, Robert Komer, and Seymour Weiss.

Both games started with a series of threats and counter-
threats between Blue and Red over Berlin. Initially, neither side
wanted to escalate the conflict. Schelling turned up the heat,
creating provocative scenarios. Blue starts flying East German refugees out of Berlin; Red tells Blue to stop; Blue persists; Red
shoots down some Blue airplanes, killing dozens; riots erupt in
East Berlin, all through East Germany; West Berlin students join
in; two Soviet divisions cut Berlin off from the rest of East Germany, proceeding "brutally and successfully"; a battalion of Blue
troops breaks through the barriers; Red aircraft attack the troops.

On it went like this for three days, the team members taking
their roles and the game very seriously, getting in only a few hours
of sleep each night. Yet for all the outlandish provocations that
Schelling hurled into the game, against both sides, all the players,
Blue and Red, civilian and military, did all they could to clamp
things down, to defuse the kegs of dynamite that Schelling had lit
and thrown their way. Schelling simply could not get a war
started, could not get either side to consider seriously the use of
nuclear weapons.

Meanwhile, reality was reflecting art, so to speak, in a quadripartite military planning group set up to deal with the crisis.

In the early fall of 1961, Paul Nitze, his Berlin aide, Colonel
DeWitt Armstrong, Harry Rowen, Seymour Weiss, Bill Kaufmann
and a few others started to meet with military representatives
from the allied countries (U.K., France and Germany) to try to
agree on a set of responses to Soviet provocation in Berlin. The
idea was to see if they could jointly plan a series of responses to a
wide variety of contingencies, so that Western moves could be
taken with expediency and mutual authority.

The premise was a condition of extreme crisis in which the
Soviets had cut off access to Berlin. Phase One involved the allied
response. Phase Two began with the assumption that the Soviets

or East Germans or both persist in their activities and have re-pelled the allies' Phase-One resistance. Phase Three asked the question: what do we do if the Soviets continue to persist? There were several answers on which the allies agreed for Phase Three operations: send three armored divisions up the *Autobahn* toward Berlin, smash East European (but not Soviet) airfields with (conventional) fighter-bombers, and other similar steps designed to demonstrate Western resolve and to buy time for the further mobilization of troops.

Then came Phase Four. The Warsaw Pact forces come back and destroy those three divisions and counterattack with, say, ten or fifteen divisions of their own. Meanwhile, they have the advantage of local superiority with ground troops. *Now* what is to be done? The answer involved using nuclear weapons—not necessarily shooting off SIOP-62, not even necessarily pulling a counterforce first-strike, but rather engaging in something like low-level tactical attacks, using nuclear weapons on the battlefield to repel the onslaught of Soviet divisions, or perhaps a "demonstration shot" to indicate Western resolve, such as setting off a big nuclear blast over one of the U.S.S.R.'s own nuclear-weapon test sites. But nobody, especially not the Europeans, wanted to talk about Phase Four, to discuss the matter of using nuclear weapons. Phases One through Three were cluttered with many different options and counterresponses. For Phase Four, the quadripartite group merely filled in, "Call Washington."

The Europeans had dissented from the Kennedy Administration's campaign to build up non-nuclear forces, objecting that conventional forces were too expensive, that the threat of using nuclear weapons, especially in the French case their own nuclear weapons, would be sufficient to deter the Soviet hordes. Now, in their own "moment of thermonuclear truth," the European allies were refusing to make any sort of commitment or assent on the first use of nuclear weapons under any circumstances.

Tentative steps toward the brink were taken in the latter half of 1961. Shortly after the Wall went up in August, the Soviets closed off all but one border crossing into Berlin. At one point, an American battalion was let in the entry checkpoint, and for several hours was not allowed out the other end. On October 27, Soviet and American tanks faced each other, at short range, along one Berlin checkpoint. After sixteen hours, the Soviet tanks finally backed off, to everyone's relief. Toward the end of the year, the crisis faded away. There were negotiations; Khrushchev backed off, for the second time in two years, from his demand for a six-month deadline on coming to terms with an East German peace treaty.

The crisis ended partly because the United States displayed more will and determination not to let Berlin go than Khrushchev had anticipated. Another reason was that all along, Khrushchev had been managing his Berlin initiatives on the assumption that the Americans believed the Soviets were ahead in the arms race; he himself had made many public statements encouraging this delusion. But now he knew the game was over, and so did his foes in the Kremlin who had long expressed skepticism of his dangerous policy of aggression backed by bluff. He knew now that the U.S. might not be taunted by his nuclear threats, might not be afraid to use nuclear weapons as a final resort themselves. The Soviets were in no position to play that game, and so Khrushchev was forced to bow out of the crisis that he had precipitated.

What Khrushchev could not possibly have known is that the Americans were not willing to go first with nuclear weapons either, that they too assessed the risks as too high, that even while they realized their own superiority they could find no practical way to exploit it.

The same phenomenon occurred a year later, during the Cuban missile crisis of October 1962. Under considerable pressure to achieve diplomatic victory and realizing that bluff could no longer support policy, Khrushchev started to move SS-4 and SS-5 intermediate-range missiles into Cuba—enough to boost the number of Soviet missiles capable of hitting U.S. territory by roughly half. For thirteen days, October 16 through 28, the crisis engulfed everything. For the last six days, an Executive Committee of Kennedy's advisers met to debate what to do. Eventually, this crisis abated as well. The United States dispersed the SAC bombers, instituted a naval blockade in the Caribbean, and concentrated an enormous amount of non-nuclear firepower in southern Florida—tripling the number of fighter aircraft on alert, transferring Marines to the point of crisis from both coasts, moving elements of the 1st Armored Division from Fort Hood, Texas, to Fort Stewart, Georgia. On Saturday, October 27, Robert McNamara and Maxwell Taylor were urging that steps be taken to prepare for an invasion of Cuba, McNamara stating that an invasion was "almost inevitable." Indeed, had the Soviets not caved in on

Sunday, American troops were ready to invade the island on Monday. Khrushchev's gamble was an atrocious mistake: the combination of geography, conventional superiority and nuclear superiority forced him to back down.

Nevertheless, during the crisis, the Americans again shied away from the controlled, deliberate use of nuclear weapons that would have been featured almost casually in a scenario written at the RAND Corporation. At one point, Dean Acheson came in and bellowed that we would have to knock out the Soviet missiles in Cuba. Someone asked what the Soviets would do in response.

"I know the Soviet Union well," Acheson responded. "I know what they are required to do in the light of their history and their posture around the world. I think they will knock out our missiles in Turkey."

"Well, then what do we do?" another queried.

Acheson replied, "I believe under our NATO treaty, with which I was associated, we would be required to respond by knocking out a missile base inside the Soviet Union."

Came the inevitable question: "Then what do they do?"

Acheson paused. "That's when we hope," he answered, "that cooler heads will prevail, and they'll stop and talk."

It was a chilling conversation for everyone in the room. As in the Berlin crisis, despite overwhelming nuclear superiority, nobody was willing to "send signals" with nuclear weapons, nobody wanted to walk up an "escalation ladder" supported by limited nuclear strikes, nobody wanted to think much about using nuclear weapons rationally.

To the extent that nuclear weapons entered into the discussion at all, their image hardly matched that associated with theories of controlled and limited options. On Monday, October 22, President Kennedy proclaimed to the nation and the world: "It shall be the policy of this nation to regard any nuclear missile launched from Cuba against any nation in the Western hemisphere as an attack by the Soviet Union on the United States requiring a full retaliatory response upon the Soviet Union." Kennedy and his advisers were gradually escalating their responses with conventional weapons, but no such distinctions were recognized, at any level of power, regarding nuclear weapons.

After the Cuban missile crisis, American superiority was obvious. It was in the aftermath of the crisis that the Kremlin made its first steps toward amassing a formidable arsenal of intercontinental ballistic missiles. Shortly after the missile crisis, Robert McNamara's five-year defense plan called for eventually deploying 1,400 ICBMs. After the Soviets completed their crash missile program over the next decade, they ended up with 1,400 ICBMs. They also built a fleet of nuclear-missile submarines, emulating the American Polaris program, and they began to bury their land-based missiles in underground concrete silos similar to those of the American Minuteman.

The Berlin and Cuban crises represented the last time that either side could seriously contemplate a "splendid first-strike." After then, he who struck first would have to expect hundreds, eventually thousands of enemy missiles thrown back on his homeland. Yet even in those halcyon days of "strategic superiority," the most determined American officials, who had firmly believed in the counterforce strategy in theory, did not even contemplate taking the awesome risk of executing the strategy in practice.

21 SHELTER MANIA

ANOTHER CASUALTY of the Berlin crisis was the nonchalance with which many strategists had previously viewed the question of fallout shelters and civil defense.

It began to emerge as an issue in the opening months of the Kennedy Administration. In December 1960, the last full month of the Eisenhower period, the Office of Civil Defense Mobilization (OCDM) proposed a program that would provide shelter spaces, as well as training, shelter stockpiling, radiometers and postwar recuperation planning to everyone potentially endangered by fallout. Initially, Kennedy was wary of such a large-scale program, and he asked his national security adviser, McGeorge Bundy, to conduct a review of the issue.

Kennedy started to come under pressure to adopt some sort of program, however, in early May when the Conference of Governors met in Washington. The chairman of the Conference's Committee on Civil Defense was New York Governor Nelson Rockefeller. Rockefeller was a staunch proponent of fallout shelters. It was Rockefeller who had persuaded Eisenhower to constitute what became the Gaither Committee of 1957. Rockefeller had instituted an enormous fallout-shelter program involving tax incentives and matching grants in the state of New York. And it was widely thought that Rockefeller might be Kennedy's Republican opponent in the 1964 election.

On May 9, Rockefeller met with Kennedy and Bundy to discuss civil defense, telling them that a strong program was needed to stiffen the public's willingness to support the American use of nuclear weapons if necessary. Kennedy expressed skepticism. Advisers had told him that a nationwide fallout-shelter program might cost $20 billion. Over the long term, with bigger and bigger bombs, would any shelter program have value?

By this time, Bundy had given two of his assistants, Carl Kaysen and Marc Raskin, the task of reviewing the OCDM civil-defense proposal. Kaysen had several years earlier participated in a

307

Cambridge "Summer Study" on civil defense and, in 1954, published an article in *World Politics* proposing a plan to reduce vulnerability to atomic attack by dispersing urban dwellers. He was initially receptive to the notion of fallout shelters.

Raskin was fervently opposed. He thought that a major civil-defense program would require a major federal propaganda effort to get public support, and he worried that such a campaign would engender a "garrison-state" mentality and transform the free and open nature of American democracy into an "authoritarian and regimented" society. He also thought that such a program would appear to the Soviets as a sign of first-strike intentions, thus accelerating the arms race and further heightening the chances of nuclear war.

The more Kaysen looked into the issue, the more skeptical he became as well, enough so to see many "troublesome questions," as he delicately put it. Kaysen recognized that the optimistic fatality estimates in the civil-defense studies by the RAND Corporation and similar think tanks resulted not "from a war game analysis of what the Soviets could in fact achieve, but only [from] a set of assumptions about 'reasonable attacks.' " But what if the attack was not "reasonable"? For example, if, instead of hitting only military targets, the Soviets diverted a mere fifteen missiles to cities, fatalities would increase by ten or twenty million even under the most favorable of assumptions regarding shelters.

There were other questions. Could the President get money from Congress for civil defense *and* his other defense priorities? Was building fifty-four million new urban fallout shelters really a good idea, since the effects of blast and fire from even a "modest" attack against cities would far exceed effects of fallout, thus negating the entire shelter plan? Conversely, building *blast* shelters on so grand a scale would cost tens of billions of dollars, and would not be effective against the damage from thermal heat and possible firestorms anyway.

Kaysen's position was that Kennedy should not approve any civil-defense plan until these sorts of questions were answered; and even then, the program should be a much more "modest" endeavor than OCDM had proposed.

One sunny Saturday afternoon in mid-May, Bundy, Kaysen and Raskin met in Bundy's office with Ted Sorensen, Sorensen's deputy, Meyer Feldman, and Elmer Staats of the Budget Bureau to discuss the civil-defense review. Kaysen and Raskin made their dissenting points. Sorensen listened, but then told them that the President had made up his mind to go with some civil-defense program.

"But it would be a political disaster," Raskin objected.

"We *have* to do it," Sorensen said. "You have to prepare a program."

At that point, Bundy, who came to the meeting dressed in shorts and carrying a tennis racket, got up, said, "I have to go play tennis," and left the room. Kaysen and Raskin were left holding the bag.

Kennedy still had questions about civil defense, but he felt he had to approve something. First, there was the pressure from Rockefeller, which could have politically disastrous consequences in the next election if Kennedy did nothing. Second, there *was* always the possibility of war, and Kennedy felt that as President he should offer the citizenry some hope for survival. Third, and most important, the Berlin crisis was beginning to heat up, and Kennedy believed that having a civil-defense program would strengthen his hand, that he could move more freely if the population could be protected from an attack that the Soviets might launch in response to actions he might be forced to take. On this fundamental point, he essentially agreed with Nelson Rockefeller and Herman Kahn. On May 25, Kennedy announced that he was stepping up federal efforts for a nationwide fallout-shelter program.

When Kennedy returned from Vienna in early June, shaken by his tense meeting with Khrushchev, he started to put still greater emphasis on civil defense. In his July 25 radio and television address to the nation, explaining the Berlin crisis and his decision to add more than $3.2 billion to the defense budget, the President also announced that he was adding $207 million to the civil-defense budget—which, on top of the $104 million already appropriated, meant a 500 percent increase over the previous year. The money would go toward identifying shelter spaces with civil-defense signs, stocking the shelters with water, biscuits and first-aid kits, and improving air-raid warning systems.

Over the summer, as Kennedy grew more and more concerned with Berlin, he became increasingly enthusiastic about civil defense. He was spurred in this direction partly by his brother Robert, the Attorney General, who was an extreme enthusiast for civil defense, urging members of the White House staff to outline a program that would require everyone to join a citizens corps that would practice evacuation-and-shelter drills once a week. The President didn't go quite that far, but on August 14, one day after the East Germans started constructing the Berlin Wall, Kennedy wrote McNamara, "I am concerned that we move . . . as quickly as possible on Civil Defense."

Life magazine was planning to run, in its September 15 issue, an enormous section on fallout shelters, replete with detailed blueprints and photographs on how to build several different types of shelters in or near your own home, with a headline reading: "You Could Be Among the 97% to Survive If You Follow Advice in These Pages." Kennedy signed a letter addressed to the magazine's readers, dated September 7, reprinted as the article's introduction, stating in part: "I urge you to read and consider seriously the contents of this issue of *Life*."

Around the same time, the Pentagon was planning to put out its own official pamphlet on fallout. Adam Yarmolinsky, McNamara's special assistant, took charge of the project and commissioned the editorial team that wrote the *Life* article to help draft it. Yarmolinsky had been given the civil-defense beat in a rather peculiar fashion. In the early spring of 1961, shortly after Kennedy ordered McGeorge Bundy to review the OCDM's civil-defense proposal, Bundy told Carl Kaysen and Marc Raskin that they would have to find a point of contact in the Defense Department. Raskin, who was out to sabotage the civil-defense campaign from the start, ran down the list of high Pentagon officials in search of the man who would most likely share his own views on the topic. He hit upon Adam Yarmolinsky. Much to Raskin's surprise, however, Yarmolinsky took the assignment for which Raskin had recommended him very seriously, transforming himself into a leader and public spokesman for civil defense, even building his own do-it-yourself family fallout shelter.

And then there was the fallout-shelter pamphlet. The Pentagon wanted Kennedy to go on TV to explain his shelter program and then, the next day, to send copies of the pamphlet to every single home in America—making it, as Raskin waggishly remarked in a memo to Bundy, "the most widely distributed piece of literature in man's history outside of the Bible." In mid-October, Yarmolinsky and his team from *Life* finished a draft of the booklet, entitled "Fallout Protection: What to Know About Nuclear Attack—What to Do About It," and circulated it throughout the

Pentagon and the White House for comment. Nearly everyone who saw it, especially outside the Pentagon, was aghast. White House staffers caustically referred to it as "Fallout Is Good for You."

One section headline in the pamphlet read "Shelter Living Will Be As Healthy As You Make It." The vision of everyone coming out of his shelters and returning to previous circumstances—"The communities that are well organized and have planned their decontamination actions will be able to return to normal life conditions"—struck most officials as "too facile." There was nothing about the uncertainties and difficulties involved in decontamination, nothing that suggested that hospitals, doctors and nurses might no longer exist in abundance, no justification for the assumption that everyone can come out of his shelter after two weeks, no references to biological hazards of consuming fresh milk or foodstuffs that might be contaminated, no details about safe levels of radiation dosage or the area of damage that would be most endangered by blast or fire or fallout, given different sizes of nuclear explosives that might be involved in the Soviet attack.

Several White House critics were also disturbed by the class bias that pervaded the pamphlet. One passage went so far as to trumpet, "The anticipation of a new market for home shelters is helpful and in keeping with the free enterprise way of meeting changing conditions in our lives." Illustrations showed office buildings and suburban homes with large basements and gardens—but no tenements or apartment buildings in cities, no workers in factories. One drawing portrayed a family evacuating themselves out to sea in a cabin cruiser. John Kenneth Galbraith, the witty, liberal Harvard economist and Kennedy's ambassador to India, was deeply offended by the whole business. In a memo to Kennedy—which he prefaced by noting, "I regard this as a matter of high importance"—Galbraith dryly remarked, "The present pamphlet is a design for saving Republicans and sacrificing Democrats. . . . I am not at all attracted by a pamphlet which seeks to save the better elements of the population, but in the main writes off those who voted for you."

Some White House officials felt that release of the pamphlet would create a public panic. Already, shelter mania was possessing large segments of the population, and the Administration was largely to blame. It was not only Kennedy's forceful advocacy of fallout shelters that nourished the fever; it was that he did so in a speech about the Berlin crisis and the concrete possibility of war with the Russians by the end of the year. *Newsweek* reported that "fallout shelters, like the Twist, have become fashionable," with some citizens "behaving as if they were cavemen already." Do-it-yourself shelter kits were selling like hamburgers.

The New York Times described incidents of people in the suburbs constructing shelters clandestinely so that neighbors won't try to invade the shelter in the event of nuclear attack. Civil-defense coordinators in Nevada and in Riverside County, California, warned their citizens to arm themselves to repel H-bomb refugees from nearby Los Angeles. The Reverend L. C. McHugh, a columnist for the Catholic magazine *America*, assured readers that it was ethically permissible to shoot your neighbors if they tried to break into your fallout shelter.

White House adviser Arthur Schlesinger wrote Kennedy, "Everywhere the shelter program seems to be emerging as the chief issue of domestic concern—and as one surrounded by an alarming amount of bewilderment, confusion and, in some cases (both pro and con) of near-hysteria." Civil defense had "become the focus of all anxieties over foreign policy." The do-it-yourself spirit of the present program was turning ugly, "at war with morality and at war with the sense of community cooperation which will be indispensable in the case of attack. It is an invitation to barbarism." For some citizens, Schlesinger continued, the program was generating "a false sense of security—a belief that . . . a nuclear war will be no worse than a bad cold," an illusion that will "encourage these people to become reckless in their foreign policy demands and to condemn negotiation and accommodation as appeasement." For others, as "they begin to visualize nuclear war concretely for the first time," they react "with horror and panic," which could generate "an increase in the cry for unilateral disarmament and in the 'better-red-than-dead' nonsense." The civil-defense campaign was also promoting a new industry "based on whipping up people's fears to the point where they will rush to buy shelters." As Ted Sorensen told Kennedy in a memo written on November 23, one day after Schlesinger's, "Civil Defense is rapidly blossoming into our number one political headache."

In this raving social context, many believed that the Yarmolinsky-*Life* fallout pamphlet would only serve to push whole factions of the population several steps closer to the brink of mass de-

tely, the Yarmolinsky pamphlet was substantially
bstance and tone, and in the first week of Decem-
e million copies were sent to 790 civil-defense of-
4 post offices around the country. Kennedy decided
not to give a TV speech and he firmly decided against sending the
much-modified booklet to every household in America. He had
begun to back off from his initial enthusiasm for the subject. First,
much to everyone's surprise, civil defense was turning into a political hot potato. Second, the Berlin crisis was cooling down, the
sense of urgency was passing. Third, the critiques from the White
House staff were starting to take their toll on Kennedy's thinking.
This process was accelerated the afternoon of November 29, when
Edward Teller, father of the H-bomb, paid a visit to the White
House.

Teller was more fanatically devoted to shelters than even
Rockefeller, and he came that day to persuade Jerry Wiesner,
Kennedy's science adviser, of their virtues. In his steely Hungarian accent, his thick eyebrows impressively jumping about, Teller
narrated his scenario for a massive civil-defense program. First we
will start with fallout shelters, he explained, but that won't cover
everybody, so we will then have to go to blast shelters. But that
won't cover everybody, either, so finally we will have to build fire
shelters. And if the Russians build bigger bombs, then we will
have to dig deeper.

In a perverse sense, Wiesner was delighted by this display. In
the past few years, Wiesner had undergone a dramatic transfor-
mation from a hardline hawk to a passionate advocate of arms
control and disarmament, and like Kaysen, Raskin and—increasingly—Bundy, he thought the shelter idea was dangerous and
self-deluding nonsense.* He thought that Teller's little lecture
was mad, and he knew that any proponent who heard it would re-
examine his own position and that anyone still unsure about civil
defense would tip decisively to Wiesner's position against it. With
this in mind, Wiesner told Teller that his comments were just fas-

---

* Wiesner began to change after serving on the Gaither Committee in 1957. The
experience taught him that purely military solutions to the security problem
would only provoke Soviet responses and further problems, and so concluded that
arms control was the only answer. A few others in the Gaither group reached the
same conclusion over the next few years, among them William Foster, I. I. Rabi,
Spurgeon Keeny, Herbert York, and Vincent McRae.

314

FRED KAⱭ

cinating, and took him to see the President. With an excited gleam
in his eye, Teller went through the same scenario with Kennedy.
As Wiesner expected, Kennedy was half shocked, half bemused,
incredulous of the spectacle before him.

After the meeting, Wiesner, again feigning enthusiasm, had
Teller repeat the tale to Bundy. Two days later, Bundy wrote a
memo to Kennedy: "I must say I am horrified by the thought of
digging deeper as the megatonnage gets bigger, which is the notion of civil defense that Dr. Teller spelled out to me after your
meeting with him the other evening. He thinks it can be done
quite easily for $50 billion spent over a period of years. This is a
position from which you will wish to be disassociated. . . ." Bundy
urged shifting to "a very low key and distinctly modest program."

In December 1961, Kennedy had submitted a budget that included $695 million for civil defense. By the summer of 1962,
Congress had it whittled down to $80 million, with scarcely a ges-
ture of protest or dismay from the Administration. The civil-defense craze, like the Berlin crisis that prompted it, simply evapo-
rated. It became all too clear that while shelters would save some
lives, nuclear war would remain a catastrophic event, an un-
wieldly instrument for displaying "national will," an irrational option. Moreover, either it proved impossible to get people seriously
interested in civil defense—or, if a major crisis and a feverish
propaganda campaign did whet their appetites, the unsavory aspects of modern democracy threatened to overwhelm the marketplace, disrupting the sense of community that sustaining nuclear
war would require and the social bonds that civil defense was designed to protect.

From the fall of 1961 through the following spring, the idea
of an effective, practical and implicitly popular civil-defense program—Herman Kahn's vision of the urban population casually
evacuating two or three times a decade to bolster national resolve—took a terrible and sobering beating. And so, with it, did
another piece of the concept of a controllable nuclear war.

22 DAMAGE UNLIMITED

EVEN BEFORE Robert McNamara's landmark speech of June 1962 in Ann Arbor, publicly declaring counterforce/no-cities as official U.S. policy, strands of the RAND strategy were already slowly starting to unravel. The speech itself set into motion a variety of reactions and reflections that made the workaday theories of the defense intellectuals still less attractive. The Russians denounced McNamara as a militaristic madman who was trying to create "rules for the holocaust." Liberal arms-control advocates in the United States criticized the policy as one that would set off an ever-spiraling arms race and create incentives for preemptive first-strikes. But the response that concerned McNamara came from the Air Force.

The Air Force was emboldened by the Ann Arbor speech, telling McNamara in one report: "The Air Force has rather supported the development of forces which provide the United States with a first-strike capability credible to the Soviet Union, as well as to our Allies, by virtue of our ability to limit damage to the United States and our Allies to levels acceptable in light of the circumstances and the alternatives available."

In his first Draft Presidential Memorandum to Kennedy of September 1961, McNamara had put counterforce targeting at the very heart of his strategic nuclear force planning; the ability to strike cities was relegated to a reserve force that was not to be used unless the Soviets struck American cities first. In the second DPM, handed to Kennedy on November 21, 1962, he wrote that the objectives in general nuclear war were "*first,* to provide the United States with a secure, protected retaliatory force able to survive any attack within enemy capabilities and capable of striking back and destroying Soviet *urban society,* if necessary, in a controlled and deliberate way." The counterforce strategy was listed *second.* McNamara still favored counterforce, but said only that it "may succeed . . . and make a substantial contribution to the damage-limiting objectives" in "some circumstances."

McNamara had never favored a full first-strike capability. In the first DPM, McNamara had spent three short paragraphs briefly listing some drawbacks to a first-strike strategy. In the second DPM, just to ensure that Ann Arbor was in no way to be confused with Air Force philosophy, he devoted four pages to describing the futility of such a strategy.

McNamara did continue to hang on to the essence of the RAND doctrine. "We might try to knock out most of the Soviet strategic nuclear forces, while keeping Russian cities intact, and then coerce the Soviets into avoiding our cities (by the threat of controlled reprisal) and accepting our peace terms. . . . I believe that the coercive strategy is a sensible and desirable option to have in second-strike circumstances in which we are trying to make the best of a bad situation." However, whereas the coercive strategy served as the main rationale for the forces McNamara had decided to buy in the 1961 DPM, he now stated, "We should stop augmenting our forces for this purpose when the extra capability the increments offer is small in relation to the extra costs."

Nevertheless, the Air Force and, by this time, the entire JCS kept up their pressure for more weapons, rationalizing their wish lists with language deliberately modeled on the Ann Arbor speech and in McNamara's DPMs. Increasingly, McNamara began to fear that the counterforce strategy presented *no* logical limit to the size of the arsenal; that as long as targets of potentially military value could be found or as long as the Soviets added more weapons to their own arsenal, someone could always claim we did not have enough; that his own endorsement of counterforce was promoting an unlimited nuclear arms buildup that he had gone out of his way to suppress.

In January 1963, McNamara instructed his staff that they were no longer to cite counterforce as the official Pentagon strategic concept. His staff proceeded to inform the military that they were no longer to use counterforce as a rationale for their weapons requirements or proposals. Meanwhile, McNamara had to find some new doctrine that could be used as a further rhetorical tool to clamp down the threat from the JCS. He found the ideal device in the 1960 study known as WSEG-50, which advocated a strategy of city destruction and "finite deterrence." McNamara's chief analysts, Charlie Hitch and Alain Enthoven, both from RAND, hadn't liked that part of WSEG-50, and had urged McNamara to hear Bill Kaufmann's counterforce briefing. McNamara ended up agreeing with Kaufmann's points on *avoiding* cities and trying to control the nuclear war; but he was still attracted to the philosophy of WSEG-50, in that it suggested a basic guideline for determining how many weapons were enough.

In the next DPM, delivered to President Lyndon B. Johnson on December 6, 1963, two weeks after John Kennedy was assassinated in Dallas, McNamara devised a criterion by which nuclear adequacy should be measured, and he called it "Assured Destruction."

The new measure put almost total emphasis on the deterrence, rather than on the fighting, of nuclear war. Essentially, it said that after a surprise Soviet counterforce strike, the United States should still have enough forces surviving to destroy the U.S.S.R.'s governmental and military controls as well as a large percentage of its population and industrial base. The idea was that as long as the Soviets knew that we could retaliate, that would deter them. McNamara's Whiz Kids calculated that the Soviets would be sufficiently deterred if we could kill 30 percent of their population and destroy half of their industrial capacity, and, further, that this task could be accomplished with the explosive power of 400 megatons.

It all appeared scientific and precise, but in fact it had little to do with any formulation of how much would be enough to deter the Soviets. It was the output of a computer program designed by Alain Enthoven, "laying down" one-megaton bombs against Soviet cities and calculating, at various points, how much additional damage one additional bomb would do. From this calculation, Enthoven generated a graph with two curves, one showing how many people would be killed, the other how much industry destroyed, as a function of "delivered one-megaton warheads." Beyond 400 megatons, by which point all major cities would be devastated, the curves began to flatten considerably. And they happened to show that 400 megatons would kill about 30 percent of the Soviet population (assuming a limited urban fallout-shelter program) and destroy about half its industrial capacity. If the U.S. doubled its megatonnage to 800, Soviet fatalities would rise by only about ten percentage points and the industrial capacity destroyed would be boosted by only three percentage points.

In short, the 400-megaton requirement was based on the concept, familiar to all economists, of "diminishing marginal returns."

"SOVIET POPULATION AND INDUSTRY
DESTROYED BY MEGATONS"*

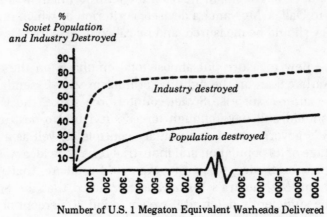

Number of U.S. 1 Megaton Equivalent Warheads Delivered

*Not including deaths caused by radiation, fallout or firestorm.

There was another reason for the 400-megaton requirement. Enthoven had calculated that after a reasonably successful Soviet first-strike, launched in 1969, and assuming that McNamara's five-year defense plan of 1964 had been adopted, the United States would be left with at least 1,200 megatons. If one stretched the Assured Destruction calculus to read that there should be 400 survivable megatons on each "leg" of the strategic "Triad"—the ICBMs, the SLBMs and the long-range bombers—that would add up to 1,200 megatons. In other words, Assured Destruction was adopted by McNamara primarily as a tool for beating back the excessive demands of the military, for proving that his own program was adequate for deterrence.

For all of McNamara's elaboration of the new counter-city strategy, the actual U.S. targeting plan remained the revised SIOP-63 that McNamara had ordered in the spring of 1961. In the 1963 DPM, just below "Assured Destruction," McNamara endorsed a strategy of "Damage-Limiting," which was another name for counterforce. And he reiterated the language from the 1962 DPM supporting the "coercive strategy" as "a sensible and desirable option to have in second-strike circumstances"—though he did add the significant proviso, in 1963, that this option did not "provide a basis for buying more missiles." McNamara also emphasized in the 1963 DPM that he was calculating "the destructive capacity of our force on the hypothetical assumption that all of it is targeted on cities, *even though in fact we would not use our forces in that manner if deterrence failed*" (italics added).

In fact, in the same 1963 DPM in which McNamara backed Assured Destruction, various charts revealed that by 1969, under his proposed program, only 18 percent of the portion of the U.S. strategic nuclear force on constant alert—or 533 missiles, including all fifty-four Titan ICBMs and about three-quarters of the Polaris SLBMs—would actually be targeted against cities. The other 2,720 weapons on alert—bombers, Minuteman ICBMs, remaining Polaris missiles at sea—would be aimed at bomber bases, missile and air-defense sites, submarine pens, weapons-storage depots, tactical interdiction targets, in short, at counterforce targets. Even the 533 missiles targeted on cities would be aimed to knock out the control centers of the Soviet government and military structure. Although at least 30 percent of the population would be killed and half the industry destroyed, that was not the actual motivation behind the targeting. Finally, these counter-city missiles were to be held in reserve for as long as possible.

McNamara talked Assured Destruction, even in Top Secret memoranda to the President; but the actual targeting strategy, which McNamara closely monitored and approved, remained mainly counterforce. In the early-to-mid 1960s, the Soviets did not have very many nuclear weapons, nor were many of them hardened to any significant degree. The 1,200-megaton alert force that McNamara proposed was rationalized as an Assured-Destruction 400-megaton arsenal times three, for each leg of the Triad; but it was also enough to deliver a powerful counterforce blow. Assured Destruction was adopted by McNamara primarily as a tool for beating back the excessive demands of the military and the JCS. In the event of war, he could still choose counterforce.

Increasingly, however, McNamara's rhetorical backpedaling from counterforce reflected more than just budgetary bouts with the JCS. He was also beginning genuinely to doubt whether the strategy was feasible. In 1962, the JCS had told him that the Soviets were beginning to deploy SLBMs, like the Polaris, and that by mid-1967 they would have 186 of them, as well as 156 sublaunched cruise missiles—none of which could be easily located, much less suddenly destroyed all at once.

Second, photoreconnaissance satellites had revealed that the Soviets were starting to follow McNamara's prudent example of encasing their ICBMs in concrete underground silos. Finally, the Whiz Kids in McNamara's Office of Systems Analysis had calculated that under very favorable circumstances, even the number of bombers and missiles proposed by the Air Force would, by 1967, "at best be able to reduce Soviet strategic forces to roughly 100 ICBMs." These, along with the 100 or so SLBMs that the Soviets would have on alert at sea, could kill fifty million Americans, assuming a modest fallout-shelter program. McNamara wrote to President Kennedy, "I do not consider this an 'acceptable' level of damage." In the December 1963 DPM, he wrote to President Johnson, "The prospects for 'Damage Limiting' by counterforce attacks may not hold great promise in the latter part of the 1960s if the Soviets harden and disperse their ICBM force and build up their missile submarine forces as we now expect them to do."

In January 1964, McNamara's skepticism was nourished by an analysis produced, interestingly enough, by an Air Force general working out of Harold Brown's Directorate of Defense Research & Engineering, or DDR&E. The study, by General Glenn Kent, was entitled *Damage Limiting: A Rationale for the Allocation of Resources by the U.S. and the U.S.S.R.* Kent was an unusual Air Force officer, a mathematician who had been director of plans in the late 1950s, took leave from 1961 to 1962 to study defense policy at Harvard, and returned to the Pentagon as an assistant to Harold Brown. Many were fooled at first by his mild manners and southern drawl, but he soon became every systems analyst's favorite general: he knew what they were talking about, he could do the calculations.

When Kent first started working in DDR&E, he noticed Harold Brown looking at the results of a JCS computer war game that attempted to examine the effectiveness of anti-ballistic missiles, ABMs, in a "nuclear exchange" between the U.S. and the U.S.S.R. The methodology of the JCS game was to assume a Soviet attack of x warheads, and then to figure out how many ABM interceptors, with what probability of kill, would be needed to shoot down a high percentage of the incoming warheads. Kent pointed out to Brown that the calculations did not take into account the likely interactions between the Soviet and the American buildup; that the construction of an American *defensive* system would almost certainly prompt the Soviets to adjust and expand their own *offensive* arsenal, in which case he would have to do the calculations all over again. A more realistic analysis, Kent continued, would display curves on a graph indicating what was necessary—in terms of interceptors, dollars, whatever—to shoot down enemy missiles, given a wide range of attack tactics that the Soviets might choose.

Kent saw the three issues of ABM, counterforce and civil defense as intertwining facets of a single strategy called "damage-limiting." Counterforce limited damage by destroying Soviet weapons before they were launched, ABMs by destroying them before they landed, shelters by protecting people from the effects of the weapons that made it through.

Brown told Kent to do a comprehensive study that would calculate what mix of these three programs would limit damage most cost-effectively and that would systematically account for the interaction between the buildup of American defense and Soviet offense, American damage-limiting and Soviet damage-inflicting.

Over the next several months, Kent worked on the calculations and drew twenty-nine graphs, plotting the relationship between the percent of surviving U.S. population and industry versus the number of attacking Soviet missiles. The graphs covered a wide variety of U.S. damage-limiting strategies and Soviet attack tactics.

The calculations revealed that damage-limiting was a fairly hopeless strategy. Kent did show that, under certain conditions, damage-limiting could make a difference of up to 55 or 60 percent in the amount of U.S. industry surviving a Soviet attack. However, if the Soviets reacted by expanding their own offensive forces, they could completely nullify the damage-limiting measures—and, moreover, do so far more cheaply than it would take for the United States to limit damage yet again. In the race between offense and defense, offense would win, and at lower cost.

When Robert McNamara read the Kent study in January 1964, he picked up on this theme immediately. Two graphs in particular riveted his attention. One plotted the cost in billions of dollars of a full fallout-shelter program, an ABM system and an anti-bomber air-defense system against the number of reliable Soviet missiles attacking the U.S. Different curves showed the relationship between cost and the number of missiles for varying percents of U.S. industry surviving the attack. The curves were hardly even curves; they looked more like straight vertical lines. If the U.S. wanted to protect 60 percent of its industry against an attack by 200 reliable Soviet missiles, it would require an $18 billion investment in damage-limiting. However, the curves showed that if the Soviets attacked with 300 missiles, a 50 percent increase in the offensive forces, the U.S. would have to double its damage-limiting budget to $35 billion. For each extra missile that the Soviets added to the attack, the U.S. would have to spend $140 million to offset its effects. If the U.S. wanted to protect 70 to 80 percent of industry (and roughly the same percentage of population), it would cost $260 million to $500 million to offset a single additional Soviet missile. If the tolerance of damage was much lower and one could stand only 50 percent surviving, the U.S. would have to spend $80 million on defenses for each missile that the Soviets added to the attack. As Kent calculated it, adding one missile to their arsenal would cost the Soviets the equivalent of only about $25 million. In other words, to limit damage so that half the industry (and about 60 percent of the population) survived an attack, the U.S. would have to spend $3.20 for each $1 paid by the U.S.S.R.—a losing proposition.

The other graph that impressed McNamara showed the cost in billions of dollars of the most economical mix of all damage-limiting measures—fallout shelters, ABMs, bomber defense and counterforce strikes—versus the cost to the Soviets of an attack against the U.S. Again, the curves measured this relationship for 70, 60, 50 and 40 percent of U.S. industry surviving the attack. The curves were only slightly less steep. For each extra dollar that the Soviets added to the attack forces, the U.S. would have to spend $3 to protect 70 percent of its industry, $2 to save 60 percent, $1.80 to defend half, and the same $1 to defend a mere 40 percent. Again, it seemed a losing battle.

Kent also warned Brown, who passed along the message to McNamara, that all of these calculations assumed extremely effective ABM systems. Specifically, they assumed that each ABM interceptor had a "kill probability" of .8—that for each ten incoming Soviet warheads, the ABMs could shoot down eight. This fig-

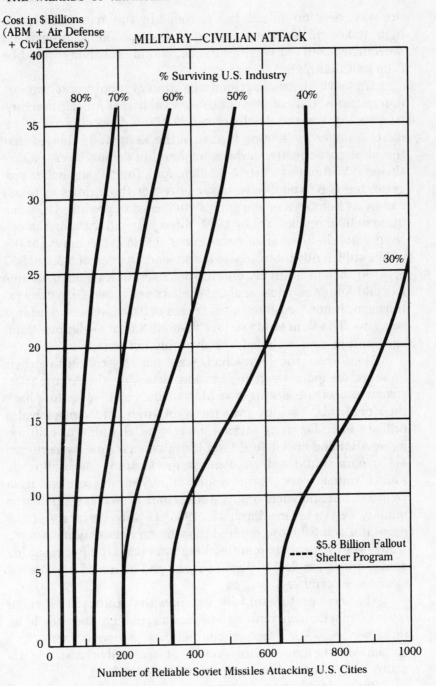

Cost in $ Billions
(ABM + Air Defense
 + Civil Defense)

MILITARY—CIVILIAN ATTACK

% Surviving U.S. Industry

80% 70% 60% 50% 40%

30%

$5.8 Billion Fallout
Shelter Program

Number of Reliable Soviet Missiles Attacking U.S. Cities

From Glenn Kent, *Damage Limiting*

ure was based on official data provided by the Army, which had high stakes in deploying vast ABM systems. Kent, Brown and McNamara doubted whether the actual kill probability would be even half that high.

In short, the damage-limiting strategy would cost way too much, and would not prevent the devastation of American industrial society and the deaths of nearly 100 million citizens, if not more. Another interesting feature of the Kent study showed that the most cost-effective devices for limiting damage were fallout shelters. Without at least $5.8 billion for a full fallout-shelter program, the U.S. would have to spend two or three times as much money as Kent's "damage curves" indicated to produce the same quite limited results. Yet by 1964, three years after the Berlin crisis and the shelter mania, it was impossible to get Congress or the public sufficiently interested to spend more than an obligatory $90 or $100 million annually on civil defense. McNamara used this fact and Kent's conclusion about shelters as a rationale to deny extravagant funds for ABMs, air defenses or additional counterforce weapons. The Kent study settled all of McNamara's doubts. Damage-limiting, he concluded, simply would not work.

Meanwhile, the Joint Chiefs were not only continuing their pressure for more weapons, but also attacking the Assured Destruction doctrine, seeing it as McNamara's tool for beating back their demands. Looking over the Kent study, McNamara had a brilliant idea. Feigning serious interest in what mix of counterforce, ABM and civil defense would limit damage most effectively, McNamara would order a Pentagon-wide study elaborating on Kent's initial work. Kent would supervise the project from DDR&E, but analytical inputs would come from officers in all the military services. On March 12, 1964, Deputy Secretary of Defense Roswell Gilpatric ordered that the services conduct such a study over the next six months. Kent integrated the five resulting studies into a single 175-page analysis, and delivered it to McNamara on September 8.

The services were initially pleased with the study. To them, it revealed that damage-limiting was feasible, that efforts made by all three services—Air Force on counterforce, Army on ABM, Navy on anti-submarine warfare—could, at reasonable cost, significantly limit damage from a Soviet nuclear attack.

But as McNamara expected, the study also revealed that if the Soviets reacted to U.S. damage-limiting measures by increasing their own offensive forces, the effects of damage-limiting would quickly reach the point of diminishing marginal returns and, in fact, that the Soviets could add to their offense far more cheaply than the U.S. could continue adding to its defense. McNamara drew conclusions exactly opposite to those that the officers involved in the study thought they had proved. And McNamara told them so.

The uniformed military was flabbergasted. LeMay accused Kent of selling the Air Force down the river and threatened to demote him to the rank of colonel. The military felt tricked by McNamara. McNamara sent the conclusions of the study to President Johnson and McGeorge Bundy, making sure that they understood his interpretation. For the next few years, as a rationale that the military could invoke to justify more weapons, damage-limiting was dead.

In his DPM of December 1964, McNamara backed off further still from counterforce, using the Kent studies as the main source of his arguments. His expressed skepticism about damage-limiting was more elaborate, his case against a new manned bomber and air-defense systems more powerfully presented than in earlier DPMs. It was in the 1964 DPM that McNamara reduced the Minuteman program from 1,400 to 1,000 ICBMs, where it remained permanently. And it was in that DPM that references to the "coercion strategy" disappeared entirely.

This was not to say, however, that counterforce disappeared from the actual targeting plan. Even in the 1964 DPM, McNamara noted that simply maximizing Soviet urban damage was not the best way to use nuclear weapons, that damage-limiting still had a role to play in that sense. As part of the compromise to reduce Minuteman to 1,000 missiles, he initiated a new Minuteman II missile program and a new inertial-guidance system that would improve the Minuteman's accuracy and thus increase Minuteman's ability to destroy "fully hardened targets," such as enemy missile silos (then hardened to resist about 300 pounds per square inch of overpressure), by 50 percent. He also ordered research to begin on a program called MIRV, Multiple Independently targetable Re-entry Vehicles—fixing several warheads on top of a single missile, giving it the ability to strike several widely separated targets—and noted that this "would permit each missile the flexibility to attack a single heavily defended urban-indus-

trial target, *or a single hardened point target,* or several unde-
fended targets. . . ."

But these points were buried in the DPM, easily overlooked.
Moreover, the 1964 DPM, unlike all the others before it, contained
no chart indicating how many U.S. weapons were aimed at what
types of Soviet targets. Such a chart would have indicated that a
counterforce strategy still ruled the actual war plan. And in his
moment of bureaucratic victory over the JCS, McNamara wanted
to keep that fact in low profile.

But these omissions also reflected McNamara's quite firm
conviction, by this time, that a counterforce or damage-limiting
strategy would not work. As early as 1962, he had recognized that
the concept counted on destroying the Soviets' will to smash our
cities, not their ability to do so. Now, if the Soviets could easily defeat our efforts to limit damage by building more offensive weapons, if whatever we did the Soviets could still inflict "unacceptable
damage" to American civilians and industry, couldn't they use
that destructive power as a bargaining tool themselves? Would a
U.S. counterforce strike that didn't much affect the Soviets' ability to devastate American society really give us so great an advantage in the game of "intrawar deterrence"? McNamara didn't
think so.

Neither, by this time, did most of the Whiz Kids. Partly
through reading the Kent studies and partly through McNamara's
own highly persuasive powers over his staff, they began to lose
faith in their old theories as well. Alain Enthoven and Harry
Rowen followed McNamara in strenuous advocacy of Assured Destruction and denial that using nuclear weapons could bring any
political gain. Bill Kaufmann never fully embraced Assured Destruction, but he too had grown tired and skeptical of his creation.
Kaufmann had always viewed counterforce/no-cities as a way of
trying to make the best of a desperate situation; now he wondered
whether it was even that. He no longer really believed that nuclear
war would start the way that the theory suggested, and seriously
doubted that the war could so easily be controlled. Increasingly,
Kaufmann shifted his attention to his much earlier interest in
non-nuclear "limited war."

As early as 1962, the Pentagon—thanks mainly to analysis
that Kaufmann helped conduct, under the supervision of Alain
Enthoven and Paul Nitze—had been coming around to realize
that the Soviet Army was not ten feet tall, that its admittedly plen-

tiful armed divisions were individually much weaker than NATO's, that facing the Soviets with only conventional weapons on the European battlefield was not a hopeless proposition and that, therefore, depending on battlefield nuclear weapons was not necessary. Even while supporting counterforce, Kaufmann had always opposed the use of nuclear weapons on the battlefield. His concept of "limited war" required rationality, mutual restraints, controlled responses and circumscribed limits on the intensity and boundaries of the conflict. If nuclear weapons came into play, limits would be much more confusing and difficult to establish; escalation would be made nearly inevitable; "limited war" would no longer be limited.

Kaufmann's ideas about limited war had had substantial impact on Enthoven, Nitze, Harry Rowen and—through them— Robert McNamara. The cumulative effect of the missile gap's sudden demise, the events of the Berlin and Cuban crises and, finally, Glenn Kent's damage-limiting studies may have put a damper on the idea that strategic nuclear war could be rationally controlled. But the disillusionment cast no dark spell on the underlying faith in the supreme powers of rational analysis, the casual ease of executing and managing "options," the controllability of other "instruments" of force. And as enthusiasm shifted from the theoretical calculus of nuclear war to a real-life "limited war" in Southeast Asia, the style of thought that had shaped the philosophy of counterforce/no-cities was given a chance to go out in the field and show what it could do.

23 VIETNAM: STALEMATE

IN HIS BOOK *On Thermonuclear War,* Herman Kahn wrote that American security must henceforth depend upon "a willingness to incur casualties in limited wars just to improve our bargaining position moderately." In the 1960s, that limited war was Vietnam.

When John Kennedy came into the White House in 1961 and scuttled massive retaliation as the nation's defense policy, it was a liberating experience for those who studied such issues. Massive retaliation, they thought, had imposed rigid shackles on America's freedom and flexibility. With its banishment, the shackles were smashed. A sort of euphoria set in, the feeling of a mighty eagle freed from its cage, a heady sense of supreme confidence that America could now control the course of events in the Free World, an impatient eagerness to dash out and meet crises head on, to prove the nation's mettle in a clash of wills and nerve.

Jack Kennedy encouraged these sentiments. He would go anywhere, fight any foe, to preserve freedom. As early as February 1, not two weeks into office, he asked Bob McNamara to examine "means for placing more emphasis on the development of counterguerrilla forces," and that he do so "promptly." In April, Kennedy appointed Maxwell Taylor as his chief adviser on paramilitary activities. The same month, he instructed McNamara to devise counterinsurgency plans that could apply to the strife in Vietnam. In January 1962, he formed a Special Group on Counter-Insurgency, with Max Taylor and Kennedy's brother, the Attorney General, Robert, spearheading the effort with—especially in Bobby's case—extraordinary enthusiasm.

In August 1961, Walt Rostow, director of the State Department's policy planning staff, wrote nonchalantly of installing some troops to defend the Mekong Delta area, while indigenous South Vietnamese troops carried out "the panhandle mop-up operations." If we needed to do more, Rostow—who helped the Eighth Air Force select strategic-bombing targets during World War II—noted that we could "increase pressure directly against North

Vietnam" through air strikes in an "interdiction operation [that] would be susceptible to flexible control at all times to meet a changing military and political situation." We might even want to introduce more ground forces so that "we could make [their] withdrawal a bargaining counter in a Vietnamese settlement," Rostow wrote to Kennedy in October 1961. The presence of such a force would also "make it clear . . . that the attempt to destroy the South Vietnamese government by force would not be carried forward to a conclusion without risking an escalation of the fight."

Upon returning from a mission to South Vietnam, Maxwell Taylor, Kennedy's chief adviser on paramilitary activities, made the same point: "Nothing is more calculated to sober the enemy and to discourage escalation in the face of the limited initiatives proposed here than the knowledge that the United States has prepared itself soundly to deal with aggression in Southeast Asia at any level."

In March 1965, the U.S. commenced a bombing campaign against North Vietnam called "Rolling Thunder." By traditional military standards, it was a bizarre campaign. Targets were initially selected not so much for their military value as for their political and psychological significance. The idea—as spelled out to President Johnson by McGeorge Bundy in May 1964, when plans were first being made for the bombing—was that the U.S. would "use selected and carefully graduated military force against North Vietnam." Air strikes "would be very carefully designed to have more deterrent than destructive impact," just as deployments of troops on the ground were intended to "maximize their deterrent impact and their menace." As Maxwell Taylor put it in a phrase that Robert McNamara felt expressed the view shared by most of those inside the Pentagon engaged in Vietnam planning, it was important not to "kill the hostage" by destroying the critical assets inside the "Hanoi donut."

By early 1965, McNamara's Vietnam strategy was essentially a conventional-war version of the counterforce/no-cities theory— using force as an instrument of coercion, withholding a larger force that could kill the hostage of the enemy's cities if he didn't back down.

The sharp parallel between Vietnam planning and the no-cities strategy was no accident. First, although McNamara had by this time rejected the strategy as a guideline for policy on nuclear weapons or nuclear war, he still viewed it as a rational approach to

the use of lesser force. Second, the counterforce/no-cities briefing
that Kaufmann gave to McNamara in February 1961 had originally grown out of Kaufmann's earlier thinking on "limited war"
at Princeton in 1955–1956. All the elements of Vietnam could be
foreseen, in retrospect, in his essays from that period: limited war
as "partial or token tests of strengths," most likely in Asia; force as
"a counter in the bargaining process"; the need for "precise, discriminating, and discreet methods of destruction"; the need to
"manage" the war by sending "messages" to induce the opponent
"to accept limitations of geography, weapons, and possibly time";
aiming not for a victory—whose prospect might compel the opponent to escalate (or, in the case of Vietnam, might bring in the
Soviets or the Chinese)—but for "a stalemate," which was "desirable" and also likely as long as we could persuade the opponent
that "the costs of fighting to him outweighed the costs to the
United States, and consequently that the advantages of terminating the conflict were greater than the advantages of continuing
it." All these principles lay at the heart of the Administration's
early Vietnam strategy.

Kaufmann himself had practically nothing to do directly with
Vietnam planning, nor did the Office of Systems Analysis. However, one of Kaufmann's former colleagues from the RAND Corporation did have an important if indirect influence, a professor of
political economy at Harvard named Thomas C. Schelling. He had
started professional life as a trade negotiator in international conferences dealing with U.S. foreign aid. From those experiences,
he learned a great deal about the art of bargaining—especially the
lesson that a good bargaining position often entails the inability to
withdraw, the deliberate establishment of an obligation to fulfill
promises and threats. This is what executive branches of government do in tariff negotiations when they plead that Congress has
tied their hands, what union negotiators do in threatening strikes
when they plead that the rank and file won't take the contract as
proposed. Schelling elaborated these ideas in a highly influential
1960 book called *The Strategy of Conflict*, focusing on war as a
case study. He saw war, essentially, as a particularly violent form
of bargaining. There were "enlightening similarities between, say,
maneuvering in limited war and jockeying in a traffic jam, deterring the Russians and deterring one's own children . . . between

the modern balance of terror and the ancient institution of hostages," he wrote.

This was the world of Game Theory. And Schelling added a spin. Most analysts figured Game Theory as a "zero-sum game": your loss is my victory; your negative "payoff" is my positive "payoff"; hence, the sum of the two payoffs is zero. Schelling thought that the more interesting and pertinent situations were "non-zero-sum games," which involve a mixture of competition and tacit cooperation. In a traffic jam, you want to pass a car, but you don't want to smash it; in limited war, you want to defeat the enemy's will without compelling him to bring nuclear weapons into play.

Schelling appealed strongly to those who felt constrained by the doctrine of massive retaliation. His book reinforced the insouciance toward force that marked the insignia of the post-Eisenhower defense intellectual. But in the process Schelling tended to make limited war appear casual, too predictable, too manageable, as if national leaders really might control their moves and countermoves in war as tightly and single-mindedly as the drivers of two cars trying to pass each other on a narrow bridge.

Far more than most of his RAND comrades, Schelling was also interested in nuclear arms control. Inspired by Albert Wohlstetter's work on the vulnerability of SAC, Schelling figured that if a nuclear war ever did spark between the superpowers, it would be because of what he called "The Reciprocal Fear of Surprise Attack." The Air Force had used Wohlstetter's arguments to justify building more bombers and missiles; Schelling inferred from those same arguments that both sides should sign arms-control agreements restricting the deployment of weapons that were both vulnerable to attack and made opposing forces vulnerable to attack. "If the advantage of striking first can be eliminated or severely reduced, the incentive to strike *at all* will be reduced." From this logic, Schelling concluded that weapons of great counterforce power upset the "stability" of the balance of terror and heighten the incentives for one side or the other to launch a pre-emptive first-strike.

Schelling's concept of nuclear stability presented a serious dilemma. If both sides were essentially invulnerable to a lethal first-strike from each other, if counterforce was destabilizing and if massive retaliation meant mutual suicide, then how would the

United States use the threat of nuclear attack to deter Soviet aggression in, say, Western Europe? Did a stable balance render nuclear weapons useless? Schelling felt that they would "still be capable of carrying out 'retaliation' in a *punitive* sense." Massive
retaliation lacked credibility as long as the Soviets could massively
retaliate in turn. But "putting pressure on the Russians" through
"limited or graduated reprisals," inflicting "civilian pain and the
threat of more"—sending signals, upping the ante in the bargaining round in a manner similar to Herman Kahn's "tit-for-tat" Type
III Deterrence strategy—would still deter limited Soviet aggression. While different from Kaufmann's counterforce idea, Schelling's strategic concept was still basically a "coercive strategy,"
demonstrating resolve, appealing to the opponent's rational calculations to back off before still more damage is done.

In his next book, *Arms and Influence,* published in 1966,
Schelling went further. "The power to hurt," he wrote, "can be
counted among the most impressive attributes of military
force. . . . To inflict suffering gains nothing and saves nothing
directly; it can only make people behave to avoid it. . . . War is always a bargaining process. . . . It is in the wars that we have come
to call 'limited wars' that the bargaining appears most vividly and
is conducted most consciously." One must use force in such a way
as to exploit "the bargaining power that comes from [the] capacity to hurt," to cause "sheer pain and damage," because they are
"the primary instruments of coercive warfare."

When, in the early months of 1964, government officials laid
plans to step up military action against North Vietnam, it was precisely this concept of coercive warfare that shaped the resulting
strategy. This was the natural outcome not only of McNamara's
own proclivity toward controlling force rationally, but also of the
coincidence that one of McNamara's closest advisers on Vietnam
strategy, one of the Pentagon's brightest theorists and most skill-
ful bureaucratic players, happened to be one of Tom Schelling's
most dedicated devotees, a Harvard Law School professor named
John McNaughton.

Tom Schelling and John McNaughton had been friends from
the late 1940s, when both were helping to administer the Marshall
Plan in Paris. In the winter of 1960–1961, Paul Nitze, the new
Kennedy Administration's Assistant Secretary of Defense for
International Security Affairs, offered Schelling a job as his

arms-control deputy. Schelling demurred, but recommended McNaughton. McNaughton thanked Schelling for the good words but said he knew almost nothing about arms control. Schelling told him not to worry, that it was easy, that he would teach McNaughton everything he would need to know. Before long, McNamara and McNaughton were hitting it off splendidly. McNamara had a penchant for brilliant Harvard lawyers. By the end of his first year, McNaughton was McNamara's general counsel and chief aide on arms control. It was mainly McNaughton who convinced the Pentagon of the merits of the Limited Test Ban Treaty of 1963. When Paul Nitze was made Secretary of the Navy that same year, McNaughton succeeded him as Assistant Secretary of Defense.

Then came Vietnam. McNaughton drifted away from Schelling's ideas on arms control and more toward his mentor's theories of limited war.

On May 22, 1964, McGeorge Bundy sent a memo to Lyndon Johnson informing him of a "small, tightly knit group" that had met at Bundy's request to prepare the plans Johnson had asked for to broaden the Vietnam War. "An integrated political-military plan for graduated action against North Vietnam is being prepared under John McNaughton at Defense," Bundy reported. "The theory of this plan is that we should strike to hurt but not to destroy, and strike for the purpose of changing the North Vietnamese decision on intervention in the south. This is easier said than done," Bundy acknowledged, "but McNamara has confidence that we have the military means as long as we have the political will." Two days later, Bundy sent Johnson a memo recommending that the U.S. "use selected and carefully graduated military force against North Vietnam," that troops be deployed "on a very large scale, from the beginning, so as to maximize their deterrent impact and their menace." He noted, "A pound of threat is worth an ounce of action—as long as we are not bluffing," and urged that the initial air strikes against the North should "be very carefully designed" to emphasize their "deterrent . . . impact, as far as possible." The Harvard professor's theory had been translated into official U.S. war strategy.

On September 3, McNaughton wrote a memo to McNamara, "Plan of Action for South Vietnam," in which he stressed, "We should watch for . . . DRV [North Vietnamese] actions which would justify a limited retaliation or the commencement of a

squeeze on North Vietnam. . . . The concept of the course of action . . . in essence is: by doing legitimate things to provoke a DRV
response and to be in a good position to seize on that response, or
upon an unprovoked DRV action, to commence a crescendo of
GVN [South Vietnam]–U.S. military actions against the DRV."

Early "actions of opportunity" had already occurred, on August 2 and 4, with allegations of a North Vietnamese gunboat attack on the U.S. destroyer *Maddox* in the Gulf of Tonkin. The next
came on November 1, three days before the 1964 Presidential
election, when the Viet Cong launched a mortar attack on the
U.S. air base at Bien Hoa, killing five Americans, wounding sev-
enty-six, and severely damaging twenty-seven of the thirty B-57
bombers that were there as a signal to Hanoi that the U.S. could
swiftly deliver a crushing air attack on the North.

The opportunity to execute the long-planned air strike had
come. An NSC interagency working group, chaired by Assistant
Secretary of State William Bundy, met to consider options. They
chose "Option C," described in a memo by John McNaughton as
"Progressive squeeze-and-talk. Present policies plus an orchestra-
tion of communications with Hanoi and a crescendo of additional
military moves against infiltration targets, first in Laos and then in
the DRV, and then against other targets in North Vietnam. The
scenario would be designed to give the U.S. the option at any point
to proceed or not, to escalate or not, and to quicken the pace or
not." The threat of greater pain and pressures was at least as important as any damage inflicted; the target was the *will* of the
North to continue its aggression, rather than its *ability* to do so.
The problem was that nobody knew quite how to make it work.

Faced with this puzzle, McNaughton consulted his old friend
Tom Schelling. McNaughton explained that there was great interest in escalating the conflict in order to intimidate the North. For
prompt results, air power was the logical instrument, but what
kind of bombing campaign did Schelling think would best ensure
that the North Vietnamese picked up on the proper signals and
responded accordingly?

Schelling first thought that the campaign should not last
more than a few weeks; it would succeed by then or, if not, the effort should be called off since it would never succeed. He and
McNaughton talked about what the U.S. might want the North to
do or stop doing: sending trained troops or supplies or both to the
South, rehabilitating sanctuaries, providing headquarters for cen-

tral communications. The question became: what could the U.S. ask the North to stop doing that they would obey, that we would soon know they obeyed, and that they could not simply resume doing after the bombing had ceased?

Schelling pondered the problem with McNaughton for more than an hour. In the end, he failed to come up with a single plausible answer to the most basic of questions. So assured, at times glibly so, when writing about sending signals with force, inflicting pain to make an opponent behave and weaving patterns of communications through tactics of coercive warfare in theory, Tom Schelling, when faced with a real-life "limited war," was stumped, had no idea where to begin.

The bombing commenced on March 2, 1965. It changed nothing in the plans or operations of the North Vietnamese or the Viet Cong. If Rolling Thunder sent signals or established a "pattern of communications," the opposition wasn't listening. The U.S. intensified the signals, dropping more bombs on a wider variety of targets, deploying more troops. The North and the VC stayed fast. When the U.S. upped the ante, so did they. The "graduated pressure" from the U.S. scarcely dented, much less conquered, their "will."

Tom Schelling had told McNaughton that the campaign should be given three weeks to produce results. On March 24, almost three weeks to the day, McNaughton wrote McNamara, "The situation in Vietnam is bad and deteriorating." To McNaughton, the most important aim at this point was merely to "avoid a humiliating U.S. defeat (to our reputation as a guarantor)." Thus, a "program of progressive military pressure" should continue, in order to affect the North's "will" and to provide the U.S. and the South "with a bargaining counter." It was essential "that the U.S. emerge as a 'good doctor.' We must have kept promises, been tough, taken risks, gotten bloodied and hurt the enemy very badly."

In April, the CIA reported, "If anything, the strikes to date have hardened [the enemy's] attitude," but then urged, "We must hit them harder, more frequently, and inflict greater damage." On April 21, McNamara, McNaughton, William Bundy, Maxwell Taylor and the Joint Chiefs met in Honolulu and agreed, as McNamara recorded in his report on the session, "that it will take more than six months, perhaps a year or two, to demonstrate VC failure in the South."

Ten years and more than 59,000 American fatalities later, it became clear that the DRV and VC had never paid much attention to our signals.

Vietnam brought out the dark side of nearly everyone inside America's national security machine. And it exposed something seamy and disturbing about the very enterprise of the defense intellectuals. It revealed that the concept of force underlying all their formulations and scenarios was an abstraction, practically useless as a guide to action.

The disillusionment for some became nearly total. Not least affected was Robert McNamara. In May 1966 in Montreal, before the American Society of Newspaper Editors, he regretted the "almost ineradicable tendency to think of our security problem as being exclusively a military problem. . . . We are haunted by this concept of military hardware." The man who, two years earlier, had written Lyndon Johnson that the Vietnam War must be "regarded as a test case of U.S. capacity to help a nation meet a Communist 'war of liberation,' " now warned that it was "a gross oversimplification to regard Communism as the central factor in every conflict throughout the underdeveloped world. . . . The United States has no mandate from on high to police the world and no inclination to do so."

McNamara was coming to believe that wars in the underdeveloped world were caused by economic impoverishment and the failure or refusal of regimes "to meet the legitimate expectations of their citizenry"; that "security means development" and development "means economic, social and political progress"; that while military force still had its place, the goal was to achieve security through world order. At the end of the Montreal speech, McNamara turned philosophical: "Who is man? Is he a rational animal? If he is, then the goals can ultimately be achieved; if he is not, then there is little point in making the effort."

McNamara was still the supreme rationalist, but he managed to move away from the notions of "graduated reprisals" and "coercive strategy" to the more fundamental rationality of sharing "international peacekeeping responsibilities."

From mid-1966 on, McNamara found it increasingly difficult to defend the Vietnam War, especially the bombing. When faced with critical questions from the press, his famous cool façade crumbled. He became increasingly moved by student protests, by calls for social change. He was very affected when John McNaughton, his close aide, died in an airplane accident in the spring of 1967. McNamara started to urge that the U.S. should train armies in the third world to be productive for their people, to assist in the development of education and agriculture. At home, he bore down on landlords who discriminated against black soldiers in providing off-base housing; he started programs in job counseling and training for men who left the military.

In November 1967, he finally told Johnson that the bombing should cease, that it was clearly useless as a bargaining chip. "McNamara's gone dovish on me," Johnson complained to a friend in the Senate. Later that month, McNamara was offered a new job as president of the World Bank, a position that had been tentatively held out the previous May when it became known that the post was about to be vacated. McNamara snapped up the offer with relish and relief. A few months later, he told friends that it was much more satisfying to be working for the development of nations than for their destruction.

The disillusioning blows of Vietnam struck a few of the defense intellectuals as well. Most notorious was the case of Daniel Ellsberg, a former hawkish Cold Warrior of unusual intensity who in 1969 turned first against the war, then against the tenets of his profession, delivered speeches likening himself and his friends to the war criminals of Nazi Germany, and cleansed his soul most dramatically by leaking the Pentagon Papers—the official Defense Department history detailing America's involvement and duplicity in the Vietnam War—to *The New York Times*. Later, Ellsberg joined fledgling socialist organizations and became an eloquent activist in the anti-nuclear movement.

Ellsberg's conversion was from one passion to another, opposite passion. But there were also less extreme though still personally disturbing and disruptive transformations among some of Ellsberg's erstwhile colleagues. Most notable was the case of Bernard Brodie.

Once considered the dean of American strategy, Brodie was conspicuously absent from the pilgrimage to Washington and power trailed by so many others from RAND in the 1960s. Brodie's first step away from the view of the world tacitly held by the strategists of RAND's economics division began in the late 1950s. Through the influence of several Soviet-affairs experts in RAND's

social science division, especially Nathan Leites, Brodie came to
realize that the Soviets were not irrational monsters, that they
were impressed by the dangers of conflict getting out of hand, that
in crises they tended to be prudent. Then, while in France for a
year in 1960, Brodie met some of the leading French strategists—
mainly Raymond Aron, Pierre Gallois, André Beaufre—and he increasingly sympathized with their views. This was when de Gaulle
was publicly proclaiming that France could no longer trust the
U.S. to defend Europe with nuclear weapons and so must build its
own independent arsenal. Meanwhile, the new Kennedy Administration in the U.S., filled with several of Brodie's old friends, was
publicly opposing such plans and encouraging the West Europeans to spend much more money to build up a conventional-weap-
ons defense.

Brodie's new French friends thought the American idea was
absurd, reflecting insensitivity toward the security interests of
France. To Pierre Gallois, the American strategy meant that
NATO would have to concentrate its troops to head off a Soviet invasion, thus creating an attractive, tightly packed target for a Soviet nuclear strike if the Russians found their aggression otherwise repelled. On the other hand, if NATO's troops were
dispersed, they would not have the strength to resist a conventional advance. Gallois, along with de Gaulle, concluded that deterring war in the first place was the only sound policy, and to do
that the West had to convince the Russians that it would use nuclear weapons to counter an invasion. McNamara's proclamation
that the U.S. would try to avoid using nuclear weapons only
blunted their deterrent value. Moreover, Gallois seriously doubted
that the Russians, after taking the enormous risk of mounting an
offensive against the West, would hesitate to use nuclear weapons
if they found themselves losing without them—no matter what
kinds of "signals" NATO might send. Brodie went to Europe a
firm believer in the strategy of conventional limited war; he had
been one of its progenitors, and the idea had gained nearly unani-
mous acceptance among his fellow American defense intellectuals. But he went home siding with his French friends.

Back in the States, his drift toward the French position was
accelerated by the growing animosity between himself and Albert
Wohlstetter. It was something that had been festering for a couple
of years, as Brodie saw the Wohlstetter style of strategic thought
gradually displacing his own preeminent position in the field. The

Brodie-Wohlstetter falling-out symbolized the clash between the old and the new—Wohlstetter the mathematical logician versus Brodie the scholar of philosophy and international relations, rigor versus softheadedness in Wohlstetter's eyes, apolitical scholasticism versus a keen historical sense in Brodie's. As Wohlstetter's star began to shine and as several of his closest acolytes took over the Pentagon as Whiz Kids, the general image of nuclear strategy changed, and Brodie's own light dimmed.

Brodie was the original nuclear strategist, the only one, except for Kaufmann and Schelling, who had given any thought to strategy before coming to RAND. Yet, in 1961, Brodie, unlike his friends and colleagues who had soared off to Washington, was offered no official position, nor even asked for his advice. He felt shunned, humiliated. And the main object of his envy was the mentor of the Whiz Kids, Wohlstetter, who became Brodie's *bête noire*. His sympathy for the French position stiffened. He would frequently take one side of an argument just because Wohlstetter had taken the other.

Those who had known Brodie for years were suddenly puzzled by the series of flip-flops that he made in the early 1960s. The Bernard Brodie who wrote in 1958 that "between the use and non-use of atomic weapons there is a great watershed of difference and distinction . . . that ought not be cavalierly thrown away if we are serious about trying to limit war," now believed that "the idea that we may not initiate use of nuclear weapons of any size or number tactically, for fear that it will precipitate a general nuclear war, seems to me to be one of the grossest forms of self-disarming that history can record." The Brodie who as late as 1960 referred to Wohlstetter's famed *Foreign Affairs* article as having "the significant name of 'The Delicate Balance of Terror' " wrote one year later that "the balance has . . . proved something other than delicate," and still later, "I think the balance of terror has never been delicate." In early 1961, Brodie observed, "It may indeed be rational for the Soviet leaders to start a total war, which is to say that they might think it rational and have fairly good reasons for thinking so." By 1965, he believed, "Unless we are dealing with utter madmen . . . it is virtually impossible to discover in the real world the considerations that could make the Soviet leaders undertake to do such a thing in the face of the enormous risks they would be incurring—risks that are certainly not slighted in their military and political doctrines."

Brodie laid out the case for theater nuclear weapons and against large conventional forces in a 1966 book, first printed as a 1965 RAND memorandum, called *Escalation and the Nuclear Option*. Clearly, there were logical inconsistencies in Brodie's new position that were sparked more by events in his personal life than by objective ruminations on strategy. However, the change in thinking was hardly without a solid intellectual base. For as Brodie departed from the traditions of his past, he opened himself up to new streams of thought. Not least was the idea, mainly inspired by the French strategists and discussions with Nathan Leites, that in a major war the Soviets might not follow America's "signals" to keep the battle confined to a certain set of rules or constraints that would serve NATO's advantage, that this fundamental premise to the strategic analysis of the preceding decade was a wish not at all supported by hard evidence.

"Everything we know about Soviet military thinking," Brodie wrote as early as February 1963, "indicates rejection of those refinements of military thought that have now become commonplace in this country, concerning, for example, distinctions between limited war and general war, between 'controlled' and 'uncontrolled' strategic targeting, and between nuclear and nonnuclear tactical operations." Even apart from considerations of Soviet doctrine, Brodie was coming to conclude that "violence between great opponents is inherently difficult to control, and cannot be controlled unilaterally. . . . Once hostilities begin, the level of violence has in modern times tended always to go up."

More important, Brodie also believed that the Soviets simply had no inclination to invade Europe, so why spend hundreds of billions of dollars to correct a problem that didn't exist? To Brodie, the very existence of nuclear weapons and an unequivocal policy to use them on the battlefield in the event of a large invasion were the best guarantees to prevent war from breaking out in the first place. What disturbed him about McNamara's conventional-war strategy was that it "tends to displace upward the level at which deterrence seems to be really important. The time to deter wars is most emphatically *before they break out,* which is entirely feasible so long as we don't spin too thick a cocoon around each nuclear weapon."

Through a long and circuitous route, Brodie had returned to the fundamental principle underlying his essays of twenty years earlier in *The Absolute Weapon:* "Thus far the chief purpose of our military establishment has been to win wars. From now on its chief purpose must be to avert them. It can have almost no other useful purpose."

The Vietnam War solidified Brodie's departure from the RAND traditions and his return to basic principles. The failure in Vietnam deeply disturbed Brodie because it raised questions about whether his own profession of twenty-five years had much to offer. In Brodie's mind, Vietnam was the Waterloo for the entire enterprise of strategic analysis. Vietnam demonstrated that options were not so manageable after all. The scenarios common to the everyday discussions of the strategic community "have almost universally assumed," Brodie wrote in December 1967 at the peak of the war, "that the United States would be free to escalate, or de-escalate, or make whatever other adjustments in policy that the President and his advisers might think desirable. Indeed, since we reached the level of some half a million troops in Vietnam, we have been essentially locked in . . . able neither to escalate nor to de-escalate in any meaningful fashion."

Vietnam taught Brodie that options may be undesirable as well. It was, after all, the obsession with options that galvanized the U.S. to intervene in Vietnam to begin with. When Kennedy expanded conventional forces, he made it possible for Johnson to intervene without having to call up the Reserves. "It is an old story," Brodie wrote, "that one way of keeping people out of trouble is to deny them the means of getting into it."

This was the ultimate heresy, the final rejection of the RAND ethos. The idea of flexibility and options had made nuclear strategy possible; it allowed the element of choice, which was the essence of strategy. Yet Brodie had come, reluctantly, to conclude that flexibility and options were illusions in the face of the massive destructiveness of nuclear weapons and the ultimate uncontrollability of modern strategic warfare.

In the final years of his life, before he died of cancer in 1978 at the age of sixty-eight, Brodie could still actively engage in discussions about strategy. But friends noticed that he quickly faded out, from gloom or boredom, when the conversation drifted far from first principles. For Brodie had been forced to conclude that nuclear strategy itself—the body of thoughts that he himself had helped formulate—was something of an illusion. The nuclear strategists, not least of them Bernard Brodie, had tried to impose order on chaos, to introduce rational choice into an area of thinking once marked by extreme rigidity. But in the wake of the Vietnam failure and the train of thinking that followed, Brodie dismissed the effort as "simply playing with words." The nuclear game could end only in stalemate. "The rigidity lies in the situation," he stated, "not in the thinking."

24 THE ABM DEBATE

A T A CONFERENCE in Chicago in June 1968, Albert Wohlstetter remarked that "of all the disasters of Vietnam, the worst may be the 'lessons' that we'll draw from it." So it was with most of the strategic community. By that summer, most of its members had given up hopes of winning the war, but still considered the RAND principles as the eternal verities, to be propagated, defended and fought for. For Wohlstetter, the battleground over the next few years was the great debate being waged over the antiballistic missile, the ABM.

The concept of the ABM—shooting down a missile with another missile—was nothing new. In May 1946, a board of scientists had recommended to the Army that one be built. In September 1956, Bell Telephone Labs declared that it was technically feasible. Two months later, the Army and the Pentagon's research and development director ordered that an ABM system be developed, under the name Nike-Zeus.

The first ABM debate got underway in the spring of 1958, when a panel of engineers and other technicians in the Pentagon, called the Reentry Body Identification Group, or RBIG, submitted a report concluding that Nike-Zeus simply would not work against a dedicated enemy attack. Nike-Zeus consisted of a battery of interceptor missiles and a set of huge radars that would track incoming enemy warheads and guide the interceptors to destroy them in their path with a nuclear explosion. The RBIG calculated that if the Soviets merely fired one missile at each defended target, the Nike-Zeus would have a decent chance of shooting it down. However, if the Soviets built a missile fitted with several warheads that separated in outer space and landed in a fairly tight cluster, the ABM would be saturated and the target destroyed.

The United States was already developing such a missile, the Polaris A-3, often called "the Claw," with just three warheads on board. In its calculations, the RBIG discovered that the Nike-Zeus would be defeated by the Polaris Claw. As William E. Bradley,

director of the RBIG and formerly director of the ABM subgroup of
the Gaither Committee of 1957, noted in a memorandum, "Such a
weapon demands such a high rate of fire from an active defense
system, in order to intercept the numerous re-entry bodies [war-
heads] which arrive nearly simultaneously, that the expense of
the required equipment may be prohibitive." Such a weapon, in
short, raised the question of an ABM's "ultimate impossibility."

The group discovered still easier ways for the Russians to defeat Nike-Zeus. Instead of wasting extra warheads, they could
send in "decoys"—metal chaff, balloons, dartlike objects—that
could trick the system into thinking they were real warheads,
forcing it to fire off all its interceptors, and then follow up with the
real weapons. More simply, the Soviets could just attack the tracking radars, which were very large and so vulnerable that they
would be disabled by a 100-kiloton bomb exploding two miles
away. Without the radar, Nike-Zeus would be blind and could not
function. If somehow the radar could be "hardened"—and nobody could figure out how to do that—there was another way to
blind it. Earlier that year, scientists observing atmospheric tests of
nuclear explosions discovered a surprising effect. At very high altitudes, the explosion's fireball was so hot that electrons were released from their atoms, ionizing the air and thus bending and absorbing electromagnetic waves. The explosion's radioactive
debris, at such altitudes, also released beta rays, which were high-
energy electrons that had the same effect. The upshot was that
the explosion would "black out" radar systems for several minutes
for miles around. Thus, the Russians could explode a missile at,
say, 100,000 feet in the air, blinding the ABM's radar, meanwhile
sending in more missiles to their targets underneath. Or, even if
the Soviets were not so clever, the first Nike-Zeus interceptor that
exploded overhead could have the same effect. In short, the ABM
was terribly vulnerable to a number of countermeasures that the
Soviets could quite easily and cheaply prepare.

These conclusions were reinforced in May 1959, with the
submission of a secret report by a panel of Eisenhower's Presidential Science Advisory Committee, or PSAC. It was an impressively
distinguished group, including Hans Bethe, director of the Theoretical Physics Division at Los Alamos during and shortly after
World War II; Wolfgang Panofsky, director of the High-Energy
Physics Lab at Stanford; Harold Brown, director of the Livermore

Lab; Jerome Wiesner and Jerrold Zacharias of MIT; and William E. Bradley, director of the RBIG.

The Army was eager to get Nike-Zeus into production, but as a result of the reports of the two expert panels, the Pentagon kept the project in research and development only.

When John Kennedy came to office, the Army, aided by Maxwell Taylor, made a big push for deployment of an enormous Nike-Zeus system: seventy batteries with 7,000 missiles defending twenty-seven areas in the U.S. and Canada. Initially, Robert McNamara endorsed Nike-Zeus, though on a lesser scale, calling for twelve batteries with 1,200 missiles defending six cities. McNamara accepted the judgment that it could never defend against a massive Soviet attack, but he thought a limited deployment might increase Soviet uncertainty, thus further deterring them from an attack. Also, it might do well against accidental attacks and discourage nuclear blackmail from smaller powers, such as China or Cuba.

Meanwhile, Jerome Wiesner, chairman of PSAC's 1959 ABM panel, was now Kennedy's science adviser, and started to educate Kennedy on the limitations of the ABM in the face of saturation, multiple warheads, radar blackout and all the rest. Wiesner talked a great deal with Kennedy's budget director, David Bell, as well, who reinforced this viewpoint in memos to the President. And Kennedy was briefed by Jack Ruina, a member of the 1958 Reentry Body Identification Group and now director of the Pentagon's Advanced Research Projects Agency. By November 1961, Kennedy had decided against any deployment of Nike-Zeus.

At the same time, the Army was coming up with a better ABM, incorporating a new "phased-array radar," which could scan a much wider area of the sky, and a dual missile system—a long-range ABM that came to be called Spartan, which would intercept incoming missiles in space, and a short-range one called Sprint, which would shoot down missiles once they entered the atmosphere. The Sprint would make the "decoy" problem more manageable, since once decoys—which are lighter than real warheads—hit the atmosphere, they descend at a different velocity, thus allowing tracking radars to distinguish them from the real objects of danger. The Army put this new technology in a new package and called it Nike-X. Still, the scientists pointed out that the fundamental problems remained.

McNamara was changing his mind about the wisdom of
ABMs generally, but pressures for some sort of ABM were mounting, from the entire Joint Chiefs of Staff and from their powerful
friends on Capitol Hill. McNamara found it politically impossible
to kill Nike-X outright, so he tried to buy its advocates off by feed-
ing them big money for research and development—nearly $500
million a year—but continually denying them funds for production.

The tactic was bound to lose. Once a few billion dollars are
spent on any weapons program, the chance of stopping it from
going into production is practically nil. By 1966, the Army had
been given enough to develop an ABM system geared for widespread deployment. All the Joint Chiefs vigorously favored such a
plan; Congress put money in the budget for ABM production,
even though McNamara had not requested it. President Lyndon
Johnson was clearly in a political bind, torn between the arguments of his Secretary of Defense and the judgment of the entire
military establishment. On December 6, 1966, at a critical meeting in Austin, Texas, with Johnson, Walt Rostow, Cyrus Vance
and the Joint Chiefs, McNamara offered a compromise: spend
some money on preproduction tooling and procurement for Nike-
X, but defer a decision on deployment and try to reach an arms-
control accord with the Soviets to prohibit all ABMs. Johnson
agreed.

In January 1967, McNamara arranged for Johnson to meet
with every past and present Presidential Science Adviser and
Director of Defense Research and Engineering. As McNamara anticipated, they all argued that defending against a massive missile
attack was impossible. In June, Johnson and McNamara met with
Soviet Premier Aleksei Kosygin in Glassboro, New Jersey, to discuss arms control. McNamara lectured Kosygin on nuclear strategy and on how ABMs would only prompt an offense-defense arms
race. But Kosygin didn't understand. "When I have trouble sleep-
ing nights," he told McNamara, "it's because of your offensive
missiles, not your defensive missiles."

Time was running out, and Johnson finally ordered McNamara to fund production of Nike-X. Still, McNamara wanted to
shape the decision in such a way that it would retard any efforts to
expand production into a full-scale nationwide system.

On July 3, McNamara called one of his aides, Morton Halperin, into his office to have him draft a speech on the ABM. The

speech should say that it was futile to spend billions on a massive ABM system because the Soviets could, at less expense, counter all such efforts with an increased offensive-missile program; that, in fact, an ABM would compel the Soviets to do so, which would prompt us to respond, which would lead to an uncontrolled arms race with no greater security for us in the end; that our greatest deterrent against a Soviet first-strike was not a thick ABM shield that could easily be penetrated anyway, but rather a surviving second-strike capability, which we had with great assurance.

Halperin, briskly taking notes, was elated. He agreed with all of it. This would be the greatest speech that anyone had ever heard, he thought. But then McNamara dropped the punch line. After that, McNamara said, explain why we have to build an ABM to defend against an attack by Red China. Halperin's dream was suddenly shattered. He looked up. "Are you sure you want that last section in?" he faintly asked.

"Yes," McNamara replied.

Halperin walked back to his office and told his boss, Paul Warnke, who had replaced John McNaughton as Assistant Secretary of Defense for International Security Affairs, about the meeting. When Warnke saw McNamara later that day, he asked, "China bomb, Bob?"

McNamara looked down, shuffled some papers around on his desk and muttered, "What else am I going to blame it on?"

As early as 1961, before he turned against the ABM, McNamara had offered the Chinese threat as a possible rationale. Since then, he had never taken it very seriously. But when pressures mounted in 1965 to spend money on Nike-X production, McNamara cited the Chinese peril once again as something against which the system might be feasible. His strategy was to make sure that if production were forced on him, the official rationale would support only limited deployment. Johnson had forced him to approve an ABM, and McNamara was determined to open that door only so wide. By this time, McNamara also thought the Chinese-threat rationale was intellectually unsupportable; there simply was no such threat. Citing it in public, he hoped, might spur additional opposition to the whole project.

McNamara delivered the speech to a conference of United Press International editors and publishers in San Francisco on September 18, 1967. Among the intended audience back in Washington, it prompted just the confusion that McNamara had desired. Five months later, when McNamara left the Pentagon and compiled his major speeches into a book entitled *The Essence of Security,* he placed only the first part of the San Francisco speech in the main body of the book. The last part, the part calling for an anti-China ABM, the part that served his purposes as a bureaucrat under pressure but embarrassed him as an intellectual, he buried in an obscure appendix at the back.

For the military and its congressional guardians, McNamara's China rationale was the first step toward the multibillion-dollar nationwide system for which they had pined. To several in the strategic community, defense against Chinese attack was, in its own right, a laudable objective. Among this group, Albert Wohlstetter was most adamant and influential.

In the early 1960s, Wohlstetter was fired from the RAND Corporation, basically for all too willingly helping his former acolytes in McNamara's Office of Systems Analysis, which often helped kill many an Air Force weapons system. He moved on to the University of Chicago and later joined the Stanford Research Institute, SRI, the Army's think tank.

Now that the notion of defending all of America's cities against a massive Soviet nuclear attack had pretty much been exploded, SRI's main business was helping the Army come up with new justifications for a large-scale ABM system. Wohlstetter had trounced the quality of SRI's work in the late 1950s at RAND, but became intrigued with ABMs in the mid-1960s and joined their cause. Wohlstetter realized that once the Soviets made their long-range missiles more accurate, hardened shelters could no longer resist the pulverizing power of a nuclear blast and the ICBM force would once again be vulnerable. An ABM, if situated to defend the ICBM bases, could do much to relieve the peril.

Wohlstetter also worried about China. He was a strong hawk on the Vietnam War, viewed North Vietnam as a puppet of Red China and foresaw the Chinese Communists carrying out further acts of aggression against American allies in Asia over the next decade. If the U.S. could not so easily intervene with troops, we would have to offer these allies the protection of our "nuclear umbrella," as with the NATO allies. But if the Chinese invaded an Asian ally, a nuclear threat by the U.S. might not be credible since China—once it amassed its own nuclear arsenal—could strike back against American cities. However, if the U.S. had a decent

ABM system, the Chinese would know that their nuclear retaliation would inflict only minor damage, and they would thus be deterred from provoking aggression. The promise of successful coercive first-strikes against the U.S.S.R. had died out as the Soviets had built up their own arsenal; with the ABM, Wohlstetter hoped to revive the strategy against China.

The notion held not only for China, but for all "lesser" powers that might build a small arsenal of bombs and threaten to use them irresponsibly. Wohlstetter was an ardent foe of the global proliferation of nuclear weapons. It was the one issue on which he and liberal arms controllers agreed. To Wohlstetter, an ABM would discourage similar nations from engaging in nuclear blackmail and, thus, from obtaining nuclear bombs at all.

A national debate broke out over the ABM in 1968. The intellectual leadership came from an assemblage of highly distinguished scientists who had worked on nuclear weapons for many years. The debate first sparked when, in reaction to McNamara's San Francisco speech, Hans Bethe and Richard Garwin wrote an article on ABMs in the May 1968 *Scientific American*. The article cited the vulnerability of the radar to blackout or to a single detonation on the ground, the effects of decoys or multiple warheads, the ability of the offense to counter the defense at lower cost. This was the first time that these points had been outlined in public, on an unclassified basis.

The debacle in Vietnam, increasingly obvious by 1968, spurred several legislators to question Pentagon policies more generally. The ABM was the most expensive weapons system up for deployment; popular protest against it was intense in those areas where the Army wished it sited; the Bethe/Garwin piece made a splash at just the right moment politically. Leading antiwar senators suddenly sought out the scientific community for advice on opposing the ABM. By the summer, John Sherman Cooper, Philip Hart and Edward M. Kennedy formed alliances with fellow Senators William Fulbright, Albert Gore, Jacob Javits, Charles Percy, Mike Mansfield, George McGovern, Frank Church, Mark Hatfield and, not least, Stuart Symington, onetime superhawk whose views on defense had changed considerably with the impact of Vietnam. As a group they consulted Bethe, Garwin, Killian, Kistiakowsky, Wiesner, Sidney Drell, Wolfgang Panofsky, Paul Doty, Jack Ruina, George Rathjens and other scientists. Vir tually all of these scientists had been members of Eisenhower's PSAC panel in 1959 or the Pentagon's Reentry Body Identification Group of 1958, both of which had concluded that ABMs were impractical for the reasons that Bethe and Garwin spelled out a decade later. In the spring of 1969, the scientists opposed to the ABM started to testify before congressional committees. It was a new phenomenon. Only Administration witnesses had testified on defense matters in the past.

In January 1969, Richard Nixon became President and almost instantly shifted the terms of the ABM debate. A few weeks into the Administration, Nixon's national security adviser, Henry Kissinger, came over to the Pentagon to talk about the ABM with the new Deputy Secretary of Defense, David Packard, and a few of his aides. Explicitly speaking for the President, Kissinger laid down the orders: first, there will be an ABM; second, it will be cheaper than the Democratic Administration's ABM; third, it will shoot down Soviet missiles, not just Chinese missiles. Packard sent the orders to John S. Foster, Jr., the Pentagon's R&D director. Foster's conclusion: defending cities would be impossible given the guidelines on how much to spend and who the enemy was; therefore, the ABM must be geared primarily to defending the Minuteman ICBM silos.

On March 14, Nixon announced that the Sentinel ABM, the Nike-X derivative to defend against Chinese attack, was now dropped, and that a new ABM to defend Minuteman, called Safeguard, was in. The new rhetoric proclaimed that defending cities would only prompt the other side to increase its offensive-missile force, inciting an arms race, and that the major threat now was a first-strike by the Soviet Union against the retaliatory forces of the Strategic Air Command.

The new rationale blunted the case of the critics somewhat. Defending Minuteman sites was easier than defending cities: if one missile made it through the defense, a city would be destroyed in the one case, but only an ICBM would be destroyed in the other; since an ICBM was much less valuable than a city, the defense would not have to be perfectly foolproof. Moreover, in the early phases of the ABM debate, many of the critics, including Hans Bethe, had testified that an ABM designed to defend ICBMs instead of cities might be acceptable.

However, the critics now noted that the new Safeguard ABM was physically the exact same system as the old Sentinel—meaning that all of the old problems still existed and made the system unworkable. Second, they argued that the Minuteman was not so vulnerable after all. Third, they maintained that even if the Soviets could knock out all of the ICBMs, the U.S. would still have enough warheads on board the Polaris submarines at sea and on alerted B-52 bombers to devastate the Soviet Union; thus, Minuteman vulnerability alone would not sufficiently tempt the Soviets to launch a first-strike. Fourth, they argued that even if Minuteman were vulnerable and even if the Soviets were thus provoked to launch a first-strike, Safeguard would not provide adequate defense: the radar was vulnerable, the ABMs themselves would probably not be so reliable, and there was something fishy about the official U.S. intelligence estimates of Soviet missile strength.

The big danger, as the Administration saw it, came from the U.S.S.R.'s gigantic SS-9 ICBMs, which were believed to carry a twenty-five megaton warhead. Recently, however, the Soviets had been observed testing the SS-9 with three warheads of smaller but still quite large size. There was some controversy within the intelligence community as to whether this new missile was merely a Multiple Reentry Vehicle (MRV), like the Polaris A-3 "Claw," or whether it was a Multiple Independently targetable Re-entry Vehicle (MIRV), meaning that each warhead on board could be guided to a completely separate target. In June, the National Intelligence Estimate judged that it was merely an MRV; but under heavy pressure from Henry Kissinger and Defense Secretary Melvin Laird, the CIA changed the NIE to read that the SS-9 was probably a MIRV. Since the CIA had previously noted that the Soviets would have 420 SS-9s by the end of 1975, only if each of the three warheads were MIRVs could they threaten all 1,000 Minuteman ICBMs. Only then would there be a rationale for Safeguard.

However, the ABM critics noted that if the SS-9 were less threatening than the CIA had projected, Safeguard would be superfluous. Conversely, if the Soviets built more SS-9s than anticipated, the Safeguard program would be drenched by an attack. George Rathjens, one of the anti-ABM scientists, calculated that just a few additional months of SS-9 production would be enough to overwhelm the interceptor missiles defending the Minuteman sites and make them vulnerable again. In short, as Rathjens put it, the "defense would be effective only if the Soviet Union were to tailor its threat to match Safeguard's limited capabilities."

Rathjens made these points in testimony before Senator Albert Gore's Foreign Relations subcommittee on March 28 and before Senator John Stennis' Armed Services Committee on April 23. Appearing on the same panel before the Stennis committee was Albert Wohlstetter. Rathjens had told the Gore subcommittee that even if the Soviets had 500 MIRVed SS-9s with accuracy and reliability comparable to American ICBMs, one-quarter of the Minuteman force would still survive an attack. Wohlstetter challenged these figures and discovered that Rathjens had assumed that the blast resistance of Minuteman silos was two-thirds higher than the official classified data indicated. Rathjens had also assumed that the SS-9's payload could hold four warheads of one megaton each when, in fact, data publicly released since Rathjens had appeared before Gore suggested that the SS-9 actually held three warheads of five megatons each—a payload much more lethal to Minuteman silos. Wohlstetter calculated that if these two assumptions were corrected, only 16 percent, rather than 25 percent, of Minutemen would survive. Like most defense analysts, Rathjens had assumed that 20 percent of Soviet missiles would fail before detonation; but, Wohlstetter noted, had he assumed that half of those failed on the launch pad, allowing the Soviets to fire other missiles in their place, then only 5 percent of Minutemen would survive.

Wohlstetter was a fervent supporter of Safeguard, even more than he had been of Sentinel. Its mission was right up his alley— to rectify the vulnerability of SAC. Wohlstetter increasingly saw the ABM debate not so much as a dispute over the feasibility of Safeguard, but rather as an argument of principle over the sorts of calculations that he had devised in R-290 and "The Delicate Balance of Terror."

Wohlstetter took up the battle against Rathjens the next day in the Stennis hearings, telling the senators that Rathjens' calculations on Minuteman vulnerability were based on false assumptions concerning the SS-9's payload and the resistance of Minuteman silos, and also failed to take into account "familiar, well-known methods of arranging it so that you can reprogram missiles to replace a very large proportion of your failures. . . ." Rathjens replied that even if he were wrong about the assumptions, this was only a minor portion of his argument: there wasn't much difference—in terms of destroying the Soviet Union in a retaliatory attack and thus deterring the Soviets from attacking in the first place—between 250 surviving Minutemen and 50 surviving Minutemen, especially considering the many hundreds of weapons surviving on Polaris submarines and alert B-52s. Furthermore, Wohlstetter's argument said nothing about whether Safeguard could defend Minuteman if the ICBMs were vulnerable; and besides, there was no basis for believing that either the Soviets or the U.S. actually had this reprogramming technique.

But Wohlstetter relentlessly waged his battle. That fall, he convinced Tom Caywood, a fellow Chicagoan and president of the Operations Research Society of America, an organization of which Wohlstetter was a prominent member, to conduct an investigation into the uses of operations research in the ABM debate, especially into the distortions committed by Rathjens and others in calculating the vulnerability of Minuteman.

Caywood wrote to Rathjens, Jerry Wiesner and an MIT physics professor named Steven Weinberg, another anti-ABM scientist, to inform them of the pending investigation. On December 22, they wrote back denouncing the project as "absurd." The ABM controversy, they said, "was not a debate between ourselves and Mr. Wohlstetter, or between any fixed group of scholars with recognized spokesmen. Rather, the burden of proof for the Safeguard deployment was carried primarily by members of the Administration, and it was their frequently shifting and contradictory statements with which ABM opponents had to deal." Any such investigation ought also, therefore, to examine the shifting rationales and selective uses of intelligence data by Melvin Laird, David Packard and Johnny Foster. And far more crucial in the debate were the analyses of Safeguard's feasibility and effectiveness, especially in the face of likely Soviet countermeasures. They also found it a bit unethical for ORSA to investigate analysts who were not even members of the Operations Research Society.

The ORSA committee's final report was approved, amid great intercouncil conflict, in a six-to-five vote on May 5, 1971, and was published in the Society's journal, *Operations Research,* in September. The majority report adopted Wohlstetter's position on every issue, and condemned the anti-ABM scientists for producing analyses that were "often inappropriate, misleading and factually in error." Every mathematical mistake made by the anti-ABM forces, however minute, was catalogued in detail; yet on the charge, for instance, that Wohlstetter's pivotal assumption concerning missile reprogramming had no empirical basis, the committee excusingly replied that Wohlstetter "does not claim that either we or the Soviets have such techniques now, but only that they are not difficult to achieve"—itself a dubious point—"and should be considered a real possibility if a force has a significantly greater effectiveness with them." On the broader issues—whether the intelligence data on the Soviet threat were valid, whether Minuteman vulnerability degraded the deterrent power of the U.S. arsenal, whether Safeguard would work—the committee, following Wohlstetter's definition of the problem to a T, said not a word.

Months before ORSA released its report, the Administration was already conceding several of the points made by the critics. Most notably, Defense Secretary Melvin Laird admitted in hearings, as early as February 20, 1970, that the Soviets could easily build a force that "could actually turn out to be considerably larger than the Safeguard defense is designed to handle." By April, George Rathjens and Herbert York wrote, "The Administration now recognizes that the radars are the Achilles' heel of the Safeguard defense of Minuteman."

The nationwide ABM system that the Soviets were alleged to be building never materialized; they had only sixty-four ABMs around Moscow. The SS-9 turned out not to be a MIRVed missile, nor was it nearly as accurate as Safeguard's proponents had claimed. Not until late 1974 would the Soviets deploy MIRVs—almost five years after the first American MIRVed ICBMs had been fielded. By 1971, the Administration was selling Safeguard to Congress mainly for its value as a "bargaining chip" in the ongoing Strategic Arms Limitation Talks with the Soviets. The Senate continued to fund Safeguard, but by very narrow margins. Finally, on May 26, 1972, the U.S. and the U.S.S.R. concluded the SALT I Agreement and signed the ABM Treaty, which limited each side to two ABM sites of no more than 100 missiles each. Two years later, they revised the terms to allow one site of no more than 100 missiles. Shortly after that, the U.S. dismantled its single site altogether; the Soviets never deployed more than the sixty-four ABMs around Moscow. Both sides had evidently concluded that the ABM didn't work well enough to justify its exorbitant cost.

Yet the ABM debate had consequences far more enduring than the immediate issue of Safeguard. It marked the first time that experts outside the Pentagon were extensively consulted on defense issues, a precedent that has since become the norm. And it also influenced what kind of expertise emerged as "respectable"—an expertise dependent on manipulation of quantitative detail often secondary, at best, to the central issues at stake. In the latter stages of the debate, even Rathjens spent so much time contending on Wohlstetter's own turf that the larger points were often left in the background.

After publication of the ORSA report, Senators Cooper, Symington and Hart asked more than a dozen scientists and strategists to comment on the document. Among them was Philip Morse, who had resigned from ORSA over the incident. Morse had been director of the U.S. Navy Operations Research Group in World War II. During the war, he and other similar OR groups took data from the weapons designers on a particular weapon's effectiveness and then devised calculations predicting how it would perform in combat—essentially what Wohlstetter and others had done with the data on the SS-9, Minuteman and Safeguard. However, the World War II OR groups then assembled operational data on how the weapons *really* performed in combat. It turned out that the weapons designers had overestimated the effectiveness usually by about three times. Until the assumptions in the OR groups' original calculations were adjusted to conform to reality rather than theory, Morse commented, "the predictions of our beautifully accurate *analyses* could be wrong by a factor of as much as ten."

What worried him, and what seemed to him symptomatic in the ABM debate, was that "a new generation of officers and analysts has come on the scene, many of whom have never had the sobering experience of seeing their optimistic predictions disproved by deaths on the battlefield. They too often are willing to take the assumptions given them by designers and 'intelligence' as gospel truth, and to base their calculations on them without adding any correction factors for the 'fog of war' . . . Strategy is still an art, not a science. . . . Anyone who tries to argue his case for the ABM on the grounds of the accuracy of his analyses is either scientifically naïve, or else he thinks it doesn't matter, that the time will never come when hard reality will provide a check on his assumptions."

With the ABM debate, this "new generation" of analysts went public and took over the field. The realm of nuclear strategy came disconnected not only from what Bernard Brodie would call "the political dimension" but also from the technical realities of the very weapons that circumscribed what strategy can do.

25 THE NEW GENERATION

 As THE NEW GENERATION occupied positions of power, the story of nuclear strategy came full circle and started all over again, as if the debates, the disillusionments and the discreditings of the early-to-mid 1960s had never occurred. Counterforce, no-cities, limited nuclear war, tit-for-tat, the coercive strategy again came to dominate the defense world. And the spirit guiding the resurrection breathed forth, once again, from the RAND Corporation.

It was the Air Force that spearheaded the revival. By the late 1960s, the upper echelon of the Air Staff had changed character dramatically. The acolytes of Curtis LeMay and Tommy Power were no longer in charge. A new generation had worked its way up the ranks, and its members had a different conception of warfare. They were more familiar with tactical bombing in Korea than with strategic bombing over Europe or Japan. Most of them had risen to power on Air Force planning staffs during the period when defense intellectuals first came into vogue; nearly all of them had read, and met, Wohlstetter, Kahn, Kaufmann, Brodie, Schelling and the rest of the RAND community; many were Air Staff colonels when Bill Kaufmann arranged his 1960 counterforce briefing with General Noel Parrish. The combination of this intellectual milieu and their general detachment from the SAC traditions led many of these new officers to move away from the all-out, max-effort, bomb-everything notions that had dominated Air Force thinking since the end of World War II and more toward thinking about how to use these weapons in a more traditionally military manner, how to *fight* with them, how to use them *rationally*.

A small nucleus of Air Staff officers who shared this line of thinking banded together on a project they called NU-OPTS, for Nuclear Options or Nuclear Operations. Its leaders were General Richard Ellis, director of plans, who had spent years in the Tactical Air Command, SAC's rival within the Air Force, and who had worked on the first NATO war plan involving tactical nuclear weapons, all of which were to be fired against strictly military targets; General Russell Dougherty, assistant director of plans, who had done tactical bombing in the Korean War; General Leslie Bray of the war plans office, a former SAC officer who then served in the Pacific and became heavily influenced by the critiques of massive retaliation in the late 1950s; and the group's intellectual master, General Richard Yudkin.

Yudkin was a most peculiar Air Force officer—short, rotund, Jewish, bookish, a bachelor with no hobbies or interests outside the Air Force, a man who had never been a pilot or a navigator, who had climbed to the rank of major general and director of Air Force policy on his brainpower. Even more than his colleagues, Yudkin had felt continually frustrated by the budget-cutting and anti-counterforce sentiments of Robert McNamara. He realized that if the Air Force was to move to the forefront again, some new concepts—justifying both a credible nuclear war-fighting capability and procurement of more Air Force weapons—would have to be formulated. In the past, Yudkin had frequently found inspiration in discussions with the strategists at RAND, and off to RAND he journeyed again, in search of new rationales.

When Yudkin called, he was taken to the director of RAND's new strategic studies division, James R. Schlesinger. Schlesinger was practically the ideal type to help launch a revival of the RAND tradition. Everything about him spelled "defense intellectual"— the slightly jaded sensibility, the whiff of arrogance, the pipe-puffing affectation of cool insouciance. Like most of the leading lights, Schlesinger was an economist by training and so fell in comfortably with the culture of calculation and the rational-marketplace assumptions of nuclear war-fighting. He had come to RAND in 1961, naturally read all the classic RAND literature and quickly befriended Andy Marshall, who passed along to him the guiding principles of the old RAND Strategic Objectives Committee and the Kaufmann counterforce briefing.

By the mid-1960s, Schlesinger, like several others, had started to wonder about the feasibility of counterforce. Since the Soviets were building more missiles and hardening them in silos or putting them in Polaris-type submarines, a counterforce campaign might not be so effective. Moreover, it would require firing so many missiles that the Soviets might not be able to distinguish a "limited" counterforce strike from an all-out attack, and retaliate accordingly with a massive blow against American cities. Since avoiding urban damage was the whole point of the RAND strat-

egy, counterforce could soon have counterproductive consequences. And yet the problem of "credible deterrence" remained.
What was the nuclear strategy that would avoid both the implausi-
bility of counterforce and the recklessness of minimum deterrence or massive retaliation? Schlesinger found his answer in the
writings of RAND alumnus Tom Schelling—the option of "limited" or "graduated reprisals," in Schelling's words: small-scale
nuclear strikes, shots across the bow, bargaining counters demonstrating American will and resolve, pricks of pain shooting a message to the Soviets that more pain will follow unless they desist
from their aggression at once.

In December 1968, under Yudkin's direction, Schlesinger
wrote a RAND memorandum called *Rationale for NU-OPTS*, very
briefly sketching the basic principles of the Schelling strategy.
Schlesinger also told Yudkin that the strategy would make an
ideal rationale for a new manned bomber. The Air Force had been
destroying its own case by painting the bomber as little more than
a manned missile; in so straightforward a comparison, the Minuteman ICBM was certainly more cost-effective than, say, the B-70.
However, if one envisioned the Soviets grabbing northern Norway
or some other region where the U.S. would find it difficult to meet
the threat with conventional forces alone, the small-strike strategy
would be an appropriate response, and the manned bomber—
more precise and reliable than the missiles of the day—would be
the ideal instrument.

Yudkin and the NU-OPTS group back in the Pentagon were
enthusiastic. However, *Rationale for NU-OPTS* merely described
a concept, not an operational plan. What types of targets should be
hit—military, economic, some mix? Where should the targets
be—on the battlefield, in the U.S.S.R.? Should the target have
some military significance, or did it matter? Would the mere act of
setting off a nuclear explosion—anywhere—send a sufficiently
clear signal to the Soviets? How many bombs should be dropped?
How many would be enough to get the signal across but not so
many as to make the Soviets see the strike as the opening volley of
an all-out assault, prompting them to respond in kind?

Over the next several months, RAND and the Air Force
embarked upon a major study. Air Force analysts worked on
the technical side, compiling three volumes of highly complex
calculations, figuring the optimal routes for the bombers, the probabilities of penetration and damage in various scenarios and cir-

cumstances. Schlesinger, aided mainly by two young RAND colleagues, Francis Hoeber and Fritz Ermarth, elaborated the politico-military angle, thinking about what the NU-OPTS strategy should accomplish and how best, in principle, to go about accomplishing it. All of the scenarios involved a conventional invasion or land-grab by the Soviets—in northern Norway, in the Middle East, in Central Europe—followed by the first use of nuclear weapons, on a very small scale, by the United States.

In the end, the project failed. The whole business was too uncertain, risky, hinged too much on dubious assumptions. If bombers were to be used in the strike—and the source of most officers' interest in NU-OPTS was the rationale it might provide for a new bomber—the only way to penetrate Soviet air defenses with high confidence was through surprise. Yet the NU-OPTS concept critically depended on telling the Soviets in advance what we were about to do and what sorts of limitations we were deliberately imposing upon our actions. Or, if we did tell them ahead of time, thus forgoing the advantage of surprise, extra bombers would have to fly the mission to compensate for those that might get shot down, those bombers would have to be escorted by jet fighters, other fighter-bombers would have to accompany them to destroy air-defense sites ahead of the attack. In short, a whole armada would be involved, as many as 100 airplanes in most cases, so many that the original intent underlying NU-OPTS would be lost. The ambiguities of such a raid would be too severe; the Soviets would have no way of distinguishing it from an all-out attack, and the hope of mutual limitation—of controlled nuclear war-fighting—would be destroyed.

Aside from this operational defect, there were conceptual problems that, months of close analysis notwithstanding, remained unsolved. It was not so difficult to identify particularly vulnerable Soviet targets that might be attacked. But then what? Would the Soviets really be coerced? What if they didn't back down? What if they fired a similar—or much larger—salvo back at the U.S. or Europe or the Middle East? What if they did nothing? How would we end the war on favorable terms?

The dissent to NU-OPTS began at RAND, among several members of the social science division who were only peripherally involved in strategy and not at all caught up in the traditions passed down by Kaufmann, Kahn, Marshall and the others in the strategic community. The debate over NU-OPTS became closely

entangled with the debate then raging at RAND over the Vietnam
War. Those who thought that the U.S. was bound to win the war
also thought that the U.S. could prevail in a limited strategic nuclear war with the Soviets, and those who were convinced that
Vietnam was a losing proposition, on the grounds that the Viet
Cong and the North were ignoring our finely wrought signals, felt
the same way about NU-OPTS. If the Soviets lacked the ability or
desire to play along with our tit-for-tat game, they could simply
threaten to raise the stakes of destruction, twisting the game to
their terms.

The Air Staff officers who originally supported NU-OPTS
were also growing increasingly wary. It just didn't seem practical.
Military officers tend to be conservative; they want to have high
confidence that a military operation will work before they endorse
it. And high confidence was the one element most conspicuously
missing from any close consideration of NU-OPTS. Most of them
felt, like Schlesinger, that the NU-OPTS strategy was "less miserable" than other options. For that reason, they worked hard, redoing the calculations, searching for better targets, more efficient
bombing techniques, more favorable scenarios, trying to make it
work. It was 1970, two years into the project, before they gave it
up. It was frustrating to see the project fall apart. Its failure meant
that, in practical terms, there might be nothing left except massive destruction after all, that maybe nuclear war *was* "unthinkable."

Their frustration was short-lived. For just as NU-OPTS
showed sure signs of failure, new technology was coming to the
forefront that, on the face of things, seemed to reinvigorate the
notion of a controllable nuclear-war-fighting force. The technology
was the Multiple Independently targetable Re-entry Vehicle, the
MIRV. During the ABM debate, it was MIRVs that the Administration feared the Soviets would soon be putting on top of their
SS-9 ICBMs, thus making the U.S. Minuteman ICBMs vulnerable
to a counterforce first-strike. In June 1970, the U.S. started to put
its own MIRVs on a new generation of Minuteman missiles, the
Minuteman III. And to many officers and civilians inside the Pentagon, the purpose was the same—to revive counterforce as a realistic option.

Very much behind the scenes, MIRV had been labored into

life in the early-to-mid 1960s just as McNamara was beginning to abandon the premises of the counterforce philosophy.

It began life as a figment inside the flighty imagination of a physicist at the RAND Corporation named Richard Latter. Latter had been one of the handful of those at RAND who had helped set up the Theoretical Division of the Livermore weapons lab to work on the H-bomb in the early 1950s, and was a perpetual promoter of a U.S. nuclear buildup to defend against the Soviet threat. In 1962, Latter fiercely opposed the atmospheric nuclear test-ban treaty that the Kennedy Administration was negotiating with Moscow, and worried intensely that someday the Soviets could launch a knockout punch against the Minuteman ICBM force.

At a cocktail party that spring at the Dupont Plaza Hotel in Washington, D.C., Latter sat chatting with an old friend from Livermore named Roland Herbst and an Air Force colonel who supported the treaty. The colonel pointed out to Latter that we had more missiles than the Soviets, that we could build more if they built more, and that we had dispersed the ICBMs and hardened them in underground silos to such a degree that even if the Soviets detonated a 100-megaton bomb in between two silos, it wouldn't destroy both. Therefore, Latter should not worry about Minuteman vulnerability. This was essentially the argument that Robert McNamara and his chief scientist, Harold Brown, had been making before Congress.

Latter objected. The number of missiles doesn't mean a thing: the Soviets could simply put lots of warheads on each missile, just as we had done with the Polaris A-3 "Claw"; but they could do it differently, devising a separate aiming mechanism for each of the warheads so that they could be released against widely separated targets. Thus we might be equal in missiles, but their warheads would outnumber our missiles, making Minuteman vulnerable. The colonel didn't know what to say; nobody had ever talked about anything like that before. Latter had mostly made it up off the top of his head, but the more he thought about it, the more plausible it sounded. Back at RAND, he wrote a report on how such a multiple-warhead missile might work and why it would make Minuteman vulnerable to attack.

The idea of a MIRV for the United States was pushed more than a year later by Latter's brother, Albert, also a RAND physicist who had made the trek to Livermore in the early 1950s, and who

was presently sitting as chairman of the Nuclear Panel of the Air
Force Scientific Advisory Board. At one panel session in early
1964, General Glenn Kent, who was then in the midst of directing
the damage-limiting study, delivered a briefing that suggested
there were more Soviet targets than there were U.S. strategic nuclear warheads, especially if one counted all the airfields in the
U.S.S.R. that might host Soviet military aircraft. Kent flashed a
slide of a typical Soviet airfield, and Al Latter noticed something
that led him to a novel observation. The field was strangely
shaped—long, narrow, twisting in several different directions.
The circle of damage caused by the explosion of a single high-yield
warhead would blow up a lot of the territory around the airfield
and would not destroy all of the airfield itself. Latter reflected on
the RAND memo that his brother had written on multiple warheads and suddenly realized that they could come in very handy in
this mission. Several small warheads could much more efficiently
destroy the entire airfield and do relatively little damage to the
surrounding area.

And there was another bonus. In the official U.S. war plan,
309 Minuteman ICBMs were aimed at 210 Soviet bomber bases,
and another 220 gravity bombs were to be dropped from B-52s on
the 110 Soviet "aircraft dispersal bases"—nearly 530 weapons in
all. Latter reasoned that if one took, say, 100 of those Minutemen
and put six warheads on each, they could destroy all the airfields
and free the other 209 missiles and the 220 gravity bombs to go
after completely different targets.

Latter assembled a group of highly respected weapons scientists, told them about his revelation and said, "Let's write a report." It was finished in June 1964, and was signed by the Latter
brothers and a gaggle of heavyweights from Livermore and Los
Alamos, among them Edward Teller, Johnny Foster, Harold
Agnew, David Griggs, Roland Herbst and others whom the Latters
had known for years. Al Latter made sure that Glenn Kent and
other Air Force generals passed the report to the right people.

Independent of Latter's efforts, the technology for MIRV was
already coming into existence. The U.S. space program had developed what was called a "post-boost control system" that, when attached to the nosecone of a rocket booster and launched into outer
space, could fire several satellites, each with its own motor, into
orbit. Such a system was first launched in October 1963. The

technology involved was very similar to the multiple-warhead system that Dick Latter originally had in mind.

Harold Brown, Robert McNamara's chief scientist and one-time director of the Livermore Lab, naturally knew about this new space technology, and when his old friend Al Latter showed him the report by the Nuclear Panel on Multiple Warheads, he found the synthesis of science and strategy irresistible. Brown made only one alteration in the recommendation: an existing warhead, called the MK-12, could hold three warheads; he proposed using that instead of some totally new six-warhead contraption that would cover only a few extra targets at much higher cost. Latter concurred.

Meanwhile, McNamara was embroiled in serious disputes with the Air Force over how many Minuteman ICBMs to deploy and with the Army over whether to fund fully the Nike-X ABM. From a bureaucratic standpoint, MIRV was a godsend: by putting multiple warheads on some of the Minutemen, he could persuade the Air Force to accept his decision to field only 1,000 missiles; and he could use the MIRV as yet another weapon in his arsenal of arguments on why an ABM could ultimately be defeated by a Soviet buildup of offensive weaponry. McNamara approved development of MIRV without hesitation, reporting to Lyndon Johnson in his DPM of December 3, 1964, "I intend to . . . provide for the development of a capability for delivering three MK-12 warheads to geographically separated targets. . . ." The next year, he approved a new version of the Minuteman, called Minuteman III, to be equipped with the MK-12 MIRV.

Publicly, McNamara rationalized MIRV as a way of penetrating enemy ABM systems, saturating them with more warheads than they could handle. But in classified memoranda, he endorsed another mission: going after counterforce targets—not just airfields, but also "hardened" missile silos. Along with his 1964 MIRV decision, as another part of his compromise with the Air Force, McNamara announced, in the DPM to Johnson, the development of a new inertial-guidance system that would improve the accuracy of Minuteman so that "the probability of destroying targets hardened up to 300 psi [pounds-per-square-inch overpressures, roughly the blast-resistance of Soviet ICBM silos at the time] would be in excess of 90 percent." In his 1965 DPM, McNamara described the Minuteman III, also called the Improved

Capability Missile, as having "much greater accuracy, payload and versatility" than its predecessors, promising a much higher "single shot kill probability" against hardened targets. In the 1966 DPM, he noted that his calculation of how many MIRVed Minuteman IIIs should be deployed "was arrived at by considering the Soviet military and urban target system *in the absence of ballistic missile defenses [ABMs].*"

MIRV saved the counterforce strategy from extinction at just the right moment. Through the mid-1960s, McNamara could talk all he wanted about assured destruction, but everyone knew that the real targeting plan was counterforce. The U.S.S.R. had so few strategic nuclear forces, and they were so vulnerable to the effects of blast, that a U.S. arsenal geared publicly toward assured destruction could just as easily execute a counterforce plan as well. But it soon became clear that the Soviets were building more and more ICBMs, meaning that the U.S. would have to build more weapons to cover them. And they were following the Pentagon's prudent example of encasing their ICBMs in underground concrete silos, meaning that the U.S. would have to make its missiles more accurate, to put the peak of explosive pressures closer to the silo. McNamara's concessions on MIRV and improved accuracy satisfied both requirements.

The irony was grim. In his efforts to clamp down on Air Force demands for more intercontinental *missiles,* McNamara gave the service more ICBM-based *weapons* than it had hoped for in years. In 1962, Air Force officers had requested 2,100 Minuteman ICBMs. By the end of the decade, they were allowed to deploy 550 Minuteman III missiles, carrying a total of 1,650 warheads, and 450 single-warhead Minuteman IIs—a grand total of 2,100 weapons. Just as McNamara was departing from the rhetoric of Ann Arbor, just as he was rejecting counterforce as an unrealistic strategy, his decision on MIRV and improved guidance systems gave the advocates of limited nuclear war fresh cause for hope and glory.

To go much further on this new hope, however, the enthusiasts of NU-OPTS would have to change the nuclear targeting plan, the SIOP. In the late 1960s, the plan still remained essentially the SIOP-63 guidance that Dan Ellsberg had written in the spring of 1961 and that Alain Enthoven and Frank Trinkl had elaborated upon that summer. The officers at SAC's Joint Strategic Target Planning Staff had kept following this guidance over the years, targeting missiles and bombs on counterforce targets as they emerged, a task for which the MIRVs, once they came on line a few years later, would be ideal. However, the expansion of the Soviet force was creating another problem. In the early 1960s, the U.S. needed to fire only a few hundred weapons to execute Option One of SIOP-63—destroying the Soviet strategic nuclear forces. Now, doing so would require firing a couple of thousand—at least one, often two, for each ICBM silo as well as one or two for each of the bomber bases, possible aircraft-dispersion bases and submarine ports. The critique of counterforce offered by Tom Schelling and, later, Jim Schlesinger—that such an attack would be so massive that the Soviets could not distinguish it from an all-out strike and, so, would respond with an all-out blow themselves—became particularly cogent. Yet this was the smallest strike option in the SIOP.

The problem had first been noticed by a young engineer in the Pentagon's Office of Systems Analysis named Ivan Selin. Selin was Alain Enthoven's deputy for strategic systems in the last two years of the Lyndon Johnson Administration, and a Whiz Kid of the highest order—fast, witty, fluent in seven languages, a brilliant computer engineer. One of his first tasks was to go down to SAC Headquarters and check out the SIOP. He discovered not only that the most limited option required firing a couple of thousand warheads, but that many of the military targets in the U.S.S.R.—especially the command-control facilities—were not too far from the downtown areas of the U.S.S.R.'s most populous cities. Even in the more limited options, there would be too much radioactive fallout, too many civilians killed. He worked with the JSTPS in Omaha to change several of the "aim points" and to remove certain targets from the limited options altogether. Still, that was not enough. If the idea behind counterforce was to signal restraint and to prompt reciprocal restraint from the Soviets, the Pentagon would have to devise new options that were much more limited in magnitude.

Selin received little encouragement from his superiors. Alain Enthoven, his immediate boss, fiercely loyal to McNamara, had embraced the tenets of assured destruction as an almost religious principle. Enthoven clearly believed that limited nuclear options were necessary if deterrence failed, but he did not want to change assured destruction as the *declaratory* policy, and certainly did not want to go mucking about in the SIOP trying to program more refined options. Like McNamara, Enthoven believed that once one trod down that road, the game was lost—the Air Force would find excuses to build more and more weapons, forcing the Soviets to respond, spurring an all-out arms race. The Whiz Kids of the early 1960s had learned that lesson after Ann Arbor, and they were not about to repeat the experience.

Selin received a boost in 1969. Administrations changed; Richard Nixon took over the White House; for one year, Selin became Acting Assistant Secretary of Defense for Systems Analysis. Nixon's national security adviser was Henry Kissinger. Kissinger had long been a critic of massive retaliation. One of his first tasks, upon entering office, was to have Nixon order a study "reviewing our military posture and the balance of power." The study was completed on May 8, 1969, and was labeled National Security Study Memorandum (NSSM) No. 3.

It was an interagency project, but the bulk of the analytic work was done by Ivan Selin and his staff at Systems Analysis. Among the deeds of NSSM-3 was to kill assured destruction. "Up to now," it read, "the main criterion for evaluating U.S. strategic forces has been their ability to deter the Soviet Union from all-out, aggressive attacks on the United States." However, a nuclear war may not take form as a series of "spasm reactions." It "may develop as a series of steps in an escalating crisis in which both sides want to avoid attacking cities, neither side can afford unilaterally to stop the exchange, and the situation is dominated by uncertainty." If during a future Berlin crisis, for example, the Soviets thought that the U.S. was about to start a nuclear war, the U.S.S.R., rather than being struck first, "might consider using a portion of its strategic forces to strike U.S. forces in order to improve its relative military position. . . ." NSSM-3 conceded that these sorts of attacks "have no precedent in Soviet military doctrine or tradition," making it "highly unlikely that such a situation would develop." Even so, an American capacity for early "war termination, avoiding attacks on cities, and selective response capabilities might provide ways of limiting damage if deterrence fails."

If the language sounded familiar to an analyst from the early McNamara years, it was no coincidence. Selin and his aides had thoroughly studied McNamara's SIOP-63 guidance and were seeking to apply its basic principles to contemporary conditions.

The military section of NSSM-3 was, in fact, composed in the summer of 1968, when Selin and his crew knew that there would soon be a new Administration. When Nixon took office, one of Selin's aides, an analyst named Larry Lynn, was moved over to the NSC staff. When Kissinger assigned the NSSM-3 study, Lynn drafted it, using his work with Selin as its foundation.

On February 18, 1970, Nixon rhetorically asked in a foreign policy address to Congress (written largely by Lynn), "Should a President, in the event of a nuclear attack, be left with the single option of ordering the mass destruction of enemy civilians, in the face of the certainty that it would be followed by the mass slaughter of Americans?" The systems analysts in the Pentagon knew that Nixon was describing a dilemma that did not exist; that the SIOP, however imperfect, was far more flexible than he was suggesting. Nevertheless, such high-level concern about the issue prompted them to undertake a much more thorough study of options.

By this time, Ivan Selin had left government, but two deputies in Systems Analysis—a former Air Force civilian analyst named Archie Wood and an operations researcher named James Martin—persuaded the new head of Systems Analysis, Gardner Tucker, to take up the cause. Together, in early 1970, the three set up a middle-level interagency group, called the Strategic Objectives Study, to examine nuclear options. Martin had worked with Selin on the SIOP and was also inspired by the McNamara guidance of 1961–1962 composed by Ellsberg, Enthoven and Trinkl. Wood was a newcomer to Systems Analysis, but he had learned about limited options from the master of options, William Kaufmann, having been a student of his at MIT from 1963 to 1965, when Kaufmann was still very active in the McNamara Pentagon. Wood and Martin, then, set out in a direction that seemed destined to revive the old traditions of the RAND Corporation.

Two other influences reinforced this tendency. Shortly after the Strategic Objectives Study was established, Jim Martin received an unannounced visit by Albert Wohlstetter. By this time, Wohlstetter was a venerated guru in the strategic world, and Martin was highly impressed that he should be paying a call on a comparative neophyte like himself. Wohlstetter had heard about the project from his contacts around the government, and randomly dropped in on Martin several times over the next few months to

chat about strategy. More than anything else, Wohlstetter emphasized that the U.S. should attack enemy cities only as a matter of
last resort, that there should be a vast array of options available
before taking that step—a point that Wohlstetter himself had
picked up a decade earlier from Andrew Marshall and Herman
Kahn.

Finally, this was the period when the RAND-Air Staff NU-
OPTS project was running full steam. Jim Schlesinger and his two
RAND aides, Frank Hoeber and Fritz Ermarth, had recently completed their memos rationalizing and elaborating upon NU-OPTS,
and Martin and Wood read them excitedly. The papers had a profound impact on Martin's thinking particularly. They described
just the sorts of options that everyone had been looking for.

But the Strategic Objectives Study was headed nowhere. The
legacy of McNamara and Enthoven had left the Systems Analysis
Office with virtually no standing in the eyes of the Joint Chiefs.
Any product with the endorsement of Whiz Kids would get no re-
spect from the military. So Gardner Tucker persuaded Defense
Secretary Melvin Laird to set up a high-level panel within the Defense Department to do the same sort of analysis that Martin,
Wood and others had already been doing. To direct the project,
Laird appointed Johnny Foster, Director of Defense Research and
Engineering, the only high-level holdover from the McNamara regime but also a well-known nuclear scientist who, dating back to
his days at the Livermore Lab, looked with favor on the development of new weapons systems and counterforce power.

The Foster Panel, as the group called itself, first met in January 1972 and worked on the problem for nearly eighteen months.
The main actors were Martin, Wood, Tucker, Foster and Foster's
deputy for strategic systems, Air Force General Jasper Welch, who
had helped Foster design weapons at Livermore in the early
1950s. Members of the Joint Chiefs' staff and other offices also
participated, though more aloofly.

A year into the project, Foster decided that someone from the
State Department should be brought on, but someone whom Foster could trust to keep it a secret and be sympathetic. Foster's
choice was an old friend named Seymour Weiss, deputy director of
State's policy planning staff. Weiss fit in perfectly. In the early
1960s, working in State's politico-military bureau, Weiss was particularly troubled about NATO, concerned that the growing Soviet
arsenal of nuclear arms made the American commitment to de-

fend Western Europe with the threat of nuclear retaliation less credible. As State's chief liaison with the Pentagon, Weiss met and befriended such defense analysts as Paul Nitze, Alain Enthoven, Harry Rowen and Bill Kaufmann, who told him all about the counterforce/no-cities strategy. Like Kaufmann, who had embraced the strategy for the same reason, Weiss saw that the concept of limited options would help revitalize the credibility of the U.S. deterrent and the cohesion of the North Atlantic alliance. Over the next several years, Weiss made several trips out to the RAND Corporation, where in the late 1960s he also became intrigued with the small-strikes idea that James Schlesinger was developing in the NU-OPTS project.

And so, among its prime movers—Weiss, Martin, Wood and Foster—the Foster Panel became a forum in which the RAND ideas of the 1950s and 1960s re-emerged as respectable in high officialdom. While these ideas were being discussed, Sy Weiss regularly met with Jim Schlesinger to debrief him and ask for further advice. By this time, Schlesinger was living in Washington. Nixon had appointed him, first, director of the national security division at the Bureau of the Budget, then chairman of the Atomic Energy Commission, then—in February 1973, as the Foster Panel entered its final months—director of the CIA.

That summer, Henry Kissinger found out about the Foster Panel and, in August, transformed it into an interagency group chaired by Philip Odeen, a former Pentagon systems analyst who now sat on the NSC staff. Virtually all that was left for Odeen to do was to ratify what the Foster Panel had already done. In line with the backgrounds and interests of its members, the Foster Panel had worked out a general perspective that was essentially a mixture of counterforce/no-cities and NU-OPTS.

In the fall of 1973, Odeen's group finished its work and wrote a single-spaced twenty-page document—called the NUWEP, or Nuclear Weapons Employment Plan—that provided detailed targeting guidance to the JCS, and a shorter, more general memorandum for the White House. This work was in response to an order written the previous summer by Henry Kissinger, known as NSSM-169, and became the basis for a Top Secret National Security Decision Memorandum, to be signed by the President, entitled *Planning the Employment of Nuclear Weapons,* and labeled NSDM-242.

NSDM-242 was a fair reflection of the work by the Foster

Panel. Its premise was that the U.S. needed "a more flexible nuclear posture," especially one that "does not preclude U.S. use of
nuclear weapons in response to conventional aggression." In the
event of conflict, the goal was "to seek early war termination on
terms acceptable to the United States and its allies, at the lowest
level of conflict feasible." Doing so "requires planning a wide
range of nuclear employment options which could be used in con-
junction with supporting political and military measures (including conventional forces) to control escalation." These options
"should enable the U.S. to communicate to the enemy a determination to resist aggression, coupled with a desire to exercise restraint." The way to accomplish this feat was to " (a) hold some
vital enemy targets hostage to subsequent destruction by survivable nuclear forces, and (b) permit control over the timing and
pace of attack execution, in order to provide the enemy opportunities to reconsider his actions."

It was the same conclusion that had been reached by a dozen
panels before it. The work by the Foster Panel and the Odeen
group was similar to these previous analyses in another sense
as well: in a crunch, nobody could quite figure out how to translate the theory into practice. MIRVs and more accurate missiles
made the task a bit easier than the NU-OPTS project had envisioned: since bombers would no longer have to be used, the war
planners would not have to worry about the implications of sending in extra airplanes to suppress enemy air defenses. However,
the fundamental problems remained. How do we know the
enemy will read the signal properly? How do we know they will, or
can, or want to, respond accordingly? What happens next? How
do we manage to coerce them any more than they coerce us?
How do we end the confrontation? In short, how does one fight a
nuclear war?

Meanwhile, the same problems were bothering Henry Kissinger in the White House. During the 1970 Jordan crisis, he had
been particularly frustrated that the SAC war plan contained
nothing with which the U.S. might threaten the Soviets in some
limited fashion. In the spring of 1974, Kissinger asked the JCS to
devise a limited nuclear option that the President might order in
the hypothetical case of a Soviet invasion of Iran. A few weeks
later, two JCS generals briefed the results to Kissinger and a few
of his aides, including an arms-control analyst named David Aaron
and a former Pentagon systems analyst named Jan Lodal. The JCS

solution was to fire nearly 200 nuclear weapons at military targets—air bases, bivouacs and so forth—in the southern region of
the U.S.S.R. near the Iranian border.

Kissinger exploded. "Are you out of your minds?" he
screamed. "This is a *limited* option?" It involved way too many
weapons. Kissinger told them to go away and come back with
something smaller.

A few weeks later, the generals returned. There were two
roads leading into Iran from the U.S.S.R. The new proposal called
for exploding an atomic demolition mine on one of the roads and
firing two nuclear weapons at the other. Again, Kissinger's eyes
impatiently rolled toward the ceiling. "What kind of nuclear attack is this?" he demanded. The U.S. takes the terrible risk of
going nuclear and then uses only two weapons? Kissinger told
Dave Aaron that if the United States carried out such a plan and if
he were Brezhnev, he would conclude that the American President was "chicken."

It was the perennial dilemma: how to plan a nuclear attack
that was large enough to have a terrifying impact but small
enough to be recognized unambiguously as a limited strike. Kissinger frequently complained to his aides that the Pentagon's options weren't sensible, that they had to press the people over there
to come up with something better. Jan Lodal, who was generally
put in charge of such tasks, would pliantly tell Kissinger that he
was absolutely right and proceed to carry out his orders.

Lodal's personal view, however, was that there was no conceivable circumstance under which using nuclear weapons would
create an advantage. He had read Bernard Brodie's 1946 book,
The Absolute Weapon, and the more engrossed he became in nuclear strategy, the more he agreed with Brodie's fundamental
conclusion: that there could be no winners. But Lodal also felt
that a nation had to behave as if it really would use nuclear weapons, or else the credibility of its power to deter aggression against
allies might erode in a crisis. And so the analysts had to keep going
back to the problem over and over again, even if the problem could
never be solved. Besides, Lodal knew that nobody wanted to be the
man to step forward in the middle of a ghastly conflict with the
Russians and say to the President of the United States, "I'm sorry,
sir, but there are no good options in a nuclear war, and there is
nothing that you can do about it."

•

When NSDM-242 was finished, nothing happened at first. Inside the NSC, Dave Aaron feared that the political consequences of the memorandum could be disastrous, that its language opened up the gates to those in the Pentagon who really wanted a counterforce first-strike policy, which Aaron considered highly dangerous. So for several months, Aaron sat on it, fidgeted with a few words here and there, raised doubts, tried to study it into oblivion.

But support for NSDM-242 was growing very strong in the Pentagon. For in July 1973, Nixon had appointed James Schlesinger as Secretary of Defense. While director of the CIA, Schlesinger had been told all about the Foster Panel's work by his old friend Sy Weiss, and had also sat in on several sessions of Phil Odeen's interagency group. He saw that throughout the national security bureaucracy, a constituency was developing for the ideas that he had helped formulate in the NU-OPTS project a few years earlier. Now was his chance to translate them firmly into policy. He hired his old friend and mentor from RAND, Andrew Marshall, to be director of the Pentagon's net assessment office, whose formal task was to compare Soviet and American military forces but which Marshall turned into an intermediate contracting house that wrangled money from other divisions of the Pentagon and handed it out to consultants for studies of strategic ideas that interested Andy Marshall. One such idea was an "improved accuracy program" to develop new technology that would make the Navy's submarine-launched missiles just as accurate as the Air Force's ICBMs, that would extend counterforce power across the entire strategic arsenal. The idea would culminate in a new missile called the Trident II.

Schlesinger also brought on board, to be his speechwriter, special consultant and general adviser, William Kaufmann. In the early 1960s, Kaufmann visited his old haunts at RAND a few times each year, spent most of his time there with Andy Marshall and, in the process, met Schlesinger. When Schlesinger became national security director in the Budget Bureau, he hired Kaufmann as a special consultant. When he moved to the CIA, so, for a brief stint, did Kaufmann. It was only natural that he bring Kaufmann back to the Pentagon as well. Kaufmann had been out of the strategic nuclear game for several years, having returned to his earlier interest in NATO and conventional warfare, which he considered more tangible, more firmly rooted in history. In retrospect,

Kaufmann saw that once he slipped into the deep, dark pit of nuclear strategy, it was easy to become totally absorbed, living, eating, breathing the stuff every hour of every day, but that once he departed from that realm for a while and scanned it from a distance, it seemed crazy, unreal. When Kaufmann joined Schlesinger in the Pentagon and Schlesinger decided to delve deeply into the nuclear world, he rekindled Kaufmann's fascination with counterforce strategy—a flame that had never completely been extinguished—and Kaufmann slipped slowly into the pit once more.

Schlesinger was frustrated by the obstructions that the NSC was mounting against NSDM-242. So, on January 10, 1974, at a lunchtime press conference before the Overseas Writers Association, he announced that he was implementing a "change in targeting strategy" in order to develop alternatives to "initiating a suicidal strike against the cities of the other side," that the old policy of assured destruction was no longer adequate for deterrence, that we needed "a set of selective options against different sets of targets" on a much more limited and flexible scale. In abbreviated form, Schlesinger was describing the strategy of NU-OPTS, the Foster Panel and NSDM-242. Henry Kissinger was infuriated by Schlesinger's ploy of going public, but it worked. Exactly one week later, NSDM-242 was signed by the President.

Meanwhile, Schlesinger's remarks were creating a furor in the press and in Congress. The inside history of nuclear strategy over the past decade had been kept largely hidden from even the most interested public. Almost everyone believed that assured destruction really was the official targeting policy, and Schlesinger's pronouncements were taken as something utterly new and possibly dangerous. Schlesinger needed to wrap his ideas in some cloak of respectability, and that was where Bill Kaufmann always came in handy.

Kaufmann had been in Cambridge the day of the press conference, teaching at MIT, as he did every Thursday and Friday, and had no forewarning of what Schlesinger would be saying. Word reached him after the event, and he didn't like it at all. Kaufmann had never found appeal in this small-strike, shot-across-the-bow business. He had argued about it with Tom Schelling in 1960 and with Schlesinger in later years. It was too abstract, it didn't mean anything. At least counterforce was something that Kaufmann knew how to do; the targets made sense, the strategy had military precedent. If you were going to use nuclear weapons, Kaufmann thought, you might as well go for broke or forget about it.

Kaufmann went down to Washington and recast Schlesinger's ideas in more presentable form. He emphasized that "flexibility" and the idea of bringing the war to a quick ending were nothing new, that they dated back to McNamara's time, but that now we should make options more flexible still, a notion to which few could object in principle. Moreover, recent intelligence data indicated that the Soviets were beginning to test MIRVed ICBMs. The age-old red flag of SAC vulnerability could be waved with new vigor. Schlesinger could justify his "new" doctrine as a response to this growing Soviet threat. "The Soviet Union now has the capability in its missile forces to undertake selective attacks against targets other than cities," Kaufmann wrote under Schlesinger's name in the "posture statement" for fiscal year 1975, the official Pentagon document that justified the annual defense budget. "This poses for us an obligation, if we are to ensure the credibility of our strategic deterrent, to be certain that we have a comparable capability in our strategic systems and in our targeting doctrine. . . ." Schlesinger repeated this rationale in testimony before congressional committees.

Actually, however, this was not what Schlesinger had in mind. Unlike those who were at RAND in the 1950s, Schlesinger carried no obsession with SAC vulnerability. Ever since the U.S. had dispersed its ICBMs, encased them in underground silos and put nuclear-missile submarines to sea, he had never taken the threat of a deliberate Soviet attack against Minuteman very seriously. Nor did Schlesinger believe that a full-scale counterforce attack—by the U.S. or the U.S.S.R.—was feasible.

During the NU-OPTS project, Schlesinger had talked a great deal with an engineer at RAND named Hyman Schulman, who had worked on ballistic missile guidance systems for many years. The ability to destroy blast-resistant targets, such as hardened ICBM silos, depended partly on a weapon's explosive power but very much more on its accuracy. Strategic analysts generally measured accuracy according to a missile's CEP, or "circular error probable," the radius within which a missile will land 50 percent of the time. Yet Hy Schulman observed that random and systematic errors occurring along the flight path of a missile could throw it off course by some distance exceeding the CEP. For years, Schulman had devised mathematical models explaining the sources of error, and had helped adjust the gyroscopes inside the computer guidance systems in several missiles to correct these errors. But there was always some amount of error that the models could not explain. Nor could the source of this error be discovered and, therefore, corrected through some new equation. Only the most precise calibration instruments available could ferret out these mysterious errors, and those instruments were inside the missile, causing some of the errors themselves.

After an ICBM was fired in tests many times, the systematic errors could be measured and the gyroscopes could be tweaked and adjusted to minimize the CEP in future tests. However, Schulman noted that the U.S. tested its missiles on a flight path from Vandenberg Air Force Base in California to the Kwajalein Islands in the Pacific Ocean, in other words from east to west. Similarly, the Soviets tested their missiles on a course from west to east. Yet in a real nuclear war each side would get only one shot, and the missiles would have to sail over the North Pole. The problem here was that along different flight paths, the earth's gravitational pull varied, and so did the degree of systematic error. One could theorize about the direction and the magnitude of error across totally untested trajectories, but one could never really *know* what they would be.

In short, determining a missile's counterforce power by observing its CEP was like gauging a marksman's talents by measuring how tightly grouped his bullet holes were on a target board, without measuring their distance from the bull's-eye. If several ICBMs were fired at the same point, they might form a nice, tight circle where they landed, but the circle might lie a good distance away from the target.

The problems of systematic error would be partly relieved by shooting two missiles at each counterforce target, but then there would be the additional problem called "fratricide." The effects of a nuclear explosion included not just blast, heat and radiation, but also scattered neutrons, considerable debris, amazingly high wind velocity, and a thick radioactive cloud of various particles swooped up from the ground. If another warhead came in shortly after the first, it would probably explode prematurely, be blown off target, be eaten away by the neutrons or be destroyed in some other fashion.

Schulman's work had had a substantial impact on Schlesinger, and had reinforced his long-standing antipathy toward strategies entailing large-scale counterforce attacks. Schlesinger felt that launching a few nuclear weapons against an aggressor using conventional weapons would probably shock him into stopping and coerce him to the negotiating tables, but that if many more weapons beyond that were used, it was all over: escalation to all-out holocaust was virtually inevitable.

In short, Schlesinger really wanted a more refined ability to use nuclear weapons first. But in early 1974, the SALT I arms-control agreement less than two years old, détente with the Russians was popular, and sentiment in Congress and among the public against the straggling Vietnam War—and, by extension, against the military establishment—was at a peak. It was hardly the time for Schlesinger to state very clearly his true intentions on this score. So, although he did tell Congress of his desire for "flexibility and selectivity . . . to shore up deterrence across the entire spectrum of risk" and for nuclear options "limiting strikes down to a few weapons," he always placed this desire in a framework of the United States responding to the development of new strategic weapons, or to a possible limited first-strike, by the Soviets.

The result, however, was exactly what McNamara had experienced after the Ann Arbor speech and what David Aaron had predicted would happen if NSDM-242 were signed: advocates of new bombers and missiles and bigger warheads were given a tremendous boost. The Air Force in particular, along with its technocratic allies in the Pentagon's R&D directorate, pushed with new vigor and legitimacy its case for a new manned bomber, the B-1, accurate cruise missiles and a new ICBM called the MX with supposedly much-improved accuracy and ten MIRV warheads, each of an explosive power twice that of the three warheads on the Minuteman III.

Even though Schlesinger had told Congress and the press that his strategy would not require additional weapons, he had no objections to funding new systems. He believed that "perceptions" were an important element of international relations. The essence of his strategic ideas was to reassure the allies of our commitment to their defense and to ensure that the Soviets understood this reassurance. If it was perceived that the Soviets were ahead of the United States in megatonnage, number of MIRVed missiles, missile throw-weight or whatever indicator one might wish to perceive—no matter whether these leads gave the Soviets any meaningful military advantage—then, Schlesinger thought, it was important to reverse these perceptions and build up our strategic force accordingly. That these perceptions had been created by analysts like Schlesinger in the first place—that throw-weight ratios didn't bother the allies a bit until some Americans told them that they ought to be bothered—went unnoticed.

Schlesinger's pronouncements affected not only weapons policy but also the direction of the strategic debate, revitalizing the arguments of those nuclear strategists who had been warning of a Soviet threat to SAC and advocating a first-class American counterforce capability for decades. The most prominent of those was Paul H. Nitze, author of NSC-68 and the Gaither Report, a man who consistently foretold the years of maximum danger for the West in the perpetually near future. Nitze had been a member of the U.S. SALT delegation since 1969 and had been chiefly responsible for negotiating the ABM Treaty of 1972. In June 1974, he quit the delegation. The Watergate scandal was nearing climax and Nitze felt that the pressures were driving Nixon to cave in on SALT just to get a politically popular treaty. Second, Nitze saw danger in the new Soviet MIRVs and thought the forthcoming SALT II treaty was not dealing with the threat. Nitze felt that he could have more impact on the outside.

His first major public statement was a widely read article in the January 1976 issue of *Foreign Affairs,* in which he argued that the SALT II treaty would not prevent the Soviets from continuing "to pursue a nuclear superiority" that was "designed to produce a theoretical war-winning capability." The Soviets were deploying MIRVed ICBMs with sufficient megatonnage and accuracy to destroy the bulk of American ICBMs in their silos; at the same time, they had a major civil-defense program. Nitze described a nightmare scenario. If the Soviets evacuated their cities and then attacked SAC with a fraction of their ICBMs, the U.S. would be left mainly with submarine-based missiles, which lacked the accuracy to hit much besides cities. Since the cities would have been evacuated, a retaliatory attack would kill only "three or four percent of the total [Soviet] population." We would probably not dare to retaliate, since the Soviets would have enough warheads in a reserve force to devastate American cities.

It was essentially a replay of the "nuclear blackmail" scenario that Herman Kahn had laid out in *On Thermonuclear War*—which was, in turn, a mirror image of the counterforce/no-cities strategy that, a few years earlier, the RAND Strategic Objectives Committee, of which Kahn was a member, had devised as a policy that the *United States* should adopt.

It was all rather odd. During the 1961 Berlin crisis, at a time when the U.S. had vast nuclear superiority over the Soviets, when the Soviets had only a few strategic weapons, all of them highly vulnerable, when America was in the grip of a civil-defense frenzy, Paul Nitze had been the official most adamantly opposed to exploiting this superiority in any manner. He had voiced the loudest objections to Harry Rowen and Carl Kaysen's counterforce first-strike plan. At the quadrapartite meetings where the British, French, Germans and Nitze outlined possible joint responses to Soviet moves, he had refused even to talk about using nuclear weapons—not even a few, not even hypothetically. Fifteen years later, he was envisioning leaders in the Kremlin coldly contemplating firing a first-strike against the American ICBM and bomber bases, an attack that would involve at least 2,000 megaton warheads, all the while knowing that the U.S. would, under the brightest of circumstances from their point of view, still have several thousand surviving warheads in its submarines alone. The Soviets would also know, from analyses done by American scientists, that their "surgical" counterforce strike would kill, mainly through radioactive fallout, anywhere from two million to twenty-two million—and, most likely, at least ten million—American civilians. Nitze was arguing that the Soviets could destroy not America's ability to retaliate, but its will to do so. Yet could he really predict—more important, could the Soviets believe with any confidence—that after thousands of nuclear warheads had exploded on American soil, after millions of Americans had been murdered, the President of the United States would do nothing?

Nitze's estimate that only 3 or 4 percent of the Soviet population would be killed by American retaliation came from an official Soviet civil-defense manual. Had he forgotten about claims during the Berlin crisis that an American civil-defense program could save 97 percent of the population and how quickly those estimates had crumbled under even casual analysis? Nitze was also aware that the U.S. nuclear war plan called not for killing civilians, but rather for destroying military and industrial facilities. Even the submarine-launched missiles could destroy many of those—and the war plan had them doing so. McNamara may have said that the U.S. must have the ability to kill 25 percent of the Soviet population to deter nuclear war. But in the SIOP, at SAC, where it counted, there was no such requirement. There, civil defense played virtually no role in the strategic equation.

With the aid of his chief technical assistant on the SALT team, a hawkish engineer from the Boeing Company named T. K. Jones, Nitze attempted to state the strategic balance between the U.S. and the U.S.S.R. in mathematical terms. In a series of graphs that accompanied the *Foreign Affairs* article and in another called "Deterring Our Deterrent" in *Foreign Policy,* Nitze and Jones showed that after a counterforce first-strike by the Soviets and a counterforce second-strike by the U.S., the Soviets would end up with far more megatonnage, missile throw-weight, missiles and warheads than the United States. But did this mean that the President would—or, for that matter, could—carefully tote up the numbers left on both sides, see that he was behind and throw in the towel? The questions that had been asked, time and again, at the end of studies and exercises on U.S. counterforce and NU-OPTS strategies applied equally to the Soviet Union: What happens next? How does the war end? How do you fight a nuclear war?

Nitze's articles hit new heights of abstraction in strategic thought. They reflected an absolute faith in the power and significance of theoretical calculations, and in the desire and ability of human beings, amid the passion and fog of war, to behave according to a standard of reason established by such calculations.

Yet over the next few years, Paul Nitze set the tenor and terms of the debate, both inside the government and out, over nuclear arms and strategy. He did this mainly through the vehicle of an organization that he helped set up called the Committee on the Present Danger. A few months before his *Foreign Affairs* piece appeared, Nitze met with some old friends—mainly Yale law professor Eugene Rostow (Walt's brother), former Deputy Defense Secretary David Packard, former Treasury Secretary Henry Fowler and corporate lobbyist Charls Walker—who were also concerned about the growing Soviet threat and the apathy in the land. They thought about starting a nonpartisan organization that would awaken the people before it was too late. They were encouraged in their efforts by Secretary of Defense Jim Schlesinger, who thought that such a group would help rouse support for his defense budget.

In November, President Gerald Ford fired Schlesinger and

replaced him with his friend Donald Rumsfeld. Henry Kissinger had convinced Ford that Schlesinger was out to torpedo SALT, and Ford had never felt comfortable with Schlesinger's condescending style. The incident finally moved Nitze and Rostow to get their organization started. In March, the Committee on the Present Danger was formed. The title was Gene Rostow's idea; he remembered another committee of that name that had been set up by eminent men during the Korean War to urge higher defense spending and a return to the draft.

Meanwhile, the leading contender for the Presidency in the 1976 Democratic primaries was turning out to be an unknown quantity named Jimmy Carter. Nitze hopped aboard Carter's campaign even before the Iowa Caucus, Carter's first electoral victory. Nitze sent Carter several of his speeches. When the two met in Washington, Carter told him that he had read not only those speeches but also a few that Nitze had not even sent him. Nitze was flattered. He sent Carter some more. In June, he and his wife each contributed $750 to the Carter campaign. After Carter won the election in November, Nitze joined his transition team.

But when Carter took office in January, Nitze was out. He was offered no job, and neither were his friends. Moreover, those who did get high positions under Carter held views diametrically opposed to Nitze's. Paul Warnke, Cyrus Vance, Harold Brown, David Aaron, Leslie Gelb, Anthony Lake—all doves, men who had opposed counterforce, who thought that nuclear weapons had little utility beyond deterring war, who held a more sanguine view toward the Soviets than Nitze felt was responsible. To Nitze's mind, dangerous men were in power at a perilous time. He began to loathe Jimmy Carter, his views on the issues, his judgment in people. He felt personally betrayed.

The Committee on the Present Danger was galvanized by the Carter Administration. Its members printed dozens of pamphlets, issued press statements, gave speeches and raised plenty of money, warning the land that the "principal threat to our nation, to world peace, and to the cause of human freedom is the Soviet drive for dominance based upon an unparalleled military buildup" and that the "Soviet Union has not altered its long-held goal of a world dominated from a single center—Moscow." It was the essential message of NSC-68, the Cold War blueprint that Paul Nitze had authored twenty-five years earlier, combined with the analysis of his *Foreign Affairs* and *Foreign Policy* articles on how the Russians could deter our deterrent.

When Jimmy Carter signed the SALT II Treaty with the Russians in June 1979, Nitze went on the warpath. SALT II was a modest treaty; its advocates maintained that it put a limit on how many warheads the Soviets could load onto their ICBMs and how large their ICBMs could be and that it constrained the expansion of their overall forces while placing virtually no constraints on the weapons that the U.S. wanted to build at the same time.* But to Nitze, the treaty was a disaster because it left the Soviets with a huge superiority in the megatonnage and throw-weight of their missiles, creating an imbalance and endangering Minuteman. Nitze testified passionately against the treaty, lambasted it in speeches and debates and on TV talk shows across the nation. For a man of seventy-two, it was a remarkably energetic crusade.

In the process, Nitze dominated the debate. That summer, during the SALT II hearings before Congress, senators, journalists and ordinary citizens got caught up in a whirlwind of esoterica on throw-weight ratios, single-shot kill probabilities, counterforce targeting and nuclear-exchange calculations. The Carter Administration contributed to the atmosphere, going along with Nitze's terms and arguments, hoping to buy off conservative senators by admitting to potential imbalances and promising to boost the budget and fix the problems if they voted for SALT II. For many ob-

---

* SALT II would have, among other things, limited both sides to 2,400 strategic missile launchers. Of them 1,320 could be either MIRVed missiles or bombers capable of firing air-launched cruise missiles, but no more than 1,200 of the 1,320 could be MIRVed missiles. At the time, the U.S.S.R. had 2,504 missile launchers while the U.S. had only 2,283. (The U.S. had more warheads, however.) Both sides had well under 1,200 MIRVed missiles. The treaty would also have limited the number of "heavy" MIRVed ICBMs, such as the U.S.S.R.'s SS-18, to 308— the exact number that the Soviets had at the time—and would have limited the number of warheads that could be placed on such missiles to ten, even though the Soviets could have loaded many more, if they so desired, without the treaty. The U.S. had no heavy missiles, nor did its military see a need for any. (The proposed MX was too light to qualify for "heavy" status, although it could do all the things that a ten-warhead SS-18 could.) In these and many other provisions, the U.S. could continue to do pretty much whatever it was planning to do already, while slight restraints were imposed on the Soviets.

After a succession of political scares in 1979—reports of Soviet troops in Cuba, the revolution in Iran and the Soviet invasion of Afghanistan—along with the ascension of the Committee on the Present Danger, Jimmy Carter, seeing that he would not get the two-thirds majority needed to pass a treaty, declined to present SALT II to the U.S. Senate. Nevertheless, two years later, even the hawks in the new Ronald Reagan Administration who had attacked the treaty in the Carter years decided it was worthwhile to abide by the provisions of this signed but unratified treaty.

FRED KAPLAN

servers, it was the first time that they had heard these concepts discussed in any detail, and they found the technology, strategies and calculations endlessly fascinating. They also found out that virtually anyone could do the calculations to determine Minuteman vulnerability. All one needed was a "bomb-damage computer," a circular slide rule readily available from RAND and other think tanks. You just assumed the explosive power and CEP of a bomb and the blast-resistance of its target—data that were commonly discussed in the SALT debate. You then spun the plastic wheels of the bomb-damage computer until the arrows lined up with those numbers. Then you looked at the appropriate window, and there was the "kill probability." If it read 0.9, that meant that 90 percent of Minuteman could be killed by a Soviet first-strike. It was easy, all too easy.

The central ideas of the nuclear strategists—that nuclear war could be calculated with precision, that SAC vulnerability was the central threat of our time, and that the U.S. had to build up a strong counterforce capability—emerged as the conventional wisdom.

The Carter Administration was headed in this direction already. When he first became President, Jimmy Carter spoke of reducing the number of nuclear weapons in the world to zero. His Defense Secretary, Harold Brown, was skeptical about the wisdom of counterforce. In a speech to the Moscow Institute of U.S.A. Affairs in March 1975, while he was president of the California Institute of Technology, Brown proclaimed that "only deterrence is feasible," that nuclear war-winning or coercive strategies were impractical.

Yet in the four years of the Carter Administration, options for nuclear war-fighting were set in policy more firmly than ever before. Carter's switch was popularly explained, at the time, as a product of his campaign to appease the hawkish right wing of the Senate so that its most influential members would vote to ratify the SALT II arms-control treaty that he had negotiated with the Soviets. Also a powerful force was the influence of Carter's Polish-born Russophobic national security adviser, Zbigniew Brzezinski, a Columbia University academic and a perennial hardliner toward Moscow. And there were the Russians themselves: their continued testing of advanced MIRVed ICBMs, their probing maneuvers in unstable areas of the third world, their invasion of Afghanistan in December 1979.

But more critical than any of these factors in turning the Carter Administration around was activity going on behind the scenes—the wave of momentum started by the Foster Panel, which at this point had reached so mighty a crest that Carter could not help but be carried along with it. At first, both Carter and Brown wanted to scrap the whole approach of NSDM-242. But then Brown was briefed on the work of the Foster Panel and the Odeen group by officials who had participated in the studies. Brown also retained the consulting services of William Kaufmann and discussed the issues with him. Before long, Brown recognized what McNamara had concluded nearly two decades earlier: that having options was better than having no options, that however unlikely it may be that a nuclear war could be kept limited, "it would be the height of folly," as Brown told a congressional committee, "to put the United States in a position in which uncontrolled escalation would be the only course we could follow."

Once that assumption was accepted, the rest was almost inevitable. On August 24, 1977, Carter signed Presidential Directive No. 18, or PD-18, which reaffirmed NSDM-242 and the NUWEP as national policy. In 1978, a new targeting study was ordered, called the Nuclear Targeting Policy Review. The end result was an official document called PD-59, signed by Jimmy Carter on July 25, 1980. It ordered options that were still more limited, a withheld reserve force that was slightly larger, a greater emphasis on using nuclear weapons to destroy conventional military targets of the Soviet military as well as its nuclear targets, including targets that might be moving on the battlefield; and it planned more explicitly for the possibility of fighting a nuclear war over an extended period of time—days, weeks or longer—a task requiring vast and highly expensive improvements in the nation's command-control-communications network, especially in satellite systems that could survive a nuclear war.

Many weapons scientists thought that the mission was impossible, that some communications facilities could be "hardened" to resist nuclear effects, but only to a degree, and that degree would not be enough to withstand the blast, radiation and electromagnetic pulses of a nuclear explosion. The communications systems were like the President's eyes and ears; if they or

their transmission links were zapped, fried or blown up, he would
have no way to *control* the war. The notion of continuing to use
nuclear weapons in a fine-tuned fashion, sending subtle signals
and gauging the opponent's response, would become practically
impossible; and the likelihood of escalation to all-out holocaust
would therefore be very high. Still, "protracted nuclear war-fighting" was the mission and the Pentagon would spend tens of billions of dollars trying to accomplish it.

Moreover, this time around, the Strategic Air Command was
cooperative. The same colonels and generals who had taken an interest in the theories of RAND in the 1960s had infiltrated SAC by
the 1970s. General Russell Dougherty, who had played a role in
the NU-OPTS project, was SAC Commander from 1974 to 1977,
and he was followed by another NU-OPTS veteran, General Richard Ellis, who held the post when PD-59 was signed. Ellis had his
doubts whether something like PD-59 could be carried out with
existing technology, but—in contrast with a Curtis LeMay or a
Tommy Power—he had no arguments with the wisdom of its
principles.

Fundamentally, there was nothing new about PD-59. It was
merely an elaboration of NSDM-242, which grew out of the Foster
Panel, which was explicitly based on McNamara's SIOP-63 guidance of 1961–1962, which was modeled on a decade of analysis at
RAND. The Nuclear Targeting Policy Review, which led to PD-59,
was handled in part through the Pentagon's office of net assessment, still run by Andy Marshall. It was ultimately directed by a
Pentagon analyst named Leon Sloss, who had worked on the Foster Panel under Seymour Weiss at the State Department. Sloss
hired dozens of consultants to work on specific aspects of the review. Among the consultants who made the deepest impression
on Sloss's own thinking about the broad strategic issues were Albert Wohlstetter, Harry Rowen and Herman Kahn—the father,
son and holy ghost of the spirit of the RAND Corporation. They
had been among the prophets, and now they at last saw their
commandments carved into stone.

26 DANCING IN THE DARK

BY THE TIME Jimmy Carter and Harold Brown left office, then, every tenet of the RAND philosophy was set in place as official U.S. policy. Counterforce was endorsed with an affirmation and refinement that exceeded even the pronouncements of James Schlesinger. Moreover, the Carter Administration made every effort to make the philosophy more practical. Carter approved the production of 200 MX missiles, which the Air Force had proposed a few years earlier as the ideal weapon for killing "hard targets," such as the latest Soviet ICBM silos. He also ordered that each of the missiles would be moved about among twenty-three silos, as in an elaborate carnival shell game, so that the Soviets could not know just where the missile was, forcing them to go to much greater efforts—firing at 4,600 holes in the ground instead of 200—if they wanted to launch a counterforce first-strike themselves. This multiple-shelter plan, reflecting a fear of "SAC vulnerability" pushed to its extreme limits, was to be put into effect at a cost of well over $40 billion.

Not everyone in the Carter Administration was fully convinced of the wisdom of these steps. There were several skeptics on the NSC staff, in the State Department, the CIA, the Arms Control and Disarmament Agency. And there was the Secretary of Defense, Harold Brown.

Brown accepted the premises, the logic and the subsequent programs dictated by the principles of PD-59. But he still felt less than completely comfortable with them. He remembered the studies by General Glenn Kent on "damage-limiting" from the McNamara years, and knew that any counterforce campaign was bound to run into unanticipated problems. In his Pentagon "posture statement" for fiscal year 1981, for example, amidst several pages (written chiefly by William Kaufmann) outlining the rationale for nuclear-war plans that called for more flexible and limited warfighting options, Brown personally inserted two sentences of his own: "My own view," he noted, "remains that a full-scale thermo-

nuclear exchange would constitute an unprecedented disaster for
the Soviet Union and for the United States. And I am not at all
persuaded that what started as a demonstration, or even a tightly
controlled use of the strategic forces for larger purposes, could be
kept from escalating to a full-scale thermonuclear exchange."
Then, adding a "But" to the next sentence, he let the Kaufmann-
composed passages roll on—just as, despite his undoubtedly sincere reservations, he let the strategists who had been pushing
these ideas for more than two decades roll on more mightily than
at any time in the previous eighteen years.

For Brown agreed with the principle of options, and by this
late date, the road of options was a steep and slippery one. It had
already been marked and paved by the tightly knit coterie of intellectuals who by now dominated strategic thinking deep inside that
hidden infrastructure of the government that every day dealt with
matters of the bomb. Once Brown started down that road, he
found himself inexorably propelled to its very end.

If during the Carter years the only missing element in the renewed triumph of the RAND tradition was an enthusiastic frame
of mind among the highest-ranking officials, that was quickly provided when Ronald Reagan won the White House in the 1980
election. For decades, Reagan had spoken out against the perils of
the Soviet threat and in favor of much higher defense spending.
The men he chose as his national security advisers leaned in the
same direction. Thirty-two members of the new Reagan Administration, including the President himself, had been members of the
Committee on the Present Danger. Among them were two of its
founders, Eugene Rostow, whom Reagan appointed as director of
the Arms Control and Disarmament Agency, and—back in power
at last—Paul Nitze, chosen to head the U.S. delegation to negoti-
ate with the Soviets on reducing nuclear weapons in Europe.

To Reagan and his national security managers, counterforce
and its various accoutrements were to be celebrated, not rhetorically qualified. They could openly express their sentiments on this
matter because the RAND traditions had long ago become the
conventional wisdom, its premises and conclusions accepted almost universally throughout the national security bureaucracy.
There was still a large minority, especially in Congress, that criticized such new and expensive weapons systems as the MX missile
and the B-1 bomber. And in the first year of the Reagan Adminis-

tration, many critics took great umbrage when the President or one of his staff let slip too blatant a remark about the possibilities of winning a nuclear war. But even among the critics, practically no one any longer took issue with the fundamentals of counter-force or the theories about SAC vulnerability. If such vital tools for counterforce as the MX missile were criticized, it was because many considered its basing scheme ludicrous or infeasible—not because the Soviet first-strike threat was widely discounted or be-cause the missile itself, with its counterforce power, was in dis-favor.

In early 1982, Reagan's Secretary of Defense, Caspar Wein-berger, signed a Top Secret document known as the "Defense Guidance," which outlined the Administration's official strategy. It called for the U.S. to have nuclear forces that could "prevail and be able to force the Soviet Union to seek earliest termination of hostilities on terms favorable to the United States . . . even under the condition of a prolonged war"—in short, to fight and win a protracted nuclear war. Lying at the heart of this guidance was the old "coercive strategy": hurt the enemy and make him quit by threatening to hurt him more with a durable reserve force held securely at bay.

This was no mere coincidence. The chief authors of this doc-ument were Andrew Marshall, the RAND veteran who had worked on counterforce studies since the early 1950s and who was, from the time Jim Schlesinger appointed him there in 1973, still director of the Pentagon's net assessment office; Fred Iklé, another former RAND strategist, now Undersecretary of Defense for Policy; and Richard Perle, onetime defense aide to Senator Henry Jackson, now Assistant Secretary of Defense for Interna-tional Security Policy. Perle had not come from RAND, but he did receive his first—and seminal—lessons on strategy in the early 1960s, when as a teen-ager in Los Angeles he held many discus-sions on the subject with his girl friend's father, Albert Wohlstet-ter. Later, during the ABM debate of 1969, Perle was hired as chief research assistant for the Committee to Maintain a Prudent Defense Policy, an outfit that Wohlstetter, Paul Nitze and Dean Acheson set up in Washington to counter the anti-ABM campaign waged by several famous scientists and the arms-control commu-nity. After that, he went to work for Jackson, became notorious for whipping up opposition to SALT treaties and grew increasingly close to the group of conservative Democrats who formed the

Committee on the Present Danger. Perle was definitely a member of the club.

The policy-makers were heavily assisted by the scientists inside the Pentagon: the Director of Defense Research and Engineering, Richard DeLauer, not a strategist but a longtime vice-president of TRW, Inc., a corporation that manufactured many of the high-tech devices that helped make counterforce seem technically feasible; his principal deputy, James Wade, who, in his own words, "learned strategy at the feet of Paul Nitze" as his senior adviser during the SALT I negotiations, and who played an active role in the Foster Panel and the sessions that formulated NSDM-242; and DeLauer's deputy for strategic and theater nuclear forces, T. K. Jones, technical assistant to Paul Nitze during SALT I, the engineer who drew the graphs and divined the calculations for Nitze's influential articles in *Foreign Affairs* and *Foreign Policy,* and who gained notoriety on his own as a fervent enthusiast for civil defense, telling one reporter that in the event of nuclear attack, Americans should "dig a hole, cover it with a couple of doors and then throw three feet of dirt on top . . . If there are enough shovels to go around, everybody's going to make it."

With Reagan and his men in power, the rules of the strategic community became the rules of the nation, and Pentagon strategy and weapons policy were geared toward total conformance to those rules. Still, there was one awkward and imposing reality: nobody knew how to follow the rules while playing an actual game—nobody really knew how to fight a protracted or limited or coercive nuclear war. This conclusion had been reached before, over and over through the years; and there had since been no new data, studies or grand technological leap to warrant any other. Yet the difference in the Reagan Administration—the difference that frightened so many otherwise apathetic citizens that a popular, broad-based anti-nuclear movement suddenly grew up apparently out of nowhere—was that no one in power seemed to have truly grasped this conclusion.

It was nothing new in the annals of strategic policy when Reagan's first Secretary of State, Alexander Haig, said that he could imagine the U.S. firing off a single nuclear weapon for "demonstration" purposes during a war in Europe, or when Reagan himself or his Vice-President, George Bush, held discourse on the conceivability of fighting or winning a limited nuclear war. Contrary to many press reports of the day, there was nothing much new about Reagan's defense program generally. Reagan was certainly spending a lot more money on defense: his first defense budget amounted to $258 billion, $43.7 billion higher than Carter's last, a 13.2 percent increase even after allowing for inflation. However, 80 percent of this increase was for more surface ships and submarines, more expensive airplanes, tanks and other weapons of conventional battle that have nothing to do with nuclear war. More money was also slated for nuclear weapons; but even though in some instances Reagan called for more or faster spending, nearly every program—cruise missiles, the Trident II submarine-launched missile, the MX, extended command-control-communications systems, weapons for space warfare, the beginnings of stepped-up activity on civil defense and a new ABM—had started in the Carter Administration or before. The one major exception was the B-1 bomber, which Carter had killed in 1977 and which Reagan revived in 1981. But the B-1 had little effect on the underlying philosophy of nuclear war-fighting—which was scarcely changed at all. Like the Reagan defense budget, it was only expressed with slightly greater exuberance.

What *was* shocking and new about many of the statements made by Reagan officials on nuclear war, however, was their baldness, the nonchalant innocence with which they were frequently uttered. Indeed, it was because these theories were *not* new that their proponents could recite them so casually. To those most deeply ensconced in the strategic community's inner circle, something like the Reagan-Weinberger "Defense Guidance" appeared simply as more of the same, as a restatement and slight refinement of a long legacy of strategic thought and policy. The insidious aspect of this legacy was that it had loomed so constantly throughout their professional lives that it was, by now, difficult for them to think of these ideas as mere theories. They had taken on all the appearances of a scientifically based reality. There were calculations that could be reproduced and documents that could be recalled or taken off the shelf—PD-59, NSDM-242, the Foster Panel's work, NU-OPTS, the McNamara SIOP-63 guidance, the work at RAND by Schlesinger, Kaufmann, Marshall, Kahn, Digby, Brodie and the Strategic Objectives Committee. It was so tangible, the ideas had been around and had been officially (if not always publicly) accepted for so long, that it was easy to forget that there was nothing more in the real world to substantiate them in 1982 than there had been in 1952, when the ideas first took form.

The "new generation," as Philip Morse called these war planners who never saw war, had taken over completely. In the absence of any reality that was congenial to their abstract theorizing, the strategists in power treated the theory as if it *were* reality. For those mired in thinking about it all day, every day, in the corridors of officialdom, nuclear strategy had become the stuff of a living dreamworld.

This mixture of habit, inertia, analytical convenience and fantasy was fueled by a peculiar logic as well. It was, after all, only rational to try to keep a nuclear war limited if one ever broke out, to devise plans and options ahead of time that might end the war quickly and favorably, to keep the scope of its damage not too far out of tune with the importance of the political objectives over which the war was declared to begin with. Yet over the years, despite endless studies, nobody could find any options that seemed practical or made sense.

In 1946, in the beginning, Bernard Brodie wrote, "Everything about the atomic bomb is overshadowed by the twin facts that it exists and that its destructive power is fantastically great." The story of nuclear strategy, from that moment on, has been the story of intellectuals—not least of them, for many years anyway, Brodie himself—trying to outmaneuver the force of those axioms, trying to make the atomic bomb and later the hydrogen bomb manageable, controllable, to make it conform to human proportions. The method of mathematical calculation, derived mainly from the theory of economics that they had all studied, gave the strategists of the new age a handle on the colossally destructive power of the weapon they found in their midst. But over the years, the method became a catechism, the first principles carved into the mystical stone of dogma. The precise calculations and the cool, comfortable vocabulary were coming all too commonly to be grasped not merely as tools of desperation but as genuine reflections of the nature of nuclear war.

It was a compelling illusion. Even many of those who recognized its pretense and inadequacy willingly fell under its spell. They continued to play the game because there was no other. They performed their calculations and spoke in their strange and esoteric tongues because to do otherwise would be to recognize, all too clearly and constantly, the ghastliness of their contemplations. They contrived their options because without them the bomb would appear too starkly as the thing that they had tried to prevent it from being but that it ultimately would become if it ever were used—a device of sheer mayhem, a weapon whose cataclysmic powers no one really had the faintest idea of how to control. The nuclear strategists had come to impose order—but in the end, chaos still prevailed.

NOTES

I have not specified material taken from interviews, since almost all of them were conducted on a confidential basis; much of the information gathered from them would not have been revealed otherwise. Virtually everything, however, has been checked with several sources; this is especially the case with historically significant facts and with anecdotes that may have been told to me for self-serving or ax-grinding reasons. If interview material was inconsistent with documents, I sided with the documents. When material was based in part on printed sources and in part on interviews, I have cited the documented source, followed by "and interview(s)." A list of those I interviewed appears after the notes.

ABBREVIATIONS

BoB. Bureau of the Budget.
CNO. Chief of Naval Operations.
C/S. Chief of Staff.
DDEL. Dwight D. Eisenhower Library, Abilene, Kans.
DoD. Department of Defense.
DPM. Draft Presidential Memorandum.
FOIA. Obtained through the Freedom of Information Act.
HSTL. Harry S. Truman Library, Independence, Mo.
JCS. Joint Chiefs of Staff.
JFKL. John F. Kennedy Library, Dorchester, Mass.
LBJL. Lyndon B. Johnson Library, Austin, Tex.
LoC. Library of Congress, Manuscripts Division, Washington, D.C.
Max. AFB. Simpson Historical Research Center, Maxwell Air Force Base, Ala.
NA/MMB. National Archives, Modern Military Branch, Washington, D.C.
NSC. National Security Council.
SAC. Strategic Air Command.
USAF. United States Air Force.
*—declassified at instigation of the author.

1: YEAR ZERO

9   King report: Letter, Brodie to Edward Mead Earle, Nov. 11, 1943, *Edward Mead Earle Papers,* Box 3, B folder, Princeton Univ.

9   drop *"Layman's"*: Thomas Schelling, "Bernard Brodie (1910–1978)" in *International Security,* Winter 1978, p. 2.

11   "move freely": "The Military Intellectuals," London *Times Literary Supplement,* Aug. 25, 1961.

12   Brodie and horses: Comments, Brodie, *Proceedings of the U.S. Military History Symposium: Science, Technology and Warfare* (Office of Air Force Historian, 1969), p. 87; and interviews.

14   Brodie fellowship: Letter, Quincy Wright to Vera Dean, Mar. 25, 1940, *Quincy Wright Papers,* 1972 Addendum, Box 11, Brodie folder, Univ. of Chicago; and interview.

14   "A-number-one man": Many letters, *ibid.*
14   "opinions and ideas": Letter, Wright to William T. R. Fox, Aug. 8, 1944, *Quincy Wright Papers,* 1972 Addendum, Box 14, Fox folder.
15   "Can Peaceful Change . . .": *Bernard Brodie Papers,* Box 21, UCLA.
16   "As you already know": Letter, Brodie to Wright, Sept. 19, 1940, *Quincy Wright Papers,* 1972 Addendum, Box 11, Brodie folder.
16   Carnegie fellowship and book: Letter, Brodie to Wright, Apr. 29, 1949, and telegram, Sept. 18, 1940, *ibid.*
17   "not merely": Earle, "National Defense and Political Science" in *Political Science Quarterly,* Dec. 1940. All passages quoted were underlined, bracketed, or otherwise highlighted by Brodie; see his copy in *Bernard Brodie Papers,* Box 24, Earle folder.
17   Leites and proofing: Letter, Brodie to Wright, Apr. 29, 1941, *Quincy Wright Papers,* 1972 Addendum, Box 11, Brodie folder; and interviews.
17   Dartmouth job: Letter, Brodie to Wright, June 14, 1941, *ibid.*
18   course outline: *ibid.*
18   15,000 copies: Letter, Brodie to Wright, Oct. 9, 1942, *ibid.*
18   "There is a rather": Letter, E. Gordon Bill to Brodie, Mar. 2, 1943, *Edward Mead Earle Papers,* Box 3, B folder.
18   Brodie to Ordnance: Letterhead, Brodie to Earle, *loc. cit.*
18   to full lieutenant: Letter, Brodie to Earle, Oct. 7, 1943, *ibid.*
18   Brodie to CNO office: Letter, Brodie to Earle, Nov. 11, 1943, *ibid.*
19   "So far as": Letter, Brodie to Earle, Sept. 23, 1943, *ibid.*
19   "my voice": Letter, Brodie to Earle, Nov. 11, 1943, *ibid.*
19   Yale trip: Letter, Brodie to Earle, Aug. 14, 1944, *Edward Mead Earle Papers,* Box 5, Brodie folder.
19   "We have": Letter, Frederick Dunn to Brodie, Mar. 14, 1945, *Bernard Brodie Papers,* Box 3, Yale Univ.-Official.
19   "It was not": "Training in International Relations at Yale University," May 1945, *Charles Seymour Papers,* Box 87, #2 folder on IIS, 1934–39, Yale Univ.
20   "The international": Nicholas Spykman, *America's Strategy in World Politics* (New York: Harcourt, Brace & Co., 1942), p. 447.
20   Dunn's views: William T. R. Fox, "Frederick Sherwood Dunn and the American Study of International Relations" in *World Politics,* Oct. 1962; and interviews.
20   "to supplement": "Report of the Yale Institute of International Studies, July 1, 1949 to June 30, 1950," A. *Whitney Griswold Papers,* Box 126, folder 1153, Yale Univ.
21   strong support of Seymour: Seymour wrote to Edmund Day of the Rockefeller Foundation on June 12, 1934: "the Spykman matter . . . is a project which I have very much at heart . . ." *Charles Seymour Papers,* Box 87, #1 folder on IIS, 1934–39.
21    $100,000: Letter, Norman Thompson to James Angell, May 23, 1945, *ibid.*
21   number of international relations majors: "Training in International Relations at Yale University," *loc. cit.*
21   Advisory Council: *Charles Seymour Papers,* Box 88, IIS Advisory Council, 1944–50 folder.
21   corporate contributors: A. *Whitney Griswold Papers,* Box 126, folder 1154.
22   "they work": Memo, V. O. Key to Mr. Furniss, Dec. 18, 1950, A. *Whitney Griswold Papers,* Box 126, folder 1153.
22   "A Security Policy . . .": Attached to letter, Earle to James Reston, Apr. 2, 1945, *Edward Mead Earle Papers,* Box 5, Rye Conference folder.
22   August 1: "A Program of Studies in International Consensus," Feb. 1949, p. 13, *Charles Seymour Papers,* Box 89, IIS, Rockefeller Foundation Grants folder.

2:   LIVING WITH THE BOMB

24   Hutchins and lab: Alice Kimball Smith, *A Peril and a Hope: The Scientists' Movement in America 1945–47* (Chicago: U. of Chicago Press, 1965), p. 94.

24   Chicago Conference participants: "List of Participants," *Edward Mead Earle Papers*, Box 5, Chicago University Atomic Energy Control Conference folder, Princeton Univ.

25   Brodie's research: See footnotes in Brodie, *The Atomic Bomb and American Security* (Yale Institute of International Studies, Memorandum #18, Nov. 1, 1945); and interviews.

25   Brodie's ideas: Brodie, "Strategic Consequences of the Atomic Bomb" (notes), *Edward Mead Earle Papers, loc. cit.*; elaborated in Brodie, *The Atomic Bomb and American Security*, except the passage on p. 32, "If those four . . . ," which comes from Brodie, *The Absolute Weapon* (New York: Harcourt, Brace & Co., 1946), pp. 29–30. The thought, if not the exact quote, is also in the earlier material.

26   Brodie outline: Brodie, "Strategic Consequences of the Atomic Bomb," *loc. cit.*

27   conference dates: Letter, Robert Hutchins to Earle, Sept. 6, 1945, *Edward Mead Earle Papers, loc. cit.*

27   "The atomic bomb": "Summary of the Meetings on Thursday, September 20: Mr. Viner's Memorandum," *ibid.*

27   "What difference": Jacob Viner, "The Implications of the Atomic Bomb for International Relations" in *Proceedings on the American Philosophical Society*, Jan. 29, 1946, p. 54.

28   "agreement not to use": Edward A. Shils, "Approach to the Problem," *Edward Mead Earle Papers, loc. cit.*

28   "Proposals for the short-run": William T. R. Fox, "Control of the Atomic Bomb Through Existing Types of International Institutions," *ibid.*

28   "There is no need": Norman Cousins, "Modern Man Is Obsolete," *Saturday Review of Literature*, Aug. 18, 1945.

29   Browning poem: Frederick S. Dunn, "The Common Problem" in Brodie, *The Absolute Weapon*, p. 3.

29   publication dates: Frederick S. Dunn, "Report of the Yale Institute of International Studies 1945–46," p. 2, *Charles Seymour Papers*, Box 87, #2 folder on IIS, Yale Univ.

29   source of title: Fox, "International Control of Atomic Weapons," in Brodie, *The Absolute Weapon*, p. 181.

30   "one of the coolest": Seymour, speech, "Yale Institute of International Studies Dinner, Jan. 29, 1946," *Charles Seymour Papers, loc. cit.*

30   admired by officials: Frederick S. Dunn, "Report of the Yale Institute of International Studies 1945–46," *loc. cit.*

30   State Department consultants and Research Council: Seymour speech, *loc. cit.*

30   "superiority is not": Brodie, *The Absolute Weapon*, p. 46; *cf.* pp. 40–45.

30   "the primary targets": *Ibid.*, pp. 46–47.

31   "the number": *Ibid.*, p. 48.

31   "If 2,000 bombs": *Ibid.*

31   "must fear": *Ibid.*, pp. 73–74.

31   "The first": *Ibid.*, p. 76.

32   "Everything about": *Ibid.*, p. 52.

3:   PLANNING FOR WAR

33   Kennan article: X, "The Source of Soviet Conduct," *Foreign Affairs*, July 1947.

33   "the fact remains": Brodie, "The Atom Bomb As Policy Maker," *Foreign Affairs,* Oct. 1948, p. 30.

33   "requires appraisal": *Ibid.,* p. 24.

34   *Times* articles: *New York Times,* Nov. 9, 1947; Brodie refers to this in Brodie, "New Techniques of War and National Policies," W. F. Ogburn, ed., *Technology and International Relations* (Univ. of Chicago Press, 1949), pp. 163–64, which consists of speeches at a May 1948 symposium.

34   eight bombs tested (as of 1948): Brodie, "The Atom Bomb As Policy Maker," *loc. cit.,* p. 16.

34   uranium scarce: Brodie, "New Techniques of War and National Policies," *loc. cit.,* pp. 163–64.

34   on three-to-one margin: Brodie, "The Atom Bomb As Policy Maker," *loc. cit.,* p. 28.

34   margin favors U.S.: *Ibid.,* pp. 28–29.

34   survey of military thinking: *Bernard Brodie Papers,* Box 3, LRS folder, UCLA; his findings were published in "War Department Thinking on the Atomic Bomb" and "Navy Department Thinking on the Atomic Bomb," *Bulletin of the Atomic Scientists,* June and July 1947.

34   War Department paper: U.S. War Department, "The Effects of the Atomic Bomb on National Security," Mar. 1947; Brodie's reaction in "The Atom Bomb As Policy Maker," *loc. cit.,* p. 31.

35   "What we need to know": *Ibid.*

35   book plans: Frederick S. Dunn, "Report of the Yale Institute of International Studies, July 1, 1949–June 30, 1950," *A. Whitney Griswold Papers,* Box 126, folder 1153, Yale Univ.; and Letter, Earle to Brodie, Jan. 30, 1950, *Edward Mead Earle Papers,* Box 10, B folder, Princeton Univ.

35   read *Survey,* talked with Anderson and Kaysen: Letter, Brodie to Earle, Aug. 15, 1950, *ibid.*

35   air power as decisive: See Generals H. H. Arnold and Ira C. Eaker, *Army Flyer* (New York: Harper & Bros., 1942); on Douhet, see Bernard Brodie, *Strategy in the Missile Age* (Princeton Univ. Press, 1959), Pt.1; and Perry McCoy Smith, *The Air Force Plans for Peace, 1943–1945* (Baltimore: Johns Hopkins Press, 1970), p. 8.

36   dwellings destroyed, people killed, but no effect: *The United States Strategic Bombing Survey, Summary Report (European War),* Sept. 30, 1945, pp. 1, 3–4. See also Solly Zuckerman, *From Apes to Warlords* (New York: Harper & Row, 1978); John Kenneth Galbraith, *A Life in Our Times: Memoirs* (Boston: Houghton Mifflin, 1981), Chaps. 13–15.

36   20 percent of bombs in target area: *The U.S. Strategic Bombing Survey, Summary Report (European War),* p. 5.

36   German economy: *Ibid.,* pp. 5–7, 12; Galbraith, *op. cit.,* pp. 204–06, 210–12; Burton H. Klein, *Germany's Economic Preparations for War* (Cambridge: Harvard Univ. Press, 1959).

37   results too late: Brodie, "Strategic Bombing: What It Can Do," *The Reporter,* Aug. 15, 1950; quote, p. 29.

37   bombing as adjunct to ground forces: Brodie, "Strategic Implications of the North Atlantic Pact," *Yale Review,* Dec. 1949, p. 206.

37   "strategic bombing would be": Brodie, "Strategic Bombing: What It Can Do," *loc. cit.,* p. 28.

37   "had given very little": *Ibid.,* p. 30.

37   "the biggest single factor": *Ibid.,* p. 28.

37   illogical aim points: *Ibid.,* p. 31.

38   "we cannot accept": *Ibid.*

38   Norstad and Vandenberg read piece: Letter, Brodie to Col. John R. Maney, Sept. 21, 1953, *Bernard Brodie Papers,* Box 9, Air War College Correspondence folder; and letter, Brodie to David A. Rosenberg, Aug. 22, 1977, *Brodie Papers,* Box 9, Pending folder.

39   "may attack": JCS 2081/1, Encl. B, Feb. 13, 1950, JCS 1954–56 File List, 471.6 USSR (11-8-49), Sec. 2, NA/MMB.

39   Korea just a ploy: See NSC-76, July 10, 1950, Collection of NSC Documents, Box 5, NA/MMB; Brodie, "Schlesinger's Old-New Ideas," unpublished paper, *Bernard Brodie Papers*, Box 33, folder 8.

39   "strategic air offensive": Cited in JCS 2056/7, Aug. 12, 1950, Records of JCS, CCS 373.11 (12-14-45), Sec. 2.

39   Offtackle and target appendix: Walter S. Poole, *The History of the Joint Chiefs of Staff*, Vol. IV, 1950–52 (JCS Historical Division, 1979), pp. 161–64. The appendix was called JCS-2056.

39   panels on whether A-attack would stop Soviets: See especially the so-called Harmon Report, JCS-1953/1, May 12, 1949, Records of JCS, CCS 373 (10-23-48), B.P., NA/MMB.

39   fewer than 300: War plan Offtackle called for using 290 A-bombs, and it is noted elsewhere that the target annex for Offtackle was not a study stating requirements, but was rather intended to provide the maximum damage possible with the small number of bombs the U.S. had at the time. For 292, see *WSEG Report #1* in JCS-1952/11, Feb. 10, 1950, p. 194, B.P., Pt. 2C; for nature of annex, see JCS-1953/12, Encl. B, Apr. 24, 1950; in JCS File List 1951–53, CCS 373 (10-23-48) and (10-23-58), respectively, NA/MMB.

39   "could complete only": Memo, Maj. Gen. S. E. Anderson to Stuart Symington, Apr. 11, 1950, Air Force OPD Papers, NA/MMB.

39   re-examine target plan: In Feb. 1950, the JCS Weapons Systems Evaluation Group noted that in view of the infeasibility of Offtackle, "a re-examination of the entire target system is desirable." See *WSEG Report #1, loc. cit.*

40   Vandenberg asked Brodie: Letter, Brodie to Rosenberg, *loc. cit.;* Memo of Record, Dec. 11, 1950, *Curtis LeMay Papers*, Box B-66, Memos & R-R's, 1950 folder, LoC;* letter, Hoyt Vandenberg to Griswold, Nov. 30, 1950, *A. Whitney Griswold Papers*, Box 86, folder 75, Yale Univ. Brodie, Vandenberg and Norstad first met over lunch Aug. 21 and again Sept. 15. See *Hoyt Vandenberg Papers*, Box 4, 1950 Appointments Book, LoC.

40   tiring of Yale: Letter, Brodie to Harvey DeWeerd, Oct. 20, 1952, *Bernard Brodie Papers*, Box 1, D folder.

41   "killing a nation": Cited in Robert Frank Futrell, *Ideas, Concepts, Doctrine: A History of Basic Thinking in the United States Air Force, 1907–64* (Maxwell AFB, Ala: Air Univ., 1971), p. 122.

41   took pages from Survey: Poole, *op. cit.,* p. 165.

41   liquid fuel and electric power: *Ibid.*

41   "electric power situation": *The U.S. Strategic Bombing Survey, Summary Report (European War)*, p. 14.

41   atomic-energy plants: JCS-2056/7, Aug. 12, 1950, Records of JCS, CCS 373.11 (12-14-45), Sec. 2, NA/MMB.

41   "Delta-Bravo-Romeo": *Ibid.*

42   Tokyo attack: Len Giovannitti and Fred Freed, *The Decision to Drop the Bomb* (New York: Coward-McCann, 1965), pp. 34–36.

43   A-bomb made point stronger: Most Air Force officers felt that the bomb would vindicate theories of air power. See Lee Bowen, *A History of the Air Force Atomic Energy Program, 1943–54*, Vol. IV (USAF Historical Division, 1955), p. 108.

44   LeMay on liquid fuel: JCS-2056/16, June 18, 1951, Encl. B, p. 120, JCS File List 1951–53, CCS 373.11 (12-14-48), Sec. 4, NA/MMB.

44   LeMay on atomic-energy and electric-power plants: Poole, *op. cit.,* pp. 165–66; Gen. LeMay's Diary, Jan. 22, 1951, *Curtis LeMay Papers*, Box B-64, Diary 1951 folder.*

44   "deliver the entire": Quoted in David Alan Rosenberg, "American Atomic Strategy and the Hydrogen Bomb Decision," *The Journal of American History*, June 1979, p. 70.

44   move aim point south of Kremlin: Letter, Brodie to Rosenberg, *loc. cit.*

44   JCS say not feasible: The plan was JCS-2056/9. See JCS-1953/12, Encl. A, Apr. 24, 1950, JCS File List 1951–53, CCS 373 (10-23-58), Sec. 7, NA/MMB; cf. Diary, Jan. 23, 1950, *Curtis LeMay Papers,* Box B-64, Diary Jan.–June 1950 folder.*

44   "condition precludes": JCS-2056/13, March 28, 1951, JCS File List, 1951–53, CCS 373.11 (12-14-48), Sec. 4, NA/MMB.

45   "collapse": Letter, Brodie to Rosenberg, *loc. cit.*

45   no ground forces: Brodie, "Changing Capabilities and War Objectives," p. 13, lecture, Air War College, Apr. 17, 1952, Max. AFB.

45–6   "Sunday punch" and "collapse": Letter, Brodie to Rosenberg, *loc. cit.;* for more on Sunday punch, see Diary, July 22, 1950, *Curtis LeMay Papers,* Box B-64, Diary July–Dec. 1950 folder.*

46   asked LeMay why the hurry: Letter, Brodie to Rosenberg, *ibid.*

46   Brodie on LeMay plan: In a speech to the Naval War College, Mar. 17, 1952, called "Characteristics of a Sound Strategy," Brodie said (p. 18), "I have seen studies which thought they were attempts at war plans, but which ended simply with putting bombs on targets." (*Bernard Brodie Papers,* Box 12.)

46   "How many bombs": Brodie, "The Atom Bomb as Policy Maker," *loc. cit.,* p. 31.

46   "may, on the one hand": Brodie, "New Techniques of War and National Policies," *loc. cit.,* p. 165; the essay is taken from a speech delivered at a conference held May 7–9, 1948.

47   reports for Vandenberg: Letter, Brodie to Rosenberg, *loc cit.* In this letter, Brodie says the second memo was written in late March or early April. Actually, since Vandenberg's Appointments Book for 1951 shows four meetings with Brodie from March 6 to 23, and since on the 23rd, Vandenberg assigned Brodie the task of directing a special advisory committee on strategic bombing objectives—which he probably would not have done if Brodie had not yet turned in his memo—one can surmise that the second report was done in March, probably mid-March. (See *Hoyt Vandenberg Papers,* Box 4, 1951 Appointments Book; Memo, Vandenberg to Brodie, "Formation of a Special Advisory Panel . . . ," Mar. 23, 1951, Box 83, Miscellaneous folder.*)

47   idea of avoiding city destruction: Letter, Brodie to Rosenberg, *loc. cit.;* Brodie, "Schlesinger's Old-New Ideas," *loc. cit.;* Brodie, "A New Kind of War," *UCLA Alumni Magazine,* Winter 1968–69.

47   "more strategic leverage": Brodie, "Schlesinger's Old-New Ideas," *loc. cit.*

47   Japanese surrender: Brodie, "Changing Capabilities and War Objectives," *loc. cit.,* p. 28.

47   city destruction and bargaining lever: *Ibid.* That he was thinking along these lines while in the Pentagon as well, see Brodie, "A New Kind of War," *loc. cit.;* and letter to Rosenberg, *loc. cit.*

47   SAC must survive attack: Brodie, "Changing Capabilities and War Objectives," *loc. cit.,* p. 29. That this was a part of the Vandenberg memo has been confirmed by a former analyst in the RAND Corporation with whom Brodie discussed his Vandenberg work shortly after the fact.

47   "sacrificing the prospect": *Ibid.,* p. 29.

47   "We have thus far given": Brodie, comment attached to Memo, Col. Parrish to Gen. McKee, Dec. 9, 1950, quoted in Noel F. Parrish, "Behind the Sheltering Bomb: Almagordo to Korea," Ph.D. dissertation, Rice Univ., 1968, p. 375.

48   "an enormous area for wisdom": Brodie, "Characteristics of a Sound Strategy," *loc. cit.,* pp. 23–24.

48   "the most important": Letter, Brodie to Rosenberg, *loc. cit.* Unfortunately, the memoranda themselves appear to have been irretrievably lost, perhaps destroyed; several people, including Alfred Goldberg, historian of

the Office of the Secretary of Defense, have valiantly hunted for them, but with no luck; the RAND Corporation threw out its copies years ago. I have inferred the contents of the documents from interviews and from letters, documents and speeches written soon after Brodie's experience, which—interviews confirm—reflect the contents of the memoranda.

48–9   Special Advisory Panel: Memo, Hoyt Vandenberg to Brodie, "Formation of a Special Advisory Panel on Strategic Bombing Objectives," *loc. cit.**

49   Norstad transferred: Brodie offers this as the main reason for his own departure in letter to Rosenberg, *loc. cit.*

49   footnote on Brodie and Earle: Earle on Brodie's criticisms: letters, Earle to Brodie, Aug. 10, 1944, and Brodie to Earle, Aug. 15, 1950, *Edward Mead Earle Papers*, Box 5, Brodie folder, and Box 10, B folder, respectively. Earle on Brodie's Chicago talk: marginalia on Brodie, "Strategic Consequences of the Atomic Bomb," *Earle Papers*, Box 5, Chicago University Conference folder. "have a word": letter, Earle to Finletter, Apr. 30, 1951, *Earle Papers*, Box 11, F folder. Talk with Vandenberg: *Hoyt Vandenberg Papers*, Box 4, 1951 Appointments Book. Brodie-Earle correspondence: see letters in B or Brodie folders, *Earle Papers*.

49   Griswold abolished Institute: In *A. Whitney Griswold Paper*, see letter, Frank Altschul to Griswold, Mar. 16, 1951, Box 126, folder 1154; Griswold, Memo to Provost on Research in International Relations at Yale, Jan. 9, 1951, and letter to Irving Olds, Apr. 19, 1959, both in Box 126, folder 1153.

50   "calls up memories": "The Study of World Affairs," *New York Herald Tribune*, Apr. 24, 1951.

50   "What kind of men": Shils, "Approach to the Problem," *Edward Mead Earle Papers, Box 5, Chicago Univ. Atomic Energy Control Conference folder.*

4:   ON THE BEACH AT RAND

52   *"operational research"*: See P. M. S. Blackett, *Studies of War* (New York: Hill & Wang, 1962), Pt. 2; James Phinney Baxter, *Scientists Against Time* (Boston: Little, Brown, 1946); R. V. Jones, *The Wizard War* (New York: Coward, McCann & Geoghegan, 1978); Solly Zuckerman, *From Apes to Warriors* (New York: Harper & Row, 1978).

52   facts, theories, predictions: Blackett, *ibid.*, p. 177.

52   U-boat campaign: *Ibid.*, pp. 188, 213–15.

53   Similar techniques: *Ibid.*, Pt. 2, *passim.*

54   "Hap" smile: Oral History Interview, Lt. Gen. Fred M. Dean, Feb. 25–26, 1978, pp. 67–68, Max. AFB.

54   "We must not": Quoted in Michael S. Sherry, *Preparing for the Next War: American Plans for Postwar Defense, 1941–45* (New Haven: Yale Univ. Press, 1977), p. 19.

55   flying lessons and license: Bio sheet attached to index of *H. H. Arnold Papers*, LoC.

55   Arnold background and Mitchell: "General of the Army Henry Harley Arnold—Bio Sheet, February 13, 1946," *Carl Spaatz Papers*, Box 256, Arnold folder, LoC.

55   "We've got to think": *Ibid.*

56   "I believe the security": Memo, Arnold to Von Karman, Nov. 7, 1944, *H. H. Arnold Papers*, Box 40, Scientific Advisory Group folder.

56   "The scientific discoveries": "Abstract of Dr. Von Karman's Report to General of the Army H. H. Arnold, 'Toward New Horizons,'" Dec. 14, 1945, pp. 1–2, *Carl Spaatz Papers*, Box 58.

56   "be advised continuously": Von Karman, "Toward New Horizons, Vol. II-I, Where We Stand," Aug. 22, 1945, p. 88, *loc. cit.*

56   "a permanent interest": Von Karman, "Toward New Horizons, Vol. I, Science, The Key to Air Supremacy," p. 114, *loc. cit.*

56   "a nucleus": "Abstract of . . . 'Toward New Horizons,' " p. 32, *loc. cit.*

57   B-29 Special Project: "A Summary of Activities, Office of Dr. Edward L. Bowles . . . April 1942 through August 1945," Nov. 1, 1945, *Edward Bowles Papers,* Box 1, folder #1 on Summary of Activities, HSTL.

58   Hamilton Field lunch: Bruce L. R. Smith, *The RAND Corporation: Case Study of a Nonprofit Advisory Corporation* (Cambridge: Harvard Univ. Press, 1966), pp. 41–42; and interviews.

59   "founding fathers": *Ibid.*

59     $10 million: R. D. Specht, *RAND: A Personal View of Its History,* RAND P-1601, Oct. 23, 1958, pp. 7–8.

59   LeMay R&D director: Smith, *op. cit.,* p. 46.

59   R&D and Von Karman report: Von Karman, "Toward New Horizons, Vol. I," p. 129, *loc. cit.*

59   "Project RAND is": Specht, *op. cit.,* p. 2.

59   contract MX-791: R. D. Little, *The History of Air Force Participation in the Atomic Energy Program, 1943–53, Vol. II* (Washington, D.C.: USAF Historical Division, 1958), p. 545.

59   rockets and ramjets: Specht, *op. cit.,* p. 6.

60   "would inflame": *Preliminary Design of an Experimental World-Circling Spaceship,* RAND SM-11827, May 2, 1946.

60   Few paid attention: J. D. Williams, *An Overview of RAND,* RAND D-10053, May 14, 1962, p. 13 (provided to author).

60   Douglas connection cracking: Letters, Bowles to Arnold, Sept. 5, 11 and 15, 1946, *H. H. Arnold Papers,* Box 214A, Correspondence 1946–1948 between Gen. Arnold and Dr. E. L. Bowles folder.

61   "when we are": Letter, Spaatz to Donald Douglas, Feb. 10, 1948, *Carl Spaatz Papers,* Box 252, Chief of Staff Correspondence, Feb. 8–13, 1948, folder.

61   Wells Fargo Bank: Smith, *op. cit.,* pp. 70, 72.

61   RAND and Ford Foundation: *Ibid.,* pp. 70–72; and interviews.

61   May 14, 1948: Little, *op. cit.,* p. 545.

62   numbered 150: *Conference of Social Scientists,* RAND R-106, June 9, 1948, p. 2.

62   "I have been": Memo, Joseph Goldsen to Social Science Department, "20 Years at RAND," May 23, 1968, *Adam Yarmolinsky Papers,* Box 9, RAND Corp. Mtgs., 1967–69, JFKL.

63   fifth employee: "Profile . . . ," *RANDom News* [in-house newsletter], May 1956 (provided to author).

63   von Neumann, "Mr. Miracle," Communism: Robert Jungk, *Brighter Than a Thousand Suns* (New York: Harcourt Brace Jovanovich, 1958), pp. 298–99.

63   "I think": Letter, von Neumann to Lewis Strauss, Nov. 21, 1951, *John von Neumann Papers,* Box 22, Strauss folder, LoC.

64   ENIAC and MANIAC: Jungk, *op. cit.,* pp. 298–300.

64   Williams thrilled: Letter, Williams to von Neumann, Dec. 16, 1947, *John von Neumann Papers,* Box 15, RAND folder.

64   von Neumann and poker: John McDonald, *Strategy in Poker, Business and War* (New York: W. W. Norton & Co., 1950), pp. 50–83.

67   Williams book: John D. Williams, *The Compleat Strategyst* (New York: McGraw-Hill, 1954).

68   LeMay meeting: Smith, *op. cit.,* p. 61.

72   conference attendants: *Conference of Social Scientists, loc. cit.,* pp. xvii–ix.

72   "to discuss": *Ibid.,* p. vii.

72   "military worth": *Ibid.,* p. 7.

72   "I assume": *Ibid.,* p. 3.

5:   THE SUPERBOMB

74   RAND and Q: R. D. Little, *The History of Air Force Participation in the Atomic Energy Program, 1943–53,* Vol. II (Washington, D.C.: USAF Historical Division, 1958).

77   thousands of square feet: See many of the RE-8 reports in Records of the U.S. Strategic Bombing Survey, 1j and 3b, NA/MMB.

77   50 and 300 square miles: Bernard Brodie, "Air National Strategies and Policies As Related to Current National Capabilities," lecture, Air War College, Apr. 16, 1953, p. 2, Max. AFB; and author's own calculations.

77   fifty-five H-bombs, fifty cities, 35 million, 10 or 11 million: Bernard Brodie, "Changing Capabilities and War Objectives," lecture, Air War College, Apr. 17, 1952, p. 19, *Bernard Brodie Papers,* Box 12, UCLA.

79   H-bomb could miss targets: Brodie, *Ibid.,* pp. 11, 18.

79   "not so absolute": *Ibid.,* p. 10.

79   "makes strategic bombing": *Ibid.,* p. 20.

79   Clausewitz: *Ibid.,* pp. 3–4; for Brodie's earlier view, see Brodie, "The Security Problem in Light of Atomic Energy," Quincy Wright, ed., *A Foreign Policy for the United States* (Univ. of Chicago Press, 1947), p. 89.

80   "national objectives": Brodie, "Changing Capabilities and War Objectives," *loc. cit.,* p. 22. *Cf.* letter, Brodie to Prof. [T.] C. Schelling, Jan. 9, 1957, *Bernard Brodie Papers,* Box 2, Schelling folder.

80   "We seem to be": *Ibid.,* p. 20. In retrospect, it appears that NATO forces were probably never so overwhelmingly outnumbered on the ground. See Andrew Cockburn, *The Threat* (New York: Random House, 1983), Chapter 6.

80   "Strategic bombing has": *Ibid.,* p. 21.

80   "if . . .": *Ibid.,* pp. 28–29.

81   Oppenheimer and Vista: Philip M. Stern, *The Oppenheimer Case* (New York: Harper & Row, 1969); U.S. Atomic Energy Commission, *In the Matter of J. Robert Oppenheimer* (Cambridge: MIT Press, 1971).

81   Brodie and Oppenheimer: In the *J. Robert Oppenheimer Papers,* LoC, see: letter, Brodie to Oppenheimer, Sept. 22, 1947, Box 18, Br folder; letter, Brodie to Oppenheimer, Feb. 26, 1951, and memo, "Proposed Study of Strategic Air Warfare," Box 1972, Strategic Air Warfare folder (the memo is unsigned and undated, but it is clear from style and substance that the author is Brodie—also the memo and the Feb. 26 Brodie letter are the only two items in the folder); letter, William T. Golden to Oppenheimer, Feb. 27, 1951, Box 36, Golden folder. Also Memo for File, Conversation with Oppenheimer, Feb. 27, 1951, in William T. Golden private papers, "Government Military-Science Research: Review for the President of the United States, 1950–51" (thanks to Mr. Golden).

81   briefing: *Implications of Large-Yield Nuclear Weapons,* RAND R-237, July 10, 1952 (FOIA/USAF).*

82   people briefed: Norman Moss, *Men Who Play God: The Story of the H-Bomb,* rev. ed. (London: Penguin, 1972), p. 60; and interviews.

82   "Ernie Plesset and I": Memo from Brodie, re: attached letter from Gen. Wilson, Mar. 24, 1952, *Bernard Brodie Papers,* Box 9, Air War College folder. Brodie notes that the "mention of Ernie's name and the omission of Charlie Hitch's was simply to help Wilson identify the subject, which apparently he did. . . ."

82   tritium: Moss, *op. cit.,* p. 60; and interviews.

83   Teller and Frisch: *Ibid.,* p. 71.

84   security risk: Stern, *op. cit.; In the Matter of J. Robert Oppenheimer.*

84   Griggs and Oppenheimer: Stern, *ibid.,* pp. 91, 182–85, 187–92, 194, 348–52, 363–64, 508; quote, p. 185.

84   "It's a boy.": Moss, *op. cit.,* p. 78.

6: THE VULNERABILITY STUDY

86   Paxson and systems analysis: RAND lecture to group of USAF officers by Dr. E. W. Paxson, "Aerial Bombing Systems Theory and Analysis," Sept. 24, 1947 (provided to author); and interviews.

88   systems analysis and uncertainties: See E. S. Quade, "Pitfalls of Systems Analysis," Quade, ed., *Analysis for Military Decisions: The RAND Lectures on Systems Analysis* (New York: American Elsevier Pub. Co., 1970).

89   Air Force on Paxson bomber: Bruce L. R. Smith, *The RAND Corporation* (Cambridge: Harvard Univ. Press, 1966), p. 105.

89   costs for 3,000 versus 3,600 miles: Chart is reproduced in A. J. Wohlstetter, F. S. Hoffman, R. J. Lutz, H. S. Rowen, *Selection and Use of Strategic Air Bases,* RAND R-266, Apr. 1954, p. 64; *cf.* pp. 23–24, 63, 65.

90   dilemmas: *Ibid.*, pp. 57–59; interviews reveal that this was the beginning point of Wohlstetter's analysis.

91   "the analysis of systems": Project RAND, Fourth Annual Report, RAND R-184, Mar. 1, 1950, p. 27, in *Curtis LeMay Papers,* Box B-101, RAND folder, LoC.*

91   McKinsey and game theory: J. C. C. McKinsey, *Introduction to the Theory of Games* (New York: McGraw-Hill, 1952); *The Annals of Mathematics Studies,* Princeton Univ., 1950, No. 24.

91   Paxson and game theory: See his correspondence with von Neumann, *John von Neumann Papers,* Box 25, RAND folder, LoC.

93   " 'Pearl Harbored' ": *WSEG Report #1,* JCS 1952/11, Feb. 10, 1950, p. K–61, JCS File List 1951–53, CCS 373 (10-23-48), B.P. Pt. 2C, NA/MMB.

93   "Soviet forces are": reprinted in *ibid.*

93   "We would be": LeMay, "The Mission, Organization and Capabilities of the Strategic Air Command," lecture, Air War College, June 1, 1950, p. 15, Max. AFB.

93   LeMay and intercontinental bomber: *Ibid.;* memo, LeMay to Thomas Finletter, Mar. 11, 1950, *Curtis LeMay Papers,* Box B-64, Diary Jan.–June 1950 folder.*

95   "Most Sophisticated": "Senior Mind," *The Campus,* Mar. 5, 1934, City College of New York Archives Library.

98   number of planes and bases: Wohlstetter *et al., op. cit.,* pp. 3, 5.

99   SAC operations: *Ibid.,* pp. 3*ff.*

99   vulnerability: *Ibid.*

99   120 bombs: *Ibid.,* p. xxiii.

99   every conceivable way: Smith, *op. cit.,* p. 207; and interviews.

99–100 conclusions: Wohlstetter *et al., op. cit.,* pp. xxii–xxiv.

100   Paxson-inspired questions: *Cf. ibid.,* p. 13.

100   cost and target comparisons: *Ibid.,* pp. xxxvi–xxxvii.

101   Carswell tornado: Memo, Vandenberg to Curtis LeMay, Sept. 11, 1952, *Hoyt Vandenberg Papers,* Box 45, Strategic Command folder;* its significance to the Wohlstetter study came from interviews.

101   wind gusts of forty-kiloton bomb: Author's calculation, based on Nuclear Bomb Effects Computer in back of Samuel Glasstone, ed., *Effects of Nuclear Weapons,* 3rd ed. (Washington, D.C.: Department of Defense, 1977).

102   R-244-S: This became the summary at the beginning of R-266, referred to above as Wohlstetter *et al.*

104   ninety-two briefings: Smith, *op. cit.,* p. 219; and interviews.

104   SAC get in first blow: see, *e.g.,* memo, Col. D. O. Monteith to Col. Watson, "A Brief Resume of RAND Report R-266, 'Selection and Use of Strategic Air Bases,' " Apr. 8, 1955, p. 3, Radford File, CJCS 381, NA/MMB; and interviews.

104   SAC resistance: Smith, *op. cit.*, p. 222; and interviews.
104   "On some Mondays": "Question and Answer Period at National War
       College," Mar. 28, 1950, *Curtis LeMay Papers*, Box B-64, Diary folder.*
104   Ad Hoc Committee: Smith, *op. cit.*, pp. 223–24.
105   White interview: *Ibid.*, pp. 224–25; and interviews.
105   Soviet H-bomb: Herbert York, *The Advisors: Oppenheimer, Teller, and
       the Superbomb* (San Francisco: Freeman Press, 1976), p. 10; and inter-
       views.
105   "That the vulnerability": Memo, Gen. Robert Burns, "Decision on AFC
       22/4b: Vulnerability of the Strategic Striking Complex," Nov. 2, 1953,
       Nathan Twining Papers, Box 103, Air Force Council Chief of Staff Deci-
       sions, Vol. I, Tab 22/4b, LoC.*
106   approval: *Ibid.**
107   "to limit": *Select Operational Exercises of Strategic Air Command,
       1954–56, Sec. VI* (SAC Headquarters, Historical Division, Historical
       Study #66), pp. 54–55, Max. AFB.
108   preemptive strike: *Ibid.*, p. 55 reads: "The ultimate objective was the abil-
       ity to launch a multiple wing strike over EWP targets in a minimum
       amount of time . . . The only way to protect the nation was to be able to
       destroy the enemy's offensive power before it could be completely un-
       leashed."

7:   THE HYDRA-HEADED MONSTER

111   RAND 1950 studies: "Long-Range Ballistic Missiles—A History," White
       House Office file, Office of Staff Secretary, Subject Series, Alpha Sub-
       series, Box 5, Ballistic Missiles 1957 folder, p. 5, DDEL.
111   Atlas: *Ibid.*
112   Convair requirements: B. W. Augenstein, *A Revised Development Pro-
       gram for Ballistic Missiles of Intercontinental Range*, RAND Special
       Memorandum No. 21, Feb. 8, 1954, p. 1.
112   lithium in Soviet explosion: Roy Neal, *Ace in the Hole: The Story of the
       Minuteman Missile* (Garden City, N.Y.: Doubleday & Co., 1962), p. 47;
       and interviews.
113   re-entry speed and warhead weight: Augenstein, *op. cit.*
113   CEP/missile-number trade off: *Ibid.*, especially p. 10.
114   by 1960: *Ibid.*, p. 38.
114   Collbohm briefings on Dec. 12: Letter, J. R. Goldstein to Herbert York,
       Mar. 7, 1973 (provided to author).
115   review of missile program: "Long-Range Ballistic Missiles—A History,"
       loc. cit., p. 6.
115   Augenstein briefing: Letter, J. R. Goldstein to Herbert York, *op. cit.*
115–16 H-bomb briefing and CEP requirements: Bernard Brodie, "Changing
       Capabilities and War Objectives," lecture, Air War College, Apr. 17,
       1952, p. 18, *Bernard Brodie Papers*, Box 12, UCLA. The Plesset-Hitch-
       Brodie study, however, thought that CEP made little difference only up
       to two miles.
116   "there is no doubt": "Professor John von Neumann's Report on Nuclear
       Weapons," lecture, USAF Scientific Advisory Board, Oct. 21, 1953, p. 8,
       Max. AFB.
116   Augenstein's RM-1191: This report is identical to the Special Memoran-
       dum No. 21, cited above. Feb. 8 date comes from letter, J. R. Goldstein to
       Herbert York, *op. cit.* Its importance is also cited in Neal, *op. cit.*,
       p. 48.
116   von Neumann, February 10: "Long-Range Ballistic Missiles—A His-
       tory," *loc. cit.*, p. 6.
116   twenty sites, 100 missiles by 1960: Memo, Trevor Gardner to Sec. Talbot
       and Gen. Twining, "Intercontinental Ballistic Missile System Accelera-

	tion Plan," Mar. 11, 1954, *Nathan Twining Papers*, Box 122, Top Secret File (3), 1950–57 folder, LoC.*
116	"agreed that it": Memo, Robert Burns, "Decision on AFC 12/8: USAF Strategic Missile Program," May 6, 1954, *Nathan Twining Papers*, Air Force Council Chief of Staff Decisions, Vol. I, Tab 12/8.*
116	Western Development Division: Neal, *op. cit.*, pp. 48, 64–65; and interviews.
117	more than twenty aides: See the various footnotes in Albert Wohlstetter and Fred Hoffman, *Protecting U.S. Power to Strike Back in the 1950s and 1960s*, RAND R-290, Sept. 1, 1956 (provided to author).
118	"The defenses programmed": A. Wohlstetter and F. Hoffman, *Defending a Strategic Force After 1960*, RAND D-2270, Feb. 1, 1954, pp. 1, 3 (provided to author).
118	destroy 80 percent with 150: *Ibid.*, pp. 5–6.
118	effects of sheltering: *Ibid.*, pp. 8, 12, 14.
120	twenty-nine and fifty-five: Wohlstetter and Hoffman, *Protecting U.S. Power to Strike Back in the 1950s and 1960s*, p. 12.
120	500 ICBMs, 500 bombers: *Ibid.*, p. 97. Wohlstetter and Hoffman refer to 500 Soviet ICBMs and 500 Bear and Bison bombers as "moderately high though not extreme Soviet offensive . . . capabilities."
120	24 missiles hit 96: *Ibid.*, p. 28.
120	fifty ways: *Ibid.*, pp. 2 and *passim*.
120	$35 billion versus $10 billion: *Ibid.*, pp. 96–97.
121	15 percent versus 90 percent: *Ibid.*, pp. 89–90.
124	"do not, of course": *Ibid.*, pp. 40–41.

8: THE GAITHER COMMITTEE

125	NSC evaluates civil defense: "Record of Actions by the NSC at Its 308th Meeting Held April 4, 1957," Ann Whitman File, NSC Series, Box 2, Record of Action by NSC 1957 (1) folder, DDEL; for FCDA proposal, see "Report by the Federal Civil Defense Administration on a Federal Civil Defense Shelter Program," Jan. 17, 1957, Annex A to NSC-5709, Mar. 29, 1957, Collection of NSC Documents, NA/MMB; for $32.4 and $28.6 billion figures, see p. A-3.
126	FCDA recommendations and numbers: NSC-5709 and Annex, *loc. cit.*, pp. 1, A-3, A-12.
126	"unable at this time": *Ibid.*, p. 2.
126	"A study by the": *Ibid.*, p. 4.
126	April 4 and 8: "Record of Actions by the NSC at Its 308th Meeting Held April 4, 1957," *loc. cit.*
127	lunch with Rockefeller: All quotes from Rockefeller, Memo for Sherman Adams and Percival Brundage, "Proposal for Study of Civil Defense Measures," Apr. 12, 1957, White House Office file, Office of Special Assistant for Science & Technology Series, Box 13, OCDM & Civil Defense (1) folder, DDEL.
127	Killian, Cutler, Gaither: James R. Killian, Jr., *Sputnik, Scientists, and Eisenhower* (Cambridge: MIT Press, 1977), p. 96; and interviews.
127	Eisenhower and Gaither: Letters, Eisenhower to Gaither, May 8, 1957, Gaither to Eisenhower, May 15, 1957, White House Office file, Office of Staff Secretary, Subject Series, Alpha Subseries, Box 23, Science Advisory Committee (1) folder, DDEL.
129	steering panel members: *Deterrence and Survival in the Nuclear Age*, Nov. 7, 1957, p. 31, declassified and published by Joint Committee on Defense Production, U.S. Congress, 1976; and interviews.
129	advisory panel and research staff: *Ibid.*, pp. 31–34.
129	Gaither to hospital: *Ibid.*, letter from steering panel to Eisenhower accompanying report.

404   FRED KAPLAN

129   mandate broadened by August: In a memo to SAC Commander Curtis
       LeMay, dated Aug. 15, 1957, USAF Chief of Staff Gen. Thomas White
       refers to a board headed by Rowan Gaither originally assigned to study
       civil defense but that "is getting into all manner of defense business,
       with the backing of the President." *Thomas White Papers*, Box 41, 1957
       Top Secret File folder, LoC.*

131   Killian Panel: *Meeting the Threat of Surprise Attack*, Feb. 12, 1955, Of-
       fice of Special Assistant for National Security Affairs file, NSC Series,
       Subject Subseries, Box 11, Technological Capabilities Panel of the Sci-
       ence Advisory Report (Killian Report) folders, DDEL; "through innova-
       tion": Vol. I, p. vi.

131   overall impact: Killian, *op. cit.*, pp. 86–93.

131   committee told of SAC plan: Sprague remarks in A. J. Goodpaster, Memo
       of Conference with President, following NSC Meeting, Nov. 7, 1957,
       White House Office file, Office of Staff Secretary, Subject Series, DoD
       Subseries, Box 6, Military Planning, 1958–61 folder, DDEL.

132   September 16 alert test: Sprague remarks in A. J. Goodpaster, Memo of
       Conference with President, *loc. cit.*; and interviews.

135   Rinehart, Teller, Luce quotes: Quoted in Killian, *op. cit.*, pp. 6–7.

135   "the American people": Memo, George Reedy to Lyndon Johnson, Oct.
       17, 1957, p. 2, Senate Office Files of George Reedy, Box 420, Reedy:
       Memos, Oct. 1957 folder, LBJL.

137   *Reexamination*: NSC-141, Jan. 19, 1953, Collection of NSC Documents,
       NA/MMB; that Nitze, Nash and Bissell wrote it comes from interviews.

137   "*The* willingness": *Ibid.*, p. 7.

138   "this would present": *Ibid.*, p. 73.

138   "adequate civil defense": *Ibid.*, p. 83.

138   NSC-68: NSC-68, Apr. 7, 1950, in U.S. Department of State, *Foreign Re-
       lations of the United States, 1950*, Vol. I (Washington, D.C.: Govern-
       ment Printing Office, 1977), pp. 234–92. For fuller treatments of
       NSC-68, see Fred Kaplan, "Our Cold War Policy, Circa '50," *New York
       Times Magazine*, May 18, 1980; Paul Y. Hammond, "NSC-68: Prologue
       to Rearmament," in Warner R. Schilling, Paul Y. Hammond, Glenn H.
       Snyder, *Strategy, Politics, and Defense Budgets* (Columbia Univ. Press,
       1962), pp. 267–378.

138   Kennan against buildup: See U.S. Department of State, *op. cit.*, pp. 164,
       278, 282.

139   "a joy": Dean Acheson, *Present at the Creation* (New York: W. W. Nor-
       ton & Co., 1969), p. 373.

139   "calculates that": U.S. Department of State, *op. cit.*, p. 266.

139   1954: *Ibid.*, pp. 251, 267, 287.

139   "of such weight": *Ibid.*, p. 287.

139   "Kremlin's design": *Ibid.*, p. 245.

139   "The Kremlin is": *Ibid.*, p. 246.

139   "the principal center": *Ibid.*, p. 238.

140   "becoming dangerously": *Ibid.*, p. 262.

140   "assault on free": *Ibid.*, p. 240.

140   "to foster": *Ibid.*, pp. 252, 258.

140   "The purpose": Acheson, *op. cit.*, p. 374.

140   "task of": *Ibid.*, p. 375.

140   Murphy scared: Daniel Yergin, *Shattered Peace* (Boston: Houghton Mif-
       flin Co., 1977), p. 403.

140   NSC-68 adopted: U.S. Department of State, *op. cit.*, p. 400.

140–41 fiscal year 1951 budget: Hammond, *op. cit.*, p. 357.

141   "The evidence clearly": *Deterrence and Survival in the Nuclear Age*,
       p. 1.

141   "to finance both": *Ibid.*, p. 4.

142   "current vulnerability": *Ibid.*, pp. 5–6.

142   "the USSR may": *Ibid.*, p. 14.

9: THE REPORT OF MAXIMUM DANGER

144   Gaither recommendations: *Deterrence and Survival in the Nuclear Age,*
        Nov. 7, 1957, pp. 6–7, declassified and published by Joint Committee on
        Defense Production, U.S. Congress, 1976.

145   "Highest" and "Lower Than Highest Value": *Ibid.,* pp. 23–24.

145   fiscal year 1954 defense budget: Glenn H. Snyder, "The 'New Look' of
        1953," in Warner R. Schilling, Paul Y. Hammond, Glenn H. Snyder,
        Strategy, Politics, and Defense Budgets (Columbia Univ. Press, 1962), p.
        396.

145   Norstad remark: Cable, Norstad to Gen. Thomas White, June 10, 1953,
        Nathan Twining Papers, Box 102, 2nd Tab 28, LoC.*

145   "single critical": Letter, Eisenhower to Charles Wilson, Ann Whitman
        File, DDE Diary Series, Box 9, DDE Diary, Jan. 1955 (2), DDEL. Ac-
        cording to the letter, Eisenhower released it publicly.

146   "a respectable posture": *E.g.,* Andrew Goodpaster, Memo of Conference
        with President, May 18, 1956, Ann Whitman File, DDE Diary Series, Box
        15, May 1956 Goodpaster folder, DDEL.

146   November 4 meeting: Account and quotes from Andrew Goodpaster,
        Memo of Conference with President, Nov. 4, 1957, White House Office
        file, Office of the Staff Secretary, Subject Series, Alpha Subseries, Box 23,
        Science Advisory Committee (3) folder, DDEL.*

146   November 7 meeting: Morton Halperin, "The Gaither Committee and
        the Policy Process," *World Politics,* Apr. 1961; and interviews.

150   Sprague private meeting: Andrew Goodpaster, Memo of Conference with
        President, Following NSC Meeting, Nov. 7, 1957, White House Office
        files, Office of Staff Secretary, Subject Series, DoD Subseries, Box 6, Mili-
        tary Planning 1958–61 folder, DDEL; and interviews.

151   Sprague comments to Goodpaster: Handwritten memo by Goodpaster la-
        beled "Gaither Advisory Group, November 7," *ibid.* (thanks to staff of
        Eisenhower Library for identifying Goodpaster's handwriting).

152   Eisenhower and intelligence: See Stephen Ambrose, *Ike's Spies* (New
        York: Doubleday & Co., 1981); and interviews.

152   detailed commentary: See NSC-5724/1, Office of Special Assistant for
        National Security Affairs file, NSC Series, Policy Papers Subseries, Box
        22, NSC-5724 folder, DDEL: for DoD and JCS response, see JCS-
        2101/289, Jan. 21, 1958, JCS 2101/296 of Mar. 3, 1958, and JCS-
        2101/302 of Mar. 26, 1958, all in Records of JCS, CCS 381 US (1-31-50),
        Secs. 74–76; and JCS Memorandum for Secretary of Defense, CM-117-
        58, May 8, 1958, Records of JCS, CCS 013.26 (6-23-49), Sec. 4; both in
        NA/MMB.

152   NSC meetings: They took place in early Jan., Jan. 16, and Apr. 24, 1958.
        "Briefing Note on Jan. 16/58 Meeting," Office of Special Assistant for
        National Security Affairs file, Special Assistant Series, Chron Subseries,
        Box 5, Jan. 1958 (1) folder; and Ann Whitman File, NSC Series, Box 10,
        363rd Meeting of NSC folder; both in DDEL.

152   Foster dinner: Halperin, *op. cit.;* "Group Discusses Threat to Nation,"
        New York Times, Dec. 11, 1957; "President Backs 'Alert' Advocates,"
        New York Times, Dec. 12, 1957; and interviews.

154   Eisenhower and leak: James R. Killian, Jr., *Sputnik, Scientists, and
        Eisenhower* (Cambridge: MIT Press, 1977), p. 97; and interviews.

154   congressmen demand release: "Senators Call for Release," *New York
        Times,* December 21, 1957; "House Unit Plans Shelter Action," *New
        York Times,* December 23, 1957; "Release of Gaither Data Is Urged by
        Legislators," *Washington Post,* December 25, 1957; Telephone Call to
        Senator [Lyndon] Johnson, December 23, 1957, *John Foster Dulles
        Papers,* Box 7, Memo TelCon, General, 11/1-12/27/57 (1) folder,
        DDEL.

406   FRED KAPLAN

10:   THE MISSILE GAP

155   "first, destroy or": "Estimate of Sino-Soviet Bloc Capabilities World-
        Wide, '59–63 and Assessment of Dimensions of Soviet ICBM Threat to
        Security of U.S.," p. 2, *Thomas White Papers,* Box 6, McConnell Report
        folder, LoC.*
155   "the Soviets might": *Ibid.,* p. 8.*
155   November 12 NIE: Summarized in memo, Lawrence McQuade to Paul
        Nitze, "But Where Did the Missile Gap Go?," May 31, 1963, p. 7, Na-
        tional Security File, Box 298, Missile Gap, Feb.–May 1963, JFKL.
155   number of Atlas missiles: Letter, Sen. Stuart Symington to Eisenhower,
        Aug. 29, 1958, White House office file, Office of Staff Secretary, Subject
        Series, Alpha Subseries, Box 24, Symington Letter [8-12/58] folder,
        DDEL.
156   1955 air-show overcount: Lawrence Freedman, *U.S. Intelligence and the
        Soviet Strategic Threat* (Boulder, Colo.: Westview Press, 1977), p. 66.
        The rest of the section on the bomber gap comes, unless otherwise speci-
        fied, from interviews.
161   November 1957 NIE: Memo, McQuade to Nitze, *loc. cit.*
161   NIE on Soviet first move: *Ibid.,* p. 9.
161   100 ICBMs by 1959: *Ibid.,* pp. 7–8.
163   Symington-Lanphier-Dulles meetings: Howard Stoertz, Jr., Memo for
        Record, "Discussion of Soviet and U.S. Long Range Ballistic Missile Pro-
        grams," Aug. 18, 1958, White House Office file, Office of Staff Secretary,
        Subject Series, Alpha Subseries, Box 24, Symington Letter folder,
        DDEL;* letter, Stuart Symington to Eisenhower, Aug. 29, 1958, *loc. cit.*
165   February 9, 1960 NIE: Memo, McQuade to Nitze, *loc. cit.;* memo, G. W.
        Rathjens, "Proposed Ban on Missile Testing," p. 4, White House Office
        file, Office of Assistant for Science and Technology, Box 1, Disarmament,
        Missiles [5/58-3/60], DDEL.
165–66 Army-Navy estimates: Memo, McQuade to Nitze, *loc. cit.,* pp. 11–12; and
        interviews.
166   Air Force reduces vulnerability: Memo to Assistant C/S, Installations,
        "Protective Construction," Nov. 13, 1956, *Nathan Twining Papers,* Box
        104, Air Force Council C/S Decisions, Vol. III, Tab 39/48a, LoC;* and
        the following from *Thomas White Papers:* letter, Thomas Power to
        White, Oct. 21, 1957, Box 41, 1957 Top Secret General folder; memo,
        Curtis LeMay to White, "SAC Airborne Alert Plan," Dec. 23, 1958, Box
        14, Air Force Council folder; memo on 1959 Annual Commanders Con-
        ference, Jan. 17, 1959, Box 29, 1959 Top Secret General folder; Decision
        Memo, "SAC Airborne Alert Plan," Mar. 31, 1959, Box 25, Air Force
        Council Decisions 1959, Tab 6; memo, Curtis LeMay to White, "Vulnera-
        bility of SAC Bombers in Early 1960," Feb. 18, 1959, Box 25, Air Force
        Council folder; memo, Thomas Power to JCS, "Establishment of an Air-
        borne Alert," June 23, 1960, Box 34, SAC folder.
167   Air Force against hardening: Memo, Gen. Thomas White to C/S, "Pro-
        tective Construction Criteria," Oct. 31, 1956, *Nathan Twining Papers,* *
        Box 82, 1956 Air Force Council folder; memo, Curtis LeMay to C/S,
        "Vulnerability of SAC Bombers in Early 1960," *loc. cit.;* and interviews.
168   Air Force on deception: After meetings held Feb. 24–27, 1959, the Air
        Force Council noted, "Soviet security measures will permit the develop-
        ment of forces under concealment, capable of neutralizing the effect of
        our programmed deterrent force." Memo for C/S, "The Threat," May 9,
        1959, *Thomas White Papers,* Box 29, 1959 Top Secret General folder;*
        and interviews.
169   Symington and Eisenhower; Andrew Goodpaster, Memo of Conference
        with President, Aug. 29, 1958, and Letter, Symington to Eisenhower,
        Aug. 29, 1958, White House Office File, Office of Staff Secretary, Subject
        Series, Alpha Subseries, Box 24, Symington Letter folder DDEL.*

169   "deterrence gap." *E.g.*, Herman Kahn, *On Thermonuclear War* (Princeton Univ. Press, 1960), pp. 201, 474.
171   "with matching": Wohlstetter, "The Delicate Balance of Terror," *Foreign Affairs*, Jan. 1959, pp. 212–13.
171   "notion that a": *Ibid.*, p. 234.
171   "*are* hard": *Ibid.*, p. 234.

11.   THE MASSIVE-RETALIATION SPEECH

174   Dulles speech: Dulles, "The Evolution of Foreign Policy," *The Department of State Bulletin*, Jan. 25, 1954, pp. 107–10.
176   "the economy": Quoted in Bernard Brodie, *Strategy in the Missile Age* (Princeton Univ. Press, 1959), p. 366.
176   "the foundation": Quoted in Glenn H. Snyder, "The 'New Look' of 1953," in Warner R. Schilling, Paul Y. Hammond, Glenn H. Snyder, *Strategy, Politics, and Defense Budgets* (New York: Columbia Univ. Press, 1962), pp. 389–90.
176   Eisenhower to Gruenther: Letter, May 4, 1953, Ann Whitman File, DDE Diary Series, Box 3, DDE Diary, 12/52-7/53 (3) folder, DDEL.
176   Dodge report: Atts. to letter, George Humphrey to Joseph Dodge, Feb. 16, 1953, Office of Special Assistant for National Security Affairs file, NSC Series, Subject Subseries, Box 8, President's Meeting with Civilian Consultants, 3/1/53 (1) folder, DDEL.
177   "the United States": Letter, Eisenhower to Gruenther, *loc. cit.*
177   Korean War deaths: Precise figures are 33,629 killed and 103,284 wounded. Bernard Brodie, *War and Politics* (New York: Macmillan, 1973), p. 106.
178   Eisenhower and Conner: Oral History Interview with Gen. Andrew Goodpaster, Columbia Univ. Oral History Project; and interviews.
178   "the great equation": Snyder, *op. cit.*, p. 392.
178   "Why, the American": Quoted by Marshall at Meeting of Secretary of Defense and Service Chiefs with Secretary of State, Oct. 10, 1948, Records of JCS, CCS 312.1 (18 Nov. 47), NA/MMB.
178   "a striking power": Cited in letter, Dulles to James Reston, Dec. 13, 1954, *John Foster Dulles Papers*, Box 84, Massive Retaliation folder, Princeton Univ.
178–79 May 5 Paris speech: Dulles, "Defense Through Deterrent Power," *Vital Speeches*, June 1, 1952, pp. 493–95. Dulles made the same point later that month in Pittsburgh and New York. See Dulles, "A Positive Foreign Policy" (Pittsburgh), May 15, 1952, *John Foster Dulles Papers*, Box 62, Massive Retaliation folder, Princeton Univ.; references to both speeches appear in letter, Richard Nixon to Dulles, May 22, 1952, *Dulles Papers*, Box 62, Nixon folder.
179   "we, a professedly": Press release, Federal Council, for Aug. 10, 1945, *John Foster Dulles Papers*, Box 26, Atomic Weapons folder, Princeton Univ.
179   "the dictates of": Dulles, "The Atomic Bomb and Moral Law," *John Foster Dulles Papers*, Box 29, Atomic Weapons folder, Princeton Univ.
180   Eisenhower and Dulles' phrase: Snyder, *op. cit.*, p. 390.
180   *Helena* trip: Robert J. Donovan, *Eisenhower: The Inside Story* (Harper & Bros., 1956), pp. 17–18; "Eisenhower Visits Korea Front; Says He Has 'No Trick Solutions'; Cruiser Bringing Him from Guam," *New York Times*, Dec. 6, 1952.
181   "would become one": Andrew Goodpaster, Memo of Conference with President, May 14, 1956, Ann Whitman File, DDE Diary Series, Box 15, May 1956 Goodpaster folder, DDEL.
181   "fatuous": Andrew Goodpaster, Memo of Conference with President, May 24, 1956, *loc. cit.*

181 Dulles' aggressive view: See Townsend Hoopes, *The Devil and John Foster Dulles* (Boston: Little, Brown, 1973); Leonard Mosley, *Dulles* (New York: Dial Press/James Wade, 1978).

181 "remind individuals": Letter, Eisenhower to Dulles, March 7, 1955, *John Foster Dulles Papers,* Box 91, D. D. Eisenhower folder, Princeton Univ.

181 "Progression from the spear": USAF, *Doctrine of Atomic Air Warfare,* Dec. 30, 1948 (declassified).

182 "It is in": Memo, Chief of Naval Operations to JCS, "U.S. Military Position on the Employment of Atomic Weapons," July 24, 1951, Records of JCS, CCS 385 (2-22-51), Sec. 2, NA/MMB.

182 "it would be": Att. to letter, Maj. George Blanchard to Joseph Short, Sept. 12, 1952, Official File, 692-A Atomic Bomb folder, HSTL.

182 Army study and Navy agreement: Memo, Dir., Strategic Plans *et al.,* on JCS 1953/11, June 25, 1952, *Arleigh Burke Papers,* A-1 folder, Navy Yard, Washington, D.C.

183 "It is United States": Att. to Memo for Secretary of Defense by Omar Bradley, "JCS Views on DoD Interest in the Use of Atomic Weapons," Dec. 11, 1951, Records of JCS, CCS 471.6 (11-3-51), Sec. 1, NA/MMB.

183 "strategic air offensive": JCS-2056/7, Aug. 12, 1950, Records of JCS, CCS 373.11 (12-14-45), Sec. 2; "Joint Outline Emergency War Plan 'Ironbark,' " July 3, 1951, p. 16, Records of JCS, CCS 381 (3-2-46), B.P., Pt. 5; both in NA/MMB.

183 "What does all": Radford, Address, "Modern Evolution of Armed Forces," May 25, 1954, Records of JCS, 045.8 Naval War College, NA/MMB.

12: THE LIMITED-WAR CRITIQUE

185 Dulles and Nitze: Leonard Mosley, *Dulles* (New York: Dial Press/James Wade, 1978), pp. 307–08; and interviews.

185 Nitze memo: Memo, Nitze to Robert Bowie, "Analysis of Dulles Speech," Jan. 13, 1954 (provided to author).

187 class of 1939: *History of the Class of 1939* (yearbook), especially p. 239, Yale Univ.; and interviews.

187 "If we are": Bundy, "Class Oration," *ibid.,* pp. 191–92.

188 Kaufmann transferred: This was due largely to his Yale connections. See letters Bemis to Seymour, Dec. 12, 1941: Seymour to Kaufmann, Dec. 15, 1941; Kaufmann to Seymour, Jan. 3, 1942: all in *Charles Seymour Papers,* Box 90, Ka 1937–50 folder, Yale Univ.

190 "As a consequence": Kaufmann, "Introduction," in Kaufmann, ed., *Military Policy and National Security* (Princeton Univ. Press, 1956), p. 7.

190 "that, despite our": Kaufmann, "The Requirements of Deterrence," Memorandum #7, Princeton Center of International Studies, 1954 (reprinted in *ibid.,* quote on p. 18; in all references to this essay, page numbers will refer to the book, not to the originally printed essay).

190 "In other words": *Ibid.,* p. 21.

191 "national objectives": Bernard Brodie, "Changing Capabilities and War Objectives," p. 22, lecture, Air War College, Apr. 17, 1952, *Bernard Brodie Papers,* Box 12, UCLA.

191 Brodie's basic thoughts: Brodie, "Nuclear Weapons: Strategic or Tactical?," *Foreign Affairs,* Jan. 1954, p. 227.

191 Brodie and battlefield nuclear: *Ibid.,* pp. 224–27; on Vandenberg and RAND work, see Chaps. 3 and 5.

191 "it is quite": Kaufmann, "The Requirements of Deterrence," p. 21.

191 "must seem worth": *Ibid.,* p. 20.

192 "we must immediately": *Ibid.,* p. 23.

192 "suggested rather": *Ibid.,* p. 21.

192 "credit": *Ibid.,* p. 22.

192   "on the cheap": *Ibid.*, p. 38.
192   "to fit": *Ibid.*, p. 29.
193   "Our effort": *Ibid.*
193   "outbreak of": *Ibid.*, p. 37.
193   Brodie's same points: Brodie, "Unlimited Weapons and Limited War," *The Reporter,* Nov. 18, 1954.
194   "intrude upon": Letters, Kaufmann to Brodie, Sept. 12, 1955; Brodie to Kaufmann, Sept. 19, 1955, *Bernard Brodie Papers,* Box 1, K folder, UCLA.
194   footnotes: See essays in Kaufmann, ed., *Military Policy and National Security;* and interviews.
195   Harvard and MIT letter: *New York Times,* Apr. 30, 1950, p. 8E.
195   Kaufmann essay and Army: Anthony Leviero, "Pentagon Armed by Savant's Data," *New York Times,* Mar. 20, 1955; and interviews.
195   "Kaufmann's contentions": Memo, Col. L. F. Paul to Gen. White, "Princeton Report on Massive Retaliation," n.d., *Thomas White Papers,* Box 1, Correspondence (1954–57) folder, LoC.*
195   "increasingly impossible": See Army statements compiled in Confidential USAF analysis, *Nathan Twining Papers,* Box 117, Army-Navy-Air Force "Interservice Rivalry" 1955–56 folder, LoC.*
196   "radical departure": Memo, Radford to Gens. Twining, Taylor, Pate and Adm. Burke, "Strategic Concept and the Use of U.S. Military Forces," Mar. 28, 1956, Records of JCS, Chairmen's File, 301 Military Strategy (Posture), NA/MMB.
196   Ridgway resigns: See his letter to Secretary of Defense Charles Wilson, leaked to *New York Times,* July 15, 1955.
196   Eisenhower versus Taylor: *E.g.,* Andrew Goodpaster, Memo for Record, Feb. 10, 1956, White House Office file, Office of Staff Secretary, Subject Series, DoD Subseries, Box 4, JCS (2) folder; Memo of Conference, May 24, 1956, Ann Whitman File, DDE Diary Series, Box 15, May '56 Goodpaster folder; both in DDEL; and Maxwell D. Taylor, *The Uncertain Trumpet* (New York: Harper & Bros., 1960), p. 123; and interviews.
196   Army case takes hold: *E.g.,* memo, Robert Cutler to Eisenhower, "Limited War in the Nuclear Age," Aug. 7, 1957, Office of Special Assistant for National Security Affairs file, OCB Series, Subject Subseries, Box 3, Limited War folder; letter, George Kistiakowsky to Thomas Gates, Sept. 30, 1959, and memo, George Rathjens to Kistiakowsky, Oct. 5, 1960, both in White House Office file, Office of Special Assistant for Science and Technology, Box 2, Limited War (Sept.–Oct. 1960) folder; all in DDEL.
197   "continuing competition": Kaufmann, "Force and Foreign Policy," Kaufmann, ed., *Military Policy and National Security,* p. 252.
197   "Whatever": *Ibid.*, p. 248.
197   "perform a function": Kaufmann, "Limited Warfare," in *ibid.*, p. 118.
197   "it must be": *Ibid.*, p. 117.
198   "the scope": *Ibid.*, p. 113.
198   "managed": *Ibid.*, p. 128.
198   "messages": *Ibid.*, p. 113.
198   "great value": Kaufmann, "Force and Foreign Policy," p. 234.
198   "as in poker": *Ibid.*, p. 256.
198   "new and strange": Kaufmann, "Limited Warfare," pp. 119–20.
198   "Limited war cannot": *Ibid.*, p. 127.
199   "the lines": Kaufmann, "Force and Foreign Policy," p. 245.
199   "that the costs": Kaufmann, "Limited Warfare," p. 113.
199   "All the emotions": *Ibid.*, p. 129.
199   "returned to its": Kaufmann, "Force and Foreign Policy," p. 260.
200   "We may not": *Ibid.*, pp. 255–56.
200   "rather unhappy": Letter, Kaufmann to Brodie, Oct. 31, 1955, *Bernard Brodie Papers,* Box 1, K folder, UCLA.

13: COUNTERFORCE

201   February 1956: Reference in letter, Kaufmann to Brodie, Oct. 31, 1955, *Bernard Brodie Papers*, Box 1, K folder, UCLA; and interview.

201   war games: For a description of RAND war-game techniques, see M. G. Weiner, *War Gaming Methodology*, RAND RM-2413, July 10, 1959; facts presented here come from interviews.

203   "all-out war": Kaufmann, "Force and Foreign Policy," in Kaufmann, ed., *Military Policy and National Security* (Princeton Univ. Press, 1956), p. 243, fn. 8.

204   Brodie on Air Staff: See chap. 3.

206   RAND targeting studies: More than a dozen studies are listed in an unclassified RAND bibliography of Targeting papers.

207   Brodie-Hitch-Marshall paper: "The Next Ten Years," RAND D-2700, Dec. 12, 1954, as footnoted in James F. Digby, *Problems in Attacking Soviet Strategic Air Power*, D-2711, Feb. 4, 1955 (provided to author), p. 4. Digby states that this paper discussed countermilitary strategies, and he also refers to "earlier papers by Brodie," which "are of interest in this regard"; and interviews.

208   Barlow-Digby study: *Staff Report: Air Defense Study*, RAND R-255, Sept. 1, 1951, and *Air Defense Study*, RAND R-227, Oct. 15, 1951; both in *Curtis LeMay Papers*, B-101 RAND folder, LoC.*

208   counterforce as alternative: Digby, *op. cit.*, p. 3.

209   "principal deterrent": Albert Wohlstetter and Fred Hoffman, *Protecting U.S. Power to Strike Back in the 1950s and 1960s*, RAND R-290, Sept. 1, 1956, p. 89.

211   ATD-751 in EWP: A letter to Loftus from Col. Gordon M. Graham, Chief of Target Analysis Division, dated May 1, 1953 (provided to author), reads: "The highest tribute which can be paid you . . . is the recent approval without modification of the results of your work by the Joint Chiefs of Staff." Digby, *op. cit.*, also refers to how counterforce "seems to have pervaded U.S. plans in the past year. SAC now accords it the highest priority, and apparently finds that the JCS agrees." (p. 3) Digby must have learned this from Loftus. (And interviews.)

214   "surprise ('sneak') attack": Herbert Goldhamer and Andrew W. Marshall with the assistance of Nathan Leites, *The Deterrence and Strategy of Total War, 1959–61: A Method of Analysis*, RAND RM-2301, Apr. 30, 1959, pp. iii, 2 (FOIA/DoD).*

214   "utilities or values": *Ibid.*, p. iv.*

215   "Very likely": *Ibid.*, p. 109.*

215   "utility to the Soviet": *Ibid.*, p. 11.*

215   "might be worthwhile": *Ibid.*, pp. 109–10.*

215   "trying to estimate": *Ibid.*, p. 64.*

216   "We believe": *Ibid.*, p. 22.*

218   "managed": William W. Kaufmann, "Limited Warfare," Kaufmann, ed., *Military Policy and National Security*, p. 128.

218   "messages": *Ibid.*, p. 113.

218   "have a good chance": *Ibid.*

219   "Constant Monitor": From Brodie, "Strategy Hits a Dead End," *Harper's*, Oct. 1955, p. 37; footnoted in Kaufmann, "Limited Warfare," p. 119.

14: DR. STRANGELOVE

220   "first came in contact": Kahn, *On Thermonuclear War* (Princeton Univ. Press, 1960), p. 484. (All page numbers refer to 1969 2nd-edition paperback published by The Free Press.)

221 Monte Carlo and H-bomb: *RAND Staff Report R-192*, June 1, 1950; and interviews.

222 Brodie and two million: Kahn, *op. cit.*, p. 169; and interview.

223 "Doomsday Machine": *Ibid.*, pp. 144*ff.*

223 44 "rungs": Kahn, *On Escalation* (New York: Frederick A. Praeger, 1965).

223 Credible-First-Strike: Kahn, *On Thermonuclear War, passim*, especially pp. 27–36; on Not-Incredible, see p. viii.

224 tit-for-tat: *Ibid.*, p. 282n. This is not actually a Kahn term, but he sticks by it.

224 I, II, III: Most lengthily discussed in *ibid.*, pp. 126–38, 138–44, and 126–37 and 285–86, respectively.

224 "If the Soviet": *Ibid.*, p. 143; for more on "blackmail," see pp. 165*ff.*, 174, 348, 463.

224 "Deterrence Gap": *Ibid.*, pp. 201, 474.

224 Munichs or Pearl Harbors: *Ibid.*, pp. 286, 377, 403*ff.*, 411*ff.*, 476, 562.

224 "our negotiators": *Ibid.*, p. 221.

224 "however the next": *Ibid.*, p. 463. Obviously, as detailed in a later chapter, the real crises of 1961 and 1962 turned out quite differently.

225 "The whole purpose": *Ibid.*, p. 647.

225 "Any power": *Ibid.*, p. 213.

225 "perfectly conceivable": *Ibid.*, p. 649.

225 "Insofar as": *Ibid.*, pp. 647–48.

225 "an adequate": *Ibid.*, p. 516; and interview.

226 Kahn civil-defense team: The resulting report was *A Report on a Study of Non-Military Defense*, RAND R-322-RC, July 1, 1958, of which Chap. 2 in *OTW* is a sort of summary.

226 radiation meters: Kahn, *On Thermonuclear War*, pp. 626*ff.*

226 Goldhamer and Marshall and counterforce: *The Deterrence and Strategy of Total War, 1959–61*, RAND RM-2301, Apr. 30, 1959, p. 124 (FOIA/DoD).*

226 "winning": Letter, Kaufmann to Gen. Thomas White, Feb. 18, 1960, p. 6, *Thomas White Papers*, Box 36, Missiles/Space/Nuclear folder, LoC.*

226 "war-fighting": Letter, Frank Collbohm to Gen. White, July 25, 1960, *Thomas White Papers*, Box 37, RAND folder; that Kaufmann wrote the letter comes from interview.*

226 "Will the Survivors": Title of Chap. 2, Kahn, *On Thermonuclear War;* "Tragic But Distinguishable," *ibid.*, p. 20.

226 5,000 people: *Ibid.*, p. xxvi.

227 30,000 copies: Norman Moss, *Men Who Play God*, rev. ed. (London: Penguin, 1970), p. 279.

227 "Now just imagine": Kahn, *On Thermonuclear War*, p. 86.

228 "War is a": *Ibid.*, pp. 45–46.

228 "the increase would": *Ibid.*, p. 21.

228 "we can imagine": *Ibid.*, p. 646.

228 "This is": James R. Newman, "On Thermonuclear War," *Scientific American*, Mar. 1961.

228 Kahn and Flanagan: Letters, Kahn to Flanagan, Mar. 6, 1961; Flanagan to Kahn, Mar. 15, 1961 (provided to author).

228 Kahn, *Thinking About the Unthinkable* (New York: Horizon Press, 1962); and interview.

229 "The one circumstance": Kahn, *On Thermonuclear War*, p. 158; Kahn even italicizes this passage.

229 "seven optimistic": *Ibid.*, p. 84.

229 "However, experience": *Ibid.*, p. 81.

229 "The A food": *Ibid.*, p. 66.

230 "comes from assuming": *Ibid.*, p. 67.

230 "a nation like": *Ibid.*, p. 91 (emphasis added).

230 "did not look": *Ibid.*

230   "all these things": *Ibid.*, p. 92.
230   "How much confidence": *Ibid.*, p. 94.
230   "We may not": *Ibid.*, p. 95.
231   *Dr. Strangelove:* In researching the film, Stanley Kubrick discussed strat-
       egy at great length with such people as Kahn, Kaufmann, Henry Kis-
       singer, Thomas Schelling and others. (Interviews.)
231   "to create a": Kahn, *On Thermonuclear War*, p. 5.
231   "more reasonable": *Ibid.*, p. 240.

15: THE REAL RIVALRY

232   "Admirals' Revolt": See Warner R. Schilling, "The Politics of National
       Defense: Fiscal 1950," in Warner R. Schilling, Paul Y. Hammond, Glenn
       H. Snyder, *Strategy, Politics, and Defense Budgets* (New York: Columbia
       Univ. Press, 1962).
232   "ruthless and barbaric": Hearings, House Armed Services Committee,
       The National Defense Program: Unification and Strategy, Oct. 1949, pp.
       183–89.
232   Radford testimony: *Ibid.*, pp. 64–65.
232   A-bomb on Washington Airport: *Ibid.*, p. 170.
233   Navy on A-bombs at outset: *E.g.*, memo, L. D. McCormick, Acting CNO,
       to JCS, "U.S. Military Position on the Employment of Atomic Weapons,"
       July 24, 1951, Records of JCS, CCS 385 (2-22-51), Sec. 2, NA/MMB.
233   "rigidly pre-planned": *E.g.*, memo, Deputy CNO (Ops) to CNO, "Atomic
       Air Operations in Support of the Joint Operational Emergency War
       Plan," Dec. 17, 1951, *Arleigh Burke Papers,* A16-10 Atomic Warfare Op-
       erations folder, Navy Yard, Washington, D.C.
234   "expressed as": Burke, introduction to NAVWAG-1, Jan. 15, 1957 (pro-
       vided to author).
234   "we shall soon": "Unclassified Summary of NAVWAG Study No. 5," Jan.
       22, 1958, White House Office files, Office of Staff Secretary, Subject Se-
       ries, Alpha Subseries, Box 21, Nuclear Exchange (1) folder, DDEL.
235   "lower levels": *Ibid.*
236   "we would be": Memo with att., Power to White, "CNO Personal Letter
       to Retired Flag Officers," May 9, 1959, *Thomas White Papers,* Box 27,
       SAC folder, LoC.*
236   "There is": Letter, Wheless to Westover, May 12, 1959, *Thomas White
       Papers, loc. cit.**
236   "will be pointed": *Ibid.**
236   "This would lead": Letter, White to Power, May 11, 1959, *Thomas White
       Papers,* Box 29, 1959 Top Secret File folder.*
237   "constitute": W. W. Kaufmann, "The Puzzle of Polaris," Feb. 1, 1960,
       att. to memo, Roscoe Wilson to Gen. White, Feb. 17, 1960, *Thomas
       White Papers,* Box 36, Missiles/Space/Nuclear folder.*
238   letter to White: Kaufmann, *loc. cit.**
238   "A strategic": Letter, Kaufmann to White, Feb. 18, 1960, *loc. cit.**
242   Air Force Intelligence: Memo, Lawrence McQuade to Paul Nitze, "But
       Where Did the Missile Gap Go?," May 31, 1963, National Security File,
       Box 298, Missile Gap, Feb.–May 1963, JFKL.
242   scenarios and fatalities: Richard Fryklund, *100 Million Lives* (New York:
       Macmillan, 1962), pp. 2–4, 13–14; and interviews. Though it doesn't say
       so, Fryklund's book is based almost entirely on Kaufmann's briefing,
       which Gen. Noel Parrish leaked to him. (Interviews.)
243   officers' questions: Noted in W. W. Kaufmann, *Counterforce IV: Sum-
       mary Briefing,* RAND DL-7880-PR, Sept. 6, 1960 (provided to author);
       and interviews. As far as I know, this document is the only written ver-
       sion of the Kaufmann briefing still extant; no actual report was ever
       composed.

244   "disturbed": White, "Military Requirements and Resources for FY60-62," lecture, Quantico Conference, June 21, 1958, *Thomas White Papers*, Box 19, 1958 Top Secret File folder.*

244   White endorsed: Letter, White to Frank Collbohm, Aug. 12, 1960, *Thomas White Papers*, Box 37, RAND folder;* and interviews.

245   "your public": "Air Force Information Policy Letter," Oct. 1, 1960, *Thomas White Papers*, Box 37, Commanders' Conference (1960) folder.*

245   "effective deterrence": "Subjects of Major Importance for Discussion at the Commanders' Conference, 17–18 November 1960," Tab A, Nov. 1, 1960, *Thomas White Papers*, Box 41, 1960 Top Secret File folder.*

246   "I endorsed": White to Power, Feb. 27, 1961, *Thomas White Papers*, Box 48, 1961 Top Secret File folder.*

16:   THE WHIZ KIDS

248   "the United": Cited in memo, Mar. 1958, *Theodore Sorensen Papers*, Box 9, Defense and Veterans, JFK Position, 3/58 folder, JFKL.

248   "We are rapidly": Reprinted in Kennedy, *The Strategy of Peace*, ed. by Allan Nevins (New York: Harper & Row, 1960), p. 34.

249   "the deterrent ratio": *Ibid.*, pp. 36–37.

249   "missile power": *Ibid.*, pp. 37–38.

249   "the problem of": Kennedy, speech, n.d. (internal evidence suggests Apr. 1959), *Theodore Sorensen Papers*, Box 22, Defense folder.

249   "Academic Advisory Group": List of members in *Dierdre Henderson Papers*, Box 1, 1st manila folder, JFKL; and interviews.

250   RAND and JFK campaign: See various letters in *Dierdre Henderson Papers*, Boxes 1 and 2; and interviews.

250   McNamara background: Henry L. Trewhitt, *McNamara: His Ordeal in the Pentagon* (New York: Harper & Row, 1971); Elie Abel, "The Thinking Man's Business Executive" in *The Kennedy Circle*, Lester Tanzer, ed. (Washington, D.C.: Luce, 1961); and interviews.

251   30 percent more flying hours: Eugene Zuckert, Oral History Interview, p. 2, JFKL.

252   McNamara and Hitch: Norman Moss, *Men Who Play God*, rev. ed. (London: Penguin, 1970), p. 290; and interviews.

253   "a certain accent": Cited in letter, Enthoven to Brodie, June 10, 1960, *Bernard Brodie Papers*, Box 1, E folder, UCLA.

253   "Fundamentally" and "I have lost": *Ibid.*

254   "General, I don't": Trewhitt, *op. cit.*, p. 13.

255   McNamara and Minuteman: He wanted 1,200 Minuteman ICBMs in 1961, 1,300 in 1962, 1,400 in 1963, and settled on 1,000 in 1964. See DPM, McNamara to Kennedy, "Recommended Long Range Nuclear Delivery Forces 1963–67," Sept. 23, 1961, p. 2 (FOIA/DoD);* DPM, McNamara to Kennedy, "Recommended FY 1964–68 Strategic Retaliatory Forces," Nov. 21, 1962, p. 2 (FOIA/DoD);* McNamara to Kennedy, Dec. 3, 1962, National Security File, Box 275, DoD, Defense Budget, FY64, Vol. I, Misc. folder, JFKL. And citation in BoB memo, "Minuteman Programs," Aug. 14, 1963, National Security File, Agency File, Box 14–17, Defense Budget, 1965, Sec. 2 folder; and memo, Cyrus Vance to Lyndon Johnson, Dec. 14, 1964, National Security File, Agency File, Box 11–21, DoD, Vol. II folder; both in LBJL.

255   Air Force 3,000: Air Force Council approved this "requirement" on May 12, 1959; memo, Jacob Smart, "USAF Tasks and Objective Force Structure," May 15, 1959, *Thomas White Papers*, Box 25, Air Force Council Decisions 1959—folder, LoC.*

255   SAC 10,000: Alain Enthoven and K. Wayne Smith, *How Much Is*

Enough? Shaping the Defense Program, 1961–1969 (New York: Harper & Row, 1971), p. 195.

255   "In common": White, "Strategy and the Defense Intellectuals," *Saturday Evening Post,* May 4, 1963.

257   Kaysen and BoB: Memos, Carl Kaysen to McGeorge Bundy, "Secretary McNamara's Memorandum on the Defense Budget dated Oct. 6, 1961," Nov. 13, 1961; Kaysen to President, "Force Structure and Defense Budget," Nov. 22, 1961; Kaysen to President, Dec. 9, 1961; all in National Security File, Box 275, DoD, Defense Budget, FY63, 11–12/61, JFKL.

257   "The term 'defense' ": White, *op. cit.*

17:   TWO BRIEFINGS

258   *WSEG-50: WSEG-50,* Dec. 27, 1960, select volumes (FOIA/DoD); and interviews.*

259   *WSEG-50* and counterforce: *WSEG-50,* Appendix E to Encl. A, "The Feasibility of Achievement of Counterforce Objectives" (FOIA/DoD);* and interviews.

259   "once an effective": *WSEG-50,* p. 12.*

18:   THE SIOP AND THE ROAD TO ANN ARBOR

263   August 16: Hq. SAC, "History of the Joint Strategic Target Planning Staff: Background and Preparation of SIOP-62," n.d., p. 1 (FOIA/DoD).

263   "Strategic Command": See following in *Thomas White Papers,* LoC:* Letter, White to Enis Whitehead, Mar. 17, 1960, Box 36, Missiles/Space/Nuclear folder; letter, White to All Major Air Commands, May 6, 1959, Box 26, Command Letters folder.* (And interviews.)

264   White fallback: Letter, White to Thomas Gates, June 10, 1960, *Thomas White Papers,* Box 41, 1960 Top Secret File folder; and interviews.*

264   June 14 briefing: SAC, "Unity in the Strategic Offensive" (FOIA/USAF).* For references to NSTL, SIOP and SAC, see Charts 40, 52, 58, 69, 72–74, 76. For delivery to Gates on June 14, see memo, White to Power, "Recommended Actions for Increasing Capabilities and Readiness Posture of SAC Forces," July 19, 1960, *Thomas White Papers, ibid.*

264   "18 Questions": JCS-2056/134, Sept. 4, 1959, with enclosure CM-386-59 of Aug. 24, 1959 (FOIA/DoD); and interviews.

264   July 6 meeting: Andrew Goodpaster, Memo of Conference with President, July 6, 1960, White House Office file, Office of Staff Secretary, Subject Series, DoD Subseries, Box 2, DoD, Vol. IV (5), DDEL.

264   "At last": Transcript, "Adm. Burke's Conversation with Gen. Lemnitzer, 10 August 1960," *Arleigh Burke Papers,* SIOP/NSTL Briefing Folder, Navy Yard, Washington, D.C.*

265   "This is just": *Ibid.*

265   "They're smart": Transcript, "Adm. Burke's Conversation with Secretary Franke, 12 August 1960," *Arleigh Burke Papers, loc. cit.*

265   "they think they": Transcript, "Adm. Burke's Conversation with Capt. Bardshar, 22 August 1960," *Arleigh Burke Papers,* Transcripts & Phonecons (NSTL) folder.*

266   Burke's understanding of war plan: *E.g.,* Burke's notes on conversation with Eisenhower, Cable, Burke to CincPacFlt, LantFlt, USNavEur, Pt. 3, August 12, 1960, *Arleigh Burke Papers,* SIOP/NSTL Briefing folder.*

266   "then our": "Minutes of CNO Deputies' Conference, 18 August 1960," *Arleigh Burke Papers,* Transcripts & Phonecons (NSTL).*

266   "paving the way": Transcript, "Adm. Burke's Conversation with RAdms. Parker and Raborn, 16 August 1960," *ibid.;* cf. "Adm. Burke's Instruc-

tions to RAdm. Parker, 21 August 1960," *ibid.;* * transcript, "Adm.
Burke's Conversation with Sec. Franke, 12 August 1960" and "Adm.
Burke's Conversation with Gen. Lemnitzer, 10 August 1960," in *Burke
Papers*, SIOP/NSTL Briefing folder.*

266   SAC 1,300: "Message, CincPacFlt (Dennison) to CNO," Feb. 1, 1961,
        Arleigh Burke Papers, NSTL/SIOP Messages, Exclusives & Personals.*

267   "will consist": Cited in memo, Op-06 to Op-00 on "JCS 2056/189, The
        Initial NSTL & SIOP" (Nov. 1960), *Arleigh Burke Papers*, Memos &
        Letters (NSTL).*

267   Smith on "minimum": Cited in Memo (by Lee, for CincLant rep.) for
        Record, "Report of Planning Conference at SAC Hq., Omaha, 24–26
        Aug. 1960, on Strategic Planning for a National Strategic Target List
        (NSTL) and a Single Integrated Operational Plan (SIOP)," Aug. 27,
        1960, *ibid.**

267   700 versus 200: Cited in memo, CincLantFlt (Dennison) to CNO, "Min-
        utes of the 21st Mtg., of JSTPS Policy Committee," Mar. 22, 1961, *Ar-
        leigh Burke Papers*, NSTL/SIOP Messages, Exclusives & Personals.*

267   airfield controversy: Memo, Op-06c to Op-00, "Suggested Key Points for
        Discussion—Adm. Burke & Adm. Parker" (Sept. or Oct. 1960), *Arleigh
        Burke Papers*, Memos & Letters (NSTL).*

267   bomber attrition: Message, CincPacFlt to CNO, Oct. 22, 1960; Message,
        Navrestracom (Hyland) to CNO, Nov. 15, 1960; Message, CincLantFlt
        to CNO, July 21, 1961; all in *Arleigh Burke Papers*, NSTL/SIOP Mes-
        sages, Exclusives & Personals.*

268   Polaris on SAMs or wasted: Memo for Record, "Report of Planning Con-
        ference at SAQ Hq., Omaha, 24–26 Aug. 1960, on Strategic Planning for
        a NSTL and a SIOP," Aug. 27, 1960, *Arleigh Burke Papers*, Memos &
        Letters (NSTL).*

268   202 with 97 percent: Message, CincLant (Lee) to CNO, Nov. 22, 1960,
        Arleigh Burke Papers, NSTL/SIOP Messages, Exclusives & Personals.*

268   7 with 97 percent: Memo, CincLantFlt to CNO, Apr. 27, 1961, *ibid.**

268   nine on four in Leningrad: Message, Navrestracomd to CNO, Nov. 3,
        1960, *ibid.**

268   2.2 weapons/target: Message, CNO to CincPacFlt, CincLantFlt, USNav-
        Eur, Nov. 24, 1960, *ibid.;* * and interview.

268   blast only: Message, CincPac to Rbepw/JCS, "Report of Preliminary Re-
        view of SIOP-62," Jan. 19, 1961, *ibid.;* * also in *Burke Papers:** Tran-
        script, "Adm. Burke's Conversation with Adm. Russell, 11 November
        1960," Transcripts & Phonecons (NSTL); and CNO to Flag & General
        Officers, "Special Edition Flag Officers Dope," Dec. 4, 1960, Memos &
        Letters (NSTL).

268   fallout exceeds limits: Message, CincLant (Lee) to CNO, Nov. 22, 1960,
        Arleigh Burke Papers, NSTL/SIOP Message, Exclusives & Personals.*

268   "our weapons": Message, CincPac to Rbepw/JCS, "Report of Prelimi-
        nary Review of SIOP-62," Jan. 19, 1961, *ibid.**

268   Kistiakowsky trip: Memos, Eisenhower to Kistiakowsky, Oct. 19, 1960,
        and Kistiakowsky to Andrew Goodpaster, Nov. 7, 1960, both in White
        House Office files, Office of Staff Secretary, Subject Series, Alpha Sub-
        series, Box 16, Dr. Kistiakowsky (6), DDEL; and interviews.

269   December 14: SAC Hq., "History of the Joint Strategic Target Planning
        Staff: Background and Preparation of SIOP-62," p. 15.

269   alert forces, 1,459 bombs: Memo, Op-06 (Ricketts) to Op-00, on "JCS-
        2056/189, The Initial NSTL & SIOP," Nov. 22, 1960, *Arleigh Burke
        Papers*, Memos & Letters (NSTL).*

269   full force and all fatality figures: Handwritten notes on SIOP-62 docu-
        ments (provided to author), confirmed by interviews.

270–71 McNamara grasps connection and "fantastic": Memo, Navrestracomd-
        Omaha to CNO, "JSTPS Briefing for McNamara on 4 February," Feb. 6,

1961, *Arleigh Burke Papers,* NSTL/SIOP Messages, Exclusives & Personals.*

271   three eighty-kiloton: *Ibid.**

272   Hitch-Enthoven-Stern paper: Richard Fryklund, "Weapon Survival Seen Aim of Defense Study," *Washington Star,* Feb. 15, 1961; and interviews.

272   "General War Offensive Package": Richard Fryklund, "U.S. Arms Plan Seen Holding Nuclear Edge," *Washington Star,* Feb. 22, 1961.

273   list of ninety-six: McNamara, Memorandum, Mar. 1, 1961, Presidential Office Files, Box 77, DoD, Defense Budget, Jan.–Mar. 1961, JFKL.

273   "McNamara's Band" and "96 Trombones": Henry Trewhitt, *McNamara: His Ordeal in the Pentagon* (New York: Harper & Row, 1971), p. 22.

273   ninety-two questions: McNamara, "Assignment of Projects within the DoD," Mar. 8, 1961 (FOIA/DoD).*

273   "that we do not": Memo, L. L. Lemnitzer to McNamara, " 'Doctrine' on Thermonuclear Attack," Apr. 18, 1961 (FOIA/DoD).*

273   McNamara's motivation: DPM, McNamara to Kennedy, Appendix I, "Recommended Long Range Nuclear Delivery Forces 1963–67," Sept. 23, 1961, p. 12 (FOIA/DoD).*

274   "the advantages": Memo, Lemnitzer to McNamara, *op. cit.**

275   Ellsberg lectures: First delivered Mar. 1959 and broadcast over WGBH-FM radio, Boston; later published by RAND, Ellsberg, *The Theory and Practice of Blackmail,* P-3883, July 1968.

276   "interference": See memo, Clarence Irvine to Gen. White, "Interaction of Air Operations in Time of Emergency," Feb. 5, 1959, *Thomas White Papers,* Box 25, Air Force Council, Tab AFC 8/1; and interviews.*

277   "A general war": Cited in memo, U. S. G. Sharp to Secretary, JCS, on changes in CINCEUR Plan 100-1 through 100-4, Aug. 21, 1958, CCS 381 (11-15-48), Sec. 19, NA/MMB.

277   "as principal": *Ibid;* and interviews.

278   "while limiting": Quotes from the final draft, which was Central War section of McNamara guidance for JCS strategic war planning, signed by McNamara, May 1961 (provided to author).

279   Enthoven/Trinkl orders: Desmond Ball, *Politics and Force Levels: The Strategic Missile Program of the Kennedy Administration* (Berkeley: Univ. of California Press, 1980), p. 191; and interviews.

281    $840 million: *Ibid.,* p. 194.

281   number of DPMs: Alain Enthoven and K. Wayne Smith, *How Much Is Enough?* (New York: Harper & Row, 1971), p. 54.

281   "They're a far": Quoted in *ibid.,* p. 58.

281   "greater survival": DPM, McNamara to Kennedy, *op. cit.,* p. 12.*

281   "ideal for": *Ibid.,* p. 14.*

281   "the extremes of": *Ibid.,* pp. 4–5.*

281   "The forces I am": *Ibid.,* p. 4.*

282   shorter budget memo: Memo, McNamara to Kennedy, "Recommended DoD FY '63 and 1963–67 Program," Oct. 6, 1961, Presidential Office Files, Box 77, Defense, 9–12/61, JFKL.

282   aides oppose: See Memo, David Bell to Kennedy, "FY 1963 Defense Budget Issues," Nov. 13, 1961; Memos, Carl Kaysen to Kennedy, Nov. 22 and Dec. 9, 1961; both in National Security File, Box 275, DoD Defense Budget, FY63, 11–12/61, JFKL; and interviews.

282   "Bob McNamara is": Cited in Trewhitt, *op. cit.,* p. 83.

282   Fryklund leak: Richard Fryklund, "New A-War Plan Would Spare Cities," *Washington Star,* Dec. 17, 1961; and interview.

282   "major mission": McNamara, testimony, Hearings, House Appropriations Committee, *DoD Appropriations for 1963,* Pt. 2, pp. 13, 249–50.

282   "be used in several": Cited in William W. Kaufmann, *The McNamara Strategy* (New York: Harper & Row, 1964), p. 74. Kaufmann's book is most interesting, in that he pretends to be simply an MIT professor attempting to explain McNamara's strategy "in his own words wherever

possible" since "McNamara is well able to speak for himself." (p. x.) Little does the reader know that Professor Kaufmann played a major role in devising the strategy and wrote several of the speeches that he quotes.

284 "the U.S. has come": "Remarks by Secretary McNamara, NATO Ministerial Meeting, 5 May 1962, Restricted Session," p. 2–3. (Thanks to David N. Schwartz, who obtained this document through FOIA/DoD and provided me with a copy.)

284 "intolerable to have": *Ibid.*, p. 11.

284 "repeat to the point": Handwritten notes from memo, McGeorge Bundy, on JFK's opinion of Athens speech (provided to author).

285 enthralled: Kaufmann, *op. cit.*, p. 114.

19: THE GAP THAT NEVER WAS

286 August 10: John Prados, *The Soviet Estimate* (New York: Dial Press, 1982), p. 109; reports of missiles at Plesetsk, p. 97; and interviews.

287 "The 'bomber gap':" *Public Papers of the Presidents, Dwight D. Eisenhower, 1960–61* (Washington, D.C.: Government Printing Office, 1961), p. 919.

287 June NIE: Memo, Lawrence McQuade to Paul Nitze, "But Where Did the Missile Gap Go?," p. 14, National Security File, Box 298, Missile Gap, Feb.–May 1963, JFKL.

288 "no more than": *Ibid.*, p. 14n.

289 "believe that our": CIA, "Current Status of Soviet and Satellite Military Forces and Indications of Military Intentions," Sept. 6, 1961, pp. 4–5, Presidential Office File, Box 117, Germany-Security, 8–12/61 folder, JFKL.

289 four SS-6, twenty SS-7/8 under construction: McQuade's memo to Nitze (*op. cit.*, p. 15) reports that the Sept. NIE cites "10–25" ICBMs. According to several interviewed, the "Codeword-classified" Annex of the NIE reported four SS-6 ICBMs, with the remainder of the "10–25" being SS-7s and SS-8s not yet deployed but whose sites were under construction.

20: THE CRISES

291 "test of": Theodore Sorensen, *Kennedy* (New York: Harper & Row, 1965), p. 657.

291 Berlin background: Material on general history mostly taken from Robert M. Slusser, "The Berlin Crises of 1958–59 and 1961," in Barry M. Blechman and Stephen S. Kaplan, *Force Without War* (Washington, D.C.: Brookings Institution, 1978); and Slusser, *The Berlin Crisis of 1961* (Baltimore: Johns Hopkins Univ. Press, 1973).

292 "peaceful coexistence": Quoted in Slusser, "The Berlin Crises of 1958–59 and 1961," p. 396.

293 "read, mark": Stewart Alsop, "Kennedy's Grand Strategy," *Saturday Evening Post*, Mar. 31, 1962, p. 12.

293 read at NSC: Arthur Schlesinger, Jr., *A Thousand Days* (Boston: Houghton Mifflin, 1965), pp. 302–03.

293 "cold winter": Schlesinger, *op. cit.*, p. 348.

293 Acheson memo: *Ibid.*, pp. 354–56.

294 Acheson critics: *Ibid.*, pp. 356–60; memo, Lucius Battle to McGeorge Bundy, National Security File, Box 81, Germany-Berlin-General, 6/30/61, JFKL.

294 "to neutralize": Schlesinger, *op. cit.*, p. 353.

296 McNamara and JCS plans: *Ibid.*, p. 361; and interviews.

296 NSC June 14: Memo, L. L. Lemnitzer to Kennedy, "Supply Levels in

Berlin," June 14, 1961, National Security File, Box 81, Germany-Berlin-General, 6/17-6/22/61, JFKL.

296   Acheson memo circulated: Memo, C. E. Johnson to Bromley Smith, "Distribution of Mr. Acheson's Memorandum on Berlin," June 29, 1961, National Security File, Box 81, Germany-Berlin-General, 6/29-6/31/61, JFKL.

296   "It is clear": Memo, Carl Kaysen to McGeorge Bundy, July 3, 1961, National Security File, Box 81, Germany-Berlin-General, 7/1-7/6/61, JFKL.

297   "all agree": Bundy, Covering Note on Henry Kissinger's Memo on Berlin, July 7, 1961, National Security File, Box 381, Germany-Berlin-General-Kissinger Report, 7/7/61, JFKL.

297   mobilize million men: Memo, McGeorge Bundy to McNamara, July 10, 1961, National Security File, Box 81, Germany-Berlin-General, 7/13/61, JFKL.

297   July 25 speech: Text in National Security File, Box 82, Germany-Berlin-General, 7/23-7/26/61, JFKL.

298   resolve and time for second thoughts: Schlesinger, op. cit., p. 361.

298   "hinges on": Quoted in ibid., pp. 360–61.

298   "nuclear war": Bundy, handwritten notes, "JFK's Berlin Agenda," National Security File, Box 81, Germany-Berlin-General, 7/19-7/22/61, JFKL.

298   "With the": Memo, Kennedy to McNamara, Aug. 14, 1961, National Security File, Box 82, Germany-Berlin-General, 8/11-8/15/61, JFKL.

299   Raskin on study: Marcus G. Raskin, Being and Doing (New York: Random House, 1971), pp. 62–63; and interviews. Raskin's is the only book or article, to my knowledge, that even mentions the existence of the first-strike study, and it does so only briefly. The material here comes from interviews with nine participants and close observers.

300   Nitze Asilomar speech: Nitze, "Power and Policy Problems in the Defense of the West," draft, Apr. 22, 1960, Roswell Gilpatric Papers, Box 8, Changes in DoD Organization 1960–61 folder, JFKL; "multilateralize," pp. 16–17.

300   Nitze Maxwell speech: Nitze, "Political Aspects of National Security," May 24, 1960, lecture, Air War College, Max. AFB.

302   Schelling Berlin game: Material derived from Documents on NATO Planning Conference (code name for the game), Sept. 8–11, 1961 (FOIA/DoD);* Memo to Participants in NATO Planning Conference and attached scenario documents, Sept. 6, 1961, National Security File, Box 82, Germany-Berlin-General, 9/6/61; Memo to Participants in ISA Conference (29 Sept.–1 Oct.), Sept. 27, 1961, National Security File, Box 83, Germany-Berlin-Vol. 5 (Partial); and "ISA Conference, Tentative Time Schedule" and "Brief Scenarios," ibid.; all but FOIA in JFKL; and interviews.

303   the brink and tanks: Slusser, in Force Without War, pp. 427–34.

304   boost by half: Memo from McCone, National Security Files, Box 313, Folder 40, NSC Mtgs., 1962, #507, 10/22/62, JFKL.

304   U.S. military alert steps: Memo, Adam Yarmolinsky, "DoD Operations During the Cuban Missile Crisis," Feb. 12, 1963, National Security File, Box 61, Cuba Testing Tab: OSD & Mil. Responses, JFKL.

304   McNamara, Taylor, invasion, "almost": Minutes, National Security File, Box 315, ExCom Mtgs., #8, 10/27, 4pm, JFKL; and interviews.

305   "I know the Soviet": Quoted in Theodore Sorensen, Oral History Interview, p. 51, JFKL.

305   "It shall be": Quoted in Theodore Sorensen, Kennedy, p. 790.

305   Kremlin first steps after crisis: This interpretation is confirmed by several participants and historians who have had full access to pertinent intelligence files.

306   McNamara 1,400: Cited in memo, BoB, "Minuteman Programs," Aug.

14, 1963, National Security File, Agency File, Box 14–17, Defense Budget, 1965, Sec. 2, LBJL.

21: SHELTER MANIA

307   OCDM plan: Memo, George McGhee to McGeorge Bundy, "Fallout Shelters for Civilians," Feb. 24, 1961, National Security File, Box 295, Folder 1-Civil Defense, 1-3/61, JFKL; memo, Carl Kaysen and Marc Raskin to Bundy, May 16, 1961, pp. 1–2, National Security File, Box 295, Folder 2-Civil Defense, 4-5/17/61, JFKL.

307   Kennedy wary: Memo, Director, BoB (Bell) to Files, "Meeting with the President and Mr. Ellis re Additional Appropriation Requests for FY 1962—OCDM," Mar. 20, 1961, National Security File, Box 83a, Office of Emergency Planning, 1-5/61, JFKL.

307   May 9 meeting: McGeorge Bundy, memo, "Civil Defense Meeting, May 9, 1961," May 13, 1961, National Security File, Box 295, Folder 2-Civil Defense, 4-5/17/61, JFKL.

308   Kaysen article: Kaysen, "The Vulnerability of the United States to Enemy Attack," *World Politics,* Jan. 1954.

308   Raskin opposition: Memos, Raskin (to Bundy), May 19, 1961, Raskin to Bundy, "Civil Defense and Berlin," July 7, 1961, and Oct. 13, 1961, in National Security File, Box 295, Folder 3-Civil Defense, 5/18-5/31/61; Folder 4-Civil Defense, 6/1-7/11/61; Folder 6-Civil Defense, 10/1-10/27/61, JFKL; and interviews.

308   "troublesome": Memo, Kaysen and Raskin to Bundy, May 16, 1961, *ibid.,* Folder 2, pp. 7–8.

308   "from a war": Memo, Kaysen to Bundy, "Berlin Crisis and Civil Defense," July 7, 1961, Appendix, p. 4, National Security File, Box 81, Germany-Berlin-General, 7/7-7/12/61, JFKL; fifteen missiles, p. 2.

308   other questions: *Ibid.;* memo, Kaysen and Raskin to Bundy, *loc. cit.;* and interviews.

309   JFK on civil defense: Theodore Sorensen, Oral History Interview, pp. 7–9, JFKL; and interviews.

309   May 25: Cited in memo, Kaysen to Bundy, July 7, 1961, *op. cit.*

309   July 25 speech: Text in National Security File, Box 82, Germany-Berlin-General, 7/23-7/26/61, JFKL; see p. 4.

310   "I am concerned": Memo, Kennedy to McNamara, Aug. 14, 1961, *ibid.,* 8/11-8/15/61 folder.

310   "I urge you": "Fallout Shelters," *Life,* Sept. 15, 1961, p. 95.

310   *Life* team: Steuart Pittman, Oral History Interview, pp. 10–11, JFKL; and interviews.

310   Yarmolinsky shelter: Adam Yarmolinsky, Oral History Interview, pp. 38–39, JFKL.

310   "the most widely": Memo, Raskin to Bundy, Oct. 17, 1961, National Security File, Box 295, Folder 6, Civil Defense, 10/1-10/27/61, JFKL.

311   "Shelter Living": Quoted in memo, Raskin to Kaysen, Nov. 15, 1961, p. 3, National Security File, Box 295, Folder 8, Civil Defense, 11/13-11/19/61, JFKL.

311   "The communities" and "too facile": Quoted in *ibid.,* p. 4; and interviews.

311   "The anticipation": Quoted in memo, Arthur Schlesinger, Jr., to Kennedy, "Reflections on Civil Defense," Nov. 22, 1961, p. 8, Presidential Office Files, Box 65, Staff Memoranda Arthur Schlesinger folder, JFKL.

311   illustrations: *Ibid.,* p. 3.

311   cabin cruiser: Letter, John Kenneth Galbraith to Kennedy, Nov. 9, 1961,

p. 2, National Security File, Box 295, Folder 7, Civil Defense, 10/28-11/17/61, JFKL.

311   "The present": *Ibid.,* p. 2.
312   "fallout shelters": "Survival: Are Shelters the Answer?," *Newsweek,* Nov. 6, 1961, p. 19.
312   shelter sales: "All Out Against Fallout," *Time,* Aug. 8, 1961, p. 11.
312   clandestine shelters: "Fallout Shelters Speeded by Hundreds in Suburbs, But Families Tend to Keep Plans Secret to Bar Use by Others," *New York Times,* Oct. 3, 1961.
312   Nevada and Riverside: "Survival: Are Shelters the Answer?," *loc. cit.,* p. 19; and memo, Schlesinger to Kennedy, *op. cit.,* p. 3.
312   shoot your neighbors: L. C. McHugh, S. J., "Ethics at the Shelter Doorway," *America,* Sept. 30, 1961.
312   "Everywhere": Memo, Schlesinger to Kennedy, *op. cit.,* pp. 1, 3, 4–5.
312   "Civil Defense": Memo, Sorensen to Kennedy, "Civil Defense," Nov. 23, 1961, *Theodore Sorensen Papers,* Box 30, Civil Defense, JFKL.
313   copies to offices: DoD Release, Dec. 30, 1961, National Security File, Box 295, Folder 11-Civil Defense, 12/61, JFKL.
313   Kennedy TV speech: Sorensen did write a draft, however. See "Civil Defense Fireside Chat—Draft," *Theodore Sorensen Papers, loc. cit.*
313   November 29: Date comes from records of JFK's appointments at JFKL; substance comes from interviews.
314   "I must say": Memo, Bundy to Kennedy, Dec. 1, 1961, National Security File, Box 295, Folder 11-Civil Defense, 12/61, JFKL.
314   Civil defense budget cut: Stanley L. Newman, "Civil Defense and the Congress: Quiet Reversal," *Bulletin of the Atomic Scientists,* Nov. 1962, p. 36.

22:   DAMAGE UNLIMITED

315   "The Air Force": Quoted in DPM, McNamara to Kennedy, "Recommended FY 1964–68 Strategic Retaliatory Forces," Nov. 21, 1962, p. 6 (FOIA/DoD).*
315   "*first,* to provide": *Ibid.,* p. 5;* emphasis added.
315   "may succeed": *Ibid.,* p. 6.*
316   McNamara against full first-strike: DPM, McNamara to Kennedy, Appendix I, "Recommended Long Range Nuclear Delivery Forces 1963–67," Sept. 23, 1961, p. 5 (FOIA/DoD).*
316   three paragraphs: *Ibid.*
316   four pages: DPM, McNamara to Kennedy, Nov. 21, 1962, pp. 7–10.*
316   "We might": *Ibid.,* p. 9.*
316   no longer to cite counterforce: Richard Kugler, "The Politics of Restraint: Robert McNamara and the Strategic Nuclear Forces, 1963–69," Ph.D. dissertation, MIT, 1975, pp. 82–83.
317   "Assured Destruction": DPM, McNamara to Johnson, "Recommended FY 1965–69 Strategic Retaliatory Forces," Dec. 6, 1963, pp. I-5, I-12, I-13 (FOIA/DoD).*
317   30 percent and half: *Ibid.,* p. I-5.*
317   400 megatons: This calculation did not appear until the next year's DPM, but interviews with those involved reveal that it had been done by the time of the 1963 DPM. See DPM, McNamara to Johnson, "Recommended FY 1966–70 Programs for Strategic Offensive Forces, Continental Air and Missile Defense Forces, and Civil Defense," Dec. 3, 1964, p. 11 (FOIA/DoD).* A similar idea appears in the 1963 DPM, p. I-14.*
317   double to 800: DPM, McNamara to Johnson, Dec. 3, 1964, p. 11.*
317   "diminishing marginal returns": *Ibid.;* and Alain Enthoven and K. Wayne Smith, *How Much Is Enough?* (New York: Harper & Row, 1971), p. 207.

318   1,200 megatons: DPM, McNamara to Johnson, Dec. 6, 1963, p. I-12.*
319   "Damage-Limiting": *Ibid.*, p. I-5.*
319   "coercive strategy": *Ibid.*, p. I-20.*
319   "the destructive": *Ibid.*, p. I-12;* emphasis added.
319   numbers and targeting: *Ibid.*, p. I-37.* (Columns labeled Force II are the
        relevant ones; see p. I-15.*)
319   held in reserve: This is specified in DPM, McNamara to Kennedy, Nov.
        21, 1962, p. 15; there is no mention of it in the '63 DPM, though inter-
        views with those involved reveal that the concept remained unchanged.*
320   Soviet SLBMs and hardening: *Ibid.*, pp. 7–8.*
320   "I do not": *Ibid.*, p. 8.*
320   "The prospects": DPM, McNamara to Johnson, Dec. 6, 1963, p. I-6.*
321   twenty-nine graphs and relationship: *Damage Limiting: A Rationale for
        the Allocation of Resources by the U.S. and the U.S.S.R.*, prepared for
        DDR&E, Jan. 21, 1964, especially pp. 3, 4 (FOIA/DoD).
321   difference of 55 or 60 percent: *Ibid.*, p. 48.
321   One plotted the cost: *Ibid.*, Figure 11 and pp. 23–24. That McNamara
        was riveted by the graph was indicated in interviews.
322   second graph: *Ibid.*, Figure 23 and pp. 40–42.
322   "kill probability" =.8: *Ibid.*, p. 8; and interviews.
324   shelters most cost effective: *Ibid.*, pp. 16, 49, 51, Figures 5, 8.
324   McNamara used shelter argument: See DPM, McNamara to Johnson,
        "Recommended FY 1966–70 Programs for Strategic Offensive Forces,
        Continental Air and Missile Defense Forces, and Civil Defense," Dec. 3,
        1964, pp. 21, 35, 65–66 (FOIA/DoD);* and interviews.
324   March 12: *A Summary Study of Strategic Offensive and Defensive Forces
        of the U.S. and U.S.S.R.*, prepared for DDR&E, Sept. 8, 1964, p. 11
        (FOIA/DoD).
324   damage-limiting feasible: *Ibid.*, p. 177.
325   McNamara to Johnson and Bundy: Kugler, *op. cit.*, p. 104.
325   '64 DPM against counterforce, bomber, air defense: DPM, McNamara to
        Johnson, Dec. 3, 1964, pp. 3–6, 12, 14–29, 31–34, 54–58, 63.*
325   1,000 Minutemen: *Ibid.*, pp. 29–30, 44–46.*
325   urban damage not best: *Ibid.*, p. 17.*
325   "fully hardened": *Ibid.*, pp. 46, 48.*
325   "would permit": *Ibid.*, p. 52; *cf.* p. 48;* emphasis added.
326   destroy will, not ability: DPM, McNamara to Kennedy, Nov. 21, 1962, p.
        9.*
326   Enthoven work on Soviet Army: Enthoven and Smith, *op. cit.*, chap. 4;
        and interviews.
327   Kaufmann against battlefield nuclears: He dealt most directly with this
        issue in a notorious review—W. W. Kaufmann, "The Crisis in Military
        Affairs," *World Politics*, Jan. 1958—of Harvard Professor Henry Kis-
        singer's best seller, *Nuclear Weapons and Foreign Policy* (New York:
        Harper & Bros., 1957). Kissinger criticized the Dulles massive-retaliation
        policy, but advocated instead the use of nuclear weapons on the battle-
        field in a war against the U.S.S.R. Kaufmann agreed with Kissinger's
        case against Dulles; indeed, it was essentially derivative of the case made
        earlier by himself and Bernard Brodie. But Kaufmann coolly and devas-
        tatingly ripped Kissinger's other arguments to shreds, pointing out a
        dozen or so internal contradictions. Kaufmann argued, in contradiction
        to Kissinger, that nuclear weapons—even those of very low yield, much
        less the half-megaton monsters that Kissinger deemed permissible for
        battle-zone use—would destroy the territory we were trying to defend.
                Kaufmann thought Kissinger was opportunistic, appearing—in his
        anti-Dulles arguments—to criticize the Eisenhower Administration,
        while in fact telling those officials just what they wanted to hear: that
        their policy of using nuclear weapons in ground wars was intellectually
        respectable. Two years later, when the Democrats seemed bound for vic-

tory in the 1960 election, waving the banner of "flexible response" and stronger conventional forces for NATO, Kissinger wrote another book, *The Necessity for Choice* (New York: Harper & Bros., 1961), renouncing his past optimism about battlefield nuclears and cheering conventional forces after all—prompting Kaufmann, then still at RAND, to compose a satirical ditty titled "I Wonder Who's Kissinger Now."

Kaufmann's point about Kissinger's opportunism—expounded more heavily still in a RAND memo, "Mr. Kissinger Builds His Dreamhouse" (RAND M-4969, Sept. 23, 1957; provided to author)—was probably correct. Kissinger's book was circulated throughout Eisenhower's national security bureaucracy and was much admired, including by Ike himself. (See Memo, Gordon Gray to Andrew Goodpaster, Nov. 20, 1957, White House Central File, Confidential File, Subject Series, Box 7, Atomic Energy & Bomb (10) folder; memo, Eisenhower to Acting Sec. of State, July 31, 1957, Ann Whitman File, DDE Diary Series, Box 25, July 1957, DDE Dictation; both in DDEL.)

327   Kaufmann impact: In 1964, the package of DPMs that McNamara sent to Johnson included, for the first time, a DPM on "Theater Nuclear Forces," which opposed tactical nuclear weapons as substitutes for conventional forces. It was drafted by Kaufmann. (DPM, McNamara to Johnson, "Theater Nuclear Forces," Dec. 1964; also for Oct. 1965, Jan. 1967, Jan. 1968, Jan. 1969; all FOIA/DoD. That Kaufmann wrote them comes from interviews.)

23: VIETNAM: STALEMATE

328   "a willingness": Kahn, *On Thermonuclear War* (Princeton Univ. Press, 1960), p. 566.

328   "means for placing": McGeorge Bundy to McNamara, NSAM #2, Feb. 3, 1961, Collection of NSC Documents, NA/MMB.

328   Taylor as adviser: NSC Action #2407, Apr. 22, 1961, *ibid.*

328   counterinsurgency Vietnam: NSC Action #2411, Apr. 27, 1961, *ibid.*

328   Special Group: NSAM #124, Jan. 18, 1962, *ibid.*

328   "the panhandle": Memo, Rostow to Kennedy, "Southeast Asia," Aug. 4, 1961, National Security File, Box 231a, Regional Security, Southeast Asia, 8/1-8/7/61, JFKL.

329   "we could make": Memo, Rostow to Kennedy, "Southeast Asia," Oct. 5, 1961, National Security File, Regional Security, Southeast Asia, General, 10/1-10/5/61, JFKL.

329   "Nothing is more": Report, Taylor to Kennedy, Nov. 3, 1961, in *Pentagon Papers: The Defense Dept. History of U.S. Decisionmaking on Vietnam,* Senator Gravel Edition, Vol. II (Boston: Beacon Press, 1971), p. 654.

329   targets political and psychological: *Pentagon Papers,* Vol. III, p. 272.

329   "use selected": Memo, Bundy to Johnson, "Basic Recommendation and Projected Course of Action on Southeast Asia," May 25, 1964, National Security File, Aides' File, Box 1, McGeorge Bundy, Memos for President, Vol. 4, LBJL.

329   "kill the hostage": McNamara, Report on Honolulu Meeting, *Pentagon Papers, III,* p. 706.

330   Kaufmann-Schelling-nuclear-Vietnam connection: Thomas Schelling notes the resemblance between his own limited-war theories and the Ann Arbor speech, and also likens them to early Vietnam strategy, in *Arms and Influence* (New Haven: Yale Univ. Press, 1966), pp. 24–26, 154, 162–65, 190–92, 75–76, 79, 83–86, 141*ff.,* 166–76; for Kaufmann statements, see chap. 12.

330   "enlightening similarities": Schelling, *The Strategy of Conflict* (Cambridge/Harvard Univ. Press, 1960), p. v.

331 "non-zero-sum games": *Ibid.*, pp. 83–118.
331 Schelling and arms control: *Ibid.*, pp. 205–229; Schelling and Morton Halperin, *Strategy and Arms Control* (New York: 20th Century Fund, 1961); "Reciprocal Fear," "if the advantage," p. 231, and Chap. 9, *Strategy of Conflict.*
332 "still be capable": Schelling, *Strategy of Conflict,* pp. 252–53.
332 "The power to hurt": Schelling, *Arms and Influence,* pp. v, 2, 3.
332 "War is always": *Ibid.,* p. 142.
332 "the bargaining power": *Ibid.,* p. 31.
333 McNaughton and Test Ban Treaty: David Halberstam, *The Best and the Brightest* (New York: Random House, 1972), p. 442 (paperback ed.).
333 "small, tightly knit": Memo, Bundy to Johnson, "Planning Actions on Southeast Asia," May 22, 1964, National Security File, Aides' File, Box 1, McGeorge Bundy, Memos for President, Vol. 4, LBJL.
333 "use selected": Memo, Bundy to Johnson, May 25, 1964, *ibid.*
333 "we should watch": Memo, McNaughton to McNamara, Sept. 3, 1964, *Pentagon Papers,* III, pp. 558–59.
334 Bien Hoa: *Ibid.,* p. 288.
334 "Option C": *Ibid.,* p. 600.
334 target was the *will: Ibid.,* p. 289.
335 March 2: *Ibid.,* p. 272.
335 "The situation": Memo, McNaughton to McNamara, "Proposed Course of Action Re Vietnam," Mar. 24, 1965, *ibid.*, pp. 694–700.
335 "If anything": *Ibid.,* pp. 352–53.
335 "that it will take": *Ibid.,* p. 706.
336 "almost ineradicable": Reprinted in McNamara, *The Essence of Security* (New York: Harper & Row, 1968), p. 142.
336 "regarded as a test": Memo, McNamara to Johnson, "South Vietnam," Mar. 13, 1964, National Security File, Aides' File, Box 1, McGeorge Bundy, Memos for President, Vol. 2, LBJL.
336 "a gross" and "The United States": McNamara, *The Essence of Security,* p. 148.
336 "to meet": *Ibid.,* pp. 148–49, 150.
336 "Who is man?": *Ibid.,* p. 158.
336 "international": *Ibid.,* p. 144.
336 cool façade crumbled: Henry L. Trewhitt, *McNamara* (New York: Harper & Row, 1971), pp. 230–31.
337 military do productive things: McNamara, *The Essence of Security,* p. 151.
337 landlords, job training: *Ibid.,* pp. 122–40.
337 "McNamara's gone dovish": Trewhitt, *op. cit.,* p. 270.
337 much more satisfying: *Ibid.,* p. 296.
337 Ellsberg and war criminals: See Ellsberg, *Papers on the War* (New York: Simon & Schuster, 1972), pp. 275–309.
337 Pentagon Papers: On the case, see Peter Schrag, *Test of Loyalty* (New York: Simon & Schuster, 1974); Harrison Salisbury, *Without Fear or Favor* (New York: Times Books, 1980).
338 Brodie and France: Letter, Brodie to William Marvel, May 9, 1960, and to Peter Caws, Sept. 17, 1965, both in *Bernard Brodie Papers,* Box 3, Carnegie Corp. folder; and interviews.
338 Gallois position: *E.g.,* Pierre Gallois, *The Balance of Terror* (Boston: Houghton Mifflin, 1961); Raymond Aron, *The Great Debate* (Garden City, New York: Doubleday, 1965), especially Chap. 4; and interviews.
339 only one who had thought about strategy before: Brodie made this point frequently: *e.g.,* Brodie, *The American Scientific Strategists,* RAND P-2979, Oct. 1964; and interviews.
339 envy of Wohlstetter: For sampler, see letter, Brodie to Colin Gray, Aug. 11, 1975, *Bernard Brodie Papers,* Box 8, G folder; see also Brodie, "The

McNamara Phenomenon," *World Politics,* July 1965, a very revealing article, a deprecating review of William Kaufmann's semiofficial chronicle,
The McNamara Strategy (New York: Harper & Row, 1964), a review that
Brodie saw as a major statement separating himself from his former
brethren. He wrote his friend Peter Paret that the review "has been
hanging over my head for months" (*Brodie Papers,* Box 2, P folder), sent
reprints of it to dozens of friends, and told Pierre Gallois, "I think you will
like it because I am mean" (*Brodie Papers,* Box 1, G folder). Kaufmann
personally considered the book a "potboiler . . . about 50% McNamara
and others, and about 50% me" (letter to Brodie, *Brodie Papers,* Box 1, K
folder). That Brodie felt this way in the early 1960s as well is confirmed
by interviews.

339   "between the use": Brodie, *The Meaning of Limited War,* RAND P-1222,
June 10, 1958, p. 19; also in Brodie, *Strategy in the Missile Age* (Princeton Univ. Press, 1959), p. 327.

339   "the idea that": Letter, Brodie to Fred Iklé, *Bernard Brodie Papers,* Box
1, I folder; he made the same point in numerous articles in the mid-
1960s, as cited below.

339   "the significant name": Brodie, "Disarmament Goals and National Security Needs," lecture, Iowa State, Mar. 17, 1960, *Bernard Brodie Papers,*
Box 17.

339   "I think the balance": Brodie, "On Predicting Weapons Systems, Especially Nuclear Strategic Systems," lecture, IIS/CEIP conference, June
17–19, 1970, *Bernard Brodie Papers,* Box 6, last folder.

339   "It may indeed": Brodie, "How Probable Is General War?," *RCAF College
Journal* (1961), in *Bernard Brodie Papers,* Box 10, Shorter Reviews
1944–65 folder; also in "Defense Policy and the Possibility of Total War,"
Daedalus, Fall 1962, p. 741.

339   "Unless we are": Brodie, *Escalation and the Nuclear Option,* RAND
RM-4544-PR, June 1965, p. 38.

340   "Everything we know": Brodie, "What Price Conventional Capabilities in
Europe?," RAND P-2696, Feb. 1963, p. 20; a shortened version appeared
in *The Reporter,* May 23, 1963.

340   "violence between": *Ibid.,* p. 28. *Cf.* pp. 19*ff.;* letter, Brodie to Eugene
Rabinowitch, June 20, 1963, *Bernard Brodie Papers,* Box 1, R folder;
Brodie, *The Political Dimension in National Strategy,* UCLA Security
Studies Paper #13, 1968, p. 40; Brodie, "The Strategic Issue: Has NATO
a Future?," lecture, Aug. 1967, *Brodie Papers,* Box 20, Book Reviews
1966–67; Brodie, "U.S. Strategic Policies," lecture, Mar. 1969, p. 26,
Brodie Papers, Box 6, last file; letter, Brodie to Stansfield Turner, Jan. 16,
1976, *Brodie Papers,* Box 9, T folder.

340   no inclination to invade: Brodie, memo, "Afterthoughts on CWE from
the Meeting (with Herr Erler) of April 16," Apr. 22, 1963, *Bernard Brodie Papers,* Box 18.

340   "tends to displace": Letter, Brodie to Thomas Schelling, Dec. 15, 1964,
Bernard Brodie Papers, Box 2, Schelling folder; *cf.* "What Price Conven-
tional Capabilities in Europe?," pp. 23, 31; *Escalation and the Nuclear
Option,* p. 46.

341   "Thus far": Brodie, *The Absolute Weapon* (New York: Harcourt, Brace,
1946), p. 76. He cites this in his last published article, "The Development of Nuclear Strategy," *International Security,* Spring 1978, p. 65.

341   Vietnam failure: Brodie, "Why Were We So (Strategically) Wrong?,"
Foreign Policy, Winter 1971–72, p. 159; and interviews.

341   "have almost universally": Brodie, "Learning to Fight a Limited War,"
Los Angeles Times, Dec. 3, 1967; and interviews.

341   "It is an old": Brodie, Japan Lecture #7, undelivered, pp. 3, 4, *Bernard
Brodie Papers,* Box 33, folder 7.

342   "simply playing" and "The rigidity": *Ibid.,* p. 6; and interviews.

24: THE ABM DEBATE

343 "of all": In Richard Pfeffer, ed., *No More Vietnams?* (New York: Harper & Row, 1968), pp. 1–6.

343 1946 and 1956 decisions: Fred A. Payne, "A Discussion of Nike-Zeus Decisions," unpublished paper, 1964 (provided to author).

344 "Such a weapon": Memo, W. E. Bradley to Dr. Killian, "Effectiveness of the Nike-Zeus System Against ICBM Attack," Oct. 29, 1958, White House Office file, Office of Special Assistant for Science & Technology, Box 4, AICBM (1), DDEL. Information about RBIG comes from Payne, *op. cit.*, and interviews.

344 "decoys," radar attacks, blackout: Memo, Bradley to Killian, *ibid.*

344 nuclear tests and blackout: James Killian reported this to Eisenhower on Feb. 25, 1958. See A. J. Goodpaster, Memo of Conference, Feb. 25, 1958, Ann Whitman File, DDE Diary Series, Box 30, Staff Notes, Feb. 1958, DDEL; for further detail, see Hans Bethe and Richard Garwin, "Anti-Ballistic-Missile Systems," *Scientific American*, May 1968.

344 PSAC report: "Report of the AICBM Panel," May 21, 1959, White House Office File, Office of Special Assistant for Science & Technology, Box 4, AICBM (1), DDEL; and interviews.

345 Army 7,000 missiles: Memo, Robert McNamara to Kennedy, Appendix II, "Program for Deployment of Nike-Zeus," Sept. 30, 1961, p. 13, National Security File, Box 275, DoD, Defense Budget, FY63, 11-12/61, JFKL.

345 McNamara twelve batteries: *Ibid.*, p. 12.

345 McNamara reasons for limited: *Ibid.*, pp. 2, 9–11. The same points were made in a report otherwise highly critical of Nike-Zeus by McNamara's R&D office, "ODDR&E Assessment of Ballistic Missile Defense Program," Apr. 17, 1961, p. 8 (FOIA/DoD).*

345 Bell memos: Memo, Bell to Kennedy, "FY 1963 Defense Budget Issues," Nov. 13, 1961, pp. 3-1, 3-2, National Security File, Box 275, DoD, Defense Budget, FY63, 11-12/61, JFKL; and interviews.

346 nearly $500 million a year: In 1964, McNamara requested $400 million for FY66 funds for Nike-X R&D; in 1965, he asked for $417 million and in 1966 for $420 million. This was in addition to money for Project Defender, an R&D program to look into technology for more advanced ABMs. Spending on Defender ranged from $113 million in 1961 to $130 million in 1965. On Nike-Zeus funding, see Memo, Cyrus Vance to Johnson, "Summary of Force Structure Changes," Dec. 14, 1964, National Security File, Agency File, Box 11-12, DoD, Vol. II, LBJL; DPM, McNamara to Johnson, "Recommended FY 1967–71 Strategic Offensive and Defensive Forces," Nov. 1, 1965, p. 3 (FOIA/DoD);* DPM, McNamara to Johnson, "Recommended FY68–72 Strategic Offensive and Defensive Forces," Nov. 9, 1966, p. 2 (FOIA/DoD).* On Defender, see memo, David Bell and Jerome Wiesner to McGeorge Bundy, "Request for DX Priority Rating for Project Defender," Sept. 25, 1962, National Security File, Box 339, NSAM 191, JFKL; and DPM, McNamara to Johnson, *op. cit.*, Nov. 1, 1965, p. 37.*

346 December 6 meeting: Edward R. Jayne II, "The ABM Debate: Strategic Defense and National Security," Ph.D. dissertation, MIT, 1969, p. 338.

346 January meeting with science advisers: *Ibid.*, p. 347; Anne Hessing Cahn, "Eggheads and Warheads: Scientists and the ABM," Ph.D. dissertation, MIT, 1971, pp. 38–39. Those present were James Killian, George Kistiakowsky, Jerome Wiesner, Donald Hornig, Herbert York, Harold Brown, John S. Foster, Jr.

347 China rationale: Memo, McNamara to Kennedy, "Program for Deployment of Nike-Zeus," Appendix II, Sept. 30, 1961, National Security File, Box 275, DoD, Defense Budget, FY63, 11-12/61, JFKL; memo, Henry Glass, "Record of Meeting on DoD FY 1967 Budget (Nov. 9, 1965)," Nov. 10, 1965, National Security File, Agency File, Box 14-17, DoD FY67

Budget Book, LBJL; memo, McNamara to Johnson, "Defense Department Budget Issues to Be Raised by the Joint Chiefs," Dec. 9, 1965, National Security File, Agency File, Box 11-12, DoD, Vol. III, LBJL; DPM, McNamara to Johnson, *op. cit.,* Nov. 1, 1965, p. 36 (FOIA/DoD);* memo, McNamara to Johnson, Dec. 13, 1966, Confidential File, Box 69, ND 10 Preparedness, LBJL.

348   San Francisco speech split in book: Robert McNamara, *The Essence of Security* (New York: Harper & Row, 1968), Chap. 4 and Appendix I; and interviews.

348   Wohlstetter China threat: Stanford Research Institute (for Army Deputy C/S, Military Operations), Report to Secretary of Defense, Nike-X Deployment Study, Oct. 1, 1965, Appendix E, Annex 6, "The Question of Bypassing BMD Through Sabotage or Clandestine Delivery," by A. Wohlstetter, p. E-6-5; *cf.* Annex 2 to the same study, "Ballistic Missile Defense and 'Asian Hostages to China,' " by A. Wohlstetter, F. C. Iklé, A. M. Jonas, L. Sloss (FOIA/Army).*

349   Wohlstetter on proliferation: *E.g.,* Wohlstetter, "Nuclear Sharing: NATO and the N+1 Country," *Foreign Affairs,* Apr. 1961; and interviews.

349   Bethe/Garwin article: "Anti-Ballistic-Missile Systems," *Scientific American,* May 1968.

350   scientists had been in PSAC, RBIG: See PSAC, "Report of the AICBM Panel," May 21, 1959, p. 15 for members, White House Office file, Office of Special Assistant for Science & Technology, Box 4, AICBM (1), DDEL. Rathjens, Kistiakowsky and Doty were not on the panel, but all were active in PSAC. They also took part in a PSAC "MIDAS Panel," which also explored ABM technology; see "Ad Hoc Midas Panel," *ibid.,* AICBM (3); and memos, Rathjens, Sept. 9, 1960, Rathjens to Panofsky, Oct. 7, 1960 and Nov. 23, 1960, Bethe to Rathjens, Oct. 26, 1960.

350   scientists testify: See especially Hearings, Senate Foreign Relations Committee, *Strategic and Foreign Policy Implications of ABM Systems,* Pt. I, Mar. 1969; Hearings, Senate Armed Services Committee, *Authorization for Military Procurement & R&D, FY 1970,* Pt. 2, 1969.

350   Nixon Safeguard rationale: John Newhouse, *Cold Dawn: The Story of SALT* (New York: Holt, Rinehart & Winston, 1973), p. 152; and interviews.

350   Bethe on ICBM defense: Hearings, Senate Foreign Relations Committee, *op. cit.,* p. 39.

350   critics on Safeguard: See various testimony in *ibid.* and Hearings, Senate Armed Services Committee, *op. cit.;* and interviews.

351   MRV or MIRV and pressure on CIA: Lawrence Freedman, *U.S. Intelligence and the Soviet Strategic Threat* (Boulder, Colo.: Westview Press, 1977), chap. 8; John Prados, *The Soviet Estimate* (New York: Dial Press, 1982), chap. 13.

351   "defense would be": George Rathjens and Herbert York, "Comments on Safeguard—1970," Apr. 5, 1970, privately distributed, summary p. 1 (provided to author).

352   one-quarter of Minuteman: Rathjens, Hearings, Senate Foreign Relations Committee, *op. cit.,* p. 359; Senate Armed Services Committee, *op. cit.,* p. 1252.

352   Wohlstetter on Rathjens' analysis: Wohlstetter, letter to Sen. John Stennis, May 23, 1969, reprinted in Senate Armed Services Committee, *ibid.,* and see p. 1264.

352   "familiar, well-known": Quoted in Paul Doty, "Can Investigations Improve Scientific Advice? The Case of the ABM," *Minerva,* Apr. 1972, p. 286.

352   Rathjens' reply: *Ibid.;* Senate Armed Services Committee, *op. cit.;* Letter to Editor, *New York Times,* June 15 and 22, 1969; interviews.

353   Wohlstetter battle: See letters between the two, *New York Times,* June 15, 22, 29, 1969.

353 Wohlstetter and ORSA: "Guidelines for the Practice of Operations Research," *Operations Research*, Sept. 1971, pp. 1246, 1248. This entire issue was devoted to the resulting ORSA report.

353 "absurd": Letter, Rathjens, Wiesner and Weinberg to Caywood, Dec. 22, 1969 (provided to author).

353 six-to-five vote: The report and "minority report" are reprinted in *Operations Research, op. cit.*

354 "could actually turn": Laird, Hearings, Senate Armed Services Committee, *Authorization for Military Procurement, R&D, FY71,* Feb., Mar. 1970, pp. 36–37.

354 "The Administration": Rathjens and York, *op. cit.,* p. 1.

354 "bargaining chip": Newhouse, *op. cit.,* pp. 187–88; Gerard Smith, *Doubletalk: The Story of SALT I* (Garden City, N.Y.: Doubleday, 1980), p. 149.

354 narrow margins: On amendments to delete funding of ABM, the vote lost 50–50 in 1969, 47–52 in 1970.

354 ABM Treaty: Text in U.S. Arms Control & Disarmament Agency, *Arms Control & Disarmament Agreements* (Washington, D.C.: Government Printing Office).

355 Rathjens on Wohlstetter's turf: Rathjens later conceded most of the math errors, but noted, "Obviously, my greatest error was in responding, even to the extent I did, to Mr. Wohlstetter's questions and charges, for it is clear that he and the [ORSA] Committee lacked the capacity or inclination or both (a) to understand what I had done, and (b) to discriminate between errors that make a difference and those that do not." G. W. Rathjens, "Errors Made By Me in the ABM Debate," Dec. 7, 1971, privately circulated memo, p. 5 (provided to author).

355 Morse comments: Letter by Philip Morse, *Congressional Record,* Feb. 17, 1972, p. S-1938.

25: THE NEW GENERATION

362 number weapons against air bases: DPM, McNamara to Johnson, "Recommended FY 1965–FY 1969 Strategic Retaliatory Forces," Dec. 6, 1963, p. I-37 (FOIA/DoD).*

362 MIRV space technology: Herbert York, "The Origins of MIRV," *SIPRI Research Report #9* (Stockholm International Peace Research Institute, Aug. 1973), pp. 9–14, 19–20.

363 "I intend": DPM, McNamara to Johnson, "Recommended FY 1966–70 Programs for Strategic Offensive Forces, Continental Air and Missile Defense Forces, and Civil Defense," Dec. 3, 1964, p. 48 (FOIA/DoD).*

363 Minuteman III: DPM, McNamara to Johnson, "Recommended FY67–71 Strategic Offensive and Defensive Forces," Nov. 1, 1965, p. 2 (FOIA/DoD).*

363 "the probability": DPM, McNamara to Johnson, Dec. 3, 1964, p. 48.*

364 "much greater": DPM, McNamara to Johnson, Nov. 1, 1965, p. 34.* See also John Foster, quoted in Ralph E. Lapp, *Arms Beyond Doubt* (New York: Cowles Book Co., 1970), p. 21: Gen. John Ryan, quoted in Philip Karber, "MIRV: Anatomy of an Enigma," *Air Force & Space Digest,* Feb. 1971, p. 83; DoD statement, quoted in Alton Frye, *A Responsible Congress* (New York: McGraw-Hill, 1975), p. 69.

364 "was arrived at": DPM, McNamara to Johnson, "Recommended FY68–72 Strategic Offensive and Defensive Forces," Nov. 9, 1966, p. A-3 (FOIA/DoD).*

364 2,100 Minutemen: Desmond Ball, *Politics and Force Levels* (Berkeley: Univ. of California Press, 1980), p. 192.

365 requires couple of thousand weapons: James Schlesinger, Hearings,

Senate Foreign Relations Committee, *U.S.–U.S.S.R. Strategic Policies,* Mar. 4, 1974, p. 9; and interviews.

365   Enthoven for options: See, *e.g.,* DPM, McNamara to Johnson, "Strategic Offensive and Defensive Forces," January 15, 1968, pp. 6, 9 (FOIA/DoD).*

366   "reviewing our military": Memo, Henry Kissinger to Secretaries of State and Defense and Director of Central Intelligence, Jan. 23, 1969 (provided to author).

366   "Up to now": NSSM-3, revised version, May 8, 1969 (provided to author).

367   "Should a President": Richard Nixon, Report to Congress, *U.S. Foreign Policy for the 1970s: A New Strategy for Peace,* Feb. 18, 1970, p. 122.

370   "a more flexible": NSDM-242, Jan. 17, 1974 (provided to author).

373   "change in targeting": "Remarks by Secretary of Defense James R. Schlesinger, Overseas Writers Association Luncheon, International Club, Washington, D.C., Thursday, January 10, 1974," DoD Public Affairs Office, pp. 5, 6.

374   "The Soviet Union": Schlesinger, *Annual Defense Department Report, FY 1975,* p. 4; that Kaufmann wrote it comes from interviews.

375   different trajectory, different error: It was with this in mind that Schlesinger testified before Congress in 1974:

   "I believe that there is some misunderstanding about the degree of reliability and accuracy of missiles. . . . [I] t is impossible for either side to acquire the degree of accuracy that would give them a high confidence first-strike because we will not know what the actual accuracy will be like in a real-world context.

   "As you know, we have acquired from the western test range a fairly precise accuracy, but in the real world we would have to fly from operational bases to targets in the Soviet Union. The parameters of the flight from the western test range are not really very helpful in determining those accuracies to the Soviet Union.

   "We can never know what degrees of accuracy would be achieved in the real world. . . .

   ". . . if you have any degradation in operational accuracy . . . counterforce capability goes to the dogs very rapidly.

   "We know that and the Soviets should know it, and that is one of the reasons that I can publicly state that neither side can acquire a high confidence first-strike capability."

   (Hearings, Senate Foreign Relations Committee, *U.S.–U.S.S.R. Strategic Policies,* March 4, 1974, pp. 15–17.)

375   "fratricide": Schlesinger, *Annual Defense Department Report, FY 1976 and 197T,* p. I-14; see also John Steinbruner and Thomas Garwin, "Strategic Vulnerability: The Balance Between Prudence and Paranoia," *International Security,* Summer 1976.

376   "flexibility": Schlesinger, Hearings, Senate Foreign Relations Committee, *op. cit.,* pp. 7, 9.

376   framework of response to Soviets: *Ibid.,* pp. 7, 18; Hearings, Senate Foreign Relations Committee, *Nuclear Weapons and Foreign Policy,* Mar. and Apr. 1974, p. 192; Schlesinger, *Annual Defense Department Report, FY 1975,* pp. 4, 6, 28; *FY 1976 and 197T,* pp. I-13, 16, II-4, 5; and interviews.

376   "perceptions": Schlesinger, *Annual Defense Department Report, FY 1975,* p. 28; *FY 1976 and 197T,* p. II-8; and interviews.

377   allies had no such perceptions: Lynn Etheridge Davis, "Limited Nuclear Options: Deterrence and the New American Doctrine," *Adelphi Paper #121* (London: International Institute for Strategic Studies, Winter 1975–76), pp. 11–13.

377   "to pursue": Nitze, "Assuring Strategic Stability in an Era of Détente," *Foreign Affairs,* Jan. 1976, p. 207.

377   "three or four": *Ibid.*, p. 212.
378   American fatalities: The analysis was done for the Senate by the Office of Technology Assessment in response to a claim by Schlesinger that as few as 25,000 Americans might be killed by a Soviet counterforce attack. Schlesinger estimate: Hearing, Senate Foreign Relations Committee, *U.S.–U.S.S.R. Strategic Policies,* p. 19. OTA estimate: Report for Senate Foreign Relations Committee, *Analyses of Effects of Limited Nuclear Warfare,* Sept. 1975; *cf.* OTA, *The Effects of Nuclear War,* June 1979, especially pp. 85–86.
378   Soviet civil defense: An unclassified summary of an extensive CIA study on the Soviet program concluded: "We do not believe that the Soviets' present civil defenses would embolden them deliberately to expose the U.S.S.R. to a higher risk of nuclear attack." (CIA, "Soviet Civil Defense," July 1978.) For other skeptical assessments, see Rep. Les Aspin, "The Mineshaft Gap Revisited," *Congressional Record,* January 15, 1979; Fred Kaplan, "The Soviet Civil Defense Myth—Parts I and II," *Bulletin of the Atomic Scientists,* Apr. and May 1978.
379   T. K. Jones assistance: Nitze, *op. cit.,* p. 225. Jones later gained notoriety for claiming that 97 percent of the Soviet population could survive nuclear war, and so could we with enough dirt and shovels. See Jones, Hearings, Joint Committee on Defense Production, *Defense Industrial Base: Industrial Preparedness and Nuclear War Survival,* Pt. I, Nov. 17, 1976; Robert Scheer, interview with T. K. Jones, *Los Angeles Times,* Jan. 16, 1982.
379   graphs: Nitze, *op. cit.,* pp. 224, 225; Nitze, "Deterring Our Deterrent," *Foreign Policy,* Winter 1976–77, pp. 201–03.
379   Committee on the Present Danger: William Delaney, "Trying to Awaken Us to Russia's 'Present Danger,'" *Washington Star,* Apr. 4, 1977; Jerry Wayne Sanders, "Peddlers of Crisis: The Committee on the Present Danger and the Legitimation of Containment Militarism in the Korean War and Post–Vietnam Periods," Ph.D. dissertation, Univ. of California, Berkeley, 1980, pt. 2.
380   $750 each: Public Records, U.S. Federal Election Commission, Washington, D.C.
380   "principal threat": Committee on the Present Danger, "Common Sense and the Common Danger," pamphlet, Nov. 1976.
382   "bomb-damage computer": An example is D. C. Kephart, *Damage Probability Computer for Point Targets with P and Q Vulnerability Numbers,* RAND R-1380-PR, Feb. 1974.
382   "only deterrence": Brown, "Strategic Force Structure and Strategic Arms Limitation," Mar. 1975, reprinted in Hearings, Joint Committee on Defense Production, *Civil Preparedness and Limited Nuclear War,* Apr. 28, 1976, p. 130.
383   "it would be": Brown, Hearings, Senate Foreign Relations Committee, *The SALT II Treaty,* Pt. 1, July 1979, p. 113.
383   PD-18: Desmond Ball, "Counterforce Targeting: How New? How Viable?," *Arms Control Today,* Feb. 1981, p. 2.
383   PD-59: *Ibid.* PD-59 received enormous attention in the press, but nearly everyone treated it as a completely new departure from the so-called American strategy of assured destruction. For an account of this, see Fred Kaplan, "Going Native Without a Field Map: The Press Embraces Limited Nuclear War," *Columbia Journalism Review,* Jan./Feb. 1981.
383   communications vulnerability: See Desmond Ball, "Can Nuclear War Be Controlled?" *Adelphi Paper #169* (London: International Institute for Strategic Studies, Fall 1981); William J. Broad, "Nuclear Pulse—Parts I, II, III," *Science,* May 29, June 5 and 12, 1981; Broad, "A Fatal Flaw in the Concept of Space War," *Science,* Mar. 12, 1982.

26:   DANCING IN THE DARK

385   200 MX missiles and shell game: See Harold Brown, DoD, *Annual Report, Fiscal Year 1981,* Jan. 29, 1980, pp. 127–30.
385   "My own view": *Ibid.,* p. 67.
386   despite reservations: It should be noted that, after quitting the Pentagon in 1980, William Kaufmann, once again let out of the nuclear-strategy pit, started to express reservations himself about the practicality of war-fighting theories. See especially Kaufmann, "The Defense Budget," in Joseph Pechman, ed., *Setting National Priorities: The 1983 Budget* (Washington, D.C.: Brookings Institution, 1982); and Kaufmann, quoted in Fred Kaplan, "Nuclear War Strategy Not New—Or Practical," *Boston Globe,* June 13, 1982.
386   Thirty-two members: Information from Committee on the Present Danger, Washington, D.C.
387   criticism of MX basing plan: Reagan scrapped the multiple-shelter plan after taking office, partly because it was Carter's plan and he had campaigned vigorously against Carter's defense program; partly because his good friend Sen. Paul Laxalt of Nevada pressured Reagan to drop it after learning that the residents of Nevada, where many MX missiles would be based, did not want it there; partly because Defense Secretary Weinberger realized the obvious, that even with 4,600 shelters, the Soviets could build enough warheads to destroy each shelter. After many starts and stops, Reagan settled on a plan called "Dense-Pack" or "Closely Spaced Basing," in which 100 MX missiles would be put in "super-hardened" shelters spaced very closely together, so close that the attacking Soviet warheads would have to re-enter the atmosphere along a very narrow corridor of sky. The effects of "fratricide"—the first warhead killing its brother warheads through its radioactive debris, blast and wind velocity—would prevent all the other warheads from destroying the MX silos. By late 1982, many officials were beginning to see serious problems with this plan as well, and it was unclear whether yet another basing plan would have to be proposed or even whether—but only because a "survivable" basing plan seemed impractical—Congress would allow the MX to be built in large numbers.
387   "Defense Guidance": Richard Halloran, "Pentagon Draws Up First Strategy for Fighting a Long Nuclear War," *New York Times,* May 30, 1982.
387   Perle and Wohlstetter: Robert Kaiser, "Senate Staffer Richard Perle: Behind-Scenes Power Over Arms Policy," *Washington Post,* June 26, 1977; and interviews.
388   "dig a hole": Jones, quoted in Robert Scheer, interview with T. K. Jones, *Los Angeles Times,* Jan. 16, 1982.
388   Haig and "demonstration": Haig, Hearings, Senate Foreign Relations Committee, *Strategic Weapons Proposals,* Pt. 1, Nov. 4, 1981, p. 74.
388   Reagan and Bush on war-fighting: Reagan, press conference, Oct. 16, 1981; Robert Scheer, interview with George Bush, *Los Angeles Times,* Jan. 24, 1980.
389   Reagan defense budget: Caspar Weinberger, DoD, *Annual Report to the Congress, FY 1983,* Feb. 8, 1982; Ronald Reagan, White House press conference, Oct. 2, 1981.
389   Carter started most of the programs: See Harold Brown, *op. cit.,* pp. 123–50.
390   "Everything about": Brodie, *The Absolute Weapon* (New York: Harcourt, Brace, 1946), p. 52.

INTERVIEWS

(Not including telephone calls or correspondence, unless they were the only form of communication.)

DAVID AARON. New York City, July 10, 1981.
GEN. ANDREW B. ANDERSON. Washington, D.C., September 2, 1981.
GEN. DEWITT ARMSTRONG. Washington, D.C., October 15, 1981.
KENNETH ARROW. Palo Alto, Cal., June 12, 1981.
LOUIS AUCHINCLOSS. New York City, July 29, 1981.
BRUNO AUGENSTEIN. Santa Monica, Cal., December 22, 1980.
ED BARLOW. Stanford, Cal., December 11, 1980.
DAVID BELL. New York City, August 5, 1981.
GEN. LESLIE W. BRAY. Arlington, Va., August 20, 1981.
BRUCE BRODIE. Century City, Cal., June 16, 1981.
FAWN BRODIE. Pacific Palisades, Cal., August 28, 1980.
HAROLD BROWN. Washington, D.C., November 13, 1981.
MCGEORGE BUNDY. New York City, May 4, 1981.
WILLIAM BUNDY. New York City, February 10, 1981.
GEN. DAVID BURCHINAL. Doylestown, Pa., August 13, 1981.
ADM. ARLEIGH BURKE. Bethesda, Md., November 13, 1980.
FRANCIS COLLBOHM. Palm Desert, Cal., December 27, 1980.
GEORGE CONTOS. Washington, D.C., February 26, 1981.
JOHN COYLE. Washington, D.C., April 6, 1981.
NORMAN DALKEY. Los Angeles, Cal., December 18, 1980.
W. PHILIP DAVISON. New York City, October 12, 1981.
JAMES DIGBY. Santa Monica, Cal., June 18, 1981.
PAUL DOTY. Cambridge, Mass., May 6, 1981.
GEN. RUSSELL DOUGHERTY. Washington, D.C., September 2, 1981.
SIDNEY DRELL. Palo Alto, Cal., June 10, 1981.
GEN. RICHARD H. ELLIS. McLean, Va., January 5, 1982.
DANIEL ELLSBERG. Stinson Beach, Cal., September 3, 1980; Washington, D.C., October 17, 1980.
ALAIN ENTHOVEN. Palo Alto, Cal., September 2, December 12, 1980; June 10, 1981.
FRITZ ERMARTH. Washington, D.C., September 8, 1981.
HUGH EVERETT. Arlington, Va., February 4, 1981.
JACK EVERNDON. Palo Alto, Cal., June 11, 1981.
JAMES FOSTER. Santa Monica, Cal., August 25, 1980.
JOHN S. FOSTER, JR. Washington, D.C., November 3, 1981.
RICHARD B. FOSTER. Arlington, Va., June 1, July 2, 1981.
WILLIAM C. FOSTER. Washington, D.C., October 21, 1981.
WILLIAM T. R. FOX. New York City, August 5, 1981.
ALTON FRYE. Washington, D.C., April 7, 1981.

RICHARD FRYKLUND. Washington, D.C., October 20, 1980.
GEN. PIERRE M. GALLOIS. Paris, France (correspondence), November 24, 1981.
RAYMOND GARTHOFF. Washington, D.C., November 20, 1980.
THOMAS S. GATES, JR. Devon, Pa., November 1, 1981.
GEN. JAMES GAVIN. Boston, Mass., May 6, 1981.
LESLIE GELB. Washington, D.C., March 9, 1981.
ALEXANDER GEORGE. Stanford, Cal. (telephone conv.), September 4, 1980.
ROSWELL GILPATRIC. New York City, July 29, 1981.
GEN. ROBERT N. GINSBURGH. Chevy Chase, Md., August 24, 1981.
ALFRED GOLDBERG. Washington, D.C., August 15, 1980.
MARV GOLDBERGER. Pasadena, Cal., June 19, 1981.
WILLIAM T. GOLDEN. New York City, August 4, 1981.
GEN. ANDREW GOODPASTER. Alexandria, Va., October 27, 1981.
MORTON HALPERIN. Washington, D.C., August 7, 1980; May 14, 1981.
BROWNLEE HAYDON. Los Angeles, Cal., August 26, 1980.
OLAF HELMER. Carmel, Cal. (telephone conv.), September 16, 1981.
DIERDRE HENDERSON. Cambridge, Mass., November 8, 1980.
ROLAND HERBST. Marina del Rey, Cal., June 17, 1981.
ALBERT HILL. Cambridge, Mass., November 7, 1980.
ROGER HILSMAN. New York City (telephone conv.), October 19, 1981.
CHARLES J. HITCH, Berkeley, Cal., September 5, December 11, 1980.
MALCOLM HOAG. Santa Monica, Cal., August 19, 1980.
FRANCIS HOEBER. Arlington, Va., July 22, August 10, 1981.
FREDERIC S. HOFFMAN. Santa Monica, Cal., August 18, 1980; June 15, 1981.
TOWNSEND HOOPES. Washington, D.C., April 27, 1981.
ARNOLD HORELICK. Santa Monica, Cal., December 23, 1981.
MICHAEL INTRILLIGATOR. Los Angeles, Cal., August 22, 1980.
GEN. WILLIAM JONES. Santa Monica, Cal., August 19, 1980; June 15, 1981.
HERMAN KAHN. Croton-on-Hudson, N.Y., February 6, August 4, 1981.
MORTON KAPLAN. Chicago, Ill., April 24, 1981.
AMROM KATZ. Los Angeles, Cal., December 15, 1980.
WILLIAM W. KAUFMANN. Washington, D.C., July 15, 1980, September 29, 1981; Cambridge, Mass., November 4, 1980, May 7, 1981.
CARL KAYSEN. Cambridge, Mass., November 4, 1980; May 5, 1981.
SPURGEON KEENY. Washington, D.C., January 22, September 17, 1981.
KONRAD KELLEN. Santa Monica, Cal., June 17, June 18, 1981.
GEN. GLENN KENT. Arlington, Va., October 10, 1980; August 14, 1981.
JAMES KILLIAN. Cambridge, Mass., October 29, 1980.
GEN. ROBERT KILMARX. Washington, D.C., May 11, 1981.
JAMES KING. McLean, Va., July 17, 1980.
WILLIAM KINTNER. Philadelphia, Pa., August 13, 1981.
GEORGE KISTIAKOWSKY. Cambridge, Mass., November 5, 1980.
KLAUS KNORR. McLean, Va., July 31, 1980.
ROMAN KOLKOWICZ. Los Angeles, Cal., August 29, 1980.
ALBERT LATTER. Marina del Rey, Cal., December 18, 1980.
RICHARD LATTER. Marina del Rey, Cal., June 15, 1981.
NATHAN LEITES. Santa Monica, Cal., December 15, 1980.
GEN. CURTIS E. LEMAY. Newport Beach, Cal., June 16, 1981.
GEN. LYMAN LEMNITZER. Washington, D.C., December 3, 1981.

JAN LODAL. Arlington, Va., October 15, 1980.
JOSEPH E. LOFTUS. Pacific Palisades, Cal., June 17, 1981.
ROBERT J. LUTZ. Rancho Bernardo, Cal., June 21, 1981.
LAURENCE E. LYNN. Cambridge, Mass., October 29, 1980; May 5, 1981.
ANDREW MARSHALL. Washington, D.C., February 11, July 28, 1981.
JAMES MARTIN. Alexandria, Va., January 26, 1981.
DAVID McGARVEY. Santa Monica, Cal., August 20, 1980.
ROBERT S. McNAMARA. Washington, D.C., July 24, 1981; January 18, 1982.
ADM. GERALD MILLER. Fairfax, Va., May 13, 1981.
WILLIAM MILLER. Washington, D.C., June 1, 1981.
ROGER MOLANDER. Washington, D.C., November 18, 1980.
RUSSELL E. MURRAY II. Washington, D.C., January 28, 1981.
WILLIAM NISKANEN. Los Angeles, Cal., December 15, 1980.
PAUL H. NITZE. Arlington, Va., July 23, 1981.
PHILIP A. ODEEN. Washington, D.C., July 1, 1981.
WOLFGANG PANOFSKY. Palo Alto, Cal., June 10, 1981.
PETER PARET. Palo Alto, Cal., December 12, 1980.
GEN. NOEL PARRISH. Alexandria, Va., October 10, 1980.
ERNST PLESSET. Woodside, Cal., June 12, 1981.
GEORGE PUGH. Arlington, Va., March 13, 1981.
EDWARD S. QUADE. Los Angeles, Cal., December 19, 1980.
MARCUS G. RASKIN. Washington, D.C., November 25, 1980.
GEORGE W. RATHJENS. Cambridge, Mass., November 5, 1980.
JOEL RESNICK. McLean, Va., March 6, 1981.
GEN. ROBERT RICHARDSON. Washington, D.C., April 1, 1981.
LEO ROSTEN. New York City, September 21, 1981.
WALT W. ROSTOW. Austin, Tex., June 9, 1981.
HENRY S. ROWEN. Palo Alto, Cal., September 2, December 12, 1980.
JOHN RUBEL. Los Angeles, Cal., December 27, 1981.
JACK P. RUINA. Cambridge, Mass., November 8, 1980.
DONALD RUMSFELD. Chicago, Ill., April 24, 1981.
ANTHONY RUSSO. Los Angeles, Cal., June 18, 1981.
WILLIAM SCHAUB. Bethesda, Md., March 18, 1981.
THOMAS C. SCHELLING. Cambridge, Mass., October 27, 1980; May 5, 1981.
JAMES R. SCHLESINGER. Washington, D.C., February 12, 1982.
GEN. BERNARD SCHRIEVER. Washington, D.C., September 30, 1981.
HY SCHULMAN, Santa Monica, Cal. (telephone conv.), May 7, 1982.
DIETER SCHWEBS. Arlington, Va., March 9, 1981.
HERBERT SCOVILLE, Jr. McLean, Va., February 3, 1981.
IVAN SELIN. Arlington, Va., October 9, 1980.
WILLIS SHAPLEY. Washington, D.C., June 3, 1981.
GUS SHUBERT. Santa Monica, Cal., December 16, 1980; June 22, 1981.
LEON SLOSS. Arlington, Va., January 21, 1981.
K. WAYNE SMITH. Washington, D.C., August 27, 1981.
LEVERING SMITH. Arlington, Va., August 10, 1981.
THEODORE C. SORENSEN. New York City, February 9, 1981.
ROBERT D. SPECHT. Los Angeles, Cal., December 17, 1980.
HANS SPEIER. Hartsdale, N.Y., August 18, 1981.
ROBERT C. SPRAGUE. North Adams, Mass., November 23, 1981.
PIERRE M. SPREY. Glen Dale, Md., October 7, 1980.
ELMER STAATS. Washington, D.C., March 11, 1981.

JOHN D. STEINBRUNER. Washington, D.C., March 3, 1981.
MARVIN STERN. Los Angeles, Cal., August 24, 1980.
SAYRE STEVENS. Bethesda, Md., November 9, 1981.
HOWARD STOERTZ, JR. Herndon, Va., December 1, 1981.
GEORGE TANHAM. Washington, D.C., July 7, 1981.
GEN. MAXWELL TAYLOR. Washington, D.C., February 23, 1981.
FRANK TRINKL. Berkeley, Cal., September 4, December 11, 1980.
JAMES WADE. Washington, D.C., July 21, 1981.
PAUL WARNKE. Washington, D.C., August 24, 1981.
PAUL WEIDLINGER. New York City, February 9, 1981.
MILTON WEINER. Santa Monica, Cal., December 16, 1980.
SEYMOUR WEISS. Bethesda, Md., April 3, 1981.
GEN. JASPER WELCH. Washington, D.C., April 9, 1981.
ROBERT WIESER. Huntington Beach, Cal., June 22, 1981.
PETER A. WILSON. Arlington, Va., August 11, 1981.
ALBERT J. WOHLSTETTER. Los Angeles, Cal., August 23, December 28,
    1980; June 20, 1981.
ROBERTA WOHLSTETTER. Los Angeles, Cal., June 20, 1981.
COL. THOMAS W. WOLFE. Falls Church, Va., December 9, 1981.
ARCHIE WOOD. Falls Church, Va., November 21, 1980.
ADAM YARMOLINSKY. Washington, D.C., August 14, 1980.
HERBERT F. YORK. LaJolla, Cal., December 24, 1980.
GEN. RICHARD YUDKIN. Washington, D.C., February 3, 1982.
CIRRO ZOPPO. Santa Monica, Cal., December 22, 1980.
EUGENE ZUCKERT. Washington, D.C., February 24, 1981.

ACKNOWLEDGMENTS

A book like this could not have been nearly so complete as it is were it not for the mountains of pertinent documents that have been declassified only in the past few years. For guiding me through many of them, I thank the wonderful staffs at the archival libraries where I spent months engrossed in boxes, files and folders—the John F. Kennedy, Dwight D. Eisenhower, Lyndon B. Johnson and Harry S. Truman Presidential Libraries in Dorchester, Mass., Abilene, Kans., Austin, Tex., and Independence, Mo., respectively; the Modern Military Branch of the National Archives, the Manuscripts Division of the Library of Congress, and the Naval Historical Center at the Navy Yard in Washington, D.C.; and the Simpson Historical Research Center at Maxwell Air Force Base in Montgomery, Ala. I also thank the talented archivists at the Special Collection Libraries at the University of Chicago and UCLA, the Sterling Library at Yale University, the Mudd Library at Princeton University, the Archives Library at City College of New York, and the Oral History Project at Columbia University. I also thank those who allowed me to look at personal papers for which I needed permission to do so—Admiral Arleigh Burke, General Curtis LeMay, Adam Yarmolinsky and, for letting me quote from the papers of their late husbands, Mrs. Edward Mead Earle and Mrs. Quincy Wright.

I especially thank John Knowlton at the Library of Congress, who helped to declassify—at my request—thousands of documents in the papers of the Air Force Chiefs of Staff (Generals Hoyt Vandenberg, Nathan Twining, Thomas White and Curtis LeMay). Equally valuable were the SIOP files in the papers of Admiral Arleigh Burke at the Navy Yard in Washington, which also appear declassified here for the first time. Without these collections, much of the material on Air Force politics and practically the entire section in Chapter 18 on the SIOP, the integrated nuclear war plan of the U.S. military, simply could not have been written.

I thank the officials in the Pentagon's Freedom of Information Office, especially Charles Hinkle and Major Henry McIntyre (Office of Secretary of Defense) and Ann Wilkinson (Air Force). Although many of my requests for material were denied, they did succeed in declassifying dozens of valuable documents, most importantly the entire set of Draft Presidential Memorandums (DPMs) on strategic and theater nuclear forces signed by former Defense Secretary Robert McNamara from 1961 to 1969. These once–Top Secret papers provide a new perspective, quite different from the one publicly disseminated and popularly believed, on the evolution of "the McNamara strategy." I thank, as well, those, whom I must for obvious reasons leave nameless, who gave me copies of documents not yet declassified.

Just as important as the documents, often more so, were the interviews that I conducted with 160 characters and close observers of this story; their names are listed after the Notes. Interviews lasted from twenty minutes to twelve hours, with most ranging from two to four hours. With few exceptions, the people involved welcomed me into their homes or offices, graciously answered all the questions they could, sometimes fed me dinner or lunch or both, supplied me with valuable information, tolerated my repeated phone calls or letters or return visits that pestered them for more, and in some cases speculated with me on the larger issues, guiding me to novel perspectives and connections that I sometimes accepted, sometimes rejected, but always found stimulating.

I also thank a few other students and scholars of strategy—Desmond Ball, Kevin Lewis, Mark Lorell and David Alan Rosenberg—for extremely useful conversations and occasional exchanges of documents. And I thank the Books and Magazines Division of Air Force Public Affairs for miscellaneous assistance.

I was fortunate enough to have friends who could give me bed and board in almost every city that I had to visit in the course of my research, some of them putting me up for days or weeks at a time and on several occasions. For making my travels much more pleasant, I warmly thank David and JoAnn Braff, Andrew and Leslie (and Chloe) Cockburn, Darby and Steven Dizard, Diane Eisenberg, Steven Freeman, George Giles, Lisa and Stacey Gladstone, Karen Goldberg, Lenny Gordon, Gary and JoAnn Kaplan, Peter Kurth, Lori Lefkovitz, Nicholas Lemann, Kevin Lewis, Donald Margulies, Terry Murray, Robin Netzer, Mark Paul, Carolyn

Skorneck, Karen Trott, Judith and Kosta Tsipis, and Mary Williams.

I must also thank the four professors at the Massachusetts Institute of Technology, where I happily attended graduate school in political science, who first plunged me into the bizarre discourse on nuclear strategy: William Kaufmann, George Rathjens, Jack Ruina and Kosta Tsipis. Kaufmann plays a major role in this book, Rathjens and Ruina minor ones; I hope that my respect for them has not tarnished the objectivity with which I have tried to tell the story of which they are a part.

Many long months went into the writing of this book, and I am forever indebted to those who helped along the way. My literary agent, Raphael Sagalyn, perused the entire manuscript, offering friendly encouragement and cogent criticism at every step, dispelling every nasty stereotype I once held of agents. Jonathan Coleman provided crucial support at an early stage of the project. My editor, Alice Mayhew, and her assistant, David Masello, cleaned up the manuscript with exceptional intelligence, insight and care. Later on, the copyeditor, Patricia Miller, checked facts and consistency with impressive diligence. Throughout, many friends listened to my tales from the typewriter with welcome patience and convincing fascination. And for all that and much more, I thank Brooke Gladstone, best friend, wise counsel, sharp eye and sensitive ear, who was always there to show me the other half of the sky.

FRED KAPLAN
Washington, D.C.
November 1982

INDEX

Aaron, David, 370–72
ABM (anti-ballistic missile), 234,
    320–24, 343–55
  Chinese A-bomb as rationale for,
      347–48
  defeat of, 344
  development of, 343–44
  futility of, 322, 347
  and McNamara, 345, 346–48
  national debate over, 349–55
  Nike-X missile, 345–48
  Nike-Zeus missile, 343–45
  operations research and, 353–54
  opposition to, 349–50
  Safeguard missile, 350–55
  as SALT bargaining chip, 354
  Sentinel missile, 350
  Spartan/Sprint missile, 345
  Wohlstetter/Rathjens debate on,
      351–55
ABM Treaty (1972), 354
Absolute Weapon, The (Yale Institute
    of International Studies), 29–32,
    34, 47, 85, 190, 235, 259, 340–41,
    371
Acheson, Dean, 82, 137–40, 183, 387
  in Cuban missile crisis, 305
  militaristic views of, 139
  in 1961 Berlin crisis, 293–94, 299,
      301
  on NSC-68, 140
Agnew, Harold, 362
Air Force, U.S., 10, 40, 44–45, 85,
    103–6
  Atlas program accelerated by, 116
  city destruction policy as weakness
      of, 236–37
  coercive strategy revived by,
      356–60
  counterforce strategy and, 245,
      315–16
  early planning in, 40
  first-strike capability and, 331
  hardened shelters resisted by, 167
  Kaufmann monograph and, 195
  MIRV deployment by, 364
  MX proposed by, 385

  Navy rivalry with, 232–46
  NU-OPTS strategy studied by,
      358–59
  SIOP and, 263–69
  see also Strategic Air Command,
      U.S.
Air Force Development Planning Of-
    fice, 115
Air Force Intelligence, 41–42, 109
  on Bison bomber production,
      156–60
  budgetary pressure on, 160–61
  CIA estimates challenged by,
      159–60
  civilians vs. military in, 212
  Discoverer photos and, 287–88
  end of deterrence predicted by,
      155
  Soviet air base data collection by,
      209–11
  Soviet missile force estimated by,
      161–66, 168, 242, 287–88
  Target Programs office of, 209–12
Air Force Project RAND, 56, 59–61,
    62
Air Force Scientific Advisory Board,
    114–16
Albania, 271–72
America (magazine), 312
America's Strategy in World Politics
    (Spykman), 20
Anderson, Orvil, 35
Annals of Mathematics Studies, The,
    91
Arms and Influence (Schelling), 332
arms control, 27–29, 32, 313n, 331,
    381n
arms race:
  counterforce targeting and, 244
  NAVWAG on, 234–35
  Prisoner's Dilemma and, 66–67
  size of forces and, 234
Armstrong, DeWitt, 296, 302–3
Armstrong, Hamilton, 171
Army, U.S.:
  atomic weapons downplayed by,
      182

conventional defense favored by,
  194–97
Kaufmann monograph and, 194–97
Nike-Zeus supported by, 345
on Soviet ground power, 182
on Soviet ICBM estimates, 288
Army Air Force, U.S., 36
  OR in, 52, 54, 56–61
Army Intelligence, 159, 165–66, 242
Arnold, Henry "Hap," 43, 54–61,
  111–12
Aron, Raymond, 338, 340
Arrow, Kenneth, 91
Assured-Destruction strategy:
  as deterrence strategy, 317
  development of, 317
  military weapons requests and, 318
ATD-751, 210–11
Atlas Missile Project, 111–16
  accuracy requirement for, 112–14,
    116
  Convair requirements for, 112–13
  projected deployment of, 155
atomic bomb:
  as absolute weapon, 29
  defenses against, 25–26
  diminishing returns from, 31, 108
  naval strategy and, 25–26
  number and use of, 34–38, 46–48
  political implications of, 26
  protection of, 31–32, 47
  strategic consequences of, 25–27,
    30–38
  surprise attacks and, 27
  target selection for, see targeting
    strategy
  wars shortened by, 25
  see also nuclear weapons; strategy,
    nuclear
Atomic Bomb and American Security,
  The (Brodie), 27, 30
Atomic Energy Commission (AEC),
  82, 84
Atwood, Harry, 54–55
Augenstein, Bruno, 112–16, 237
Aurand, E. P., 268

B-1 bomber, 389
B-29 Special Bombardment Project, 57
B-36 bomber, 232–33
B-47 bomber, 255
B-52 bomber, 106, 255
Baldwin, Hanson, 34
Barlow, Ed, 208, 216
basing, bomber:
  Ad Hoc Committee recommenda-
    tions on, 105–6
  location dilemma in, 90–91, 97–102
  post-strike support from, 107

Soviet H-bomb and, 105–6
  vulnerability in, 86, 92–94, 97–102
Baxter, James Phinney, III, 128–29,
  136
Beaufre, André, 284, 338, 340
Bell, David, 254, 345
Berlin airlift (1948), 291
Berlin crisis (1958–59), 291–92
Berlin crisis (1961), 293–304, 378
  allied responses planned in, 302–3
  Berlin Wall begun in, 298
  border crossings closed in, 303
  civil defense and, 309
  ending of, 303–4
  mobilization plans ordered in,
    297–98
  nuclear war as option in, 298–301,
    304
  Soviet conventional force advantage
    in, 295
  U.S. contingency plan for, 299–301
  U.S. simulation war game on,
    301–2
Bethe, Hans, 220, 344–45, 349
Bison bomber, 156–60
Blackett, P. M. S., 52–53
bomber gap, 155–61
bombers:
  air-defense system for, 322
  intercontinental, 106
  see also basing, bomber; specific
    bombers
bombing:
  mean area of effectiveness in, 71
  reserve force in, 46–47
  roof damage as effectiveness indica-
    tor in, 71
  target selection in, see targeting
    strategy
  Uniform Random Drops Model of,
    241
  in World War II, 35–37, 41–43,
    70–71
  see also strategy, nuclear; specific
    bombs
Bowie, Robert, 185
Bowles, Edward, 54, 56–61
Bradbury, Norris, 75
Bradley, William E., 343–45
Bray, Leslie, 357
Brewer, Keith, 166
Brodie, Bernard, 9–50, 72, 76, 81–82,
  84, 197, 222–23, 226, 253, 390
  on A-bomb, 25–27, 30–32
  as Air Force consultant, 40, 45–49
  background of, 11–16
  change in views of, 337–40
  controlled use of nuclear weapons
    and, 191

Brodie, Bernard (*cont.*)
  at Dartmouth, 17–18
  European defense as seen by,
    337–38
  on H-bomb strategy, 79–81, 85
  Kaufmann monograph and, 193–94
  on limited war, 340
  on mutual use of nuclear weapons,
    191
  nuclear strategy rejected by,
    339–42
  on peaceful change, 15–16
  at Princeton, 16–17
  selective bombing proposed by,
    204–5, 207
  sex-war plan connection seen by,
    222–23
  on theater nuclear weapons, 340
  in U.S. Navy, 18–19
  Vietnam War and, 341
  Wohlstetter and, 338–39
  at Yale, 22–24, 186–89
  see also Absolute Weapon, The
Brown, Harold, 256, 320–21, 344–45
  on counterforce strategy, 382
  flexibility supported by, 383
  MIRV development and, 363
  on nuclear war, 385–86
Browning, Robert, 29
Bundy, McGeorge, 187, 195, 279, 325
  fallout shelters studied by, 307–10
  1961 Berlin crisis and, 296–99, 302
  Teller civil defense program and,
    314
  Vietnam War escalation and, 329,
    333
Bundy, William, 187, 334–35
Burchinal, David, 299
Burke, Arleigh, 234, 236
  SIOP and, 264–70
Bush, George, 388

Cabell, Charles P., 45, 49
Calkins, Robert, 128
"Can Peaceful Change Prevent War?"
  (Brodie), 15–16
Capehart, Homer, 248
Carney, Robert, 129
Carter, Jimmy, 380–85
  Committee on the Present Danger
    and, 380
  counterforce endorsed under, 385
  NSDM-242 reaffirmed by, 383–84
  nuclear war-fighting options of,
    382–84
  nuclear weapons elimination advo-
    cated by, 382
  protracted nuclear war and, 383–84
Caywood, Tom, 353

Central Intelligence Agency (CIA),
  157
  Air Force Intelligence dispute with,
    159–60
  economic division of, 157–60
  on "Rolling Thunder" bombing
    campaign, 335
  Soviet missiles estimated by,
    162–66, 287–89
  see also National Intelligence Esti-
    mates
Chicago, University of, 11–16
Chicago Conference on Atomic Energy Control (1945), 24–27, 50
China, People's Republic of, 269–70,
  347–49
Christian News Letter, 179
civil defense, 125–29, 145, 225,
  307–14
  cost of, 225–26, 309, 314
  difficulties of, 308
  strategic value of, 225
  see also fallout shelters
Clausewitz, Karl von, 79, 191, 261
Coddington, L. C., 103
Cohen, Bernard, 50
Cohen, Sam, 74, 220–21
Collbohm, Frank, 56–63, 68, 75, 105,
  114–16, 240–41
COMINT (communications intelli-
  gence), 211
Commission on a Just and Durable
  Peace, 179
Committee on the Present Danger,
  379–80
Committee to Defend America by Aid-
  ing the Allies, 15
Committee to Maintain a Prudent De-
  fense Policy, 387
Compton, Karl, 61
Congress, U.S.:
  ABM system supported in, 346
  "Admirals' Revolt" and, 232–33
  SAC supported in, 233
  SALT II hearings in, 381
Conner, Fox, 177
Contos, George, 258
Convair Missile Division, 112–14
Cooper, John Sherman, 355
Corbett, Percy, 29, 188
Corson, John, 128, 149–50
Council on Foreign Relations, 171,
  174–75
counterforce strategy, 203–19,
  260–62, 278–85
  arms race and, 244
  in ATD-751, 210–11
  as bargaining scheme, 240
  casualties from, 222, 241–43

damage-limiting strategy as, 318–19
deterrence and, 243–44
as dynamic disarmament, 260
ending of war in, 260–61
endless weapons requirements in,
    261
MIRVs and, 363–64
missile gap and, 289–90, 295
1961 Berlin crisis and, 295–304
reality and, 300–306
systems analysis of, 208–9
WSEG on, 259
Cousins, Norman, 28
Cowles, John, 152
Cox, Archibald, 249
Coyle, John, 234
Cragg, Ernie, 276–77
Cuban missile crisis (October, 1962),
    304–6
Cutler, Robert, 127, 132, 146–47

Damage Limiting (Kent), 320–24
damage-limiting strategy, 318–26
    ABMs, counterforce, and civil de-
        fense in, 321, 324
    cost of, 322–24
    hopelessness of, 321
    military support for, 324–25
David, Donald, 61
Davison, W. Philip, 204–5
Dean, Gordon, 82
Deane, Larry, 260
Decker, George, 270
*Defending a Strategic Force After
    1960* (RAND), 118
Defense Department, U.S.:
    Army strength supported in, 196
    basing briefing at, 103
    Brodie's views scorned in, 48
    damage-limiting strategy studied in,
        324–25
    Directorate of Defense Research &
        Engineering in, 320–25
    fallout pamphlet of, 310–13
    limited war strategy in, 326–27
    Special Advisory Panel on Strategic
        Bombing Objectives in, 48–49
    Systems Analysis Office in, 254,
        257, 320, 368
    Whiz Kids at, 254–57, 274, 317,
        320
de Gaulle, Charles, 283–85, 338
DeLauer, Richard, 388
"Delicate Balance of Terror, The"
    (Wohlstetter), 171–73, 249, 339
deterrence:
    Assured Destruction as, 317
    basing systems and, 109
    counterforce and, 243–44

credibility in, 191–93
finite, 259–60
intrawar, 223–24
massive retaliation threat as, 175,
    178–81, 191–92
missile gap and, 169–73
mutual, 236
Polaris missile as, 234–36
risk in, 190–91
versatility needed in, 192–93
*Deterrence and Strategy of Total War,
    1959–61* (Marshall-Goldhamer),
    213–16, 219
*Deterrence and Survival in the Nu-
    clear Age* (Gaither Report),
    141–42, 144–54
"Deterring Our Deterrent" (Nitze-
    Jones), 379
Digby, James, 207–9, 212–13
Discoverer satellite, 286–89
Doctrine of Atomic Air Warfare,
    181–82
Dodge, Joseph, 176–77, 180
Dougherty, Russell, 276–77, 357–58,
    384
Douglas, Donald, 56–61
Douglas, Jim, 105–6, 150–51
Douglas Aircraft, 58–61
Douhet, Giulio, 35–36, 69
Draft Presidential Memorandums
    (DPM), 281–82, 315–30, 325–26,
    363–64
Dr. Strangelove (Kubrick), 11, 231
Dulles, Allen, 150–51, 159, 163–64,
    168
Dulles, John Foster, 136, 149–51,
    174–75, 178–81
    atomic weapon use accepted by,
        178–80
    "massive-retaliation speech" of,
        174–75, 181, 185–86, 190
    New Look and, 175, 181
Dunn, Frederick Sherwood, 19–22,
    29–30, 50, 186, 188–89

Earle, Edward Mead, 16–17, 25
East Germany, 291–98
    1961 Berlin crisis and, 294–98
    population exodus from, 291–92
    Soviet treaty with, 292–93
Eckert, C. A., 103
*Economics of Defense in the Nuclear
    Age, The* (Hitch), 252
Eisenhower, Dwight D., 126–27, 131,
    145–47, 149–54, 251, 256
    on Army use in "big war," 196
    budget tightness under, 145, 176
    defense buildup rejected by,
        145–47, 176–77

Eisenhower, Dwight D. (cont.)
  foreign aid under, 177
  on Gaither Report, 146–47, 152,
    154
  "great equation" of, 178, 180
  Khrushchev met by, 292
  massive retaliation and, 180–81
  military decisions and, 177–78
  missile gap and, 168–69, 172–73,
    287
  "New Look" defense plan of, 175,
    180–81, 183–84
  Nitze paper rejected under, 137
  SAC vulnerability and, 150–52
  SIOP and, 264, 266
  on strong defense, 145–46
  election, of 1960, 248–50
Ellis, Richard, 356, 384
Ellsberg, Daniel, 123–24, 249–50,
    253, 275–79, 285
  counterforce option suggested by,
    278–79
  JSCP and, 277–78
  Pentagon Papers leaked by, 337
  SIOP-63 and, 275–79
Emergency Action Message (EAM),
    276
Enthoven, Alain, 124, 250, 252–54,
    256, 259–62, 272, 285, 316
  Assured Destruction criterion and,
    317–18, 326, 365–66
  DPMs and, 281–82
  limited war strategy and, 327
  military officers and, 254
  in 1961 Berlin crisis, 299, 302
  on RAND climate, 253
  Soviet targets categorized by, 279
  style of, 253–54
Ermarth, Fritz, 359, 368
Escalation and the Nuclear Option
    (Brodie), 340
Evaluation of Strategic Offensive
    Weapons Systems (WSEG-50),
    258–62

fallout, 126, 261, 268, 271, 310–14
"Fallout Protection: What to Know
    About Nuclear Attack—What to
    Do About It," 310–13
fallout shelters, 145, 307–14, 322–24
Federal Civil Defense Administration
    (FCDA), 126
Federal Housing Administration, 126
Feldman, Meyer, 308–9
Felt, Harry, 275
Fili Plant (Moscow), 156–60
Fisher, R. E., 71
Flanagan, Dennis, 228
Ford, Gerald, 379–80

Ford, Henry, II, 61, 251
Ford Foundation, 61
Foreign Affairs, 33, 171, 191, 377–79
Foreign Policy, 379
Foster, John S., Jr., 350, 353, 362,
    368–69
Foster, William C., 128–29, 132,
    146–47, 149–51, 152–53
Foster Panel, 368–70
Fowler, Henry, 379
Fox, William T. R., 19, 21–25, 27–30,
    50, 72, 188
France, 302, 338
Franke, William, 265
Fryklund, Richard, 282
Fullhouse Concept, 107–8

Gaither, H. Rowan, 60–61, 125,
    127–29, 146–47, 171
Gaither Committee, 125–43, 225–26
  advisory panel for, 129
  fallout shelter program recom-
    mended by, 145
  IRBM abandonment urged on,
    144–45
  LeMay challenged by, 132–34
  Marshall and, 213
  national security issues as mandate
    of, 129
  NSC briefing by, 149–50
  priorities of, 145
  report of, see Gaither Report
  R-290 report and, 128, 130–31, 144
  SAC readiness studied by, 131–34
  Sputnik and, 136
  steering committee of, 129, 132,
    134, 136, 148
Gaither Report, 141–42, 166–67
  defense spending recommended by,
    145, 149–50
  J. Dulles on, 150
  missile program acceleration recom-
    mended by, 144
  press stories on, 153–54
  public relations for, 152–53
Galbraith, John Kenneth, 195, 249,
    311
Gallois, Pierre, 284, 338, 340
game theory, 63–68, 91, 178, 214
  initial conception of, 64–65
  limitation of, 67
  limited war and, 199
  minimax solution in, 66
  Prisoners' Dilemma in, 65–67
Gardner, Trevor, 115–16
Garwin, Richard, 349
Gates, Thomas, 168, 252, 263–70
  SIOP-62 and, 269–70
Gavin, James, 249

Germany, Nazi:
  post-war division of, 291
  World War II bombing of, 35–37,
    41, 70–71
Germany, see also East Germany;
  West Germany
Gilpatric, Roswell, 152, 270–72, 279,
    287, 324
Goldhamer, Herbert, 202, 213–16,
    219, 226
Goodpaster, Andrew, 146–47, 150–51,
    169
Gray, Gordon, 128, 146–47, 150–51
Graybeal, Sidney, 162
Great Britain, 36, 53, 302
Griggs, David, 57–58, 74, 84, 111,
    115, 221, 362
Griswold, A. Whitney, 50
Gruenther, Alfred, 176
Guided Missiles Intelligence Commit-
    tee (GMIC), 163–65

Halperin, Morton, 346–47
Hanounian, Norman, 261
Harlan, John Marshall, 52
Hart, Philip, 355
Helmer, Olaf, 62, 97
Henderson, Dierdre, 249
Henderson, Larry, 61, 68, 82, 104–5
Herbst, Roland, 361–62
Hershleifer, Jack, 206
Hiroshima, atomic bombing of, 22,
    179
Hitch, Charles, 70–72, 76–78, 81–84,
    90, 97, 191, 206–7, 253, 316
  in Defense Department, 252–56,
    259–62, 272, 285
  in 1961 Berlin crisis, 299
Hoeber, Francis, 359, 368
Hoffman, Frederic S., 98–104, 106,
    118–24, 209, 250, 253
Hull, John, 129
Humphrey, George, 176, 180
Hunt, Victor, 205–7, 222
Hutchins, Robert, 24
hydrogen bomb:
  CEP of, 113–14
  deterrence power of, 85
  development of, 74
  manufacturing cost of, 82
  power of, 77–80
  rational use of, 79–81
  research on, 64
  size of, 111
  see also nuclear weapons; strategy,
    nuclear

ICBM (intercontinental ballistic mis-
    sile), 111–24, 255

ABM defenses for, 350
accuracy of, 374–75
fratricide of, 375
Killian Panel and, 131
protection from, 118–21
SAC vs. RAND defense systems for,
    120–21
systematic error in, 375
Iklé, Fred, 387
"Implications of Large-Yield Nuclear
    Weapons" (RAND), 82
Introduction to the Fleet Ballistic
    Missile (NAVWAG-1), 234
IRBM (intermediate-range ballistic
    missile), 131, 144–45

Japan, World War II bombing of,
    42–43
Johnson, Louis, 138–40
Johnson, Lyndon B., 317, 325, 329
  on McNamara, 337
  on Nike-X production, 346
  Vietnam War and, 333
Joint Chiefs of Staff, U.S. (JCS), 22,
    39, 41–42, 44, 85, 149–50,
    182–83, 335
  ABM advocated by, 346
  ABM war game of, 320–21
  Assured Destruction attacked by,
    324
  atomic weapon use planned by,
    183
  Berlin crisis contingency plans of,
    296
  counterforce strategy as weapons
    rationale in, 316
  Joint Strategic Capabilities Plan of
    (1956), 196
  limited nuclear option of, 370–71
  McNamara's questions for, 273
  National Strategic Target and At-
    tack Plan (NSTAP) of, 267–68
  SIOP-62 and, 269–70
  on Soviet SLBMs, 320
  targeting questions for, 264
  war plan of, 277–79
Joint Intelligence Committee, 39,
    44–45, 93
Joint Strategic Capabilities Plan
    (JSCP), 277–79
Joint Strategic Operational Plan
    (JSOP), 277
Joint Strategic Survey Committee (of
    JCS), 22
Joint Strategic Target Planning Staff
    (JSTPS), 269, 365
Jones, Ed, 107
Jones, T. K., 379, 388
Jordan crisis (1970), 370

Kahn, Herman, 76, 101, 119, 123, 129–30, 207, 219–31, 237, 328, 377–78, 384
  background of, 220
  civil-defense program advocated by, 225–26, 309
  on counterforce targeting, 222
  Credible-First-Strike Capability advocated by, 223–25
  "Doomsday Machine" of, 223
  escalation theory of, 223
  free-market system and, 229–30
  as Gaither Committee consultant, 129–30, 225–26
  interwar deterrence plan of, 223–24
  multi-option war plan advocated by, 223–25
  nuclear strategy studied by, 222–27
  on post-nuclear war society, 227–30
  public lectures by, 226–28
  SAC and, 222–23
  Soviet nuclear blackmail threat seen by, 224
  style of, 222, 226–27
  systems analysis and, 221–22
Kaplan, Abraham, 69
Kaufmann, William, 50, 123, 144, 186–200, 217–20, 226, 237–46, 367
  on arms race, 244
  Assured Destruction strategy and, 326
  background of, 186–89
  "bonus" strategy as seen by, 219
  Clausewitzian outlook of, 199–200
  as consultant to Schlesinger, 372–74
  counterforce study at RAND by, 217–19, 237–45
  in Kennedy administration, 253, 256–58, 260–62, 272, 283–85, 294–97
  on limited war, 197–200, 326–27
  McNamara's Athens speech written by, 283–85
  on massive retaliation, 190–92
  1961 Berlin crisis and, 294–97, 299, 302–3
  on Polaris, 237–39
  at Princeton, 189
  at RAND, 189, 201–4, 217–19, 238–47
  reserve force advocated by, 218–19
  on Soviet reaction to counterforce strategy, 244
  strong conventional forces advocated by, 191–92
Kaysen, Carl, 35, 206, 249, 257
  fallout shelters studied by, 307–10
  in 1961 Berlin crisis, 296–300, 302

Keegan, George, 167–68, 288
Keeny, Spurgeon, 130, 209
Kellogg-Briand Pact, 13
Kennan, George, 33, 138–39, 195, 197
Kennedy, John F., 11, 248–52, 256–57
  Academic Advisory Group of, 249–50
  civil defense and, 307, 309–14
  Communist expansionism and, 292–93
  counterforce strategy and, 282
  counterinsurgency plans under, 328
  in Cuban missile crisis, 305
  defense appropriations supplement requested by, 297
  Khrushchev met by, 293
  massive retaliation rejected by, 328
  on missile gap, 248–49
  Nike-Zeus and, 345
  in 1961 Berlin crisis, 293–99
  on nuclear war, 284–85
  as RAND's ideal candidate, 250
  SAC vulnerability decried by, 249
Kennedy, Robert, 282, 309–10, 328
Kennedy Administration, 248–62
  Berlin crisis options in, 295–304
  European nuclear arms opposed in, 338
  fallout shelters studied in, 307–14
  missile gap rejected in, 286–88
Kenney, George, 43
Kent, Glenn, 276–77, 320–25, 362
Kent, Sherman, 157
Khrushchev, Nikita, 135, 142, 160, 292–94
  on Berlin occupation, 292
  in Cuban missile crisis, 304–6
  Kennedy met by, 293
  1961 Berlin crisis and, 293–94, 304
Killian, James R., Jr., 127, 146–47
Killian Panel, 130–31
King, Ernest J., 18
Kirk, Grayson, 22
Kissinger, Henry, 249, 296–99, 302, 373, 380
  ABM deployment and, 350–51
  Foster Panel and, 369
  limited nuclear option and, 370–71
  massive retaliation opposed by, 366
  Soviet SS-9 missiles and, 351
Kistiakowsky, George, 115, 268–69
Klein, Burt, 206
Knorr, Klaus, 21, 188
Komer, Robert, 302
Korean War, 39, 81, 140, 177, 185–86, 193
Kosygin, Aleksei, 346

Laird, Melvin, 351, 353–54, 368–69
Lanphier, Thomas, 163–64
Lasswell, Harold, 25, 72
Latter, Albert, 221, 361–62
Latter, Richard, 221, 361–62
Lay, James, 126
Layman's Guide to Naval Strategy, A
    (Brodie), 9, 18
Leach, Barton, 249
League of Nations, 12–13
Leites, Nathan, 17, 213, 338, 340
LeMay, Curtis E., 42–44, 57, 59, 68,
    74, 148, 210, 280
  on bomber basing, 93
  counterforce targeting rejected by,
    240
  Gaither Committee and, 132–34
  intercontinental bomber favored by,
    106
  Japan bombed by, 42–43
  preemptive strike as policy of, 134
  SAC competence under, 43–44,
    132–34
  SAC independence guarded by, 104
  on Soviet capabilities, 142–43
  Whiz Kids and, 255–56
Lemnitzer, Lyman, 270–74
Library of Congress, 34
Life, 310
Lilienthal, David, 24
limited war strategy, 197–200,
    326–27, 330–32
  counterforce and, 218–19
  game theory and, 199
  management of, 198
  nuclear weapons in, 191, 198
  real-life problems in, 334–35
  stalemate as goal of, 198–99
Lindsay, Franklin, 152
Lipp, Jim, 76–78, 114, 207
Livermore Laboratory, 220–21
Lodal, Jan, 370–71
Loftus, Joseph, 209–13, 216–17, 219,
    240
  at RAND, 212–13, 216–17, 219
  Soviet air base vulnerability studied
    by, 209–11
Los Alamos scientists, H-bomb op-
    posed by, 83
Lovett, Robert, 82, 129, 137, 251
Luce, Clare Booth, 135
Lukeman, Bob, 276–77
Lutz, Robert J., 97, 104, 106
Lynn, Larry, 367

McCloy, John, 129, 146–47, 149–50
McCormick, L. D., 182
McElroy, Neil, 149–51, 168
McFarland, Earl, 163–64

McGarvey, Dave, 237, 240–43
McHugh, L. C., 312
McKinsey, J. C. C., 91, 97
McNamara, Robert S., 11, 250–62,
    270–73
  Assured Destruction criterion of,
    317–19
  Athens-Ann Arbor speech of,
    283–85, 315–16
  background of, 250–51
  on causes of wars, 336
  counterforce strategy and, 262,
    274, 281–83, 315, 319, 325–26
  in Cuban missile crisis, 304
  damage-limiting strategy of,
    318–19, 321–26
  disillusionment of, 336–37
  DPMs of, 281–82, 315–20, 325–26,
    363–64
  on effects of "Rolling Thunder,"
    335
  first-strike capability and, 316
  "General War Offensive Package"
    of, 272–73
  ICBM production increased by, 306
  limited war strategy and, 327
  NcNaughton and, 333, 337
  Minuteman program reduced by,
    325
  MIRV and, 325–26, 363–64
  missile gap rejected by, 286–88
  Nike-X opposed by, 346–48
  Nike-Zeus endorsed by, 345
  in 1961 Berlin crisis, 297–99
  "96 Trombones" of, 273–79
  on SIOP-62, 270–72
  on Soviet SLBMs, 320
  Vietnam War and, 329–30, 336–37
  vulnerability lessened by, 273–74
  world growth and development sup-
    ported by, 337
  WSEG-50 and, 258–59
McNaughton, John, 302, 332–35
  on failure of "Rolling Thunder,"
    335
  McNamara and, 333, 337
  Vietnam War plans of, 333–35
Makers of Modern Strategy (Earle),
    17
Malenkov, Georgi, 105
Marshall, Andrew, 92, 123
  counterforce and, 205–7, 209,
    212–17, 219, 222, 226, 372, 384
  in Defense Department, 372
  Gaither Committee and, 213
  in Kennedy campaign, 250
  in Reagan administration, 387
Marshall, George C., 178
Martin, James, 367–69

Massachusetts Institute of Technology (MIT), 56–57, 126
Meeting the Threat of Surprise Attack (Killian Panel), 131
Merriam, Charles, 13
Military Policy and National Security (Kaufmann), 197–200
Millikan, Clark, 115
Minuteman missiles, 255, 257
  inflexible programming in, 280
  modification of, 280–81
  reduction of, 325
  vulnerability of, 351–54, 361
Minuteman II missiles, 325
Minuteman III missiles, 363–64
MIRVs (Multiple Independently targetable Re-entry Vehicles), 325–26, 351, 354, 360–64
  as counterforce weapon, 363–64
  Soviet target shape and, 362
  technology developed for, 362–63
  vulnerability from, 361
missile gap, 155, 161–73, 248–49, 286–90
  as "deterrence gap," 169–73
  lack of evidence for, 155, 162–66, 287–90
  Wohlstetter on, 171–73
missiles:
  defenses for, *see* ABMs
  support equipment for, 164–65
  see also specific missiles
Mitchell, Billy, 35–36, 54–55
MK-12 warhead, 363
Morgenstern, Oskar, 66
Morse, Philip, 355, 390
Mosley, Phil, 171
Murphy, Charles, 140
"Must We Shoot from the Hip?" (Brodie), 207
MX (Missile Experimental), 385–87

National Intelligence Estimates (NIE):
  1956, 156–60
  1957, 155, 161
  1959, 161, 164–65
  1960, 287–89
  1969, 351
National Policy Implications of Atomic Parity (NAVWAG-5), 234–36
National Security Council, 125–27, 140
  Army strength and, 196
  civil defense studied by, 126–27
  Gaither Report and, 149–50
  NSDM-242 and, 372–73
  Planning Board of, 126

National Security Decision Memorandum (NSDM) 242, 369–70, 372–73
National Security Study Memorandum (NSSM) No. 3, 366–67
National Strategic Target List (NSTL), 264, 267
NATO, *see* North Atlantic Treaty Organization
Naval Warfare Analysis Group (NAVWAG), 234–36
  on arms race, 234–35
  conventional forces supported by, 235
  SAC dominance denounced by, 234
Navy, U.S.:
  A-bomb denounced by, 232–33
  "Admirals' Revolt" in, 232–33
  Air Force rivalry with, 232–46
  atomic weapons acquired by, 182, 233
  Brodie's books used by, 17–18
  mutual deterrence policy of, 236
  Pacific Command (PacCom) of, 275–76
  Polaris project of, 131, 233–38, 244
  Soviet ground power and, 182–83
  on Soviet ICBM estimates, 288
  see also Office of Naval Intelligence
Neumann, Franz, 72
Newman, James R., 228
Newsweek, 312
New York *Herald Tribune*, 50
New York Times, 9, 34, 76, 153, 195, 312, 337
"Next Ten Years, The" (Brodie-Hitch-Marshall), 207
Nitze, Paul Henry, 136–41, 152–53, 183, 185–86, 195, 197, 249, 285, 326, 332–33, 387
  in Committee on the Present Danger, 379–80
  on counterforce strategy, 300–301, 379
  in Defense Department, 252–53, 275, 279
  J. Dulles disliked by, 185
  on flaw in cities targeting, 377–78
  and Gaither Report, 136–41, 145
  limited war strategy and, 327
  massive-retaliation speech rejected by, 185–86
  military buildup recommended by, 140
  in 1961 Berlin crisis, 299–303, 378
  NSC-68 and, 139–41
  nuclear blackmail feared by, 377
  nuclear debate controlled by, 379–81

in Reagan administration, 386
SALT II opposed by, 377–78, 381
on Soviet military intentions,
   139–40, 377
writing skill of, 138
Nixon, Richard M., 152–53, 366–67,
   369
   ABM system under, 350–55
no-cities strategy, *see* counterforce
   strategy
Norstad, Lauris, 38, 45, 49, 145
North Atlantic Treaty Organization
   (NATO):
   American strategy for, 338
   counterforce and, 217–19
   independent nuclear forces for,
      283–85
   IRBMs deployed by, 291
   joined by West Germany, 291
   McNamara speech to, 283–85
   1961 Berlin crisis and, 294
   U.S. nuclear shield and, 182,
      283–85
   U.S.-supplied nuclear weapons for,
      202
NSC-68, 140
Nuclear Targeting Policy Review,
   383–84
nuclear war:
   controlled response in, 273–74
   deaths from, 125–26
   food after, 229–30
   post-war conditions, 227–30
   protracted, 383–84
   rational control of, 327
   strategies for, *see* strategy, nuclear;
      and specific strategies
   two-way nature of, 48, 274
nuclear weapons:
   controlled use of, *see* counterforce
      strategy
   proliferation of, 202–3
   see also specific weapons
Nuclear Weapons Employment Plan
   (NUWEP), 369
"Nuclear Weapons: Strategic or Tactical?" (Brodie), 191
NU-OPTS project, 356–60, 368
   dissent to, 359–60
   operational defects of, 359
   targeting in, 358–59

Odeen, Philip, 369
Office of Civil Defense Mobilization
   (OCDM), 307
Office of National Estimates (ONE),
   157, 159
Office of Naval Intelligence, 18–19,
   165–66, 242

Ofstie, Ralph, 232
Oliver, Edward P., 128, 216–17
On Thermonuclear War (Kahn),
   227–28, 230–31, 328, 377
*Operational Code of the Politburo,
   The* (Leites), 76
operations research, 52–57
   reality as test of, 355
   in World War II, 53–54
Operations Research, 353–54
Operations Research Society of
   America (ORSA), 353–55
Oppenheimer, J. Robert, 63, 81, 84

Packard, David, 350, 353, 379
Panofsky, Wolfgang, 344–45
Parrish, Noel, 239–40, 243, 245, 261,
   282
Patterson, Robert, 58
Paxson, Ed, 78, 86–91, 206
   bomber design attempted by, 88–90
   style of, 86
Pearl Harbor, Japanese attack on, 17,
   92, 109
Pearl Harbor: Warning and Decision
   (Wohlstetter, R.), 92
Pentagon Papers, 337
Perkins, James, 128, 171
Perle, Richard, 387–88
Plesset, Ernst, 74–78, 81–84, 111,
   115, 123, 191, 220
Polaris A-3 missile, 343–44
Polaris submarine, 131, 233–38, 244
   SIOP and, 263–68
   Whiz Kids' support of, 255
Power, Thomas S., 68, 102, 166, 236,
   245–46, 262
   counterforce briefings and, 246
   McNamara briefed on SIOP-62 by,
      270–72
   SIOP and, 266–69
   Soviet ICBM force estimate and,
      287
   style of, 245–46
Powers, Francis Gary, 286–87
*Preliminary Design of an Experimen-
   tal World-Circling Spaceship*
   (RAND), 60
Presidential Directive (PD)-18, 383
Presidential Directive (PD)-59,
   383–84, 389
Presidential Science Advisory Commit-
   tee (PSAC), 344–45
Prim, Robert, 128
Princeton Center of International
   Studies, 50, 186, 189, 193,
   201
Princeton Institute for Advanced
   Study, 16–17

Princeton University Press, 9, 16, 17, 18, 227
Proctor, Ed, 157–59
Project East River, 126
Project Vista, 81, 84
Protecting U.S. Power to Strike Back in the 1950s and 1960s (RAND), 121, 125, 129–31, 144, 166–67, 209

Quade, Edward S., 88, 206
Quarles, Don, 150–51

Rabinowitch, Eugene, 24
Radford, Arthur W., 175–76, 180, 183–84, 194, 196, 232–33
  on atomic weapon use, 196
  on New Look policy, 183–84
Ramo, Simon, 115, 117
RAND Conference of Social Scientists, 70, 72
RAND Corporation, 10–11, 50–52, 58–124
  air base location studied at, 90–94, 97–110
  Air Force-Navy conflict and, 237–46
  atmosphere at, 51, 62
  basing briefings by, 103–4
  bomber design study at, 88–90, 98
  counterforce studied at, 204–9, 212–19, 240–44
  Douglas Aircraft and, 58–61
  economic division of, 63, 68, 70–73, 203
  Fourth Annual Report of, 91
  game theory at, 67–68, 91, 214
  H-bomb briefings by, 81–82
  H-bomb consequences researched by, 74–81, 108
  ICBM research at, 111–24
  as independent non-profit corporation, 61–62
  Kennedy campaign and, 249–50
  legacy in 1980s, 386–89
  missile gap discussed at, 169–70
  new generation of strategy at, 357–58, 390
  NIEs withheld from, 170
  NU-OPTS strategy studied at, 357–60
  origins of, 52, 58–59
  physics division at, 74–76, 220–21
  publicity eschewed by, 170
  quantitative analysis dominant at, 121
  SAC vulnerability studied at, 117–21
  simulation games at, 201–2
  social science division of, 63, 68–70, 72–73, 76, 201–2, 228–29
  strategic community at, 123–24
  Strategic Objectives Committee at, 207–9, 222, 378
  Strategic Offensive Forces study of, 216–17, 237
  systems analysis at, 86–91
  Uniform Random Drops Model at, 241
  Vietnam War debate at, 360
Raskin, Marcus, 299–300, 307–10
Rathjens, George, 269, 351–55
Rationale for NU-OPTS (Schlesinger), 358
Raymond, Arthur, 56–59, 61
Reagan, Ronald, 386–89
Reagan Administration:
  Committee on the Present Danger and, 386
  counterforce strategy in, 386–87
  defense spending in, 389
  nuclear strategy of, 387–90
  nuclear war conceivability in, 388–89
Reedy, George, 135
Reentry Body Identification Group, 343
Reexamination of United States Programs for National Security (Bissell-Nash-Nitze), 137–38
Reporter, The, 38, 193
"Requirements of Deterrence, The" (Kaufmann), 186, 193–97
Revised Development Program for Ballistic Missiles of Intercontinental Range, A (RAND), 116
Rinehart, John, 135
Rockefeller, Nelson, 127, 307, 309
Roper, Elmo, 152
Rosten, Leo, 68–70, 72
Rostow, Eugene, 379–80, 386
Rostow, Walt, 279, 328–29, 346
Rowe, David, 22
Rowen, Henry, 97–104, 106, 240, 250, 252–53, 256, 262, 275, 283, 285, 294, 384
  Assured Destruction strategy and, 326
  limited war strategy and, 327
  1961 Berlin crisis options and, 296–99, 302–3
R-290, *see Protecting U.S. Power to Strike Back in the 1950s and 1960s*
Ruina, Jack, 345
Rumsfeld, Donald, 380
Rusk, Dean, 297

SAC Intelligence:
  SIOP and, 267–68
  Soviet missile forces estimated by,
    288–89
SALT I, 354, 377
SALT II, 377, 380–82
Samuelson, Paul, 249
satellites, reconnaissance, 286
Saturday Evening Post, 255, 257
Saturday Review of Literature, 28
Schelling, Thomas, 302, 330–33, 358
  arms control and, 331
  limited war advocated by, 330–32
  on Vietnam War escalation, 334–
    335
  war and bargaining as seen by,
    330–31
Schlesinger, Arthur, Jr., 195, 249,
    298, 312
Schlesinger, James R., 357–59,
    368–69
  Committee on the Present Danger
    and, 379
  counterforce feasibility doubted by,
    357–58
  as Defense Secretary, 372–79
  flexibility and selectivity supported
    by, 374, 376
  graduated reprisals strategy and,
    358
  NSDM-242 supported by, 372–73
  on perceptions in international rela-
    tions, 376–77
  refined first-strike capability sought
    by, 375–76
  style of, 357
  targeting strategy change publi-
    cized by, 373
Schriever, Bernard, 103, 115–16
Schulman, Hyman, 374–75
Scientific American, 228, 349
Scoville, Herbert (Pete), Jr., 162, 269
Sea Power in the Machine Age (Bro-
    die), 16–17
"Security Policy for Postwar America,
  A" (Rye conference), 22
*Selection and Use of Strategic Air
  Bases* (RAND), 106
Selin, Ivan, 365–67
Senate, U.S., 12, 349
  ABM funding by, 354
  Armed Services Committee of, 352
  Foreign Relations subcommittee of,
    352
  missile gap and, 168–69
sensitivity analysis, 170
Shils, Edward, 24–25, 28, 50
Shoup, David, 270
simulation games, 201–2

Single Integrated Operational Plan
  (SIOP), 262–72
  civilian casualties from, 365
  first Planning Conference for,
    266–67
  increasing Soviet strength and,
    364–65
  "minimum number" of targets in,
    267–68
  multiple bombing of targets in,
    268–69
  origin of, 263–66
  weapons requirements exaggerated
    in, 268–69
SIOP-62, 269–72
  Albania in, 271–72
  China in, 269–70
  fallout anticipated from, 268, 271
  Plan 1-A of, 271
SIOP-63, 279
Skifter, Hector, 128, 130
SLBMs (submarine launched ballistic
    missiles), 320
  see also Polaris; Trident II
Sloss, Leon, 384
Smith, Bob, 267
Smyth, H. D., 25
Smyth Report, 25, 26
Social Science Research Council, 30
Sorensen, Theodore, 299, 308–9, 312
Soviet Union, 33–42
  A-bomb acquired by, 39, 99
  air base vulnerability in, 209–11
  atomic-energy plants in, 41
  bombing targets in, 39–48, 78
  East Germany and, 291–94
  expansionist ideology of, 33–34
  Gaither Committee on, 141–42
  ground power of, 80, 182–83,
    326–27
  H-bomb first exploded by, 105, 112
  ICBM force of, 155, 160–68,
    286–89, 294–95, 320
  ICBMs tested by, 162, 164
  massive retaliation threat and, 192
  military objectives of, 155, 157,
    161
  MIRVs tested by, 374
  missile building program in, 305–6,
    365
  potential first strike by, 86, 92–93,
    155
  SLBMs of, 320
  strategic vulnerability of, 295
  underground missile silos of, 320
  U.S. secret intelligence on, 211,
    213, 216–17
  see also specific events and weapons
Spaatz, Carl, 61

Speier, Hans, 50, 70, 72, 76, 189,
    201–2, 205
Sprague, Robert C.:
    Eisenhower briefed on SAC by,
        150–51
    Gaither Committee and, 127, 129,
        132–34, 136, 146–53
    R-290 and, 130
Sprout, Harold, 22
Sputnik, 135–36, 160
Spykman, Nicholas, 19–21, 186
SS-9 ICBM, 351–54
Staats, Elmer, 308–9
Stearns, Joyce, 24
Stern, Marvin, 253, 260, 270–72,
    280–81
Stoertz, Howard, Jr., 163
Strategic Air Command, U.S. (SAC),
    39–48, 85
    airborne alert begun in, 166–67
    ATD-751 in EWP of, 211–12
    "Bonus" targeting by, 211–12
    confusion in war plan of, 276–77
    Delta-Bravo-Romeo plan and,
        41–42, 44–45, 209
    Emergency War Plans (EWP) of,
        44, 209, 211–12, 277
    Gaither Committee and, 131–34
    independence guarded for, 104
    intelligence estimates used by,
        167–68
    Kahn and, 222–23
    mass destruction as goal of, 212,
        246, 277
    Optimum Mix bombing plan of, 242
    overseas refueling bases recom-
        mended for, 100–101
    PD-59 and, 384
    Polaris as threat to, 236–37
    readiness lacking for, 132–33
    SIOP created by, 264, 266,
        276–77
    "Sunday Punch" plan of, 204
    survivability as imperative for, 47
    vulnerability of, 86, 92–94, 97–102,
        142, 166–67, 171–73, 249, 374
    Wohlstetter's basing briefing for,
        102–3
    World War II-type planning in,
        98–99
"Strategic Bombing: What It Can Do"
    (Brodie), 38, 46
Strategic Missile Evaluation Commit-
    tee (Teapot Committee), 114–16
Strategic Objectives Study, 367–68
Strategic Offensive Forces (SOF)
    study (RAND), 216–17
strategy, military, 17
strategy, naval, 25–26

strategy, nuclear, 203
    ABM debate and, 355
    civil defense in, 225
    first-strike, 316
    graduated reprisals as, 358
    illusory nature of, 341–42
    intrawar deterrence as, 223–24
    new generation in, 356
    NU-OPTS as, 356–60
    public debate of, 381–82
    reserve force in, 215, 218–19
    superiority in, 30–31
    targeting in, see targeting strategy
    see also specific strategies
Strategy of Air Power (Brodie), 35
Strategy of Conflict, The (Schelling),
    330
Strauss, Lewis, 63, 150–51
Study of War, A (Wright), 13–15
Summer Studies, the, 126
Super-Powers, The (Fox), 22
Symington, Stuart, 163–64, 168–69,
    355
systems analysis, 86–88, 221–22
Szilard, Leo, 24

Tanham, George, 237–39
targeting strategy, 37–48
    atomic-energy facilities in, 41, 44
    cities in, 26, 30–31, 44, 47, 78–81,
        214, 236, 329
    counterforce, 203–19
    Delta-Bravo-Romeo as, 41–42,
        44–45
    electric-power systems in, 41, 44
    H-bomb and, 79–81
    liquid-fuel industries in, 37, 41,
        44
    Marshall-Goldhamer study of,
        213–16
    selective, 204–6
    see also counterforce strategy;
        SIOP; SIOP-62; SIOP-63; NU-
        OPTS; strategy, nuclear
Taylor, Maxwell, 255, 299, 335
    in Cuban missile crisis, 304
    versus Eisenhower, 196
    Nike-Zeus pushed by, 345
    as paramilitary activities advisor,
        328–29
Teller, Edward, 75, 83–84, 114–15,
    220, 362
    background of, 83
    civil defense program of, 313–14
    H-bomb and, 83–84
    on Sputnik, 135
Theory of Games and Economic Be-
    havior (Morgenstern-von Neu-
    mann), 66

Thinking About the Unthinkable (Kahn), 228
Trinkl, Frank, 240–43, 252–53, 261, 299–300
  Soviet targets categorized by, 279
Truman, Harry S, 25, 82
Truman Administration:
  conventional forces supported under, 183
  defense spending under, 138–41
Tucker, Gardner, 367–69
Twining, Nathan, 128, 150–51, 264

Ulam, Stanislaw, 75
United States Objectives and Programs for National Security (NSC-68), 138–41
United States Strategic Bombing Survey, 35, 41, 45, 71
"Unlimited Weapons and Limited War" (Brodie), 193–94
Urey, Harold, 24
U-2 spy plane, 131, 165, 286–87

Vance, Cyrus, 187, 280, 346
Vandenberg, Hoyt, 38, 40–41, 45, 48–49, 82, 101, 116
Victory Through Air Power, 69
Vietnam War, 328–36, 341
  escalation planned in, 333–35
  "Rolling Thunder" bombing campaign in, 329, 335–36
Vigner, Eugene, 24
Viner, Jacob, 14–15, 21, 25, 27, 72, 188
Von Karman, Theodore, 56
von Neumann, John, 63–66, 91, 114–16, 178, 220

Wade, James, 388
Walker, Charls, 379
Wallace, Henry, 25
Walsh, James, 167, 210, 212, 288
War Department, U.S., 34–35
"Warning and Bombing" (RAND), 204–5
Warnke, Paul, 347
Warsaw Pact:
  formation of, 291
  in 1961 Berlin crisis, 296–97, 303
Washington Post, 153–54
Weapons System Evaluation Group (WSEG), 93, 258–60, 264–65
  on counterforce strategy, 259
  finite deterrence strategy recommended by, 259–60, 316–17
Weaver, Warren, 63, 72
Webster, William, 128, 132, 149–50
Weidlinger, Paul, 96, 119

Weinberg, Steven, 353
Weinberger, Caspar, 387
Weiss, Seymour, 299, 302–3, 368–69
Welch, Jasper, 368–69
Western Development Division of the Air Research and Development Command (WDD), 116–17
West Germany, 291–93, 302
Westover, Charles "Westy," 236
Wheless, Hewitt, 236
Whisenand, Jim, 103
White, Thomas D., 104–6, 150–51, 155, 166, 195, 216, 236, 238, 240, 270
  counterforce strategy embraced by, 244–46
  Strategic Command advocated by, 263–64
  on Whiz Kids, 255, 257
Wiesner, Jerome, 115, 128, 130, 132, 142, 149–50, 195, 249, 345, 353
  Nike-Zeus and, 345
  Teller's civil defense program and, 313–14
Williams, John Davis, 62–73, 76, 206–7, 252
Wilson, Charles, 82, 115, 128, 180, 250
Wohlstetter, Albert J., 86, 89–110, 117–24, 206, 209, 237, 240, 384, 387
  ABMs supported by, 348–49, 352–54
  background of, 94–97
  Brodie and, 338–39
  on China, 348–49
  Gaither Committee and, 128–31, 144–45
  ICBMs and, 117–21
  influence of at RAND, 121–22
  IRBMs rejected by, 144–45
  in Kennedy campaign, 250
  on lessons of Vietnam, 343
  missile gap discussed by, 170–73
  nuclear weapon proliferation opposed by, 202–3
  overseas base selection studied by, 90–94, 97–102
  on Soviet SS-9 missiles, 352–53
  Strategic Objectives Study and, 367–68
  style of, 122–23
  vulnerability studies by, 110, 117
Wohlstetter, Roberta, 86, 92, 96–97, 122–23
Wolfers, Arnold, 19–22, 29, 186, 188
Wood, Archie, 367–69
Wooldridge, Dean, 115, 117
world government, 28–29, 32

World Politics, 308
World War II:
  beginning of, 12, 16
  German U-boats in, 52–53
  Germany bombed in, 35–37, 41,
    70–71
  Japan bombed in, 42–43
  rocket bombing of London in, 26
Wright, Quincy, 13–16

Yale Institute of International Studies,
  19–23, 27, 29, 186–89

abolishment of, 49–50
Advisory Council for, 21
aim of, 20–21
interaction at, 21–22
power of, 21–22
Yarmolinsky, Adam, 285, 310–13
York, Herbert, 115, 142, 270–72, 354
Yudkin, Richard, 234, 357–58

Zacharias, Jerrold, 195, 345
Zuckert, Gene, 280

ABOUT THE AUTHOR

FRED KAPLAN writes regularly on defense policy for *The Boston Globe* and has also written for *The New York Times, The Atlantic, American Heritage, Scientific American, The New Republic* and many others. He graduated from Oberlin College and has a doctorate in political science from MIT. He is 28 and lives in Washington, D.C.